THE REALITIES OF AGING

SIXTH EDITION

THE REALITIES OF AGING

An Introduction to Gerontology

CARY S. KART

The University of Toledo

JENNIFER M. KINNEY

Miami University

ALLYN AND BACON

Boston ■ London ■ Toronto ■ Sydney ■ Tokyo ■ Singapore

Series Editor: *Sarah L. Kelbaugh*
Editor in Chief, Social Sciences: *Karen Hanson*
Editorial Assistant: *Lori Flickinger*
Editorial-Production Administrator: *Annette Joseph*
Editorial-Production Coordinator: *Holly Crawford*
Editorial-Production Service: *Lynda Griffiths, TKM Productions*
Photo Researchers: *Marla Feuerstein and Katharine Cook*
Composition Buyer: *Linda Cox*
Electronic Composition: *Omegatype Typography, Inc.*
Manufacturing Buyer: *Julie McNeill*
Cover Administrator: *Linda Knowles*

Between the time Website information is gathered and then published, it is not unusual for some sites to have closed. Also, the transcription of URLs can result in unintended typographical errors. The publisher would appreciate being notified of any problems so that they may be corrected in subsequent editions. Thank you.

Library of Congress Cataloging-in-Publication Data

Kart, Cary S. (Cary Steven)
    The realities of aging: an introduction to gerontology / Cary S. Kart, Jennifer M. Kinney. — 6th ed.
        p.   cm.
    Includes bibliographical references and index.
    ISBN 0-205-31802-9
    1. Gerontology.   I. Kinney, Jennifer M.   II. Title.

HQ1061 .K36 2000
305.26—dc21

00-025103

Printed in the United States of America
10   9   8   7   6   05

Photo credits:

p. 10: courtesy of Pearson Education/PH College; p. 34: Gary Conner/PhotoEdit; p. 54: Stone/David Young Wolff; p. 73: courtesy of Pearson Education/PH College; p. 97: Jim Whitmer/FPG; p. 118: Jennifer Kinney; p. 153: Will Faller; p. 197: Robert Harbison; p. 226: Gary Conner/PhotoEdit; p. 271: Z. Michael Nagy; p. 311: Elizabeth Crews/Stock, Boston; p. 334: courtesy of Pearson Education/PH College; p. 361: Martha Tabor/Impact Visuals; p. 374: Owen Franklin/Stock, Boston; p. 397: Will Faller; p. 428: courtesy of Pearson Education/PH College; p. 459: Ron Chapple/FPG; p. 488: Michael Weisbrot/The Image Works; p. 517: H. Armstrong Roberts; p. 539: courtesy of Pearson Education/PH College

To the memories of
Eleanor and Irving Kart
and
Ethel Martin Kinney and Cline Kinney

CONTENTS

PART II   BIOMEDICAL ASPECTS OF AGING

CHAPTER 4

What Are the Results of Aging?   64
by Cary S. Kart, Eileen S. Metress, and Seamus P. Metress

CHAPTER 5

Why Do People Become Old?   89
by Cary S. Kart and Eileen S. Metress

CHAPTER 9
Sociological Theories of Aging   208

PART IV   THE AGED AND SOCIETY

CHAPTER 10
Aging and Family Life   243

Epilogue: Education and Careers in the Field of Gerontology   536

Allyn and Bacon deserves a thank you for providing a sixth opportunity to present *The Realities of Aging.* The field of gerontology continues to grow. Efforts to keep current are considerably more difficult than in the past, as gerontology continues to strengthen its multidisciplinary identity. With a coauthor, this endeavor becomes more manageable. Dr. Jennifer M. Kinney, Professor of Gerontology at Miami University (OH), has made invaluable contributions to this text. She had primary responsibility for Chapters 7, 8, 10, and the Epilogue and provided assistance in rewriting and updating a number of other chapters. I expect that readers will recognize the overall improvement to the book. Welcome aboard, Dr. Kinney!

An introductory course in gerontology is in the core curriculum of most academic gerontology programs and an available elective for those in many human service and other programs. From my biased perspective, this sixth edition of *The Realities of Aging* remains the text of choice for such a course, because it has strengths in social gerontology and the sociology of aging, the biology/physiology of aging, and the psychology of aging, and it reflects the multidisciplinary identity of the field.

The basic structure of this book has been retained from the prior edition. Part I introduces the study of aging and consists of three chapters. Chapter 1 discusses 10 myths about aging. Chapter 2 defines the field of gerontology, presents a history of aging, and includes updated material on methodological issues current in aging research. Chapter 3 presents the population dynamics and demographic characteristics of the aged, updated to include the most current data. Part II discusses material on the biomedical aspects of aging. Chapters 4 and 5 are devoted to the biological aspects of aging. Chapter 6 describes the health status of the elderly population, including mental health.

Part III places aging in psychological and sociological perspective. Separate chapters are devoted to the psychological aspects of aging (Chapter 7) and to sociological theories of aging (Chapter 9). Chapter 8 bridges the psychological and sociological approaches to aging. Part IV looks at the relationship between the aged and society. Chapter 10 presents material on the family life of older people, whereas Chapters 11, 12, and 13 deal, respectively, with the economics of aging; work, retirement, and leisure; and the politics of aging; respectively. Chapter 14 deals with the relationship between religion and aging.

Part V deals with special issues of concern for older people: the problems of racial and ethnic aging (Chapter 15); living environments (Chapter 16); long-term care (Chapter 17); health policies for the aged in the United States (Chapter 18); and death and dying (Chapter 19). The Epilogue has been rewritten to reflect the current educational and career opportunities in gerontology.

An additional feature of this edition is the selective placement throughout the book of website addresses. These are used to provide ease of access to additional information about aging, the aged, and social policy issues from government agencies, professional organizations, nonprofit and proprietary associations, and the like. Typically, a website address will appear only once after the first reference in the book to a government agency or other organization. We recognize that, as time passes between when website information is gathered and then published, some sites will have closed or moved to new addresses. Still, we hope that students and their professors alike will find this feature useful and that it will help both groups stay connected to the study of aging!

Eileen and Seamus Metress, Ruth Dunkle, and Van Luong are important contributors to this book through coauthorship of important chapters. I also wish to thank the reviewers of this edition: Chris Adamski-Mietus, Western Illinois University; Peggy Franklin, California State University, Fullerton; Donna Iams, University of Arizona, Tucson; William C. Lane, State University of New York at Cortland; and Marjorie Starrels, Colorado State University.

These are not the best of times in higher education. Budgets are tight and resources scarce. Nevertheless, the University of Toledo continues to be a productive environment for me. What is now the Department of Sociology and Anthropology has a hard-working, productive faculty and staff, as well as conscientious and congenial students. I have given up the Chair position and have already started to reap benefits from the time away from administrative matters.

By the time this edition appears, Michelle will have put up with over 30 years of this—we were in Alaska for our thirtieth anniversary! Through it all, she has remained a caring and loving partner, while at the same time pursuing her own career. I really have been lucky! In the preface to an earlier edition, I wrote that Renee was old enough for me to start thinking about her using this text in a college course. That time has long come and gone, as has her graduation from law school. She is creating a legal career in Atlanta. Jeremy has graduated with a B. A. in Anthropology and, with educational experiences in Ecuador and Costa Rica behind him, looks forward to starting graduate training in anthropology. The future is his to create. I have reason to be a proud father!

With the death of my mother, my family circle narrowed. May Ina (my sister) and Charlie remain healthy, happy, and prosperous; Stacey and Jamie are in the process of being "launched," and Illisa (State University of New York at Albany) is still hitting "winners." Carol (Michelle's sister) and Vincent were with us in Alaska and have already seen the joy of grandparenthood. With some bumps along the road, Grandpa Max and Grandma Sylvia stay active and in relatively good health. As with prior editions of this text, the sixth edition is formally dedicated to the memory of my mother and father, Eleanor and Irving Kart.

Cary S. Kart

My introduction to *The Realities of Aging* occurred in 1990, when I used the third edition in an introductory gerontology course that I taught as an assistant professor at Bowling Green State University. At that time, I admired the text for its comprehensive coverage of gerontological issues and respected the author's obvious commitment to capturing the complexity inherent in the processes of aging. It never occurred to me that fewer than 10 years later, I would be given the opportunity to join the author in this endeavor! I offer my sincere thanks to Dr. Cary S. Kart for sharing *Realities* with me, and for proving to be both an understanding colleague and a valued friend.

Although my involvement in this edition was initiated at a lunch meeting in February 1998, it was not until that summer, after I relocated to the Department of Sociology, Gerontology, and Anthropology, and the Scripps Gerontology Center at Miami University in Oxford, Ohio, that my efforts began in earnest. Writing is oftentimes a solitary pursuit. My new colleagues offered support and encouragement; I have found my "gerontological family"!

Formally, this book is dedicated to the memory of the only set of grandparents I knew, Ethel Martin Kinney and Cline Kinney, who taught me so very much, especially in their later years. I gratefully acknowledge the support of my parents, Pat and Jack Kinney, both of whom I appreciate more with each passing year, and Z. Michael Nagy, my partner for the past 10 years.

Jennifer M. Kinney

THE REALITIES OF AGING

FIRST THE GOOD NEWS...
THE MYTHS OF AGING

According to Greek mythology, Aurora, the goddess of the Dawn, was in love with Tithonus, a Trojan. Aurora asked Zeus to make Tithonus immortal, and Zeus agreed. But Aurora did not think to ask Zeus to allow Tithonus to retain his youthfulness. For a while, the lovers lived happily, but then the consequences of Aurora's error began to appear. Tithonus's hair turned gray, and soon he could move neither hand nor foot. He prayed for death, but there was no release for him. At last, in pity, Aurora left him alone in his room, locking the door behind her. As one version of the story goes, Tithonus still lies in that room, babbling endlessly (Hamilton 1942, p. 428).[1]

The myth of Tithonus reflects a number of themes relevant to contemporary life in the United States, not the least of which is the prevalent fear of old age and its concomitant hardships and infirmities. Some see this fear of growing old as the root of a negative attitude toward aging and old age, and of the tendency on the part of many Americans to avoid the word *old* and substitute euphemisms such as *golden years.* Surveys of individuals aged 18 years and over conducted by the National Council on the Aging <http://www.ncoa.org> show that, on average, Americans believe that the problems of older people are more severe than their own problems. Further, Ferraro (1992) reports that these surveys show that most Americans believe the problems of older people are more serious than do older persons themselves.

Dr. Robert N. Butler, winner of the Pulitzer prize for his 1975 book *Why Survive? Being Old in America,* coined the term **ageism** to describe this negative attitude toward aging and the aged. He equates ageism with racism and sexism and defines it as "a process of systematic stereotyping and discrimination against people because they are old" (Butler 1987, p. 22). Just as racism has generated unfortunate stereotypes of members of different racial groups, so too has ageism fostered unfortunate myths about old people and the aging process. Moreover, like racism, ageism has roots in the early American experience.

---

[1]Another version of the story maintains that Tithonus shrank in size until Aurora, with a feeling for the natural fitness of things, turned him into a skinny and noisy grasshopper.

According to historian David Hackett Fischer (1977), colonial America was a place in which age, not youth, was exalted and venerated, honored, and obeyed. This respect for older people found expression in a variety of forms, including the iconography of Puritanism, the distribution of honored seats in the meetinghouses of Massachusetts, and the patterns of office holding in church and state. Fashions were also designed to flatter age, and census data suggest that people attempted to enhance their status by reporting themselves as older than they actually were.

This era of *gerontophilia* was succeeded by a period of transformation (1780–1820) during which attitudes toward old age began to change. In the nineteenth century, Fischer (1977) argues, there was truly a revolution in age relations in the United States, evidenced by new expressions of contempt for the aged (such as *old fogey* and *geezer*), by the appearance of mandatory retirement policies, and by the development of a cult of youth in literature.

Fischer (1977) attributes the beginnings of this era of *gerontophobia* to two important factors. The first is demographic. Declines in both birth and death rates along with increases in life expectancy—long-term trends beginning in the colonial period—changed the age composition of the population in the United States. Old people increased in numbers as well as in the proportion of the population they constituted. Second, and perhaps more important according to Fischer, is the radical expansion of the ideas of equality and liberty that occurred during the late eighteenth and early nineteenth centuries. These ideas altered forever the conception of the world on which the old order had rested. Not only did the aged suffer the apparent misfortune of being identified with the old order but they were also a constant reminder of what the new order hoped to avoid: dependence, disease, failure, and sin.

Ageism is a cultural phenomenon whose long-standing acceptance crosscuts differences in age, region, and social class. Some theories of prejudice against racial and religious minorities also seem to help explain ageist attitudes in the United States. According to Levin and Levin (1980), people who hold unfavorable attitudes toward the aged are also apt to dislike blacks, the mentally ill, and the physically disabled. Laws (1995) argues that, more than prejudice, ageism is a form of oppression that limits those who are the object of that oppression and shapes the perceptions of those who hold ageist attitudes.

Ageism may be passed from generation to generation by means of *socialization* and other processes of transmission of culture. For example, Covey (1991) analyzes the extent to which older people have historically been characterized as avaricious and miserly in Western art and literature. He reminds his readers of Dickens's 1843 classic, *A Christmas Carol*, which introduces the character of Ebenezer Scrooge, who has become the contemporary archetype of the old miser.

In examining the artworks of the "old-age painter," European artist Hubert von Herkomer (1849–1914), McLerran (1993) argues that the positive images of aged seamstresses depicted in his popular late-nineteenth-century woodcuts and paintings were ageist in nature. They provided support for the view in England at that time that individuals could be redeemed by the work they performed. McLerran asserts that these images promoted the idea that the elderly were as able-bodied and capable of their own support as anyone else. Consequently, aged individuals who could not support themselves were deemed immoral and undeserving of help unless they agreed to a life of enforced labor in a squalid poorhouse. Seemingly, no account was made for diminishment of physical capacity that might accompany advanced age. From McLerran's perspective, the presentation of positive stereotypes of the aged were used in Victorian England to support an ageism that allowed for the institutionalization of the aged poor. The aged poor women in Herkomer's paintings were "doomed to conditions of squalor by an ideology of labor which allows no compromise" (p. 770). They were, in Victorian eyes, "saved by the hand that is not stretched out" (p. 770).

Cohen and Kruschwitz (1990) have examined popular sheet music published in the United States between 1830 and 1980 and found considerably more negative than positive sentiment about aging and old age. The 1912 song "Old Joe Has Had His Day" reflects a sad acceptance of old age:

> The marks are creeping on
> My hair is turning grey
> The springtime of life has faded
> With the flow'rs that grow by the way
> We, like roses, must wither and fade
> There's nothing comes to stay
> The allotted time is drawing near
> "Old Joe has had his day."

In a more contemporary vein, Paul Simon's song "Old Friends" presents an equally sad view of old age:

> Old friends,
> Sat on their park bench like bookends,
> A newspaper blows through the grass
> Falls on the round toes
> Of the high shoes
> Of the old friends...
> Can you imagine us
> Years from today
> Sharing a park bench quietly?
> How terribly strange to be 70,
> Old friends,
> Memory brushes the same years,
> Silently sharing the same fears.[2]

How is ageism perpetuated today? One way is through so-called commonsense observations. Everyday aphorisms ("You can't teach an old dog new tricks") reflect a common sense that is negative as well as inconsistent with scientific knowledge. Scientific knowledge can also reinforce negative stereotypes about old people. This was especially the case in the early post–World War II period, as

---

[2]Copyright © 1968 Paul Simon. Used by permission of the Publisher.

the study of aging began to develop (see Chapter 2). As Steffl (1978) points out, "Early research described characteristics of...aged congregated in poor farms, nursing homes, and state mental hospitals leading to a general picture of impaired elderly." Add to this picture the testimony of physicians and social workers, whose elderly clients were (and are) often physically and socially dependent. Finally, as Tibbitts (1979) suggests, the private agencies and public program bureaucracies helped perpetuate negative stereotypes by pleading with Congress for legislation on behalf of "the impaired, deprived, dependent elderly."

Myths and stereotypes of the elderly may also be transmitted through the mass media. Virtually all analyses of the content of television programming show an underrepresentation of older people in comparison to their numbers in the total population, as well as a striking imbalance in the ratio of older males to females. With few exceptions, it seems that most older characters portrayed on television are males, whereas, in reality, in the United States and virtually every other setting in the world, elderly women outnumber elderly men. Moreover, with some exceptions, the image of older people in television has been generally negative. Network and TV news shows often portray the elderly as victims of disasters (e.g., hurricanes or tornadoes) or as having some serious problem (e.g., homelessness or lack of access to health care) that is the basis for a human-interest story or editorial commentary. Even when TV advertisers make an appeal to older consumers, they often present overidealized images of exceptional health and involvement in vigorous activity. Public affairs and talk shows have been an island of exception in the sea of negativity. Generally, they have presented the greatest percentages of older people and the most positive image of the elderly (e.g., Hugh Downs and Barbara Walters). Still, this is not much of a middle ground. Television seems intent on denying the inevitability of old age. Old people are portrayed either as victims or as ideal types that too few could really hope to emulate.

Television is not the only mass medium in which stereotypes about old people have been found. Researchers have examined themes of aging as they have appeared in diverse media from children's books and fairy tales (Chinen 1987), to print advertising (DeRenzo & Malley 1992) and literature (Holstein 1994).

Images of Grandpa Simpson (from the cartoon show *The Simpsons*) notwithstanding, some research does indicate a positive shift in attitudes toward older persons. Austin (1985) reports a sample of midwestern university students more accepting of close relationships with older people than of close relationships with people who are disabled, including the blind, paraplegics, and the mentally retarded. Austin proposes that people have developed more positive attitudes toward old age in recent years as more older people have become visible in productive roles. This does not suggest that ageist attitudes have disappeared in U.S. society, only that, vis-à-vis other groups, older people are seen as productive and conforming to societal values.

Some exceptions to the generally negative television image of older people have also appeared in recent years. Bell (1992) analyzes the images of aging presented in five prime-time television programs in which older persons played a major character. These included *The Golden Girls; Murder She Wrote; In the Heat of the*

Night; Matlock; and *Jake and the Fatman.* (A number of these programs continue to appear in syndication on local television as well as cable stations.) Rather than appearing "comical, stubborn, eccentric, and foolish," Bell argues that the older characters portrayed in these programs are stereotyped more positively, appearing powerful, affluent, healthy, socially and mentally active, and widely admired. Also, during the late 1980s and into the 1990s, Hollywood put forth successful films with themes related to aging. These included *Driving Miss Daisy* (1989), *Fried Green Tomatoes* (1991), *The Joy Luck Club* (1993), *Nobody's Fool* (1994), *Down in the Delta* (1998), and *The Straight Story* (1999). A number of these films also gave esteemed older actors and actresses an opportunity to display their creative talents.

Many of today's aging TV and movie stars serve as as inspiration to middle-aged Baby Boomers. Harrison Ford (age 55), Goldie Hawn (52), Robert Redford (60), Morgan Freeman (60), and Barbra Streisand (56),[3] among many others, may help create new stereotypes of aging well. The risk is that these new images of aging will marginalize older people who are less successful, ill, or very old.

Ageism is likely to persist, however. Whether TV or movies or children's books are implicated or not, some research suggests that many young children already possess well-defined negative attitudes toward older people and the aging process (Corbin, Kagan, & Metil-Corbin 1987). Programmatic efforts may help overcome these attitudes. Fernandez-Pereiro and Sanchez-Ayendez (1992) report on a project in the Dominican Republic that focuses on early childhood development but enlists older people as an important educational resource. The project includes specific activities to give children a positive view of older people and of the aging process. The theory is that knowledge of the aging process and the development of positive attitudes toward old age can contribute to the improvement of intergenerational relationships, combat stereotypes that promote ageism, and prepare children for a more realistic approach to their own aging.

The theory may work. Aday, Sims, and Evans (1991) matched fourth-graders with elderly participants from a center for senior citizens in a nine-month intergenerational project on aging. Students developed significantly more positive views toward the elderly and these were maintained after a one-year follow-up. One student summarized what had been learned in the project as follows: "Older people are basically the same as us. They have a heart, they have feelings, and they depend on someone to help them when they need help" (p. 380).

Still, ageism can be a subtle and flexible foe. According to Binstock (1983), a past president of the Gerontological Society of America <http://www.geron.org>, new distortions of the reality of older people provided the foundation for the emergence of the aged as a scapegoat for a variety of economic and political frustrations in U.S. society. These distortions, identified by Binstock as classic examples of "tabloid thinking," included the belief that annual federal budget deficits in the United States in the range of $200 billion and more during the 1980s and into the

---

[3]These ages are reported on pages 32–40 of the March–April 1998 issue of *Modern Maturity.* Also identified in this article are individuals 65 years of age or older who are starring in TV and movies, including Clint Eastwood (67), Sean Connery (67), Lauren Bacall (73), and Sidney Poitier (71).

1990s resulted from insatiable demands by older people for additional Social Security <http://www.ssa.gov> and health benefits. From this view, generations of younger workers were to be taxed at burdensome levels in order to support social programs for the elderly (Villers Foundation 1987).

According to the Budget Committee of the U.S. House of Representatives (1986), however, were it not for Medicare and Social Security, the budget deficit would have been *substantially greater*. The committee notes that Social Security and Medicare <http://www.hcfa.gov> swung substantially out of deficit to balance and then surplus during the 1980s and into the 1990s, while the rest of the budget plunged deeply into deficit. Quadagno (1996) blames lack of funding for government programs for these deficits and cites two measures in particular: President Reagan's Economic Recovery Tax Act (ERTA) of 1981, which substantially cut taxes for individuals and corporations, and the Budget Enforcement Act (BEA) of 1990, which placed caps on spending for government social programs.

The increase in the elderly population has created demand for federal, state, and local programs to benefit this group. It is important to remember, however, that the biggest of these programs—Social Security, Medicare, and veterans' and civil service pensions—are not welfare programs. They are legal entitlements the elderly have earned with contributions made throughout their working years. Old people and the programs that benefit them cannot be held accountable for the massive federal budget deficits that have burdened the economy in recent decades. As Quadagno (1996) points out, entitlement spending in the United States has shown almost no growth since the mid-1970s; it was 11.3 percent of the gross domestic product (GDP)[4] in 1976 and 11.9 percent in 1994. Social Security has also remained steady at just over 4 percent of GDP since 1975.

Binstock (1983) identifies three important consequences for U.S. society of this scapegoating of the aged. First, it diverts attention from other public policy issues, including unemployment, poverty, and violence in society. Second, it produces conflict between generations as representatives of the young and the old battle for scarce resources. Third, it diminishes confidence in government and diverts attention from long-standing issues of equity and justice in public programs of support for people of all ages.

One aim of this book is to refute negative stereotypes and present a more realistic view of aging in the United States—a view that is more positive than many students of aging have admitted. Treat the following list of 10 statements about old people and the aging process as a quiz. Read each item carefully and indicate whether you believe it to be true or false.

_____   **1.** Senility inevitably accompanies old age.
_____   **2.** Most old people are alone and isolated from their families.
_____   **3.** The majority of old people are in poor health.
_____   **4.** Old people are more likely than younger people to be victimized by crime.
_____   **5.** The majority of old people live in poverty.

---

[4]The GDP is the total market value of all the goods and services produced and consumed in the United States in a given year.

    _____   **6.** Old people tend to become more religious as they age.

    _____   **7.** Older workers are less productive than younger ones.

    _____   **8.** Old people who retire usually suffer a decline in health and early death.

    _____   **9.** Most old people have no interest in, or capacity for, sexual relations.

    _____   **10.** Most old people end up in nursing homes and other long-term care institutions.

If you answered "false" to all 10 statements, you have a perfect score; "true" responses indicate misconceptions about old people and the aging process.

DEBUNKING THE MYTHS

MYTH 1: *Senility Inevitably Accompanies Old Age*

Cervantes wrote the second part of *Don Quixote* in his sixty-eighth year. Verdi composed the opera *Falstaff* in his eightieth year. Barbara McClintock, a noted geneticist, won a National Medal of Science at age 68, the first MacArthur Laureate Award at age 79, and a Nobel prize in physiology at age 81. Goethe completed *Faust* when he was 83 years old; Bach dictated the final chorale to *Art of the Fugue* from his death bed in his mid-sixties; Marcel Duchamp, considered by many art professionals to be the greatest artist of the twentieth century, was productive right up to his death in his eighty-first year (Simonton 1990; Pritikin 1990); and heartthrob actor Paul Newman received an Academy Award nomination for Best Actor for the 1994 movie, *Nobody's Fool,* in his seventieth year.

    These are individuals whose quality of achievement was not diminished by age. This myth is part of the conventional view that aging brings with it a decline in intelligence, memory, learning, and creativity. Yet, empirical evidence shows that these relationships are quite complex, and decline is anything but inevitable. Age-related changes in learning ability appear to be quite small, even after the keenness of the senses has begun to decline. Similarly, although creativity seems to peak in the forties, the age-related decline thereafter is such that creators in their sixties and seventies will still be generating new ideas at a rate exceeding their rate in their twenties (Dennis 1966; Simonton 1990). Memory and learning are functions of the central nervous system. Thus, when there is impairment, it is often due to some disease (e.g., arteriosclerosis) or an associated condition; one should not assume that some typical process of normal aging is at work.

MYTH 2: *Most Old People Are Alone and Isolated from Their Families*

Research on the history of family relations in the United States and Europe has contradicted myths about a so-called Golden Age in the family relations of older people in days past. Apparently, those extended families (three or more generations living together) that have become part of the folklore of modern society rarely existed in the past (Laslett 1977). Historical research has similarly dispelled the myth of the contemporary American nuclear family isolated from adult children and other kin. Nuclear family members continue to maintain strong traditional and reciprocal relations, and the expectation that family and kin carry the major responsibilities for the care of aged relatives is still strong in the United States. However, there is growing concern that families do not have the necessary supports available to discharge these responsibilities (Litwak 1985).

As Hareven (1994) asserts, the family has ceased to be the only available source of support for dependent members. Starting in the nineteenth century and continuing through today, the family has surrendered to the public sector functions of social welfare it previously controlled. Increasingly, there are ambiguities about who exactly provides what for the elderly.

> On the one hand, family members assume that the public sector carries the major responsibilities of care for the aged; on the other hand, the public sector assumes that the family is responsible for the major supports. This confusion in the assignment of responsibilities often means that old people are caught between the family and the public sector without receiving proper supports from either. (Hareven 1994, p. 456)

Compounding these ambiguities is a revolution in the demography of intergenerational family life, with individuals growing older in more diverse familial settings than ever before (Bengtson, Rosenthal, & Burton 1990). Shanas (1980) estimates that about 50 percent of people over age 65 are members of four-generation families, and Hagestad (1988) reports that 20 percent of women who died after the age of 80 were great-great-grandmothers, members of five-generation families.

Changes in the configurations of families have also resulted from increases in divorce and remarriage. However, as many readers know from their own experience, divorce does not necessarily reduce the extent or strength of ties between older family members and kin. For example, ties with grandparents do survive divorce, especially when the grandparents have had close contact with the grandchildren before divorce. Also, with remarriage, the kinship pool expands with the addition of new relatives, without the relinquishment of existing ones.

Most older people live near, but not with, their children and interact with them frequently. And most older people prefer it this way. Assistance in the form of goods and services, as well as financial aid, flows both from adult children to their parents and from the parents to their children. Grandparents and older family members may provide care for young children within the extended family network, and adult children may act as caregivers to parents and other relatives with chronic illnesses and/or cognitive deficits.

Despite the commitment to independent living in nuclear households, in virtually all ethnic and racial groups, these households expand to include other kin in times of need, especially when older parents and widowed mothers are unable to maintain themselves in separate households (Hareven 1994). In the National Survey of Families and Households, only 7 percent of Americans aged 55 and older with a surviving parent reported that the parent was living with them at the time of the survey, yet about one in four of those in their late fifties had an aged parent live with them for some time in their lives (Hogan, Eggebeen, & Snaith 1994). Pelham and Clark (1987) state that Latino American and Asian American widows are more likely to be living with other family members than white and African American widows. The large household size and larger number of offspring among Latino American widows suggests that they may have more active support systems than do other racial and ethnic groups.

MYTH 3: *The Majority of Old People Are in Poor Health*

I recently asked a group of third-year medical students what proportion of older people they believed were sick and institutionalized. The consensus was that more than half the older population are in ill health, and perhaps half of that population (25 percent of the total) are in institutions. *This simply is not the case.* These answers reflected the fact that in their clinical experiences, these medical students come into contact with only sick and disabled elderly persons.

The majority of older people do *not* have the kinds of health problems that limit their ability to be employed or manage their own households. Only about 5 percent of those age 65 and over can be found in an old-age institution on a given day. Data from the National Health Interview Surveys <http://www.cdc.gov/nchswww/about/major/nhis/nhis.htm>, conducted annually by the National Center for Health Statistics to assess the health status and needs of the noninstitutionalized population in the United States, consistently show about two-thirds of those 65 years of age and older reporting their health status in positive terms (good, very good, or excellent); about one-third report themselves as being in fair or poor health (Cohen, Van Nostrand, & Furner 1993). Although the proportion of older adults who rate their health in positive terms seems to decline with age, more than 60 percent of the oldest-old (those 85 years of age and over) continue to evaluate their health status positively.

Self-assessment of health status is one important measure of the health condition of a population; another is how that population is functioning. Wiener and associates (1990) explain that across 11 different national surveys, 5 to 8 percent of community-dwelling elderly receive help in one or more of the activities of daily living (ADLs): bathing, dressing, moving out of beds and chairs, toileting, and eating. Hing and Bloom (1990) define *functional dependency* as needing help in at least one of seven ADLs or one of seven instrumental activities of daily living (IADLs). IADLs include preparing meals, shopping, managing money, using the telephone, getting outside, and doing light or heavy housework. Under this definition, Hing and Bloom (1990) estimate that 6.7 million elderly, or less than one in four, are functionally dependent. Functional dependencies are more prevalent

In later life, many older adults enjoy themselves more than they did in their middle years.

among women than men, among African Americans and Latino Americans than whites, and increase with age. Still, it is clear that the vast majority of individuals 65 years of age and older live independently in the community with no functional dependencies!

MYTH 4: *Old People Are More Likely than Younger People to Be Victimized by Crime*

Concerns about crimes against elderly Americans are quite high—especially among elderly Americans themselves. Many surveys show that old persons are more fearful of crime than younger persons. This concern appears to stem from the popular belief that elderly persons are victimized more often than others and suffer more serious consequences as a result. Yet, no evidence supports this belief.

National and local surveys show that the elderly are actually *less* likely to be victimized than are younger persons, in all crime categories. Data from the U.S. Bureau of Justice Statistics <http://www.ojp.usdoj.gov/bjs>, for example, show that when compared with rates of victimization against persons 12 years old and over, the elderly have lower rates of victimization in all categories of crime (U.S. Bureau of the Census 1998, Table 347). Further, differences in rates of victimization of the elderly and the general population are so great that even factoring in substantial underreporting by older people does not equalize the rates of victimization. For example, the rate of victimization of the elderly by robbery was only about one-fifth that for the total 12-year-old and over population in 1996. The elderly were victimized by personal theft at a rate only 47 percent of that for the total population in 1996, and at a rate only 21 percent of that for adolescents 12 to 15 years of age.

Despite these comparisons of rates of actual criminal victimization between the elderly and the general population, there is no getting away from the fact that many older people are fearful of crime. For some, this fear is so great that they can be described as living under virtual house arrest. And, for certain subgroups of elderly people, there is some reality to these fears. Many urban aged persons, including minority elderly, live in central-city neighborhoods where the crime rate is high. Many of these same elderly persons live alone and rely on public transportation, which makes them available for victimization. Add reduced strength and diminished vision to the equation, and it is easy to understand why some elderly people feel particularly vulnerable to crime, even though national data suggest such fears are disproportionate to the reported levels of victimization.

MYTH 5: *The Majority of Old People Live in Poverty*

It used to be easy to write about the economic problems of the old. The situation today, though more complex, is much improved. For example, in 1996, while 10.8 percent of those 65 years of age and older in the United States had incomes below the poverty threshold, 13.7 percent of the total U.S. civilian noninstitutionalized population could be similarly characterized. Many private and public programs have been developed in recent decades to deal with the economic problems of old age. According to Schulz (1995), these programs include the following:

1. Substantial increases in Social Security old-age benefits in recent years—a faster rate of climb than inflation in the same period
2. Widespread and rapid growth of private pension plans, with increased benefit levels
3. Creation of public health insurance and nutrition programs
4. Legislation of property tax and other tax-relief laws in virtually all states
5. Increased benefit levels within the Supplemental Security Income (SSI) Program <http://www.ssa.gov/pubs/11000.html>, which now covers more than twice as many low-income elderly as did the now abolished old-age assistance plan

However, certain subgroups among the elderly continue to show relatively high rates of impoverishment: Approximately one in four (25.3 percent) elderly African Americans had incomes below the poverty threshold in 1996, and this rate expanded to 29.0 percent among African Americans aged 75 years and older.

Part of the complexity in analyzing the economic situation of the aged stems from the fact that they receive money income from so many available sources. Wages and salaries, retirement benefits, veterans' benefits, unemployment insurance, workers' compensation, public assistance, dividends, interest, rents, royalties, private pensions, and annuities are only some of their sources of money income. In recent years, the composition of total income of the elderly has shifted slightly toward earnings and pensions and away from property income and Social Security benefits (Radner 1991). Approximately three out of four aged Americans own homes, and most have substantial equity in these homes. Finally, the elderly receive indirect or in-kind income in the form of goods and services that they obtain free or at reduced cost. Medicare, food stamps, and housing subsidies are examples of programs that provide in-kind benefits to older people.

MYTH 6: *Old People Tend to Become More Religious as They Age*

Religion serves a variety of functions in human societies. It defines the spiritual world and provides explanations for events and occurrences that are difficult to comprehend. Further, it helps integrate people into the broader community in at least two ways. First, institutionally based religious services provide a physical meeting ground for unattached and disaffiliated people. Second, religious ideas arise out of the collective experience of individuals. As a result, the content of religious belief systems expresses a vision of a shared fate of believers, a community of individuals with otherwise diverse interests and aspirations. Thus, religion functions both to maintain social control and to provide social support in times of need.

Do these functions change over time, as individuals and their families age and move through individual and family developmental periods? Much research supports a lifetime stability model (Levin 1989). On the one hand, findings suggest that *organizational* religious involvement, such as attendance at religious services, is stable over the life course, with some slight decline at advanced ages, especially among those who are disabled. On the other hand, indicators of *nonorganizational* religious involvement, such as watching religious television shows or praying at home, remain stable as people age, with some slight chance of increase among the very old and disabled to offset declines in organizational involvement.

MYTH 7: *Older Workers Are Less Productive than Younger Ones*

This myth, based on misconceptions about the aging process and the employment of older people, is often raised by proponents of mandatory retirement. The argument assumes that older persons, as a group, may be less well suited for work than younger workers because older people do not learn new skills as well as younger persons do, older workers are less flexible with respect to changes in work schedules and regimens, and declining physical and mental capacity are found in greater proportion among older persons.

These arguments are not based on fact. Many studies indicate that older workers produce a quality of work that is as good as or better than that of younger workers. In addition, older workers bring significant benefits to the workplace, including flexibility in scheduling, low absenteeism, high motivation, and mentoring of younger workers. There is no reason to expect a decline in intellectual capacities with age and every reason to assume that older workers in good health are capable of learning new skills when circumstances require it.

Still, the employment situation of older Americans is quite varied (Quinn & Burkhauser 1990). Since 1950, when nearly half of all men aged 65 and over were in the labor force, the rates of labor-force participation have decreased dramatically. Today, only about 17 percent of older men are in the labor force. The trends for older women are less dramatic, with a modest increase evident in work-force participation since 1980 (from 8.1 to 8.6 percent). Those elderly people who do work are likely to work part time, and the proportion of the elderly working part time has increased over the last 20 years to almost 50 percent of men and 60 percent of women. The elderly people still in the labor force are three times more likely to be self-employed than is the general population, and almost twice as likely as those aged 55 to 64. One study suggests that the official counts greatly underestimate the actual number of self-employed elderly persons (Haber, Lamas, & Lichtenstein 1987).

Interestingly, the declining birthrate means a proportionately smaller labor force will be supporting a larger retiree population. The potentially problematic economics of this situation could be alleviated by inducing older workers to *remain* in the labor force and retirees to *return* to the workplace. According to one study, reported on in *Working Age*, a newsletter published by the American Association of Retired Persons (AARP) <http://www.aarp.org>, less than 10 percent of U.S. companies have formal hiring policies or programs to recruit retirees to return to the workplace. Nevertheless, as recently as 1991, 46 percent of U.S. businesses reported employing retirees. Most of these people had retired from other firms (AARP 1993).

Obstacles to change in the labor-force participation rates of the elderly remain great, however. Jondrow, Brechling, and Marcus (1987) argue that many, perhaps most, workers would like to retire gradually. Most do not because they cannot. Part-time wage rates are generally much lower than full-time compensation, and only a small minority of firms permit phased retirement.

MYTH 8: *Old People Who Retire Usually Suffer a Decline in Health and an Early Death*

It is widely held that retirement has an adverse affect on health. Most people have heard at least one story about a retiree who "went downhill fast." The way the story usually goes is that the individual carefully plans for retirement, only to become sick and die within a brief period of time—and the story is the same regardless of whether the retirement is mandatory or voluntary.

One problem with such stories is that they are never clear as to what the health status of the retiree was before retirement. Another problem is that most retirees themselves are older, and although the majority of old people do not have major health problems, it is true that older people have a greater risk of illness than younger people do. In a classic study in gerontology, *Retirement in American Society,* Streib and Schneider (1971) concluded that retired people were no more likely to be sick than were people of the same age who remained on the job. That is, *health declines appear to be associated with age, not with retirement!* In fact, as some researchers have pointed out, unskilled workers and others who work in harsh environments and in high-risk occupations may show *improvements* in health following retirement.

MYTH 9: *Most Old People Have No Interest in, or Capacity for, Sexual Relations*

Sexual interests, capacities, and functions change with age. Nevertheless, older men and women in reasonably good health can have active and satisfying sex lives. Verwoerdt, Pfeiffer, and Wang (1969a, 1969b) at Duke University studied 254 men and women ranging from 60 to 94 years of age and found no age-related decline in the incidence of sexual interest. In fact, interest may persist indefinitely. Most important, these researchers found that sexual behavior patterns of the later years correlate with those of the younger years. If there was interest and satisfying activity in the early years, there is likely to be continuing interest and satisfying activity in the later years as well.

Some decline in sexual activity among the old is due to old people's acceptance of stereotypes about the sexless older years. Elderly people may feel shame and embarrassment about having sexual interests. Further, some older people relate normal changes in sexual functioning and impotence, and so avoid sexual opportunities because they fear failure. Fulton (1988) suggests that some responsibility for acceptance of sexuality among the aged must rest with those in the helping professions: "Support and encouragement of sexual behavior should be given without embarrassment or evangelization" (p. 282).

Older people need not duplicate the sexual behavior of youth in order to enjoy their sexual experiences. Sex is qualitatively different in the later years. Sexual activity in the elderly may fulfill the human need for the warmth of physical closeness and the intimacy of companionship. Older people should be encouraged to seek this fulfillment.

MYTH 10: *Most Old People End Up in Nursing Homes and Other Long-Term Care Institutions*

Most old people do *not* end up in nursing homes. The 1990 U.S. Census reports about 5 percent of the elderly population residing in old-age institutions of one kind or another. Still, this does not mean that the odds of being institutionalized are 1 in 20. The Census merely gives a picture of the institutional population at only one point in time.

In 1976, Palmore of Duke University reviewed the cases of 207 individuals from the Piedmont, North Carolina, area who were studied in the Duke First Longitudinal Study of Aging beginning in 1955 until their deaths prior to the spring of 1976. He observed that 54 of the 207 persons, or 26 percent, had been institutionalized in some type of extended-care facility one or more times before death. On the basis of this and other findings, Palmore concluded that, among normal elderly persons living in the community, the chance of institutionalization before death would be about one in four. Other researchers, using different populations and different methods, have substantiated these findings. This suggests that three in four aged persons have no reason to view a nursing home stay as inevitable.

SUMMARY

This brief chapter opened with a look at the mythological Tithonus, an unfortunate man who suffered the infirmities of old age endlessly. Actually, this myth appears in the middle of a Homeric hymn describing an adventure of Aphrodite, the goddess of Love (Evelyn-White 1936). It seems that Aphrodite had considerable power over other gods. She was often able to beguile them into mating with mere mortals, an act considered demeaning. To temper her arrogance, Zeus managed to infect her with desire for Anchises, a handsome Trojan (and a mortal himself).

Aphrodite arranged a rendezvous with Anchises, but after the lovemaking, Anchises, concerned about his ability to sustain a love affair with the goddess, begged Aphrodite to do something to preserve his good health. At first, Aphrodite seemed sympathetic to Anchises, but then she recounted to him the myth of Tithonus. She emphasized that she would not want Anchises to be deathless if he had to suffer the fate of Tithonus. Unwilling to grant him "youthful immortality," Aphrodite finally turned down Anchises's request with these words: "But as it is, harsh old age will soon enshroud you—ruthless old age which stands someday at the side of every man, deadly, wearying, dreaded even by the gods" (cited in Evelyn-White 1936).

Although most people in U.S. society *do* live to experience old age (about 80 percent of those born today can expect to reach age 65), not many expect to endure as Tithonus has. And although some in the United States do experience the harsh and ruthless old age that Aphrodite described for Anchises, many do not. Further, the debunking of prevalent myths about aging and the aged does not require that old people reflect the mirror opposite of ageism: Old people do not have to be intellectually gifted, happy, wealthy, and sexually active. Rather, the myths of aging discussed here simply suggest the diversity of aging experiences represented in society. The rest of this book explores the biological, psychological, and social factors that contribute to this wide range in the experience of old age.

STUDY QUESTIONS

1. Is the myth of Tithonus relevant to aging in contemporary society? How so?

2. Define the term *ageism*. What are its origins and how is it perpetuated today? In what ways do the mass media (e.g., TV, movies, books) play a special role in maintaining myths about the aged?

3. Why do gerontologists argue that senility is not an inevitable part of the aging process?

4. A common misconception is that most old people are alone and isolated from their families. Present evidence to the contrary.

5. What is the health status of people 65 years of age and older in the United States? Discuss this in terms of their ability to work and carry out other daily activities, their risks of being institutionalized, and their capacity for sexual relations.

6. Why has analyzing the economic position of older people become so complex? What has occurred in recent decades to improve the economic position of older people relative to the population as a whole?

REFERENCES

Aday, R. H., Sims, C. R., & Evans, E. (1991). Youth's attitudes toward the elderly: The impact of intergenerational partners. *Journal of Applied Gerontology, 10* (3), 372–384.

American Association of Retired Persons. (1993). Small businesses hire retirees. *Working Age, 9* (3), 2.

Austin, D. R. (1985). Attitudes toward old age: A hierarchical study. *Gerontologist, 25* (4), 431–434.

Bahr, H. (1970). Aging and religious disaffiliation. *Social Forces, 49,* 59–71.

Bell, J. (1992). In search of discourse on aging: The elderly on television. *Gerontologist, 32* (3), 305–311.

Bengtson, V., Rosenthal, C., & Burton, L. (1990). Families and aging: Diversity and heterogeneity. In R. H. Binstock & L. K. George (Eds.), *Handbook of aging and the social sciences* (3rd ed.). San Diego, CA: Academic.

Binstock, R. H. (1983). The aged as scapegoat. *Gerontologist, 23* (2), 136–143.

Butler, R. (1975). *Why survive? Being old in America.* New York: Harper & Row.

Butler, R. (1987). Ageism. In G. Maddox (Ed.), *The encyclopedia of aging.* New York: Springer.

Chinen, A. B. (1987). Fairy tales and psychological development in late life: A cross-cultural hermeneutic study. *Gerontologist, 27* (3), 340–352.

Cohen, E. S., & Kruschwitz, A. L. (1990). Old age in America represented in nineteenth and twentieth century popular sheet music. *Gerontologist, 30* (3), 345–354.

Cohen, R. A., Van Nostrand, J. F., & Furner, S. E. (1993). *Health data on older Americans, 1992.* DHHS Publication No. (PHS) 93-1413. Hyattsville, MD: National Center for Health Statistics.

Congressional Budget Office. (1994). *Reducing the deficit.* Washington, DC: U.S. Government Printing Office.

Corbin, D. E., Kagan, D. M., & Metil-Corbin, J. (1987). Content analysis of an intergenerational unit in aging in a sixth grade classroom. *Educational Gerontology, 13,* 403–410.

Covey, H. C. (1991). Old age and historical examples of the miser. *Gerontologist, 31* (5), 673–678.

Dennis, W. (1966). Creative productivity between the ages of 20 and 80 years. *Journal of Gerontology, 21,* 1–8.

DeRenzo, E. G., & Malley, J. (1992). Increasing use of ageist language in skin-care product advertising: 1969 through 1988. *Journal of Women and Aging, 4* (3), 105–126.

Evelyn-White, H. G. (1936). *Hesiod, The Homeric hymns and Homerica.* London: William Heinemann.

Fernandez-Pereiro, A., & Sanchez-Ayendez, M. (1992). LinkAges: Building bridges between children and the elderly. *Ageing International, 19* (2), 10–14.

Ferraro, K. F. (1992). Self and older-people referents in evaluating life problems. *Journal of Gerontology, 47* (3), S105–S114.

Fischer, D. H. (1977). *Growing old in America.* New York: Oxford.

Fulton, G. B. (1988). Sexuality in later life. In C. S. Kart, E. K. Metress, & S. P. Metress. *Aging, health and society.* Boston: Jones and Bartlett.

Haber, S. E., Lamas, E. J., & Lichtenstein, J. H. (1987). On their own: The self-employed and others in private business. *Monthly Labor Review, 72,* 716–724.

Hagestad, G. O. (1988). Demographic change and the life course: Some emerging trends in the family realm. *Family Relations, 37,* 405–410.

Hamilton, E. (1942). *Mythology.* Boston: Little, Brown.

Hareven, T. (1994). Aging and generational relations: A historical and life course perspective. In J. Hagan & K. S. Cook (Eds.), *Annual review of sociology* (Vol. 20). Palo Alto, CA: Annual Reviews.

Hing, E., & Bloom, B. (1990). *Long-term care for the functionally dependent elderly.* Vital and Health Statistics, Series 13, No. 104, DHHS Pub. No.

(PHS) 90-1765. Hyattsville, MD: Public Health Service.

Hogan, D. P., Eggebeen, D. J., & Snaith, S. M. (1994). The well-being of aging Americans with very old parents. In T. K. Hareven (Ed.), *Aging and generational relations over the life course: A historical and cross-cultural perspective.* Berlin: Walter de Gruyter.

Holstein, M. (1994). Taking next steps: Gerontological education, research, and the literary imagination. *Gerontologist, 34* (6), 822–827.

Jondrow, J., Brechling, F., & Marcus, A. (1987). Older workers in the market for part-time employment. In S. H. Sandell (Ed.), *The problem isn't age: Work and older Americans.* New York: Praeger.

Laslett, P. (1977). *Family life and illicit love in earlier generations.* Cambridge, England: Cambridge University Press.

Laws, G. (1995). Understanding ageism: Lessons from feminism and postmodernism. *Gerontologist, 35,* 112–118.

Levin, J. (1989). Religious factors in aging, adjustment and health: A theoretical review. In W. M. Clements (Ed.), *Religion, aging and health.* New York: Haworth (for the World Health Organization).

Levin, J., & Levin, W. C. (1980). *Prejudice and discrimination against the elderly.* Belmont, CA: Wadsworth.

Litwak, E. (1985). *Helping the elderly: The complementary roles of informal networks and formal systems.* New York: Guilford.

McLerran, J. (1993). Saved by the hand that is not stretched out: The aged poor in Hubert von Herkomer's *Eventide: A Scene in the Westminster Union. Gerontologist, 33* (6), 762–771.

Palmore, E. (1976). Total chance of institutionalization among the aged. *Gerontologist, 16,* 504–507.

Pelham, A. O., & Clark, W. F. (1987). Widowhood among low income racial and ethnic groups in California. In H. Lopata (Ed.), *Widows, Vol. 2: North America.* Durham, NC: Duke University Press.

Pritikin, R. (1990). Marcel Duchamp, the artist, and the social expectations of aging. *Gerontologist, 30* (5), 636–639.

Quadagno, J. (1996). Social Security and the myth of the entitlement "crisis." *Gerontologist, 36* (3), 391–399.

Quinn, J. F., & Burkhauser, R. V. (1990). Work and retirement. In R. H. Binstock & L. K. George (Eds.), *Handbook of aging and the social sciences* (3rd ed.). San Diego, CA: Academic.

Radner, D. (1991). Changes in incomes of age groups, 1984–89. *Social Security Bulletin, 54* (12), 2–28.

Schulz, J. H. (1995). *The economics of aging* (6th ed.). Westport, CT: Auburn.

Shanas, E. (1980). Older people and their families: The new pioneers. *Journal of Marriage and the Family, 42,* 9–15.

Simonton, D. K. (1990). Creativity in the later years: Optimistic prospects for achievement. *Gerontologist, 30* (5), 626–631.

Smith, M. C. (1976). Portrayal of elders in prescription drug advertising: A pilot study. *Gerontologist, 16,* 329–334.

Steffl, B. M. (1978). Gerontology in professional and pre-professional curricula. In M. Seltzer, H. Sterns, & T. Hickey (Eds.), *Gerontology in higher education: Perspectives and issues.* Belmont, CA: Wadsworth.

Streib, G., & Schneider, C. (1971). *Retirement in American society.* Ithaca, NY: Cornell University Press.

Tibbitts, C. (1979). Can we invalidate negative stereotypes of aging? *Gerontologist, 19* (1), 10–20.

U.S. Bureau of the Census. (1998). *Statistical abstract of the United States: 1998* (118th ed.). Washington, DC: U.S. Government Printing Office.

U.S. House of Representatives, Committee on the Budget. 1986. *President Reagan's fiscal year 1987 budget.* Washington, DC: U.S. Government Printing Office.

Verwoerdt, A., Pfeiffer, E., & Wang, H. S. (1969a). Sexual behavior in senescence. I. *Journal of Geriatric Psychiatry, 2,* 163–180.

Verwoerdt, A., Pfeiffer, E., & Wang, H. S. (1969b). Sexual behavior in senescence. II. *Geriatrics, 24,* 137–154.

Villers Foundation. (1987). *On the other side of easy street: Myths and facts about the economics of old age.* Washington, DC: Author.

Wiener, J. M., Hanley, R. J., Clark, R., & Van Nostrand, J. F. (1990). Measuring the activities of daily living: Comparisons across national surveys. *Journals of Gerontology: Social Sciences, 45* (6), S229–S237.

CHAPTER TWO

THE STUDY OF AGING

Concerns about aging and death are found in the written and oral records of societies dating back many thousands of years. One of the most prominent themes reflects the belief that extended life is neither possible nor desirable; another, by contrast, refers to the desirability of attempting to lengthen life. Clearly, the latter has been the most prevalent throughout history.

Three different themes represent the quest for the prolongation of life (Gruman 1966). The *antediluvian theme*—the belief that in the past, people lived much longer—is best exemplified in the book of Genesis, which records the life spans of 10 Hebrew patriarchs who lived before the Flood. Noah lived for 950 years, Methuselah for 969 years, Adam for 930 years, and so on. The *hyperborean theme* involves the idea that in some remote part of the world there are people who enjoy remarkably long lives. According to the traditions of ancient Greece, a people live *hyper Boreas* ("beyond the north wind"): "Their hair crowned with golden bay-leaves they hold glad revelry; and neither sickness nor baneful eld mingleth among the chosen people; but, aloof from toil and conflict, they dwell afar" (Pindar in Gruman 1966, p. 22).

Finally, the *fountain theme* is based on the idea that there is some unusual substance that has the property of greatly increasing the length of life. The search for the Fountain of Youth in 1513 by Juan Ponce de Leon (who accidentally discovered Florida instead) is a good example of this rejuvenation theme. According to the earliest account of Ponce de Leon's adventure, published by a Spanish official in the New World in 1535, the explorer was "seeking that fountain of Biminie that the Indians had given to be understood would renovate or resprout and refresh the age and forces of he who drank or bathed himself in that fountain" (Gruman 1966).

These themes remain current. The fascination with reportedly long-lived peoples such as the Abkhasians of the Georgian Republic of Russia (see Chapter 5) reflects a modern-day hyperborean theme. Similarly, any student of U.S. billboard and television advertising will recognize the fountain theme. Skin creams, hair colorings, body soaps, foods, and vitamins are all depicted as unusual substances that one may use to remain eternally young.

The persistence of these themes suggests that throughout history and up to the present, it has been difficult to distinguish between myth and history, between magic and science. The development of the systematic study of aging can be seen in this light, for it is these very distinctions that it attempts to make clear.

WHY STUDY AGING?

Why study aging? At first, the question may seem odd, but that is because individuals are so rarely asked to explain why they chose to work in a particular substantive area or why they chose one discipline over another (e.g., gerontology instead of demography). The answer comes in five parts.

1. Despite what has been written about the long history of aging, aging itself is a relatively new phenomenon. Never before have so many people lived to be old. Historian Ronald Blythe (1979) suggests that if a Renaissance or Georgian man could return, he would be just as astonished by the sight of so many elderly people as he would be by a computer. In his world, it was the exception to go gray, to retire, to grow old. Today, this process is ordinary, but that does not make it any less novel. This is a real-life experiment of sorts. As Blythe points out, these "are the first generations of the full-timers and thus the first generations of old people for whom the state…is having to make special supportive conditions." The novelty, the experimentation, and the uncertainty all make gerontology an exciting field today, and that excitement has drawn many people to the study of aging.

2. Students of gerontology have come to view aging as a lifelong process in which humans and all other living things participate. From this perspective, aging is seen as ongoing, starting at conception and ending with death. Aging is not reserved for senior citizens or Golden Agers; it is shared by infants, children, teenagers, and young adults, as well as the more mature. It occupies the total life span, not merely the final stage of life. Without knowledge and understanding of the entire life span, it is difficult to understand the events of any one life phase. In this sense, one studies the aged to learn not only about the final phase of life but also about youth and the middle years.

3. Many sociologists, psychologists, and others study aging because they see the later years as a strategic site for examining a wide range of scientific issues of fundamental importance in their disciplines. Examples of these issues include status maintenance (Henratta & Campbell 1976), role multiplicity (Moen, Dempster-McClain, & Williams 1992), and social support (Hogan & Eggebeen 1995).

4. Another reason to study aging has to do simply with the dramatic increase in interest in the problems of old people in the United States. Although it has been said sardonically that people admire aging only in bottles, in recent decades, as more people have encountered old age, many elaborate programs have been promoted and financed on behalf of elderly citizens. One reason for the promotion of these governmental and nongovernmental programs is that the situation of the elderly has come to be defined by many as the responsibility of society as a whole. The burden of this responsibility is reason enough for studying the aged. Only by knowing more about elderly people and the difficulties and changes they face can society realistically come to grips with its problems.

5. Different matters hold intrinsic fascination for different scientists. This may explain, in part, why some choose the field of gerontology. We find the study of aging intrinsically exciting and interesting. For us, as for many others, one answer to the question "Why study aging?" is "Because the study of aging can become an end in itself."

DEFINING THE FIELD

Gerontology is the term used to describe "the study of aging from the broadest perspective" (National Institute on Aging 1986). Though gerontology may include the study of aging in plants and animals below humans on the evolutionary scale, the term generally refers to the study of later adulthood among humans.

Gerontology is an interdisciplinary study. Its major elements are drawn from the physical and social sciences, although the humanities and arts, business, and education are also represented in the content of gerontology. In 1954, Clark Tibbitts, a pioneer in the modern scientific era of gerontology, introduced the term *social gerontology* to describe the study of the impact of social and sociocultural factors on the aging process. Tibbitts and others recognized that aging does not occur in a vacuum. Rather, the aging process occurs in some social context—a social context that helps determine the meaning of aging as both an individual and a societal experience. Gerontology is not only an academic discipline but it is also a field of practice that involves aspects of public policy and human service. In 1909, a Vienna-born physician, I. L. Nascher, coined the term *geriatrics* to describe one subfield of gerontological practice: the medical care of the aging.

The student of aging faces three main tasks: theoretical, methodological, and applied (Bromley 1974). The *theoretical* task involves confirming and extending the conceptual frameworks that explain the observed facts of aging. The *methodological* task involves developing suitable methods of research for examining the nature of aging. The *applied* task involves attempts to prevent or reduce the adverse effects of aging. Some gerontologists specialize in one or another task area; others find it difficult to separate theory, research, and practice. Gerontology is not a disinterested science. For many gerontologists, apparently, understanding the aging process is not enough. They must also address the practical and immediate problems of old people.

Gerontology is a complex field, encompassing a wide variety of substantive areas of study—health, family life, political economy, and retirement, among others. Yet, there are no dominant paradigms in the broader field; and standardization of measurement, a common conceptualization of issues, and systematic testing of hypotheses derived from theory are often lacking (Maddox & Wiley 1976). As Maddox and Wiley point out, applied, problem-oriented studies of the societal consequences of aging have dominated the field. This book reflects these facts; it introduces undergraduate and beginning graduate students to the major concepts and issues in the field of gerontology. In doing so, however, this text recognizes the current state of affairs in gerontology. It recognizes, first, the importance of making the connection between basic and applied research without downplaying the role applied research has played in the development of gerontology or the need for additional research at a basic level. Second, it recognizes the need to bring diverse disciplinary and interdisciplinary approaches to the study of aging.

THE HISTORY OF AGING

The study of aging is now considered to be scientific. As has been seen, however, particular nonscientific themes in concepts of human aging have persisted with some consistency through the prescientific and into the scientific era. This is especially clear when one looks at the imagery in discussions of the causes of aging. Bromley (1974) summarizes this imagery in three categories. In the first, the body is a container full of some essential substance or spirit. This substance is gradually depleted or destroyed, leading to diminished capacities and increased vulnerability to disease and death. In the second image, aging represents a conflict within each person between positive and negative forces. Eventually, the negative forces of evil, disease, corruption, and the like prevail. Finally, aging is seen as symbolizing a process of renewal of life. Like the seed within the dry decaying shell, or the reptile that sheds its outer skin, aging represents the casting off of one's "mortal coil" in preparation for life after death.

The astute reader of this brief history will recognize these images in theories of aging from Greco-Roman medicine to modern times. The similarity of imagery employed by different theorists at different times reflects the enormous difficulty involved in conceptualizing human aging—for example, in distinguishing between aging as a cause and aging as an effect. The careful reader may also conclude that much of what passes for new knowledge in gerontology today is not new at all but rather is the result of a systematizing and "scientizing" of ideas that have been in circulation for a long time.

Greece and Rome

In the Western world, the first full explicit theory of the causation of aging is found in Greco-Roman medicine and the Hippocratic theory (about the fourth century B.C.) (Grant 1963). According to the Hippocratic theory, the essential factor in life is heat. At that time, the common belief was that individuals have a fixed quantity of some life force. This material, characterized by Hippocrates as "innate heat," is used up during the course of a lifetime, although the rate of utilization varies with the individual. In general, old age was equated with a continuous diminishing of innate heat, and aging was seen as a consequence of a natural course of events. The latter point in itself constitutes a remarkable breakthrough, because many writers of the time confused the aging process with diseases in the old.

About a century after Hippocrates, Aristotle expanded on the "innate heat" theory of aging in his book *On Youth and Old Age, On Life and Death and On Respiration.* Aristotle likened the heat to a fire that had to be maintained and provided with fuel. Just as a fire could run out of fuel or be put out, innate heat could also be exhausted (as in the case of a natural death due to aging) or extinguished (as in a death due to violence or disease). The contributions of Greek philosophers reached their peak with Galen (circa A.D. 130–200), who clearly differentiated between aging and dying and who was perhaps the first to characterize aging as a process beginning with conception (Grant 1963). To Aristotle's innate heat, Galen added the elements of blood and semen. Blood and semen were sources of generation; drying in the form of heat produced the tissues.

> By this means, then, the embryo is first formed and takes on a little firmness; and after this, drying more, acquires the outlines and faint patterns of each of its parts. Then, drying even more, it assumes not merely their outlines and patterns, but their exact appearance. And now, having been brought forth, it keeps growing larger and drier and stronger, until it reaches full development. Then all growth ceases, the bones elongating no more on account of their dryness, and every vessel increases in width, and thus all the parts become strong and attain their maximum power.
>
> But in ensuing time, as all the organs become even drier, not only are their functions performed less well but their vitality becomes more feeble and restricted. And drying more, the creature becomes not only thinner but also wrinkled, and the limbs weak and unsteady in their movements. This condition is called old age.... This, then, is one innate destiny of destruction for every mortal creature....
>
> These processes, then, it is permitted no mortal body to escape; but others, which ensure, it is possible for the forethoughtful to avoid. Moreover, the source of these is from attempting to correct the aforesaid inevitable processes. (Galen, quoted in Grant 1963, p. 7)

It is interesting that, for Galen, the very element that appears to bring life (drying) leads quite naturally (and unequivocally) to its end.

The attitude of the Greeks expressed their ambivalence toward aging. They emphasized family love and the wisdom of age, but they also recognized the weaknesses and eccentricities of the aged. Aristotle condemned old age and presented youth and old age as opposites. He characterized youth as a time of excess and later life as a time of conservativeness and small-mindedness. Plato had a somewhat positive view of old age. In *The Republic*, he referred to two important features of late life: the persistence of characteristics from earlier life and the relief of having outgrown some of life's difficulties (including frustrated ambition and unfulfilled sexual desire).

Cicero (106–43 B.C.), in his *De Senectute*, has become a favorite source for contemporary writers on aging; nevertheless, he was typical of his day. Although Cicero recognized that advanced age brought biological degeneration, he emphasized the relationship between aging and development, including the continuing capacity for psychological growth, and placed great value on experience accumulated over time. In fact, Cicero recommended intellectual activity as part of a regimen to resist premature aging.

The Greek influence persisted. Freeman, a noted historian of aging, writes of the physician Villanova and the Franciscan friar Roger Bacon, thirteenth-century experts on aging, who essentially "followed the Galenic thought that aging was due to the loss of innate heat" (1965). In many respects, however, Bacon was a precursor of the scientific era to come. He argued that three factors tended to hasten the diminution of heat: infection, negligence, and ignorance of matters related to health. He proposed a method of hygiene that would allow men and women to achieve their rightful term of years in good health.

The Early Scientific Era

The scientific method, born during the sixteenth and seventeenth centuries, involved a radical break from earlier modes of thought. Magic, faith, and speculation no longer sufficed; observation, experimentation, and verification were the order of the day. One of the chief proponents of this new way of thinking, Francis Bacon, also wrote about aging. He attempted to dispel prior theories of aging because he believed them "corrupt with false opinion." Bacon wrote that "for both these things, which the vulgar physicians talk(e), of radical moisture, and natural heat, are but meer [sic] fictions." Unfortunately, Bacon himself was unable to escape completely the old ways of thinking. He simply replaced the Greek notion of innate heat with that of "spirit" or "pneuma" and argued that every body part (bones, blood, etc.) has such a spirit enclosed within it. With use, these spirits were consumed or dissolved—hence, old age. As might be expected, Bacon was unable to verify this idea; yet, he believed that with the proper method, the "secrets of nature" could be discovered (Grant 1963).

Despite the new scientific approach, many people's basic ambivalence toward old age did not change. Bacon reflected this ambivalence in his discussion of the qualities intrinsic to youth and age:

> Men of age object too much, consult too long, adventure too little, repent too soon, and seldom drive business home to the full period, but content themselves with a mediocrity of success...[yet] age doth profit rather in the powers of understanding, than in the virtues of the will and affections. (quoted in Hendricks & Hendricks 1977)

A more positive sixteenth-century view was put forth by Paleotti, who, in terms reminiscent of Cicero 16 centuries before, concluded that "wisdom, maturity, and a cooling down of certain emotional currents give old age its peculiar form of creativeness unobtainable at other life periods" (quoted in Hendricks & Hendricks 1977).

In Europe and America, many books were written on and advances made in physiology, anatomy, pathology, and chemistry during the seventeenth and eighteenth centuries, although pre-Enlightenment ideas were still around in abundance. One of the first Americans to write about aging was Cotton Mather (1663–1728). His orientation was theological: Illness was conceived as punishment for original sin, and only through temperance could longevity be achieved. Longevity was also the issue in what, perhaps, was the first complete American work on aging. William Barton, in his *Observations on the Progress of Population and the Probabilities of the Duration of Human Life, in the United States of America* (1791), attempted to show that people in the United States lived longer and were healthier than people in Europe. He deduced that the likelihood of a person living past age 80 was greater in the United States than abroad.

The first American work in geriatrics, *Account of the State of the Body and Mind in Old Age,* was published in 1793 by the physician Benjamin Rush. Perhaps more accurately than anyone before him, Rush described the changes in the body and the mind that accompany old age. A historian of aging describes Rush as striking one of the last blows at the idea that old age is itself a disease: "Few persons appear to die of old age. Some of the diseases which have been mentioned generally cuts [sic] the last thread of life" (Rush, quoted in Grant 1963). Rush and his contemporaries— Hufeland in Germany and Bichat in France, for example—represent the beginning of a more modern period. Science flowered, and writers of the time believed the principles of life would be discovered by scientific observation and experimentation.

The nineteenth century experienced an increase in the capacity for scientific research and some outstanding technological innovations, including advances in microscopy and thermometry. Lister, Pasteur, and Metchnikoff revolutionized public health by their discoveries of methods to control epidemic diseases and infection. Medical specialization was increasing, and one could begin to envision the outlines of a fledgling branch dealing with old age. The French physician Charcot attended particularly to the clinical aspects of old age; he believed that management of diseases of aging and the aged should be based on an established clinical regimen. According to Freeman (1965), Charcot was responsible for dividing the study of aging into two permanent lines of inquiry. One investigates the facts of aging, describes its effects, and measures its changes in capacities. The other looks for principles of aging, for a central theme or cause.

This distinction may have been anticipated by the Belgian mathematician Quetelet, considered by some to be the first gerontologist. Quetelet, one of the earliest statisticians, helped discover the concept of the normal distribution. The *normal distribution* indicates that there is an average or central tendency around which are distributed higher and lower measurements. Quetelet applied this notion to various traits, such as hand strength and weight, records of birth and death rates, and the relationship between age and productivity (Birren & Clayton 1975).

Sir Francis Galton, an English statistician responsible for developing the index of correlation, was influenced by Quetelet's work. Galton's fundamental contribution to the study of aging is the data gathered by his Anthropometric Laboratory at the International Health Exhibition in London in 1884. Over 9,000 males and females ranging in age from 5 to 80 were measured on 17 different characteristics, including hearing, vision, and reaction time. Galton used these data to show how human characteristics change with age. This was the first large survey related to aging, and the data were still being analyzed in the 1920s.

The Twentieth Century and Today

In the early part of the twentieth century, interest in aging involved including old age in a developmental psychology framework (Birren & Clayton 1975). G. Stanley Hall, president of Clark University and founder of the Psychology Department of Johns Hopkins University, had specialized in childhood and adolescence, but concern with his own retirement led him to write *Senescence, the Last Half of Life,* published in 1922. Although he may have been tempted to characterize the second half of life as a regression occurring among the same lines as development, Hall struck a new note:

> As a psychologist I am convinced that the psychic states of old people have great significance. Senescence, like adolescence, has its own feeling, thought, and will, as well as its own psychology, and their regimen is important, as well as that of the body. Individual differences here are probably greater than in youth. (Hall 1922, p. 100)

Hall used questionnaire data to investigate the relationship between religious belief and fear of death. The conventional wisdom at the time was that, with age, fear of death increased and people became more religious in an attempt to reconcile themselves to an uncertain future. Hall argued that religious fervor did not increase with age, nor were old people more fearful of death than were the young. In fact, he said, fear of death seemed to be a young person's concern.

During the early part of the twentieth century, biologists such as Child, Metchnikoff, Minot, Pearl, and Weismann were writing prolifically on aging. An internist at Johns Hopkins University, William Osler, while considering the high frequency of cases of arteriosclerosis among the elderly, discovered that aging was closely related to the state of the blood vessels, and he realized how the hardening of the arteries had an impact on brain functioning. Clearly, the locus of aging study was shifting to the United States during this period, although important research was being carried out by Pavlov in Russia and Tachibana in Japan.

By the 1930s, a new attitude toward old age had emerged, one that had enormous impact on the growth of gerontology as a scientific discipline. Stimulated by the changing demographics of modern societies, by an increased life expectancy, and by a growing older population, and perhaps by an economic depression, people began to see old age as a social problem. Recognizing the prevalence of incapacity, isolation, and poverty among aged citizens, Western society's concern turned toward social action on behalf of the aged. Interestingly, this concern and the accompanying perceived need for collective social action were reflected not only in legislation (such as the passage of the Social Security Act in 1935) in the United States but also in a new institutional approach to aging as a social scientific problem.

In the late 1930s and early 1940s, conferences on aging were sponsored by professional and governmental organizations, such as the American Orthopsychiatric Association <http://www.amerortho.org> and the National Institutes of Health <http://www.nih.gov>. Private foundations, including the Josiah Macy Foundation <http://www.josiahmacyfoundation.org/jmacy1.html>, also provided assistance in conducting conferences on aging. Many of the issues raised at these early conferences anticipated some of the current concerns in gerontology: mental health and aging, aging and intellectual functioning, and aging and worker productivity. One of the earliest reports on the implications of the changing demographic structure of U.S. society was initiated by the Social Science Research Council <http://www.ssrc.org> (Pollak 1948).

World War II interrupted the continuing development of gerontology. When the war ended in 1945, however, gerontologists resumed activity and founded the Gerontological Society (now the Gerontological Society of America). The Society publishes two influential journals in the field of aging: the *Journal of Gerontology* and *The Gerontologist*. Other professional associations soon appeared. The American Psychological Association <http://www.apa.org> established a division on maturity and old age in 1946; the American Geriatric Society <http://www.americangeriatrics.org> was founded in 1950; and the American Society on Aging <http://www.asaging.org>, organized initially as the Western Gerontological Society, was founded in 1954.

The founding of a gerontological unit of the National Institutes of Health in 1946 led to the creation of the National Institute of Aging <http://www.nih.gov/nia> in 1974. Robert Butler, a psychiatrist and gerontologist, became its first director. The International Association of Gerontology <http://www.cas.flinders.edu.au/iag> was organized in 1948 and had its first meeting in Liege, Belgium. Today, many other professional societies, including the American Sociological Association <http://www.asanet.org> and the American Public Health Association <http://www.apha.org>, maintain sections for those members with a specific interest in aging.

By the 1950s, the volume of gerontological literature had increased dramatically, and it continues to increase unabated. The major journals of gerontology were started between 1946 and the early 1970s. In addition to those mentioned previously, these include *Geriatrics* (1946), *Gerontologia* (1956), *Experimental Gerontology* (1966), *Journal of Geriatric Psychiatry* (1967), *Aging and Human Development* (1971), *Ageing and Society* (1981), *Journal of Aging and Health* (1989), and *Journal of Applied Gerontology* (1982). An attempt to create a definitive bibliography of biomedical and social science research in aging for the years 1954 to 1974 yielded 50,000 titles (Woodruff & Birren 1975). This number has grown exponentially since 1974. Many gerontologists express both joy and dismay at this explosive increase in gerontological research. The joy comes with being able to participate in an exciting and growing scientific enterprise; the dismay comes with trying to keep pace with the growth of gerontological knowledge.

Several attempts have been made to synthesize this growing body of literature. Landmarks in this regard are Birren's *Handbook of Aging and the Individual: Psychological and Biological Aspects* (1959), Tibbitts's *Handbook of Social Gerontology: Societal Aspects of Aging* (1960), and Burgess's *Aging in Western Societies* (1960). This effort was later matched in three volumes edited by Matilda W. Riley and colleagues and supported by the Russell Sage Foundation: *Aging and Society: An Inventory of Research Findings* (Riley & Foner 1968), *Aging and the Professions* (Riley, Riley, & Johnson 1969), and *A Sociology of Age Stratification* (Riley, Johnson, & Foner 1972). More recent reviews of the field are provided in the fourth editions of the Handbook of Aging Series: *Handbook of the Biology of Aging* (Schneider & Rowe 1996), *Handbook of the Psychology of Aging* (Birren & Schaie 1996), and *Handbook of Aging and the Social Sciences* (Binstock & George 1996).

Almost every discipline involved in gerontology has had its pioneer through this modern period, and clearly all cannot be listed here. E. V. Cowdry, considered by some to be the founder of modern gerontology, led the way with his seminal volume, *Problems of Aging,* published in 1939. Early on, he recognized the interdisciplinary nature of gerontology, synthesized a variety of materials in his field, and contributed significantly to the establishment of the International Association of Gerontology (Kaplan, in Schwartz & Peterson 1979). Social psychologist Bernice Neugarten began teaching the psychology of aging at the University of Chicago in the early 1930s. She and her students have contributed immeasurably to the development of gerontology, as well as to the broader study of human development. Other outstanding work was produced in psychology by Birren and Schaie, in sociology by Shanas and Rosow, in anthropology by Simmons and Clark, in economics by Kreps, and in history (more recently) by Fischer and Achenbaum. These people and others not named here have also contributed to the development of strong university centers at Chicago <http://www.spc.uchicago.edu/coa/index.html>, Duke <http://cds.duke.edu>, Southern California <http://www.usc.edu/dept/gero>, and elsewhere.

The study of aging continues to grow in the twenty-first century, in part fueled by funding from federal government sources. The National Institutes of Health, including the National Institute of Mental Health <http://www.nimh.nih.gov> and the newer National Institute on Aging, and the Administration on Aging <http://www.aoa.dhhs.gov>, through state and area offices on aging, provide the primary funding for interdisciplinary research and training in gerontology. Other governmental agencies (e.g., the Department of Labor <http://www.dol.gov>), as well as private organizations such as the American Association of Retired Persons, also fund research and training programs related to aging.

If one were to write a more detailed history of the last three or four decades in gerontology, an important point to develop would be the extent to which it has been institutionalized on the U.S. academic scene. Today, courses on aging are taught on almost every college and university campus; students who major in gerontology as well as professors who teach the relevant courses identify themselves as gerontologists. The Association for Gerontology in Higher Education (AGHE) <http://www.aghe.org> was established in 1974 for the purpose of advancing gerontology as a field of study within institutions of higher learning. The 1994 AGHE Directory lists 354 formal gerontology programs at member colleges and universities. A *formal gerontology program* is defined as one offering a degree, certificate, concentration, specialization, emphasis, or minor in gerontology, or is identified as a research and/or clinical training center in gerontology/geriatrics.

Still, there remains much debate over whether gerontology ought to be recognized as a discipline in its own right, as are psychology, physics, and philosophy. Some argue that gerontologists have not really succeeded in creating a body of theory all their own, that gerontology is just a consumer of theories from other sciences, and that gerontologists should be satisfied to have the field function as an applied social science. One contributing factor in this argument involves the lack of consensus over what constitutes the common core of knowledge in gerontology. In addressing this issue, AGHE (Peterson, Douglass, & Lobenstein 1996) reports that most faculty agree that there are four core courses that should be offered to every student of gerontology: Introduction to Social

Gerontology, Biology/Physiology of Aging, Psychology of Aging, and Sociology of Aging. In addition, most gerontology programs require a practicum or field placement. Beyond these requirements, there is apparently less consensus concerning the electives that should comprise the remainder of a gerontology curriculum. What do people working in the field think? Peterson, Douglass, and Lobenstein (1996) offer results from a survey of graduates of college- and university-based gerontology programs in 10 midwestern states. Interestingly, alumni reported that the most useful courses included Bilogy of Aging, Health and Diseases, Long-Term Care, Psychology of Aging, Administration, Program Planning and Evaluation, Supervision, and Public Relations.

Thomas Jefferson and many of the American Founding Fathers argued for a style of agrarian democracy which, in Jefferson's picturesque phrase, was based on no man living so close to his neighbor that he could hear his dog bark. Unfortunately, the way gerontology is sometimes practiced in colleges and universities in the United States allows the appropriate paraphrase to be that "no gerontologist lives so close to his academic neighbor that he reads his work" (Kart 1987, p. 86).

The future of gerontology continues to be dependent on the willingness of traditional academic departments (e.g., psychology, sociology, and biology, among others) to cooperate in the gerontological enterprise. If academic competition becomes the order of the day, the field will surely suffer. If these traditional disciplines make a commitment to interdisciplinary activity, the field will surely flourish. Some in the field are optimistic, for they (and we) understand that no discipline by itself is capable of providing adequate education in gerontology.

METHODOLOGICAL ISSUES IN AGING RESEARCH

Earlier, *gerontology* was defined as the study of aging from the broadest perspective. In addition, it was described as an interdisciplinary study with *major* elements drawn from the physical and social sciences. In this regard, active researchers in gerontology have relied and continue to rely on scientific methods of investigation. Actually, as Popenoe (1991) points out, scientists can take one of three pathways in the pursuit of knowledge. One path, involving reasoning from the general to the specific or from certain premises to a logically valid conclusion, is referred to as the use of **deductive logic.** A second path, involving the direct perception of truth apart from any reasoning process or logic, can be referred to as **intuition.** Gerontologists do not reject deductive logic and intuition as pathways to knowledge, but they do rely more heavily on a third path—the empirical method. The **empirical method** involves the use of human senses (e.g., sight and hearing) to observe the world. This method is public; the observations of one researcher can be checked for accuracy by others using the same process. Gerontological "truths" cannot be accepted on the basis of logic and/or intuition. They must be subjected to empirical investigation.

Most students reading this text have limited experience with empirical research (and likely even less experience with such research carried out by gerontologists). Moreover, much of this experience comes from reading research reports required for fulfilling course assignments. Typically, what the student sees is a finished product, which includes a statement of the problem to be investigated, some theoretical justification, discussion of the research methods employed, presentation of the data, and discussion of the findings. Rarely does the student get a chance to observe firsthand the problems involved in carrying out the research process. These include how the project may have changed in the course of the research process and the judgments that the researcher was forced to make as difficulties were encountered.

The research problems gerontologists encounter are much like those encountered by scientists working in a wide array of scientific disciplines. Common concerns include the appropriateness of research technique and design, the validity and reliability of measurement devices, and the problems of sampling and data analysis. The following brief description of the most frequently used methods in gerontological research provides examples from the social sciences (with particular emphasis on sociology and psychology) to show how research is currently carried out in the field of aging.

Field Research

Field research is generally observation centered. It is most useful in the study of relatively small groups of individuals or well-defined social settings and may allow the researcher to establish and maintain close, firsthand contact with subjects and their actions (Williamson, Karp, & Dalphin 1977). Zelditch (1962) distinguishes among three types of strategies for field research: (1) participant observation, (2) informant interviewing, and (3) enumeration and samples.

Participant observation includes observing and participating in events, interviewing other participants during the events, and maintaining stable relationships in the group. *Informant interviewing* involves interviewing an informant about others in the group and about events that have happened in the past. *Enumerations and samples* include small surveys and structured observations that require a low level of participation in group events.

Field work requires what Smith (1975) describes as "distinctive methodological attitudes." In general, this means that the researcher must be comfortable with the lack of standardization and the unstructured nature of the field research process. Field research must be quite flexible and adaptable to changing environmental conditions as well as to emerging theoretical concerns. In this regard, field methods are much more conducive to description than inferential analysis and more conducive to hypothesis generation than to hypothesis testing. As Keith (1986, p. 1) argues, with regard to the use of participant observation for old-age research, so little is known about the quality of older people's lives that many other research approaches simply cannot be used before some preliminary field work identifies the relevant questions.

A significant problem the field researcher faces has to do with the possible influence or effect the research itself may have on the field setting. For example,

Smith (1975) indicates that the more the researcher finds it necessary to participate in the field setting, the more the research role will depend on the ability to establish successful relationships of trust with individuals in the field setting. The fact
that informant contacts are established with some subjects and not others may
affect the relationships among these subjects. Also, such relationships with informants may bias data collection toward one point of view and away from others.

A number of gerontological researchers have employed field research methods, principally participant observation, with considerable success in the study of
retirement communities (Keith 1977/1982; Jacobs 1974; Hochschild 1973; Johnson 1971), nursing homes (Gubrium 1975), and single-room-occupancy (SRO)
hotels (Stephens 1976). Keith (1977/1982) and her husband took an apartment at
Les Floralies, a high-rise retirement residence with a planned capacity of 150,
which was built by the French national retirement fund for construction workers
and is located in a suburb outside of Paris. Residents included those who had
worked in the construction trades and their spouses. The average age of residents
was 75 years old, almost two-thirds were female, and 90 percent received some
form of government assistance to meet the costs of living in the residence. Keith
immersed herself in the activities of the retirement community, as she attempted to
outline a map of social relations within the residence:

> I participated in every possible aspect of community life.... Access to organized ac-
> tivities was easy: committee meetings once a week, a weekly sewing and knitting
> group, daily work with volunteer residents in the kitchen, the laundry or the re-
> search office, and the afternoon *belote* game. These activities...led to invitations
> to...people's apartments. Neighbors invited us too, and the head of the Commu-
> nist faction became my knitting teacher. (1977/1982, pp. 29–30)

Les Floralies was not just an apartment house for elderly retirees. Rather, as
Keith states, it was inhabited by people who were engaged together in the process
of creating community. A number of factors contributed to the creation of community among these people. First, residents shared many characteristics in common, such as age, occupation, educational level, income, ethnicity, and social
class. Second, these old people believed that their alternatives were few. Thus,
they made considerable financial and emotional investment in the move. Being
"here for the rest of our lives" was certainly an important source of identification
with the community. Third, they entered this setting in small enough numbers
that they got to know each other personally; the physical arrangements, in particular those in the dining room, helped promote a greater sense of participation in
the residence. The dining facility employed small round tables as opposed to the
long, institutional tables (familiar to university student cafeterias) often used in
nursing homes and other residences. This allowed the "possibility for immediate,
primary ties which consistently appear in studies of human groups as essential for
linking the individual to a larger community" (Keith 1977/1982, p. 157).

Keith believes that these factors allowed residents to turn to each other for
the fulfillment of their social needs. They supported each other in illness and

emergency, just as they laughed and danced together at parties. Further, they were able to evaluate each other in terms of the life they shared in the residence, rather than according to the status system of the outside world. In this regard, they identified themselves as members of a community of age-mates sharing refuge from an outside world fraught with physical, financial, social, and psychological dangers for them.

Keith's insightful work involves the study of only one specific retirement community—a fact that makes generalization to other communities problematic. However, it can be added to a body of field research on retirement communities that suggests that the factors important for community formation among old people in the suburbs of Paris may be the same for communities of old people in the United States.

Use of Existing Records

Examination of existing records of individual behavior or social conditions can serve as a useful method of research for the gerontologist. Such records include personal written accounts, such as diaries or letters; public documents, such as birth, death, marriage, and probate records; and print media, film records, and sound recordings. Another kind of existing record that can be very useful to a researcher is the statistical compilation. Although the best and most widely used statistical compilations are the official publications of the U.S. Bureau of the Census <http://www.census.gov>, other organizations provide additional sources of statistical information.

In recent years, considerable growth has occurred in the number of machine-readable data files available for statistical analysis. Archival organizations have become important in making these data files available to researchers. Two of the largest machine-readable data archives in the United States serving the general social science community are the Inter-University Consortium for Political and Social Research (ICPSR) <http://www.icpsr.umich.edu> at the University of Michigan and the Roper Center <http://www.ropercenter.uconn.edu>.

Many universities and research institutes serve their social science researchers by providing facilities for ordering data from these two repositories. Such data can be used for *secondary analysis*, a term that describes a reanalysis of data produced by someone else, and often for other purposes. One problem with secondary analysis is that the current researcher is at the mercy of the original researcher in terms of what questions were asked to collect the data. Nevertheless, secondary analysis can be quite fruitful and, given the prohibitive costs of doing research, is likely to become even more popular in the future.

Researchers who use existing records not provided in some statistical format are likely to engage in some kind of *content analysis*. Here, the researcher establishes a number of categories, each of which refers to some repeated or patterned occurrence in the content of the record. Tabulations made of the frequency of each element or combination of elements may constitute the basic data in the research.

It is important in content analysis that the categories used are precisely defined and well tailored to the research problem at hand.

Engler-Bowles and Kart (1983) engaged in a content analysis of 60 wills sampled from Wood County, Ohio, probate records filed between 1820 and 1967. They were interested in the extent to which inheritance practices reflected changes in the family relationships of older people in a largely rural area of northwest Ohio during this time period. Testamentary documents commend themselves for such use because of their public and permanent accessibility as well as the demands for legal accuracy (Bryant & Snizek 1975). In addition, the will represents a particularly candid and forthright form of communication. Nevertheless, testamentary records do have some limitations. Systematic bias may be introduced as a result of the number of people who die intestate (without a will). Also, the wills themselves often do not contain relevant demographic, social, and economic information that is important for addressing certain research questions.

In order to categorize the way elderly testators disposed of their estates, Engler-Bowles and Kart used a typology of inheritance patterns adapted from Rosenfeld (1979) to identify the presence or absence of family obligation. This typology was used to measure the relative degree of that obligation, as indicated by the following three categories of inheritance patterns: familistic inheritance, articulated inheritance, and disinheritance.

Familistic inheritance represents the strongest degree of obligation by the testator to family ties. Wills in this category generally distribute the estate among family members only. *Articulated inheritance* is the dual recognition of kin and nonkin, with priority placed on nonkin heirs in testamentary disposition. *Disinheritance* is the total exclusion of family members from testamentary disposition, and therefore the apparent absence of family obligation as perceived by the testator.

The familistic inheritance pattern dominated the time period explored by Engler-Bowles and Kart. Articulated wills appeared rarely; several wills seemed equally divided between familistic and articulated bequests, and no examples of total family disinheritance were evident in this population of wills. Across this lengthy time span, married testators emphasized their conjugal relations, showing the strong emphasis placed on the nuclear family throughout the period. In the early part of this time period, direct bequests to children were usually unequal, sometimes reflecting differences in sex and individual circumstances, such as advancements made to certain children. Starting in the latter part of the nineteenth century, sons and daughters were equally likely to receive testamentary bequests.

Misconceptions about the family lives of elderly Americans past and present abound. Stereotypical images of alienated families and the isolated elderly are popular topics for research and mass media reports. The study by Engler-Bowles and Kart presents a different picture. Their analysis suggests that elderly Wood County, Ohio, testators were active participants in family life and maintained strong ties to their children from the early nineteenth century until the mid-twentieth century. Still, additional historical research is necessary to determine whether the results of this study are idiosyncratic to a small sample of will writers in rural northwest Ohio.

Survey Research

Survey research differs from other methods of data collection in two important ways. First, the focus is generally on a representative sample of a relatively large population. Second, data are collected from respondents directly, often at their homes, through the use of either interviews or questionnaires, or both. The major elements that combine to make up the survey research process include sampling procedures, questionnaire or interview schedule construction and testing, interviews carried out by trained interviewers, and data preparation and analysis.

Studies that employ a survey research approach may follow a cross-sectional or a longitudinal design. A *cross-sectional study* is carried out at one time and examines the relationships among a set of variables as they occur at that time. A *longitudinal study* involves repeated contacts with the same respondents over a period of time and is particularly attentive to changes that occur with time. This type of research design is frequently referred to as a *panel study.*

Panel studies are found increasingly preferable by gerontological researchers, but they pose special methodological problems, not the least of which is referred to as the *age/period/cohort problem (APC).* Interest in this problem first developed among psychologists attempting to understand what happens to intellectual functioning in old age (Schaie 1976) and among political scientists interested in voting behavior across the life cycle (Hudson & Binstock 1976). Both groups of researchers came to realize the importance of distinguishing, both conceptually and empirically, among changes in individuals that were a function of individual maturation (aging), those that were a function of biographical factors (cohort), and those that resulted from environmental and/or historical factors (period).

Identifying the relative importance of age, period, and cohort effects is no easy task. Maddox and Campbell (1985) offer as an example the introduction of vitamin D into milk supplies. This innovation was made instantaneously and thus can be thought of as a period effect that cut across all age groups. Yet, certain cohorts of newborns received the benefits of vitamin D supplements in their milk almost immediately from birth, whereas preceding cohorts received the benefits no earlier than the date of introduction. Thus, the period effect had potentially different consequences for different cohorts. Some received the vitamin supplements throughout their childhood years; others received the supplements for a smaller proportion of those years. Is this nutritional innovation a period or a cohort effect, or both?

Important differences exist between questionnaires and interviews as data-collecting tools in survey research. Questionnaires, delivered to respondents at work or school or mailed to them at home, are filled out by the respondents themselves. This permits access to many people who are spread over a large geographical area as well as saves time and money. Disadvantages include the need for a literate population and the low response rate that can be expected (30 percent is not uncommon). Also, questionnaires must be relatively brief, as respondents may lose interest quickly. Thus, questionnaires often cannot provide for an in-depth probing of respondents' attitudes.

What gerontological concept might explain why this young person finds herself in the role of tutor?

Interviews can be carried out either face to face or over the telephone. The latter method is less expensive, as interviewer travel time is virtually eliminated. A serious obstacle to the personal interview is the initial resistance to being interviewed. Nevertheless, as Blalock and Blalock (1982) point out, refusals to be interviewed once a contact has been made are relatively rare, and most respondents are cooperative, seem to enjoy the experience, and appear to take it seriously. Among older people, the response rate does appear to be lower for telephone surveys than for face-to-face interviews. Also, people seem more willing to respond "I don't know" on the telephone than in face-to-face interviews (Herzog & Rodgers 1988). Still, Herzog, Rodgers, and Kulka (1983) conclude that telephone interviews are about as effective for older adults as are personal interviews, which are prohibitively expensive for most studies.

With funding from the AARP Andrus Foundation, Kart and Engler (1994) attempted to identify and describe self-health care practices and attitudes within a national sample of older people. In particular, these authors sought to specify characteristics of older people that may predispose them to provide health care to themselves. In the fall of 1991, trained interviewers completed over 700 extensive telephone interviews with a national probability sample of noninstitutionalized adults age 55 years and older. By the definition offered earlier, this study represents a cross-sectional research design.

According to these authors, self-health care is a multifaceted concept that includes self-evaluation and treatment of illness symptoms, as well as overall assessment of the capacity to take care of one's own health. Although elements of this study are too numerous to identify here, among other methods employed to assess self-health care, respondents were presented with a list of 20 illness symptoms ranging from minor to potentially serious in consequence. They were asked if they had experienced the symptom in the past six months and, if yes, what they did about the symptom. For example, 6 in 10 (60.4 percent) had experienced pain or stiffness in a joint; at the other extreme, only 12.3 percent experienced frequent constipation during the past six months.

For each symptom experienced, respondents were categorized as using professional care only for treatment (e.g., physician care, prescription medicine), some combination of self-care plus professional care, or self-care only to deal with the symptom (e.g., home remedy, over-the-counter medication, doing nothing). More than five of six respondents (86.3 percent) indicated experiencing at least one of the 20 symptoms within the past six months for which they employed self-care only. An index of actual self-care revealed that, on average, across these 20 symptoms, study respondents employed self-health care responses 14.3 percent of the time.

Being female, white, perceiving an inability to maintain control over one's own health, having vision and/or hearing problems, and having one or more serious chronic illnesses (e.g., heart disease, cancer) were characteristics of respondents most likely to respond to illness symptoms with self-care. Kart and Engler conclude that researchers and health care policymakers can no longer ignore the phenomenon of self-health care among the elderly and how it interfaces with patterns of utilization of the formal health care system.

> Self-health care is an often overlooked component of the total health care received by older individuals in the United States…. Still, too little is known about this…. The question remains, do different illness symptoms lend themselves to self-care more than others, or is it that certain groups of individuals, more than others, are predisposed to undertake self-health care, regardless of illness symptoms and comorbidities? (Kart & Engler 1994, pp. S305–S307)

Laboratory Experimentation

Laboratory experimentation, used primarily by psychologists, involves the systematic observation of phenomena under controlled conditions. In the simplest experiment, there is a single independent variable *(I)* and a single dependent variable *(D)*. The research hypothesis is that *I* leads to *D*. However, although the effect of the independent variable on the dependent variable need not be viewed as causal, it ordinarily is in experiments. The primary objective of the experimental procedure is to eliminate the possibility that any variable other than the independent variable will affect the dependent variable.

The operationalization of the independent variable acts to define experimental and control groups in the simple laboratory experiment. These groups are composed of subjects who are alike in every way except that those in the experimental group are exposed to *I*, whereas those in the control group are not. Assuming initial equality, any observed differences between the two groups on the dependent variable can be attributed to the influence of the experimentally introduced independent variable. A variation on this model is that subjects in the experimental and control groups are alike in every way except one—age, for example. The two groups are exposed to the same stimuli; differences in their responses (the dependent variable) are assumed to result from age (the independent variable). Other variations on this uncomplicated model have been developed and are represented in the gerontological literature. An example follows.

Everybody experiences memory failures. How these failures are evaluated and what causal attributions are made can have important implications. A memory failure in a young adult may be ignored or joked about, but the same failure in an aged person may be taken as a sign of mental decline or the onset of dementia. Erber, Zsuchman, and Rothberg (1990) refer to this difference in appraisal of memory failure as a "double standard." More recently, Erber and Rothberg (1991) speculate that judgments of the attractiveness of the person experiencing the failure might have consequences for the causal attribution made. Further, the researchers devised an experiment to test whether the memory failures of elderly adults and unattractive adults would be evaluated differently from those same failures in young adults and attractive adults.

Of the 72 women who were subjects for the experiment, 36 were young adults, ages 19 to 32, recruited from a local university; 36 were elderly adults, ages 64 to 81, recruited from the community. The women were asked to read vignettes describing short-term (e.g., immediately forgetting material), long-term (e.g., forgetting material learned 30 minutes to several hours ago), and very long-term memory failures (e.g., forgetting very familiar and overlearned information).

Each vignette was accompanied by a photograph of an attractive or unattractive young or elderly female target person. These photos were selected from a large pool of magazine and yearbook photos on the basis of evaluations by young and old female raters. There was a high level of agreement about the photographs among the raters. Subjects judged each vignette for possible reasons for the memory failure, including each target's effort, motivation, attention, and ability. Subjects also rated whether they believed the failure was a sign of mental difficulty and whether medical and/or psychological intervention was indicated.

Erber and Rothberg (1991) report an unequivocal demonstration of the double standard. The memory failures of elderly targets were attributed more to lack of ability, whereas the failures of young targets were attributed to lack of effort. Also, the memory failures of older targets were seen as indicating greater mental difficulty and a more urgent need for medical/psychological evaluation than were the identical failures of younger targets. Similar findings were reported on the attractiveness dimension. Generally, attractive targets were evaluated in a more positive light than unattractive targets. Target age, however, was more important than target attractiveness in evaluating the memory failures. Young subjects, in particular, considered very long-term memory failures to be more indicative of mental difficulty and need for evaluation than short-term or long-term failures. Clearly, more research is needed to understand the different criteria for judgment used by younger and older people in order to identify the basis for leniency in the evaluations made by older adults.

SUMMARY

Several reasons exist for studying aging, not the least of which is the intrinsic fascination of the field. There have been students of aging for several thousand years. In the past, perhaps the most prominent concern was the quest to prolong life, as reflected in the antediluvian, hyperborean, and fountain themes, all still represented today.

The scientific study of the aging process is a recent phenomenon that arose out of a need to make clear distinctions between myth and history, magic and science. The first full and explicit theory of the causation of aging is found in Greco-Roman medicine and the Hippocratic theory. The Greek influence persisted, and a radical break with earlier modes of thought did not occur until the scientific method was born during the sixteenth and seventeenth centuries.

By the nineteenth century, capacity for scientific research increased; by the latter part of the century, a fledgling science of old age could be envisioned. During the early part of the twentieth century, the locus of aging study shifted toward the United States. By the 1930s, a new attitude toward old age emerged—a perception of old age as a social problem. Recognition of the prevalence of incapacity, isolation, and poverty among elderly people had enormous impact on the growth of gerontology as both a scientific and applied discipline.

In the 1970s, gerontology was institutionalized on the U.S. academic scene. There is still much debate over whether gerontology can be recognized as a discipline in its own right. Some argue that gerontologists have not created a body of theory of their own and should therefore be satisfied to see gerontology function as an applied social science. Nevertheless, gerontologists today show a strong research orientation and employ a variety of research procedures in their efforts, including field research, use of existing records, survey research, and laboratory experimentation. Gerontologists are also concerned with a number of special methodological issues in aging research, including issues of design and, in particular, the age/period/cohort problem, as well as the common concerns shared by scientists in a wide array of scientific disciplines.

STUDY QUESTIONS

1. Describe the antediluvian, hyperborean, and fountain themes of aging. How are these themes reflected in modern society?

2. What does it mean to describe gerontology as an interdisciplinary study?

3. Identify the three main tasks confronting the student of aging.

4. The Hippocratic theory of "innate heat" was the first explicit theory of aging in the Western world. Describe this theory, and explain why it is considered a breakthrough in the study of aging.

5. With the advent of the scientific era, thinking about aging both changes and remains the same. How is this the case?

6. Changing attitudes in the 1930s resulted in a major growth of the field of gerontology. Old age was increasingly recognized as a social problem. Discuss some social and demographic factors that influenced this change in attitude.

7. Discuss the application of field research in the study of gerontology. Distinguish between (a) participant observation, (b) informant interviewing, and (c) enumeration and samples.

8. Explain how survey research differs from other methods of data collection. What are the major elements of the survey research process?

9. Why is it important to distinguish age, period, and cohort effects in gerontological research?

10. Identify the following:
    a. secondary analysis
    b. content analysis
    c. cross-sectional study design
    d. longitudinal study design
    e. experimental group
    f. control group

REFERENCES

Achenbaum, W. A. (1978). *Old age in the new land.* Baltimore, MD: Johns Hopkins University Press.

Binstock, R., & George, L. K. (1996). *Handbook of aging and the social sciences* (4th ed.). San Diego, CA: Academic.

Birren, J. (1959). *Handbook of aging and the individual: Psychological and biological aspects.* Chicago: University of Chicago.

Birren, J., & Clayton, V. (1975). History of gerontology. In D. Woodruff & J. Birren (Eds.), *Aging: Scientific perspectives and social issues.* New York: Van Nostrand.

Birren, J., & Schaie, W. (1996). *Handbook of the psychology of aging* (4th ed.). San Diego, CA: Academic.

Blalock, A. B., & Blalock, H. M., Jr. (1982). *Introduction to social research* (2nd ed.). Englewood Cliffs, NJ: Prentice-Hall.

Blythe, R. (1979). *The view in winter: Reflections on old age.* New York: Harcourt Brace Jovanovich.

Bromley, D. B. (1974). *The psychology of human aging* (2nd ed.). Middlesex, England: Penguin.

Bryant, C., & Snizek, W. (1975). The last will and testament: A neglected document in sociological research. *Sociology and Social Research, 59,* 219–230.

Burgess, E. (1960). *Aging in Western societies.* Chicago: University of Chicago Press.

Engler-Bowles, C. A., & Kart, C. S. (1983). Intergenerational relations and testamentary patterns: An exploration. *Gerontologist, 23* (2), 167–173.

Erber, J. T., & Rothberg, S. T. (1991). Here's looking at you: The relative effect of age and attractiveness on judgements about memory failure. *Journal of Gerontology, 46* (3), P116–P123.

Erber, J. T., Zsuchman, L. T., & Rothberg, S. T. (1990). Everyday memory failures: Age differences in appraisal and attribution. *Psychology and Aging, 5,* 236–241.

Freeman, J. (1965). Medical perspectives in aging (12–19th century). *Gerontologist, 5,* 1–24.

Grant, R. L. (1963). Concepts of aging: An historical review. *Perspectives in Biology and Medicine, 6,* 443–478.

Gruman, G. (1966). *A history of ideas about the prolongation of life.* Philadelphia: American Philosophical Society.

Gubrium, J. F. (1975). *Living and dying at Murray Manor.* New York: St. Martin's.

Hall, G. S. (1922). *Senescence, the last half of life.* New York: Appleton.

Hendricks, J., & Hendricks, C. D. (1977). *Aging in mass society: Myths and realities.* Cambridge, MA: Winthrop.

Henratta, J., & Campbell, R. (1976). Status attainment and status maintenance: A study of satisfaction in old age. *American Sociological Review, 41,* 981–992.

Herzog, A. R., & Rodgers, W. L. (1988). Interviewing older adults: Mode comparison using data from a face-to-face survey and a telephone survey. *Public Opinion Quarterly, 52,* 84–99.

Herzog, A. R., Rodgers, W. L., & Kulka, R. A. (1983). Interviewing older adults: Comparison of telephone and face-to-face modalities. *Public Opinion Quarterly, 47,* 405–418.

Hochschild, A. R. (1973). *The unexpected community.* Englewood Cliffs, NJ: Prentice-Hall.

Hogan, D. P., & Eggebeen, D. J. (1995). Sources of emergency help and routine assistance in old age. *Social Forces, 73* (3), 917–936.

Hudson, R., & Binstock, R. (1976). Political systems and aging. In R. Binstock & E. Shanas (Eds.), *Aging and the social sciences.* New York: Van Nostrand Reinhold.

Jacobs, J. (1974). *Fun City: An ethnographic study of a retirement community.* New York: Holt, Rinehart and Winston.

Johnson, S. K. (1971). *Idle Haven: Community building among the working class retired.* Berkeley: University of California.

Kart, C. S. (1987). The end of conventional gerontology? *Sociology of Health and Illness, 9* (1), 77–87.

Kart, C. S., & Engler, C. A. (1994). Predisposition to self-health care: Who does what for themselves and why? *Journal of Gerontology, 49* (6), S301–S308.

Keith, J. (1977/1982). *Old people, new lives.* Chicago: University of Chicago Press.

Keith, J. (1986). Participant observation. In C. L. Fry, J. Keith, & contributors (Eds.), *New methods for old age research.* South Hadley, MA: Bergin & Garvey.

Maddox, G., & Campbell, R. T. (1985). Scope, concepts and methods in the study of aging. In R. Binstock & E. Shanas (Eds.), *Aging and the social sciences* (2nd ed.). New York: Van Nostrand Reinhold.

Maddox, G., & Wiley, J. (1976). Scope, concepts and methods in the study of aging. In R. Binstock & E. Shanas (Eds.), *Aging and the social sciences.* New York: Van Nostrand Reinhold.

Moen, P., Dempster-McClain, D., & Williams, R. M. (1992). Successful aging: A life-course perspective on women's multiple roles and health. *American Journal of Sociology, 97* (6), 1612–1638.

National Institute on Aging. (1986). *Age words: A glossary on health and aging.* NIH Publication No. 86-1849. Washington, DC: U.S. Government Printing Office.

Peterson, D. A., Douglass, E. B., & Lobenstein, J. C. (1996). *Careers in aging: Opportunities and options.* Washington, DC: Association for Gerontology in Higher Education.

Pollak, O. (1948). *Social adjustment in old age: A research planning report.* New York: Social Science Research Council.

Popenoe, D. (1991). *Sociology* (8th ed.). Englewood, Cliffs, NJ: Prentice-Hall.

Riley, M. W., & Foner, A. (1968). *Aging and society: An inventory of research findings.* New York: Russell Sage Foundation.

Riley, M. W., Johnson, M., & Foner, A. (1972). *A sociology of age stratification.* New York: Russell Sage Foundation.

Riley, M. W., Riley, J., & Johnson, M. (1969). *Aging and the professions.* New York: Russell Sage Foundation.

Rosenfeld, J. (1979). *The legacy of aging: Inheritance and disinheritance in social perspective.* Norwood, NJ: Ablex.

Schaie, W. (1976). Quasi-experimental research design in the psychology of aging. In J. Birren & W. Schaie (Eds.), *The psychology of aging.* New York: Van Nostrand Reinhold.

Schneider, E. L., & Rowe, J. W. (1996). *Handbook of the biology of aging* (4th ed.). San Diego, CA: Academic.

Schwartz, A., & Peterson, J. (1979). *Introduction to gerontology.* New York: Holt, Rinehart and Winston.

Smith, H. W. (1975). *Strategies of social research: The methodological imagination.* Englewood Cliffs, NJ: Prentice-Hall.

Stephens, J. (1976). *Loners, losers, and lovers: Elderly tenants in a slum hotel.* Seattle: University of Washington Press.

Tibbitts, C. (1960). *Handbook of social gerontology: Societal aspects of aging.* Chicago: University of Chicago.

Williamson, J. B., Karp, D. A., & Dalphin, J. R. (1977). *The research craft: An introduction to social science methods.* Boston: Little, Brown.

Woodruff, D., & Birren, J. (1975). *Aging: Scientific perspectives and social issues.* New York: Van Nostrand.

Zelditch, M., Jr. (1962). Some methodological problems of field studies. *American Journal of Sociology, 67,* 566–576.

CHAPTER THREE

THE DEMOGRAPHY OF AGING

As of this writing, about 35 million people in the United States are age 65 years and older. This group represents the fastest-growing age group in the nation's population: If the U.S. population of those 65 years and over were all grouped together, they would make up the most populous state in the nation, exceeding the population of California. Actually, there are more people age 65 and older in the United States than the combined total resident populations of New England (Maine, New Hampshire, Vermont, Massachusetts, Rhode Island, and Connecticut) and the Mountain States (Montana, Idaho, Wyoming, Colorado, New Mexico, Arizona, Utah, and Nevada).

Assessing the circumstances of old people in the United States requires an understanding of how this group is currently constituted, how the elderly population has changed from the past, and how it may change in the future. Developing such understanding through systematic study of population attributes defines the mission of **demography,** the scientific study of population materials. Population attributes—*fertility, mortality,* and *migration*—influence and are influenced by social and economic conditions. High birthrates in the first decades of the twentieth century yielded large numbers of elderly people 65 to 75 years later. Progress in public health and medicine has reduced the rates of illness and mortality in the population, especially among the young, allowing more of the population to live to be old. Immigration to the United States has also had an impact on the growth of the elderly population in recent years. Migrants who were young adults at the time of their immigration in the first two or three decades of the twentieth century increased the numbers of persons in their respective age groups, leading to large numbers of older people decades later.

This chapter presents a systematic study of population trends for the aged and phenomena in relation to their social setting. Much of the available data in the United States define the elderly as those 65 years of age and older. Although 65+ is an imprecise identifier of the older population, it is a useful designation for gerontologists, and it is followed in this chapter. This definition, however, is not universal. Most everyone can recognize the differences between 20-year-olds and 40-year-olds, but that same 20-year difference between 55-year-olds and 75-year-olds is often overlooked. Neugarten (1974) makes the distinction between the **young-old** (55 to 74 years of age) and the **old-old** (75 years of age and older). Recently, the National Institute on Aging has sought research proposals to study those individuals 85 years of age and older. This activity suggests the usefulness of further subdividing the old-old into those 75 to 84 years *(the elderly)* and those 85 years and over *(the very-old* or *the oldest-old)*. The young-old are healthier, wealthier, and better educated than the old-old, and their family and career experiences and expectations are quite different.

NUMBER AND PROPORTION OF THE ELDERLY

The elderly population of the United States has grown consistently since the turn of the twentieth century, when about 3.1 million men and women were aged 65 and over. In the year 2000, estimations are that this population has increased more than elevenfold to 34.7 million (see Table 3.1). This is much greater than the rate of increase for the total U.S. population, which increased about 3.6 times, from 76 million to 275 million, in the same period.

As Table 3.1 shows, the absolute and proportional increases in the aged population are expected to continue well into the twenty-first century, though at a slowed pace until the 2010–2020 decade. Between 1990 and 2000, the increase in the aged population was estimated to be about 3.63 million, or a 11.7 percent decennial increase. This compares with the 5.5 million (or 21.6 percent) decennial increase between 1980 and 1990. This slowed growth rate in the elderly population is a reflection of the small **cohorts** caused by the low birthrate during the Great Depression and up to World War II.[1] The earliest of these small cohorts reached age 65 during the 1990s. When the post–World War II babies, sometimes referred to as **Baby Boomers,** begin to reach age 65 shortly after the year 2010, the growth rate in the elderly population will again increase. Table 3.1 shows this; the projected increase in the elderly population between 2010 and 2020 is 35 percent. Later, this growth rate will likely fall, to 4.8 percent between 2040 and 2050, reflecting a decline in birthrates that began in the 1960s. Still, the elderly population is expected to more than double between now and the year 2050, to almost 80 million. Most of this growth, approximately 30 million, will occur between the years 2010 and 2030.

Demographers have considerable confidence in these projections, because all those who will be elderly by 2050 have already been born. The accuracy of these projections will be determined ultimately by how accurately demographers predict mortality among these maturing individuals. This is not an easy task. For a time, demographers employed a single assumption of regular small declines in **mortality rates** among older adults (Siegel 1979). This may no longer be a safe course to follow. Death rates can decline at different rates in successive periods, or may even rise occasionally as they have in the last several decades. Some suggest that the nation has entered a new era of mortality decline due primarily to reduced death rates from cardiovascular diseases and reduced death rates generally

---

[1]All persons born during the same year who are analyzed as a unit throughout their lifetime constitute a *cohort* (Petersen, 1975).

TABLE 3.1   Total Aged Population and Percentage of Total Population That Is Aged: 1980–2050

				PROJECTIONS				
	1980	*1990*	*2000*	*2010*	*2020*	*2030*	*2040*	*2050*
65 years and older (thousands)	25,550	31,080	34,710	39,408	53,220	69,378	75,233	78,859
Percentage of total population (%)	11.3	12.5	12.6	13.2	16.5	20.0	20.3	20.0
Increase in preceding decade (%)	—	21.6	11.7	13.5	35.0	30.4	8.4	4.8

Note: These middle series Census Bureau projections are based on the following assumptions: (1) Total fertility rate = 2.25; (2) life expectancy in 2050 = 82.0 years; and (3) annual net immigration = 820,000.

Source: U.S. Bureau of the Census, *Statistical Abstract of the United States: 1997* (Washington, DC: U.S. Government Printing Office, 1997), Tables 14 and 17.

at older ages. If this is so, there will be a substantial increase in the number of people over age 65 in the population.

How accurate have past projections of the older population been? Until 1975, estimates for the older population of 2000 were in the range of 28 to 29 million. In 1975, the Census Bureau increased the estimate to about 30.5 million. As Table 3.1 shows, the projection for year 2000 (made in 1997) is for 34.7 million people age 65 and over, a 13.7 percent increase over the estimate made in 1975. These newly revised estimates reflect lower-than-anticipated mortality since 1975 and the use of these more favorable mortality rates in making future estimates.

The first year in which over two million Americans died was 1983. It is likely that there will never again be a year in which there is fewer than two million deaths in the United States. Between 2010 and 2020, when Baby Boomers begin to reach age 65, the number of deaths should rise quickly and exceed three million. Generally, however, death rates are expected to continue to decline. There is also the possibility of marked future reductions in death rates at the older ages, at the same time that increases are seen in the proportion of deaths in the United States that come in old age. By 2020, the Census Bureau estimates that 76.4 percent of all deaths will be of individuals 65 years of age or older.

Such changes in the trends of death rates could bring a somewhat larger elderly population and greater increases than are shown by the Census Bureau's middle series of population projections used in this book. As Table 3.1 indicates, the middle series of population projections used by the Census Bureau assumes mortality rates consistent with achieving an ***average life expectancy at birth*** of 82 years in the year 2050. Using the highest series of population projections (not shown in Table 3.1), including the assumption that life expectancy in 2050 will be 89.4 years, the Census Bureau projects 35.2 million elderly in the year 2000 and

58.4 million by the year 2020. The highest series projects an aged population that is about 500,000 or 1.4 percent larger than that projected by the middle series for 2000, and 5.2 million, or 9.7 percent larger for 2020.

The proportion of the total population that older people will make up in the future will be determined in great part by the *fertility rate* (birthrate). The middle series of population projections used by the Census Bureau includes an assumption of 2.25 lifetime births per woman. As Table 3.1 indicates, under this assumption, the elderly are expected to constitute about 16.5 percent of the total U.S. population by the year 2020 and 20 percent by 2050.

AGING OF THE OLDER POPULATION

Not only did the older population of the United States grow in absolute size and in its proportion of the total population during the twentieth century but it also aged. The median age of the 65-and-over population in the United States was 73.3 years in 1990, up from 71.9 in 1960. Table 3.2 shows that since 1980, the proportion of the aged who are 65 to 74 years of age has been getting smaller and that it will continue to do so until 2010. The proportion of people ages 75 to 84 has been getting larger, and this trend is also expected to continue until 2010. By 2010, the percentage of persons who are 65 to 74 years of age will be about 53.4 percent. After 2010, the aging trend of the population 65 years and over should reverse itself, as larger cohorts born in the post–World War II period enter the younger segment (65 to 74 years) of the elderly population.

The oldest-old, those 85 years of age and over, are the most rapidly growing elderly age group. Today, they likely number more than 4 million, or 12.3 percent of the elderly. Thanks to expected high rates of survivorship among the Baby Boom generation, it is expected that the oldest-old will number over 18 million in 2050, or 23.1 percent of elderly Americans and about 5 percent of all Americans.

TABLE 3.2   Percentage Distribution of the Population Age 65 and Over: 1980–2050

			PROJECTIONS			
	1980	*1990*	*2000*	*2010*	*2020*	*2050*
65 years and over	100.1	100.0	100.1	100.0	100.0	99.9
65–74 years	61.0	58.1	52.3	53.4	59.0	44.0
75–84 years	30.3	32.2	35.5	32.2	28.9	32.8
85 years and over	8.8	9.7	12.3	14.4	12.1	23.1

Note: Based on middle series Census Bureau projections. See Table 3.1 for an explanation of assumptions.

Source: U.S. Bureau of the Census, *Statistical Abstract of the United States: 1997* (Washington, DC: U.S. Government Printing Office, 1997), Tables 14 and 17.

Clearly, a pervasive trend throughout the latter part of the twentieth century, one that is expected to continue throughout the twenty-first century, is the overall aging of the population. The median age of the U.S. population was 32.8 years in 1990 and is expected to rise to 35.5 years by 2000 (middle series projections). This figure is projected to rise to 39.0 years by 2050.

The aging of the older population that is expected to occur over the next two decades or so has important policy implications for local, state, and federal agencies. One example involves the question of whether quality health service will be available to the growing population of elderly and very old people at an affordable cost.

THE DEMOGRAPHIC TRANSITION

The pattern of an increasing number and proportion of elderly persons in the U.S. population is no real surprise to students of demography. In fact, it is predictable from a theory of population change used by many demographers to explain the growth in a society's population. This theory is concerned with the relationship between birthrates and death rates (as well as migration rates) and the resulting effects on the age composition of populations. It allows one to understand and predict changes in the age composition of a society. The theory, which describes a three-stage process whereby a population moves from high fertility and high mortality to low fertility and low mortality, is often called the ***demographic transition***.[2] Most industrialized societies today have gone through the entire process of the demographic transition. They began to do so around 250 to 300 years ago, which is about the time the world's population began to grow rapidly.

The first stage of the demographic transition is characterized by high birthrates and high death rates. ***Preindustrial societies,*** with their very high death rates, were examples of populations in the first stage. They were extremely vulnerable to crop failure and famine, possessed very limited environmental health controls, and had no health technologies for caring for the sick and disabled. Individuals in such societies usually had a life expectancy of no more than 35 or 40 years, on average. Fertility was also necessarily high, as mortality took such a substantial toll that the continued existence of the society required high birthrates. As a result, there was little or no population growth in this stage of the demographic transition.

The second stage, sometimes called the stage of *transitional growth,* is characterized by continued high birthrates but a declining mortality. In this second stage of demographic transition, the population grows very rapidly and undergoes changes in age composition. Typically, the declining death rates are due to technological changes: increased food production, distribution, and availability; and reduced vulnerability to crop failures and famine. The ***age composition*** changes

---

[2]Zopf (1984), among others, offers a version of the demographic transition that allows for identifying more refined variation among societies and includes seven stages. For purposes of simplicity, a three-stage version of the demographic transition is offered here.

accompanying the technological changes usually involve a slightly increased proportion of the elderly (increased longevity being the likely cause) and a marked increase in the proportion of the population that is young (resulting from a significant decline in infant and child mortality).

Today, the less-industrialized countries of the world, which account for over 80 percent of the world's population, are in the middle stage of the demographic transition. Their death rates have fallen, but their birthrates remain high. Thus, their populations are growing rapidly, and, because they represent most of the world's population, the world's population is also growing rapidly.

The third stage, characterized by *low mortality and low or controlled fertility,* is most often descriptive of modern Western societies. Populations experiencing this stage are capable of controlling birthrates so that very low or no population growth may eventually occur. Birthrates in the United States and other industrialized countries have fallen for a number of reasons. These include social and economic changes that came with a rising standard of living. For example, individuals increasingly put off having children to attain more education and career advancement. Postponement of childbearing usually means having fewer children, because the number of years during which a woman can give birth is limited. In agricultural societies, children remain an important source of labor; in industrialized nations, the cost of raising and educating children is substantial. Birth-control techniques have improved dramatically and are available to more women. Finally, the decline in mortality itself has contributed to lower birthrates. As rates of survivorship into adulthood increase, the pressure to give birth to a large number of offspring has declined.

Some demographers believe that demographic transition theory is a useful tool only for analyzing population change in the West. Petersen (1975), for example, argues that today's so-called underdeveloped nations and totalitarian societies exhibit patterns of fertility, mortality, and migration that make them difficult to analyze in terms of a three-stage transition process. Typically, underdeveloped countries interested in rapid development have imported Western health programs and medical technology on a wholesale basis. This has resulted in significant declines in their death rates. Unfortunately, efforts to cut fertility have been less successful, with enormous population growth as a result. Some nation-states have attempted intervention in an effort to achieve specific demographic goals. Policies such as family subsidies, creation of state-controlled abortion centers, forced migration, and immigration or emigration restrictions have been employed to affect population dynamics.

The Population Pyramid

One graphic technique that is often employed to depict the demographic transition process is the population pyramid. The ***population pyramid*** is a special type of bar graph, with the various bars representing successive age categories, from the lowest at the bottom to the highest at the top. The population represented in this graphic device is usually broken down into 5-or 10-year intervals, with each bar divided between males at the left and females at the right. The length of the bars represents the population either in absolute figures or as a percentage.

Figure 3.1 shows population pyramids for the United States in 1995, 2010, and 2030. The reason for the basic shape of the pyramid is that among those born in a given year—1940, for example—some have died in each year since then, thus reducing the length of the bars representing successively higher ages. However, the shape is not ordinarily pyramidal because birthrates, death rates, and rates of migration all vary from year to year. The 1995 pyramid is somewhat bottom-heavy, with the largest age groups being 30 to 34 and 35 to 39 years of age and birthrates somewhat lower since 1967 or thereabout (Spencer 1989). The narrowness of the top of the 1995 pyramid (from 65 to 69 years and up) is a result of (1) lower birthrates during the Depression and up to World War II and (2) deaths that have already occurred within the early twentieth-century birth cohorts.

Today, the large Baby Boom cohorts are all over age 35, increasing the median age of the population, as was already indicated. The pyramid for 2010 reflects continuing expectation of lower birthrates into the first decade of the twenty-first century. After 2010, the Baby Boom cohorts no longer have such disproportionate influence on the shape of the pyramid; the median age of the population will begin to rise at a much slower rate. If it is possible to maintain the consistently low birthrates and death rates required in the third stage of the demographic transition, the pyramid would come to look like a rectangle turned on its end (e.g., see the pyramid for the year 2030), with relatively no population growth over the long term. Under such hypothetical conditions, the proportion of the aged population would rise steadily and become stationary toward the end of the twenty-first century. By 2080, almost 25 percent of the population could be expected to reach age 65 years; the Census Bureau projects 5 to 7 percent of the total population at age 85 years and over in the year 2080, and 0.5 percent of the population at 100 years of age or over (Spencer 1989).

THE DEPENDENCY RATIO

The growth of the elderly population has led gerontologists to look to the demographic relationship between it and the rest of the population. To the degree that the old are to be supported by the society to which they have contributed, this relationship may suggest the extent of social, economic, and political effort a society may be asked to make in support of its elderly.

One crude measure used to summarize this relationship is known as the *dependency ratio*. Arithmetically, the ratio represents the number or proportion of individuals in the dependent segment of the population divided by the number or proportion of individuals in the supportive or working population. Although the dependent population has two components, the young and the old, students of gerontology have especially concerned themselves with the *old-age dependency ratio*. Definitions of *old* and *working* are "65 and over" and "18 to 64" years of age, respectively. Thus, the old-age dependency ratio is, in simple demographic terms,

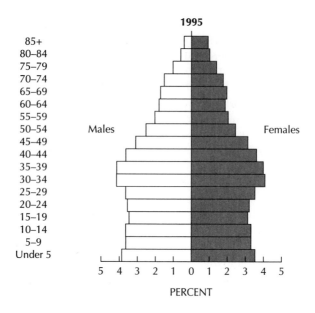

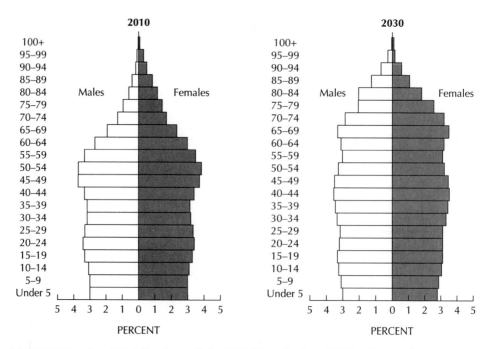

FIGURE 3.1   Age Distribution of the U.S. Population: 1995, 2010, and 2030

Sources: U.S. Senate Special Committee on Aging, *Aging America: Trends and Projections, 1991 ed.* (Washington, DC: U.S. Department of Health and Human Services, 1991), Figure 1; Current Population Reports p. 25–1104 (Washington, DC: U.S. Government Printing Office, 1993), Table 2.

65+/18–64.[3] This does not mean that every person aged 65 and over is dependent or that every person in the 18 to 64 range is working. However, these basic census categories are used to depict the relationship between these two segments of the society's population.

Table 3.3 shows old-age dependency ratios for the United States from 1980 to 2050. The ratio has increased slowly since 1980 and is expected to continue to do so until the year 2020, when a dramatic increase is projected. During the decade between 2010 and 2020, the oldest Baby Boomers will begin reaching retirement age, thus increasing the numerator; and a relatively low birthrate (such as now exists) means a relatively smaller work-force population (ages 18 to 64), reducing the denominator. Another dramatic increase is projected between 2020 and 2030. The projected old-age dependency ratio of 35.7 in 2030 indicates that every 36 individuals 65 years of age or over will hypothetically be supported by 100 working persons between the ages of 18 and 64. This constitutes a ratio of less than 1 to 3. In 1930, this ratio was about 1 to 11, and in 1980, it was about 1 to 5.4.

Some demographers have begun to distinguish between a *societal* old-age dependency ratio (discussed previously) and a *familial* old-age dependency ratio.

TABLE 3.3   Societal Old-Age Dependency Ratios in the United States: 1980–2050

YEAR	RATIO
1980	18.6
1994	20.2
Projections	
2000	20.5
2010	21.2
2020	27.7
2030	35.7
2040	36.5
2050	36.0

Note: Based on middle series Census Bureau projections. See Table 3.1 for an explanation of assumptions. The societal old-age dependency ratio is computed as follows: (population ages 65 years and over/population ages 18 to 64 years) × 100.

Source: U.S. Bureau of the Census, *Statistical Abstract of the United States: 1997* (Washington, DC: U.S. Government Printing Office, 1997), Tables 14 and 17.

[3]Actually, in order to ensure the presentation of the old-age dependency ratio in whole numbers, compute as follows: (those 65+ years of age/those 18 to 64 years of age) × 100.

The *familial old-age dependency ratio* can be used to illustrate the shifts in the ratio of elderly parents to children who would support them. This ratio is also defined in simple demographic terms: population aged 65 to 84/population aged 45 to 54. This does not mean that all persons aged 65 to 84 need support or even have children, or that every person in the 45 to 54 age range is willing or able to provide. Yet, these age categories are used to depict the ratio of the number of elderly persons to the number of younger persons of the next generation.

Table 3.4 shows familial old-age dependency ratios for the United States from 1980 to 2050. The ratios increased from 1980 to 1990 and then are projected to decline until 2020 when a dramatic increase is expected. In 1980, there were 102 persons aged 65 to 84 for every 100 persons aged 45 to 54. This figure reached 112 in 1990. A higher figure of 124 is projected for 2020, with a figure of 156 projected for 2030. Changes in the familial old-age dependency ratio result mainly from past trends in fertility. For example, the relatively high ratio in 1990 reflects the combination of high fertility (and in-migration) in the early part of the twentieth century (population aged 65 to 84 years) and reduced birthrates during the 1930s and 1940s (population aged 45 to 54 years). The higher ratio expected in 2020 and 2030 results from high fertility during the post–World War II Baby Boom years and the lower birthrates of the 1970s and early 1980s.

Shifts in the societal and familial old-age dependency ratios suggest that support of the aged will become especially serious after 2010, as Baby Boomers

TABLE 3.4   Familial Old-Age Dependency Ratios: 1980–2050

YEAR	RATIO
1980	102
1990	112
Projections	
2000	82
2010	77
2020	124
2030	156
2040	142
2050	139

Note: Based on middle series Census Bureau projections. See Table 3.1 for an explanation of assumptions. The familial old-age dependency ratio is computed as follows: (population ages 65 to 84 years/population ages 45 to 54 years) × 100.

Source: U.S. Bureau of the Census, *Statistical Abstract of the United States: 1997* (Washington, DC: U.S. Government Printing Office, 1997), Tables 14 and 17.

begin to turn age 65. It would seem that unless the elderly of the future are better able to support themselves than are current cohorts of elderly, an increasing burden will fall on the working population, requiring government to play a larger part in providing health and other services to the aged. Further, low fertility, low or no population growth, and aging of the population may predict no or slow economic growth. Such a scenario would increase the burden on the working population and make it more difficult to support rising public retirement and health care expenditures (Palmer & Gould 1986).

Some would disagree, however. It may be argued that the dependency burden of the elderly should not be measured in a vacuum and that the level of the child- or "young-age" dependency ratio should be taken into account, because the share of society's support available for the elderly is affected by the level of young-age dependency (Siegel & Davidson 1984). Table 3.5 presents the young- and old-age dependency ratios for the United States from 1980 and projected through the year 2050. The child- or young-age dependency ratio,[4] which is the number of children under age 18 per 100 persons 18 to 64 years, is expected to decline from 46.5 in 1980 to 39.0 in 2010 and slowly increase to 43.9 in 2050. This results from a continued expectation of reduced fertility and implies a marginally declining burden on the working population.

The combination of old- and young-age dependency ratios, representing an overall dependency burden on the working-age population, declined between 1980 and 1990 and is projected to be relatively stable through the year 2020. The

[4]The child- or young-age dependency ratio is computed as follows: (those less than 18 years of age/those 18 to 64 years of age) × 100.

TABLE 3.5   Old- and Young-Age Dependency Ratios: 1980–2050

YEAR	TOTAL DEPENDENTS	YOUNG-AGE RATIO	OLD-AGE RATIO
1980	65.1	46.5	18.6
1990	61.8	41.6	20.2
Projections			
2000	62.3	41.8	20.5
2010	60.2	39.0	21.2
2020	68.1	40.4	27.7
2030	78.7	43.0	35.7
2040	79.6	43.1	36.5
2050	79.9	43.9	36.0

Note: Based on middle series Census Bureau projections. See Table 3.1 for an explanation of assumptions.

Source: U.S. Bureau of the Census, *Statistical Abstract of the United States: 1997* (Washington, DC: U.S. Government Printing Office, 1997), Tables 14 and 17.

total dependency burden in 2020, projected to be 68.1, is close to the figure (65.1) used to describe the total burden in 1980. Between 1980 and 2020, the projected proportion of the total dependency burden accounted for by those under 18 years of age declines from 71.4 to 59.3 percent. By 2030, when the total dependency ratio is projected to increase to 78.7 (it was 79.0 in 1965), those under 18 years of age will account for only 54.6 percent of the total dependency burden.

Presumably, this decline would permit the conversion of some funds and other support resources from use by children to use by the elderly. Support costs for the elderly are generally thought to be greater than for the young and historically more likely to become a public responsibility; in the United States, support for children tends to be a private family responsibility (Clark & Spengler 1978). As a result of the expected shift in dependency burden between 1980 and 2030 from the young to the old, future governments may play a larger part in providing health and other support services to the aged.

Richard Easterlin (1991), a noted demographer, has attempted to place concern about the total dependency burden in the United States and other advanced industrial countries in some historical context. Using data from the Organization for Economic Cooperation and Development (OECD) <http://www.oecd.org> and the United Nations <http://www.un.org>, Easterlin plotted separately the total dependency burden, actual and projected, from 1880 to 2050 for the United States and 10 other western industrial nations. Two questions emerge from the projections: Will the process of technological invention and innovation slow as a result? and Will the working population be able to support rising public retirement and health care expenditures?

Over the long term, from 1870 to 1986, population growth has shown a downward trend in Austria, Belgium, Denmark, Germany, the Netherlands, Norway, Sweden, Switzerland, United Kingdom, and the United States. Only France shows a higher rate of population growth in the period from 1973 to 1986 than the period from 1870 to 1913. At the same time, the rate of real per capita income growth in these nation states has shown an upward trend. Only Sweden and Switzerland show real per capita income growth rates in 1973 to 1986 that are lower than the rates in 1870 to 1913. According to Easterlin, any future negative effects of an aging labor force will likely be offset by a more educated work force (and older population) and by continued increases in female labor-force participation.

When viewed in historical perspective, projections for the total dependency burden are not unique either. Figure 3.2 shows total and projected dependency ratios, actual and projected, for 11 different nations (including the United States) for 1880 to 2050. Ratios are calculated as the total number of persons aged 14 and under and aged 65 and over to those aged 15 to 64. On average, projected total dependency rates in 2050 are about the same as in 1880. In part, this results from a rising old-age dependency that is offset by a declining youth dependency. Only France and Switzerland show significantly higher dependency ratios projected for 2050 than experienced in 1880. Several nations—the United States, the United Kingdom, and Norway—show projections for 2050 to be noticeably lower than was actually experienced in 1880. Thus, working populations should be able to

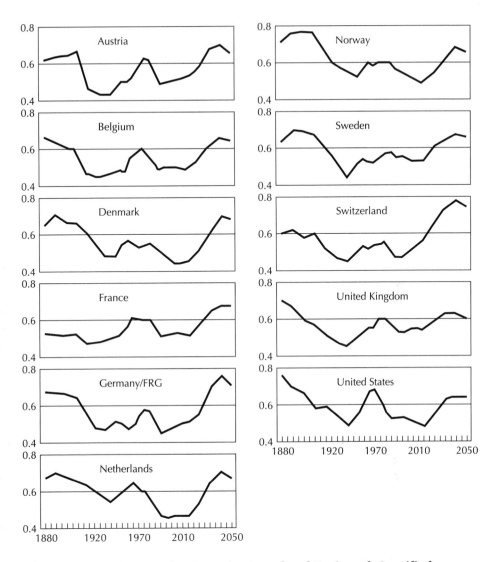

FIGURE 3.2   Total Dependency Ratio, Actual and Projected, Specified Country: 1880–2050 (ratio of persons ages 0 to 14 and 65+ to those ages 15 to 64)

Source: R. A. Easterlin, "The Economic Impact of Prospective Population Changes in Advanced Industrial Countries: An Historical Perspective," *Journal of Gerontology, 46* (6) (1991). Copyright © The Gerontological Society of America. Reproduced by permission of the publisher via Copyright Clearance Center, Inc.

handle the tax burdens related to programs for older dependents because there will be reduced need to support younger dependents.

Two caveats are in order, however. First, more research is needed on the issue of how private funds are used to support younger and older dependents. After all, tax burdens are about public monies, and public funds represent only a portion of the total available monies to support dependent populations. Second, shifting public expenditures from support of younger dependents to older dependents is a political problem. Projecting the feasibility of such a transfer is considerably more problematic than projecting the dependency rates!

SEX, RACE, AND ETHNIC COMPOSITION

Elderly women outnumber elderly men in virtually all settings within which aging takes place, despite the fact that the number of male births in a population consistently exceeds the number of female births (Matras 1973, pp. 145–146). Typically, after the earliest ages, the male excess is reduced by higher male mortality; at the most advanced ages, the number of females exceeds the number of males.

In the United States, the number of males for every 100 females—the *sex ratio*—in the over age 65 population declined throughout the twentieth century. In 1900, the sex ratio was 102; by 1930, it had declined to 100.4. The sex ratio in these years, however, was still heavily influenced by the predominantly male immigration prior to World War I. As Table 3.6 shows, in 1997, the sex ratio in the

Among older adults, chronological age is more indicative of diversity than disability.

TABLE 3.6   Males per 100 Females by Age: 1980–2050

	1980	1990	2000	2025	2050
All ages	94.5	95.1	95.5	96.0	96.3
65+ years	67.6	67.2	70.4	82.9	84.3

Source: U.S. Bureau of the Census, *Statistical Abstract of the United States: 1997* (Washington, DC: U.S. Government Printing Office, 1997), Tables 15 and 17.

older population in 2000 was projected to be 70.4 (it was 95.5 for the total population), and increases are expected through the first half of the twenty-first century. Principally, the sex ratio of the aged population is explained in terms of the higher mortality of males, particularly at ages below 65. This higher mortality among males reduces the relative number of survivors at the older ages. The projected increase in the sex ratio through 2050 reflects a projected narrowing of mortality rate differences between older males and females.

Until recently, the female population aged 65 and over grew more rapidly than the male population in this age stratum. Between 1980 and 1990, the aged female population increased about 22 percent, whereas the increase for the aged male population was about 21 percent; between 1990 and 2000, the aged female population was expected to increase by 9.6 percent, whereas the increase in aged males was expected to be 14.8 percent. This differential in growth rates, significant for the change in pattern it represents, added to the continued excess of males among the newborns, continues to yield a proportion of those age 65 and over among females that is considerably above that for males. In 2000, aged females constitute about 14.5 percent of the total female population, and aged males constitute about 10.7 percent of the total male population. The sex ratio of the elderly population in 2000 corresponds to about 6 million more women than men, or about 17.3 percent of the total aged population. In 1960, the excess was about 1.6 million women, accounting for about 9.5 percent of the aged population.

Because of enumeration problems, statistics on minority elderly should be viewed with some caution. In 1998, 12.7 percent of the total U.S. population was African American; however, African American elderly made up about 8.3 percent of the total elderly population. In general, the African American population in the United States is younger than the population of whites. The proportion of the black population that is 65 years of age and over is considerably smaller than that of the white population, for both males and females. Smaller proportions of blacks than whites survive to old age, although survival rate differences between the races narrow somewhat in old age. For example, according to *life tables* for 1990, 76 percent of white males survive from birth to age 65, as compared with 57 percent for African American males; for survivorship to age 65 among females, these percentages are 86 and 75 percent, respectively.

The key factor in the relative youthfulness of the African American population is their higher fertility. On average, black women have 2.4 children, compared to the 2.0 recorded for white women. Approximately 43 percent of all African Americans are under age 25, but only about 34 percent of all whites are in this age grouping. The median age of blacks is roughly 6.2 years less than that of whites. In 1998, for example, African Americans had a median age of 29.9 years; the comparable figure for whites was 36.3 years.

Next to Africans Americans, Latinos make up the largest minority in the United States, and this population is fast growing. In 1998, Latinos constituted about 11.2 percent of the U.S. population, or about 30.3 million people. Officially, this population increased by almost 14 million, or 93.5 percent, since 1980. The actual rate of growth, however, has probably been higher as a result of illegal immigration. The Census Bureau forecasts a substantial increase in the Latino population by 2000, with Latinos approaching about 88 percent of the size of the African American population in the United States. By 2010, the number of individuals of Latino origin in the United States is projected to be larger than the African American population.

The Latino population is a heterogeneous group. About 60 percent are of Mexican origin. One in eight Latinos is of Puerto Rican background (12.2 percent), 4.7 percent are Cuban, and 23 percent are of other Hispanic heritage. About half of the Latino elderly were not born in the United States. Cubans and Puerto Ricans are more recent immigrants than Mexican Americans, many of whom are descendants of original settlers of territories annexed by the United States in the Mexican-American War. The Latino population is an even younger population than that of African Americans (about 47 percent under 25 years of age versus 41 percent, respectively). High fertility and large family size, in addition to immigration of the young and repatriation of the middle-aged, contribute to the youthfulness of this group.

Many *ancestry groups* are represented within the U.S. population. Table 3.7 presents some data on single and multiple ancestry groups collected through surveys conducted by the Census Bureau in 1990. German, Irish, and English ancestry groups are the largest in the United States. Ancestry groups, large and small, are likely to have substantial proportions of elderly. For example, groups of Polish, Russian, and Italian ancestry are likely to have high proportions of elderly, resulting from the considerable *migration* to the United States that occurred early in the twentieth century, mostly before the mid-1920s. English and Irish migration largely took place in the nineteenth century. Thus, the high proportion of elderly in these groups is likely a result of declining fertility during the twentieth century. Recent immigrants, most of whom are relatively young, are most likely to have come from Mexico, the Caribbean (e.g., Dominican Republic and Cuba), the former Soviet Union, and Asia (e.g., the Philippines, Vietnam, and China).

Migration has had great impact on the age distribution of the foreign-born population in the United States. Before World War I, immigration was relatively unrestricted. After that war, changes in policy brought a sharp curtailment to immigration. In 1970, a relatively high proportion of the elderly were themselves foreign-born—among those 65 years of age and older, 15.3 percent were born

TABLE 3.7   Population by Selected Ancestry Groups, and Persons 65 Years and Over Speaking a Language Other than English at Home: 1990

ANCESTRY	TOTAL (1,000)	ANCESTRY	TOTAL (1,000)
German	57,947	Dutch	6,227
Irish	38,736	Asian[a]	5,904
English	32,652	Scotch-Irish	5,618
African American	23,777	Scottish	5,394
Italian	14,665	Swedish	4,681
Mexican	11,587	Norweigian	3,869
Polish	9,366	Russian	2,953
American Indian	8,708	Spanish	2,024

Persons 65 years old and over	31,195,000
Speak only English	27,381,000
Speak other language (total)	3,814,000
Speak Asian or Pacific Island language	355,000
Speak Spanish or Spanish Creole	1,057,000
Speak some other language	2,402,000

[a]Includes Asian Indian, Chinese, Filipino, Japanese, Korean, and Vietnamese.

Source: U.S. Bureau of the Census, *Statistical Abstract of the United States: 1995* (Washington, DC: U.S. Government Printing Office, 1995), Tables 56 and 57.

outside the United States. The proportion of the elderly population that is foreign-born will likely continue to decline in the near future.

GEOGRAPHIC DISTRIBUTION

The elderly population, like the total population, is not distributed equally across the United States. Generally, the elderly are most numerous in the states with the largest populations. California (3.6 million), Florida (2.7 million), New York (2.4 million), and Texas (2.0 million) have the largest elderly populations with more than two million each. Pennsylvania, Ohio, Illinois, Michigan, and New Jersey each have over 1 million aged residents. Together, these nine states account for 52.3 percent of the entire 1998 aged population in the United States. Table 3.8 lists the states by percentage of population aged 65 and over for 1998.

In all states, the aged population increased between 1980 and 1998 though at widely differing rates. By 1998, Florida showed the highest proportion of its population 65 years of age and older (18.3 percent), with 2.7 million elderly residing in the state. On the other end of the continuum, Alaska showed the smallest proportion of its population 65 years of age and older (5.5 percent), or about 34,000 elderly residing in the state.

TABLE 3.8   States by Percentage of Population Aged 65 Years and Over, 1998

PERCENTAGE		STATE
18.3	1	Florida
15.1–15.9	4	Iowa, Pennsylvania, Rhode Island, West Virginia
13.5–14.4	11	Arkansas, Connecticut, District of Columbia, Kansas, Maine, Massachusetts, Missouri, Nebraska, New Jersey, North Dakota, South Dakota
13.0–13.4	10	Arizona, Alabama, Delaware, Hawaii, Montana, New York, Ohio, Oklahoma, Oregon, Wisconsin
12.0–12.5	11	Kentucky, Illinois, Indiana, Michigan, Minnesota, Mississippi, New Hampshire, North Carolina, South Carolina, Tennessee, Vermont
11.1–11.5	9	California, Idaho, Louisiana, Maryland, Nevada, New Mexico, Virginia, Washington, Wyoming
8.8–10.1	4	Colorado, Georgia, Texas, Utah
5.5	1	Alaska
	51	

Source: U.S. Bureau of the Census, *Statistical Abstract of the United States: 1999* (119th ed.) (Washington, DC: U.S. Government Printing Office, 1999), Table 33.

According to the U.S. Census Bureau, eight of the nation's states are projected to double their elderly population by the year 2020. Nevada is expected to increase the fastest (by 116 percent), followed by Arizona (112 percent), Colorado (108 percent), Georgia (104 percent), Washington (104 percent), Alaska (103 percent), Utah (102 percent), and California (101 percent). Seven of the states are located in the West; only Georgia is located outside the Western region. By 2020, Arizona, Georgia, and Washington will join the nine states that currently have more than one million elderly residents.

Residential Mobility

Some of the growth in state elderly populations is due to natural increase, but some is the result of interstate migration. Compared to younger persons, the elderly are much less likely to be residentially mobile. Between 1992 and 1993, movers age 65 years and older were only one-half as likely as the total U.S. population to move to a different county (3 vs. 6 percent) and only one-third as likely to move to a different state (1 vs. 3 percent). About one-half of the elderly who move remain within the same metropolitan area.

The proportion of women movers is comparable to those of men for all elderly age groups and mobility types. Elderly African Americans and Latinos changed residence within the United States in proportions similar to their representation within the total elderly population (Hansen 1994). Rogers (1988) identified two age-based patterns in his analysis of elderly migration data from selected developed countries, including the United States. One pattern is characterized by *intercommunity* (amenity-motivated, long-distance migrations) and the other by *intracommunity* (assistance-motivated, short-distance moves). According to the U.S. Census Bureau, in the 1985–90 period, those 85 years of age and older were more likely to have moved within the United States than those age 65 to 84 years. The moves of the oldest-old may be related to health problems; perhaps nursing homes or residence of near relatives (e.g., adult children, siblings) are their destinations. Add widowhood to health declines and the probability of a residential move increases dramatically (Bradsher et al. 1992).

Most elderly migrants who move to a different county stay in the same region of the country as where they previously lived. Between 1992 and 1993, only 18 percent of migrants in the Northeast came from some other part of the country; about one-fourth of migrants in the Midwest (23 percent), the South (26 percent), and the West (30 percent) came from other regions. Longino (1995) reports that interstate migration of persons 60 years of age and over tends to be concentrated among relatively few origin and destination states. Florida was the state with the largest net elderly in-migration, whereas New York had the largest elderly out-migration, during 1965–70, 1975–80, and 1985–90.

Using data from the 1990 census to derive elderly net migration rates by state between 1985 and 1990, the U.S. Census Bureau identified several revealing geographic patterns. For example, the 13 states with the highest net elderly in-migration rates are in the South and Southwest, the so-called **Sunbelt.** Among the 23 states with net in-migration of elderly, 21 were in the Sunbelt. Only New Hampshire and Vermont had net in-migrants of elderly among the 21 Northeast and Midwest states.

Planners are concerned about the economic implications of elderly interstate migration. Substantial amounts of retirement income may be transferred between States as a result of retirement migration. Based on the 1990 census data, we would expect Sunbelt states such as Florida and Arizona to benefit from interstate migration of the aged, while Frostbelt states in the Midwest lose as a result of elderly interstate income transfers. Silverstein (1995) reports that older persons moving from the Sunbelt to the Frostbelt are disproportionately disabled and widowed in comparison with older persons moving in the opposite direction. This pattern seems consistent with a "second" elderly move after the "first" retirement move. The second move, motivated by the onset of disability and widowhood, represents an effort to move closer to the supportive efforts of adult children and other relatives. This type of move may represent a double whammy in income transfer for many Midwest and Northeast "sending" states. For example, states such as Florida and California may benefit by receiving relatively healthier and wealthier migrants, while "sending" states first lose well-off consumers and then may later gain back migrants more likely to need costly social and health services.

Residential Concentration

Increasingly, the elderly have become an urbanized population, locating in central cities or in places that structurally and functionally are parts of larger metropolitan areas. In 1990, only 26.4 percent of the elderly in the United States lived outside of large metropolitan areas in cities with fewer than 50,000 people, small towns, rural areas, or farms. According to Frey (1992), the growth in the urban elderly population is largely the result of younger cohorts aging "in place" and of residential relocations made earlier in the life span, rather than of relocation made after retirement. These aging-in-place metropolitan areas are found disproportionately in the Northeast and Midwest, and among moderate and smaller-sized metropolitan areas in the South. This is reflected in the fact that for the year 2000, these regions project the highest proportion of population aged 65 years and older. Within the Middle Atlantic states (New York, New Jersey, and Pennsylvania), people 65 years of age and older are projected to constitute 13.9 percent of the total population in the year 2000. Similarly, in the West North Central (Iowa, Minnesota, and the Dakotas, among others) and the South Atlantic (Virginia, Georgia, Florida, among others) regions, 13.6 percent of the total population in year 2000 is expected to be 65 years of age or older. This contrasts with the Pacific and Mountain regions, where only 10.8 and 11.6 percent of the respective populations are projected to be age 65 years or older in 2000.

Still, it is important to remember that more than 20 states have at least 40 percent of their older population in rural areas; and in 9 states (Alaska, Arkansas, Mississippi, North Carolina, North Dakota, South Carolina, South Dakota, Vermont, and West Virginia), more than half of the older population is rural. Also, a number of these states have 10 percent or more of their older populations living on farms (here, for the moment, the elderly is defined as those 60 years of age and over). This fact has important policy implications, given that so many government programs are designed to serve an urban population.

In 1990, 79 percent of the U.S. population resided within a metropolitan area; the comparable figure was about 74 percent (about 23 million people) for the population age 65 years and over. Metropolitan population growth in the United States has been a function of the growth of suburbs, however—the fastest growing sites for the elderly population in recent decades. Elderly American Indians, Eskimos, and Aleuts (AIEA) were the only racial group in 1990 more likely to live outside metropolitan areas than inside. Elderly Asian Americans were most likely to be found living inside metropolitan areas (almost 13 living inside a metropolitan area to every 1 living outside a metropolitan area in 1990), followed by elderly Latinos (about 8 to 1), elderly African Americans (about 4 to 1), and elderly whites (about 3 to 1). Also, in each of the racial groups, the oldest-old were somewhat more likely to be found residing outside metropolitan areas than those aged 65 to 84 years.

SUMMARY

The elderly population of the United States increased throughout the twentieth century and continued substantial growth is projected through the first half of the twenty-first century. Changes in fertility, mortality, and migration have and will continue to contribute to this growth. In addition, the aged population is itself aging. By 2010, approximately 46.6 percent of the aged will be 75 years of age or over; and by 2050, more than 55 percent of the aged are projected to be 75 years of age or older.

The old-age dependency ratio is a measure often used to summarize the demographic relationship between the elderly and the rest of the population. It is expected to increase slowly in the coming years, with dramatic increases by 2020 and again by 2030. Continued expectations for reduced fertility during this same period should allow for a projected decline in the young-age dependency ratio. Thus, the total dependency burden over the next 20 years or so should be relatively stable, with the projected dependency ratio in 2020 approximating the figure for 1980. However, the total dependency ratio is projected to rise by 2030, with most of the increase coming from the old-age dependency ratio.

Elderly women outnumber elderly men, a difference that has been increasing for the past several decades. Because of enumeration problems, data on minority elderly must be evaluated cautiously. African Americans constitute the largest group of nonwhite elderly, although they represent a smaller proportion of the total elderly population than of the total general population. The Latino elderly population has undergone dramatic increase in recent decades, and this trend is expected to continue. This population, however, is even more youthful than the black population.

In general, the elderly population is concentrated in the largest states. Florida, California, and New York have the largest elderly populations, with more than two million each. Some growth in state populations of elderly is due to interstate migration. Sunbelt states rank among the most popular destinations for elderly migrants. Streams of elderly migrants seem to come to the Sunbelt principally from the Northeast and Midwest. Recently, gerontologists have identified streams of out-migrants returning home from the Sunbelt states. For individual elderly persons, this may be a consequence of widowhood or of the onset of health and/or financial problems. Increasingly, planners are concerned about the economic implications of elderly interstate migration.

Like the rest of the U.S. population, the elderly have become increasingly urbanized, locating in central cities or places that structurally and functionally are part of a larger metropolitan area. This pattern reflects the aging "in place" of populations that may have relocated earlier in life more than the migration of those over 60 years of age. The suburbs have been a fast-growing site for the elderly population in recent decades. Also, among racial groups in 1990, only elderly American Indians, Eskimos, and Aleuts were more likely to live outside metropolitan areas than inside.

STUDY QUESTIONS

1. Discuss the roles fertility, mortality, and migration have played in the growth of the elderly population in the United States during the twentieth century.

2. Should people have confidence in U.S. Census Bureau projections of the growth in numbers and proportion of the elderly population in the United States in the future? Why or why not?

3. What is a *dependency ratio*? Distinguish between the *societal* old-age dependency ratio and the *familial* old-age dependency ratio. How is the mix of old-age and young-age dependency ratios expected to change in the United States in the future?

4. Try to put dependency ratios in some historical and cross-national perspective. How does what is projected to occur in the United States compare with the projections for other nations? Assume these projections about the future are accurate and discuss their consequences. What, if any, are the caveats about dependency ratios in the future?

5. Define *sex ratio*. Applying the concept to the elderly population, how did the sex ratio change during the twentieth century? Why did it change?

6. Why is recognition of minority elderly issues likely to increase in the future? Why may the importance of ancestry groups diminish among the elderly in this same future?

7. Describe the residential mobility patterns of the elderly in the contemporary United States. What role do the Sunbelt states play in elderly migration? In this context, what is meant by aging "in place"?

8. How has the residential concentration of the elderly population changed in recent decades? Why?

REFERENCES

Bradsher, J. E., Longino, C. F., Jackson, D. J., & Zimmerman, R. S. (1992). Health and geographic mobility among the recently widowed. *Journal of Gerontology: Social Sciences, 47* (5), S261–S268.

Clark, R. L., & Spengler, J. J. (1978). Changing dependency and dependency costs: The implications of future dependency ratios and their composition. In B. Herzog (Ed.), *Aging and income: Programs and prospects for the elderly.* New York: Human Sciences Press.

Easterlin, R. A. (1991). The economic impact of prospective population changes in advanced industrial countries: An historical perspective. *Journal of Gerontology: Social Sciences, 46* (6), S299–309.

Frey, W. H. (1992). Metropolitan redistribution of the U.S. elderly: 1960–70, 1970–80, 1980–90. In A. Rogers and others (Eds.), *Elderly migra-* *tion and population redistribution.* London: Bellhaven Press.

Hansen, K. A., U.S. Bureau of the Census (1994). *Geographic mobility: March 1992 to March 1993.* Current Population Reports, P20–481. Washington, DC: U.S. Government Printing Office.

Longino, C. F. (1995). *Retirement migration in America.* Houston, TX: Vacation Publications.

Matras, J. (1973). *Populations and societies.* Englewood Cliffs, NJ: Prentice-Hall.

Neugarten, B. (1974, September). Age groups in American society and the rise of the young-old. *Annals of the American Academy,* pp. 187–198.

Palmer, J. L., & Gould, S. G. (1986). Economic consequences of population aging. In A. Pifer & L. Bronte (Eds.), *Our aging society: Paradox and promise.* New York: Norton.

Petersen, W. (1975). *Population* (3rd ed.). New York: Macmillan.

Rogers, A. (1988). Age patterns of elderly migration: An international comparison. *Demography, 25* (3), 355–370.

Siegel, J. S. (1979). *Prospective trends in the size and structure of the elderly population, impact of mortality trends and some implications.* Current Population Reports, Special Studies Series P-23, No. 78. Washington, DC: U.S. Department of Commerce, Bureau of the Census.

Siegel, J. S., & Davidson, M. (1984). *Demographic and socioeconomic aspects of aging in the United States.* Current Population Reports, Special Studies Series P-23, No. 138. Washington, DC: U.S. Department of Commerce, Bureau of the Census.

Silverstein, M. (1995). Stability and change in temporal distance between the elderly and their children. *Demography, 32* (1), 29–45.

Spencer, G. (1989). *Projections of the population of the United States, by age, sex, and race: 1988 to 2080.* Current Population Reports, Population Estimates and Projections Series P-25, No. 1018. Washington, DC: U.S. Department of Commerce, Bureau of the Census.

U.S. Bureau of the Census. (1997). *Statistical abstract of the United States: 1997* (117th ed.). Washington, DC: U.S. Government Printing Office.

Zopf, Paul, Jr. (1984). *Population: An introduction to social demography.* Palo Alto, CA: Mayfield.

CHAPTER FOUR

WHAT ARE THE RESULTS OF AGING?

CARY S. KART

EILEEN S. METRESS

SEAMUS P. METRESS

The physician Alexander Leaf (1973) quotes Frederic Verzar, the Swiss gerontologist, as saying, "Old age is not an illness. It is a continuation of life with decreasing capacities for adaptation." Some students of aging would disagree. It has been a popular view that if old age is not an illness in and of itself, there is at least a strong relationship between biological aging and pathology. This view posits that biological deterioration creates a state of susceptibility to disease, and susceptibility to particular diseases leads to death.

One way to resolve this disagreement may be to distinguish between *biological* and *pathological* aging. It is difficult to say at what point in life a person is old, but it is clear that everyone becomes so. Everyone ages. Genetic and other prenatal influences set the stage for the aging sequence and factors in the postnatal environment (demographic, economic, psychological, and social) act to modify this sequence. The changes that accompany aging occur in different people at different chronological ages and progress at different rates. Changes in physical appearance are the most easily recognized; it is also well known that some physical capabilities diminish. These changes may be placed in the category of **biological aging.**

Disease is another matter. As individuals grow older, they are more likely to become afflicted with certain diseases, many of which prove fatal. Changes that occur as a result of disease processes may be categorized as **pathological aging.** Kohn (1985) offers three ways to define disease:

1. Some diseases are universal, progressive, and inevitable with age. Atherosclerosis, a chronic disease of the blood vessels, exemplifies this type of dis-

ease. It increases a person's vulnerability to other diseases, but in many respects is indistinguishable from normal aging.

2. Some diseases are age related, but are neither universal nor inevitable. For example, the risks of contracting many forms of cancer increase with age, but not all elderly people contract cancer.

3. Some diseases are not age related, but their impact is greater as the individual ages. Death rates from respiratory diseases, for example, are dramatically higher in older age groups than in younger and middle-aged groups.

We begin this chapter by discussing recent progress in mortality and life expectancy among the elderly. This is followed by a description of the results of biological aging—those important bodily changes that occur as age increases. Current theories or explanations of biological aging are evaluated in Chapter 5. Disease processes related to pathological aging are reserved for discussion in Chapter 6.

For those who wonder why a social gerontologist needs to know so much about biology, gerontologist Robert Atchley has an answer: Understanding the physiological changes that accompany aging is important for the social gerontologist "because they represent the concrete physiological limits around which social arrangements are built" (Atchley 1972, p. 47). Broadly interpreted, Atchley's statement means that changes fundamental to aging do not occur in isolation. Psychological and social changes both affect and are affected by the physiological changes taking place. The social gerontologist who is ignorant about the biological aspects of aging cannot hope to comprehend the important relationships among the physical, psychological, and social changes that accompany aging.

MORTALITY

Gerontologists use the term *senescence* to describe all postmaturational changes and the increasing vulnerability individuals face as a result of these changes. Senescence describes the group of effects that lead to a decreasing expectation of life with increasing age (Comfort 1979). Strehler (1962) distinguishes senescence from other biological processes in four ways: (1) Its characteristics are universal, (2) the changes that constitute it come from within the individual, (3) the processes associated with senescence occur gradually, and (4) the changes that appear in senescence have a deleterious effect on the individual.

Is senescence a fundamental, inherent, biological process? Comfort (1979) is doubtful. He believes that attempts to identify a single underlying property that explains all instances of senescent change are misplaced. Yet, there does appear to be some pattern to one's increased vulnerability through the life course. Roughly speaking, it appears that the probability of dying doubles every eight years.

This phenomenon has been recognized since 1825, when Benjamin Gompertz observed that an exponential increase in the death rate occurred between the ages of 10 and 60. After plotting age-specific death rates on a logarithmic scale and finding an increase that was nearly linear, Gompertz suggested that human mortality was governed by an equation with two terms. The first accounted for chance deaths that would occur at any age; the second, characteristic of the species, represented the exponential increase with time. These observations, sometimes referred to as *Gompertz's law,* reasonably seem to describe human mortality in many human societies (Fries & Crapo 1981). However, although the principle that the probability of dying increases with age is a valid one, it is important to emphasize that the probabilities themselves differ for males and females, vary by race, and change through time.

During 1997, an estimated 2.3 million deaths occurred in the United States. The preliminary death rate for that year was 8.6 deaths per 1,000 population. The majority of these deaths involved elderly people. Over 1.7 million (or about 74 percent) of the deaths occurred among individuals who had passed their 65th birthday.

The leading cause of death among the elderly is heart disease, which accounts for almost 37 percent of all deaths in old age. Malignant neoplasms (cancer) account for 23 percent of the deaths (26 percent for men, 20 percent for women) and cerebrovascular diseases account for another 8 percent of deaths among the elderly. Together, these three categories accounted for about 68 percent of all deaths of elderly people and approximately 62 percent of all deaths in the United States in 1994. Obviously, the high proportion of deaths of elderly people due to these three causes is an expression of vulnerability to these afflictions that begins earlier in the life cycle.

Table 4.1 shows the pattern of death rates for these three leading causes of death among the elderly between 1960 and 1995. Death rates for the elderly have declined overall since 1960; between 1970 and 1990, death rates for males ages 65 to 74 years declined by 28 percent, and the decline for comparably aged females was 23 percent. The death rate for elderly men is considerably higher than that of elderly women, continuing a long-term trend. Among whites ages 65 to 74 years of age, for example, the death rate from all causes was 95 percent higher for males than females in 1970, and 77 percent higher in 1990.

As Table 4.1 indicates, the death rates for two of the three leading causes of death, heart disease and stroke (cerebrovascular disease), declined significantly between 1960 and 1995. The death rate for cancer, the second leading cause of death in 1995, has increased over the years (21.6 percent for individuals 65 to 74 years of age in the 1960–95 period). Sex differences in death (not shown in this table) are pronounced for different forms of cancer; in 1990, among individuals 65 to 74 years old, males had a death rate for respiratory cancer approximately 2.5 times higher than that for females. Since 1970, however, large annual increases in respiratory cancer mortality, associated with cigarette smoking, have occurred for older women. The increase from 1970 to 1990 in mortality rates from respiratory cancer among women ages 65 to 74 was 307 percent. This compares with a 15.8 percent increase in mortality rates from breast cancer for comparably aged women over the same time period. In 1990, for women ages 65 to 74 years and 75 to 84 years, the death rates from respiratory cancer were higher than those from breast cancer.

TABLE 4.1   U.S. Death Rates for Diseases of the Heart, Cerebrovascular Diseases (including stroke), and Malignant Neoplasms (cancer), by Age: 1960–1995

AGE	1960[a]	1970	1980	1990	1995
Diseases of the Heart					
55–64 years	737.9	652.3	494.1	357.0	322.9
65–74 years	1,740.5	1,558.2	1,218.6	872.0	799.9
75–84 years	4,089.4	3,683.8	2,993.1	2,219.1	2,064.7
85+years	9,317.8	8,468.0	7,777.1	6,618.4	6,484.1
Cerebrovascular Diseases					
55–64 years	147.3	115.8	65.2	46.4	46.1
65–74 years	469.2	384.1	219.5	139.6	137.2
75–84 years	1,491.3	1,254.2	788.6	479.4	481.4
85+ years	3,680.5	3,234.6	2,288.9	1,587.7	1,636.5
Malignant Neoplasms					
55–64 years	396.8	423.0	436.1	448.4	416.0
65–74 years	713.9	754.2	817.9	871.6	868.2
75–84 years	1,127.4	1,168.0	1,232.3	1,351.6	1,364.8
85+ years	1,450.0	1,417.3	1,594.6	1,773.9	1,823.8

Note: Deaths per 100,000 population in specified group.

[a]Includes deaths of nonresidents of the United States.

Sources: National Center for Health Statistics, *Health, United States, 1988,* DHHS Publication No. (PHS) 89-1232, Public Health Service (Washington, DC: U.S. Government Printing Office, 1989); U.S. Bureau of the Census, 1994, Table 128. 1995 data taken from <http://www.cdc. gov/nchswww/datawh/statb/unpubd/mortabs/gmwk290.htm>.

Most elderly people die as a result of some long-standing chronic condition, which is sometimes related to personal habits (e.g., smoking, drinking, poor eating patterns) or environmental conditions (e.g., harsh work settings, air pollution) that go back many years. Preventing illness and death from these conditions must begin before old age. Some deaths, such as those from accidents, have declined significantly. The death rate from accidents and violence, for example, for white males age 65 years and over in 1990 was 8 percent lower than that in 1980; the comparable decline for elderly African American males during this period was 18.7 percent.

Sex Differences in Mortality

As can be seen from Table 4.2, comparisons by race show that men have higher death rates than women in every age category. Some of this difference is almost certainly attributable to biological factors. For example, the larger proportion of males who die in infancy is apparently not explainable by any systematic variation

TABLE 4.2 Age-Specific Death Rates, by Race and Sex: 1995

| | DEATHS PER 1,000 | | | |
| | Whites | | African Americans | |
AGE	Male	Female	Male	Female
All ages	9.3	8.9	9.8	7.6
Age-adjusted	6.1	3.7	10.1	5.7
Under 1	7.2	5.7	15.9	13.4
1–4	0.4	0.3	0.8	0.6
5–14	0.3	0.2	0.4	0.3
15–24	1.2	0.4	2.5	0.7
25–34	1.8	0.6	4.2	1.7
35–44	2.9	1.3	7.2	3.3
45–54	5.3	2.9	12.7	6.2
55–64	13.3	7.9	24.4	13.5
65–74	32.0	19.2	46.1	28.2
75–84	73.2	48.3	87.8	58.4
85+	181.5	146.4	167.3	134.7

Source: U.S. Bureau of the Census, *Statistical Abstract of the United States: 1998* (Washington, DC: U.S. Government Printing Office, 1998), Tables 131 and 132.

in physical and/or social environmental factors. For most adults, however, it may be difficult to distinguish between biological and environmental contributors to death. Male/female differences in mortality may be due, in part, to sex differences in the use of physician services. Typically, women report using health services more frequently than men do. This may result in earlier and more effective treatment of their illnesses and may contribute to lower death rates relative to men. The child-bearing experience of females and the overrepresentation of males in dangerous occupations are two additional factors that make it difficult to determine the relative effect on mortality of biological and environmental or sociocultural factors.

Francis Madigan (1957) attempted to differentiate between biological and environmental factors in mortality. His classic study compared the mortality experience of Catholic brothers and nuns who were members of teaching communities. Madigan argued that the life patterns of these two groups are quite similar and that, over time, brothers and nuns are subjected to the same sociocultural stresses. Of particular importance here is the absence of sex-linked activities that are relevant to mortality—namely, childbearing for females and participation in dangerous occupations for males. Madigan found that the difference in death rates between brothers and nuns was greater than between males and females in the population as a whole and that this difference had been increasing during the decades under study. From this, he argued that biological factors are more important than sociocultural ones. Further, Madigan hypothesized that the death rate advantage enjoyed by women was bound up in their greater constitutional resistance to degenerative diseases.

Such a hypothesis is difficult to test empirically. Table 4.3 presents ratios of male to female death rates for the population 65 years of age and over, by age and race, for 1995. In general, the table shows a decline in male/female death ratios by age for whites and African Americans. Among people ages 55 to 64, the male death rate is about 70 percent higher than that of females (80 percent for African Americans), whereas the death rate of men in the group 85 years and older is only 24 percent higher than that of women.

The general increase in mortality differences between the sexes very likely reflects a major shift in the cause pattern of mortality. During the twentieth century, the contribution of infectious and parasitic diseases and maternal mortality to overall mortality rates diminished relative to that of chronic degenerative diseases, such as diseases of the heart, malignant neoplasms, and cerebrovascular diseases (Siegel 1979). However, changes in recent decades in the male/female mortality ratio appear to be more closely associated with social and environmental factors than with biological ones. For example, according to Petersen (1975), the age-adjusted death rate from cancers was 65 percent higher for females than males in 1900, about equal between the sexes in 1947, and 20 percent higher for males by 1963. This changing pattern would seem to have more to do with technological advancements than with innate biological factors. The diagnosis and cure of the cancers most frequently occurring among females (i.e., breast and uterine) have improved at a more rapid rate than those for cancers most frequently occurring among males (i.e., lung and digestive system).

Can the pattern of increasing male/female death rate ratios among the elderly continue? Among those of all races and of whites ages 65 to 69, ratios actually fell between 1970 and 1980, and again between 1980 and 1990. This deceleration suggests that the death rate differential between older men and women will not increase in the future as it has in the past (Zopf 1986). This is especially the case for the young-old.

TABLE 4.3   Male-Female Death Ratios among the Elderly, by Age and Race: 1995

	AGE			
RACE	*55–64*	*65–74*	*75–84*	*85+*
Whites	1.68	1.67	1.52	1.24
African-Americans	1.81	1.63	1.50	1.24

Note: Ratios computed from data in Table 4.2.

Source: U.S. Bureau of the Census, *Statistical Abstract of the United States: 1998* (Washington, DC: U.S. Government Printing Office, 1998), Tables 131 and 132.

Race Differentials in Mortality

The large racial differential in mortality rates often does not receive the attention it deserves because it is a hidden factor. Return to Table 4.2 and look across the first row ("All ages"). Note that the death rate for African American males is slightly *higher* than that for white males (9.8 versus 9.3), whereas the death rate for African American females is slightly *lower* than that for white females (7.6 versus 8.9). Nevertheless, because of higher birthrates, African Americans have a younger age structure, and this tends to mask true mortality. By examining mortality across the second row ("Age-adjusted") and in individual age groups, the full impact of race emerges. For example, infant mortality in the United States in 1995 was 135 percent higher among African American than white females (13.4 vs. 5.7 percent, respectively) and 121 percent higher among African American than white males (15.9 vs. 7.2 percent, respectively). Death rates among young adults 25 to 34 years of age are 133 percent greater for African American males and 183 percent greater for African American females than for whites. Only among those 85 years of age and over does the racial differential in death rates tend to decline precipitously.

Although there has been some longer-term progress in reducing the racial differential in mortality, most recently this trend has reversed itself. In 1980, the age-adjusted death rate for African Americans was 50 percent higher than the comparable figure for whites. For 1990, this differential was 61 percent, and by 1995, it was 58 percent.

The race differential in mortality is greater for males than for females. As Table 4.2 shows, in 1995, African American males had an age-adjusted death rate that was 66 percent higher than the rate for white males (10.1 vs. 6.1 percent, respectively); this differential for females was 54 percent (5.7 vs. 3.7 percent, respectively). Also, the sex differential in mortality is greater for African Americans on a proportional basis than for the white population. Among whites, males have an age-adjusted death rate that is 65 percent higher than that among females; among African Americans, this difference is 77 percent. It appears that African American women have been able to achieve a greater share of the available advancements in death control than have African American men.

Two additional points need to be stressed when dealing with racial differentials in mortality. First, there is no reason to believe that African Americans, in particular, or nonwhites, in general, are biologically less fit than whites in their capacity to survive. What this point emphasizes is that racial differentials in mortality reflect unnecessarily high mortality among nonwhites. Second, other factors, not the least of which is socioeconomic status, confound mortality data. Over 25 years ago, Kitagawa and Hauser (1973) showed that age-adjusted mortality rates for Japanese Americans were about one-third the corresponding rates for whites and one-half the rate for African Americans. Their analysis of median family income among these groups suggests that socioeconomic status may account for a considerable proportion of the race differentials in mortality.

How does low socioeconomic status contribute to higher illness and mortality rates? A number of different mechanisms can be identified through socioeconomic status or position that may influence health status and even likelihood of death. These include differential susceptibilities to illness from the physical and social environment, variations in health habits and behaviors, as well as differential access to and/or response to health services (Hertzman, Frank, & Evans 1994).

Although it may be impossible to quantify precisely the role biological and social/cultural factors play as contributors to mortality differentials among different population groups in U.S. society, it is apparent that aging, even biological aging, does not occur in a sociocultural vacuum. Age-adjusted death rates in the U.S. population are, for example, only about one-third what they were at the beginning of the twentieth century. Additionally, even when considering those who, as a group, are already chronologically old, a significant decline in death rates has been seen since 1960. For males ages 65 to 74 years, for example, the reduction from 1960 to 1990 is about 27 percent; for comparably aged females, the reduction is 23 percent. These reductions in the death rates of the population reflect at least four factors, all of which involve attempts begun in the nineteenth century to increase control over the environment (Dorn 1959): (1) increased food supply, (2) development of commerce and transportation, (3) changes in technology and industry, and (4) increased control over infectious disease.

LIFE EXPECTANCY

Progress in the reduction of mortality is also reflected in figures for average life expectancy at birth. *Average life expectancy at birth,* defined as the average number of years a person born today can expect to live under current mortality conditions, has shown great improvement since 1900. It rose from 49.2 years in 1900–02 to 75.8 years in 1995 (see Table 4.4). This change constitutes a 54 percent increase in life expectancy at birth, or an average annual gain of almost 0.3 year in this period. Still, just as there are significant sex and racial differentials in mortality, there are similar differentials in life expectancy. As Table 4.4 shows, the population group with the highest life expectancy at birth in 1995 is the white female (79.6 years); nonwhite males have the lowest life expectancy (67.5 years). All groups have substantially increased life expectancies since 1900. Better sanitary conditions, the development of effective public health programs, and rises in the standard of living are three factors often cited to explain increased life expectancy in the twentieth century.

Life expectancy at birth is a function of death rates at all ages. Thus, the statistic does not reveal at what specific ages improvement has occurred. Gerontologists are particularly interested in judging progress in "survivorship" for those age 65 and over. One technique for judging such progress is to look at actual survivorship rates. For example, in 1900–02, 40.9 percent of newborn babies could be expected to reach age 65; by 1994, 86 percent of the female birth cohort and 75 percent of the male birth cohort could be expected to experience age 65.

A second technique for measuring changes in survivorship involves looking at changes in *age-specific life expectancy.* Table 4.5 presents life expectancies at various

TABLE 4.4   Years of Life Expectancy at Birth, by Race and Sex: 1900–02 to 1995

YEARS	ALL GROUPS	WHITE		OTHER RACES	
		Male	*Female*	*Male*	*Female*
1900–1902	49.2	48.2	51.1	32.5	35.0
1909–1911[a]	51.6	50.3	53.7	34.2	37.7
1919–1921[a]	56.6	56.6	58.6	47.2	47.0
1929–1931	59.3	59.2	62.8	47.5	49.5
1939–1941	63.8	63.3	67.2	52.4	55.4
1949–1951	68.2	66.4	72.2	59.1	63.0
1959–1961	68.9	67.6	74.2	61.5	66.5
1969–1971	70.7	67.9	75.5	61.0	69.1
1980–1981	73.9	70.8	78.4	65.7	74.8
1990	75.4	72.7	79.4	67.0	75.2
1995	75.8	73.4	79.6	67.5	75.8

[a]Death registration states only.

Sources: National Center for Health Statistics, *Vital Statistics of the United States, 1978,* Vol. 2, Sec. 5, *Life Tables* (1980), Tables 5-A and 5-5; Annual Summary of Births, Deaths, Marriages, and Divorces: United States, 1981, *Monthly Vital Statistics Report,* Vol. 30, No. 13 (1982), pp. 3–4, 15. Data for 1990 & 1995 taken from U.S. Bureau of the Census, 1997, Table 117.

TABLE 4.5   Years of Life Expectancy at Ages 65 and 75: 1900–02, 1985, 1996

YEAR AND AGE	WHITES		AFRICAN AMERICANS	
	Male	*Female*	*Male*	*Female*
1900–1902[a]				
65 years	11.5	11.2	10.4	11.4
75	6.8	7.3	6.6	7.9
1985				
65 years	14.5	18.7	13.0	16.9
75	9.0	11.7	8.7	11.1
1996				
65 years	15.8	19.1	13.9	17.2
75	9.8	12.0	9.0	11.2

[a]Death registration states only.

Source: National Center for Health Statistics. *Health, United States, 1998 with Socioeconomic Status and Health Chartbook* (Hyattsville, MD: Author, 1998), Table 29.

elderly ages by sex and race in the United States for 1900–02, 1985, and 1996. In particular, gains in life expectancies for aged males (both whites and African Americans) have not kept pace with those for aged females. With the exception of white females, life expectancy at age 65 has moved ahead more slowly than has life expectancy at birth since 1900. The relatively small increase of "expectation" values for those age 65 and over between 1900–02 and 1996 is, in part, a function of the relative lack of success the health sciences have had in reducing adult deaths caused by heart disease, cancer, and cerebrovascular diseases. These have been the leading causes of death among persons 65 years and over since 1950. Although some modest progress in reducing death rates due to heart disease and cerebrovascular diseases has been made in the last 40 years, the death rate from malignant neoplasms (cancer) has increased by more than 11 percent since 1980.

AGE-RELATED PHYSIOLOGICAL CHANGES[1]

It is important to recall that all people age, but not at the same rate. Some individuals show symptoms of aging before they are chronologically old. Others, who are chronologically old, do not yet show all of the results of senescence. According to

[1]Materials presented in this section are adapted from Kart, Metress, and Metress (1992).

Across the life course, which changes are more significant—those that are internal and psychological or those that are external and observable?

Leaf (1973, p. 52), the average person at age 75, compared with the same person at age 30, will have 92 percent of his or her former brain weight, 84 percent basal metabolism, 70 percent kidney filtration rate, and 43 percent maximum breathing capacity. Still, the loss of function reflected in these figures does not occur at the same rate in every individual. More important, these changes do not, in and of themselves, bring dysfunction. Yet, these figures do provide empirical support for something many of us (even those under age 75) have long suspected: We are not the people we once were!

What happens physiologically as people age? What are the specific results of senescence?

The Skin

To most people, the condition of the skin, hair, and connective tissue collectively represents the ultimate indicator of age. People are often judged to be of a certain age on the basis of visible wrinkles or the degree of graying of the hair. Many older people (as well as younger people) invest in so-called miracle creams and hair dyes in an attempt to disguise these signs of age. Although perceptions of age, like those of beauty, are in the eyes of the beholder, one's outward appearance does change as one ages.

The speed and degree of some age-associated skin changes are related to a number of factors such as heredity, hormone balances, and life-style, including smoking, nutrition, and exposure to sun, wind, or chemicals. Long-term exposure to sunlight accelerates time's metamorphosis of the skin. It is the major environmental/modifiable factor contributing to cosmetic alteration and cancer of the skin. Thus, recreational and occupational pursuits can hasten age-associated skin changes. Likewise, the rate of melanoma, the most serious form of skin cancer, differs geographically on the basis of sun exposure and among ethnic groups.

Most of these skin changes are not life threatening. However, they are those that many in this highly youth-oriented society equate with dreaded old age. Such changes, cosmetic and benign (as they are described here), may affect an individual's self-concept. Older people have pride in their appearance, and such concerns should not be dismissed because of their age.

The skin is a marvelous organ that generally serves its owner well throughout life, including old age. Its elasticity, suppleness, and musculature allow freedom of movement and expression. It also protects one against various physical and chemical injuries while serving as an important heat regulator and sensory device. As a protective sheath, skin limits water loss and prohibits the entrance of countless numbers of disease-causing microorganisms. These various functions of the human skin are aided by the presence of subcutaneous fat tissue, sweat- and oil-secreting glands, pigment cells, and blood vessels. Changes in these structures lead to various age-associated changes in the form and function of the skin.

Certainly the most obvious age-associated skin change is wrinkling, which begins during one's twenties and continues throughout life. Wrinkling is influenced by several factors. The human face, because of its musculature, is capable of tremendous movement and expression of emotions. Indeed, facial expressions represent an extremely important component of human communication. Smiles, laughter, frowns, disappointment, anger, rage, and surprise are all recorded. The hand of time captures these expressions and outlines them on the face. The lines that begin to form in areas of greatest movement proliferate and become deeper as the years pass. By the age of 40, most people bear the typical lines of their expressions.

Wrinkling is also caused by a loss of subcutaneous fat tissue as well as skin elasticity. The latter is significantly affected by chronic exposure to ultraviolet radiation. The loss of fat tissue is generalized but is usually most obvious in the face and the upper and lower extremities. The entire body becomes wrinkled and thus changed in appearance. Diminished subcutaneous fat tissue is also largely responsible for the characteristic emaciated look of old age. A once filled-out form gives way to a frame that seems to exhibit many of the constituents of which it is made. The hands prominently display the bones, tendons, and blood vessels that make them up. Likewise, bony prominences and vessels of the face, trunk, and extremities become more apparent.

A loss of padding, normally provided by subcutaneous fat tissue, predisposes many older persons to the development of pressure sores. These sores develop in areas between bony prominences and overlying skin areas when pressure is unrelieved. These serious lesions represent an important problem in the health care of older persons.

The loss of subcutaneous fat tissue alters certain normal functions of the skin. Subcutaneous fat serves as an important insulator of the body; as it diminishes, greater amounts of body heat escape, often leaving an individual feeling chilly. Older people often complain of being cold when others around them are comfortable. Complaints of being cold are caused largely by a loss of body insulation and, in part, by a diminished blood flow to the skin and extremities.

Older people are also more likely to suffer from heat exhaustion because of changes in their capacity to perspire as a result of atrophy of the sweat glands. Thus, elderly individuals should avoid being in hot, stuffy rooms, spending too much time in the sun on a warm day, or overexerting themselves. Furthermore, atrophic changes in the sweat glands make the use of deodorants and antiperspirants unnecessary for many older people.

As has already been noted, aging is accompanied by a reduction of blood flow to the skin. The diminished blood supply contributes to the coolness of the surface of the aged skin as well as to thickened fingernails and toenails and a generalized loss of body hair, including a reduction of head hair.

The hair also grays with age—one of the most noted age-associated physical changes. Loss of hair color as well as loss of one's previously characteristic skin color occur as a result of a decrease in the number of functioning pigment-producing cells. As if to compensate for their loss, some pigment cells of the skin enlarge. These enlarged areas are responsible for many of the pigmented blotches seen on aged skin.

Various factors contribute to increased skin infections in the elderly—for example, blood vessel changes, an altered immune response, and atrophy of the sebaceous or oil-secreting glands. Blood vessels supply the body with the nutrients and chemicals that help repair tissue and combat foreign invaders, such as infectious microorganisms. If blood flow is decreased, so is the important supply of these substances. Furthermore, skin may dry and crack because of the atrophy of the oil-secreting glands. Cracks and breaks in the skin not only lead to discomfort but also can serve as portals of entry for bacteria, viruses, and fungi.

The elderly are susceptible to the same skin disorders as are persons in younger age groups. Still, certain skin disorders are more common among older persons, such as senile pruritus (itching), keratosis (a localized thickening of the skin), skin cancer, and pressure sores.

The Skeletomuscular System

One's bones and muscles provide support, stability, and shape to the body; protect vital organs; and allow freedom of movement and locomotion. These provisions of the skeletomuscular system are very much taken for granted. As one ages, however, many of these functions become limited and, on occasion, denied. Joint changes, along with diminished bone and muscle mass, can give way to increased falls and fractures, stooped posture and shortened stature, loss of muscle power, misshapen joints, pain, stiffness, and limited mobility.

Arthritis and allied bone and muscular conditions are among the most common of all disorders affecting people 65 years of age and over. In fact, joint and muscular aches and pains, as well as stiffness, are often expected in old age. Frequently, all such symptoms are lumped together as discomforts of arthritis or rheumatism. Such a practice can be dangerous. The stiff limbs of Parkinson's disease and the bone pain of osteomalacia may be dismissed, thereby causing a delay in needed medical attention. Chronic, recurrent muscular and joint pain is *not* natural; in response to such symptoms, people of all ages should seek prompt medical attention.

Bone and muscle changes are significant in that they can greatly alter an individual's life-style by making certain tasks of daily living much more difficult. It should be emphasized that even though certain degenerative changes occur, they need not necessarily be disabling if proper diagnosis, treatment, and maintenance are given. Changes or disease states of the skeletomuscular system rarely serve directly to shorten the life span. Nevertheless, if a person is bedridden and immobilized as a result of pain, stiffness, falls, or fractures, complications can result that lead to death.

Arthritis is a generic term that refers to an inflammation or a degenerative change of a joint. It occurs worldwide and has occurred throughout time; it is one of the oldest known diseases. Indeed, the cartoon image of Neanderthal man as a stooped brute with a bent-knee gait represents a caricature of an arthritic relative who lived over 40,000 years ago. This condition is still very prevalent today; it represents the number-one crippler of all age groups in the United States.

Osteoarthritis, the most common joint disease, is a degenerative joint change that takes place with aging. Its cause is not definitely known. It is also referred to as "wear-and-tear arthritis" and "degenerative joint disease." With this condition, there is a gradual wearing away of joint cartilage. The resultant exposure of rough underlying bone ends can cause pain and stiffness. Bony outgrowths known as osteophytes may appear at the margin of the affected bone. Long-standing osteoarthritis can also do damage to the internal ligaments, resulting in abnormal movements of the bones and joint instability or disorganization. The joints reflecting such involvement are most generally those associated with weight bearing. Differences in severity may be related to differences in life-styles, occupation, and/or participation in certain leisure activities.

Although osteoarthritis affects more people (perhaps as many as 40 million in the United States), *rheumatoid arthritis* is the more serious disease and carries the greatest potential for pain, disfigurement, and crippling. It may commence at any age, but persons most commonly develop initial symptoms somewhere between the ages of 20 and 50. The disease is not typically a condition of old age per se; most people carry it into old age.

Rheumatoid arthritis is a chronic, systemic, inflammatory disease of connective tissue that is two to three times more common among women than men. This condition is most commonly characterized by persistent and progressive joint involvement leading to disorganized joints and great pain and discomfort. Symptoms include malaise, fatigue, weight loss, fever, joint pain, redness, swelling, stiffness, and deformity. Many joints are affected. Extra-articulated tissue—especially that of the heart, lungs, eyes, and blood vessels—is also involved. The disease is characterized by acute episodes or flares alternating with remissions or periods of relative inactivity. Within 10 to 15 years, most rheumatoid arthritis victims will develop moderate to marked decline in functional capacity.

The cause of rheumatoid arthritis is not fully understood. It is now viewed as an autoimmune disease—that is, one that results from the production of antibodies that work against the body's own tissues. The autoantibody known as rheumatoid factor (RF) is present in 85 percent of rheumatoid arthritis patients. Multiple factors that probably lead to the development of this condition include possible previous exposure to an infectious agent and genetic factors that program a given immune response.

Associated with the aging process is a gradual loss of bone that reduces skeletal mass without disrupting the proportions of minerals and organic materials. This general loss of bone is known as *osteopenia.* When the condition advances to undermine the actual structural integrity of bone, *osteoporosis* is said to occur. Osteoporosis has been recognized for many years, since it was first described by German anatomists. The quantitative decrease in bone mass can result in diminished height, slumped posture, backache, and a reduction in the structural strength of bones that makes them more susceptible to fracture. For many persons, however, bone loss is asymptomatic.

Osteoporosis can involve most bones of the body; those most critically involved, however, include the vertebra, wrist, and hip. Some diminution in the density of the vertebral column eventually occurs in most individuals beyond a certain age, resulting in vertebral compression and an age-associated shortening of the trunk and loss of stature. Osteoporosis of the spine is a common cause of backache in the elderly, with symptoms of vertebral involvement ranging from minor to severe back pain. A more severe consequence of osteoporosis is a femoral neck fracture. The neck of the femur is forced to bear much weight, and osteoporosis can so diminish its mechanical integrity that a fracture results. It is now believed that many of the falls and associated hip fractures of old age actually represent an osteoporotic femoral neck that broke under its weight-bearing task. In fact, radiographic evidence indicates that approximately three out of four of those elderly individuals who suffer from a broken hip express evidence of osteoporotic involvement of the femoral neck. Osteoporosis can be ameliorated in old age with a solid bone structure based on sufficient calcium intake during the younger years.

Sarcopenia is the loss of muscle that occurs with age. The condition is not completely understood, but it is known to be influenced by multiple factors, including a sedentary life-style. Much muscle loss that occurs with age in so many individuals is both preventable and reversible with regular physical activity. Resistance training or weight lifting can help maintain and even increase muscle mass and strength.

The Neurosensory System

The nervous system is important in controlling the functioning of the body—including activities such as smooth and skeletal muscle contractions—and in receiving, processing, and storing information. The special senses of vision, hearing, taste, smell, and touch provide an individual with a link to the outside world. Neurosensory changes that can influence an individual's functioning, activities, response to stimuli, and perception of the world do occur with age. It is also true that the world's perception of an individual may be unduly influenced by neurosensory changes that he or she has undergone. For example, the older person with impaired hearing or vision may be labeled as stubborn, eccentric, or even senile.

Recent work maintains that, contrary to what was once widely conjectured, normal aging is not accompanied by a significant loss of brain cells. Although there is some decline and shrinkage in neurons and some loss of synapses (connections between them), these changes do not translate into major declines in learning ability or memory. However, some specific brain parts do lose substantial numbers of neurons. Such losses can be accelerated by other factors, such as stress. The hippocampus serves as an example in this matter. Located deep within the brain, this structure is essential to cognitive functioning and memory. Its sustained exposure to high concentrations of stress hormones may contribute to hippocampus cell loss and cognitive decline. Hence, the importance of stress prevention and management is significant.

The brain's ability to adapt continues well into old age. Despite some losses in cell numbers, mental activity encourages the branching of nerve fibers establishing new synaptic connections. This increased "hard wiring" of the brain allows communication between neurons to maintain cognitive functioning. Such information underscores the importance of intellectual stimulation from the cradle to the grave. Furthermore, the surplus brain capacity provided by mental activity and the concomitant increase in the number of synaptic connections carries implications for the treatment of stroke and the possible postponement or circumvention of the onset of Alzheimer's disease. Theoretically, it may be possible to reroute brain messages whose normal pathways would otherwise be blocked by brain injury or disease.

It should be noted that although the capacity for brain adaptation continues with age, it does decrease somewhat and is influenced in some degree by genetics. As a result of aging, there is an inevitable slowing of reaction time, which is a measure of how quickly an individual can respond to a stimulus.

The Gastrointestinal System

The gastrointestinal tract is the product of millions of years of biocultural evolution. The human species evolved from primate ancestors who were primarily vegetarians but capable of omnivorous alimentation. The omnivorous nature of the species helped it expand and evolve to fit a wide variety of ecological conditions. Judging from the development of a great variety of cultural traditions with dissimilar eating customs, it seems that the gastrointestinal system has served the species well.

Like other body systems, the gastrointestinal system is subject to the aging process. Age-associated changes include atrophy of the secretion mechanisms, decreasing motility of the gut, loss of strength and tone of the muscular tissue and its supporting structures, changes in neurosensory feedback on such things as enzyme and hormone release, innervation of the tract, and diminished response to pain and internal sensations. Although the indisputable evidence for the relationship between these changes and aging is still not overwhelming, there is certainly enough circumstantial evidence to warrant a consideration of the possibilities.

Gastrointestinal symptoms such as indigestion, heartburn, and epigastric discomfort increase with age, although identifying and evaluating these symptoms is difficult. For example, age changes in the teeth and gums increase the likelihood of periodontal disease, which itself may cause pain in chewing, thereby resulting in less chewing of food. This can increase the chance of choking on food as well as lead to greater likelihood of indigestion. Many gastrointestinal symptoms are caused by normal functional changes in the tract. With increasing age, however, they often are associated with serious pathological conditions, such as cancer. The threat or fear of cancer can exert a great deal of psychological pressure on individuals. Stress of this type not only affects mental health but it can also affect other body systems to cause or exacerbate problems such as hypertension and chronic respiratory disease.

The signs and symptoms often associated with one part of the gastrointestinal tract may actually be associated with another part of the tract. This is caused by the phenomenon of *referral,* as well as by the fact that the organs are part of an integrated system and thus are interrelated. The tract includes the mouth, esophagus, stomach, small intestine, gall bladder, liver, pancreas, and large intestine. Discomfort perceived as originating in the stomach may actually be coming from the lower gastrointestinal tract. An organ-based survey of the gastrointestinal system and its age-related problems is beyond the scope of this chapter. Still, several caveats are in order. Health professionals who deal with gastrointestinal disorders of the aged must be flexible in their approach. Disorders should be carefully evaluated before being dismissed as functional manifestations. Symptoms of the gastrointestinal tract often have their origins in pyschosocial factors, not biological malfunction. If evaluation indicates a functional disorder, the health professional should explain the problem to the patient in clear, jargon-free terms. A sympathetic attitude and a face-to-face discussion of the situation can sometimes do more for people than medical intervention.

The Cardiopulmonary System

Generally, the anatomical and physiological changes that take place in the aging heart still allow it to function adequately if the coronary artery system is not greatly damaged by disease. Because coronary artery disease is prevalent among older Americans, however, it is difficult to determine the extent to which the heart ages independently of the disease. In the absence of disease, the heart tends to maintain its size; in some individuals, it may become smaller with age. In particular, the left ventricular cavity, that chamber of the heart that sends oxygenated blood to the body, may decrease in size because of a reduction in activity and physical demands in old age. Older people who are malnourished, confined to bed, or experiencing extended illness may show additional atrophy of the heart. Accompanying this reduction in heart size is a reduction in heart muscle strength and cardiac output. Still, without disease or additional alteration in heart function, cardiac output should be quite adequate, as the body's requirements are reduced because of the atrophy of other body tissues and a decreased basal metabolism rate.

The heart valves tend to increase in thickness with age, and certain valves may be the sites of calcium salt deposits. These changes are not clinically significant unless there is a modification in the normal closing of a heart valve, which may stimulate more serious heart disease. Although blood pressure tends to increase with age, this is often related to changes in underlying mechanisms, including kidney and heart functions, among others. Systolic pressure—associated with the phase of the cardiac cycle in which the heart contracts, expelling blood—tends to stabilize at approximately 75 years of age. Diastolic pressure, involving the phase of the cardiac cycle during which the heart relaxes and its chambers fill with blood—tends to stabilize at age 65 and then may gradually decline.

Coronary artery disease increases in incidence with age and represents the major cause of heart disease and death in older Americans. In this condition, there is a deficiency of blood to the heart tissue because of the narrowing or constricting of the cardiac vessels that supply it. Tissue that is denied an adequate blood supply is called *ischemic;* hence, coronary artery disease is also known as ***ischemic heart disease.***

An overwhelming number of persons living in industrialized nations develop a condition known as ***atherosclerosis,*** a narrowing of arterial passageways as a result of the development of plaques on their interior walls. These plaques—which contain an accumulation of smooth muscle cells and fat and cholesterol crystals in combination with calcium salts, connective tissue, and scar tissue—serve to reduce the size of the passageway in such a manner that the vessel may eventually become totally closed off. The closing of an artery can cause ischemic heart tissue.

Arteriosclerosis, a generic term referring to the loss of elasticity of the arterial walls, is sometimes called "hardening of the arteries." This condition, which occurs in all populations, is progressive and age related. Ultimately, this age-associated loss of elasticity of arteries can contribute to reduced blood flow to an area. Unfortunately, the terms *arteriosclerosis* and *atherosclerosis* are often confused or used interchangeably. Arteriosclerosis is a general aging phenomenon, whereas atherosclerosis is variable in individuals and populations.

A number of aging changes collectively exert an effect on the respiratory system. These changes, which serve to reduce maximum breathing capacity, cause elderly people to become fatigued more easily than younger persons. Nevertheless, these changes are not sufficient to cause apparent symptoms at a resting state. In the absence of disease, they do not significantly affect the life-style of an older individual. Changes do occur, but they are not necessarily incapacitating.

The airways and tissues of the respiratory tract, including the air sacs, become less elastic and more rigid with age. Osteoporosis may alter the size of the chest cavity as a result of the downward and forward movement of the ribs. Also, the power of the respiratory muscles becomes reduced along with that of the abdominal muscles, which can hinder the movement of the diaphragm.

Respiratory diseases are more prevalent in older individuals than in the general population. The threat of serious respiratory infection increases with age, as does the threat of the obstructive conditions of chronic bronchitis, emphysema, and lung cancer. Some researchers believe the threat of respiratory infection is related to age-associated reductions in resistance to infectious microorganisms. Others suggest that age simply allows for an increased number of exposures as well as an increased cumulative time of exposure to disease-promoting factors. Nevertheless, obstructive pulmonary conditions and lung cancer are not solely the results of inherent age factors. Environmental conditions such as exposure to secondhand cigarette smoke and polluted air play an important role in their development. Recently, data from the Department of Health and Human Services show that death rates from lung cancer increase fourfold throughout the adult life of a nonsmoker. Nevertheless, the risk of developing lung cancer in an elderly moderate smoker (one-half to one pack of cigarettes a day) is 10 times as great as in a nonsmoker. With additional increase in the degree of exposure to tobacco, the risk increases still further.

The Urinary System

The bladder of an elderly person has a capacity of less than half (250 milliliters) that of a young adult (600 ml) and often contains as much as 100 ml of residual urine. Moreover, the onset of the desire to urinate, referred to as the *micturition reflex,* is delayed in older persons. Normally, this reflex is activated when the bladder is half full, but in the elderly, it often does not occur until the bladder is near capacity. The origin of this alteration of the micturition reflex is unclear, but it may be related to age changes in the frontal area of the cerebral cortex or to damage associated with a cerebral infraction or tumor. Changes in sensory neurons are probably more important than bladder changes and cause more frequent voiding at lower bladder volumes.

Reduced bladder capacity, coupled with a delayed micturition reflex, can lead to problems of frequent urination and extreme urgency of urination. These conditions, even if they do not render an individual incontinent, are an annoyance to older persons. In spite of the gradual decline of many kidney functions, in general, most people enter adulthood with enough reserve capacity so that ample functioning is maintained regardless of age. Even in the event of persistent bladder problems, programs do exist to physically retrain older people in the control of bladder function.

There appears to be a decrease in average renal function with age, with some variation attributed to changes in diet as well as psychosocial factors. This may result from a loss of nephrons, the basic cell unit in the kidneys. With increasing age, the kidneys themselves are found to be smaller, and the nephrons are smaller in size and fewer in number. Despite these apparently dramatic changes, loss of renal tissue is probably secondary in importance to the structural vascular changes that occur in the aging kidneys. In general, the arterial tree atrophies, and blood flow to the kidneys is reduced, decreasing the functional efficiency of the system. These vascular changes likely contribute to the loss of nephrons, and this is especially significant when the kidney is seriously malfunctioning or when severe atherosclerosis is superimposed on the aging process.

SEXUALITY AND AGING

Late-Life Sexuality: Myth and Reality

The reputedly "long-lived" **Abkhasians** attribute their longevity to their practices in sex, work, and diet (Benet 1971). They normally do not begin regular sexual relations before the age of 30, the traditional age of marriage. They believe such self-discipline is necessary to conserve energy, including sexual energy, in order to enjoy prolonged life. Anthropologist Sula Benet (1971) reports that one medical team investigating the sex life of the Abkhasians concluded that many men retain their sexual potency long after the age of 70 and almost 14 percent of the women continue to menstruate after the age of 55.

Although there is no hard evidence to link Abkhasian sexual practices with longevity, it is fair to say that the relationship between sexuality and age expressed in Abkhasian society is quite different from the norm in U.S. society. In the latter, sex and aging are often linked to negative humor that is filled with disdain and an apprehensiveness about growing older. Popular themes for such humor often include the impotence of older men and the unquestioned unattractiveness of older women. Examples abound:

> An eighty-five-year-old man was complaining to his friend, "My stenographer is suing me for breach of promise." His friend answered, "At eighty-five, what could you promise her?" (Adams 1968)

It may be that life begins at forty but everything else starts to wear out, fall out, or spread out. (*Reader's Digest* 1972)

Such jokes may reflect basic attitudes, thoughts, and feelings that are not commonly stated, which makes one wonder why most attitudes are so negative about sex in later life. Certainly some of this reflects negative feelings about old people and aging in general—what is referred to in this book as *ageism.* Among the stereotypes of ageism is the myth of **desexualization:** If a person is old (or getting old), he or she is alleged to be finished with sex. This myth is part of what Butler and Lewis (1976) refer to as the "aesthetic narrowness" about sex that prevails in U.S. society. Stated simply, the widespread assumption in the United States (and in most of the Western world) is that sex is only for the young and beautiful. Unfortunately, it is not just the young who believe this but many older people as well.

Misinformation surrounds the issue of late-life sexuality. For example, there is a common presumption that sexual desire diminishes with age, but this is not necessarily the case. Verwoerdt, Pfeiffer, and Wang (1969a, 1969b) found the following:

1. The incidence of sexual interest does not show an age-related decline—interest may persist into the eighties.
2. The incidence of sexual activity declines from a level of more than 50 percent in the early sixties to a level between 10 and 20 percent for people in their eighties.
3. The sexual behavior patterns of the later years correlate with those of the younger years. If there was interest and satisfying activity in the early years, there is likely to be interest and satisfying activity in the later years as well.

Sexual interest, capacities, and functions change with age. For the most part, like many biological and psychological functions discussed in this book, these dimensions of sexuality decline with increasing age. This decline can be seen as part of the normal aging process, but it does *not* mean that older men and women in reasonably good health should not be able to have active and satisfying sex lives.

Age-Related Changes in the Genital System[2]

The genital system is characterized by a number of age-related changes in physiology and anatomy. On the whole, very few age-specific disorders are associated with this body system. With the exception of declining levels of testosterone, most of the problems of sexuality and aging are sociogenic or psychogenic.

The Female Genital System.   The female reproductive system becomes less efficient with age, with a reduction in secretion of sex hormones (*estrogen* and

[2]This section relies heavily on Katchadourian (1972) and Fulton (1992).

progesterone), in ovulation, and in the ability of the uterine tube (where fertilization occurs) and the uterus (womb) to support a young embryo.

Many physical changes occur in the female genital tract. The external genitalia of the female, known as the *vulva,* include the major and minor lips, the clitoris, and the vaginal orifice. With age, the folds of the major and minor lips become less pronounced, and the skin becomes thinner. Vascularity and elasticity decrease, and the area becomes more susceptible to tissue trauma and the development of pruritus (itching). Glands decrease in number, as does the level of secretion, leading to shrinking and drying of the area.

Among the internal female reproductive organs, the uterus decreases in size, becomes more fibrous, and has fewer endometrial glands. The cervix, or lower portion of the uterus, is reduced in size, and the cervical canal (which is surrounded by the upper end of the vagina) decreases in diameter. The uterine tubes (where ova pass and are fertilized) become thinner, and the ovaries take on an irregular shape. Ovulation becomes irregular and finally stops, and there is a drastic reduction in the production of female hormones.

The latter changes, along with irregular or absent menstruation, often characterize *menopause,* a term used to describe the conclusion of a 20- to 30-year period of change in the female genital system that progresses differently in each individual. Approximately 50 percent of all women go through menopause between ages 45 and 50, about 25 percent before age 45, and about 25 percent after age 50 (Hafez 1976). The age of onset can be accelerated by debilitating disease, endocrine disorder, or both.

A number of symptoms are associated with menopause, although they appear to be less common than is popularly thought. These include irritability, anxiety, depression, loss of appetite, insomnia, and headache. Some of these symptoms are more psychologically than physiologically based. It has been observed that these symptoms are found more often in women with a history of psychotic behavior. Hot flashes, patchy redness on the face and chest, and sweating are associated with vasomotor instability, which causes irregularity in blood vessel diameter and thus irregularity of blood flow to the surface. There is a tendency for fat deposits in the abdominal and pelvic areas. Pubic hair becomes abundant, and breasts may atrophy. The nipples become smaller and less erectile. Still, postmenopausal women can continue to be interested and active sexually.

How do these changes affect female functioning in sexual relations? According to Masters and Johnson (1970):

1. Older women take a longer time to respond to sexual stimuli.
2. Lubrication takes longer and is generally less effective than in younger women.
3. The vagina has reduced elasticity and expansive qualities. The tissues lining the vagina are more easily irritated.
4. The clitoris is reduced in size, though still responsive to stimulation.
5. Orgasms are generally less intense and of shorter duration.

A special note is in order about disorders of the female genital system. The uterus and breast are frequent sites of cancer. Breast cancer is the leading cause of death among women between the ages of 40 and 60. Cervical cancer peaks during these same ages, whereas uterine cancer does so at about 65 years of age. Cancer of the vulva is more a disease of older women; over 50 percent of all cases occur in those over age 60. These are all good reasons that sex organs should not be cloaked in myth and mystery. All these disorders give early warnings that should be taken seriously. Not every swelling of the breast indicates breast cancer, and not every vaginal discharge is evidence of carcinoma. These are some of the early signs of cancer, however, and are *not* normal age-related changes. Women can be alert to them without becoming preoccupied. Often, the difference between alertness and ignorance may be one of life and death.

The Male Genital System.   The male reproductive system continues to produce germ cells *(sperm)* and sex hormones *(testosterone)* well into old age. Production of both declines with advancing age, although testosterone production is maintained at a higher level longer than is estrogen production in women. The decrease of testosterone has definite effects on older men, including a possible waning of sexual desire, although other physiological changes such as decreased sensitivity of the penis may be even more responsible for the decline.

A number of major physical changes occur in the genital system. The size and the firmness of the testes decrease. Sperm production takes place within the testes in seminiferous or sperm-bearing tubules, which thicken and decrease in diameter with age. This reduces sperm production, although abundant spermatozoa are found even in old age. The production of sex hormones also takes place in the testes but is independent of the sperm-producing structures. The cells responsible for hormone production, located between the seminiferous tubules in proximity to blood vessels, are called *interstitial cells.* Age-related fibrosis, involving an increase in the amount of fibrous connective tissue in the testes, constricts the blood supply and reduces production capacities of the sperm and hormone-producing structures.

Fibrosis may also affect the penis, the male organ for sexual intercourse and for the delivery of semen for reproductive purposes. The penis has no bone and no intrinsic muscles; its components are sheathed in fibrous coats and enclosed within a loose skin. Erection is a purely vascular phenomenon, and age-related increase in fibrous tissue can affect blood supply.

Secretions of the prostate gland account for much of the volume of semen as well as its characteristic odor. The prostate gland often enlarges in older men. The ejaculatory duct, which empties into the urethra (the tube that leads out of the bladder), and the urethra itself traverse the prostate gland. Thus, prostatic enlargement often has the dual effect of making ejaculatory contractions less forceful and urination more difficult. Cancer of the prostate is a frequent neoplasm among older men and is not necessarily immediately life threatening. All older men should have regular physical examinations to monitor the condition of the prostate.

Masters and Johnson (1970) have translated these physical changes into their impact on the sexual functioning of the older male. Summarized, these impacts include the following:

1. It takes longer to achieve a full erection, which may not be as full or as firm as for a younger man.
2. It usually takes longer to achieve an orgasm. There is a reduction in the force and amount of the ejaculation and fewer genital spasms are experienced.
3. Erection subsides more rapidly after ejaculation.
4. It takes longer to have a second erection and orgasm.

The changes described here are a normal part of aging, but individual variations should be recognized. Individuals should understand these age-related changes and not be alarmed when they occur. With proper education, the aging person may be assured that competent sexual function and fulfillment can continue into the later years.

Sexual dysfunction is certainly not an inevitable result of the aging process. The same factors that lead to sexual problems in the younger years are also important in the elderly, especially when superimposed on the changing genital system. These factors include drug abuse, fatigue, emotional problems, disease, urogenital surgery, alcoholism, overeating, and sociocultural pressures. In the elderly, these factors are compounded by fear of failure and society's expectations concerning sexual behavior and the older adult.

SUMMARY

Senescence describes the effects that lead to the increasing vulnerability individuals face with increasing age. Is senescence an inherent biological process? That may be difficult to say, yet as long ago as 1825, Gompertz identified a pattern of increased vulnerability through the life course.

A variety of factors influence the point at which people become old and, in particular, the time when they show the kind of vulnerability to aging processes that result in mortality. These include not only differences in biological potential but also in social and environment factors that may limit the expression of biological potential. The leading cause of death among the elderly is heart disease, followed by cancer and stroke. Death rates differ significantly by sex and race. Average life expectancy at birth has increased more than 50 percent since the turn of the twentieth century, and survivorship rates to old age have improved even more dramatically. In 1994, the proportion of newborn babies expected to reach age 65 was 75 percent for males and 86 percent for females, almost twice the proportion in 1900–02. With the exception of white females, age-specific life expectancy at 65 years has moved ahead more slowly than has life expectancy at birth during the twentieth century.

What are the specific results of senescence? Age-related physiological changes affect the skin and the skeletomuscular, neurosensory, gastrointestinal, cardiopulmonary, and urinary systems.

Misinformation surrounds the issue of sexuality and aging. Some people may experience declines in sexual desire and activity with advancing age. Such a decline can be seen as part of the normal aging process. Nevertheless, older people in reasonably good health should be able to have active and satisfying sex lives.

STUDY QUESTIONS

1. Distinguish between *biological aging* and *pathological aging*. Define *senescence*. How can it be distinguished from other biological processes?

2. Taking biological and socioenvironmental factors into consideration, explain the impact of sex on mortality rates. What role do socioeconomic factors play in the racial differences in mortality rates observed in the United States today?

3. Explain (a) increased life expectancy at birth in the twentieth century and (b) the small increase in life expectancy from age 65 in the twentieth century.

4. Discuss the changes in the form and function of the skin that are associated with the aging process.

5. Define and distinguish *osteoarthritis, rheumatoid arthritis, osteopenia, osteoporosis,* and *sarcopenia*. Describe the resulting complications for those afflicted with these conditions.

6. How is the neurosensory system subject to aging? The gastrointestinal system?

7. Discuss coronary heart disease, making the distinction between *atherosclerosis* and *arteriosclerosis*.

8. Why are attitudes generally so negative about sex in later life? Discuss the impact on the sexual functioning of older males of physical changes associated with the aging process. Do the same for older females.

REFERENCES

Adams, J. (1968). *Joey Adams' encyclopedia of humor.* New York: Bonanza Books.

Atchley, R. (1972). *Social forces in later life.* Belmont, CA: Wadsworth.

Benet, S. (1971, December 26). Why they live to be 100, or even older in Abkhasia. *New York Times Magazine.*

Butler, R., & Lewis, M. (1976). *Love and sex after sixty.* New York: Harper & Row.

Comfort, A. (1979). *The biology of senescence* (3rd ed.). New York: New American Library.

Dorn, H. (1959). Mortality. In P. Hauser & O. Duncan (Eds.), *The study of population.* Chicago: University of Chicago Press.

Fries, J. F., & Crapo, L. M. (1981). *Vitality and aging.* San Francisco: Freeman.

Fulton, G. B. (1992). Sexuality and aging. In C. Kart, E. Metress, & S. Metress (Eds.), *Human aging and chronic disease.* Boston: Jones and Bartlett.

Gonnella, J. S., Louis, D. Z., & McCord, J. J. (1976). The staging concept: An approach to the assessment of outcome of ambulatory care. *Medical Care, 14,* 13–21.

Hafez, E. (1976). *Aging and reproductive physiology.* Ann Arbor, MI: Ann Arbor Science.

Hertzman, C., Frank, J., & Evans, R. G. (1994). Heterogeneities in health status and the determinants of population health. In R. G. Evans, M. L. Barer, & T. R. Marmor (Eds.), *Why are some people healthy and others not? The determinants of health of populations.* New York: Aldine de Gruyter.

Kart, C., Metress, E., & Metress, J. (1992). *Human aging and chronic disease.* Boston: Jones & Bartlett.

Katchadourian, H. (1972). *Human sexuality: Sense and nonsense.* New York: Norton.

Kitagawa, E. M., & Hauser, P. M. (1973). *Differential mortality in the United States: A study in socioeconomic epidemiology.* Cambridge, MA: Harvard University Press.

Kohn, R. R. (1985). Aging and age-related diseases: Normal aging. In H. A. Johnson (Ed.), *Relations between normal aging and disease.* New York: Raven.

Leaf, A. (1973). Getting old. *Scientific American, 299* (3), 44–52.

Madigan, F. C. (1957). Are sex mortality differentials biologically caused? *Milbank Memorial Fund Quarterly, 35* (2), 202–223.

Masters, W., & Johnson, V. (1970). *Human sexual response.* Boston: Little, Brown.

Petersen, W. (1975). *Population* (3rd ed.). New York: Macmillan.

Reader's Digest. (1972). *Treasury of American humor.* New York: American Heritage.

Siegel, J. S. (1979). *Prospective trends in the size and structure of the elderly population, impact of mortality trends, and some implications.* Current Population Reports, Special Studies Series P-23, No. 78. Washington, DC: U.S. Department of Commerce, Bureau of the Census.

Strehler, B. (1962). *Time, cells and aging.* New York: Academic.

U.S. Office of Health Resources Opportunity. (1979). *Health status of minorities and low-income groups.* DHEW Publication No. (HRA) 79-627. Health Resources Administration. Washington, DC: U.S. Government Printing Office.

Verwoerdt, A., Pfeiffer, E., & Wang, H. S. (1969a). Sexual behavior in senescence. I. Changes in sexual activity and interest of aging men and women. *Journal of Geriatric Psychiatry, 2,* 163–180.

Verwoerdt, A., Pfeiffer, E., & Wang, H. S. (1969b). Sexual behavior in senescence. II. Patterns of change in sexual activity and interest. *Geriatrics, 24,* 137–154.

Zopf, P. E., Jr. (1986). *America's older population.* Houston, TX: Cap and Gown.

CHAPTER FIVE

WHY DO PEOPLE BECOME OLD?

CARY S. KART

EILEEN S. METRESS

Why do people become old? Potential answers to this question are being researched at both the cellular and physiological levels. According to Comfort (1979), there are four classical hypotheses that attempt to explain the mechanism of aging. These include the beliefs that vigor declines as a result of the following: (1) changes in the properties of multiplying cells, (2) loss of or injury to nonmultiplying cells (e.g., neurons), and (3) primary changes in the noncellular materials of the body (e.g., collagen). A fourth hypothesis locates the mechanism of aging in the so-called software of the body—"in the overall program of regulation by which other aspects of the life cycle are governed" (Comfort 1979, p. 17). These hypotheses are not mutually exclusive. After all, aging is a complex phenomenon. Different explanations may be required for different aspects of the aging process; diverse phenomena may act together to account for biological aging. Comfort points out that although some of these hypotheses have been around for 200 years, none has yet been eliminated by convincing experimental data. The alert reader may recognize these classic hypotheses in the brief summaries of research in biological aging that follow.

Differentiating between normal aging and superimposed disease is vital to understanding why people become old. The ultimate cause of the majority of deaths in older adults is physiological decline that increases the risk of disease. Mortality results when the ability to withstand the challenge of disease is overwhelmed. For instance, the increased risk of death from pneumonia among older persons is associated with age-related declines in the body's immune defense system and reduced pulmonary reserve and function (Rothschild 1984).

Unlocking the mystery of aging and extending the human life span has been the dream of many. As noted in Chapter 2, efforts at prolonging life have been described in the written and oral records of societies dating back many thousands of years. Research efforts in biogerontology continue. There are no magic potions to cure or prevent aging, despite the fact that books on longevity and its promotion have appeared on best-seller lists in recent years.

This chapter presents an overview of some of the important research in the biology of aging. We distinguish cellular theories of aging from physiological theories of aging. The goal of this research, regardless of whether it is aimed at understanding aging from the cellular or the organismic level, is not to grant immortality but to understand the aging process and improve the quality of life for the growing number of people who are being added to the ranks of the aged.

CELLULAR THEORIES OF AGING

In the early twentieth century, it was widely believed that if some cells were not immortal, at the very least they could grow and multiply for an extended time. Child (1915) "showed" that senescence in planarians (small flatworms that move by means of cilia) is reversible; Carrel (1912) "demonstrated" that tissue cells taken from adult animals could be propagated indefinitely *in vitro* (in a test tube or other artificial environment). In the same vein, Bidder (1925, 1932) "identified" a number of instances in fish where the life span was not believed to be fixed—that is, general vigor appeared to persist indefinitely. Such work had a significant impact on the field of gerontology. During most of the first half of the twentieth century, aging was not considered a characteristic of cells (Cristofalo 1985).

Since the late 1950s, Leonard Hayflick has shown that *fibroblast cells* (which give rise to connective tissue) from human fetal tissues cultured *in vitro* undergo a finite number of divisions and then die. Across several experiments, Hayflick and Moorhead (1961) observed that such cells undergo an average of 50 divisions *in vitro*, with a range from about 40 to about 60, before losing the ability to replicate themselves. In 1965, Hayflick reported that fibroblasts isolated from human adult tissue undergo only about 20 divisions *in vitro*. On the basis of these and other studies, he argued that (1) the limited replicative capacity of cultured normal human cells is an expression of programmed genetic events and (2) the limit on normal cell division *in vitro* is a function of the age of the donor. Hayflick's (1977) work noted an inverse relationship between the age of a human donor and the *in vitro* cell division capacity of fibroblasts derived from the skin, lung, and liver.

Although it appears that normal (noncancerous) cells have a finite lifetime, this is not the case for abnormal cells. Cancer cells, which are distinguishable from normal cells in genetic makeup and gene expression, are capable of unlimited division. Cancer cells are able to divide indefinitely in tissue culture. A famous line of human cancer cells named HeLa (after Henrietta Lacks, the woman from whom they were taken after her death in 1951) is still being cultured for use in standardized cancer cell studies (Gold 1981). Tissue culture studies have limitations, and these experiments almost certainly do not literally replicate the aging process. Yet, the experiments have been analyzed by many investigators, and all confirm the findings. Fries and Crapo (1981) report that in 1962, Hayflick froze many vials of embryo cells that had completed several divisions. Each year since that time, some vials have been thawed and cultured; they always go on to complete their natural growth to the same roughly 50 divisions.

Continued research has uncovered further information regarding cell division, aging, and cancer. When cells divide, their chromosomal tips, known as *telomeres,* shorten (Harley 1991). This shortening is progressive, occurring with each cell division. Consequently, cells taken from older donors show shorter telomeres. Laboratory studies demonstrate that once telomere length is critically shortened, cells cease to divide. The key to understanding the maximum capacity for cell division is ultimately linked to telomere length and the production of the enzyme *telomerase.* Most human cells cease manufacturing the enzyme once embryonic development is complete—with one important exception: Cancer cells produce it, maintain telomere length, and achieve immortality.

The relationship between telomeres, aging, and cancer is an important area of research today (Bodnar et al. 1998). At a practical level, many questions are being asked: Is it possible to extend telomere length without causing cancer? Will telomere extension increase the life span? Will cancer one day be treated by arresting telomerase production?

Researchers continue to suggest that aging may be genetically programmed into cells. Bernard Strehler has hypothesized that programmed loss of genetic material could cause aging. As Strehler (1973) points out, most cells contain hundreds of repetitions of the same *DNA* (the molecule of heredity in nearly all organisms—*deoxyribonucleic acid*) for the known genes they contain. This simply means that the cell does not have to rely on a single copy of its genetic blueprint for any one trait. In experiments done on beagles, Strehler found that, as cells age, a considerable number of these repetitions are lost (Johnson, Crisp, & Strehler 1972). This is especially true for brain, heart, and skeletal muscle cells. How the loss occurs is not specifically known, although there is some speculation that it results from age-related changes in cell metabolism. Strehler suspects that cells may be programmed, at a fixed point in life, to start manufacturing a substance that inhibits protein synthesis.

Another school of thought claims that senescence is largely a result of the accumulation of accidental changes that occur to cells over a period of time. Sinex (1977) thinks that random mutations may produce aging by causing damage to DNA molecules. Although the cell has DNA repair mechanisms, it is likely that either some mutational changes are too subtle for the repair process to detect or that mutations occur too rapidly for all of them to be repaired. It is theorized that as cellular mutations accumulate, cells begin to lose their ability to function, including even a loss of the ability to divide.

Orgel (1963, 1973) has also hypothesized that random errors or mutations could show up in the transcriptions of DNA into *RNA* (*ribonucleic acid,* which carries instructions from the DNA) or through errors in the translation of RNA into proteins. He suggests that random errors in the synthesizing of information-carrying proteins would lead to a cascade of other errors. This *error cascade* (sometimes referred to as an *error catastrophe*) results in cell deterioration. This hypothesis has not been confirmed experimentally. No one has yet been able to detect errors at the protein level, although efforts continue to be made (Fries & Crapo 1981). This error or mutation theory may not be incompatible with the theory of genetic programming. It is certainly possible that a shutoff of cellular repair mechanisms is a programmed genetic event. Cell mutations may also be the result of extrinsic factors—air or water pollutants, as well as toxins in food. At this time, it may be safe to summarize by saying that although changes in DNA do occur, their causes and consequences are uncertain (Ricklefs & Finch 1995).

Another explanation of aging involves the belief that *free radicals,* highly unstable molecule fragments containing an unpaired electron, reduce cellular efficiency and cause an accumulation of cellular waste. Free radicals may be produced by radiation, extreme heat, or oxidation reactions. They are created in small quantities as part of the normal oxidant cell metabolism. Over time, free radicals, regardless of their source, may damage cellular membranes and other cellular components contributing to aging. Some believe that the fatty "age pigment" *lipofuscin,* which accumulates to an appreciable extent in neurons and cardiac and skeletal muscle cells, may be an end product of cellular membrane damage caused by free radicals (Cristofalo 1990). It should be emphasized, however, that current thinking holds that lipofuscin is an indicator rather than a cause of aging.

Harman (1961, 1968), among others, has done work attempting to reduce the source of free radicals. Certain chemicals, called **antioxidants** (a common one is the food preservative known as BHT), have been used to combine with and disarm free radicals. Harman reports that the inclusion of antioxidants in the diet of experimental animals increased their average life span by 15 to 30 percent. The animals receiving the antioxidants showed lower weight, suggesting the possibility that dietary restriction itself may prolong the average life span. Another effect of adding antioxidants to the diet of experimental animals was a reduction in tumor production (Harman 1968).

A well-known antioxidant is vitamin E. Although there is some evidence that vitamin E deficiency reduces the life expectancy of experimental animals, no experimental evidence is available to show that supplementing the diet with vitamin E extends average life expectancy (Tapple 1968). In addition, there is no current evidence to support the idea that dietary supplementation of other vitamins (A and C) and minerals (e.g., silenium) with antioxidant properties can extend human life (Ames 1983; Schneider & Reed 1985; Willet & MacMahon 1984). There is evidence, however, that eating foods rich in vitamin C and beta carotene, or taking antioxidant supplements, is linked with decreased risk of various cancers. The role of free radical reactions in aging and human disease and the avoidance of their excess formation remains an area of significant interest. Free radicals have been suggested to play a role in at least 50 diseases, including atherosclerosis, cancer, stroke, and Parkinson's disease (Aruoma, Kaur, & Halliwell 1991).

Higher organisms do possess sophisticated biochemical systems for scavenging free radicals. The enzyme *superoxide dismutase* is a part of such a system. A relationship has been noted between superoxide dismutase activity and life span in varying species and species strains (Bartosz, Leyko, & Fried 1979; Kellogg & Fridovich 1976; Munkres, Rana, & Goldstein 1984; Tolmasoff, Ono, & Cutler 1980). It is possible that the regulation of superoxide dismutase is under the control of the same genes that dictate the life span of a particular species (Schneider & Reed

1985). Superoxide dismutase tablets have been touted for their so-called antiaging effect. Nevertheless, there is no evidence that oral administration of the enzyme prolongs life. In fact, one report demonstrates that blood and tissue levels of this enzyme are not affected by its ingestion (Zidenburg-Cherr et al. 1983).

The aforementioned theories are concerned with aging at the cellular (and molecular) level; it is a long leap from cell biology to studying aging in the total organism. Several of the physiological theories that attempt to relate aging to the performance of the total organism deserve attention.

PHYSIOLOGICAL THEORIES OF AGING

One physiological theory of aging involves the *autoimmune* mechanism. This theory postulates that many age-related changes can be accounted for by changes in the immune response. Normally, the immune system, through the action of special immune cells and the production of antibodies, protects the body from material that it reads as foreign, including cancer cells. With age, immune cell function declines, and increased levels of autoantibodies are found in the blood (Goidl, Thorbecke, & Weksler 1980; Walford, 1982; Weksler, 1982). *Autoantibodies* are substances that are produced against host tissues. In usual circumstances, the body's immune system is able to distinguish between host body cells and foreign substances subject to attack.

The significance of age-associated increases in autoantibodies is not well understood, but it is believed that they contribute to inefficiencies in physiological functioning. Why these antibodies are produced against one's own tissue is not known. Perhaps it is because once-normal body cells begin to look different as a result of accumulated changes resulting from mutation or free-radical damage. If immune cells undergo similar changes, this might cause production of aberrant antibodies. Also, body constituents may break down from disease or other damage and present as new substances that the body's defense mechanism will not tolerate. Potentially, all of these factors may interact to produce autoimmunity.

Diminished immunocompetence has been established as an age-related change. Schneider and Reed (1985) suggest that the decline in immune function may have evolved as a protective mechanism against the ravages of autoimmunity. Presumably, a vigorous immune reaction might allow for an even greater production of autoantibodies.

The immune system is not organ specific. It is in constant contact with all body cells, tissues, and organs. Any alteration in the immune system could be expected to exert an effect on all body systems (Kay & Baker 1979; Kay & Makinodan 1982). Thus, as immune competence decreases, the incidence of autoimmunity, infection, and cancer can be expected to increase (Good & Yunis 1974; MacKay, Whittington, & Mathews 1977).

In humans, the immune system begins to decline shortly after puberty. This decline includes beginning atrophy of the thymus, the gland thought by many to be the structure central to the aging of the immune system. Thymic hormone influences immune functioning. Its progressive age-related loss is associated with declines in the reactivity of certain immune cells. The percentage of immature immune cells increases in association with the lack of thymic hormone. Other substances, called *lymphokines,* are also important in activating and maintaining the immune response. One lymphokine, interleukin-2 (IL-2), undergoes limited production with age (Thoman 1985).

Thompson and associates (1984) report on the immune status of a group of healthy **centenarians.** This study population withstood the risk of cancer and an assortment of other diseases for at least 100 years. Their immune systems appeared to function in a fashion similar to the immune systems of much younger individuals. The researchers were left asking (1) when changes in the immune cells of these centenarians began, (2) whether these changes represent irreversible programmed aging that simply began later in this group, and (3) whether other outside factors are responsible for immune decline.

This last question is particularly important, given that recent work in the area of *psychoneuroimmunology* has shown that stressful social situations—such as being in a troubled marriage (Kiecolt-Glaser, Fisher, et al. 1987) or caring for someone with Alzheimer's disease (Kiecolt-Glaser, Glaser, et al. 1987)—can cause suppression of the immune system. Interestingly, immune system function may be increased as a result of positive social situations (Kennedy, Kiecolt-Glaser, & Glaser 1990).

Another theory with a long history is the **wear and tear theory of aging.** In effect, this theory posits an inverse relationship between rate of living and length of life—that is, those who live too hard and fast cannot expect to live very long. In the early part of the twentieth century, Rubner (described in Comfort 1979) carried out calorimetric experiments to determine the energy requirements necessary for the maintenance of body metabolism. He suggested that senescence might reflect the expenditure of fixed amounts of energy used to complete particular chemical reactions. An important question then arises: Can an individual live a life that causes a speedup or slowdown in the expenditure of such energy?

Many theorists using this model employ machine analogies to exemplify the theory's underlying assumption that an organism wears out with use. Nevertheless, these analogies often fail to take into account two important characteristics of living organisms: (1) living organisms have mechanisms for self-repair that are not available to machines and (2) functions in a living organism may actually become more efficient with use.

Hans Selye's work on stress has been used by some to support the wear and tear theory. Selye (1966), on the basis of his experiments with animals, identified three stages of responses to continued stress. Each stage of response parallels a phase of aging. Stage 1 is characterized by an alarm reaction in which the body's adaptive forces are being activated but are not yet fully operational. This stage is reminiscent of childhood, in which adaptability to stress is growing but in which adaptability is still limited. Stage 2 is the stage of resistance—mobilization of the defensive reactions to stress is completed. This phase parallels adulthood, during which the body has acquired resistance to most stress agents likely to affect it.

Stage 3, the stage of exhaustion, results eventually in a breakdown of resistance and, at last, in death. This final stage parallels the process of senescence in human beings.

Although it makes intuitive sense that an old animal is less able to withstand the same stress that can be tolerated by a young animal, there is some empirical evidence that accumulated stress may be implicated in age-related functional decrements. For example, stress and the subsequent elevation of the hormone cortisol (a glucocorticoid), if sustained for long periods, can injure brain cells in the hippocampus. It is possible that diminished cognitive function and memory may be affected by stress. Selye's work remains important in showing the relationship between stress and disease, and it may yet prove helpful in efforts to understand the mechanisms of aging.

Collagen, an extracellular component of connective tissue, has also been implicated in age-related changes in physiological functions. Widely scattered throughout the body, collagen is included in the skin, blood vessels, bone, cartilage, tendons, and other body organs. With age, collagen shows a reduction in its elastic properties as well as an increase in cross-linkages. *Cross-linkage* is a process whereby proteins in the body bind to each other.

According to the cross-linkage theory of aging, alteration in collagen plays an important role in impairing functional capacities. For example, the reduced efficiency of cardiac muscle may be the result of increasing stiffness. Connective tissue changes in small blood vessels may lead to the development of hypertension. Less elastic vessels may alter permeability, affecting nutrient transport and waste removal. Such changes could have far-reaching effects on all body organs.

Diabetics may be susceptible to excessive cross-linking. They undergo many complications that are similar to age-related changes, such as cataract formation and atherosclerosis. Diabetes is often referred to as a model for studying the aging process. Elevated blood sugar levels promote cross-linkage formation (Cerami 1985). It is now believed that many of the long-term complications of diabetes are related to glucose-induced cross-linkage, especially the cross-linkage of collagen.

Excess blood glucose reacts with many different proteins in a chemical reaction known as *nonenzymatic glycation (NEG).* It is suggested that this process contributes to several events that are age-related, including the formation of cataracts, the cross-linkage of collagen, and the reduced elasticity of arteries. The ability to metabolize glucose efficiently declines with age. Thus, most older adults demonstrate some degree of elevated glucose.

Nathan Shock, a noted gerontologist, suggests that there is sufficient evidence to entertain the possibility that aging results from some breakdown or impairment in the performance of endocrine and neural control mechanisms (Shock 1961, 1962, 1974). Studies carried out by the Gerontology Research Center of the National Institutes of Health show that age-related declines in humans are greater for functions that are complex and require the coordinated activity of whole organ systems. Measurements of functions related to a single physiological system, such as nerve conduction velocity, show considerably less age decrement than do functions such as maximum breathing capacity, which involve coordination between systems (in this case, between the nervous and muscular systems).

The relationship between age and task performance also shows greater age-related decline that is most likely associated with task complexity. For example, simple motor performance, as demonstrated by the time it takes an individual to push a button in response to a signal of light, increases only modestly across the human life span. Complex motor performance, on the other hand, does show significant decrement with age. Complex motor performance can involve having an individual select one of several possible responses after the presentation of a complex stimulus. Although simple motor performance involves the transmission of nerve impulses over short distances and through relatively few synapses, complex motor performance requires transmission through many synapses and is influenced by other factors in the central nervous system. Interestingly, however, elderly people often show significantly improved motor performance with practice (Botwinick 1973).

PROLONGEVITY

Some information presented in this and previous chapters may lead readers to believe that length of life has been increased and will continue to increase almost automatically as a by-product of technological and social changes. Whether this is really so is unclear and points up the necessity of distinguishing between the concepts of life expectancy and life span. Whereas *life expectancy* refers to the average length of life of persons, **life span** refers to the longevity of long-lived persons. Life span is the extreme limit of human longevity, the age beyond which no one can expect to live (Gruman 1977). Gerontologists estimate the life span at about 110 years; some argue that it has not increased notably in the course of history.

Is the human life span an absolute standard? Or should people expect a significant extension of the length of life? Those who have always believed that human life should be lengthened indefinitely are proponents of **prolongevity,** the significant extension of the length of life by human action (Gruman 1977). Others believe that new treatments and technology, as well as improved health habits, may continue to increase life expectancy but that the human life span is unlikely to increase. In attempting to estimate the upper limits of human longevity, Olshansky, Carnes, and Cassel (1990) suggest that it is highly unlikely that life expectancy at birth would ever exceed the age of 85. They argue that to achieve an average life expectancy at birth of 85 years in the U.S. population, mortality from all causes of death would need to decline at all ages by 55 percent and at ages 50 and over by 60 percent.

Prolongevitists often point to the peoples in mountain regions of Ecuador (the Andean village of **Vilacabamba**), Pakistan (the **Hunza** people of Kashmir), and the former Soviet Union (the Abkhasians in the Russian Caucasus) as examples of populations that have already extended the human life span (Leaf 1973). Each of these groups purportedly shows a statistically higher proportion of cente-

Although aging is inevitable, certain lifestyle choices are associated with more successful aging.

narians in the population, with many individuals reaching 120, 130, and even 150 and 160 years. Unfortunately, there are many reasons for doubting the validity of these claims (Kyncharyants 1974; Mazess & Forman 1979; Medvedev 1974, 1975). Russian gerontologist Medvedev says that none of these cases of superlongevity is scientifically valid. He offers the following case as explanation of why many in the Caucasus claim superlongevity:

> The famous man from Yakutia, who was found during the 1959 census to be 130 years old, received especially great publicity because he lived in the place with the most terrible climate.... When...a picture of this outstanding man was published in the central government newspaper, *Isvestia*, the puzzle was quickly solved. A letter was received from a group of Ukrainian villagers who recognized this centenarian as a fellow villager who deserted from the army during the First World War and forged documents or used his father's.... It was found that this man was really only 78 years old. (Medvedev 1974, p. 387)

There continues to be interest—even mass interest—in increasing human longevity. A good part of this interest originates in the antediluvian theme found in tradition and folklore that people lived much longer in the distant past. Noah, after all, supposedly lived to be 950 years old.

What are the prospects for continued reduction in death rates and life extension? As already seen, death rates have declined and are likely to continue to do so. Nevertheless, some research suggests that there is little room for improvement, unless some significant breakthrough eliminates cardiovascular diseases. In any case, small improvements would seem to be attainable. According to Siegel (1975), if the lowest death rates for females in the countries of Europe are combined into a single table, the values for life expectancy at birth and at age 65 exceed those same values for the United States by 4.3 and 1.4 years, respectively. Table 5.1 shows the projected average life expectancy at birth in selected countries for the years 1997 and 2000. Although the United States experienced gains in life expectancy during the twentieth century, it is clear that Canada, France, Italy, the Netherlands, Spain, Hong Kong, Japan, and Australia have life expectancies at birth that exceed those of the United States in 1997 and are projected to continue to do so into the beginning of the twenty-first century.

Most elderly people die as a result of some long-standing chronic condition that is sometimes related to personal habits (e.g., smoking, drinking alcohol, eating an unhealthy diet) or environmental conditions (e.g., harsh work environments, air pollution) that go back many years. Attempts to prevent illness and death from these conditions must begin before old age. But what if death from these conditions could be prevented? Table 5.2 gives a partial answer to this question. Using available life table data, notice that the elimination of all deaths in the United States caused by accidents, influenza and pneumonia, infective and parasitic diseases, diabetes mellitus, and tuberculosis would increase life expectancy at birth by 1.6 years and at age 65 by 0.6 year. Even the elimination of cancer as a cause of death would result in only a 2.5-year gain in life expectancy at birth and little more than half that (1.4 years) at age 65. This is because cancer affects individuals in all age groups, although the risk of developing cancer increases with age. If the major cardiovascular-renal diseases were eliminated, there would be an 11.8-year gain in life expectancy at birth, and even an 11.4-year gain in life expectancy at age 65.

Work by Olshansky, Carnes, and Cassel (1990) supports these data. These researchers estimate that if all mortality attributable to the combination of all circulatory diseases, diabetes, and cancer were eliminated, life expectancy at birth would increase by 15.8 years for females and 15.3 years for males. Such a decline in mortality from these diseases would represent approximately three-fourths of all deaths in the United States. These diseases are not likely to be eliminated in the near future, although death rates as a result of them may be reduced. There remains substantial room for improvement in death rates and life expectancies in the United States among men and nonwhites. As has already been pointed out in Chapter 4, the death rate for aged men is considerably higher than the rate for aged women. Controlling for sex, the death rate for elderly African Americans is higher than for their white counterparts.

Perhaps the focus on simply extending life or life expectancy at birth is misplaced and we should be concentrating on how to increase active life expectancy. *Active life expectancy (ALE)* is operationally defined by Katz, Branch, and Banson (1983) as that period of life free of limitations in activities of daily living (ADLs

TABLE 5.1   Life Expectancy at Birth for Selected Countries, 1997 and 2000 (projected)

COUNTRY	1997	2000
North America		
Canada	79.3 years	80.0 years
Cuba	75.2	75.6
Mexico	74.0	75.0
United States	76.0	76.3
Europe		
France	78.6	79.1
Italy	78.2	78.6
Netherlands	77.9	78.2
Poland	72.2	72.6
Romania	69.6	70.0
Russia	63.8	65.4
Spain	78.5	79.1
United Kingdom	76.6	77.1
Asia		
China	70.0	71.1
Hong Kong	82.4	82.8
India	60.2	61.5
Japan	79.7	80.0
Vietnam	67.4	68.5
South America		
Argentina	74.7	75.0
Brazil	61.4	60.9
Chile	74.7	75.5
Colombia	73.1	74.2
Peru	69.6	70.8
Africa		
Algeria	68.6	69.6
Burundi	49.0	48.1
Ethiopia	46.6	46.0
Nigeria	54.7	55.9
South Africa	56.3	51.9
Tanzania	41.7	40.0
Other Areas		
Australia	79.6	80.4
Saudi Arabia	69.5	71.1

Source: U.S. Bureau of the Census 1997, Table 1336.

TABLE 5.2   Gain in Life Expectancy if Various Causes of Death Were Eliminated

	GAIN IN YEARS	
VARIOUS CAUSES OF DEATH	*At Birth*	*At Age 65*
1. Major cardiovascular-renal disease	11.8	11.4
2. Malignant neoplasms	2.5	1.4
3. Motor vehicle accidents	0.7	0.1
4. Influenza and pneumonia	0.5	0.2
5. Diabetes and mellitus	0.2	0.2
6. Infective and parasitic diseases	0.2	0.1

Source: U.S. Public Health Service data of life tables by cause of death for 1969–1971, U.S. Bureau of the Census, *Current Population Reports,* Series P-23, No. 59, January 1978 (revised).

will be discussed in Chapter 6). A basic tenet of ALE as a measure is that simple longevity (as reflected in average life expectancy at birth or age-specific life expectancy) is not a sufficient criteria for assessing the quality of life of older people; freedom to pursue their daily activities, or independence, may be more important in defining health and quality of life. This begs the question of whether it should matter that other countries have higher life expectancy at birth than does the United States (see Table 5.1). What would seem to matters more is: Is there variation in the United States in ALE? By gender? By geography? How does active life expectancy in the United States compare with other industrialized nations?

With data from 10,000 Caucasian men and women from three disparate geographic areas (East Boston, MA; New Haven, CT; and two largely rural Iowa counties), Branch and colleagues (1991) calculated ALEs using life table techniques developed by the U.S. Bureau of Labor Statistics. For example, at age 65, men in the three sites who were ADL independent had ALEs ranging from 11.3 to 12.9 years; similarly ADL-independent women had ALEs ranging from 15.4 to 17.0 years. For both men and women, the low values were from East Boston and the high values was from rural Iowa.

Active life expectancy may also be presented as a percent of remaining life that is independent in ADLs. This calculation may be expressed by dividing the ALE by age-specific life expectancy (and multiplying by 100 to yield a percent). Interestingly, despite the fact that it is well known that women have greater life expectancy than do men at every age, the data provided by Branch and colleagues (1991) show women to have approximately equal percentages of ALE in comparison with men at age 65 years. For example, men and women in East Boston who were 65 years of age showed ALEs of 85.6 percent and 83.2 percent, respectively; for New Haven, these values were 77.2 percent and 79.9 percent, respectively.

However, given that, on average, women have a greater life expectancy than do men, these comparable percentages point to the fact that women can expect a greater number of years of dependency than can men. In rural Iowa, at age 65, the average woman can expect 17.1 years of ALE and 4.3 years of dependency, whereas the average man can expect 12.9 years of ALE and 3.8 years of dependency. In addition, the data suggest that, all other things being equal, a pattern of increasing life expectancy in the United States will likely create additional dependency and thus impose additional pressure for an adequate supply of long-term care services (Branch et al. 1991).

Recently, Tsuji and associates (1995) calculated ALEs for elderly residents of Sendai City, Japan, the eleventh largest city in Japan with a population of approximately 900,000. The ALE for those age 65 in Sendai City was longer than among comparably aged Americans in the previously mentioned three U.S. sites. Japanese men had an ALE of 14.7 years, or 91.3 percent of age-specific life expectancy, whereas Japanese women had an ALE of 17.7 years, or 86.8 percent of age-specific life expectancy. These data suggest that the Japanese live longer than Americans (see Table 5.1), with a longer duration of ADL-independent functioning. Why would this be the case? Are differences between the United States and Japan real or artifacts of differences in study methods? At least two reasons exist for exhibiting caution in the interpretation of these differences.

First, there are slight differences in the studies related to the criteria for ADL independence. In the U.S. study, people were asked if they needed help to perform one or more of the following ADLs: bathing, dressing, transferring from a bed or a chair, and eating. In the Japan study, ADLs included toileting instead of transferring from a bed to a chair, because the use of a bed is less common among elderly Japanese (Tsuji et al., 1995, p. M175). Different criteria would cause different estimates of ADL independence or dependence, and perhaps this accounts for at least a portion of the differences in ALE between the U.S. and Japanese samples.

Second, the data do not allow one to determine whether the differences between the U.S. and Japanese samples of elderly reflect true differences in ADL independence or merely reflect the differences in willingness in the populations to report their problems. After all, ADLs are measured by self-report. Tsuji and colleagues (1995) suggest the possibility that Japanese elderly may be *less* likely than U.S. elderly to admit their own functional limitations at age 65, although they do not explain why this might be so.

Extending active life expectancy is now considered a major goal for the future in the United States (U.S. Department of Health and Human Services 1990). As a measure of the health and quality of life of elderly Americans, it may be a more important measure than average life expectancy at birth or even age-specific life expectancy. Standardized measures of ALE need to be established and international comparisons made in order to evaluate and promote improvements in the quality of life of older people in the United States and around the world.

Much more discussion of biogerontological research on prolongevity is needed. Improving death rates and life expectancies in the United States (or anywhere else, for that matter) do not necessarily translate into an extension of the life span. On the other hand, if major advances in genetic engineering and new life-extending technologies are forthcoming, as some believe (Olshansky, Carnes, & Cassel 1990), then significant declines in mortality and extensions of longevity will likely follow. Should people live to be 120 or 130 years of age? Before the reader answers, assume first that this would involve more than a simple increase in time at the end of life. Imagine that researchers could alter the rate of aging in such a way as to add extra years to all the healthy and productive stages of life. Under these conditions, extra years might be difficult to turn down. But what if a longer life meant a longer "old age"? Many readers, while considering whether the human life span should be extended, will think about pollution, overpopulation, dwindling energy resources, retirement policies, Social Security benefits, and the like. The long list of negative implications may simply reflect one's negative characterization of old age. Those readers who think of old age in terms of the continuation of productive possibilities may very well accept those extra years, however and whenever they come.

SUMMARY

Answers abound to the question, "Why do people become old?" They reflect the commitment of biogerontologists to aging research at both the cellular and the organismic levels. Clearly, more research is needed to understand biological aging and to improve the quality of life for increasing numbers of the aged. Attempts should be made to test the relative merits of genetic programmed theory, mutation theory, autoimmune theory, cross-linkage theory, and stress theory, among others. Perhaps the expectation that there is one overall theory of biological aging should be discarded. Aging is a complex phenomenon, and it may well be that different explanations are required for different aspects of the aging process.

What would be the effect of a solution to the riddle of biological aging? Should prolongevity be welcomed? Have people thought sufficiently about its potential impact on themselves, others, and society as a whole?

STUDY QUESTIONS

1. List the four classical hypotheses, identified by Comfort, that attempt to explain the mechanisms of aging. Can you link any of the theories of biological aging discussed in this chapter with these classical hypotheses? How?

2. Which cellular theories suggest that aging may be genetically programmed into cells? Which cellular theories of aging appear to implicate diet or nutrition in the aging process?

3. Identify the following physiological theories of aging: (a) autoimmune theory, (b) wear and tear theory, and (c) collagen theory. How may a breakdown in endocrine or neural mechanisms influence the aging process?

4. Define *prolongevity*. Distinguish between *life expectancy* and *life span*. Do the Abkhasians of the Russian Caucasus really live as long as they claim? Explain your answer.

5. Compare the life expectancy at birth of people in the United States with that of citizens of other industrialized nations. Which groups in the United States show the greatest potential for improvement in the values of life expectancy and death rates?

6. How much gain in life expectancy in the United States could be realized through

the elimination of certain diseases? Where would the greatest gain come from?

7. Eliminating certain diseases and thereby extending life expectancy would seem to

be an inherently positive thing. Is the idea of extending the human life span equally positive? Explain your answer.

REFERENCES

Ames, B. (1983). Dietary carcinogens and anticarcinogens: Oxygen radicals and degenerative disease. *Science, 221,* 1256–1264.

Aruoma, O. I., Kaur, H., & Halliwell, B. (1991). Oxygen free radicals and human diseases. *Journal of the Royal Society of Health, 111* (5), 172–177.

Bartosz, G., Leyko, W., & Fried, R. (1979). Superoxide dismutase and life span of Drosophila melanogaster. *Experientia, 35,* 1193.

Bidder, G. P. (1925). The mortality of Plaice. *Nature, 115,* 495.

Bidder, G. P. (1932). Senescence. *British Medical Journal, 115,* 5831.

Bodnar, A., Ouellette, M., Frolkis, M., et al. (1998). Extension of life-span by introduction of telomerase into normal human cells. *Science, 279,* 349–352.

Botwinick, J. (1973). *Aging and behavior.* New York: Springer.

Branch, L. G., Guiralnik, J. M., Foley, D. J., Kohout, F. J., Wetle, T. T., Ostfeld, A., & Katz, S. (1991). Active life expectancy for 10,000 Caucasian men and women in three communities. *Journal of Gerontology: Medical Sciences, 46* (4), M145–M150.

Calle, E. E., Martin, L. M., & Thun, M. J. (1993). Family history, age, and risk of fatal breast cancer. *American Journal of Epidemiology, 138* (9), 675–681.

Carrel, A. (1912). On the permanent life of tissues. *Journal of Experimental Medicine, 15,* 516.

Cerami, A. (1985). Hypothesis: Glucose as a mediator of aging. *Journal of American Geriatrics Society, 33,* 626–634.

Child, C. M. (1915). *Senescence and rejuvenescence.* Chicago: University of Chicago Press.

Comfort, A. (1979). *The biology of senescence* (3rd ed.). New York: New American Library.

Cristofalo V. (1985). The destiny of cells: Mechanisms and implications of senescence. *Gerontologist, 25,* 577–583.

Cristofalo, V. (1990). Biological mechanisms of aging: An overview. In W. Hazzard, R. Andres, E. Bierman, & J. Blass (Eds.), *Principles of geriatric medicine and gerontology.* New York: McGraw-Hill.

Fries, J. F., & Crapo, L. M. (1981). *Vitality and aging.* San Francisco: Freeman.

Garfinkel, L. (1995). Probability of developing or dying of cancer, United States, 1991. *Statistical Bulletin, 76* (4), 31–37.

Goidl, E., Thorbecke, G., & Weksler, M. (1980). Production of auto-anti-idiotypic antibody during the normal immune response. *Proceedings of National Academy of Science, 77,* 6788.

Gold, M. (1981). The cells that would not die. *Science 81, 2* (3), 28–35.

Good, R., & Yunis, E. (1974). Association of autoimmunity, immunodeficiency and aging in man, rabbits and mice. *Federal Proceedings, 33,* 2040–2050.

Gruman, G. (1977). *A history of ideas about the prolongation of life.* New York: Arno Press.

Harley, C. (1991). Telomere loss: Mitotic clock or genetic time bomb? *Mutation Research, 26,* 1271–1282.

Harman, D. (1961). Prolongation of the normal lifespan and inhibition of spontaneous cancer by antioxidants. *Journal of Gerontology, 16,* 247–254.

Harman, D. (1968). Free radical theory of aging. *Journal of Gerontology, 23,* 476–482.

Hayflick, L. (1965). The limited in vitro lifetime of human diploid cell strains. *Experimental Cell Research, 37,* 614–636.

Hayflick, L. (1977). The cellular basis for biological aging. In C. Finch & L. Hayflick (Eds.), *Handbook of the biology of aging.* New York: Van Nostrand Reinhold.

Hayflick, L., & Moorhead, P. S. (1961). The serial cultivation of human diploid cell strains. *Experimental Cell Research, 25,* 585–621.

Johnson, R., Crisp, C., & Strehler, B. (1972). Selective loss of ribosomal RNA genes during the aging of post-mitotic tissues. *Mechanisms of Aging and Development, 1.*

Katz, S., Branch, L. G., & Banson, M. H. (1983). Active life expectancy. *New England Journal of Medicine, 309,* 1218–1224.

Kay, M., & Baker, L. (1979). Cell changes associated with declining immune function: Physiology and cell biology of aging. In A. Cherkin et al. (Eds.), *Aging* (Vol. 8). New York: Raven.

Kay, M., & Makinodan, T. (1982). The aging immune system. In A. Viidik (Ed.), *Lectures on gerontology, Vol. 1: On biology of aging, Part A.* London: Academic.

Kellogg, E., & Fridovich, I. (1976). Superoxide dismutase in the rat and mouse as a function of age and longevity. *Journal of Gerontology, 31,* 405–408.

Kennedy, S., Kiecolt-Glaser, J. K., & Glaser, R. (1990). Social support, stress, and the immune system. In B. R. Sarason, I. G. Sarason, & G. R. Pierce (Eds.), *Social support: An interactional view.* New York: Wiley.

Kiecolt-Glaser, J. K., Fisher, L. D., Ogrocki, P., Stout, J. C., Speicher, C. E., & Glaser, R. (1987). Marital quality, marital disruption, and immune function. *Psychosomatic Medicine, 49,* 13–34.

Kiecolt-Glaser, J. K., Glaser, R., Shuttleworth, E. C., Dyer, C. S., Ogrocki, P., & Speicher, C. E. (1987). Chronic stress and immunity in family caregivers of Alzheimer's disease victims. *Psychosomatic Medicine, 49,* 523–535.

Kyncharyants, V. (1974). Will the human life-span reach one hundred? *Gerontologist, 14,* 377–380.

Leaf, A. 1973. Getting old. *Scientific American, 299* (3), 44–52.

MacKay, I., Whittington, S., & Mathews, J. (1977). The immunoepidemiology of aging. In T. Makinodan & E. Yunis (Eds.), *Immunity and aging.* New York: Plenum.

Mazess, R., & Forman, S. (1979). Longevity and age exaggeration in Vilacabamba, Ecuador. *Journal of Gerontology, 34,* 94–98.

Medvedev, Z. A. (1974). Caucasus and Altay longevity: A biological or social problem? *Gerontologist, 14,* 381–387.

Medvedev, Z. A. (1975). Aging and longevity: New approaches and new perspectives. *Gerontologist, 15,* 196–210.

Munkres, K., Rana, R., & Goldstein, E. (1984). Genetically determined conidial longevity is positively correlated with superoxide dismutase, catalase, gluthathione peroxidase, cytochrome peroxidase and ascorbate free radical reductase activities in Neurospora crass. *Mechanisms of Aging and Development, 24,* 83–100.

Olshansky, S. J., Carnes, B. A., & Cassel, C. (1990, November 2). In search of Methuselah: Estimating the upper limits to human longevity. *Science, 250,* 634–640.

Orgel, L. E. (1963). The maintenance of the accuracy of protein synthesis and its relevance to aging. *Proceedings of the National Academy of Sciences, 49,* 517.

Orgel, L. E. (1973). The maintenance of the accuracy of protein synthesis and its relevance to aging. *Proceedings of the National Academy of Sciences, 67,* 496.

Ricklefs, R., & Finch, C. (1995). *Aging: A natural history.* New York: Scientific American Library.

Rothschild, H. (1984). The biology of aging. In H. Rothschild (Ed.), *Risk factors for senility.* New York: Oxford University Press.

Schneider, E., & Reed, J. (1985). Life extension. *New England Journal of Medicine, 312,* 1159–1168.

Selye, H. (1966). *The stress of life* (2nd ed.). New York: McGraw-Hill.

Shock, N. (1961). Physiological aspects of aging in man. *Annual Review of Physiology, 23,* 97–122.

Shock, N. (1962). The physiology of aging. *Scientific American, 206* (1), 100–111.

Shock, N. (1974). Physiological theories of aging. In M. Rockstein (Ed.), *Theoretical aspects of aging.* New York: Academic.

Siegel, J. S. (1975). Some demographic aspects of aging in the United States. In A. Ostfeld & D. Gibson (Eds.), *Epidemiology of aging.* Bethesda, MD: National Institutes of Health.

Sinex, F. M. (1977). The molecular genetics of aging. In C. Finch & L. Hayflick (Eds.), *Handbook of the biology of aging.* New York: Van Nostrand Reinhold.

Strehler, B. (1973, February). A new age for aging. *Natural History.*

Tapple, A. L. (1968). Will antioxidant nutrients slow aging processes? *Geriatrics, 23,* 97.

Thoman, M. (1985). Role of interleukin-2 in the age-related impairment of immune function. *Journal of American Geriatrics Society, 33,* 781–787.

Thompson, J., Wekstein, D., Rhoades, J., Kirkpatrick, C., Brown, S., Rozman, T., Straus, R., & Tietz, N. (1984). The immune status of healthy centenarians. *Journal of American Geriatrics Society, 32,* 274–281.

Tolmasoff, J., Ono, T., & Cutler, R. (1980). Superoxide dismutase: Correlation with life span and specific metabolic rate in primate species. *Proceedings of the National Academy of Sciences, 77,* 2777–2781.

Tsuji, I., Minami, Y., Fukao, A., Hisamichi, S., Asano, H., & Sato, M. (1995). Active life expectancy among elderly Japanese. *Journal of Gerontology: Medical Services, 50A* (3), M173–M176.

U.S. Department of Health and Human Services. (1990). *Healthy people 2000: National health promotion and disease prevention objectives.* Washington, DC: Author.

Walford, R. (1982). Studies in immunogerontology. *Journal of American Geriatrics Society, 30,* 617.

Weksler, M. (1982). Age-associated changes in the immune response. *Journal of American Geriatrics Society, 30,* 718.

Willet, W., & MacMahon, B. (1984). Diet and cancer—An overview. *New England Journal of Medicine, 310,* 633–638, 697–703.

Zidenberg-Cherr, S., Keen, C., Lonnerdal, B., & Hurley, L. (1983). Dietary superoxide dismutase does not affect tissue levels. *American Journal of Clinical Nutrition, 37,* 5–7.

CHAPTER SIX

HEALTH STATUS
OF THE ELDERLY

Human organs gradually diminish in function over time, although not at the same rate in every individual. By itself, this gradual diminution of function is not a real threat to the health of most older people. Diseases are another matter. Diseases represent the chief barriers to extended health and longevity. And when they accompany normal changes associated with biological aging, maintaining health and securing appropriate health care becomes especially problematic for older people.

This chapter begins with a discussion of the physical health status of older people. Of particular interest are the patterns of chronic illness among the elderly, the variation in their self-assessments of health, and the functional decrements they experience. The text then focuses on whether patterns of morbidity among the elderly are changing such that there is compression of the length of illness before death. This is followed by a discussion about the mental health of older adults. Finally, the chapter concludes by identifying two additional factors that may contribute to the difficulty older persons face in maintaining their health status: (1) the medical model and (2) expectations held by older people and others about what aging means.

Efforts at maintaining health and functioning in old age include the formidable task of assessing health status. This assessment task is described as formidable for three related reasons (Kane & Kane 1981). First, the elderly are often subject to multiple illnesses and thus to multiple diagnoses. Second, the physical, mental, and social health of elderly individuals are closely interrelated; as a result, assessment must be multidimensional. Finally, measures of functioning that allow for assessment of an individual's ability to carry on independently, despite disease or disability, are probably the most useful indicators for practitioners.

The concept of *physical health* can be divided into at least three subcategories: (1) general physical health, or the absence of illness; (2) the ability to perform basic self-care activities, including what are known as *activities of daily living (ADLs)*; and (3) the ability to perform more complex self-care activities that allow for greater independence, including what are known as *instrumental activities of daily living*

(IADLs). These subcategories are thought to reflect a hierarchical order in that each level generally requires a higher order of functioning than the preceding one.

Most health survey data show a pattern in which vigorous old age predominates, but there is a clear association of poorer functioning with advancing age. Manton (1989) suggests that function can be maintained well into advanced old age and that people vary greatly in the rate at which functional loss occurs. The potential for rehabilitation exists even where a decline in functioning is the result of a currently untreatable disease (Besdine 1988). An active approach to preserving function with increasing age includes changing medical and institutional responses to disabilities and chronic diseases among the elderly. It also includes altering negative attitudes about normal aging, even though these attitudes are accepted by many elderly persons themselves.

The great majority of older Americans live in the community and are cognitively intact and fully independent in their activities of daily living. The individuals who remain active may be those who exercise, eat nutritiously, and have a positive psychological view of life. Still, many older Americans have had or currently have a serious illness. Today, chronic illnesses are the key health problems affecting middle-aged and older adults. In fact, when compared with younger age groups, middle-aged and older adults generally present lower rates of acute conditions, including infective and parasitic conditions, respiratory conditions, conditions of the digestive system, and injuries.

Not only are chronic conditions long lasting but their progress most often causes irreversible pathology. Generally, the prevalence of chronic conditions among the elderly is higher than among younger persons. The reported prevalence rates among the elderly for a wide array of chronic conditions—including heart conditions, hypertension (high blood pressure), arthritis, diabetes, and visual and hearing impairments—show the most substantial differences for both females and males when compared with the prevalence rates of chronic conditions among those in the younger age groups (see Table 6.1).

What is the impact of all this chronic illness? Table 6.2 shows the average number of days spent inactive in bed in the past 12 months for people 55 years of age and older as reported from the 1993 National Health Interview Survey (NHIS). Although the majority of respondents 55 years of age and older report spending no time inactive in bed due to illness during the previous 12 months, there does seem to be a linear relationship between age and "bed days." With advancing age, the proportion of individuals spending more time inactive in bed increases, so that those 75 years and older are about 40 percent more likely than those 55 to 64 years to spend more than seven days in bed during the past 12 months (18 vs. 13 percent). Females, African Americans, people with family income below $20,000, and central-city dwellers were most likely to report having spent time inactive in bed as a result of illness during the previous 12 months.

Table 6.3 reports on the self-assessment of health status made by 1993 NHIS respondents 55 years of age and older. A positive correlation exists between subjective health status and measures of functional status in aged adults (Ferraro

TABLE 6.1   Prevalence of Selected Chronic Conditions, by Age and Sex: 1994

CHRONIC CONDITION	CONDITIONS (1,000)	MALE				FEMALE			
		Under 45 Years Old	45–64 Years Old	65–74 Years Old	75 Years and Over	Under 45 Years Old	45–64 Years Old	65–74 Years Old	75 Years and Over
Arthritis	33,446	27.4	176.8	430.8	424.9	38.2	297.0	513.6	604.4
Dermatitis	9,192	29.3	21.8	25.3	na	46.3	44.6	38.6	40.2
Visual impairments	8,601	29.5	52.7	78.4	113.7	12.9	38.0	48.0	110.7
Hearing impairmerts	22,400	43.2	191.9	298.8	447.1	30.4	87.5	183.3	307.8
Orthopedic impairments	31,068	93.5	166.7	144.4	169.3	101.3	173.2	161.8	189.9
Ulcer	4,447	11.3	27.4	27.1	na	13.3	23.3	42.8	22.3
Diabetes	7,766	7.3	63.3	102.4	115.6	8.9	63.0	101.0	91.8
Heart conditions	22,279	27.0	162.0	319.3	429.9	33.1	111.0	250.8	361.4
Hypertension	28,236	31.9	220.0	307.7	329.2	32.4	224.5	378.8	417.5
Chronic bronchitis	14,021	43.6	43.8	41.7	68.0	56.5	82.7	79.0	51.7
Asthma	14,562	57.1	32.3	39.3	70.3	60.0	68.0	62.8	34.1
Hay fever	26,146	98.0	107.3	79.6	36.6	99.2	133.4	92.2	78.8

Note: Rate per 1,000 persons.

Source: U.S. Bureau of the Census 1997, Table 218.

1985) and between self-assessment of health by older adults and health ratings by physicians (LaRue et al. 1979; Maddox & Douglas 1973). Whereas almost four out of five (78.1 percent) persons ages 55 to 64 years assessed their health in positive terms, only about two of three (68.1 percent) of those 75 years and older did similarly.

Variable correlation exists between other demographic measures and self-assessment of health among the aged. For example, 1993 NHIS respondents 55 years of age and older with family incomes under $20,000 were more than twice as likely as were more affluent age peers (36.6 vs. 17.1 percent, respectively) to assess their health as fair or poor. Whites are more likely than African Americans

TABLE 6.2   Number of Days Spent Inactive in Bed in the Past 12 Months: 1993 National Health Interview Survey

	BED DAYS			
	None *(%)*	*1–7 Days* *(%)*	*8–30 days* *(%)*	*31+ days* *(%)*
Age				
55–64 years	64.5	22.6	8.3	4.7
65–74	67.9	18.0	9.2	4.8
75+ years	65.4	16.6	11.0	7.0
Gender				
Male	67.2	19.2	8.7	4.8
Female	64.9	19.7	9.7	5.7
Race				
White	65.6	19.7	8.9	4.9
African American	61.7	18.2	11.6	8.5
Family Income				
Under $20,000	63.6	17.6	11.1	7.7
$20,000 or more	67.7	20.9	7.9	3.5
Residence				
Central City	63.9	19.9	10.1	5.1
Suburban	67.0	19.9	8.4	4.7
Farms	70.7	19.5	5.8	4.0

Source: 1993 National Health Interview Survey (Hyattsville, MD: National Center for Health Statistics, 1993).

to assess their health positively; 32.9 percent of African Americans and 23.3 percent of whites assess their health as fair or poor. This differential is consistent with prior research (Schlesinger 1987). Black/white differences in self-assessment of health status reflect real differences in health status and health service utilization (Gibson & Jackson 1987). Geographic locale is also an important consideration. Elderly suburbanites have more positive assessments of their health than do elderly residents of central-city and rural areas. Gender differences in self-assessments of health status among the aged are quite modest. This is particularly interesting in light of the significant female advantage over males in mortality rates and life expectancy (Zopf 1986).

TABLE 6.3   Self-Assessed Health Status by Selected Characteristics: 1993 National Health Interview Survey

	SELF-ASSESSED HEALTH STATUS			
	Excellent or Very Good (%)	Good (%)	Fair (%)	Poor (%)
Age				
55–64 years	48.0	30.1	14.8	7.1
65–74	41.7	33.3	17.6	7.4
75+ years	35.4	32.7	22.0	10.0
Gender				
Male	44.4	30.8	16.4	8.4
Female	41.5	32.7	18.3	7.5
Race				
White	44.7	32.0	16.3	7.0
African American	28.6	31.1	18.3	14.6
Family Income				
Under $20,000	32.5	30.9	23.9	12.7
$20,000 or more	50.5	32.6	12.7	4.3
Residence				
Central City	39.4	31.8	19.7	9.1
Suburban	47.0	31.7	15.5	5.8
Farms	45.1	31.7	17.2	6.1

Source: 1993 National Health Interview Survey (Hyattsville, MD: National Center for Health Statistics, 1993).

CHRONIC ILLNESS

In contrast to an *acute illness* that is temporary in nature, a *chronic illness* is a long-lasting illness or disease. Three chronic illnesses already identified as causing the great proportion of mortality among the elderly, and that contribute as well to functional deficits and activity limitations, are heart disease, cancer, and cerebrovascular disease (stroke). These conditions are briefly discussed in this section.

Heart Disease

Heart disease is the principal cause of death among the elderly; it also accounts for a great deal of morbidity, disablement, and inactivity in older people. The dominant factor associated with the incidence of heart disease is *atherosclerosis*—a condition characterized by a buildup of fatty deposits within the arterial walls.

With this buildup, arteries supplying heart tissue become narrowed, reducing blood flow to the heart. Tissue that is denied an adequate blood supply is described as *ischemic.* Heart disease is also known as ***ischemic heart disease,*** coronary heart disease (CHD), and coronary artery disease.

A common form of ischemic heart disease is ***myocardial infarction,*** or heart attack. In time, if a deficient blood supply to the heart persists, heart tissue will die. The dead area is known as an *infarct.* The extent of heart tissue involved determines the severity of the heart attack. Most often, only a small portion of heart muscle is affected, and cardiac reserves allow the work of the heart to be continued. In some older persons, however, there may not be sufficient heart reserve to withstand the attack. Heart attack may also result from a cardiac arrest, resulting from some interruption in the normal pattern of cardiac contractions.

In an older adult, a heart attack may be triggered by an array of different mechanisms. A coronary artery may be suddenly blocked by a blood clot (***coronary thrombosis***) or other fibrous debris released into an arterial channel. Hemorrhaging near the site of already obstructive arterial plaque may further constrict blood flow and cause the death of heart tissue and heart attack. Finally, strenuous exercise or activity, such as snow shoveling, can suddenly increase the oxygen needs of the heart, resulting in severe ischemia and heart attack.

Mortality associated with myocardial infarction for persons over 70 years of age is twice that of those under age 70. With advanced age, there may be insufficient cardiac reserve to withstand the attack. Still, the direct effect of age itself is not clearly understood. Poor prognosis following a heart attack is predicted by dysfunction in the left ventricular chamber of the heart and multivessel coronary artery disease. These predictors are more likely to be present in the elderly than in younger heart attack victims (Morley & Reese 1989).

Brocklehurst and Hanley (1981) point out that, in many respects, heart disease is no different in old age than in youth. The symptoms and presentation of myocardial infarction, however, may be an exception. These authors indicate, for example, that whereas complete absence of chest pain is very rare in acute myocardial infarction up to middle age, it is a "mundane occurrence" in old people. In fact, only about one-third of elderly patients present with a classical prolonged episode of chest pain. Other atypical presentations (representing about another one-third of the cases) include (1) development of acute brain failure, (2) severe breathing difficulty, (3) severe fall in blood pressure, (4) formation of an arterial embolism or clot in the area of the infarction, and (5) vomiting and weakness.

Some myocardial infarcts in the aged are completely "silent" and may be discovered only with an electrocardiograph (EKG) (Brocklehurst & Hanley 1981). It is not precisely clear why this occurs, although it is speculated that age-associated desensitivity to ischemic pain is involved. This desensitivity may also result from reduced blood flow to the brain, which is secondary to the related reduction in cardiac output.

Prevention of morbidity and mortality associated with heart disease must take into account certain modifiable risk factors. For example, cigarette smokers have twice the rate of heart attack of nonsmokers and are most at risk for sudden death from heart attack (American Heart Association 1990). High blood pressure is also associated with increased risk of CHD mortality, as are high-serum cholesterol levels. Both are modifiable with proper diet, exercise, and medication, if necessary. Diabetes, obesity, sedentary life-style, and excessive stress are also contributing factors to heart disease that may be modified. Heredity, gender (male), race (black), and age are additional risk factors that cannot be changed. The more risk factors present, the greater the chance of development of serious atherosclerotic lesions and heart disease.

The U.S. Department of Health and Human Services' (1992) report, *Healthy People 2000,*[1] spells out health promotion and disease prevention objectives for the U.S. population for the year 2000. Risk-reduction objectives related to heart disease and stroke include:

1. Increase the proportion of people whose high blood pressure is under control.
2. Reduce the mean-serum cholesterol level among adults, in part, by increasing the proportion of adults with high blood cholesterol who are aware of their condition.
3. Reduce dietary fat intake and average unsaturated fat intake among children and adults.
4. Reduce the prevalence rates of obese and overweight adults.
5. Increase the proportion of children and adults who engage in regular, preferably daily, light to moderate physical activity for at least 30 minutes a day.
6. Reduce cigarette smoking among people age 20 and older.

None of these risk-reduction objectives is specific to older people. They all suggest that reducing deaths in old age from coronary heart disease, stroke, and end-stage renal disease requires health promotion and illness-prevention behaviors that begin much earlier in the life course.

Cancer

Cancer is the second-leading cause of death in the United States. Over 535,000 Americans died of cancer in 1995. The incidence of cancer increases with age such that the death rate in 1995 among males 65 years of age and over was 60 times that among those ages 25 to 44 and more than 5 times that among males ages 45 to 64 years of age. In part, these facts reflect two important understandings that have been developed about the etiology of cancer: (1) Most forms of cancer have a long latent period, and initiating factors start during youth; and (2) increasing age and the accompanying physiologic changes make the patient more susceptible to the actions of carcinogens.

The death rate from cancer for women 65 years of age and older was about 62 percent that for aged men in 1994. Table 6.4 shows the differences in death

---

[1]A status report on *Healthy People 2000* and information on the new *Healthy People 2010* initiatives are available at <http://www.health.gov/healthypeople>.

TABLE 6.4   **Death Rates from Cancer, by Sex, Age, and Selected Type, for Persons 65 Years and Over: 1994**

	MALE	FEMALE
Total U.S. rate	220.8	188.2
AGE AT DEATH AND SELECTED TYPE OF CANCER		
Persons 65–74 Years Old		
Respiratory, intrathoracic	434.5	203.6
Digestive organs, peritoneum	260.8	149.7
Breast	1.4	105.6
Genital organs	115.1	69.2
Lymphatic and hematopoietic tissues (excl. leukemia)	59.0	42.5
Urinary organs	52.1	20.9
Lip, oral cavity, pharynx	18.0	7.9
Leukemia	35.6	19.1
Persons 75–84 Years Old		
Respiratory, intrathoracic	576.7	236.4
Digestive organs, peritoneum	437.2	284.0
Breast	2.0	145.9
Genital organs	350.7	96.7
Lymphatic and hematopoietic tissues (excl. leukemia)	107.8	78.4
Urinary organs	105.3	39.9
Lip, oral cavity, pharynx	23.5	10.6
Leukemia	71.5	38.3
Persons 85 Years Old and Over		
Respiratory, intrathoracic	556.1	171.8
Digestive organs, peritoneum	661.4	477.2
Breast	3.9	197.5
Genital organs	822.5	115.3
Lymphatic and hematopoietic tissues (excl. leukemia)	145.6	95.5
Urinary organs	189.6	67.3
Lip, oral cavity, pharynx	30.0	16.9
Leukemia	118.5	68.1

Note: Deaths per 100,000 population in specified age groups.

Source: U.S. Bureau of the Census, 1997, Table 135.

rates from cancer for persons 65 years and older by sex and the site of cancer in that year. Cancer of the lungs (respiratory), digestive organs, and genital and urinary organs are primary sites for men. Digestive, breast, respiratory, and genital (cervical) cancers are primary sites among women.

The onset and management of many cancers do not vary greatly in the old and young (Brocklehurst & Hanley 1981). Prevention is still the order of the day regarding cancer. Where possible, known causes of cancer should be avoided and removed from the environment. This includes (1) avoiding unnecessary exposure to ionizing and ultraviolet radiation, (2) implementing hygienic measures in occupations involving exposure to cancer-producing chemicals and dusts, and (3) avoiding exposure to tobacco and cigarette smoke.

Older people, especially, should be encouraged to have periodic preventive medical examinations. Any predisposing factors or premalignant conditions should not be misattributed to old age. Even in the oldest patients, cancer can be cured if it is detected early and diagnosed at a localized stage.

Lung cancer, among a number of diseases related to cigarette smoking, is probably the most preventable health problem in the United States. Lung cancer is principally a disease of older persons who have smoked cigarettes (Tockman & Ball 1990). Risk of the disease increases with the intensity and duration of cigarette smoking, the depth of inhalation, and the tar and nicotine content of the cigarettes. Lung cancer risk decreases with smoking cessation. The reduced risk will approach that of a nonsmoker 10 to 15 years after smoking has ceased (Doll & Peto 1976).

Risk-reduction objectives for cancer specified in the *Healthy People 2000* report by the U.S. Department of Health and Human Services include:

1. Reduce cigarette smoking among people age 20 and older. (Special population targets are offered for high-risk populations: the less well educated, blue-collar workers, military personnel, blacks, Hispanics, American Indians, Southeast Asian men, women of reproductive age, pregnant women, and women who use oral contraceptives.)
2. Reduce dietary fat and average unsaturated fat intake among children and adults.
3. Increase complex carbohydrates and fiber-containing foods in the diets of children and adults.
4. Increase the proportion of people of all ages who limit sun exposure, use sun screens and protective clothing when exposed to sunlight, and avoid artificial sources of ultraviolet light.

Stroke

Just as heart tissue can be denied adequate blood supply, changes in blood vessels that serve brain tissue, cerebral infarction, or cerebral hemorrhage can reduce nourishment carried to the brain and result in a malfunction or death of brain cells. Such impaired brain tissue circulation is referred to as ***cerebrovascular disease.***

When a portion of the brain is completely denied blood, a *cerebrovascular accident (CVA)*, or stroke, results. The severity of the accident is determined by the particular area affected as well as by the total amount of brain tissue involved. A stroke may affect such a small area of the brain that it goes unnoticed or such a large area that it causes death. After diseases of the heart, malignant neoplasms (cancers), and accidents, cerebrovascular disease is the fourth-leading cause of death in the United States today.

Cerebral thrombosis, a main cause of stroke in the elderly, occurs when a formed clot becomes lodged in an already narrowed artery. There may be no transient symptoms before the stroke occurs, or there may be what Brocklehurst and Hanley (1981) describe as a *stroke-in-evolution.* In the latter case, the stroke may develop over hours or even days. Symptoms may appear within minutes or hours after the onset of a stroke. Mini-strokes, referred to as **transient ischemic attacks (TIAs),** may also precede a CVA. TIAs are warning signs of an impending stroke. Sudden motor weakness, speech dysfunction, dizziness, sudden changes in vision (especially in one eye), and sudden falls are possible transitory symptoms that may accompany TIAs and precede a major stroke.

A cerebral embolism may also be responsible for a CVA. In this instance, the thrombus does not form locally but is derived from elsewhere in the body and travels to obstruct a vessel supplying the brain. In such cases, the stroke and its damage appear almost instantly.

When a stroke does occur, varying degrees of damage may result. Disorders of motor function, including weakness or paralysis on one side of the body, sensory disturbances, aphasia (speech disorders), and mental symptoms, among others, are possible clinical features of a CVA. Rehabilitation efforts should begin immediately. Success in these efforts is a function of area and degree of brain damage as well as support of a rehabilitative team of family, friends, and medical professionals.

Aphasia, which refers to impaired ability to comprehend or express verbal language, is a clinical feature of stroke in many elderly victims. The condition is emotionally disturbing to the victim, especially to those persons who were very verbal before a stroke, as well as to family members and friends. In *receptive aphasia,* a person has difficulty processing external stimuli. Because of damage within the speech center of the brain, the individual may not understand others' speech or what is read; also, familiar objects may become unrecognizable. When a person understands what is said but cannot form the words or gestures to respond to stimuli, *expressive aphasia* has resulted. Frequently, an aphasiac suffers from a mixed condition.

Tragically, aphasia may be incorrectly associated with mental deterioration. In such cases, people may assume that comprehension is impaired when it is not, and the person may be infantilized (treated as a child) while being fully aware of the situation. Individuals should be encouraged to speak, and those around them should listen patiently and should not rush the person or cut him or her off in the middle of an attempt. Such behavior on the part of a listener can cause an individual to feel awkward and self-conscious, and it may foster depression and withdrawal.

The extent of the damage and the degree of deficit that has taken place determine to what extent functional language skills can be regained. Unless the aphasia lasts only a few days, it may be difficult for geriatric patients ever to regain their former level of articulation. This is not to say that they cannot reestablish functional language patterns, but they and their families should not set goals too high. Every attempt should be made at language rehabilitation, and every gain should be recognized. The success of small forward steps should not be discounted because of failure to meet great expectations. A paternalistic or overly

helpful attitude toward the stroke victim, although well intended, may slow recovery and make the patient feel helpless or even useless. Any gain in independent living can only enhance a person's sense of self-worth and dignity.

ACTIVITIES OF DAILY LIVING

Practitioners and researchers have sought to develop measures that reflect the
practical aspects of physical functioning. ***Activities of daily living (ADLs)*** scales
have developed as the ultimate indicators of the elderly individual's capacity to
deal with basic self-care. With some variation across different instruments, items
used to measure basic self-care or activities of daily living include bathing, dressing, going to the bathroom, getting into or out of a bed or chair, walking, getting
outside the house or apartment, and feeding. These are ordered in terms of decreasing dependency (Katz et al. 1963). That is, it is generally found that bathing
is the least restrictive and most common problem, whereas lack of the ability to
feed oneself is indicative of the most severe restriction of function. Difficulty in
feeding oneself is highly associated with the presence of other problems and is the
least common ADL difficulty.

Generally, as Figure 6.1 shows, problems with ADLs increase with advancing age. In the age 65 to 74 category, 5.6 percent of males and 6.6 percent of females report difficulty with at least one ADL lasting six months or longer. By age

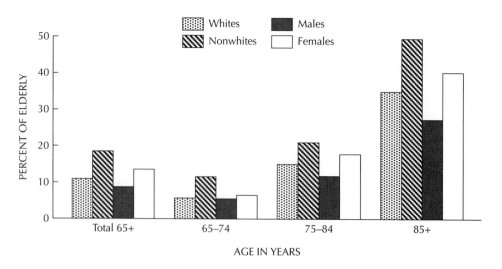

**FIGURE 6.1   Community Residents 65 Years and Older with Activity of
Daily Living (ADL) Limitations Lasting Six Months or Longer, by Age, Race,
and Sex: 1989**

Source: Data compiled by the National Aging Information Center from the National Long-Term Care
Survey and taken from the Administration on Aging website at <http://www.aoa.dhhs.gov/aoa/stats>.

85 and over, 27 percent of the males and 40 percent of the females report having long-term difficulty performing at least one ADL. Differentials between aged whites and nonwhites are substantial, as well. Among those 65 to 74 years, nonwhites report long-term limitations with ADLs at twice the rate of whites (11.6 vs. 5.7 percent); and almost half (49.4 percent) of nonwhites 85 years of age and older report similar long-term limitations in ADLs. Data from the Supplement on Aging (SOA) confirms this pattern. In that data set, the oldest-old, women, those elderly with a family income under $15,000, nonwhites, and those residing in rural areas report the most limitations in ADLs.

Age brings an increase in the likelihood of multiple ADL limitations. For example, data from the 1989 National Long-Term Care Survey reveal that only 3.2 percent of respondents ages 65 to 74 reported having three or more ADL limitations, but the figure goes up to 22 percent for those 85 years and older. Figure 6.2 shows the proportion of community residents with ADL limitations lasting three months or longer by age and type of limitation. For each ADL, advancing age brings an increased likelihood of limitation. And, for each age group, the order in which limitations occur seems to be the same. Limitations with bathing occurs most frequently; 9.4 percent percent of all respondents 65 years and older report

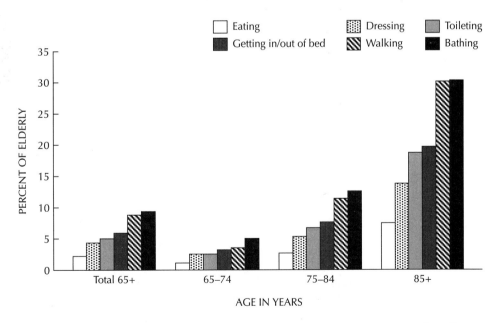

FIGURE 6.2   Community Residents 65 Years or Older with Activity of Daily Living (ADL) Limitations Lasting Three Months or Longer, by Age and Type of Limitation: 1989

Source: Data compiled by the National Aging Information Center from the National Long-Term Care Survey and taken from the Administration on Aging website at <http://www.aoa.dhhs.gov/aoa/stats>.

at least some difficulty carrying out this activity. Difficulty with eating or feeding oneself occurs least frequently; only 2.1 percent of respondents 65 years and older report experiencing this limitation.

INSTRUMENTAL ACTIVITIES OF DAILY LIVING

Instrumental activities of daily living (IADLs) include both the personal self-care reflected in the ADL measures and more complex activities. For example, going shopping, a commonly used IADL indicator, requires being able to get out of bed, dress, walk, and leave the house. Because the IADL tasks are more complicated and multifaceted, functional decrements are expected to show up first in the IADL items, and more older people are expected to report limitations in carrying out these instrumental activities than in performing the more basic activities of daily living. IADLs typically include home-management activities, including preparing meals, shopping, managing money, using the telephone, doing light housework, and doing heavy housework.

Difficulties in performing IADLs are related to age, as is revealed in Figure 6.3. For both males and females, the percent reporting difficulty with only IADLs as well as those with IADLs and ADLs increased with advancing age. Even among the oldest-old, those 85 years and older, only 8.3 percent reported IADL limitations

Although the probability of functional impairment increases with age, many older adults are able to perform both basic and instrumental activities of daily living well into their eighties.

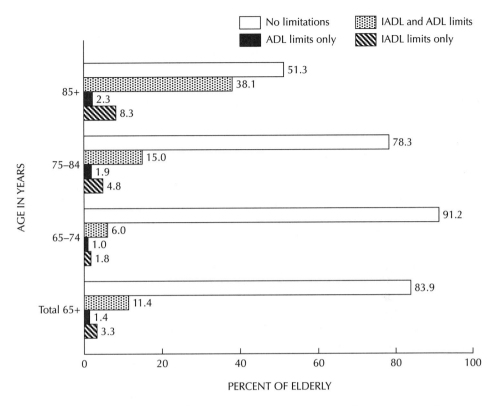

FIGURE 6.3   Community Residents 65 Years or Older with Instrumental Activity of Daily Living (IADL) and Activity of Daily Living (ADL) Limitations Lasting Three Months or Longer, by Age: 1989

Source: Data compiled by the National Aging Information Center from the National Long-Term Care Survey and taken from the Administration on Aging website at <http://www.aoa.dhhs.gov/aoa/stats>. A person had an IADL limitation if he or she could not get around outside or shop for groceries, or could only do so with the aid of a person or special equipment.

only; however, an additional 38.1 percent reported having both IADL and ADL limitations. Among those 65 to 74 years, a total of 7.8 percent had either IADL limitations only or some combination of IADL and ADL limitations.

A greater percent of women than men reported difficulty in performing IADLs, among those 65 years and older. Whereas 17.3 percent of older females experienced IADL limitations (either alone or in some combination with ADL limitations), only 10.9 percent of older males reported similar experiences. However, according to Furner (1992), these sex differences may not be the result of true functional differences between men and women, but rather may be the result of differences in role socialization (with men typically performing fewer IADLs than women, thus causing men's reports of difficulty to be underestimated). Conceivably, these sex differences may also be the result of age bias within each subgroup (on average, within any given age subgroup, women had higher mean ages than men).

Nathanson (1975) offers three categories of explanation for why women report more illness and limitation and use more medical services than do men:

1. It is culturally more acceptable for women to be ill.
2. Women's social roles are more compatible with reports of illness and use of medical services than is the case for men.
3. Women's social roles are, in fact, more stressful than those of men; consequently, they have more real illness and need more assistance and care.

The merits of these explanations continue to be debated (Verbrugge & Madans 1985). Kane and Kane (1981) suggest that, because of the complexity and multifaceted nature of IADLs, the way respondents report on the individual items may be biased by variations in motivation, mood, and overall emotional health. For instance, a depressed older person might be more likely to neglect IADLs (e.g., managing money or doing the housework) than basic aspects of personal self-care (e.g., dressing or using the toilet).

It can also be argued that social structural and environmental factors contribute to IADL limitations. A widower who never performed certain IADL tasks when his spouse was alive and fit may report limitations because he never learned the skills, not because he is unable to perform the function. Similarly, an older woman may report limitations in shopping because markets are scarce in her inner-city neighborhood and she lacks transportation to area stores.

As Lawton and Nahemow (1973) reported in the early 1970s, when the fit between an individual's competence and the environment in which the individual resides is good, adaptation is positive. This may be the case for the great majority of older people. When environmental demands are too great, adaptation is poor and the outcome (including self-care capacity) is likely to be negative.

IS THERE COMPRESSION OF MORBIDITY?

What if the time spent in chronic mental or physical illness or with functional limitations in the ADLs or IADLs before death could be reduced from current levels? Presumably, this would mean more years of a higher-quality old age, even in an absence of further improvements in life expectancy. Fries (1980, 1987) argues that this *compression of morbidity* may already be occurring. According to Fries (1987), a compression of morbidity may be considered to occur if the length of time between onset of disease and death is shortened.

One way in which compression of morbidity may reveal itself is through a decline in the disability rate. At least three different research teams employing different data sources have shown that disability rates in the United States have declined since the early 1980s (Manton, Corder, & Stallard 1997; Freedman & Martin 1998; Crimmins, Reynolds, & Saito 1999). Using data from the National Long-Term Care Survey (NLTCS), Manton and colleagues (1997) show that if disability rates had remained unchanged between 1982 and 1994, the number of older Americans with chronic functional limitations would have increased by 1.9 million people, as a result of the increased overall population of older people. The actual number of functional disabled people increased by only about 700,000 people. The decrease in chronic disability occurred in every age category among the elderly. Also, the rate of decrease in chronic disability accelerated over time during the period under study.

In contrast, Olshansky and associates (1991) suggest the possibility of an expansion of morbidity through two hypothetical mechanisms. First, medical technology may continue to improve survival from disabling conditions associated with fatal diseases, but the progress of the diseases themselves may remain unchanged. Second, as mortality from fatal diseases at older ages is reduced, the morbidity and disability resulting from nonfatal diseases could continue unabated. Thus, the trade-off becomes reduced mortality in middle and older ages for a redistribution of causes of disability and an expansion of morbidity (Olshansky et al. 1991). Much work remains to determine whether reductions in risk factors such as smoking and improvements in medical treatments lead to a compression of morbidity or whether causes of disability are redistributed with a resulting longer life with worsening health.

House and colleagues (1990) argue that people need to move beyond the dispute over whether compression of morbidity is occurring in the total population and instead determine whether certain subgroups of the population are experiencing greater postponement of morbidity and functional limitations than others. The researchers express surprise at the extent to which socioeconomic differentials in the relation of aging and health have been neglected in the compression of morbidity debate. They point out how, even as average life expectancy has advanced, socioeconomic differences in mortality and health have persisted in the United States and elsewhere. They hypothesize that the higher socioeconomic strata in U.S. society already approximate the compression of morbidity scenario (that is, low levels of morbidity and functional limitations until quite late in life), whereas levels of morbidity and functional limitations increase steadily throughout middle-age and early old age for those in the lower socioeconomic strata.

Data from the Americans' Changing Lives (ACL) survey, including 3,617 respondents ages 25 and over interviewed in 1986, was used to test the hypothesis. The key dependent variables were three self-reported indicators of physical health. Four different levels of socioeconomic status (SES), defined in terms of education and income, were identified for purposes of the analyses. Respondents in the lowest level of SES had both 0 to 11 years of education *and* income below $20,000; those in the highest level of SES had 16+ years of education *and* income of $20,000 or more.

The results of the analyses show a particularly striking pattern of differences in the relation of age to health for all three indicators across four levels of socio-economic status defined by education and income. Only the specific pattern for one indicator of physical health—number of chronic conditions experienced in the past year—is described here.

Among young-adult survey respondents ages 25 to 34, there are no socio-economic differences in prevalence of chronic conditions. Marked differences become evident for those in early middle-age (35 to 44 years), and these differences become larger still among those 45 to 54 years and those in early old age (55 to 64 years and 65 to 74 years). The differences are much smaller among persons 75 years and older. More important, the lowest socioeconomic stratum shows a prevalence of chronic conditions at ages 35 to 44 that is not seen in the highest stratum until after age 75. The prevalence of chronic conditions peaks at ages 55 to 64 in the lowest SES group, at ages 65 to 74 in the next group, but not until age 75 and over for the two highest SES groups.

In sum, considerable postponement of morbidity seems to be occurring in the highest socioeconomic group, where the mean number of chronic conditions remains below 1.0 until age 75. In contrast, the mean number of chronic conditions in the lowest socioeconomic group rises sharply between ages 25 and 54 and exceeds 2.0 by age 55. On the basis of this research, House and colleagues (1990) identify the vast amount of "excess" or preventable morbidity and functional limitations as being located in the lowest SES groups in U.S. society. Clearly, efforts to postpone morbidity, disability, and even mortality in U.S. society must include serious efforts to reduce socioeconomic differentials in health in middle-age as well as early old age.

MENTAL DISORDERS AND MENTAL HEALTH

Definitions of mental illness in older adults include objective limitations in cognitive, emotional, and social functioning, as well as subjective feelings of distress. Qualls and Smyer (1995) suggest that mental health/illness for older adults can be thought of along a continuum that ranges from "optimal psychological vitality" (p. 630) to serious mental illness. But mental illness is more than just a list of disorders and mental health is more than the absence of such a list. Mental health must also take into account how individuals adjust to the normative and non-normative events that occur in later life (Katz 1995).

Mental disorders in later life include chronic, neurologically based conditions (e.g., Alzheimer's disease and related disorders), symptoms that are secondary consequences of physical conditions or medical interventions (e.g., delirium), and understandable reactions (e.g., depressive symptomatology) to identifiable stressors (e.g., retirement, death of a spouse) (Gatz 1995). These disorders vary widely in terms of severity and symptoms, but each can impact a number of life domains, including well-being, life satisfaction, morbidity, self-care behavior, health care utilization, and mortality (Katz 1995).

Mental disorders are not a normal part of aging. However, when mental disorders are present in later life, they are the result of one of three patterns (Gatz, Kasl-Godley, & Karel 1996):

1. An individual who had been diagnosed with a mental disorder early in life grows old and the mental disorder either continues or reoccurs
2. An individual was exposed to particular stressors throughout his or her life that result in the development of a mental disorder in later life
3. An individual grows old and develops a mental disorder in later life

Diagnostic Criteria for Mental Disorders: The *DSM-IV*

What criteria are used to determine whether someone has a mental disorder? The criteria currently used to diagnose mental disorders for people of all ages are contained in the fourth edition of the American Psychiatric Association's (1994) <http://www.psych. org> *Diagnostic and Statistical Manual of Mental Disorders (DSM-IV)*. The **DSM-IV** provides sets of observable symptoms for approximately 300 specific diagnoses that are classified into 17 major groups of mental disorders (Koenig & Frances 1995). Although the *DSM-IV* is used to diagnose mental disorders in individuals of all ages, there are several aspects of *DSM-IV* that are especially relevant to the diagnosis of mental disorders in older adults (Koenig & Frances 1995).

The *DSM-IV* classifies disorders as either *primary* (i.e., idiopathic, a morbid state or condition not the result of another disease) or *secondary* (i.e., symptomatic, the result of an identifiable medical condition or substance). Thus, for example, according to *DSM-IV,* an older adult can be diagnosed with "major depressive disorder" or "secondary major depressive episode due to Parkinson's disease."

The diagnosis of psychopathology in older adults is complicated by the fact that it is oftentimes difficult to distinguish among medical conditions, the side-effects of medications, and actual psychiatric disorders (Koenig et al. 1993). As such, the *DSM-IV* provides guidelines as to when symptoms should be counted toward the diagnosis of a mental condition. Basically, if a symptom is thought to be a physiological consequence of a medical illness or a medication, the symptom does not contribute to the diagnosis of a mental disorder. If, however, the symptom is thought to be a psychological reaction to the physical illness, then it does contribute to such a diagnosis (American Psychiatric Association 1994).

Distinguishing medical conditions and side-effects of medications from mental disorders is especially difficult among older adults. Because older adults metabolize medications differently than do younger adults, they commonly experience adverse psychological reactions to medications. To emphasize the impact that medications can have on mental health, and the importance of distinguishing reactions to medications from primary mental disorders, the *DSM-IV* has developed categories for substance-induced mental disorders (e.g., "substance-induced mood disorder" or "substance-induced anxiety disorder").

Some evidence shows that psychopathology may present differently as a function of demographic and other characteristics, such as age. As a result, for each major diagnostic category, the *DSM-IV* includes information on how age, gender, and cultural factors might influence the presentation of the disorder. For example, the criteria for major depressive disorder specify that, in older adults, "cognitive symptoms (e.g., disorientation, memory loss, and distractibility) may be particularly prominent" (American Psychiatric Association 1994, p. 325).

Mental Disorders in Later Life

It is estimated that 22 percent of all older adults have a mental disorder (Gatz & Smyer 1992; Park et al. 1993), although estimates among institutionalized older adults are higher than 50 percent (Burns et al. 1988; Rovner et al. 1990). The major mental disorders observed among older adults include dementia, delirium, mood disorders (e.g., depression, mania), anxiety/phobia, schizophrenia and other psychotic disorders, and substance-related disorders (e.g., Gatz 1995; Katz 1995; Schneider 1995).

Dementia.   According to the *DSM-IV, dementia* is characterized by memory impairment (which can include either difficulty in learning new material or recalling previously learned material) and at least one of the following cognitive difficulties: (1) aphasia (language difficulty), (2) apraxia (impaired ability to perform motor activities), (3) agnosia (inability to recognize/identify objects), (4) disruption in executive functioning (i.e., complex behaviors that require planning and organization). In order to be diagnosed with dementia, additional criteria are that these symptoms must be characterized by a gradual onset and continuing decline, represent significant decline from previous levels of functioning, and be severe enough to impair social and/or occupational functioning. Finally, in order to be diagnosed as dementia, these symptoms must not occur during the course of a delirium.

The lifetime risk of developing dementia is 14 to 16 percent (Terry, Katzman, & Beck 1994), and the incidence of dementia increases with age. It is estimated that 5 percent of adults over age 65 and 30 percent of adults over age 85 have some type of dementia. Females are at greater risk for dementia than are males, and African Americans are at greater risk than are whites (Heyman et al. 1991). Given that the segment of the population age 85 and older is the most rapidly growing, and that dementia is age related, it can be expected that increasing numbers of older adults will exhibit dementia.

Figure 6.4 presents the criteria that the National Institute of Neurological Disorders and Stroke (NINDS) <http://www.ninds.nih.gov> recommends to diagnosis "probable Alzheimer's disease." Alzheimer's disease is characterized as "probable" because it is an exclusionary diagnosis. A comprehensive diagnostic examination that includes a medical workup, blood tests, brain imaging, and neuropsychological tests determines whether a cause for the dementia can be identified. If a cause cannot be identified, then a diagnosis of probable Alzheimer's disease is made.

FIGURE 6.4   Criteria for the Diagnosis of Probable Alzheimer's Disease

1. Criteria for clinical diagnosis of *probable* Alzheimer's disease include:
   a. Dementia established by clinical examination and documented by the Mini Mental State Test, Blessed Dementia Scale, or some similar examination and confirmed by neuropsychological tests
   b. Deficits in two or more areas of cognition
   c. Progressive worsening of memory and other cognitive functions
   d. No disturbance of consciousness
   e. Onset between ages 40 and 90, most often after age 65
   f. Absence of systemic disorders or other brain diseases that in and of themselves could account for progressive deficits in memory and cognition
2. Diagnosis of probable Alzheimer's disease is supported by:
   a. Progressive deterioration of specific cognitive functions, such as language (asphasia), motor skills (apraxia), and perception (agnosia)
   b. Impaired activities of daily living and altered patterns of behavior
   c. Family history of similar disorders, particularly if confirmed neuropathologically
   d. Laboratory results of normal lumbar puncture as evaluated by standard techniques; normal pattern or nonspecific changes in EEG, such as increased slow-wave activity; and evidence of cerebral atrophy on CT with progression documented by serial observation
3. Other clinical features consistent with diagnosis of probable Alzheimer's disease, after exclusion of causes of dementia other than Alzheimer's disease, include:
   a. Plateaus in the course of progression of illness
   b. Associated symptoms of depression; insomnia; incontinence; delusions; illusions; hallucinations; catastrophic verbal, emotional, or physical outbursts; sexual disorders; and weight loss
   c. Other neurological abnormalities in some patients, especially with more advanced disease and including motor signs, such as increased muscle tone, myoclonus, or gait disorder
   d. Seizures in advanced disease
   e. CT normal for age
4. Features that make the diagnosis of probable Alzheimer's disease uncertain or unlikely include:
   a. Sudden, apoplectic onset
   b. Focal neurological findings such as hemiparesis, sensory loss, visual field deficits, and uncoordination early in the course of the illness
   c. Seizures or gait disturbance at onset or very early in the course of the illness
5. Clinical diagnosis of probable Alzheimer's disease:
   a. May be made on the basis of dementia syndrome, in the absence of other neurological, psychiatric, or systemic disorders sufficient to cause dementia and in the presence of variations in onset, in presentation, or in the clinical course.
   b. May be made in the presence of a second systemic or brain disorder sufficient to produce dementia, which is not considered to be the cause of dementia.
   c. Should be used in research studies when single, gradually progressive severe cognitive deficit is identified in the absence of other identifiable cause.
6. Criteria for diagnosis of definite Alzheimer's diseases are:
   a. Clinical criteria for probable Alzheimer's disease
   b. Histopathological evidence obtained from biopsy or autopsy
7. Classification of Alzheimer's disease for research purposes should specify features that may differentiate subtypes of the disorder, such as:
   a. Familial occurrence
   b. Onset before age 65
   c. Presence of trisomy-21
   d. Coexistence of other relevant conditions, such as Parkinson's disease

Source: National Institute of Neurological, Communication Disorders and Stroke, undated.

The specific type of dementia that an individual is diagnosed with has implications for treatment. If the cause of the dementia proves to be substance induced, it is possible that the dementia is reversible. On the other hand, if the dementia is disease specific or is vascular in etiology, then it is not reversible. Because there is no cure for irreversible dementia, one set of treatment strategies typically centers on behavioral and environmental interventions designed to encourage appropriate behavior, minimize inappropriate behavior, maintain current levels of functioning, and ensure the safety of the individual with the diagnosis. The second set of treatment strategies revolves around providing family caregivers with the educational and emotional support necessary for them to sustain their caregiving efforts.

Delirium.   *Delirium* is a direct physiological consequence of a medical condition that is characterized by disruptions in consciousness (which can include difficulty in focusing, maintaining, or shifting attention) and a change in cognitive abilities or the development of perceptual difficulties that are not due to a dementia. Delirium develops over a short period of time (usually within hours or a day) and fluctuates over the course of a day (American Psychiatric Association 1994). Among the medical conditions that can cause delirium are substance abuse, substance withdrawal, toxins due to infections, and a host of medications (e.g., sedative-hypnotics, anxiolytics, antidepressants, antiinflamatories) (Schneider 1995).

It is estimated that 10 to 30 percent of hospitalized patients have delirium. Risk factors for delirium include advanced age, medical illness, medication use, dementia, and being postoperative (Schneider 1995). The primary treatment strategy is to identify and treat the underlying cause of the delirium. In addition, it is helpful to provide a predictable, stable environment for the person who suffers from delirium (Rabins 1991).

Mood Disorders.   *Mood* refers to how people experience emotion as well as their sustained and predominant internal emotional state. The *DSM-IV* categorizes disorders that involve extremes in individuals' moods, or affective functioning, as *mood disorders*. Mood disorders can involve blunted mood and diminished interest or pleasure in events (i.e., depression); elevated or expansive mood (i.e., mania); or a combination of the two (i.e., bipolar disorder). Although there are several additional mood disorders, only depression and mania are included here.

Depression is the most common mental health problem confronting older adults. The *DSM-IV* criteria for depression vary as a function of the severity and frequency of the symptoms. In general, the symptoms of a major depressive disorder are:

1. Depressed mood that is either reported by the individual or observed by others
2. Diminished interest or pleasure in activities
3. Weight loss or weight gain of 5 percent of body weight within a month without trying to lose/gain weight
4. Insomnia or hypersomnia

5. Psychomotor retardation or agitation that is observable by others
6. Fatigue or loss of energy
7. Feelings of worthlessness or guilt
8. Diminished ability to concentrate or indecisiveness
9. Recurrent thoughts of death, suicidal ideation without a specific plan, a suicide plan, or a suicide attempt

In order to be classified as a major depressive disorder, the individual must exhibit five or more of the symptoms, one of which must be either depressed mood or diminished interest/pleasure. The symptoms have to have lasted for greater than two weeks, represent a departure from previous functioning, and result in impaired social, occupational, and/or other important domains of functioning. In addition, there must be no evidence that the symptoms are due to the physiological effects of a substance, a general medical condition, or bereavement over the loss of a loved one. Specific diagnoses include "major depressive episode," "major depressive disorder, single episode," and "major depressive disorder, recurrent."

More common than older adults who have a diagnosis of depression are older adults who do not meet the criteria for a diagnosis of depression but who nonetheless report some of the symptoms (Blazer 1993). Older adults who report depressive symptomatology should be monitored and their concerns should be taken seriously.

Regardless of whether an older person is experiencing depressive symptoms or a full-blown depressive disorder, the elderly talk about their feelings of depression differently than do younger adults. In fact, many depressed older adults do not consider themselves to be depressed. They are much less likely than younger adults to talk about feelings of depressed mood. In contrast, older people are more likely to talk about not being interested in things going on around them (Gallo, Anthony, & Muthen 1994) and to express their concerns as somatic complaints.

Among community-dwelling people age 65 and older, more of this population exhibits depressive symptoms than major depressive disorder (15 vs. 3 percent, respectively) (Friedhoff 1994). It is estimated that 12 percent of older adults in primary care settings have a major depressive disorder (Koenig et al. 1988), and estimates for older adults in nursing homes range from 12 percent (Parmelee, Katz, & Lawton 1989) to 23 percent (Burns et al. 1988). Friedhoff (1994) reports that 13 percent of older adults admitted to nursing homes develop a new episode of major depression over a one-year period, and that an additional 18 percent develop new symptoms of depression during that same time period.

The lifetime risk of developing depression is estimated to be between 20 and 25 percent (Schneider 1995). The risk factors of depression and depressive symptomatology for older adults include being female; being unmarried, widowed, or recently bereaved; experiencing various stressful life events, and having lower levels of social support (Zisook, Schucter, & Schledge 1994). A serious physical illness also increases the risk of developing depression (Reynolds et al. 1994). In fact, it is estimated that 50 percent of older adults who have a chronic physical illness may have a major depressive disorder (Schneider 1995). This is not to suggest that such older adults should not receive treatment for their depression. To the contrary, when it is thought that depression might coexist with other medical conditions, careful diagnosis and treatment are critical.

Depression is generally unrecognized/undiagnosed in older adults. It is estimated that only approximately 10 percent of older adults who could benefit from treatment actually receive it (Schneider 1995). In part, this might stem from the fact that many mental health professionals believe that depression is a normal response to aging-related changes (Friedhoff 1994).

The issue of suicide among older adults is typically raised in the context of discussions on depression. It surprises many people to learn that the suicide rate for older adults is twice the rate for the population in general. The rate of suicide among the general population is 12.4 per 100,000, whereas the rate is 26.5 per 100,000 among adults between the ages of 80 and 84 (Conwell 1994).

Older white males show the highest suicide rate of any group. Among males ages 65 to 74, their rate is almost 3 times that of African American males, more than 5 times that of older white females, and almost 12 times that of older African American females (U.S. Bureau of the Census 1995, Table 136). Older females in the United States have among the lowest suicide rates in the world. Older U.S. males fall in the middle of the range represented by selected countries. Older males have higher suicide rates in Austria, Denmark, France, and West Germany; countries in which older adults have lower suicide rates than in the United States include England and Wales, Australia, Canada, Italy, Poland, and the Netherlands (U.S. Bureau of the Census 1994, Table 1360).

Interestingly, three-fourths of older adults who committed suicide visited their primary care physician in the month prior to the suicide act (Conwell 1994). Most of these older adults were suffering from a first episode of a major depressive disorder that was moderately severe in nature. Nonetheless, the symptoms went undiagnosed and untreated.

The goals of treatment for depression are to reduce symptoms, decrease the risk of relapse and/or recurrence, improve the individual's quality of life, improve the individual's general and medical health status, and decrease mortality (Schneider 1995). Schneider suggests that treatment for depression can be either acute or maintenance, and identifies two general categories of treatment: biological therapies (including pharmacotherapy/drug therapy and electroconvulsive therapy) and psychosocial therapies (including cognitive/behavioral, interpersonal, and psychodynamic psychotherapy). The type and severity of the depressive disorder determine which treatment approach is most effective. In the most extreme cases, hospitalization and a combination of therapies is warranted.

According to the *DSM-IV,* **mania** is characterized by an abnormally and consistently elevated, expansive, or irritable mood that lasts for at least one week (American Psychiatric Association 1994). During this time, the individual must demonstrate at least three out of the following seven symptoms: (1) inflated self-esteem/grandiosity, (2) decreased need for sleep, (3) increased talkativeness, (4) racing thoughts, (5) distractibility, (6) increased goal-directed activity, and (7) excessive involvement in activities that could have negative consequences (e.g., making foolish purchases). In order for a diagnosis of mania to be made, the symptoms must be severe enough to impair social and/or occupational functioning, and the physiological effects of medical conditions and substance abuse must be ruled out as causes. Mania often occurs in individuals who also have episodes of depression.

Mania is relatively uncommon in older adults. It is estimated that 1 percent of older adults exhibit acute mania, although 5 percent of hospitalized geropsychiatric patients do so (Stone 1989). Mania can present differently in older than in younger adults (Schneider 1995). For example, symptoms in older adults can include confusion, irritability, distractibility, and paranoid ideation. Secondary mania may result from medical illness, prescription medications, and illicit drugs. Treatment for mania involves psychopharmacologic (i.e., drug) therapies.

Anxiety/Phobic Disorders.   The *DSM-IV* classifies anxiety states (i.e., anxiety in response to no particular stimulus), *panic disorders* (i.e., recurrent anxiety attacks and anxiety about additional attacks), *phobic disorders* (i.e., excessive or unreasonable fear of a particular object or situation that causes anxiety), *obsessive-compulsive disorder* (i.e., recurrent and persistent thoughts that are inappropriate and that cause anxiety), and *post-traumatic stress disorder* as related disorders (American Psychiatric Association 1994). Regardless of the underlying disorder, anxiety is characterized by impaired concentration, attention and memory; dizziness; fear; insomnia; and hypervigilence (Schneider 1995).

Situational anxiety, which is common in older adults, is an understandable response to a major life change (e.g., relocation to a retirement community, a major illness), but anxiety disorders are not. Regier and colleagues (1988) estimate that the combined prevalence of panic, phobic, and obsessive-compulsive disorders among older adults is 5.5 percent. Similarly, Cohen (1990) reports that anxiety disorders are diagnosed in 5 percent of older men and 10 percent of older women.

It is important to diagnose and treat anxiety in older adults for at least two reasons (Schneider 1995): (1) Treatment of an anxiety disorder can increase an older adult's daily functioning and (2) the symptoms of anxiety disorders can be confused with more serious disorders, such as dementia and major depression. Depending on the type of anxiety disorder, various psychopharmacologic, psychosocial, and behavioral therapies have been shown to be effective.

Schizophrenia and Other Psychotic Disorders.   The primary characteristics of schizophrenia and other psychotic disorders are hallucinations (i.e., distortions in perceptions) and delusions (i.e., belief systems that are not based on reality) (American Psychiatric Association 1994). Typically, schizophrenia and other psychotic disorders do not have a late-life onset. It is estimated that only 1 percent of the population develops a psychotic disorder in later life (Gurland & Cross 1982). In contrast, 90 percent of older adults with schizophrenia were age 45 or younger at its onset, and fewer than 35 percent of older adults had an onset after age 40 (Harris & Jeste 1988). Nonetheless, the symptoms of schizophrenia and other psychotic disorders are oftentimes secondary problems of other disorders, such as Alzheimer's disease (Jeste et al. 1995). As such, it is important that the symptoms and diagnoses of these disorders be understood. Treatment is disorder specific and can include antipsychotic and antidepressant medications (Schneider 1995).

Substance Abuse.   The *DSM-IV* identifies two main groups of substance-related disorders: substance-use disorders and substance-induced disorders (American Psychiatric Association 1994). Basically, the *substance-use disorders* include dependence on and abuse of a particular substance. The *substance-induced disorders* are those disorders that can result from the use of the substances. Examples of substance-induced disorders include delirium, persisting dementia, psychotic disorder, mood disorder, and anxiety disorder. The substances that are included in the *DSM-IV* classification are alcohol; amphetamines; caffeine; cannabis; cocaine; hallucinogens; inhalants; nicotine; opioids; phencyclidine; sedatives, hypnotics, or anxiolytics; polysubstance; and "other" (American Psychiatric Association 1994).

Although the rates of substance-related disorders among older adults are relatively low, it has been suggested that many substance-abuse disorders are overlooked in the elderly. For example, Cummings (1993) estimates that the incidence of alcohol dependence is stable at approximately 10 percent of the population across the life course. Nonetheless, 60 percent of older adults' secondary hospital diagnoses are alcohol related. These data, combined with predictions that substance-related disorders will be more common in future cohorts of older individuals (Schneider 1995), suggest that more attention will be devoted to these disorders in upcoming years.

Mental Health Service Utilization

The one-year prevalence of all mental disorders among people over age 65 is 20 to 22 percent (Gatz & Smyer 1992), and it is estimated that today, 7.5 million older adults have mental health problems that require professional attention (Gatz & Finkel 1995). Nonetheless, many older adults do not take advantage of the mental health services that are available to them. Older people are consistently identified as being unserved, underserved, or inappropriately served by the mental health system.

A number of factors that contribute to older adults' underutilization of mental health services have been identified. For example, it is well documented that the elderly are more apt to conceptualize their problems in terms of physical rather than mental health (Heller 1993), and that they are hesitant to use traditional mental health settings (Gatz & Smyer 1992). These two factors at least partially explain findings regarding community-dwelling older adults' use of various treatment settings. Burns and Taube (1990) and George and colleagues (1988) found that, of those community-dwelling older adults who needed mental health treatment, 32 percent received the treatment from mental health professionals, 31 percent received treatment (usually pharmacotherapy) from a primary care physician, and 37 percent did not receive any treatment for their mental health condition.

Additional factors that contribute to underutilization of mental health services include the stigma associated with mental illness among members of the current cohort of older adults, limited knowledge regarding the availability of services, low referral rates by general practitioners, ageism on the part of mental health providers, inadequate detection, and economic disincentives (Colenda & van Dooren 1993; Feinson 1990). Ethnic minority elders are especially underserved as a function of the stigma regarding mental health needs, the perception of discrimination on the part of mental health providers, language barriers, economic factors, and limited knowledge regarding providers and services (McCombs 1993; Smith 1993).

Mental Health: Prevention and Promotion

Increasingly, professionals are emphasizing the importance of mental health prevention for older adults (Horne & Blazer 1992; Katz, Streim, & Parmelee 1994). The goal of prevention in mental health is "to help older adults find pleasure and meaning in their lives, use appropriate supports, and retain or assume as much control over their lives as possible" (Waters 1995, p. 183). This goal is consistent with the six criteria for positive mental health that Jahoda (1958) advocated over four decades ago:

1. Positive self-attitude
2. Growth and self-actualization
3. Integrated personality
4. Autonomy
5. Reality perception
6. Mastery of the environment

The mental health challenge for older adults is to strive to achieve and/or maintain these six criteria in the face of normative and non-normative biological, psychological, and social changes. Mentally healthy older adults develop the coping strategies that enable them to adapt to the challenges they encounter (Qualls & Smyer 1995).

Two additional factors contribute to the difficulty the elderly face in maintaining both physical and mental health, and these deserve a brief mention here. One has to do with the basic orientation of modern medicine, the so-called medical model. The other pertains to the attitudes and expectations that older people, their family and friends, and health care providers have about what aging means.

THE MEDICAL MODEL

The concept of the ***medical model*** describes the basic paradigm that rules medical practice. Eliot Freidson employs the term *medical-intervention pattern* to describe what is meant here:

> The medical man is prone to see the patient's difficulty as a transitory technical problem that can be overcome by some physical or biochemical intervention

which only the physician is qualified to perform. The assumption is that the patient can be cured and discharged. (1988, pp. 132–133)

In this model, attention is aimed at obtaining a diagnosis of a condition and developing a treatment regimen for its cure. Efforts are almost always geared at identifying just one condition or dysfunction. Among the elderly in ill health, however, a single condition is unusual. More often, elderly patients have multiple conditions, including degenerative changes associated with biological aging and diseases associated with pathological aging. In addition, specific disease states may manifest themselves differently among the elderly than is the case among the young. These multiple changes, along with age-based differences in symptom manifestation, can lead to confusion in trying to diagnose accurately and to further difficulty in generating an appropriate treatment plan.

This confusion would occur even if the presence of disease, its diagnosis, and its treatment could be defined objectively. There is considerable evidence, however, that such objectivity is a questionable assumption underlying the medical model (Wolinsky 1988). Zola (1962, 1966) has demonstrated that the differing worldviews of patients and the differences in their cultural backgrounds affected how they presented symptoms to attending physicians. For example, Zola found that Irish patients tended to understate their symptoms, whereas Italians were more likely to generalize and even embellish their symptoms. Wolinsky summarizes the sociological principle in effect here:

> The selection, salience, and presentation of symptoms are at least partially determined by sociocultural factors and conditioning…. If the symptoms of disease are socioculturally relative, then disease itself must be in part defined relative to sociocultural phenomena. (1988, p. 77)

Even if symptoms of illness were presented in some objective fashion, there is a serious question about whether all physicians would or could identify the signs and presence of disease. As Wolinsky (1988) points out, although physicians are comparably trained, there is no uniform mechanical procedure for examining all patients or even all elderly patients. Some physicians routinely check blood pressure, pulse, and respiration during an examination or office visit; others do not. Also, diseases linked to sociocultural traits (e.g., obesity and hypertension among older black women or osteoporosis among elderly white women) may cue physician attention toward or away from particular diagnoses.

Kovar addresses the fact that the medical model treats all older people as if they were representatives of a homogeneous grouping.

> The range in health status is just as great in this age group as in any other, even though the proportion of persons who have health problems increases with age and a minor health problem that might be quickly alleviated at younger ages tends to linger. Aging is a process that continues over the entire lifespan at differing rates among different persons. The rate of aging varies among populations and among individuals in the same population. It varies even within an individual because different body systems do not age at the same rate. (1977, p. 9)

ATTRIBUTION OF ILLNESS

Health is as much a subjective as an objective phenomenon. Individuals assess their health on the basis of various factors, including their own expectations about how people like themselves should feel. People experiencing changes in usual body functioning try to make sense of their experiences, often by hypothesizing about the possible causes of symptoms. A central issue in most perceptions of causality is whether to attribute a given experience to internal or external states (Freedman, Sears, & Carlsmith 1978). External attribution ascribes causality to anything external to the individual, such as the general environment, role constraints or role losses, stressful tasks being worked on, and so on. Internal causes include such factors as disease states, biological aging, personality, mood, and motivation (Freedman, Sears, & Carlsmith 1978).

Potentially, the development of illness attribution and misattribution can be affected by many factors both internal and external to the individual. These include the perceived seriousness of symptoms, the extent of disruption of normal activities involved, the frequency and persistence of the symptoms, the amount of pain and discomfort to which a person is accustomed, the extent of the person's medical knowledge, the need to deny the illness, the nature of competing needs, the availability of alternative explanations, and the accessibility of treatment (Mechanic 1978).

According to Jones and Nisbett (1971), actors and observers tend to make different causal attributions. *Actors* usually see their behavior as a response to an external situation in which they find themselves; typically, *observers* attribute the same response to factors internal to the actor. This difference between an actor's and an observer's attributions can lead to misunderstanding, perhaps especially so in a health care context. Patients and their physicians may see the same event from different perspectives. The patient attributes his or her response to environmental factors (e.g., stress at home) that are out of the purview of the physician, but the physician attributes the patient's response to internal physical processes (e.g., disease states or biological aging). These internal processes are, for the most part, the only causal explanations available to the physician, who may be handicapped by a lack of information about those factors to which the patient is responding in the environment.

This is the basis for problems in the doctor/patient relationship. The noncompliant patient may be deemed uncooperative or recalcitrant by the physician ("The patient has a personality problem"), whereas the patient may attribute noncompliance to situational factors ("The medication made me sick") (Janis & Rodin 1979).

The elderly themselves seem overly ready to make attributions to internal physical processes rather than to the environment (Janis & Rodin 1979). Their perceptions often include grossly exaggerated notions of what happens during normal aging. Too many associate pain and discomfort, debilitation, or decline in intellectual function with aging in itself. These are not normal accompaniments of aging. Unfortunately, such associations are supported by significant others (e.g., "What do you expect at your age?") as well as by physicians. In fact, the aged patient/doctor relationship may be a special case of actor/observer interaction, when both agree that events are attributable to internal physical processes (e.g., biological aging).

This consensus may reinforce a set of consequences that are essentially negative. First, elderly individuals may assume that aging has had a greater impact on them than it really has. For example, Kahn and associates (1975) found that only a small amount of memory loss was evident in an elderly sample; yet, patients perceived a high degree of loss. These perceptions were highly correlated with depression. Second, the elderly may attribute all negative changes in health and mood to aging in itself. Chest pain as a warning signal of heart disease may be considered another attack of heartburn; bone pain, which may herald a fracture or bone cancer, may be ascribed to age-related rheumatism. A change in bowel habits is a well-known danger signal of cancer but such an alteration may easily be ignored by an older person who seems to be plagued by bowel problems. Even rectal bleeding may be attributed to hemorrhoids.

Attributing illness or biological changes to so-called normal aging may incorrectly focus an elderly person (and his or her physician) away from situational and social factors that are stress inducing and that affect health. Much of the remainder of this book is concerned with the impact on health and other aspects of the lives of older people of events and processes, including retirement, widowhood, and changing living environments, among others.

SUMMARY

Disease is the chief barrier to extended health and longevity in older people. Today, chronic illnesses—including heart disease, cancer, and stroke—represent the key health problems affecting middle-aged and older adults. The prevalence of chronic conditions varies by age, sex, race, income, and residence. Chronic illness can be burdensome in terms of days spent in bed and deficits in the elderly individual's capacity to engage in activities of daily living (ADLs) and instrumental activities of daily living (IADLs). The oldest-old, women, those elderly with family incomes under $15,000, nonwhites, and those residing in rural areas report the most limitation in ADL score. The pattern is similar for IADLs.

Fries (1980, 1987) offers a hypothesis of "compression of morbidity," suggesting the likelihood that people can expect to live longer and healthier with a shorter duration of illness and disability in old age before death. House and colleagues (1990) suggest that considerable postponement of morbidity seems already to be occurring in the highest socioeconomic groups. However, at this point, evidence in support of the compression of morbidity hypothesis is mixed, and some projections into the twenty-first century suggest increases in the numbers of elderly who are disabled.

Estimates vary as to the proportion of the elderly population with mental health problems. Perhaps as many as 25 percent of the elderly have some mental health problems, with the percentage being lower for those residing in the community and as high as 50 percent for those in long-term care institutions. The major mental disorders observed among older adults include dementia, delirium, mood disorders (e.g., depression, mania), anxiety, schizophrenia and other psychotic disorders, and substance-related disorders. In 1992, older white males showed the highest suicide rate of any group. Among males ages 65 to 74, their rate was almost 3 times that of African American males, more than 5 times that of older white females, and almost 12 times that of older African American females. Older females in the United States have among the lowest suicide rates in the world.

The most common cause of dementia is Alzheimer's disease. It is estimated that more than 50 percent of adults with a diagnosis of dementia have Alzheimer's disease; that 10 to 15 percent have vascular dementia; and that an additional 10 to 15 percent have a combination of Alzheimer's disease and vascular dementia. At present, there is no known cure for Alzheimer's disease, and little is known about the extent to which social and psychological experiences may contribute to the onset of the disease. Regardless of the cause of a dementia, individuals with dementia ultimately are not able to care for themselves, and most typically rely on family members.

Two additional factors that affect the health status of older people are the orientation of modern medicine and the attitudes and expectations of old and young alike toward the difficulty of maintaining health in the later years. The elderly, along with health care professionals, may be too ready to attribute illness or biological changes to supposedly normal aging.

STUDY QUESTIONS

1. What does the concept of *physical health* encompass? Distinguish among the absence of illness, basic self-care activities, and more complex indicators of functioning.

2. What is the relationship between sociodemographic characteristics of the elderly (such as age, sex, race, family income, and residence) and self-assessment of health, ADLs, and IADLs?

3. Discuss the dominant causes or forms of heart disease and their impacts on the elderly.

4. What understandings have developed about the etiology of cancer? Describe the death rate differences from cancer between older men and women. What are the primary sites of cancer for men? For women?

5. What social and psychological problems does aphasia create for the stroke victim?

6. Identify and describe the major mental disorders experienced by older people. How do suicide rates vary by sex and race among the elderly?

7. Distinguish between *primary* and *secondary* mental disorders. What are the diagnostic problems in determining prevalence rate of psychopathology among the elderly?

8. What is Alzheimer's disease? Describe its symptoms. What is known about the causes and cures for Alzheimer's?

9. What does the concept of *compression of morbidity* describe? Is there evidence for this phenomenon? If so, what is it?

10. Explain the medical model as it is applied to the elderly. What are its primary limitations?

11. How does the attribution (or misattribution) of illness to the normal aging process pose serious health and social problems for older individuals?

REFERENCES

American Heart Association. (1990). *Heart facts— 1990.* Dallas, TX: National Office.

American Psychiatric Association. (1987). *Diagnostic and statistical manual of mental disorders* (3rd ed., rev.). Washington, DC: Author.

American Psychiatric Association. (1994). *Diagnostic and statistical manual of mental disorders* (4th ed.). Washington, DC: Author.

Besdine, R. (1988). Dementia and delirium. In J. W. Rowe & J. W. Besdine (Eds.), *Geriatric medicine.* Boston: Little, Brown.

Blazer, D. G. (1993). *Depression in late life* (2nd ed.). St. Louis, MO: Mosby.

Brocklehurst, J. C., & Hanley, T. (1981). *Geriatric medicine for students.* Edinburgh: Churchill Livingstone.

Burns, B. J., Larson, D. B., Goldstrom, I. D., Johnson, W. E., et al. (1988). Mental disorders among nursing home patients: Preliminary findings from the National Nursing Home Survey. *International Journal of Geriatric Psychiatry, 3,* 27–35.

Burns, B. J., & Taube, C. A. (1990). Mental health services in general medical care and nursing homes. In B. S. Fogel, A. Furino, & G. Gottlieb (Eds.), *Protecting minds at risk* (pp. 63–84). Washington, DC: American Psychiatric Association.

Cohen, G. D. (1990). Psychopathology and mental health in the mature and elderly adults. In J. E. Birren & K. W. Schaie (Eds.), *Handbook of the psychology of aging* (3rd ed., pp. 359–371). San Diego: Academic Press.

Colenda, C. C., & van Dooren, H. (1993). Oportunities for improving community mental health services for elderly persons. *Hospital and Community Psychiatry, 44,* 531–533.

Conwell, Y. (1994). Suicide in the elderly. In L. S. Schneider, C. F. Reynolds, B. D. Lebowitz, & A. J. Friedhoff (Eds.), *Diagnosis and treatment of depression in late life: Results of the NIH Consensus Development Conference* (pp. 397–418). Washington, DC: American Psychiatric Association.

Crimmins, E., Reynolds, S., & Saito, Y. (1999). Trends in health and ability to work among the older working-age population. *Journal of Gerontology: Social Sciences 54B* (1): S31–40.

Cummings, N. A. (1993). Chemical dependency among older adults. In F. Lieberman & M. F. Collen (Eds.), *Aging in good health: A quality lifestyle for the later years* (pp. 107–113). New York: Plenum.

Doll, R., & Peto, R. (1976). Mortality in relation to smoking: Twenty years' observation on male British doctors. *British Medical Journal, 2,* 1525–1536.

Exton-Smith, A. N., & Overstall, P. W. (1979). *Geriatrics.* Baltimore: University Park Press.

Feinson, M. C. (1990). Underutilization of community mental health services by elders: Examining policy barriers. *Medicine and Law, 9,* 1044–1051.

Ferraro, K. F. (1985). The effect of widowhood on the health status of older persons. *International Journal of Aging and Human Development, 21,* 9–25.

Freedman, V., & Martin L. (1998). Understanding trends in functional limitations among older Americans. *American Journal of Public Health 88* (10): 1457–1462.

Freedman, J., Sears, D., & Carlsmith, J. (1978). *Social psychology* (3rd ed.). Englewood Cliffs, NJ: Prentice-Hall.

Freidson, E. (1988). *Profession of medicine.* Chicago: University of Chicago Press.

Friedhoff, A. J. (1994). Consensus Development Conference statement: Diagnosis and treatment of depression in late life. In L. S. Schneider, C. F. Reynolds, B. D. Lebowitz, & A. J. Friedhoff (Eds.), *Diagnosis and treatment of depression in late life: Results of the NIH Consensus Development Conference* (pp. 491–512). Washington, DC: American Psychiatric Association.

Fries, J. F. (1980). Aging, natural death and the compression of morbidity. *New England Journal of Medicine, 303,* 130–135.

Fries, J. F. (1987). An introduction to the compression of morbidity. *Gerontologica Perspecta, 1,* 5–7.

Furner, S. E. (1992). Health status. In R. A. Cohen, J. F. Van Nostrand, & S. E. Furner (Eds.), *Chartbook on health data on older Americans: United States, 1992.* Washington, DC: National Center on Health Statistics.

Gallo, J. J., Anthony, J. C., & Muthen, B. O. (1994). Age differences in the symptoms of depression: A latent trait analysis. *Journal of Gerontology: Psychological Sciences, 49,* P251–P264.

Gatz, M. (1995). Introduction. In M. Gatz (Ed.), *Emerging issues in mental health and aging* (pp. xv–xx). Washington, DC: American Psychological Association.

Gatz, M., & Finkel, S. I. (1995). Education and training of mental health service providers. In M. Gatz (Ed.), *Emerging issues in mental health and aging* (pp. 282–302). Washington, DC: American Psychological Association.

Gatz, M., Kasl-Godley, J. E., & Karel, M. J. (1996). Aging and mental disorders. In J. E. Birren & K. W. Schaie (Eds.), *Handbook of the psychology of aging* (4th ed., pp. 365–382). San Diego: Academic.

Gatz, M., & Smyer, M. (1992). The mental health system and older adults in the 1990s. *American Psychologist, 47,* 741–751.

George, L. K., Blazer, D. G., Winfield-Laird, I., Leaf, P. J., & Fishbach, R. L. (1988). Psychiatric disorders and mental health service use in later life: Evidence from the Epidemiologic Catchment Area Program. In J. Brody & G. Maddox (Eds.), *Epidemiology and aging* (pp. 189–219). New York: Springer.

Gibson, R., & Jackson, J. (1987). The health, physical functioning, and informal supports of the black elderly. *Milbank Memorial Fund Quarterly, 65* (Suppl.), 421–454.

Gurland, B. J., & Cross, P. S. (1982). Epidemiology of psychopathology in old age: Some implications for clinical services. *Psychiatric Clinics of North America, 5,* 11–26.

Harris, M. J., & Jeste, D. V. (1988). Late-onset schizophrenia: An overview. *Schizophrenia Bulletin, 14,* 39–55.

Heller, K. (1993). Prevention activities for older adults: Social structures and personal competencies that maintain useful social roles. *Journal of Counseling and Development, 72,* 124–130.

Heyman, A., Fillenbaum, G., Prosnitz, B., Raiford, K., et al. (1991). Estimated prevalence of dementia among elderly Black and White community residents. *Archives of Neurology, 48,* 594–598.

Horne, A., & Blazer, D. G. (1992). The prevention of major depression in the elderly. *Clinical Geriatric Medicine, 8,* 159–172.

House, J. S., Kessler, R. C., Herzog, A. R., et al. (1990). Age, socioeconomic status and health. *The Milbank Quarterly, 68* (3), 383–311.

Jahoda, M. (1958). *Current concepts of positive mental health.* New York: Basic Books.

Janis, I., & Rodin, J. (1979). Attribution, control and decision making: Social psychology and health care. In C. G. Stone et al. (Eds.), *Health psychology—A handbook.* San Francisco: Jossey-Bass.

Jeste, D. V., Naimark, D., Halpain, M. C., & Lindamer, L. (1995). Strengths and limitations of research on late-life psychoses. In M. Gatz (Ed.), *Emerging issues in mental health and aging* (pp. 72–96). Washington, DC: American Psychological Association.

Jones, E., & Nisbett, R. (1971). *The actor and the observer: Divergent perceptions of the causes of behavior.* Morristown, NJ: General Learning Press.

Kahn, R., Zarit, S., Hilbert, N., & Niederehe, G. (1975). Memory complaint and impairment in the aged. *Archives of General Psychiatry, 32,* 1569–1573.

Kane, R. A., & Kane, R. L. (1981). *Assessing the elderly: A practical guide to measurement.* Lexington, MA: D. C. Heath.

Katz, I. R. (1995). Infrastructure requirements for research in late-life mental disorders. In M. Gatz (Ed.), *Emerging issues in mental health and aging* (pp. 256–281). Washington, DC: American Psychological Association.

Katz, I. R., Streim, J., & Parmelee, P. A. (1994). Prevention of depression, recurrences, and complications in later life. *Preventive Medicine, 23,* 743–750.

Katz, S., Ford, A., Moskowitz, R., Jackson, B., & Jaffee, M. (1963). Studies of illness in the aged. The index of ADL: A standardized measure of biological and psychosocial function. *Journal of the American Medical Association, 185,* 914–919.

Koenig, H. G., Cohen, H. J., Blazer, D. G., Krishnan, K. R. R., & Silbert, T. E. (1993). Profile of depressive symptoms in younger and older medical inpatients with major depression. *Journal of the American Geriatrics Society, 41,* 1169–1176.

Koenig, H. G., & Frances, A. (1995). Psychiatric diagnosis and DSM-IV. In G. L. Maddox (Ed.), *The encyclopedia of aging* (2nd ed., pp. 772–774). New York: Springer.

Koenig, H. G., Meador, K. G., Cohen, H. J., & Blazer, D. G. (1988). Depression in elderly hospitalized patients with medical illness. *Archives of Internal Medicine, 148,* 1929–1936.

Kovar, M. G. (1977). Health of the elderly and use of health services. *Public Health Reports, 92,* 9–19.

LaRue, A., Bank, L., Jarvik, L., & Hetland, M. (1979). Health in old age: How do physicians' ratings and self-ratings compare? *Journal of Gerontology, 8,* 108–115.

Lawton, M., & Nahemow, L. (1973). Ecology and the aging process. In C. Eisdorfer & M. P. Lawton (Eds.), *Psychology of adult development and aging.* Washington, DC: American Psychological Association.

Maddox, G., & Douglas E. (1973). Self-assessment of health, a longitudinal study of elderly subjects. *Journal of Health and Social Behavior, 14,* 87–92.

Manton, K. (1989). Epidemiological, demographic, and social correlates of disability among the elderly. *The Milbank Quarterly, 67,* 13–57.

Manton, K., Corder, L., & Stallard E. (1997). Chronic disability trends in elderly United States Populations: 1982–1994. *Proceedings of the National Academy of Sciences 94* (6): 2593–2598.

McCombs, H. G. (1993). Access of minority elderly to mental health services. *Mental health and aging* (Forum before the U.S. Senate Special Committee on Aging, No. 103-10, pp. 67–73). Washington, DC: U.S. Government Printing Office.

Mechanic, D. (1978). *Medical sociology* (2nd ed.). New York: Free Press.

Morley, J., & Reese, S. (1989). Clinical implications of the aging heart. *American Journal of Medicine, 86,* 77–86.

Nathanson, C. (1975). Illness and the feminine role: A theoretical review. *Social Science and Medicine, 9,* 57–62.

Olshansky, S. J., Rudberg, M. A., Carnes, B. A., Cassel, C. K., & Brody, J. A. (1991). Trading off longer life for worsening health: The expansion of morbidity hypothesis. *Journal of Aging and Health, 3* (2), 194–216.

Park, D., Cavanaugh, J., Smith, A., & Smyer, M. (1993). *Vitality for life: Psychological research for productive aging.* Washington, DC: Public Policy Office, American Psychological Association.

Parmelee, P. A., Katz, I. R., & Lawton, M. P. (1989). Depression among institutionalized aging: Assessment in prevalence estimation. *Journals of Gerontology: Medical Sciences, 44,* M22–M29.

Qualls, S. H., & Smyer, M. A. (1995). Mental health. In G. L. Maddox (Ed.), *The encyclopedia of aging* (2nd ed., pp. 629–631). New York: Springer.

Rabins, P. V. (1991). The impact of care delivery settings and patient selection in shaping research questions and results: Psychosocial and management aspects of delirium. *International Psychogeriatrics, 3,* 319–324.

Regier, D. A., Boyd, J. H., Burke, J. D., Rae, D. S., Myers, J. K., Kramer, M., Robins, L. N., George, L. K., Karno, M., & Locke, B. Z. (1988). One month prevalence of mental disorders in the United States. *Archives of General Psychiatry, 45,* 977–986.

Reynolds, C. F., Schneider, L. S., Lebowitz, B. D., & Kupfer, D. J. (1994). Treatment of depression in the elderly: Guidelines for primary care. In L. S. Schneider, C. F. Reynolds, B. D. Lebowitz, & A. J. Friedhoff (Eds.), *Diagnosis and treatment of depression in late life: Results of the NIH Consensus Development Conference* (pp. 463–490). Washington, DC: American Psychiatric Association.

Rovner, B., German, P., Broadbent, J., Morriss, R. K., et al. (1990). The prevalence and management of dementia and other psychiatric disorders in nursing homes. *International Psychogeriatrics, 2,* 13–24.

Sartorius, N., & Ustun, B. (1994). Functional psychiatric disorders in ICD-10. In E. Chiu & D. Ames (Eds.), *Functional psychiatric disorders of the elderly* (pp. 3–15). Cambridge: Cambridge University Press.

Schlesinger, M. (1987). Paying the price: Medical care, minorities, and the newly competitive health care system. *Milbank Memorial Fund Quarterly, 65* (Suppl.), 270–296.

Schneider, L. S. (1995). Efficacy of clinical treatment for mental disorders among older persons. In M. Gatz (Ed.), *Emerging issues in mental health and aging* (pp. 19–71). Washington, DC: American Psychological Association.

Smith, M. (1993). Access to mental health services in rural settings. *Mental health and aging* (Forum before the U.S. Senate Special Committee on Aging, No. 103–10, pp. 78–82). Washington, DC: U.S. Government Printing Office.

Stone, K. (1989). Mania in the elderly. *British Journal of Psychiatry, 155,* 220–224.

Terry, R. D., Katzman, R., & Beck, K. L. (Eds.) (1994). *Alzheimer's disease.* New York: Raven.

Tockman, M., & Ball, W., Jr. (1990). Lung cancer. In W. Hazzard, R. Andres, E. Bierman, & J. Blass (Eds.), *Principles of geriatric medicine and gerontology.* New York: McGraw-Hill.

U.S. Bureau of the Census. (1994). *Statistical abstract of the United States, 1994* (114th ed.). Washington, DC: U.S. Government Printing Office.

U.S. Bureau of the Census. (1995). *Statistical abstract of the United States: 1995* (115th ed.). Washington, DC: U.S. Government Printing Office.

U.S. Department of Health and Human Services. (1992). *Healthy people 2000: Summary report of national health promotion and disease prevention objectives.* Boston: Jones & Bartlett.

Verbrugge, L., & Madans, J. (1985). Social roles and health trends of American women. *Milbank Memorial Fund Quarterly, 63* (4), 691–735.

Waters, E. (1995). Let's not wait till it's broke: Interventions to maintain and enhance mental health in later life. In M. Gatz (Ed.), *Emerging issues in mental health and aging* (pp. 183–209). Washington, DC: American Psychological Association.

Wolinsky, F. D. (1988). *The sociology of health.* Belmont, CA: Wadsworth.

Zisook, S., Schucter, S. R., & Schledge, P. (1994). Diagnostic and treatment considerations in depression associated with late life bereavement. In L. S. Schneider, C. F. Reynolds, B. D. Lebowitz, & A. J. Friedhoff (Eds.), *Diagnosis and treatment of depression in late life: Results of the NIH Consensus Development Conference* (pp. 419–436). Washington, DC: American Psychiatric Association.

Zola, I. K. (1962). *Sociocultural factors in the seeking of medical care.* Unpublished Ph.D. dissertation, Harvard University.

Zola, I. K. (1966). Culture and symptoms: An analysis of patients presenting complaints. *American Sociological Review, 31*, 615–630.

Zopf, P. E. (1986). *America's older population.* Houston, TX: Cap and Gown Press.

CHAPTER SEVEN

PSYCHOLOGICAL ASPECTS OF AGING

The physical and mental changes that accompany aging have already been discussed in some detail. This chapter discusses the study of aging with respect to mental vitality—the psychology of aging. The psychology of aging concerns psychological development and change throughout the adult years. It is a broad field that includes, among other substantive areas, personality, sensory processes and psychomotor responses, and cognitive processes. Members of Division 20 of the American Psychological Association <http://www.iog.wayne.edu/apadiv20/apadiv20.htm> are dedicated to studying the psychology of adult development and aging.

In some contexts, it is difficult to distinguish between *biological* and *psychological aspects of aging.* Biological changes do affect an individual's psychological state of being, and psychological and psychosocial changes may affect biological functioning. More than 60 years ago, the philosopher-educator John Dewey (1939) addressed the problems of aging and made this very point:

> Biological processes are at the root of the problem and of the methods of solving them, but the biological processes take place in economic, political, and cultural contexts. They are inextricably interwoven with these contexts so that one reacts upon the other in all sorts of intricate ways. We need to know the ways in which social contexts react back into biological processes as well as to know the ways in which the biological processes condition social life.

The interplay between biology and psychology continues to be acknowledged today. For example, Schroots (1996) identifies three general approaches to studying psychological aspects of aging:

1. The psychology of *the aged* studies a particular phenomenon of interest among older adults (e.g., life satisfaction, hearing loss, creativity).
2. The psychology of *age* studies differences in behavior between people of different ages, using cross-sectional research (e.g., compares young and old adults on anxiety, visual abilities, intelligence).
3. The psychology of *aging* integrates the psychology of the aged and the psychology of age in longitudinal research to study patterns of behavior change that occur with age.

These three approaches yield different types of information about psychological aspects of aging, with the latter approach being the most encompassing. In the following sections, we use theory and research from these approaches to examine what is currently known about personality, cognitive processes (i.e., intelligence, wisdom, and creativity; learning and memory), and age-related changes in sensory processes and psychomotor responses. Finally, we conclude with several models of successful aging.

PERSONALITY

Personality has been defined in a variety of ways. One recent definition is that *personality* refers to the "psychological organization of the individual as a whole and especially to those features that distinguish the individual from others" (Mc-Crae 1995, p. 735). This definition of personality includes an internal component (i.e., characteristics or qualities) and an external component (i.e., behavior).

Just as there are many definitions of personality, there is no shortage of personality theories, nor of methodologies and research tools designed to measure personality. Kogan (1990) and Ruth (1996) discuss three major traditions in personality theory and research:

1. The *trait tradition* focuses on the adjectives that people use to describe themselves and others. The emphasis is on the description of internal characteristics/qualities rather than on observable behavior. Data are collected using tests and self-report measures.
2. The *developmental tradition* focuses either on qualitatively different stages or phases that occur during development, or on continuous development around certain themes throughout life. The emphasis is on changes in both internal characteristics/qualities and in behavior. Data are collected using self-report measures or observations of behavior.
3. The *experiential-contextual tradition* focuses on how people's lives evolve, and the meaning that they place on the things that happen to them. The emphasis is on the mutual importance of individual, social, and historical forces that shape personality development. Data derive from self-reports of past, current, and anticipated situations.

Implicit in these traditions are differences in responses to two important questions about personality: Is personality stable over the course of the life span? and How much of personality is influenced by internal versus external factors? Differences in responses to these questions are important to keep in mind while reviewing the contributions of each tradition to our understanding of personality in later life.

Personality Research: The Trait Tradition

The trait tradition in personality theory and research assumes that there are relatively enduring aspects of people's personalities (i.e., traits or characteristics) that influence how they behave across a variety of situations. Various models of personality development within this tradition hypothesize that different units are the "building blocks" of personality (e.g., traits, motives, control beliefs), but each model maintains that personality is the result of these internal building blocks.

Probably the most widely cited personality theory and research that derives from the trait tradition is the *five-factor model of personality* (Costa & McCrae 1994, 1998; McCrae & Costa 1990). This theory has been explored in a number of empirical investigations, including the Baltimore Longitudinal Study of Aging, which began in 1958 with a sample of well-educated, community-dwelling men between the ages of 18 to 69 years (women were added to the sample in 1978). Additional waves of participants continue to be recruited for the study, the purpose of which is to examine biomedical and psychosocial aspects of aging.

Based on data from the Baltimore Longitudinal Study of Aging, Costa and McCrae conceptualize personality in terms of five factors, each of which includes six facets and subsumes a number of personality traits that were generated by earlier research. The five factors that comprise the model are:

1. *Neuroticsm:* Includes traits that suggest maladjustment, such as anxiety, hostility, self-consciousness, depression, impulsiveness, and vulnerability
2. *Extraversion:* Includes traits that reflect both interpersonal qualities (e.g., warmth, gregariousness, and assertiveness) and temperament (e.g., activity, excitement seeking, and positive emotions)
3. *Openness:* Includes traits that reflect openness in a number of domains, such as fantasy, aesthetics, action, ideas, values, and experiences)
4. *Agreeableness:* Includes traits such as tender-mindedness and compliance
5. *Conscientiousness:* Includes traits such as orderliness, self-discipline, and need for achievement

This five-factor model has been used to study personality traits in a number of cross-sectional, longitudinal, and cohort-sequential studies. Many of these studies have been concerned with the stability of personality traits over time, and the results have been quite consistent. Cross-sectional studies show that older adults report slightly lower levels of neuroticism, extraversion, and openness than do younger adults, and slightly higher levels of agreeableness and conscientiousness. Of course, in these cross-sectional studies it is not possible to determine whether these results reflect age differences (i.e., due to cohort effects) or are due to actual age changes.

Results from a number of longitudinal and cohort-sequential studies, which do reveal age changes, suggest that there is little if any change in neuroticism, extraversion, and openness over more than a decade in later life (Costa & McCrae 1994, 1998; McCrae & Costa 1990). Taken together, then, there is ample evidence—at least with respect to neuroticism, extraversion, and openness—that personality traits remain relatively stable in later life.

Another area of personality theory and research that derives from the trait tradition concerns beliefs about control. Originally formulated by Rotter (1966), *locus of control* refers to the extent to which a person believes that he or she can influence the outcomes in his or her life. Rotter originally conceptualized locus of control as being either internal (i.e., belief that outcomes are within one's control) or external (i.e., beliefs that outcomes are outside of one's control).

Rhee and Gatz (1993) compared the general control beliefs of 60 college students and 97 adults between the ages of 65 and 85. They found that older adults reported higher levels of internal control than did college students. In addition, college students viewed older adults as having more external control beliefs than older adults reported for themselves, and older adults viewed college students as having more internal control beliefs than college students reported for themselves.

Gatz and Karel (1993) studied perceptions of control among four generations of 560 family members who were participating in an ongoing longitudinal investigation of family relationships. Cross-sectional, longitudinal, and sequential analytic strategies were employed to analyze the data. Over the 20-year period from 1971 to 1991, participants' control beliefs became more internal. Developmental changes toward greater internality were indicated for young adults as they progressed into middle age. Cross-sectional differences in middle-aged and older adults did not reveal developmental differences. The oldest generation of women was consistently the most external subgroup.

More recent conceptualizations have expanded on the dichotomy between internal and external control. For example, Levenson (1981) conceptualizes control as comprising three separate components: internal, powerful others, and chance. In another elaboration, Brandstaedter (1989) has demonstrated that beliefs of control are domain specific. That is, he showed that individuals can have one set of control beliefs for the domain of health and physical well-being, and different control beliefs about domains such as assertiveness, intellectual competence, and self-development. However, Brandstaedter and Greve (1994) found high levels of generalized control beliefs over an eight-year period among middle-aged adults.

Thus, when personality is conceptualized in terms of beliefs about control, there is some evidence of change as one progresses from young to older adulthood. Once individuals reach middle age, however, it is not clear whether control beliefs change substantially. Additional analyses regarding domain-specific control beliefs over the life course will provide valuable information on this issue. Some researchers question whether perceptions of control truly are traits, and maintain that it makes more sense to conceptualize control beliefs as a developmental process, rather than a relatively stable dimension of personality. Presumably, additional research will assist in resolving this debate.

Despite a long-standing tradition of theory and research based on the trait/characteristic approach to personality, the approach is not without critics (Ruth 1996). The major criticism of this approach concerns ecological validity (i.e., the extent to which the results of the research apply in the "real world"). For example, this approach focuses on the internal component of personality and overlooks the external, or behavioral, component of personality. Relatedly, it is not clear whether self-reports of traits have any relationship with actual, everyday behavior.

Personality Research: The Developmental Tradition

The developmental tradition of personality theory and research is rooted in Sigmund Freud's notion that development in the early years significantly influences one's later life. Although Freud did not believe that development occurred beyond infancy and childhood, several theorists in the developmental tradition have used Freud's stages of childhood development as a point of departure for their own work.

The developmental tradition of personality theory and research focuses either on qualitatively different stages or phases that occur during development, or on continuous development around certain themes throughout life. Some of these models hypothesize that stages or phases progress in a fixed order, with each resulting in qualitatively different behavior. Other models are linked more closely to chronological age and to socially expected transitions.

Personality as General Development.   Carl Jung initially studied with Freud, but then left the psychoanalytic tradition to pursue his interest in development beyond childhood and adolescence. Jung began his discussion of the stages of life with youth—a period extending from after puberty to about age 35. In general, this period involves giving up childhood and widening the scope of one's life. The next stage begins at about age 35 and continues to old age.

Jung (1971) identified two shifts in personality as an individual matures from youth into old age. First, Jung believed that each person has both feminine and masculine aspects of personality. He said that in youth and early adulthood, individuals express the socially stereotypic aspect of their personality. That is, women do not express their more masculine qualities and men do not express their more feminine qualities. In middle and later age, however, individuals begin to express the features of their personalities that they had earlier "held in check." Second, Jung believed that each person maintains a balance between an interest in the external world (i.e., extraversion) and an interest in his or her own inner world and subjective experiences (i.e., introversion). According to Jung, young adults are more extraverted in their orientation, and during middle age, there is a shift toward introversion, or greater self-reflection. Both of these shifts are reflected in Jung's statement: "We cannot live the afternoon of life according to the programme of life's morning; for what was great in the morning will be little at evening and what in the morning was true will at evening have become a lie" (Jung 1971).

Results from the Kansas City Studies of Adult Life are relevant here. These studies took place over a 10-year period and were among the first longitudinal studies of personality in adulthood. Carried out on a large sample of adults ages 40 to 80, measures included projective tests, self-administered questionnaires, and interviews. Based on this research, Neugarten (1973, 1977) concludes that, in most respects, personality is relatively stable across the years.

Coping styles, methods of attaining life satisfaction, and goal directedness were among the most stable characteristics. However, Neugarten and colleagues did document some age-related changes that are not inconsistent with Jung's notions. The relevant age-related changes found in the Kansas City studies included feelings about the extent to which the social environment could be controlled. For example, 40-year-olds expressed considerable active control over the environment and a greater willingness to take risks; 60-year-olds were more likely to perceive the environment as threatening and thus avoided risk taking. Neugarten described this personality change as moving from active to passive mastery. Gutmann (1977) notes a similar pattern among Navajo Indians, isolated groups in Israel, and the Mayans of Mexico. Such passive mastery seems to reflect a greater orientation toward introspection and self-reflection, sometimes referred to as ***interiority***.

Although Jung did not provide empirical data to support his claims, the research of Neugarten (1973, 1977), Gutmann (1977), and several others lend some support to the claim that there are several predictable shifts that occur in people's general orientations as they progress from adulthood into later adulthood.

Personality Development as Eras and Transitions.   A second area of personality research that derives from the developmental tradition is Levinson and colleagues' model of personality (Levinson et al. 1978). These researchers propose that the life cycle evolves through a sequence of eras, each lasting approximately 20 to 25 years. In the broadest sense, each *era* is a "time of life" with its own distinctive qualities. Personal crises and developmental tasks characterize the transition from one era to the next. Unlike some other developmental models, Levinson and colleagues believe that relationships and personal commitments through which tasks of one period are accomplished may not serve the needs of the individual beyond that period. Levinson and colleagues based their model on secondary analyses of published biographies and on interviews with middle-aged men. According to this model, a primary developmental task of late adulthood (which begins at about age 60) is to find a new balance between involvement with society and with the self. This new balance is necessary because individuals begin to see a physical decline in self and age-mates and because they are now viewed as "old" in the eyes of society.

In addition, employing the same extensive biographical interviewing techniques they used to study men, Levinson and colleagues turned their attention to 39 women who occupied a range of occupations, including homemakers, businesswomen, and women from academia (Brown 1987). One substantial difference between men and women, and between groups of women, concerns the life plans envisioned by women between the ages of 22 and 28. Typically, young men organize a "tentative life structure" around occupation. Young women have more difficulty forming their plans for the life course. According to Levinson, "Everything in society supports men having an occupational dream, but for a woman, there is still a quality of going into forbidden territory" (Brown 1987, p. 23). For many women, the themes of career and family are viewed as two mutually exclusive choices. These differences are understood, in part, as consequences of the greater complexity of women's dreams and the problems encountered in living them out. As Levinson points out, there is no preponderance of cultural wisdom to aid women with these choices. In many respects, these women can be thought of as pioneers. Clearly, given the extent to which the sociocultural level of the life structure influences these eras and transitions, additional research will be required to understand this process for the generations of women (and men) who follow these pioneers.

Personality Development as Epigenetic Stages.   One of the most popular models in the developmental tradition is Erik Erikson's model of psychosocial development (Erikson 1950, 1982). Erikson outlines eight ages of humanity that stretch from birth to death, with each representing a choice or a crisis. The model hypothesizes that biological, psychological, and sociocultural processes are the basis for development. The model is intrinsically *psychosocial,* in that these crises occur within the context of relationships with other people. The model is also *epigenetic,* in that each psychosocial crisis has a period when it is especially important, which determines the order in which the crises are faced. If decisions are made well during one age, then successful adaptation can be made in the subsequent age. Whereas Freud believed a person became fixated at a particular stage, Erikson sees each stage as reworking elements of the prior stage. Thus, people could act as their own therapists and rework difficult areas of their personalities (Kermis 1986). Erikson believes that age leads to further differentiation of the personality, and each new accomplishment is integrated into experiences and may be drawn upon in later years.

Erikson's first five ages rely heavily on the work of Freud and deal largely with childhood development, whereas the last three ages focus on adult development. The eight ages are:

1. In early infancy, the development of a sense of basic trust versus a sense of mistrust
2. In later infancy, when some anal muscular maturation has occurred, a growing sense of autonomy versus a sense of shame and doubt
3. In early childhood, a developing sense of initiative versus a sense of guilt
4. In the middle years of childhood, a sense of industry versus a sense of inferiority
5. In adolescence, a sense of ego identity (involving certainty about self, career, sex role, and values) versus role confusion
6. In early adulthood, the development of intimacy (including more than simply sexual intimacy) versus a sense of ego isolation
7. In middle adulthood, the development of generativity (the desire to become a caring and productive member of society) versus ego stagnation
8. In late adulthood, a sense of ego integrity (including a basic acceptance of one's life as having been appropriate and meaningful) versus a sense of despair

In an effort to document age changes in generativity, McAdams, de St. Aubin, and Logan (1993) examined age differences in **generativity,** or the goal of providing for the next generation, among young, midlife, and older adults. Data were collected on four dimensions of generativity:

1. Generative concern described the extent to which an individual expresses concern about the future generation.
2. Generative commitments described the specific actions an individual would like to take to help nurture the next generation.
3. A listing of specific actions that an individual has already carried out would describe generative actions.
4. The degree to which past memories reflect the theme of generativity is described in the concept of generative narration.

According to Erikson, generativity should peak in middle-age and progressively decline throughout old age. Results were partially supportive of Erikson's theory. Younger adults (22 to 27 years) showed the lowest levels of generativity. Middle-aged adults (37 to 42 years) scored higher than younger adults but not higher than older adults. Thus, generativity would seem to be more characteristic of middle-age and older adulthood than younger adulthood. Interestingly, McAdams, de St. Aubin, and Logan (1993) report that, within each age group, study participants showed a strong positive relationship between generativity and life satisfaction and happiness.

The sense of ego integration generated in late adulthood is very much a function of what took place in the previous ages. Erikson contends that good adjustment in this age comes only when important matters have been placed in proper perspective and when the successes and failures of life have been seen as inevitable. According to Erikson (1963), "Only in him who in some way has taken care of things and people and has adapted himself to the triumphs and disappointments adherent to being, the originator of others or the generator of products and ideas—only in him may gradually ripen the fruit of these seven stages." A deficit in this accumulated ego integration is often characterized by a failure to accept one's life and ultimately by fear of death.

A careful reading of the conceptual schemas of development and aging offered by Erikson and Levinson reveals considerable agreement between the two, despite the fact that the labels for stages and transitions are different. Both seem to characterize adulthood as reflecting the change from career considerations to generativity, with older adulthood marked by a shift toward the search for meaning and final integration.

Personality Development as Gerotranscendence.   Gerotranscendence is one of several emerging humanistic models of personality development that extend the work of earlier theorists and researchers in the developmental tradition. Tornstam (1989) posits that anyone who lives into old age will experience a shift toward gerotranscendence. *Gerotranscendence* refers to a shift in overall perspective from a rational and materialistic vision of the world to a more transcendent one. Tornstam (1994) believes that this shift is accompanied by an increase in life satisfaction and hypothesizes three levels of change:

1. *Cosmic level:* Includes changes in the perception of time, space, and objects; increasing affinity with other generations; changes in the perception of life; loss of the fear of death; acceptance of the mystery of life; and increase in communion with the spirit of the universe
2. *Self-level:* Includes discovery of hidden positive and negative aspects of the self; decrease in self-centeredness; transcendence from egoism to altruism; rediscovery of the child within; and ego integrity
3. *Social and individual relations level:* Includes less interest in superficial relations; increasing need for solitude; more understanding of the distinction between self and role; decreasing interest in material things; and increasing self-reflection

Although Peck (1968) did not set out to test the notion of gerotranscendence, he did find some support for the concept. Based on his efforts to refine Erikson's work, Peck identified three issues as being central to old age:

1. The individual must establish a wide range of activities so that adjustment to loss of accustomed roles such as those of worker or parent is minimized (ego differentiation versus work-role preoccupation).
2. Because nearly all elderly individuals suffer physical decline and/or illness, activities in the later years should allow them to transcend their physical limitations (body transcendence versus body preoccupation).
3. Although death is inevitable, individuals may, in various ways, make contributions that extend beyond their own lifetimes; this may provide meaning for life and overcome despair that one's life was meaningless or should have been other than it was (ego transcendence versus ego preoccupation).

More recently, Tornstam (1997) conducted qualitative interviews with 50 Swedish men and women between the ages of 52 and 97 in order to examine developmental changes in worldview and self-attitudes. Retrospective changes were reported by some (but not all) of the respondents, reflecting an awareness of a more cosmic dimension of reality as well as attitudes reflecting a less narcissistic view of the self.

Although models in the developmental tradition typically are more difficult to test empirically than are models in the trait/characteristic tradition, there is some evidence to suggest that, when personality is conceptualized in terms of development, people do demonstrate changes in adulthood.

Although most of the empirical work on personality research has derived from the developmental tradition, the tradition has been criticized along several dimensions. One major criticism is that these models are difficult to verify. Reported data are typically rich in anecdotal material, but cannot be quantified. Thus, although the models are interesting, it is difficult to assess the extent to which they accurately describe personality development. A second criticism specific to the stage theories is that they have a tendency to focus too extensively on developmental crises. Third, personality theorists and researchers are increasingly aware of the importance of cohort and period effects on development. For example, most of the individuals originally studied by Levinson and colleagues were born around the time of the Great Depression, and thus were in formative adolescence during World War II. What were the pressures faced by members of those birth cohorts in light of the historical period in which they grew up? And, will what was true for these individuals when they reached age 40 be true for today's college students when they reach age 40?

Personality Research: The Experiential-Contextual Tradition

Within the experiential-contextual tradition, there are two approaches: the constructionist approach and the life-story approach (Ruth 1996). Both approaches emphasize the mutual importance of individual, social, and historical forces in shaping personality development. The *constructionist approach* acknowledges that people's identities both create and are created by one another and society, whereas the *life-story approach* seeks to learn how people integrate past, current, and anticipated experiences into a cohesive life story. As such, the emphasis is on how people actively create and modify their personalities. The importance of context underlies both approaches, and represents an advantage over the trait and developmental traditions. Although the experiential-contextual tradition has not generated a lot of data on the development of personality, the data that are available are quite interesting.

Personality as Types.   Data from the Kansas City Study of Adult Life (Neugarten 1973, 1977) were examined to identify personality types in adulthood. Based on measures including projective tests, self-administered questionnaires, and interviews, Neugarten and colleagues identified four personality types:

1. *Integrated:* Self-actualized older adults who have complex lives, have competent egos, and report high levels of life satisfaction
2. *Armoured-defensive:* Individuals who are thought to be fighting an internal battle against aging and death, and who are not particularly insightful; people who are in a "holding pattern" and do not demonstrate good adjustment
3. *Passive-dependent:* Individuals who are content to let others take care of them; includes people who are isolated and withdrawn, and who report moderate to high levels of life satisfaction
4. *Unintegrated:* People who have diagnosable cognitive or emotional disorders and who are not very well adjusted and report low levels of life satisfaction

Obviously, these personality patterns likely did not emerge for the first time in old age. For most participants, they were carryovers of adjustment and coping styles from the younger years. Some achieved successful aging through activity; others achieved it through disengagement. In general, those whose personal adjustment was high were effective in overcoming frustrations; they were able to resolve conflicts and remain socially active and accepted. The poorly adjusted, however, were unhappy, fearful of contact with others, withdrawn, and incompetent.

Personality as Life Stories.   Within the experiential-contextual tradition of personality development, several researchers (e.g., McAdams 1993, 1994, 1996; Whitbourne 1987) rely on the life-story approach to examine development over time. Whitbourne (1987) argues that people build their own conceptions of how their lives should proceed, and this is part of a life-span construct, a person's unified sense of the past, the present, and the future. There are two important components of this construct. The *scenario* consists of the expectations an individual has for the future. It is the game plan of how a person expects and wants his or her life to be in the future. The *life story* is a personal narrative history that organizes past events into a coherent sequence, giving them meaning and continuity. One characteristic of life stories is that they are frequently rewritten over the course of a lifetime.

McAdams (1993, 1994) maintains that each life story has seven features:

1. *Narrative tone:* The emotional feel of the story
2. *Imagery:* Characteristic pictures, symbols, and metaphors in the story
3. *Themes:* Repeated attempts to meet certain goals throughout the course of the story
4. *Ideological setting:* The beliefs and values held by the individual constructing the story
5. *Nuclear episodes:* Key defining events, both positive and negative, that occur in the story
6. *Characters:* Idealized versions of the self (e.g., "the perfect spouse") that are important to the story
7. *Ending:* The legacy that the individual hopes to leave at the end of the story

The life story, what a person tells others when he or she is asked about the past, can become too rehearsed and stylized. Distortions occur with time and retelling (Neisser & Winograd 1988). Theorists and researchers who conceptualize personality in terms of life stories believe that life-story distortions are actually ways of coping that allow a person to feel that he or she was "on time" rather than "off time" in past events. Such distortions may allow people to feel better about their plans and goals, and make them less likely to feel a sense of failure.

An example of the rich detail that the life-story approach offers can be found in McAdams and colleagues (1997). These researchers examined two groups of people with similar demographic characteristics, but who differed in terms of how generative they were: 40 were highly generative adults and 30 were less generative adults. The purpose of the research was to determine the extent to which the two groups constructed different identities, or life stories. Results indicated that the highly generative adults were more likely to reconstruct the past and anticipate the future as variations on a prototypical commitment story. The themes of this prototype were that protagonist enjoys an early family blessing or advantage, is sensitized to others' suffering at an early age, is guided by a clear and compelling personal ideology that remains stable over time, transforms or redeems bad scenes into good outcomes, and sets goals for the future to benefit society. McAdams and colleagues conclude that such commitment stories sustain and reinforce the adult's efforts to be generative.

Clearly the life-story approach is premised on the notion that personality development is an ongoing process—one in which the individual is actively engaged as he or she constructs an identity on the basis of his or her perceptions of interactions with the environment. Longitudinal research will contribute to a better understanding of the extent to which life stories change over time, and document the extent to which life stories demonstrate commonalities as a function of the aging experience.

Personality as Self-Concept.   One way to think about personality is in terms of a person's self-concept. *Self-concept* consists of the attitudes that a person has about himself or herself as an object. Self-concept consists of three components (Giarrusso & Bengtson 1996):

1. *Cognitive:* How a person describes himself or herself and the roles that he or she plays
2. *Evaluative:* The extent to which a person likes (or does not like) his or her identity
3. *Conative:* A person's motivations to reduce discrepancies between his or her real self and the self that he or she would like to be

One popular way to conceptualize self-concept is in terms of ***possible selves*** (Markus & Nurius 1986). Possible selves represent individuals' ideas of what they might become, and can include both hoped-for selves (i.e., what they would like to become) and feared selves (i.e., what they are afraid of becoming). Markus and Nurius hypothesize that possible selves function as incentives for future behavior and provide an evaluative and interpretive context for the current view of self; as such, possible selves can motivate an individual to change certain characteristics and aspects of his or her behavior.

Cross and Markus (1991) examined hoped-for (e.g., powerful, glamorous) and feared (e.g., out-of-shape, unwanted) possible selves among 173 adults between the ages of 18 and 86. Results indicated that participants who reported low levels of life satisfaction generated different possible selves than did participants who reported high levels of life satisfaction. In addition, the most frequently reported hoped-for and feared selves differed between participants of different ages. For example, traditional college-aged students and middle-aged adults reported more hoped-for selves that dealt with family issues than did respondents between the ages of 25 and 39. Based on these results, Cross and Markus conceptualize possible selves as psychological resources that are instrumental in motivating and defending the self throughout the course of adult development.

Hooker and Kaus (1994) used possible selves to determine when health-related goals become dominant in adulthood. They predicted that by middle age, most adults would have health-related possible selves, and that health-related possible selves would be associated with greater use of health behaviors. Comparisons of the possible selves of young (ages 24 to 39 years) and middle-aged (ages 40 to 59 years) adults indicated that health-related possible selves did become predominant in midlife. In addition, both young and middle-aged adults reported more feared than hoped-for selves in the realm of health. Supporting the notion that possible selves can serve as motivators of behavior, participants did engage in health behaviors in an effort to avoid feared health-relevant selves.

The experiential-contextual tradition of personality research and theory is relatively new, and attempts to include individual, social, and historical influences are quite complicated. Nonetheless, initial theory and research in this tradition is very exciting, and the results of longitudinal work is eagerly awaited. The strength of the experiential-contextual tradition is also its major limitation. That is, any approach that attempts to incorporate individual, social, and historical forces in an effort to understand human behavior is undertaking a tremendous challenge. Further, because research in this tradition is relatively new, additional data must be collected before definitive judgments about the merit of this approach can be made.

In summary, the trait, developmental, and experiential-contextual traditions of research and theory have all made contributions to the understanding of personality development in later life. The trait/characteristic tradition assumes that personality is relatively stable over time, and does not conceptualize the self as being particularly active in shaping personality. Research in this tradition is especially rich in data and lends support to the argument that personality is relatively stable over time, although the degree of stability that is demonstrated depends on what trait characteristic is measured (i.e., traits, motives, control beliefs), the age ranges that are studied (i.e., there appears to be greater stability in later adulthood than in earlier adulthood), and the length of the time interval that is examined (i.e., there is greater stability at shorter intervals than at longer intervals).

The developmental tradition assumes that there is continued personality development in adulthood, and certain models within this tradition believe that some developmental stages are linked to chronological age. Given that many of the developmental stage theories, such as those proposed by Jung and Erikson, were formulated in the early to middle part of the twentieth century, it is surprising that more empirical tests of these models are not available. Although this tradition is more rich in theory than in empirical data, the data that are available do support the existence of developmental shifts in personality across the life span.

Finally, the experiential-contextual tradition conceptualizes personality as an ongoing process of development that results from individuals' interactions with their environments. Further, it is assumed that development can be understood only in the context of sociocultural and historical parameters. As such, the potential for continued growth and development in later life is greatest in this tradition. Despite the difficulty associated with research in this tradition, it represents an exciting new way to better understand personality development in later life.

COGNITIVE PROCESSES

Cognitive processes have been defined as the activity that occurs between the time a person experiences something in the environment and the time that he or she responds to that experience. In this section, theory and research based on different approaches to the study of cognitive process are used to examine what is known about intelligence, wisdom, and creativity, as well as learning and memory.

Intelligence, Wisdom, and Creativity

Intelligence.   Although not all people enter old age with equal levels of intelligence, there is no question that all people hope to retain their intellectual abilities for as long as possible. So what, exactly, is intelligence? Over the years, psychologists have defined *intellectual abilities* in a number of different ways, many of which are still acknowledged today. For example, more than 50 years ago, Thurstone (1938) identified 10 primary intellectual abilities, some of which continue to be examined among older adults today (e.g., verbal meaning, spatial orientation, inductive reasoning, number frequency, and word frequency; Schaie 1995a).

Individuals may, in various ways, make contributions that extend beyond their own lifetimes.

More than 30 years ago, Guilford (1967) conceptualized the structure of intelligence as involving the components of operation, products, and content. Among the most useful of the early conceptualizations of intelligence is Catell's (1963) distinction between two categories of intelligence—fluid mechanics and crystallized pragmatics—which has been elaborated on by Horn and Hofer (1992).

Fluid mechanics refers to a person's ability to solve novel problems, whereas *crystallized pragmatics* refers to the knowledge that a person acquires as a result of his or her socialization into, and experiences as part of, a given culture. Using a computer analogy, Baltes and Graf (1996) equate fluid mechanics with computer hardware and crystallized pragmatics with computer software. Fluid mechanics is thought to be influenced by sensory process, such as how quickly and accurately information is entered into the system and processed, and is determined by biological-genetic factors, including health. In contrast, crystallized pragmatics includes a variety of skills, ranging from reading and writing to professional and life skills, and is thought to be determined by environmental-cultural factors, including learning (Baltes & Graf 1996).

Given everyone's interest in maintaining intellectual functioning in later life, it is not surprising that many researchers have examined what happens to intellectual abilities as people age. Much of the early research on intelligence focused on Thurstone's primary mental abilities. Decades of research on these intellectual abilities indicate that the "typical" trajectory consists of stability in intellectual functioning until the age of 60 or so, with increasing, but not dramatic, declines in each successive decade until the 80s, and more substantial declines thereafter. However, this typical trajectory hides the fact that although changes do occur with age, the changes occur at different rates for different abilities, and that the rates of change differ from cohort to cohort.

Much of what is known about intelligence in later life comes from Schaie's Seattle Longitudinal Study of Aging (Schaie 1995b). The Seattle Longitudinal Study began in 1956 as a cross-sectional study with four cohorts of adults between the ages of 22 and 67. Participants completed extensive tests of intellectual functioning. In 1963, Schaie reassessed the original participants and added new groups of participants between the ages of 20 and 70, resulting in the sequential design. Schaie continues to reassess current participants and add new cohorts of participants to the study, resulting in the longest-running studies of intellectual functioning in adulthood.

Schaie (1995a) cautions that studies that conclude that older adults demonstrate poorer intellectual functioning than younger adults might not be due to intellectual decline at all. First, it is possible that, either through personal choice or environmental constraints, older adults might not use certain intellectual skills, and the resulting decline in functioning is due to a lack of use rather than to age. Second, it is possible that older adults' performance on intellectual assessments may be disadvantaged by sociocultural and technological change.

Lending support to these hypotheses, Schaie (1995a) reports that both cross-sectional and longitudinal research demonstrate that older adults' intellectual performance can be modified through cognitive training. Specifically, using a longitudinal design, Willis and Schaie (1994) found that decrements in intellectual performance can be reversed in 40 percent of older adults who completed cognitive training, and that performance improved in an additional 25 percent of older participants. Further, the effects of this training were maintained over a period of seven years.

The reality is that intellectual decline in primary mental abilities is not inevitable (Schaie 1995a). Based on data from the Seattle Longitudinal Study, Schaie (1983, 1984) found that approximately 67 percent of older adults did not demonstrate intellectual decline between the ages of 60 and 67, approximately 60 percent did not decline between the ages of 67 and 74, and among 81-year-olds, approximately 50 percent maintained their intellectual functioning over a seven-year period.

Given the tremendous individual differences in intellectual decline in later life, it is important to identify the factors that explain why some people are able to maintain their primary intellectual abilities, whereas others experience decrements as they age. Based on a review of the literature, Schaie (1995a) identifies six factors that are associated with the maintenance of intellectual functioning in later life:

1. Genetic factors
2. Being free from cardiovascular disease
3. Having less than average decline in perceptual speed
4. Being of average or higher socioeconomic status
5. Having a stimulating and engaging life-style
6. Having flexible attitudes and behaviors in middle age

Taken together, these factors suggest that life-style choices made earlier in life can affect the stability of primary intellectual abilities in later life.

Additional useful information on the relationship between intelligence and age derives from research on fluid mechanics and crystallized pragmatics, or the two-component model of intellectual development. Figure 7.1 depicts the major assumptions underlying fluid mechanics and crystallized pragmatics, and the relationship between the two types of intellectual abilities and age, as hypothesized by Baltes and Graf (1996). As can be seen in the figure, Baltes and Graff hypothesize that there is a decrease in fluid mechanics as people age, whereas they hypothesize that crystallized pragmatics remain constant throughout adulthood. Applying the computer analogy, Baltes and Graf believe that the hardware of intelligence (i.e., fluid mechanics) shows signs of wear, whereas the software of intelligence (i.e., crystallized pragmatics) retains its functionality. Data from a number of studies confirm Baltes and Graf's hypotheses (Hertzog & Schaie 1988; Horn & Hofer 1992; Salthouse 1991). Nonetheless, these authors conclude that the major risk for intellectual decline occurs after the age of 80.

Just as computer hardware and software work together to determine performance, fluid mechanics and crystallized pragmatics also work together to determine intellectual functioning. A number of researchers have demonstrated that crystallized pragmatics can compensate for some of the decrements in fluid mechanics that accompany age (Baltes & Baltes 1990; Backman & Dixon 1992).

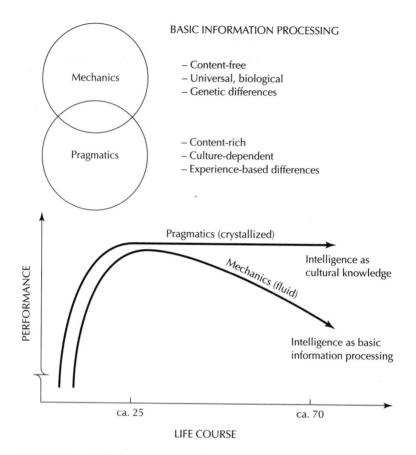

FIGURE 7.1   Life-Span Research on Two Categories of Human Intelligence: Fluid Mechanics versus Crystallized Pragmatics (top section defines the categories; bottom section illustrates the postulated life-span trajectories)

Source: From P. B. Baltes and P. Graf, "Psychological Aspects of Aging: Facts and Frontiers," in D. Magnusson (Ed.), *The Lifespan Development of Individuals: Behavioral, Neurobiological, and Psychosocial Perspectives* (p. 442) (New York: Cambridge University Press, 1996). Reprinted with the permission of Cambridge University Press. Based on Baltes 1993 and on Horn and Hofer 1992.

Therefore, it is possible for some older adults to maintain their current levels of intellectual performance despite some decrements in fluid mechanics.

Wisdom and Creativity.   Baltes and Staudinger (1995) describe wisdom as "one of the highest forms of knowledge and skill" (p. 971). They report that wisdom has been conceptualized in a variety of ways, including as a personality characteristic, as an advanced stage of intellectual development, and as the ability to solve difficult life problems (i.e., as a life skill). Consistent with this latter conceptualization, **wisdom** has been defined as "an expert knowledge system in the fundamental pragmatics of life permitting exceptional insight, judgment, and advice involving complex and uncertain matters of the human condition" (Baltes & Smith 1990, p. 95).

When wisdom is conceptualized as a life skill, an individual must meet the following five criteria in order to be considered wise (Baltes & Staudinger 1995):

1. Have a good understanding of the practical aspects of day-to-day life (i.e., factual knowledge)
2. Have a good understanding of how to tackle problems (i.e., procedural knowledge)
3. Understand that life problems differ depending on an individual's stage in the life course
4. Appreciate that an individual's particular and historical context must be considered when deciding on a course of action
5. Have an awareness of and be able to deal with uncertainty

Wisdom is assessed by having individuals respond to various dilemmas. An example of such a dilemma presented by Baltes and Staudinger (1990) is: "Sometimes when people think about their lives, they realize that they have not achieved what they had once planned to achieve. What should one/they do and consider in such a situation?" (p. 973) Individuals' responses to such dilemmas are evaluated using the five criteria just mentioned. Comparison of the responses of older and younger adults indicate that, much like their performance on tests of crystallized pragmatics, the two groups demonstrate similar levels of ability. And, when older adults' wisdom is evaluated in particular contexts with which they have experience, older adults exhibit more wisdom than do younger adults (Baltes & Smith 1990; Baltes & Staudinger 1993).

Just as older adults demonstrate comparable, and sometimes greater, levels of wisdom than do younger adults, older adults also "hold their own" with respect to creativity (Simonton 1995, 1996). When creativity over the life span is viewed in terms of the creation of products such as art, literature, music, and inventions, research indicates that creativity increases with age and, after a certain point, begins to decline. But this does not mean that there is no potential for creativity in later life. In fact, based on research on creativity, Simonton (1995) reports seven important findings:

1. Individual differences in creativity are huge (i.e., some people are simply more creative than others).
2. Typically, creative individuals in their 70s will be more productive than they were in their 20s, although their level of creativity will be below their peak levels of creativity.
3. The trajectory of creativity for a given person depends on the type of creative activity in which he or she engages.

4. Creativity is more a function of career age (i.e., experience with a particular creative activity) than of chronological age.
5. When decreases in creativity occur, it is usually due to factors other than age.
6. The quality of creativity is relatively stable across the life span.
7. Although older adults might produce a lower number of creative products, the works that are produced tend to be more ambitious than earlier works.

In summary, older adults do not inevitably experience declines in intellectual functioning. Although declines in fluid mechanics accompany advanced age, crystallized pragmatics remains stable into later life, and in some instances compensates for declines in fluid mechanics. Further, later life presents opportunities to develop wisdom and to produce creative works.

Learning and Memory

Learning.   You can't teach an old dog new tricks. This adage refers to the notion that older people are set in their ways and are unable and/or unwilling to learn new things. But is this really the case? Based on a comprehensive review of the literature, Poon (1995) identified four general findings about older adults' ability to learn new information, remember, solve problems, and make decisions:

1. Cross-sectional studies that compare older to younger cohorts of adults as well as longitudinal studies that compare the performance of the same cohort over time demonstrate that older adults take longer and have greater difficulty in learning new information than do young people.
2. Some of the difficulty that older adults have in learning new information is due to factors other than age.
3. Older adults' ability to learn new information can be enhanced by providing them with instructions and strategies, and through practice.
4. Older adults perform quite well on tasks that require expertise; however, they are disadvantaged, relative to young adults, on tasks that require new skills.

A major question surrounds the cause of decreased learning abilities in later life. Whereas early researchers were quick to attribute decrements to chronological age, researchers now know that learning (and memory) are influenced by a number of factors—including environmental, biomedical, cognitive, and psychological factors, among others—in addition to age (Poon 1995). In fact, consistent with the contextual approach, Poon, Krauss, and Bowles (1984) found that when variables such as task characteristics, gender, health, education, and intellectual functioning are taken into account, chronological age does not significantly influence learning and memory.

Memory.   Probably one of the most pervasive stereotypes about, and biggest fears of, older adults is that memory loss is inevitable in later life. Although there are age-related declines in some aspects of memory, not all older adults are forgetful or have serious memory problems. As is the case with intelligence, both internal processes and environmental adjustments can compensate for normal, age-related memory loss when it does occur.

Memory is frequently conceptualized as consisting of two major subsystems: semantic (or general) memory and episodic memory (Kausler 1995). The two subsystems differ in terms of the type of information for which they are responsible. *Semantic* (or general) *memory* consists of the processes whereby people access words, concepts, and facts, independent of the context in which they were learned. In contrast, *episodic memory* consists of the processes whereby people encode, store, and retrieve information about events that happen to them personally.

Semantic (or General) Memory.   Research indicates that once an individual has learned specific words, concepts, and facts, there are no major changes in the internal structure of this information, nor in the individual's ability to access this information (Kausler 1995). Once it is part of semantic memory, information can be recalled in one of two ways: automatically or purposefully. Regardless of which method is used to recall information, research indicates that there is no major change in semantic memory across the life span.

Episodic Memory.   Episodic memory consists of two components: working memory and long-term store. *Working memory* consists of a limited capacity processing center and a short-term, temporary storage center. As such, working memory is analogous to a desktop, a workbench, or the RAM in a computer (Salthouse 1995c). That is, working memory can process and store only a certain amount of information; a commonly used example of the type of information that is processed and stored in working memory is an unfamiliar telephone number (Kausler 1995). Information that is temporarily stored in working memory can be used directly or it can be sent to the second component of episodic memory, the long-term store.

The *long-term store* of episodic memory holds memories until they are retrieved into the working memory. The long-term store holds two types of memories: long-term explicit memories and long-term implicit memories (Kausler 1995). *Long-term explicit memory* concerns memories that must be explicitly, or purposefully, recalled from the long-term store (Graf & Schachter 1985). Examples of long-term explicit memories include being able to remember the name of a person you met several months ago when you unexpectedly see him or her at the mall and to remember the items that you went to the store for in the first place. In contrast, *long-term implicit memory* concerns memories that do not require conscious recollection to be recalled from the long-term store.

Memory Performance.   The laboratory research on working memory, long-term explicit memory, and long-term implicit memory in later life is relatively optimistic. Kausler (1995) reports that there is relatively little decline in the storage capacity of working memory over the life span, citing research that indicates there is a 10 percent or less decline in the amount of information that can be kept in working memory. Similarly, there are few deficits in long-term implicit memory among older adults. Deficits are greatest for long-term explicit memory.

Research shows that it takes older adults longer than young adults to learn the information used in tests of long-term explicit memory. Also, although some researchers report comparable long-term explicit memory for younger and older adults, other researchers report deficits in older adults' abilities. Kausler (1995) and Salthouse (1995c) hypothesize that these deficits in long-term explicit memory among older adults are due to a general cognitive resource deficit that affects both the storage and processing (or encoding and retrieval) of the information.

When it comes to memory performance, one important issue is whether age-related declines in memory are due to irreversible brain mechanisms or to older adults' less efficient learning and the strategies they use to remember information. Verhaeghen, Marcoen, and Goossens (1992) reviewed the data from over 30 studies that included more than 1,500 participants. These studies documented that older adults can be taught strategies that result in improved memory. Examples of successful strategies include instructions on effective strategies, feedback, and practice.

Sugar (1996) identifies four specific types of memory strategies:

1. *Formal mnemonics:* Developing complex systems for organizing and remembering information (e.g., acronyms and linking items through a story)
2. *Image-based memory strategies:* Creating bizarre or interacting internal visual images of the information to be remembered
3. *General internal memory strategies:* Creating internal mental associations between something familiar and the information to be remembered (e.g., rehearsal, categorization, elaboration)
4. *External memory strategies:* Relying on external, physical aids or cues (e.g., lists, calendars, diaries, times)

In an evaluation of the efficacy of the four strategies, Sugar (1996) concludes that the latter two strategies are best. The reason is that formal mnemonics and image-based strategies are quite complicated and do not tend to be used spontaneously by older adults. In contrast, older adults tend to use general internal memory strategies spontaneously and report that these are the strategies that are most preferred. Finally, although external memory strategies are quite effective and used frequently, many older adults think that relying on external memory strategies is "cheating."

A second important issue in memory performance is the practical significance of decrements in the day-to-day functioning of older adults. Evidence from the area of problem solving sheds light on this issue.

Problem Solving.   *Problem solving* is "the process by which an individual attempts to discover how to achieve a goal" (Denney 1995, p. 759). According to Denney, the three steps involved in problem solving are as follows:

1. Analyze the current situation.
2. Determine what new condition or goal is desired.
3. Generate and evaluate alternative strategies for achieving the desired condition or goal state.

Denney reports that when older adults and younger adults are presented with novel, abstract problems to solve, older adults are less efficient at problem solving than are younger adults. In contrast, when adults of various ages are presented with practical, everyday types of problems to solve rather than novel, abstract problems (i.e., with more ecologically valid tasks), the differences between younger and older adults are not as extreme (Blanchard-Fields 1996; Parks 1995; Willis 1995). In fact, research indicates that middle-aged adults generate more effective solutions to everyday problems than do either younger or older adults (Blanchard-Fields & Chen 1996; Denney 1995). This is attributed to the fact that middle-aged adults have a greater accumulation of life experiences (i.e., practice) and coping skills to draw on than do younger adults. This is yet another example of how experience can compensate for the effects of aging. It is only much later in life, when neurological and/or motor performance deficits arise, that practical problem-solving abilities begin to decline (Denney 1995; Welford 1995).

In summary, cognitive processes and the determinants of cognitive performance are quite complex, and there is evidence that declines in one aspect of the process can be compensated for by other aspects of the process (Hoyer 1995a). Perhaps nothing illustrates this complexity better than the concept of metamemory. **Metamemory** refers to "one's perceptions, knowledge, and beliefs about the functioning and development" of the content of memory (i.e., what is remembered) and the mechanics of memory (i.e., how that information is stored and retrieved) (Perlmutter 1995, p. 636). Thus, metamemory includes people's perceptions about memory in general, and about their own memory in particular (Sugar 1996). Perlmutter maintains that each individual has a sense of how his or her memory works and his or her idiosyncratic needs and abilities. Individuals then use this information to organize, navigate, and monitor their memory processes to tackle a particular memory challenge. Such a comprehensive conceptualization—which includes task characteristics, the availability and usefulness of memory strategies, the relevance of information that is stored within the memory, and the experiences and characteristics of the individual—highlights the reality that cognitive functioning is highly variable, especially in later life.

AGE-RELATED CHANGES IN SENSORY PROCESSES AND PSYCHOMOTOR RESPONSES

Regardless of their age, people actively respond to their environment. Oftentimes, overt behavior is the result of a series of processes, beginning with perception of some aspect of the environment and ending with the movement of muscles and joints (i.e., psychomotor responses). This entire process, from perception to psychomotor response, and everything in between, falls within the domain of the psychology of aging. This section examines aging-related changes in the inputs and the outputs of this process—the major sensory processes (i.e., vision, hearing, taste, smell, touch) and psychomotor responses, including reaction time and the speed-accuracy trade-off.

Sensory Processes

The senses of vision, hearing, taste, smell, and touch provide links with the outside world. However, as aging occurs, neurosensory changes can influence an individual's functioning, activities, response to stimuli, and perception of the world. Similarly, the world's perception of an individual may be influenced by age-related neurosensory changes that he or she has undergone. Witness, for example, the older person with impaired hearing or vision who may be labeled as stubborn, eccentric, or senile.

In traditional preindustrial societies, old people have often been found to be held in high esteem. In many cases, however, this lasted only as long as they were able to retain their faculties and a semblance of their previous strength. Old people who lost their sight, their hearing, or their speed of hand or foot—who became less able to pull their own weight and contribute to the group—were more likely to be neglected, abandoned, or even killed outright. Barash (1983) points out that although such treatment seems harsh, even vicious, it reflects the hard realities of primitive life, not the hardness of the hearts of primitive people.

Anthropologist John Moffat once found an old Hottentot woman left by herself in the South African desert. She spoke as follows: "Yes, my children, three sons and two daughters, are gone to yonder blue mountain and have left me to die. I am very old you see, and am not able to serve them. When they kill game, I am too feeble to help in carrying home the flesh. I am not able to gather wood and make a fire and I cannot carry their children on my back as I used to" (Barash 1983, p. 178). Why was this old woman abandoned by her children? It was, as Barash indicates, for the same reason a resident of the United States might discard any possession that was worn out and no longer worked. Many will recognize this attitude in themselves when it comes to old things. But what about attitudes toward old people who do not work quite as well as they once did?

Vision.   Two categories of changes can occur to the structure and function of the eye in later life: inevitable, age-related changes that happen to everyone as they age; and changes that are due to conditions or diseases that affect only some people (Hoyer 1995b; Roberts 1995).

With respect to inevitable, age-related changes, four changes in the anatomy of the eye are experienced by older people (Spear 1993):

1. The lens becomes less malleable, resulting in decreased accommodative ability.
2. The lens becomes less transparent, making it difficult to discern "cool" colors.
3. The cornea flattens, resulting in less refractory power.
4. The photoreceptors in the retina become less efficient.

These changes have several practical consequences. First, from childhood into early adulthood, the lens of the eye naturally changes shape so that individuals can see things at both close and far distances. With age, the lens becomes less able to change its shape, and people lose the ability to focus on close objects. This is known as **presbyopia.** Presbyopia is not a disease but a normal, age-related change that occurs in the aging eye. As a result of presbyopia, almost all adults at around age 45 require glasses or bifocals to be able to read comfortably (Kane, Ouslander, & Abrass 1999). The glasses mechanically compensate for the loss of accommodation and allow individuals to focus on objects both near and far.

Changes in the lens of the eye also lead to farsightedness (Abrams, Beers, & Berkow 1995). Thus, there is a marked tendency for older persons to hold things at a distance in order to see them. A newspaper or letter from a loved one may be held at arm's length because the print cannot be discriminated at closer range. Reading glasses allow a person to discern objects that are in the field of near vision.

As the lens becomes less transparent, there is a yellowing effect. This change is significant in that it becomes more difficult for the person to discern certain color intensities, especially the cool colors (blue, green, and violet), which are filtered out. Warm colors (yellow, red, and orange) are generally seen more easily; thus, it is advisable to mark objects such as steps and handrails with these colors, which tend to stand out.

There are several additional practical consequences of normal, age-related changes (Abrams, Beers, & Berkow 1995). One such consequence is decreased perception related to glare because the light that passes through the lens is scattered. This can particularly be a problem when driving at night. In addition, older eyes secrete fewer tears than do young eyes, which can result in irritation and discomfort. This is especially the case in postmenopausal women. Certain types of eye drops can temporarily lessen these conditions.

Some older adults experience visual disabilities in addition to the normal, age-related changes in vision. The four most common visual disabilities that are associated with aging are cataracts, glaucoma, age-related macular degeneration, and diabetic retinopathy.

Cataracts.   Cataracts are the most common disability of the aged eye. Although fewer than 15 percent of older adults between the ages of 65 and 74 have cataracts, the percentage increases to approximately 40 percent of adults who are age 85 and older (Havlik 1986). A **cataract** is an opacity of the lens, and frequently a yellowing of the lens, that decreases visual acuity to 20/30 or less (Abrams, Beers, & Berkow 1995). The opaqueness of the lens interferes with the passage of light to the retina. Depending on the degree of cataract development, an individual will suffer dimmed and blurred or misty vision. A person may need brighter light to read and may need to hold objects extremely close in order to see them. As the cataract advances, useful sight is lost. Surgical removal of the opaque lens provides safe and effective treatment for cataracts. Eyeglasses, contact lenses, or intraocular lens implants are used to compensate for the loss of the lens. The latter consists of a plastic lens permanently implanted in the eye. It has become the most common means of compensating for the loss of the natural lens.

Glaucoma.   Glaucoma is the second most common cause of blindness in the United States. **Glaucoma** is a generic term for a build up of pressure in the eye that is severe enough to damage the optic nerve (Abrams, Beers, & Berkow 1995). The disease generally develops somewhere between the ages of 40 and 65. Glaucomas are divided into primary glaucomas and secondary glaucomas. Primary glaucomas account for approximately 90 percent of all glaucomas (Abrams, Beers, & Berkow 1995).

Angle-closure glaucoma is an acute form of primary glaucoma; it appears suddenly and runs a short course. This type of glaucoma, which accounts for approximately 10 percent of glaucomas in the United States, can be treated (Abrams, Beers, & Berkow 1995). Symptoms include nausea, vomiting, eye pain, redness of the eye, and clouded vision. Prompt medical attention is imperative if severe vision loss or blindness is to be prevented.

Open-angle glaucoma, which accounts for 80 percent of primary glaucomas in the United States, is the chronic form of glaucoma (Abrams, Beers, & Berkow 1995). It develops slowly and is often referred to as the "sneak thief of vision." A gradual loss of peripheral vision is one of the earliest indications of glaucoma. This loss of side vision may cause its victim to bump into things or to fail to see passing cars in the next highway lane. The initial symptoms are so subtle that much damage may be done before medical attention is sought. In time, so much of the normal range of vision becomes eliminated that the victim is said to suffer from "tunnel vision." Left untreated, this limited field of sight will also disappear, leaving the person totally blind.

Persons over 40 years of age should have periodic eye examinations that include glaucoma testing. The irreparable damage the disease causes makes its prompt diagnosis and management imperative. There is no cure for glaucoma, but there are treatments to reduce the intraocular pressure and to keep it at a safe level. Drugs and eye drops may be used to control the pressure within the eye. Surgery is also an option in the most severe cases.

Age-Related Macular Degeneration (AMD).   AMD is one of the most frequent causes of visual impairment and is the leading cause of legal blindness among older adults in the United States (Kane, Ouslander, & Abrams 1999). **Age-related macular degeneration** involves damage to the macula, the key focusing area of the retina, and results in decreased visual acuity (Abrams, Beers, & Berkow 1995). Peripheral vision is retained, but with this disease, there is typically a decline in central visual acuity, making tasks dependent on discrimination of detail difficult to impossible. Early treatment proves to be much more effective than late treatment for certain types of AMD; for others, there is no treatment. Tasks such as reading or watching television can be accomplished with the use of magnifiers, but driving can be quite problematic, even with adaptive technology. Age-related macular degeneration is not a particularly well understood disease. Research suggests that, over time, familial/genetic and environmental factors make this an age-related condition.

Diabetic Retinopathy.   The third leading cause of adult blindness (Abrams, Beers, & Berkow 1995), **diabetic retinopathy** is a complication of diabetes that affects the capillaries and arterioles of the retina. The prevalence of diabetic retinopathy is 7 percent in those who have had diabetes for less than 10 years, and is 63 percent in those who have had diabetes for over 15 years (Stefansson 1990). A ballooning of these tiny vessels can eventually give way to hemorrhaging, neovascular growth, scarring, and blindness. Vascular changes of diabetic retinopathy occur in and around the macula, leading to macula edema. The retina swells, absorbing the fluid from leaking vessels, and eventually loses its shape so that the image it receives is distorted.

The symptoms of diabetic retinopathy are subtle, and can include minimal loss of vision, spots, or cloudy vision. Because diabetic retinopathy can be slowed or prevented in the early stages, early diagnosis is critical. As such, diabetics should have an annual examination. Laser therapy, used to seal off hemorrhaging vessels, has proved beneficial in the treatment of this disability (Abrams, Beers, & Berkow 1995).

Despite the normal, age-related changes that happen to everyone as they age and the conditions or diseases that affect a subset of older adults, many persons maintain near-normal sight well into old age, especially when aided by glasses. However, data clearly indicate that the prevalence of visual impairments is associated with increased age and is more prevalent among men than among women. In fact, adults over age 75 have a prevalence rate of visual impairments that is more than twice the prevalence rates for adults between the ages of 45 and 64. For example, the specific prevalence of visual impairments (not including cataracts) among noninstitutionalized males between the ages of 45 and 64 is 60.3 per 1,000, compared to a prevalence rate of 135.6 per 1,000 for males who are age 75 and older. The comparable prevalence rates for women are 37.1 per 1,000 and 88.7 per 1,000 (U.S. Bureau of the Census 1998, Table 231).

Age-related visual impairment may produce alterations in behavior as well as in feelings of self-esteem. The older person who is impaired may suffer from serious communication problems. Vision represents one of the most important links with the outside world. During a lifetime, an individual becomes dependent on vision for receiving and processing information about the world and for functioning in his or her surroundings. Information about the local and world scene is offered to people through newspapers, magazines, books, and television. Carrying out activities of daily living involves the ability to master various chores that characteristically depend on visual acuity: sewing on a button, turning on the stove, stirring the sauce until it is bubbly, getting dressed in the morning, matching socks of the same color, and so on. A person may be hesitant to perform tasks, especially new ones, because of self-consciousness about the problematic situation.

Special efforts can and should be carried out to help make independent living possible among older adults who are visually impaired. For example, coding schemes can be employed in the home setting to help make independent living possible. Fluorescent tape around electric outlets, light switches, door handles, and keyholes can make things much easier for someone who suffers some visual impairment.

An older person who is sent home from a hospital or a neighborhood pharmacy with a vial of medicine may not be able to read the dosage instructions printed on the bottle. All too often, such a situation and its possible consequences are not comprehended. Large-print instructions can sometimes help solve the problem. Many elderly people take a number of different drugs, and impaired vision may make it difficult to differentiate one bottle of pills from another. Taping different-colored pieces of paper to the various medicine vials might help alleviate the problem. For persons not able to discriminate the colors, other coding methods can be employed. For instance, the medicine with the piece of sandpaper on the cap can be identified as the pain reliever, the one with the felt-cap top might be the antihypertensive medication, and so on.

A final point that is useful for family members, friends, and health care workers to remember is that people who have been blind since birth have had a lifetime to adjust to living in a world that assumes everyone can see. For those who suffer visual impairments after having depended on their sight for many years, the adjustments may be quite difficult.

Hearing.   A number of changes occur in the auditory system in later life (Kane, Ouslander, & Abrass 1999). Among these changes are atrophy and cell loss throughout the system, calcification of the membranes in the middle ear, and bioelectrical and biomechanical imbalances in the inner ear. The practical consequences of these changes include hearing loss for pure tones; difficulty understanding speech; problems in localizing sounds, hearing sounds with both ears, and hearing sounds from different sources; and language problems and problems with difficult speech.

The three major types of hearing loss are conductive hearing loss, sensorineural hearing loss, and mixed hearing loss involving both conductive and sensorineural losses.

Conductive Hearing Loss.   **Conductive hearing loss** results from changes in the outer and middle ear. Two specific types of hearing loss are an accumulation of cerumen and otosclerosis (Abrams, Beers, & Berkow 1995). A common cause of conductive hearing loss in older adults occurs when excessive ear wax, or *cerumen,* blocks the external ear canal. This condition is reversible. Older persons should be checked for a buildup of cerumen, which can be removed by irrigating the canal with a wax-dissolving solution. Hardening of the middle ear bone can also impede the transmission of sound waves. This condition, known as *otosclerosis,* actually begins during youth but may not become evident until later life. Although its cause is not fully understood, it can sometimes be corrected surgically and with a special hearing aid.

Sensorineural Hearing Loss.   **Sensorineural hearing loss** results from changes in the inner ear, where sound vibrations are transformed into electrical impulses by the cochlea. This type of hearing loss in older adults may be due to presbycusis, environmental/occupational noise, drug toxicity, or disease. **Presbycusis** is the most common cause of bilateral, sensorineural hearing deficit in older adults (Corso 1995). It may involve permanent loss of the ability to detect high-frequency tones and is due to senescent changes that occur within the structures of the ear. Presbycusis is not a disease; rather, it is a normal, age-related change that occurs in the aging auditory system (Corso 1995).

Presbycusis influences the ability to hear high-pitched tones, yet varies in its effects on other aspects of hearing. At first, the loss of the ability to perceive higher frequencies does not involve the perception of normal speech patterns, but as the condition progresses, the capacity to engage in conversation becomes af-fected. Because consonant sounds are typically in the higher frequencies and vowel sounds are in the lower frequencies, speech discrimination becomes poor. Speech can be heard but words cannot be detected. The victim may hear an unin-telligible collection of vowel sounds. As the condition advances, middle and lower tones may also be lost. There is variability in the progression of presbycusis and it can coexist with other factors that impede hearing acuity.

Noise-induced hearing loss, known as *acoustic trauma,* can be a common cause of irreversible hearing decline in older persons (Kane, Ouslander, & Abrass 1999). Exposure to excessive noise induces hair-cell loss and sensorineural hearing defi-cit. The fact that older men have tended to exhibit slightly more hearing loss than older women may be related to workplace noise. Perhaps, as noise exposure be-comes more uniform, fewer gender-based differences in hearing decline will be seen.

Medications toxic to the ear can compromise hearing; these are known as *ototoxic drugs* (Kane, Ouslander, & Abrass 1999). Because older adults often take several different drugs, their hearing should be monitored. Likewise, because the elderly may already have some degree of hearing loss, known ototoxic drugs should be used with caution. It is sometimes possible to reverse the toxic effects of certain medications if early intervention takes place.

Given the changes that occur in the auditory system with age, hearing loss is a significant problem in later life (Corso 1995). Hearing impairments are two to three times more prevalent in later life than are visual impairments, and are more prevalent among men than among women. For example, the specific prevalence of hearing impairments among males between the ages of 45 and 64 is 203.6 per 1,000, compared to a prevalence rate of 423.5 per 1,000 for males who are age 75 and older. The comparable prevalence rates for women are 89.7 per 1,000 and 307.3 per 1,000 (U.S. Bureau of the Census 1998, Table 231).

Despite the prevalence of hearing loss in later life, and the difficulties it can present, many older adults attempt to hide such loss (Abrams, Beers, & Berkow 1995). This is especially unfortunate, in that hearing impairment can lead to social isolation, fear, frustration, embarrassment, low self-esteem, and anxiety.

An elderly individual with a permanent hearing loss should be evaluated for amplification via a hearing aid and should have the benefit of aural rehabilitation. Hearing aids are not a perfect substitute for normal hearing, however. They cannot restore the full frequency range of more severe losses. Sounds are made louder, but not necessarily clearer. Hearing aids also pose adjustment problems.

Many new users claim that the devices seem unnatural. For many people who have insidiously lost their hearing over a long period of time, the new sounds delivered by the hearing aid are surely "unnatural" to them. Hearing aids amplify all sounds, not just those of speech. Thus, the new hearing aid user may have a difficult time separating restaurant noises, car horns, or television sounds from conversational sounds. Hearing aid users and their families need to be counseled appropriately.

There are various helpful principles and common courtesies for communicating with people who have hearing impairments. In general, shouting should be avoided. It does nothing to aid in the delivery of lost frequencies and it results in a booming and distortion of intelligible sounds. One should speak in a normal tone of voice, a little louder, perhaps, but without shouting. Shouting often conveys a speaker's apparent annoyance and can lead to defensive or withdrawn behavior. A speaker should also talk slowly. A message is much easier to understand if it is delivered at a slower pace. Besides, talking rapidly can create an impression of being in a hurry. If a message is not understood the first time, finding other words to say the same thing may also be helpful. It not only gives the person who is hearing impaired an additional set of sounds from which to understand a message but it also gives more context from which meaning can be derived.

With or without a hearing aid, lip reading can help with communication. A complicating factor is that some persons do not form words normally when speaking to those who are hard of hearing. Exaggeration can serve to confuse the lip reader. The lip reader can be helped by facing him or her directly, by letting the light fall on the speaker's face, and by not exaggerating lip movements. For some with impaired vision, the lip-reading task may be more difficult.

Patient compliance can be greatly affected by hearing loss. Health workers may perceive a patient's limited reaction to the important information they are imparting as apparent disinterest. In the early stages of progressive hearing loss, an individual may appear preoccupied, inattentive, irritable, unsociable, and absentminded (Voeks et al. 1990). Also, health workers may not be aware of a patient's hearing loss, not having known the person before admission to the health care facility. In some cases, confusion associated with hearing loss may be falsely attributed to senility in the older patient.

When planning for discharge from an institution, hearing loss must be acknowledged so that instructions about the use of mechanical devices or drug therapy are understood. Failure to hear such instructions may mean delayed recovery and even tragedy in the home situation. Written instructions can be provided to the patient. The person may have also suffered visual losses, however, so the writing should be in large print. Also, a health worker or a family member might ask the patient to repeat instructions to make certain that the instructions were properly heard and understood.

Hearing aids are most useful when background noise is at a minimum, as in a quiet theater, a lecture hall, or a private conversation in person or over the telephone. In noisy gatherings, the wearer may be better assisted by switching off the aid.

Problems associated with a new hearing aid may be caused by improper fit. In order to serve the wearer, the ear mold must closely fit the anatomic structure of the individual's ear canal. Thus, prolonged complaints about a hearing aid should be investigated, for the difficulty may be due to more than just a long adjustment period—perhaps the ear mold does not fit.

Gates and colleagues (1990) indicate that the potential need for hearing aids exceeds their actual use. This situation may be related to a number of factors. An older person may perceive that a hearing loss is an irreparable and normal part of getting old. Some researchers suggest that physicians, too, regard hearing loss as normal aging and intervention as futile. The individual may not want to admit that a hearing loss exists. Likewise, a hearing aid may be rejected for cosmetic purposes and for the social stigma associated with it. Also, hearing aids are expensive. Neither routine hearing exams nor hearing aids are reimbursed under Medicare.

As losses advance, hearing aid amplification may become less useful. Cochlear implants are being tested and refined in order to bypass the cochlea and its faulty hair cells so that the auditory nerve can be directly stimulated. A *cochlear implant* is an electronic prosthetic device that utilizes electrodes that are microsurgically implanted into or near the cochlea to stimulate the nerve. They are intended for those with profound sensorineural hearing loss.

Taste, Smell, and Touch.   Three categories of changes can occur in taste and smell in later life (Schiffman 1995a, 1995b):

1. The inevitable, age-related changes that happen to everyone as they age generally result in decreased taste and olfactory acuity. These losses typically begin in the sixth decade of life and are caused by degeneration of nerve cells throughout these systems, although the losses are exacerbated among smokers (Abrams, Beers, & Berkow 1995).
2. Certain conditions or diseases affect only some people. Nervous, nutritional, endocrine, local, and other conditions/disorders can result in a loss of taste and olfactory acuity.
3. The use of certain medications—including local anesthetics, antimicrobial agents, and muscle relaxants—can result in decreased taste and olfactory acuity.

With respect to taste, there are small but clearly measurable increases in detection thresholds (concentration at which subjects can first detect a difference between a stimulus and water) as well as recognition thresholds (concentration at which subjects can first recognize a quality such as sweet). As such, older adults perceive tastes less intensely than do younger adults, and prefer stronger, more tart, and less sweet tastes than do younger adults. There is also a general decline in olfactory functioning with age. There are many smells that older adults perceive with less intensity than do younger adults, and older adults are also less proficient at identifying odors than are younger adults.

Although there is debate as to the exact anatomical and physiological cause of decreases in older adults' taste and olfactory acuity, the practical implications of these changes are straightforward. Because of declines in taste and olfactory acuity, older adults may not maintain interest in food, and their nutritional intake might suffer. It is also possible that they might overuse salt and sugar. Probably the most serious implication of declines in olfactory acuity is that older adults might not be able to detect dangers such as gas leaks or fires as readily as people with normal acuity (Abrams, Beers, & Berkow 1995).

Less is known about the sense of touch than any of the other senses. It is known, however, that receptors are lost as people age. As a result, the ability to make discriminations regarding touch, temperature, and pressure gradually declines with age, although the amount of decline is highly variable (Saxon & Etten 1994). Some evidence also shows that there is a decrease in the efficiency of the nerve cells in the skin as people age (Hayflick, 1994). One consequence of these changes is ***presbyalgos,*** which refers to age-related changes in sensitivity, perception, and affect regarding pain (Harkins & Scott 1996).

The practical consequences of changes in touch have to do primarily with safety (Saxon & Etten 1994). For example, mobility can become more difficult, and falls more likely, as a result of decreased receptors in the feet. Further, because of the reduced ability to perceive changes in temperature and pain, older adults are at increased risk for burns (Hayflick 1994; Saxon & Etten 1994).

Psychomotor Responses

Perception refers to the processes that enable people to acquire and interpret information from their environment (Salthouse 1995a). This text has already examined the "inputs" of this process—the major sensory processes. Psychomotor responses represent the "outputs" of the process.

If the concept of psychomotor response were represented diagrammatically, the diagram would show the organism taking in sensory input (or information), giving meaning to this new information through perceptual and integrative processes, determining whether this new information calls for any action, sending instructions to the appropriate activity center (e.g., a muscle), and activating the appropriate response. Psychomotor performance may be limited by a weakness at any point in this chain of events. It may be limited by changes in the sensory threshold, in the processes dealing with perception, in the translation from perception to action, in the strength of the sensory signal, and in muscular output. More optimistically, there is evidence that physical exercise and practice can result in increased motor performance for older adults (Welford 1995).

Psychomotor performance is typically measured in terms of reaction time. ***Reaction time*** is the interval between the presentation of a stimulus and the individual's motor response to that stimulus (Cerella 1995). Two specific types of reaction time have received a lot of research attention: simple reaction time and complex choice reaction time.

Simple reaction time tasks involve responding to one stimulus, such as pressing a button as fast as possible when a light comes on. Simple reaction time has two component parts: decision time (the time from the onset of the stimulus until the response is initiated) and motor time (the time needed to complete the physical part of the response). Welford (1995) reports that the most noticeable age difference is in the decision-time component. However, it is important to realize that responses to simple reaction time tasks do not increase more than 13 percent between the ages of 25 and 65 (Cerella 1995).

Choice reaction time tasks involve presenting people with more than one stimulus and requiring them to choose from among several responses, depending on what stimulus was presented. As such, choice reaction time tasks demand more mental processing than do simple reaction time tasks. Cerella (1995) concludes that responses to choice reaction time tasks increase gradually until age 60 or so, and then increase more quickly. Compared to younger adults, it takes older adults longer to respond, especially for nonverbal tasks and for tasks that are complex and/or difficult.

Given the complexity of the process that results in psychomotor responses, it is not surprising that variability in motor performance is greater among 70-year-olds than it is among 20-year-olds (Welford 1995). However, reaction time (i.e., speed of responding) is only one indicator of performance. A second indicator of performance is accuracy.

Although speed and accuracy are two common measures of performance, the two are not independent. The *speed-accuracy trade-off* refers to the fact that speed and accuracy are often compensatory responses, or are inversely related to one another (Salthouse 1995b; Welford 1995). That is, attempts to maximize speed often result in lower accuracy, and attempts to maximize accuracy often result in slower speed. For example, when reading this chapter for an exam, the reader can make a decision to read the material as quickly as possible (i.e., use speed as the measure of performance) or to read the material to learn it as thoroughly as possible (i.e, use accuracy as the measure of performance). Although speed might seem to be the better measure on a weekend evening, on the day of the test, accuracy will probably prove to be the better measure.

Research indicates that older adults tend to perform at higher levels of accuracy than do younger adults (Salthouse 1995b). Thus, although older adults generally respond more slowly than do younger adults, their responses tend to be more accurate. This is especially true after an older adult makes an error in performance (Welford 1995).

The impact of an age-related decline in psychomotor performance on social functioning should be obvious. In general, such decline—especially in combination with sensory and perceptual decline—reduces the aged individual's ability to exert control over his or her environment. Although Welford (1995) reports that changes in motor performance do not typically limit normal activities until a person is in his or her 60s at the earliest, after that time, tasks that were formerly nonproblematic, such as driving a car or using a sewing machine, may become hazardous with advancing age. Some work activities may also suffer, mainly in jobs relying on exceptionally speedy reactions or responses to incoming information. Activities directly related to health maintenance and care may also become more difficult to carry out.

Although the text has focused on sensory processes and psychomotor responses as the inputs and outputs of a very complex process, it is important to remember that the nervous system is responsible for everything that happens between the inputs and outputs. The nervous system plays a major role in controlling body functioning—especially in controlling smooth and skeletal muscle contractions—and in receiving, processing, and storing information. Nerve cells, or neurons, are lost during the process of aging, and the cells that comprise the nervous system cannot reproduce (Abrams, Beers, & Berkow 1995). The number of the basic functioning units begins to decline at around the age of 25. This decline brings a decreased capacity for sending nerve impulses to and from the brain, a decrease in conduction velocity, a slowing down of voluntary motor movements, and an increase in reflex time for skeletal muscles. In addition, the weight of the brain decreases by approximately 10 percent from early adulthood until the age of 90 (Abrams, Beers, & Berkow 1995).

At least three characteristics of the brain minimize the adverse effects of these changes in the nervous system (Abrams, Beers, & Berkow 1995):

1. The brain has more nerve cells than are needed.
2. If one area of the brain is damaged, in some instances other areas of the brain can compensate for the damage.
3. There is plasticity in nerve cells, such that surviving nerve cells can compensate for nerve cells that die.

In addition to these "internal" compensatory mechanisms, it is important to remember the adaptive aids and strategies that can compensate for some of the deficits in sensory processes, and that the functional significance of many of the decrements in motor responses is relatively negligible until quite late in life. Thus, for sensory processes, psychomotor functioning, and cognitive functioning, later life is not necessarily characterized by significant loss and decline.

SUCCESSFUL AGING

In U.S. society, some people typically think that *aging* and *productivity* are contradictory terms. In fact, many think of aging as being characterized by inevitable decline and the loss of the ability to be productive (Butler & Schechter 1995). This is not the case, however.

Within the category of "normal aging," Rowe and Kahn (1987, 1998) distinguish usual aging from successful aging. *Usual aging* refers to aging in which external factors heighten the effects of internal aging processes, resulting in normal decrements in functioning. *Successful aging* refers to aging in which external factors either have a neutral role or counteract the effects of internal aging processes, resulting in little or no decrements in functioning. A number of models of successful aging have been proposed during the past several decades. Different psychological aspects feature prominently in each of them. This section reviews three models of successful aging that Hansson and Carpenter (1994) identify as being particularly useful.

Pfeiffer's Model of Successful Aging

Pfeiffer (1977) conceptualizes successful aging in terms of how well older adults adapt to the challenges associated with aging. Although this conceptualization reinforces the idea that aging is inevitably associated with loss, Pfeiffer does believe that it is possible for older adults to adapt—that is, to continue to function physically, psychologically, and socially—in the face of losses. Pfeiffer identifies four tasks associated with successful aging:

1. Replace what has been lost (e.g., work roles can be replaced with volunteer roles; relationships with former colleagues and friends who relocate can be replaced with new relationships).
2. Retrain the capacities that have been lost following an illness or accident (e.g., occupational and physical therapies can reteach skills and abilities).
3. Learn to make do with less.
4. Retain the functioning that remains (e.g., "use it or lose it").

Despite the negative assumptions regarding aging from which this model originates, and the rather fatalistic tone of the third task, the notion of adaptation is an important one. Pfeiffer hypothesizes that failure to adapt will result in psychopathology. This model encourages older adults to use cognitive and emotional processes to help them adapt—Pfeiffer's definition of successful aging.

Baltes and Baltes's Model of Successful Aging: Selective Optimization with Compensation

Similar to Pfeiffer (1977), Baltes and Baltes (1990) also emphasize adaptation as a key component to successful aging. However, whereas Pfeiffer assumes that aging is characterized by loss and decline, the Baltes and Baltes model is guided by more optimistic assumptions about the aging process. This model is based on research from the Berlin Aging Study, which demonstrates that older adults not only have the ability to compensate for losses and declines but they also have the potential for further growth and development. In the Baltes and Baltes model, successful aging is conceptualized in terms of attaining and maximizing desired outcomes (i.e., gains) and avoiding and minimizing undesired outcomes (i.e., losses) (Baltes 1997).

Baltes and Baltes (1990) believe that the key process in successful aging is selective optimization with compensation, which is a three-part strategy that is hypothesized to help older adults age successfully. The three steps in the process are:

1. Select the responsibilities and activities that are of greatest importance and then concentrate effort on maintaining them.
2. Find ways to optimize performance on the selected responsibilities and activities.
3. Find ways to compensate for any declining competencies or losses in stamina (e.g., use available technology, enlist the assistance of others, identify alternative strategies to maximize performance).

In many of their writings, Baltes and Baltes use Arthur Rubinstein, a concert pianist, as an example of selective optimization with compensation (e.g., Baltes 1997; Baltes & Baltes 1990). When asked during an interview how he managed to still be an expert piano player at the age of 80, Rubinstein explained that he chose to perform fewer pieces (i.e., selection), that he practiced the selected pieces more frequently than he had in the past (i.e., optimization), and that he used "impression management." That is, before playing a "fast" segment of a piece, Rubinstein would intentionally slow his playing so that when he came to the fast segment, his playing would appear to be faster than it actually was (i.e., compensation).

A number of researchers have investigated whether use of selective optimization with compensation is associated with successful aging using data from the Berlin Aging Study (e.g., Baltes & Smith 1997; Freund & Baltes 1998). The Berlin Aging Study was designed to examine age differences and levels of functioning of older adults between the ages of 70 and 100 residing in the former city of West Berlin, Germany (Nuthmann 1995). Among the constructs included in the study are individual and family variables, social resources, and economic conditions; intelligence and cognition, self and personality, and social functioning; depression and other psychiatric disorders; and physical health. The study was designed as a cohort-sequential longitudinal study. The first wave of data gathering began in 1990, and several subsequent waves of data have already been collected.

Using data from the Berlin Aging Study, Freund and Baltes (1998) tested the hypothesis that older adults who use selective optimization with compensation to manage their life would report greater desired outcomes and fewer undesired outcomes. Examples of selective optimization strategies included items such as "I concentrate all of my energy on a few things," "I make every effort to achieve a given goal," and "When things don't go as well as they used to, I keep trying other ways of doing it until I can achieve the same result as I used to" (p. 533). Subjective well-being and positive emotions were assessed as desired outcomes, and loneliness was assessed as an undesired outcome. Freund and Baltes tested the hypothesis with 206 participants from the Berlin Aging Study who were between the ages of 72 and 102 (the mean age was 83.5, and 51 percent of the respondents were female).

Freund and Baltes's results were consistent with their hypothesis. Older adults who used selective optimization with compensation reported higher levels of subjective well-being, greater levels of positive emotions, and lower levels of loneliness. These associations remained even after the effects of age, subjective health, intelligence, and personality characteristics (e.g., neuroticism, extraversion, openness, and control beliefs) were taken into account.

Selective optimization with compensation represents a strategy that people of any age can employ to maximize desired outcomes and minimize undesired outcomes (Hansson & Carpenter 1994). Nonetheless, maximizing desired outcomes and minimizing undesired outcomes becomes increasingly difficult in advanced later life (Baltes 1997). As such, a major challenge for future generations is to identify the conditions that will enable even the very old to benefit from this strategy.

Rowe and Kahn's Model of Successful Aging: The MacArthur Studies of Successful Aging

As mentioned earlier, Rowe and Kahn (1987) define *successful aging* as aging in which external factors either have a neutral role or counteract the effects of internal aging processes, resulting in little or no decrements in functioning. More specifically, Rowe and Kahn (1998) conceptualize successful aging as a hierarchy that consists of three tasks:

1. Decreasing the risk of disease and disease-related disability
2. Increasing physical and mental functioning
3. Being actively engaged with life

Rowe and Kahn conceptualize these tasks as a hierarchy, because they believe that it is much easier to accomplish a higher-order task when the lower-order tasks have been accomplished. Thus, for example, it is much easier to increase physical and mental functioning when disease and disease-related disability are minimal. As such, true successful aging is a combination of these three tasks.

The distinction made by Rowe and Kahn (1987) between usual and successful aging stimulated two questions (Hansson & Carpenter 1994): (1) How much of usual aging is really due to external factors such as life-style choices, health behavior, and social integration? and (2) How do successful agers differ from usual agers on these factors? It is the goal of the MacArthur Community Study of Successful Aging to explore these very questions. The MacArthur study began in 1988 as a longitudinal study of 1,192 women and men between the ages of 70 and 79 who, based on their participation in other research projects in Durham, North Carolina, East Boston, Massachusetts, and New Haven Connecticut, had been identified as aging successfully (i.e., they scored in the top third of research participants in terms of cognitive and physical functioning). At the time of the initial data collection, the mean age of participants was 75.3 years, 44 percent were male, 18.7 percent were black, and 53.5 percent had not graduated from high school (Rowe 1995).

Participating in the MacArthur Studies involves assessing cognitive and physical functioning; providing information on sociodemographic characteristics, health status, productive activities, social support, and psychological characteristics; and allowing blood and urine samples to be collected (Rowe 1995; Rowe & Kahn 1998). Data collection occurred in 1988 and again in 1991.

Results from the studies indicate that there was great variability in participants' levels of cognitive and physical functioning between 1988 and 1991 (Rowe 1995). Some participants experienced declines in functioning over the three-year period, whereas some remained stable and others actually showed improvements in functioning. Participants whose physical functioning was maintained over the three-year period tended to be younger; have higher educational and income levels, lower weight, blood pressure, and other physiological measures; not have diabetes in 1988; and have avoided health conditions or hospitalization between 1988 and 1991. The only predictor of improved physical functioning over the three-year period was being black.

In terms of cognitive functioning, predictors of maintaining functioning were being younger, being white, having higher levels of education, engaging in more strenuous activity levels, having higher peak expiratory flow, and having stronger self-efficacy beliefs (Rowe 1995). Additional data from the MacArthur Studies have documented the importance of disease and disability, sociodemographic and personality variables, as well as life-style choices, health behavior, and social integration in achieving successful aging (e.g., Kubzansky et al. 1998; Rowe & Kahn 1998).

These three examples are not the only models of successful aging that have been developed. The earliest model by Pfeiffer (1977) is premised on the notion that successful aging involves adaptation to inevitable losses and declines. The latter two models were developed approximately a decade after Pfeiffer's early work. Although Baltes and Baltes (1990; Baltes 1997) primarily emphasize cognitive processes and Rowe and Kahn (1987, 1998) emphasize life-style factors in promoting successful aging, both models adopt a more positive view of aging. It is true that selective optimization with compensation represents a strategy designed to compensate for losses and declines, but a major component of the Baltes and Baltes model is older adults' potential for further growth and development. Similarly, a major focus of the Rowe and Kahn model is the identification of specific behaviors that will enable older adults to demonstrate successful, rather than merely usual, aging.

In many ways, these models reflect the development of the psychology of aging in general. Early research focused on inevitable loss and decline. When researchers and scholars began to consider that aging might include opportunities and potentials, they were rewarded with the discovery that many declines associated with aging were less extreme than originally thought. Today, it is becoming increasingly accepted that the development of maximal psychological growth and development requires a lifetime.

SUMMARY

The psychology of aging concerns psychological development and change throughout the adult years. The three general approaches to studying psychological aspects of aging include the psychology of the aged, the psychology of age, and the psychology of aging. These approaches yield different types of information about psychological aspects of aging.

The trait/characteristic, developmental, and the experiential-contextual traditions have been used to study personality. The traditions differ in terms of the extent to which personality is considered stable in later life, with the trait approach suggesting the greatest degree of stability, and the experiential-contextual tradition suggesting the least.

Psychologists distinguish fluid mechanics (i.e., a person's ability to solve novel problems) from crystallized pragmatics (i.e., knowledge that a person acquires as a result of socialization and experiences in a given culture). Research indicates that fluid mechanics decreases as people age, whereas crystallized pragmatics remains constant throughout adulthood. In some instances, crystallized pragmatics compensates for declines in fluid mechanics.

Wisdom has been defined as one of the highest forms of knowledge and skill. Older adults demonstrate comparable, and sometimes greater, levels of wisdom than do younger adults; they also maintain high levels of creativity. Fortunately, later life presents opportunities to develop wisdom and to produce creative works. However, a major question surrounds the cause of decreased learning abilities in old age. When variables such as task characteristics and gender, health, education, and intellectual functioning are taken into account, chronological age does not significantly influence learning and memory.

Memory consists of two major subsystems: semantic (or general) memory (i.e., the processes whereby one accesses words, concepts, and facts) and episodic memory (i.e., the processes whereby one encodes, stores, and retrieves information about specific events). There is little age-related decline in semantic memory, and somewhat greater decline in episodic memory. Among the strategies that can assist in memory performance are general internal memory strategies and external memory strategies.

The senses of vision, hearing, taste, smell, and touch provide links with the outside world. However, as people age, neurosensory changes can influence an individual's functioning. Although many of the senses undergo normal, age-related changes, the practical consequences of many of these changes are not noticeable until quite late in life. In addition, a range of adaptive strategies and technologies can minimize the consequences of sensory impairments in later life.

Perception refers to the processes that enable people to acquire and interpret information from their environment. Sensory processes represent the "inputs" of this process, and psychomotor responses represent the "outputs." Variability in motor performance is greater among 70-year-olds than it is among 20-year-olds. Although speed and accuracy are two common measures of performance, the two are not independent. The speed-accuracy trade-off refers to the fact that speed and accuracy are often compensatory responses. That is, older adults demonstrate lower reaction times, but greater accuracy, than younger adults on some tasks.

Successful aging refers to aging in which external factors either have a neutral role or counteract the effects of internal aging processes, resulting in little or no decrements in functioning. According to Pfeiffer, successful aging involves adaptation to inevitable losses and declines. In contrast, Baltes and Baltes's principle of selective optimization with compensation emphasizes cognitive processes, and Rowe and Kahn's model emphasizes life-style factors in promoting successful aging.

STUDY QUESTIONS

1. For what theoretical and methodological reasons, if any, is it important to distinguish between the psychology of age, the psychology of the aged, and the psychology of aging?

2. What are the theoretical and methodological strengths and limitations of each of the three traditions to studying personality?

3. Summarize what is known about the stability of personality in later life.

4. Identify a situation that illustrates how crystallized pragmatic abilities in later life might compensate for decrements in fluid mechanic abilities.

5. How similar are the findings regarding intelligence and memory in later life, and what is the role of compensation in each?

6. What sensory loss in later life would require the most accommodation?

7. Think about an older adult who you know fairly well. What, if any, accommodations has that person made to adjust to sensory and/or psychomotor limitations that he or she experiences?

8. Consider the assumptions underlying different conceptualizations of successful aging. Which set of assumptions are most consistent with your views of how others age? With how you personally hope to age?

REFERENCES

Abrams, W. B., Beers, M. H., & Berkow, R. (Eds.). (1995). *The Merck manual of geriatrics* (2nd ed.). Whitehouse Station, NJ: Merck Research Laboratories.

Backman, L., & Dixon, R. (1992). Psychological compensation: A theoretical framework. *Psychological Bulletin, 112,* 259–283.

Baltes, P. B. (1993). The aging mind: Potential and limits. *The Gerontologist, 33,* 580–594.

Baltes, P. B. (1997). On the incomplete architecture of human ontogeny: Selection, optimization, and compensation as foundations of developmental theory. *American Psychologist, 52,* 366–380.

Baltes, P. B., & Baltes, M. M. (Eds.). (1990). *Successful aging: Perspectives from the behavioral sciences.* New York: Cambridge University Press.

Baltes, P. B., & Graf, P. (1996). Psychological aspects of aging: Facts and frontiers. In D. Magnusson (Ed.), *The lifespan development of individuals: Behavioral, neurobiological, and psychosocial perspectives* (pp. 427–460). New York: Cambridge University Press.

Baltes, P. B., & Smith, J. (1990). Toward a psychology of wisdom and its ontogenesis. In R. J. Sternberg (Ed.), *Wisdom: Its nature, origins, and development* (pp. 87–120). New York: Cambridge University Press.

Baltes, P. B., & Smith, J. (1997). A systemic-holistic view of psychological functioning in very old age: Introduction to a collection of articles from the Berlin Aging Study. *Psychology and Aging, 12,* 395–409.

Baltes, P. B., & Staudinger, U. M. (1995). Wisdom. In G. L. Maddox (Ed.), *The encyclopedia of aging* (2nd ed., pp. 971–974). New York: Springer.

Barash, D. (1983). *Aging: An exploration.* Seattle: University of Washington Press.

Blanchard-Fields, F. (1996). Decision making and everyday problem solving. In J. E. Birren (Ed.), *Encyclopedia of gerontology: Age, aging, and the aged* (Vol. 1, pp. 373–381). San Diego: Academic.

Blanchard-Fields, F., & Chen, Y. (1996). Adaptive cognition and aging. *American Behavioral Scientist, 39,* 231–248.

Brandstaedter, J. (1989). Personal self-regulation of development: Cross-sequential analyses of development-related control beliefs and emotions. *Developmental Psychology, 25,* 96–108.

Brandstaedter, J., & Greve, W. (1994). The aging self: Stabilizing and protective processes. *Developmental Review, 14,* 52–80.

Brown, P. L. (1987, September 14). Studying seasons of a woman's life. *New York Times,* p. 23.

Butler, R. N., & Schechter, M. (1995). Productive aging. In G. L. Maddox (Ed.), *The encyclopedia of aging* (2nd ed., pp. 763–764). New York: Springer.

Catell, R. B. (1963). Theory of fulid and crystallized intelligence: An initial experiment. *Journal of Educational Psychology, 105,* 105–111.

Cerella, J. (1995). Reaction time. In G. L. Maddox (Ed.), *The encyclopedia of aging* (2nd ed., pp. 792–795). New York: Springer.

Corso, J. F. (1995). Hearing. In G. L. Maddox (Ed.), *The encyclopedia of aging* (2nd ed., pp. 449–452). New York: Springer.

Costa, P. T., Jr., & McCrae, R. R. (1994). Set like plaster? Evidence for the stability of adult personality. In T. F. Hetherton & J. L. Weinberger (Eds.), *Can personality change?* Washington, DC: American Psychological Association.

Costa, P. T., Jr., & McCrae, R. R. (1998). Trait theories of personality. In D. F. Barone & M. Hersen (Eds.), *Advanced personality* (pp. 103–121). New York: Plenum.

Cross, S., & Markus, H. (1991). Possible selves across the life span. *Human Development, 34,* 230–255.

Denney, N. W. (1995). Problem solving. In G. L. Maddox (Ed.), *The encyclopedia of aging* (2nd ed., pp. 759–760). New York: Springer.

Dewey, J. (1939). Introduction. In E. V. Cowdry (Ed.), *Problems of aging.* Baltimore: Williams and Wilkins.

Erikson, E. (1950). *Childhood and society.* New York: Norton.

Erikson, E. (1963). *Childhood and society* (2nd ed.). New York: Norton.

Erikson, E. H. (1982). *The life cycle completed: Review.* New York: Norton.

Freund, A. M., & Baltes, P. B. (1998). Selection, optimization, and compensation as strategies of life management: Correlations with subjective indicators of successful aging. *Psychology and Aging, 13,* 531–543.

Gates, G., Cooper, J., Kannel, W., & Miller, N. (1990). Hearing in the elderly: The Framingham cohort, 1983–1985. Part I. Basic audiometric test results. *Ear and Hearing, 11,* 247–256.

Gatz, M., & Karel, M. J. (1993). Individual change in perceived control over 20 years. *International Journal of Behavioral Development, 16,* 305–322.

Giarrusso, R., & Bengtson, V. L. (1996). Self-esteem. In J. E. Birren (Ed.), *Encyclopedia of gerontology: Age, aging, and the aged* (Vol. 2, pp. 459–466). San Diego: Academic.

Graf, P., & Schachter, D. L. (1985). Implicit and explicit memory for new associations in normal and amnesic subjects. *Journal of Experimental Psychology: Learning, Memory, and Cognition, 11,* 501–518.

Guilford, J. P. (1967). *The nature of human intelligence.* New York: McGraw-Hill.

Gutmann, D. L. (1977). The cross-cultural perspective: Notes toward a comparative psychology of aging. In J. E. Birren & K. W. Schaie (Eds.), *Handbook of the psychology of aging.* New York: Van Nostrand Reinhold.

Hansson, R. O., & Carpenter, B. N. (1994). *Coping with the challenges of transition.* New York: Guilford.

Harkins, S. W., & Scott, R. B. (1996). Pain and presbyalgos. In J. E. Birren (Ed.), *Encyclopedia of gerontology: Age, aging, and the aged* (Vol. 1, pp. 247–260). San Diego: Academic.

Havlik, R. J. (1986). Aging in the eighties: Impaired senses for sound and light in persons age 65 years and over. *NCHS Advance Data,* No. 125.

Hayflick, L. (1994). *How and why we age.* New York: Ballantine.

Hertzog, C., & Schaie, K. W. (1988). Stability and change in adult intelligence: 2. Simultaneous analysis of longitudinal means and covariance structures. *Psychology and Aging, 3,* 121–130.

Hooker, K., & Kaus, C. R. (1994). Health-related possible selves in young and middle adulthood. *Psychology and Aging, 9,* 126–133.

Horn, J. L., & Hofer, S. M. (1992). Major abilities and development in the adult period. In R. J.

Sternberg & C. A. Berg (Eds.), *Intellectual development* (pp. 44–99). New York: Cambridge University Press.

Hoyer, W. J. (1995a). Knowledge utilization. In G. L. Maddox (Ed.), *The encyclopedia of aging* (2nd ed., p. 534). New York: Springer.

Hoyer, W. J. (1995b). Vision and visual perception. In G. L. Maddox (Ed.), *The encyclopedia of aging* (2nd ed., pp. 956–957). New York: Springer.

Jung, C. (1971). The stages of life. In J. Campbell (Ed.), *The portable Jung.* New York: Viking.

Kane, R. L., Ouslander, J. G., & Abrass, I. B. (1999). *Essentials of clinical geriatrics* (4th ed.). New York: McGraw-Hill.

Kausler, D. H. (1995). Memory and memory theory. In G. L. Maddox (Ed.), *The encyclopedia of aging* (2nd ed., pp. 612–615). New York: Springer.

Kermis, M. D. (1986). *Mental health in late life: The adaptive process.* Boston: Jones & Bartlett.

Kogan, N. (1990). Personality. In J. E. Birren & K. W. Schaie (Eds.), *Handbook of the psychology of aging* (3rd ed., pp. 330–346). New York: Academic.

Kubzansky, L. D., Berkman, L. F., Glass, T. A., & Seeman, T. F. (1998). Is educational attainment associated with shared determinants of health in the elderly? Findings from the MacArthur Studies of successful aging. *Psychosomatic Medicine, 60,* 578–585.

Levenson, H. (1981). Differentiating among internality, powerful others, and chance. In H. M. Lefcourt (Ed.), *Research with the locus of control construct* (Vol. 1, pp. 15–63). New York: Academic.

Levinson, D. J., Darrow, C. N., Klein, E. B., Levinson, M. H., & McKee, B. (1978). *The seasons of a man's life.* New York: Knopf.

Markus, H., & Nurius, P. (1986). Possible selves. *American Psychologist, 41,* 954–969.

McAdams, D. P. (1993). *The stories we live by: Personal myths and the making of the self.* New York: Morrow.

McAdams, D. P. (1994). Can personality change? Levels of stability and growth in personality across the life span. In T. F. Heatherton & J. L. Weinberger (Eds.), *Can personality change?* (pp. 299–313). Washington, DC: American Psychological Association.

McAdams, D. P. (1996). Narrating the self in adulthood. In J. E. Birren & G. M. Kenyon (Eds.), *Aging and biography: Explorations in adult development* (pp. 131–148). New York: Springer.

McAdams, D. P., de St. Aubin, E., & Logan, R. L. (1993). Generativity among young, midlife and older adults. *Psychology and Aging, 8,* 221–230.

McAdams, D. P., Diamond, A., de St. Aubin, E., & Mansfield, E. (1997). Stories of commitment: The psychosocial construction of generative lives. *Journal of Personality and Social Psychology, 72,* 678–694.

McCrae, R. R. (1995). Personality. In G. L. Maddox (Ed.), *The encyclopedia of aging* (2nd ed., pp. 735–736). New York: Springer.

McCrae, R. R., & Costa, P. T., Jr. (1990). *Personality in adulthood.* New York: Guilford.

Murray, H. A. (1938). *Explorations in personality.* London: Oxford University Press.

Neisser, U., & Winograd, E. (Eds.). (1988). *Remembering reconsidered.* New York: Cambridge University Press.

Neugarten, B. (1973). Personality change in late life: A developmental perspective. In C. Eisdorfer & M. P. Lawton (Eds.), *The psychology of adult development and aging.* Washington, DC: American Psychological Association

Neugarten, B. (1977). Personality and aging. In J. Birren & K. Schaie (Eds.), *Handbook of the psychology of aging.* New York: Van Nostrand Reinhold.

Nuthmann, R. (1995). Berlin Aging Study. In G. L. Maddox (Ed.), *The encyclopedia of aging* (2nd ed., pp. 108–111). New York: Springer.

Parks, D. C. (1995). Everyday memory. In G. L. Maddox (Ed.), *The encyclopedia of aging* (2nd ed., pp. 344–346). New York: Springer.

Peck, R. (1968). Psychological developments in the second half of life. In B. Neugarten (Ed.), *Middle age and aging: A reader in social psychology.* Chicago: University of Chicago Press.

Perlmutter, M. (1995). Metamemory. In G. L. Maddox (Ed.), *The encyclopedia of aging* (2nd ed.)(pp. 636–638). New York: Springer.

Pfeiffer, E. (1977). Psychopathology and social pathology. In J. E. Biren & K. W. Schaie (Eds.), *Handbook of the psychology of aging* (pp. 650–671). New York: Van Nostrand Reinhold.

Poon, L. W. (1995). Learning. In G. L. Maddox (Ed.), *The encyclopedia of aging* (2nd ed.). New York: Springer.

Poon, L. W., Krauss, I., & Bowles, N. L. (1984). On subject selection in cognitive aging research. *Experimental Aging Research, 10,* 43–49.

Reichard, S., Livson, F., & Peterson, P. G. (1962). *Aging and personality.* New York: Wiley.

Rhee, C., & Gatz, M. (1993). Cross-generational attributions concerning locus of control beliefs.

International Journal of Aging & Human Development, 37, 153–161.

Roberts, J. C. (1995). Eye: Structure and function. In G. L. Maddox (Ed.), *The encyclopedia of aging* (2nd ed., pp. 357–359). New York: Springer.

Roberts, P., & Newton, P. M. (1987). Levinsonian studies of women's adult development. *Psychology and Aging, 2,* 154–163.

Rotter, J. B. (1966). Generalized expectancies for internal versus external control of reinforcement. *Psychological Monographs, 80.*

Rowe, J. W. (1995). MacArthur Community Study of Successful Aging. In G. L. Maddox (Ed.), *The encyclopedia of aging* (2nd ed., pp. 593–594). New York: Springer.

Rowe, J. W., & Kahn, R. L. (1987). Human aging: Usual and successful. *Science, 237,* 143–149.

Rowe, J. W., & Kahn, R. L. (1998). *Successful aging.* New York: Pantheon.

Ruth, J.-E. (1996). Personality. In J. E. Birren (Ed.), *Encyclopedia of gerontology: Age, aging, and the aged* (Vol. 2, pp. 281–294). San Diego: Academic.

Ryff, C. D. (1991). Possible selves in adulthood and old age: A tale of shifting horizons. *Psychology and Aging, 6,* 286–295.

Salthouse, T. A. (1991). *Theoretical perspectives on cognitive aging.* Hillsdale, NJ: Erlbaum.

Salthouse, T. A. (1995a). Perception. In G. L. Maddox (Ed.), *The encyclopedia of aging* (2nd ed., pp. 733–734). New York: Springer.

Salthouse, T. A. (1995b). Speed-accuracy trade-off. In G. L. Maddox (Ed.), *The encyclopedia of aging* (2nd ed., pp. 897–898). New York: Springer.

Salthouse, T. A. (1995c). Working memory. In G. L. Maddox (Ed.), *The encyclopedia of aging* (2nd ed., pp. 977–978). New York: Springer.

Saxon, S. V., & Etten, M. J. (1994). *Physical change and aging: A guide for the helping professions* (3rd ed.). New York: Tiresias Press.

Schaie, K. W. (1983). The Seattle Longitudinal Study: A 21-year exploration of psychometric intelligence in adulthood. In K. W. Schaie (Ed.), *Longitudinal studies of adult psychological development* (pp. 64–135). New York: Guilford.

Schaie, K. W. (1984). Midlife influences upon intellectual functioning in old age. *International Journal of Behavioral Development, 7,* 463–478.

Schaie, K. W. (1995a). Abilities. In G. L. Maddox (Ed.), *The encyclopedia of aging* (2nd ed., p. 2). New York: Springer.

Schaie, K. W. (1995b). *Intellectual development in adulthood: The Seattle longitudinal study.* New York: Cambridge University Press.

Schiffman, S. S. (1995a). Smell. In G. L. Maddox (Ed.), *The encyclopedia of aging* (2nd ed., pp. 867–869). New York: Springer.

Schiffman, S. S. (1995b). Taste. In G. L. Maddox (Ed.), *The encyclopedia of aging* (2nd ed., pp. 920–922). New York: Springer.

Schroots, J. J. F. (1996). Theoretical developments in the psychology of aging. *The Gerontologist, 36,* 742–748.

Simonton, D. K. (1995). Creativity. In G. L. Maddox (Ed.), *The encyclopedia of aging* (2nd ed., pp. 241–243). New York: Springer.

Simonton, D. K. (1996). Creativity. In J. E. Birren (Ed.), *Encyclopedia of gerontology: Age, aging, and the aged* (Vol. 1, p. 341–351). San Diego: Academic.

Smith, A. D. (1995). Cognitive processes. In G. L. Maddox (Ed.), *The encyclopedia of aging* (2nd ed., pp. 186–188). New York: Springer.

Spear, P. D. (1993). Neural bases of visual deficits during aging. *Vision Research, 33,* 2589–2609.

Stefansson, E. (1990). The eye. In W. Hazzard, R. Andres, E. Bierman, & J. Blass (Eds.), *Principles of geriatric medicine and gerontology.* New York: McGraw-Hill.

Sugar, J. A. (1996). Memory strategies. In J. E. Birren (Ed.), *Encyclopedia of gerontology: Age, aging, and the aged* (Vol. 1, pp. 119–124). San Diego: Academic.

Thurstone, L. K. (1938). *The primary mental abilities.* Chicago: University of Chicago Press.

Tornstam, L. (1989). Gero-transcendence: A reformulation of the disengagement theory. *Aging, 1,* 55–63.

Tornstam, L. (1994). Gero-transcendence: A theoretical and empirical exploration. In L. E. Thomas & S. A. Eisenhandler (Eds.), *Aging and the religious dimension* (pp. 203–226). Westport, CT: Auburn House.

Tornstam, L. (1997). Gerotranscendence: The contemplative dimension of aging. *Journal of Aging Studies, 11,* 143–154.

U.S. Bureau of the Census. (1998). *Statistical abstract of the United States: 1998* (118th edition). Washington, DC: U.S. Government Printing Office.

Verhaeghen, P., Marcoen, A., & Goossens, L. (1992) Improving memory performance in the aged through mnemonic training: A meta-analytic study. *Psychology and Aging, 7,* 242–251.

Welford, A. T. (1995). Motor performance. In G. L. Maddox (Ed.), *The encyclopedia of aging* (2nd ed., pp. 651–653). New York: Springer.

Whitbourne, S. K. (1985). *The aging body.* New York: Springer.

Whitbourne, S. K. (1987). Personality development in adulthood and old age: Relationships among identity style, health, and well-being. In K. W. Schaie (Ed.), *Annual review of gerontology and geriatrics* (Vol. 7). New York: Springer.

Whitbourne, S. K. (1996). *The aging individual: Physical and psychological perspectives.* New York: Springer.

Willis, S. L. (1995). Competence. In G. L. Maddox (Ed.), *The encyclopedia of aging* (2nd ed., pp. 207–208). New York: Springer.

Willis, S. L., & Schaie, K. W. (1994). Cognitive training in the normal elderly. In F. Forette, Y. Christen, & F. Boller (Eds.), *Cerebral plasticity and cognitive stimulation* (pp. 91–113). Paris: Foundation Nationale de Gerontologie.

Voeks, S., Gallagher, C., Langer, E., & Drinka, P. (1990). Hearing loss in the nursing home: An institutional issue. *Journal of the American Geriatrics Society, 38,* 141–145.

CHAPTER EIGHT

SOCIAL ASPECTS OF AGING

A number of perspectives exist that explain how people develop and change over time. This chapter begins with a discussion of three of these perspectives: life stage, life span, and life course. The first two perspectives are primarily rooted in psychology, whereas the latter is primarily rooted in sociology. These perspectives are not mutually exclusive. For example, each approach assumes that development is a process that occurs from the "cradle to the grave" (Kastenbaum 1995, p. 553). However, these perspectives differ along a variety of dimensions, including the origin of change, the amount of change that is possible, and the extent to which development is predictable, malleable, and determined by multiple influences. Each approach is described here, with the greatest attention devoted to the life-span and life-course perspectives. Table 8.1 compares these perspectives. In the second and third sections of the chapter, concepts such as *socialization, social roles*, and *role transitions* are used to help explain the sequencing of the life course. Although the life course may include predictable, socially recognized transitions, it also includes events and circumstances over which people have little or no control. Learning to cope with all of these types of situations and developing successful strategies for adapting to them are important elements of the life course. The final section of the chapter presents research on the process of coping with and adapting to predictable and unpredictable events and traditions over the life course. Chapter 9 deals with sociological theories of aging.

THREE PERSPECTIVES ON HUMAN DEVELOPMENT

The Life-Stage Perspective

The *life-stage perspective* of human development contends that development proceeds through a set pattern of sequential stages that most individuals experience. Levinson and colleagues (1974) summarize this approach: "We are interested in generating…hypotheses concerning *relatively universal, genotypic, age-linked, adult* developmental periods within which variations occur" (p. 244; emphasis in original). Kastenbaum (1995) identifies three principal characteristics of theories that adopt a life-stage perspective:

TABLE 8.1 Conceptualizations of Change and Individual Development through the Lifetime According to Life-Stage, Life-Span, and Life-Course Perspectives

CHANGE ISSUES	AMOUNT OF CHANGE POSSIBLE	ABRUPTNESS OF CHANGE	DIRECTION OF CHANGE	UNIVERSALITY OF CHANGE	ORIGIN OF CHANGE
Perspectives:					
Life stage	Change between stages; little change within.	Abrupt between stages	Unidirectional	Universal	Largely internal
Life span	Change throughout life, but amount varies depending on individual characteristics, life experiences, and history.	Varies	Reversible	Relative	Internal and external, emphasis on latter
Life course	Change throughout life, but amount varies depending on individual experiences, age norms, cohort effects, and history.	Varies	Reversible	Relative	Internal and external, much emphasis on latter

Source: From "Socialization Processes over the Life Course" by D. M. Bush and R. G. Simmons, in *Social Psychology: Sociological Perspectives*, edited by Morris Rosenberg and Ralph H. Turner. Copyright © 1981 by The American Sociological Association. Reprinted by permission of Basic Books, Inc., Publishers.

1. Individuals progress from one stage or level of development in a fixed order or sequence.
2. There are qualitative differences between each stage or level of development.
3. Transitions to a subsequent stage or level of development are based at least in part on how successful individuals were in the earlier stage.

Examples of theories that adopt a life-stage perspective include Erickson's stages of psychosocial development and Levinson's developmental periods in early and middle adulthood.

A strength of the life-stage perspective is that it acknowledges that development is an ongoing process. However, the approach has been criticized on a number of dimensions, such as the perspective assumes that development proceeds in only one direction through the stages, that it does not allow for individual differences in the progression of development, and that development is too often tied to chronological age (Bush & Simmons 1981).

The Life-Span Perspective

Originally referred to as the *life-span developmental psychology perspective*, the **life-span perspective** developed as a counterpoint to life-stage (or life-cycle) theories that posited irreversible, unidirectional, age-determined change through the lifetime (Bush & Simmons 1981). This perspective is devoted to "the description and explication of ontogenetic (age-related) behavioral changes from birth to death" (Baltes & Goulet 1970, p. 12). Baltes (1987) and Baltes and Graf (1996) outline seven characteristics of the life-span perspective:

1. Development is a life-long process.
2. Development is a multidirectional, not a unidirectional, process.
3. Development consists of both positive and negative changes in adaptive capacity. In fact, development always involves gains and losses.
4. There is a great deal of intraindividual variability, or plasticity, in development.
5. Development is embedded within a historical context.
6. Development is dependent on a host of contextual factors, including social and cultural conditions.
7. In order to attempt to understand development, it is necessary to employ a multidisciplinary approach.

Although this perspective was originally referred to as the life-span developmental psychology approach, it is not limited to consideration of intrapsychic phenomena. Rather, this perspective emphasizes the interaction of individual and social characteristics in explanations of behavioral change.

Baltes (1979) identifies three sets of factors that influence development: normative age-graded influences, normative history-graded influences, and nonnormative influences. *Normative age-graded influences* refer to biological and environmental factors that are typically correlated with chronological age. Examples of these in-fluences include puberty and menopause. *Normative history-graded influences* refer to biological and environmental factors that are experienced by all members of a cultural unit at the same time. Examples include the AIDS epidemic and the Great Depression. *Nonnormative influences* refer to biological and environmental factors that do not affect everyone, but that can have significant effects on partic-ular individuals' lives. Examples of nonnormative influences include the illness or death of a family member and winning the lottery.

There are two major areas of interest for proponents of the life-span per-spective (Hoyer, & Rybash 1996). One is the extent to which development dem-onstrates continuities versus discontinuities over time. A second area concerns the nature of development itself. That is, interest centers on how the processes and mechanisms of development in later life might differ from those of earlier life. Examples of theorists whose work is consistent with the life-span perspective include Erikson's psychosocial stages of development, and Neugarten's research on personality, and Baltes and Schaie's research on intellectual functioning.

The Life-Course Perspective

The *life-course perspective* "concentrates on age-related transitions that are *socially created, socially recognized,* and *shared"* (Hagestad & Neugarten 1985, p. 35; emphasis in original). Life-course researchers focus on the ways in which social norms and definitions influence the pattern or sequence of role changes and role transitions in the life course. One major theme of the life-course perspective is that aging is a life-long process that is influenced by, as well as influences, social processes. A second major theme is that age structures change over time and are experienced differently by different cohorts of individuals (Riley, Foner, & Waring 1988).

According to Hareven (1996), the life-course perspective emphasizes the "timing by which individuals and families make their transitions into and out of various roles and developmental tasks in relation to the social time clocks" (p. 31). Elaborating on this idea, Elder (1998) identifies four principles of the life-course perspective:

1. The principle of historical time and place
2. The principle of timing in lives
3. The principle of linked lives
4. The principle of human agency

The *principle of historical time and place* refers to the idea that the life course is both "embedded in and shaped by the historical times and places that individuals experience over their lifetimes" (Elder 1998, p. 3). The *principle of timing in lives* re-flects the notion that the impact that a series of events or life transitions has on an individual depends on when in an individual's life they occur. The *principle of linked lives* refers to the idea that lives are not led independently; rather, people are inter-dependent on one another. As a result, the historical events and situations that are experienced by one individual "ripple" through their networks of families and close friends. Finally, the *principle of human agency* maintains that, within the particular historical and social context, individuals have a role in shaping their life courses through the choices they make and the behaviors in which they engage.

Generally speaking, proponents of the life-course perspective are not particularly interested in intraindividual or biological phenomena. Rather, they are interested in the historical and social forces that differentially shape the development of different cohorts of individuals. Among the most prolific researchers who adopt a life-course perspective are Tamara Hareven and Glen Elder, Jr. Hareven (1978, 1982, 1996) has applied the life-course perspective to analyze of the role of the family throughout changing historical and social conditions. Her research focuses on how people synchronize individual life transitions with family transitions, and she examines the impact of such transitions on intergenerational relationships within the family. Elder has applied the life-course perspective to a number of developmental issues, including the impact of the Great Depression on different cohorts of older adults (Elder 1974) and the legacy of war on mens' lives (Elder, Shanahan, & Clipp 1994).

The life-stage, life-span, and life-course perspectives are not mutually exclusive, although they do differ along a number of dimensions. As summarized in Table 8.1, the three perspectives differ in terms of the amount of change that is possible, the abruptness of the change, and the direction, universality, and origin of change. As can be seen from the table, the life-stage perspective represents the most simplistic perspective of development. The life-span and life-course perspectives are most closely aligned. Because of the inclusion of age norms and cohort effects in the life-course perspective, it represents the most complex perspective of development.

HISTORICAL AND CULTURAL VARIATIONS IN THE SEQUENCING OF THE LIFE COURSE

Consistent with the life-course perspective, all societies divide the life course into recognized seasons of life—what Zerubavel (1981) describes as a *sociotemporal order*—that regulate the structure and dynamics of social life. Passing from one "season" to another often marks multiple changes in social identity. The way the lifetime is divided or segmented differs in different cultures, and can differ within the same culture over time. Typically, periods of life are identified and defined; age criteria are used to channel people into positions and roles. Rights, responsibilities, privileges, and obligations are assigned on the basis on these culturally specific definitions (Hagestad & Neugarten 1985).

Early in the seventeenth century, Shakespeare's character Jaques in *As You Like It* limited life's script to seven acts or ages:

> All the world's a stage,
> And all the men and women merely players.

> They have their exits and their entrances,
> And one man in his time plays many parts,
> His acts being seven ages.
>   (act 2, scene 7, lines 139–143)

The seven acts or ages (applicable to a woman's life script as well) constitute the sequence of roles that make up a life course, each role symbolizing age-appropriate behaviors.

> ...At first the infant,
> Mewling and puking in the nurse's arms.
> Then the whining schoolboy with his satchel
> And shining morning face, creeping like snail
> Unwillingly to school. And then the lover,
> Sighing like furnace, with a woeful ballad
> Made to the mistress' eyebrow. Then a soldier,
> Full of strange oaths, and bearded like the pard,
> Jealous in honor, sudden and quick in quarrel,
> Seeking the bubble reputation
> Even in the cannon's mouth. And then the justice,
> In fair round belly with good capon lined,
> With eyes severe and beard of formal cut,
> Full of wise saws and modern instances;
> And so he plays his part. The sixth age shifts
> Into the lean and slippered pantaloon,
> With spectacles on nose and pouch on side;
> His youthful hose, well saved, a world too wide
> For his shrunk shank; and his big manly voice
> Turning again towards childish treble, pipes
> And whistles in his sound. Last scene of all,
> That ends this strange eventful history,
> Is second childishness and mere oblivion,
> Sans teeth, sans eyes, sans taste, sans everything.
>   (act 2, scene 7, lines 143–166)

For Shakespeare, life begins with a helpless dependency and ends absent sensory capabilities that make it worth living. The course between these endpoints is described in terms of social roles. But understanding how the "mewling, puking infant" becomes the schoolboy, the lover, the soldier, and the justice, and then finally enters "second childishness" and "mere oblivion" requires some familiarity with the process of socialization.

Linton (1942) suggests that four is the minimal number of age groupings in a society: infancy, childhood, adulthood, and old age. Keith (1982) reports studying 60 traditional societies and finding a range of 2 to 8 categories or age-grades used to "slice" up the life course. Cowgill (1986) identifies at least 10 age-grades in the contemporary United States: infancy, preschool age, kindergarten age, elementary school age, intermediate school age, high school age, young adult, middle-aged, young-old, and old-old.

Researchers often assume that the layperson views the world as they do. Just how do ordinary people visualize the life course? Do they set age boundaries for different stages or age-grades? And how do they characterize the behaviors assigned to these different stages? A team of anthropologists (Ikels et al. 1992)—using cross-cultural studies in Hong Kong, the United States, Ireland, and Botswana—sought to identify how different people perceive old age and its place in the life course.

The research strategy used to elicit people's perceptions of the life course involved use of the *Age Game*. In this game, informants were provided a deck of cards containing descriptive material on individuals in terms of sex, marital status, participation in various activities, and the like. The cards contained culture-specific information based on extensive pretesting. Informants read the cards themselves or, in the cases of nonliterate participants primarily in Hong Kong and Botswana, had card descriptions read to them aloud by the researcher. The individuals in the study were asked to group cards that described people who were in the same stage of life and to order the groupings by age.

The great majority of informants across all research sites recognized between three and six age groupings. Most Hong Kong Chinese used a simple three-stage age scheme—youth, the middle years, and old age—and then modified these categories to make further accommodations. Many informants simply divided the middle years and old age into two stages each. Informants could usually assign an age range to an age category, but age was not really the most salient issue that defined membership in a particular category. For example, for Hong Kong Chinese, grandparenthood, reduced responsibilities, increased leisure, and retirement were all seen as markers of becoming old.

In Blessington, Ireland, just south of Dublin, residents perceived a four-stage life course. The first stage, 18 to 30 years of age, was characterized by freedom from responsibility for finances and family. In the second stage, 30 to 50 years of age, people settle down and accept responsibilities for employment and family. The third stage, including those from age 50 to 65, was characterized by a reaping of the fruits of labor and family rearing. Grandparenthood is a marker for this stage. The last stage of life (70 years of age or more) is viewed by many in Blessington as a return to a youthlike carefree state.

Common to Hong Kong and Blessington, Ireland, is the extent to which responsibility is viewed by residents as a central theme in the life course. Although the aged are characterized in different terms in the two societies (physically weak and out of touch in Hong Kong and fearful of ill health and the consequences of living alone in Blessington), the life stage of old age is actually described in similar terms in these two societies—relief from the burdens and struggle of middle-age.

SOCIALIZATION AND SOCIAL ROLES

The human animal is distinguished by its capacity to learn, and this capacity underlies the efforts in human society to develop and institutionalize modes of instruction designed to prepare individuals to function as members of society.

Stated more succinctly, human behavior is primarily learned. The learning process, called *socialization,* involves the transmission, by language and gesture, of the culture into which people are born. As Clausen reminds us, socialization is a lifelong process: "the process of transmitting the skills and knowledge needed to perform roles that one will (or may) occupy as one moves along the life course" (1986, p. 17).

Much socialization effort is directed toward the developing child. The function of early socialization is to present a single world of meaning as the only possible way to organize perceptions (Berger & Luckman 1990). But socialization goes on long after physical maturity has been achieved. Early socialization is insufficient to prepare a person for the many different roles of adulthood in a modern industrial society. When focused on the adult life course, socialization stresses the importance of the demands that institutions and other members of the society make on the individual (Brim 1968). These demands shape attitudes, interests, and opinions. Because socialization occurs over the life course, it requires *desocialization* (learning to give up a role) and *resocialization* (learning new ways to deal with the old role partners). Such changes carry with them the potential for major reorganization of the self (Hess, Markson, & Stein 1988).

A *social role* refers to a "set of patterned, functionally interdependent relations between a person and his/her social circle involving duties and personal rights" (Lopata 1995, p. 874). The concept of social role describes society's expectations for individuals who occupy a given social position or status. Each distinctive social status has a set of role, or behavioral, expectations attached to it. It is the concept of social role that leads one to expect that college students submit their assignments on time, that accountants be familiar with current tax law, and that police officers respond to a citizen in distress. It is also the concept that helps one understand how the same individual can juggle the different expectations associated with being a mother, professor, community volunteer, friend, spouse, and theater patron all in the same day.

Roles are not acted out in a social vacuum. They are usually defined in the context of interacting social roles performed by others. Thus, the expectations we fulfill in our role as professors are often carried out in association with someone else fulfilling the role of student. Only with the cooperation of individuals fulfilling their roles of daughter and son can a person carry out the expectations associated with being a parent. Many social roles come in pairs or sets such as these (professor-student; father-child). Such role pairs or sets are known as *complementary roles* because they require that the behavior of two or more persons interact in specific ways.

Social roles, including complementary roles, are not defined in specific or uniform terms throughout a society. Some of this lack of uniformity comes from variation in actual performance across individuals. One professor may befriend students and provide advice and counsel on personal matters, whereas another may focus strictly on duties related to the coursework at hand. In one family, the father may play a strong role as decision maker, whereas in another, the mother may take responsibility for most decisions. Generally speaking, to operate effectively, the roles people assume must complement the roles of those with whom they interact most of the time.

Social roles are a significant component of the social structure. They allow people to anticipate the behavior of others and to respond or pattern their own actions accordingly. The individual acquisition of social roles is a key element in the socialization process.

ROLE TRANSITIONS

In theory, at least, anticipatory socialization could cushion the shock associated with a role or status change such as retirement, divorce and/or remarriage, or the advent of grandparenthood. *Anticipatory socialization* describes socialization prior to or in preparation for successfully taking on a new role. The concept can also be applied to the transition to occupational and professional careers. Medical sociologists, for example, have used the concept to speak to the "training for uncertainty" (Fox 1957) and "loss of idealism" (Becker et al. 1961) experienced by those preparing for entry into the medical profession.

Some literature suggests that negative effects of role or status transitions can be offset by ***rites of passage,*** rituals that help individuals move from one known social position to another and provide signals to the rest of society that new expectations are appropriate. Ceremonial rituals can be used to mark losses or gains in privilege, responsibility, influence, or power. Typical status passages marked by ceremonial ritual in U.S. society include that from child to adult (confirmation or bar or bas mitzvah), from high school to college student (graduation), from single to married person (marriage), from worker to retiree (retirement party), and from living person to ancestor (funeral).

Are status changes in society (such as those itemized here) made easier by rites of passage? Foner and Kertzer (1978) offer that most of the evidence for the advantage of such rites of passage comes from studies of non-Western cultures. Some of their own work with African societies, however, shows that the absence of firm rules of transition encourages conflict over the timing of such transitions. Thus, those in powerful positions may attempt to delay ceremonial rites of passage because they do not want to give up their privileges, whereas those who will gain from the transition make an effort to hasten the rites of passage.

Keith argues that the most distinctive characteristics of rites of passage for old people in the United States is in their absence or incompleteness: "At most, an older person and the others who have social ties to him or her are offered *exit* signs. The separation phase of a rite of passage may be there in retirement parties or gold watches, but there is no clear pathway back to social reincorporation" (1982, p. 30). The lack of public ceremonial ritual to mark transitions experienced by the old may be further evidence of their roleless roles. Older people themselves, however, may be creating transition rituals. This is exemplified by the extended retirement trip, which makes it easier to change expectations on return, or the change in residence, which also makes it easier for some people to face changed expectations.

The Timing of Role Transitions

The timing of role transitions is not static over time within a given society. That is, cohort differences and historical period effects have contributed to changes in the timing of **role transitions** throughout the twentieth century. Schoen and colleagues (cited in Siegel & Davidson 1984) have developed some measures of important events occurring in later segments of the family life cycle (see Table 8.2). Comparing cohorts born in the years from 1908 to 1912 to those born between 1938 to 1942, the researchers observed a decline in the average duration of a first marriage that is slightly greater for men (28.7 years versus 26.1 years) than for women (29.5 years versus 27.4 years). This decline for men and women is clearly a function of an increase in the proportion of first marriages ending in divorce. Whereas 25 percent of men born between 1908 and 1912 had their first marriages end in divorce, almost 40 percent of those born between 1938 and 1942 had first marriages end in that fashion.

The mean age at widowhood has increased more dramatically for men (64.5 versus 68.4 years) than for women (64.7 years versus 66.1 years), but the average duration of widowhood has remained about the same (6.6 years for men and 14.3 years for women). Much smaller proportions of husbands outlive their wives than is the case for wives who outlive their husbands. Increases in the mean age at widowhood just described are likely a function of the greater increase in longevity of women over men experienced in the period in question. In addition, to date, the percentage of first marriages ending in widowhood has declined. Whereas 53 percent of women born from 1908 to 1912 had their first marriages end in widowhood, 45.3 percent of women born in 1938 to 1942 had their marriages end similarly.

At any given time, most societies appear to have a timetable for the ordering of life events and (almost by definition) role transitions. Describing empirical studies begun by Neugarten and colleagues in the 1950s, Neugarten and Hagestad (1976) report that interviewees were easily able to respond to questions such as "What is the best age for a man to marry?" and "What is the best age for a woman to become a grandmother?" There was greatest agreement in response to questions dealing with the timing of major role transitions. For example, most middle-class men and women agreed that the best age for a man to marry was from 20 to 25; most men should be settled in a career by age 24 to 26; they should hold their top jobs by age 40; and they should be ready to retire by age 60 or 65 (Neugarten & Hagestad 1976).

More recently, Settersen and Hagestad (1996a, 1996b) examined what they call **cultural age deadlines** among 319 adults over the age of 18. Cultural age deadlines refer to "the age by which people think certain family transitions ought to occur in men's and women's lives" (1996a, p. 179). Settersen and Hagestad were interested in both family transitions (i.e., leaving home, returning home, marriage, parenthood, completing childbearing, grandparenthood) and educational and work transitions (i.e., completing full-time schooling, beginning full-time work, settling on career/job, the peak of work career, retirement).

TABLE 8.2 Measures of the Marital Life Cycle of Men and Women, for Selected Birth Cohorts: 1908–1912 to 1938–1942

ITEM (YEARS)	MALES COHORT (YEAR OF BIRTH)				FEMALES COHORT (YEAR OF BIRTH)			
	1908–1912	1918–1922	1928–1932	1938–1942	1908–1912	1918–1922	1928–1932	1938–1942
Average age at first marriage	26.2	25.0	23.8	23.3	23.3	22.3	21.1	21.2
Average duration of first marriage	28.7	28.9	28.5	26.1	29.5	29.2	29.7	27.4
Outcome of first marriage (%)								
Divorce	25.1	29.3	33.2	39.4	23.8	27.3	31.5	36.7
Widowhood	22.8	21.1	19.6	17.6	53.0	50.3	48.5	45.1
Death	52.0	49.6	47.3	43.0	23.2	21.2	19.9	18.3
Mean age at								
Widowhood	64.5	66.7	67.8	68.4	64.7	65.6	66.0	66.1
Divorce	40.7	39.7	40.1	38.7	37.4	36.5	37.1	36.5
Mean duration of								
Widowhood	6.6	6.7	6.7	6.6	14.4	14.3	14.4	14.3
Divorce	4.4	4.4	4.5	4.2	8.9	8.7	9.7	9.6

Source: J. Siegel & M. Davidson, *Demographic and Socioeconomic Aspects of Aging in the United States*, U.S. Bureau of the Census, *Current Population Reports*, Series P-23, No. 138, Table 7–8 (1984), p. 97.

For most of the transitions that were examined, the majority of respondents perceived that there were cultural age deadlines, although the deadlines were not necessarily the same for men and women. The average cultural deadlines for the family transitions are presented in Figure 8.1, and the deadlines for the educational and work transitions are presented in Figure 8.2. With respect to family transitions, as can be seen in Figure 8.1, the deadlines for men to marry and complete family formation were significantly later than were the deadlines for women. With respect to educational/work transitions, as can be seen in Figure 8.2, the deadlines for men to enter full-time work and to retire were significantly later than were the deadlines for women.

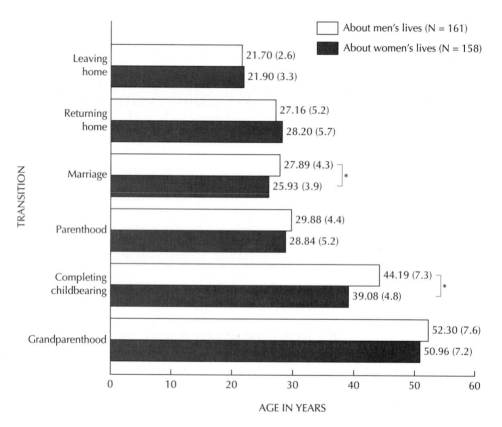

FIGURE 8.1   Average Age Deadline (and standard deviation) for Each Family Transition.

*Note: *p < .001.*

Source: Republished with permission of the Gerontological Society of America, 1030 15th Street, NW, Suite 250, Washington, DC 20005. *What's the Latest? Cultural Age Deadlines for Family Transitions* (Figure), R. A. Settersten & G. O. Hagestad, *The Gerontologist,* Vol. 36. Reproduced by permission of the publisher via Copyright Clearance Center, Inc.

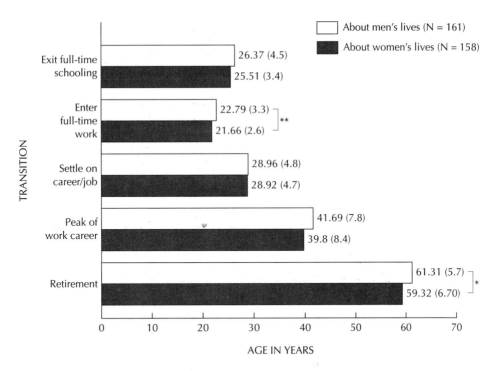

FIGURE 8.2   Average Age Deadline (and standard deviation) for Each Educational and Work Transition.

*Note: *p < .05; **p < .01.*

Source: Republished with permission of the Gerontological Society of America, 1030 15th Street, NW, Suite 250, Washington, DC 20005. *What's the Latest? Cultural Age Deadlines for Family Transitions* (Figure), R. A. Settersen & G. O. Hagestad, *The Gerontologist,* Vol. 36. Reproduced by permission of the publisher via Copyright Clearance Center, Inc.

Because Figures 8.1 and 8.2 present the average cultural age deadline for each transition, it is not possible to determine how much variability there was in respondents' perceptions of deadlines. Although there was some variability in respondents' perceived cultural age deadline for each transition, Settersen and Hagestad (1996a, 1996b) report that for most transitions, deadlines were concentrated fairly narrowly around the average deadline.

When asked to indicate the consequences of missing cultural age deadlines, most respondents reported that there were no consequences whatsoever. When consequences were identified, they tended to center on issues of psychological development (i.e., development of the self and/or personality) and physical development (i.e., health-related concerns).

For both family and educational/work transitions, Settersen and Hagestad found that nonwhites, nonprofessionals, and those with lower levels of education were more likely to perceive that cultural age deadlines existed for the various transitions, and they identified earlier deadlines. These findings suggest that there might actually be multiple cultural age deadlines within a society regarding these transitions. Further, the finding that there are no clear consequences for missing the deadlines suggests that these deadlines function more as what Nydegger (1986) called "personal timetables" that help individuals monitor their progress over their life course rather than prescriptive dictates as to how individuals should live their lives. Thus, although there are age norms associated with various aspects of social life, the extent to which these age norms affect actual behavior is less clear.

Flexibility in cultural age deadlines makes it difficult to assess the importance of being "on time" or "off time" in taking on new roles or disengaging from old ones. Some authors suggest that being off time (early or late) in taking on new roles or exiting old ones may create additional stresses. The source of such stresses may be *internal*, emanating from the individual's internalization of age norms, or *external*, from the reactions of peers and/or friends (Sales 1978). Based on Settersen and Hagestad's work, the former is probably more likely to be the source of stress. In opposition to the hypothesis that being off time is stressful, several authors offer evidence of the benefits of being off time. Nydegger (1973), for example, shows that men who were fathers relatively late in life were more effective and more comfortable in the role than those who entered the role early or on time. One explanation for the greater comfort and effectiveness of these "late" fathers is that the demands of parenthood did not compete with the demands of early career building. Along similar lines, Neugarten and Hagestad (1976) cite interviews carried out by Likert with women returning to school in their middle years. These women saw themselves as having an advantage over younger women because they were taking one thing at a time and had fewer role changes to negotiate.

Old Age and Social Roles

Is old age a social role? Do people have behavioral expectations for those who achieve old age? These are difficult questions to answer. Some have suggested that old age is a formal status or position in society and that expectations for behavior are attached to that position. Others, arguing that the problems of older people in society revolve around the absence of expectations others have for them, have characterized old age as the "roleless role." Clearly, when people become old, when they achieve some chronological or even functional definition of old age, they continue to occupy many of the social roles they occupied during the life course. They continue to be family members, community members, and volunteers, and some continue to be employed. Perhaps a more appropriate strategy, then, is to ask: How does age affect the social roles one occupies?

Rosow (1985) maintains that as people age, they are removed from important roles and statuses in society. Unfortunately, this role loss is typically based on age rather than an individual's ability to perform the given role. For example, as Keith (1982) points out, in many societies, when people can no longer work, they are defined as old, but in the United States, the situation is reversed—when

In what ways can the role of volunteer be a great equalizer?

people are defined as old, they can no longer work. Thus, in the United States, chronological age is used to mark the border between work and retirement. Age is employed as an eligibility criterion for social roles. At the same time, it makes one ineligible to work but eligible to occupy the status of retiree. When social role loss does occur, it results in older adults being excluded from various aspects of social life, which reduces their social value. If lost roles are not replaced with new ones, then social identity is sacrificed.

Chronological age also influences people's ideas about the appropriateness of certain behaviors. Neugarten, for example, argues that perceptions in the United States about behaviors appropriate at given ages have relaxed considerably:

> There is no longer a particular year—or even a particular decade—in which one marries or enters the labor market, or goes to school or has children.... It no longer surprises us to hear of a 22-year old mayor or a 29-year old university president— or a 35-year old grandmother or a retiree of 50. No one blinks at a 70-year old college student or at the 55-year old man who becomes a father for the first time—or who starts a second family. I can remember when the late Justice William Douglas, in old age, married a young wife. The press was shocked and hostile. That hostility would be gone today. People might smirk a little, but the outrage has vanished. (1980, p. 66)

Settersen and Hagestad's (1996a, 1996b) research on cultural age deadlines is consistent with Neugarten's claim that there is flexibility in age norms. Nonetheless, a relaxation of age norms should not be equated with the absence of age norms. Justice Douglas notwithstanding, one need only view the 1971 film *Harold and Maude* to gauge the characters' attitudes, as well as one's own attitudes, about age norms in U.S. society.

In contrast to Rosow's (1985) conceptualization, other social scientists maintain that although older adults might lose some of their formal social roles, informal roles can serve as meaningful substitutes (George 1995). As such, freedom from certain social roles (e.g., employee, parent to dependent child) allows older adults to occupy new social roles and to develop new roles, skills, and social relationships (Lopata 1995).

LIFE STRESS: COPING AND ADAPTATION

Much of the discussion about the social aspects of aging highlights the challenges associated with role transitions and changing behavioral expectations. Consistent with the life-span development and life-course perspectives, the ***stress process framework*** hypothesizes that how an individual deals with challenges (i.e., potential stressors) is influenced by the timing of the challenges over the life-course trajectory, by the individual's unique biography, and by the social and historical contexts in which that person finds himself or herself (Pearlin & Skaff 1995). For a number of years, Pearlin and colleagues (e.g., Pearlin et al. 1981; Pearlin & Schooler 1978; Pearlin & Skaff 1995) used the stress process framework to gain a better understanding of how people deal with and adapt to various types of stressful situations, ranging from major role transitions to more day-to-day challenges. The stress process framework consists of three main components:

1. Stressors/life events (undesirable events) and chronic strains (more enduring problems)
2. Moderators (internal and external resources that are brought to bear on stressors)
3. Outcomes (the direct and interactive effects of stressors and moderators on individuals' levels of well-being)

Stressors/Life Events in the Stress Process

The focus of much stress research throughout the life course is on stressors/life events (e.g., marriage, birth of a child, change in job, serious illness, death of a loved one). Compared to younger adults, older adults experience life events less frequently (Ensel 1991) and are less stressed by these events when they do occur (Murrell, Norris, & Grote 1988). Further, research indicates that normative life events that occur "on time" (e.g., planned retirement, the "empty nest" period) can be anticipated and prepared for. As such, they are less stressful than are unanticipated life events, whether they be "off time" or nonnormative influences (Murrell, Norris, & Grote 1988). In addition, "on time" events are more likely to result in positive rather than negative outcomes (Pearlin & Skaff 1995).

The life events experienced most often by older adults involve losses in roles and/or status (Pearlin & Skaff, 1995). Among the most common are health-related events and the death of a spouse (Ensel 1991). Despite the relatively straightforward definition of stressors, it is important to point out that there is great variability in individuals' appraisals of what is stressful. As such, a role transition or life event that is appraised as stressful by one older adult will not necessarily be similarly appraised by another older adult. Further, because of the variability in individuals' appraisals and the importance of context, role loss can be positive rather than negative. Thus, for example, a normative life event such as the death of a spouse can be viewed positively by a wife who had been unhappily married for years.

An important element of the stress process framework is the notion of **stress proliferation,** or the idea that there is a tendency for one serious stressor to lead to additional stressors. As such, Pearlin and colleagues distinguish primary stressors from secondary stressors. A *primary stressor* is the initial stressor that an older adult experiences, and a *secondary stressor* is any additional stressor that results from the primary stressor. Thus, for example, an older adult who is forced to retire against his or her wishes might experience retirement as a primary stressor, and might experience a host of secondary stressors, including financial difficulty and social withdrawal. Similarly, an older adult might experience a broken hip as a primary stressor; not being able to perform certain activities of daily living (ADLs) would be the secondary stressor.

Chronic Strains in the Stress Process.   In contrast to life events, which are discrete stressors, strains are recurrent, enduring problems (Pearlin & Skaff 1995). Pearlin and Skaff identify three types of **chronic strains:** (1) ambient strains, (2) role strains, and (3) quotidian strains.

Ambient strains refer to problematic interactions that older adults have with their community and neighborhood. As older adults age and become increasingly frail, it becomes increasingly difficult for them to maintain their previous level of functioning. Typical ambient concerns include not feeling safe in one's neighborhood, difficulties with transportation and/or accessing services, and concerns regarding relocation.

Role strains refer to difficulties that arise in the context of institutionalized roles, especially within the family. Pearlin and Skaff (1995) suggest that the high degree of interdependence among family members can result in unrealistic expectations and perceived obligations that lead to conflict among members. In addition, they point out that older adults' financial difficulties and health problems can limit their ability to perform various roles within the family and other social institutions.

Quotidian strains refer to the logistical problems that older adults face on a day-to-day basis as they carry out their everyday activities. With increasing frailty, even the most basic ADL tasks, let alone instrumental activities of daily living (IADLs) tasks, can become very salient for the older adult. Thus, for example, for an extremely arthritic older woman, bathing and dressing can consume a morning rather than be a quick prelude to a full day's work.

Moderators of the Stress Process

Regardless of whether an older adult is experiencing a stressor or a chronic strain, certain conditions regulate the impact that event/experience will have on his or her well-being. As such, these moderators help explain why people respond to stress differently, and why the same event/experience can affect two people differently (Cohen & Edwards 1989). The major internal and external resources that older adults bring to bear on stressors and strains are coping, social support, and their sense of mastery (Pearlin & Skaff 1995).

Coping refers to behavioral strategies that are designed to modify the problem or situation that is causing the stress (i.e., *problem-focused coping*) and cognitive/emotional strategies that are designed to manage the negative emotions that result from the stress (i.e., *emotion-focused coping*) (Lazarus & Folkman, 1984). Similarly, Pearlin and Schooler (1978) identify three broad categories of coping: (1) responses that modify situations (which corresponds to problem-focused coping), (2) responses that are used to reappraise the meaning of problems, and (3) responses that help individuals manage tension. The latter two categories of coping are subsumed under emotion-focused coping.

Not all problem-focused and emotion-focused coping strategies are necessarily adaptive. For example, most would agree that an older man who attempts to eliminate crime in his neighborhood by shooting alleged gang members is not engaging in adaptive problem-focused coping. An older adult who copes with the loss of a spouse by drinking to excess is engaging in a nonadaptive, albeit emotion-focused coping strategy. Even when the coping strategies that are engaged in are adaptive, there is evidence to suggest that the efficacy of a particular coping strategy depends, in part, on the type of stressor with which a person is attempting to cope. Problem-focused strategies appear to be most effective when the particular stressor is modifiable. In contrast, emotion-focused coping is most effective when used with stressors that lie outside of the individual's control (Forsythe & Compas 1987; Vitaliano et al. 1990). Given that many of the stressors and strains that confront older adults (e.g., retirement, death of a spouse, relocation to a retirement community, frailty) do not lend themself to modification (Pearlin & Skaff 1995), perhaps it is not surprising that Chiriboga (1992) finds that older adults are more likely to use emotion-focused coping strategies when dealing with these events.

Social support consists of instrumental and/or emotional assistance that is provided by family members and/or friends, and represents a second resource that older adults can mobilize to help moderate the negative consequences of stressors and strains (Pearlin & Skaff 1995). Hansson and Carpenter (1994) suggest that social support can be especially helpful to older adults who are dealing with stressors/strains that are unmodifiable and/or ongoing. But not all support is equally helpful.

In summarizing the literature on social support as a moderator of stressors/strains, Pearlin and Skaff (1995) conclude that the efficacy of social support depends on who is providing the support and whether the type of support is appropriate for the particular stressor/strain. They present results from some research that suggests that social support from someone who has experienced the particular stressor/strain is perceived as particularly helpful. In addition, instrumental and emotional support might differentially affect various indicators of outcomes, or adaptation.

Mastery, the third moderator in Pearlin and Skaff's (1995) stress process framework, refers to the extent to which people believe that they can control what happens to them in the world. Mastery has been found to buffer people from the negative consequences of stressors/strains (Cohen & Edwards 1989). Pearlin and Skaff offer several hypotheses as to why mastery can serve as a buffer to stressors/strains. Among these hypotheses are that having a strong sense of mastery prevents one from feeling like a victim. A second hypothesis identified by Pearlin and Skaff is that having a strong sense of mastery enables people to activate their own coping efforts and to engage the social support of others (Brandstaedter & Baltes-Goetz 1990).

Outcomes of the Stress Process

The stress process framework examines the impact of stressors/strains and moderators on outcomes. The outcomes that are most frequently examined among older adults include life satisfaction, morale, depression, and functional abilities (Pearlin & Skaff, 1995). It is important to underscore that, despite experiencing stressors and/or strains, most older adults maintain positive well-being and functioning. But the relationships among stressors/strains, moderators, and different indices of well-being are complex.

For example, Pearlin and colleagues (1995) examined the relationship between social support and various indices of well-being among family members who were experiencing the stress of caring for a relative with dementia. They found that instrumental support from trained professionals was associated with one index of role overload, that instrumental support from family and friends was associated with lower levels of a different index of role overload, and that emotional support helped to moderate the effects of depression among caregivers.

A hallmark of the stress process framework lies in the notion of *process.* Rather than hypothesizing static associations among stressors/strains, moderators, and outcomes, the three components of the framework are conceptualized as evolving, interactive phenomena. As such, over time, prolonged stress might result in changes in moderators, such as individuals' coping strategies and/or the amount and type of social support that they receive from family and friends (Aldwin 1992). Similarly, moderators such as mastery are not only resources that can lead to better outcomes but they may also increase as a function of well-being (Ryff 1989; Skaff, Pearlin, & Mullan 1996).

Continuing with the example of the family member who is caring for a relative with dementia, prolonged caregiving experience might result in the caregiver changing his or her coping strategy from trying to deny the relative's disease to learning how to structure the environment so that confusion is minimized. Similarly, over time, family members and friends might be less (or more) willing to spend time with the individual so that the caregiver can get some much needed respite from his or her caregiving responsibilities. Respite may improve the caregiver's morale, which in turn enhances his or her sense of mastery.

Models of Proactive Aging

Researchers from the fields of sociology and psychology are exploring models of proactive aging that supplement the more traditional stress process framework (Baltes & Baltes 1990; Kahana & Kahana 1996; Lawton 1989). That is, because the stress process framework examines how individuals manage and adapt to undesirable events and more enduring problems (i.e., stressors and strains), one might assume that older adults passively wait until they are required to respond to an environmental circumstance. A more accurate conceptualization is that older adults both respond to environmental demands and are also proactive in seeking resources and determining their environment (Lawton, 1989). As defined by Kahana and Kahana (1996), *proactive aging* refers to preventive and corrective adaptations that older adults make as they confront (or anticipate confronting) normative stresses of aging. The Kahanas maintain that even frail older adults can successfully respond to stress (or potential stress) by modifying their own activities or their environment. In their model, stressors/strains serve as the stimuli that activate the adaptation process.

The Kahanas and their colleagues (Kahana 1992; Kahana et al. 1997) are longitudinally investigating the concept of proactive aging among 1,000 older adults who migrated from the Midwest to three Florida retirement communities in their postretirement years. The purpose of the research is to gain a better understanding of the full range of adaptation to old age. At the time of the initial data collection in 1990, participants had to be at least 72 years old, live in Florida at least nine months out of the year, and be in relatively good health. Participants are interviewed every other year. Based on these interviews, the researchers distinguish preventive from corrective adaptations. *Proactive preventive adaptations* are specific behaviors that, when routinely engaged in, delay the onset of physical frailty and enhance older adults' social resources before a stressor/strain arises. The researchers have identified three constellations of proactive preventive adaptations:

1. Health promotion (e.g., regular exercise, healthy diet)
2. Planning for the future (e.g., exploring social and health care services, financial planning)
3. Helping others (e.g., helping others in need, social participation)

In contrast, *proactive corrective adaptations* are behaviors that are used to manage specific stressful situations or life events. The researchers have identified three constellations of proactive corrective adaptations, some of which are discussed in other sections of this chapter and some of which are moderators that are discussed in the stress process framework:

1. Marshalling support (i.e., social support can buffer the negative effects of a particular stressor)
2. Role substitution (i.e., substituting a new role for a lost role can lessen the loss of the former role)
3. Environmental modifications (i.e., changing a particular environmental problem through architectural redesign, the use of prosthetics, modifying one's activities, or leaving the environment)

In order to test the generalizability of their model of proactive aging to other groups of older adults, the Kahanas have extended their research to include comparisons of African American and white elderly living in urban environments (Kahana 1999). In general, results indicate that there are few differences between the two groups with respect to proactive preventive adaptations. When differences were observed, African Americans demonstrated greater proactive adaptations. For example, comparable percentages of African Americans and whites exercised regularly (although there were differences in the specific types of exercises engaged in). However, African Americans were less likely to drink alcoholic beverages, more likely to plan for the future, and more likely to provide support to family and friends in serious times of need.

Taken together, the stress process framework and concept of proactive aging provide models that can be applied to understand more clearly the processes whereby older adults anticipate, confront, deal with, and adapt to the biological, psychological, and social changes that may accompany aging. As ambitious as this sounds, such efforts are necessary if the goal is to understand the richness of development that is captured in the life-span and life-course perspectives.

SUMMARY

Three major perspectives are used to explain how people develop and change over time: life stage, life span, and life course. Each of the perspectives assumes that development is a process that occurs from the "cradle to the grave." However, these perspectives differ along a variety of dimensions.

The life-stage perspective of human development contends that development proceeds through a set pattern of sequential stages that most individuals experience. The life-span perspective emphasizes the interaction of individual and social characteristics in explanations of behavioral change. Finally, the life-course perspective focuses on the ways in which social norms and definitions influence the pattern or sequence of role changes and role transitions in the life course.

All societies divide the lifetime into different periods. Typically, age criteria are used to place people into positions and roles. How many periods or age-grades there are in a society may depend on its level of modernization.

Human behavior is primarily learned through a process of socialization. This lifelong process involves transmitting skills and knowledge needed to perform social roles across the life course. The concept of *social role* describes the expectations society has for individuals who occupy a given social position or status. Social roles are a significant component of the social structure. They allow people to anticipate the behavior of others and to respond or pattern their own actions accordingly. The individual acquisition of social roles is a key element in the socialization process.

In most societies, social role transitions are ordered along a timetable. The timing of these transitions changes as a function of cohort or historical effects. Role transitions can be stressful, although stresses may be reduced by anticipatory socialization and rites of passage. The most distinctive characteristics of rites of passage for older people in the United States is in their absence or incompleteness.

Although there is evidence of cultural age deadlines concerning family and educational/work transitions in society, there are no clear consequences associated with not conforming to these deadlines. As such, these deadlines serve more as personal timetables against which people monitor their development than as directives for behavior.

Is old age a social role in the United States? Some disagreement seems to exist on this point. Age is employed as a criterion for certain social roles, including employment and retirement. Age also influences the ideas people have about the appropriateness of certain behaviors. Much of the discussion about the social aspects of aging highlights the challenges associated with role transitions and changing behavioral expectations. The stress process framework hypothesizes that how an individual deals with stressors is influenced by the timing of the events/experiences over the life course trajectory, by the individual's unique biography, and by the social and historical contexts in which that person finds himself or herself. The stress process framework consists of three main components: (1) stressors/life events and chronic strains, (2) moderators (i.e., coping, social support, mastery), and (3) outcomes.

Researchers who employ the stress process framework, as well as proactive models of aging, have documented the adaptive capabilities of older adults. *Proactive aging* refers to preventive and corrective adaptations that older adults make as they confront (or anticipate confronting) normative stresses of aging. Taken together, the stress process framework and concept of proactive aging provide models that can be applied to better understand the processes whereby older adults anticipate, confront, deal with, and adapt to the biological, psychological, and social changes that may accompany aging.

STUDY QUESTIONS

1. What are the major age-normative, history-normative, and nonnormative influences that you have experienced? That your parents and grandparents have experienced?

2. What are the major assumptions of the three perspectives of human development (i.e., life stage, life span, life course), and which do you think offers the richest conceptualization of development? Why?

3. How do historical and cultural variations in the sequencing of the life course lend support to the life-course conceptualization of development?

4. What social roles are in operation in your extended family?

5. Are status changes in U.S. society made easier by anticipatory socialization and rites of passage? Explain. What does Keith argue is the most distinctive characteristic of rites of passage for old people in the United States. Why?

6. Provide several examples to show that the timing of role transitions is not static in the United States. How do such timing changes make it more difficult to assess the importance of being "on time" or "off time" in assuming new roles or exiting old ones?

7. Is old age a social role? Explain. How does age affect the social roles people occupy?

8. Identify a normative, primary stressor that confronts older adults and the secondary stressors that typically result from that primary stressor.

9. Identify a stressor/role strain typically experienced by older adults, and discuss the specific moderators that an older adult might use to facilitate adaptation to that stressor/strain.

REFERENCES

Aldwin, C. M. (1992). Aging, coping, and efficacy: Theoretical framework for examining coping in life-span developmental context. In M. L. Wykle, E. Kahana, & J. Kowal (Eds.), *Stress and health among the elderly* (pp. 96–113). New York: Springer.

Baltes, P. B. (1979). Life-span developmental psychology: Some converging observations on history and theory. In P. B. Baltes and O. G. Grim (Eds.), *Life-span development and behavior* (Vol. 2, pp. 255–279). New York: Academic.

Baltes, P. B. (1987). Theoretical propositions of life-span developmental psychology: On the dynamics between growth and decline. *Developmental Psychology, 23*, 611–626.

Baltes, P. B., & Baltes, M. M. (1990). Psychological perspectives on successful aging: The model of selective optimization with compensation. In P. B. Baltes & M. M. Baltes (Eds.), *Successful aging: Perspectives from the behavioral sciences* (pp. 1–34). New York: Cambridge University Press.

Baltes, P. B., & Goulet, L. R. (1970). Status and issues of a life-span developmental psychology. In L. R. Goulet & P. B. Baltes (Eds.), *Life-span developmental psychology.* New York: Academic.

Baltes, P. B., & Graf, P. (1996). Psychological aspects of aging: Facts and frontiers. In D. Magnusson (Ed.), *The lifespan development of individuals: Behavioral, neurobiological, and psychosocial perspectives* (pp. 427–460). New York: Cambridge University Press.

Becker, H., Greer, B., Hughes, E. C., & Strauss, A. (1961). *Boys in white: Student culture in medical school.* Chicago: University of Chicago Press.

Berger, P. L., & Luckman, T. (1990). *The social construction of reality: A treatise in the sociology of knowledge.* New York: Anchor Books.

Brandstaedter, J., & Baltes-Goetz, B. (1990). Personal control over development and quality of life perspectives in adulthood. In P. B. Baltes & M. M. Baltes (Eds.), *Successful aging: Perspectives from the behavioral sciences* (pp. 197–224). Cambridge: Cambridge University Press.

Brim, O. G. (1968). Adult socialization. In J. A. Clausen (Ed.), *Socialization and society.* Boston: Little, Brown.

Bush, D. M., & Simmons, R. G. (1981). Socialization processes over the life course. In M. Rosenberg & R. H. Turner (Eds.), *Social psychology: Sociological perspectives.* New York: Basic Books.

Chiriboga, D. A. (1992). Paradise lost: Stress in the modern age. In M. L. Wykle, E. Kahana, & J. Kowal (Eds.), *Stress and health among the elderly* (pp. 35–71). New York: Springer.

Clausen, J. A. (1986). *The life course: A sociological perspective.* Englewood Cliffs, NJ: Prentice-Hall.

Cohen, S., & Edwards, J. R. (1989). Personality characteristics as moderators of the relationship between stress and disorder. In R. W. J. Neu-feld (Eds.), *Advances in the investigation of psychological stress* (pp. 235–283). New York: Wiley.

Cowgill, D. O. (1986). *Aging around the world.* Belmont, CA: Wadsworth.

Elder, G. H., Jr. (1974). *Children of the great depression.* Chicago: University of Chicago Press.

Elder, G. H., Jr. (1998). The life course as developmental theory. *Child Development, 69,* 1–12.

Elder, G. H., Jr., Shanahan, M. J., & Clipp, E. C. (1994). When war comes to men's lives: Life-course patterns in family, work, and health. *Psychology & Aging, 9,* 5–16.

Ensel, W. M. (1991). "Important" life events and depression among older adults. *Journal of Aging and Health, 3,* 546–566.

Foner, A. (1996). Age norms and the structure of consciousness: Some final comments. *The Gerontologist, 36,* 221.

Foner, A., & Kertzer, D. (1978). Transitions over the life course. *American Journal of Sociology, 83,* 1081–1104.

Forsythe, C. J., & Compas, B. E. (1987). Interaction of cognitive appraisals of stressful events and coping: Testing the goodness of fit hypothesis. *Cognitive Therapy and Research, 11,* 473–485.

Fox, R. C. (1957). Training for uncertainty. In R. K. Merton, G. Reader, & P. L. Kendall (Eds.), *The student-physician.* Cambridge, MA: Harvard University Press.

George, L. K. (1995). Socialization. In G. L. Maddox (Ed.), *The encyclopedia of aging* (2nd ed., pp. 870–872). New York: Springer.

Hagestad, G. D., & Neugarten, B. L. (1985). Age and the life course. In R. H. Binstock & E. Shanas (Eds.), *Handbook of aging and the social science* (2nd ed., pp. 35–61). New York: Van Nostrand Reinhold.

Hansson, R. O., & Carpenter, B. N. (1994). *Relationships in old age: Coping with the challenge of transition.* New York: Guilford.

Hareven, T. K. (1978). *Transitions: The family and the life course in historical perspective.* New York: Academic.

Hareven, T. K. (1982). *Family time and industrial time.* New York: Cambridge University Press.

Hareven, T. K. (1996). Life course. In J. E. Birren (Ed.), *Encyclopedia of gerontology: Age, ageing, and the aged* (Vol. 2, pp. 31–40). San Diego: Academic.

Hess, B., Markson, E., & Stein, P. (1988). *Sociology* (3rd ed.). New York: Macmillan.

Hoyer, W. J., & Rybash, J. M. (1996). Life span theory. In J. E. Birren (Ed.), *Encyclopedia of gerontology: Age, ageing, and the aged* (Vol. 2, pp. 65–71). San Diego: Academic.

Ikels, C., Keith, J., Dickerson-Putnam, J., Draper, P., Fry, C., Glascock, A., & Harpending, H. (1992). Perceptions of the adult life course: Across-cultural analysis. *Ageing and Society, 12,* 49–84.

Kahana, B., Kahana, E., Namazi, K., Kercher, K., & Stange, K. (1997). The role of pain the the the cascade from chronic illness to social disability and psychological distress in late life. In J. Lomaranz & D. Mostofsky (Eds.), *Pain in the elderly* (pp. 185–206). New York: Plenum.

Kahana, E. (1992). Stress research and aging: Complexities, ambiguities, paradoxes, and promise. In M. L. Wykle, E. Kahana, & J. Kowal (Eds.), *Stress and health among the elderly* (pp. 239–256). New York: Springer.

Kahana, E., & Kahana, B. (1996). Conceptual and empirical advances in understanding aging well through adaptation. In V. L. Bengtson (Ed.), *Adulthood and aging: Research on continuities and discontinuities* (pp. 19–40). New York: Springer.

Kahana, E., Kercher, K., Kahana, B., King, C., Lovegreen, L., & Chirayath, H. (1999). Evaluating a model of successful aging for urban African-American and White elderly. In M. Wykle (Ed.), *Serving minority elders in the 21st century.* New York: Springer.

Kastenbaum, R. (1995). Life course. In G. L. Maddox (Ed.), *The encyclopedia of aging* (2nd ed., pp. 553–556). New York: Springer.

Keith, J. (1982). *Old people as people: Social and cultural influences on aging and old age.* Boston: Little, Brown.

Lawton, M. P. (1989). Environmental proactivity and affect in older people. In S. Spacapan & S. Oskamp (Eds.), *The social psychology of aging* (pp. 135–163). Newbury Park, CA: Sage.

Lazarus, R. S., & Folkman, S. (1984). *Stress, appraisal, and coping.* New York: Springer.

Levinson, D. J., Darro, C. M., Klein, E. B., Levinson, M. H., & McKee, B. (1974). The psychosocial development of men in early adulthood and the mid-life transition. In D. F. Ricks, A. Thomas, & M. Roth (Eds.), *Life history research in psychotherapy.* Minneapolis: University of Minnesota Press.

Linton, R. (1942). Age and sex categories. *American Sociological Review, 7,* 589–603.

Lopata, H. Z. (1995). Social roles. In G. L. Maddox (Ed.), *The encyclopedia of aging* (2nd ed., pp. 874–876). New York: Springer.

Murrell, S. A., Norris, F. H., & Grote, C. (1988). Life events in older adults. In L. H. Cohen (Ed.), *Life events and psychological functioning: Theoretical and methodological issues* (pp. 96–122). Newbury Park, CA: Sage.

Neugarten, B. (1980, April). Acting one's age: New rules for the old. *Psychology Today* , pp. 66–74, 77–80.

Neugarten, B., & Hagestad, G. (1976). Age and the life course. In R. H. Binstock & E. Shanas (Eds.), *Handbook of aging and the social sciences.* New York: Van Nostrand Reinhold.

Nydegger, C. (1973, October). *Late and early fathers.* Paper presented at the annual meeting of the Gerontological Society of America, Miami Beach.

Nydegger, C. N. (1986). Age and life-course transitions. In C. L. Fry & J. Keith (Eds.), *New methods for old research: Strategies for studying diversity* (pp. 131–161). South Hadley, MA: Bergin and Garvey.

Pearlin, L. I., Aneshensel, C. S., Mullan, J. T., & Whitlatch, C. J. (1995). Caregiving and its social support. In R. H. Binstock & L. K. George (Eds.), *Handbook on aging and the social sciences* (4th ed., pp. 283–302). San Diego: Academic Press.

Pearlin, L. I., Lieberman, M. A., Menaghan, E. G., & Mullan, J. T. (1981). The stress process. *Journal of Health and Social Behavior, 22,* 337–356.

Pearlin, L. I., & Schooler, C. (1978). The structure of coping. *Journal of Health and Social Behavior, 19,* 2–21.

Pearlin, L. I., & Skaff, M. M. (1995). Stress and adaptation in late life. In M. Gatz (Ed.), *Emerging issues in mental health and aging* (pp. 97–123). Washington, DC: American Psychological Association.

Riley, M. W., Foner, A., & Waring, J. (1988). Sociology of age. In N. J. Smelser (Ed.), *Handbook of sociology* (pp. 243–290). Newbury Park, CA: Sage.

Rosow, I. (1985). Status and role change through the life cycle. In R. H. Binstock & E. Shanas (Eds.), *Handbook of aging and the social sciences* (2nd ed., pp. 62–93). New York: Van Nostrand Reinhold.

Ryff, C. D. (1989). Happiness is everything, or is it? Explorations on the meaning of psychological well-being. *Journal of Personality and Social Psychology, 57,* 1069–1081.

Sales, E. (1978). Women's adult development. In I. H. Frieze, J. E. Parsons, P. B. Johnson, D. N. Ruble, & G. L. Zellman (Eds.), *Women and sex-roles: A social psychological perspective.* New York: Norton.

Settersten, R. A., Jr., & Hagestad, G. O. (1996a). What's the latest? Cultural age deadlines for family transitions. *The Gerontologist, 36,* 178–188.

Settersen, R. A., Jr., & Hagestad, G. O. (1996b). What's the latest? II. Cultural age deadlines for educational and work transitions. *The Gerontologist, 36,* 602–613.

Siegel, J., & Davidson, M. (1984). *Demographic and socioeconomic aspects of aging in the United States.* Current Population Reports, Special Studies Series P-23, No. 138. Washington, DC: U.S. Department of Commerce, Bureau of the Census.

Skaff, M. M., Pearlin, L. I., & Mullan, J. T. (1996). Transition in the caregiving career: Effects on sense of mastery. *Psychology and Aging, 11,* 247–257.

Vitaliano, P. P., DeWolfe, D. J., Maiuro, R. D., Russo, J., & Katon, W. (1990). Appraised changeability of a stressor as a modifier of the relationships between coping and depression: A test of the hypothesis of it. *Journal of Personality and Social Psychology, 59,* 582–592.

Zerubavel, E. (1981). *Hidden rhythms: Schedules and calendars in social life.* Chicago: University of Chicago Press.

CHAPTER NINE

SOCIOLOGICAL THEORIES OF AGING

The field of social gerontology has been criticized for its emphasis on practical issues and problems confronting the elderly. Many scholars believe that this concern, admirable as it may be, has grown at the expense of the development of statements of a theoretical orientation. As a result, these scholar-critics contend, no current comprehensive theoretical framework exists within which to address the question: What happens to human beings socially as they grow old?

This is not to say, however, that there have been no attempts to answer this important question. This chapter presents some answers—theoretical statements that have been placed in two broad categories: (1) theories that attempt to conceptualize the adjustment of individuals to their own aging and (2) theories that deal with the relationship between a society's social system and its older members. Some of these approaches show considerable overlap and often differ only in emphasis.

Readers may have difficulty identifying with the overconcern for theory expressed by gerontologists, perhaps because of a misunderstanding of theory. Most students think of theory as boring and not down to earth. But in fact, just the opposite is true. Theory is the way people accumulate knowledge and make sense of the world. It allows people to see more clearly and logically what they sometimes perceive only vaguely. Strictly speaking, theory differs from vague perception in that it is presented in the form of a generalized statement (or set of systematically organized statements) that can be tested through empirical research.

Theories are created to be rejected. A theory that, in principle, cannot be rejected is of little use because its acceptance must be on faith. However, a theory that is rejected actually advances the state of the art by reducing the number of possible answers by one. Those theories that survive the rejection process provide, for the present at least, the best answer to a question. In this regard, a theory is never really proven; the next empirical test might always disprove it.

Theorizing in social gerontology has a long way to go. In part, this is the case because theory has become "devalued" in gerontology. For many researchers, the diverse ways in which people experience aging makes pursuit of universal or general theories of aging seem without merit. Also, students and professionals are attracted to gerontology precisely because it provides an opportunity to help people in need, not because it provides an opportunity to develop social theory! In addition, as Bengtson, Rice, and Johnson (1999) point out, the postmodernist critique of science as truth as well as the resistance to interdisciplinary investigation in gerontology have also contributed to the devaluing of theory development in gerontology.

Still, Bengtson, Rice, and Johnson (1999) offer four pragmatic justifications for the usefulness of theory in gerontology:

1. *Integration of knowledge:* A good theory summarizes findings from different empirical studies and describes linkages among key constructs.
2. *Explanation of knowledge:* A useful theory describes in a logically sound way how and why empirically observed phenomena are related.
3. *Predictions about what is not yet known or observed:* Research based on theory can lead to new discoveries based on principles proposed in earlier theories.
4. *Interventions to improve human conditions:* Theory is valuable when applied to existing knowledge in order to solve problems or alleviate human suffering. Theory can inform public policy.

Some of the theories examined in this chapter are not theories in the strictest sense. Few, for example, are presented in the form of a set of systematically organized statements. Some are more descriptive than explanatory and might more accurately be referred to as orientations or perspectives rather than theories. None has been sufficiently tested so as to be completely rejected. Each theory suggests some important factor or set of factors that may be related to aging. In doing so, the theories act as continuing guides to further research. The continuation of such research increases the potential for theory building in social gerontology.

AGING AND THE INDIVIDUAL

Role Theory

The earliest attempt in social gerontology to understand the adjustment of the aged individual was placed within a ***role-theory*** framework (Cottrell 1942). Generally speaking, research done within this framework was practically oriented. Researchers were concerned with the problems of adjustment due to role changes in later life. The changes individuals undergo in the aging process fall into two categories: (1) the relinquishment of social relationships and roles typical of adulthood and (2) their replacement by retirement and the acceptance of social relationships typical of the later years, such as dependency on offspring (Cavan et al. 1949). The special dilemma of role change for older people is that they are more likely to lose roles than to acquire new ones. Further, these losses, such as the loss of the worker role with retirement, are largely irreversible and may lead to erosion of social identity and decline in self-esteem (Rosow 1985).

In an example of empirical research carried out within the role-theory framework, Phillips (1957) shows the relationship between role loss and adjustment to old age. In his study of almost 1,000 individuals age 60 and over, he found significantly more maladjustment to old age in the retired when compared with the employed, in the widowed when compared with the married, and in people over age 70 when compared with those age 60 to 69. Maladjustment is measured by self-reports on the amount of time spent daydreaming about the past, thinking about death, and being absentminded.

Another important variable used by Phillips is labeled *identification as old.* This item, a measure of self-image, simply asks, "How do you think of yourself as far as age goes—middle-aged, elderly, old?" Individuals who perceive themselves as elderly or old are significantly more maladjusted than are those who perceive themselves as middle-aged. In addition, age identification appears to reverse the relationship between role loss and maladjustment. Thus, for example, those who are employed but identify themselves as old are more likely to be maladjusted than are those who are retired but identify with middle age. The means by which some elderly individuals, even those who have suffered role loss, identify with middle age are still open to empirical investigation.

Researchers have looked at the relationship between sex-role differentiation and life satisfaction in old age. Sex-role differentiation has traditionally been quite strong in U.S. society. Men are expected to be aggressive and independent, whereas women are expected to be passive-dependent and nurturant. Sinnott (1977), after reviewing many studies on middle and old age, came to the conclusion that survival and satisfaction in old age often accompany flexibility in sex roles.

Reichard, Livson, and Peterson (1962) studied how 87 men between the ages of 55 and 84 adjusted to aging. The best adjusted exhibited personalities *not* dominated by male traits. The researchers concluded that growing old may make it possible for a man to integrate formerly unacceptable feminine traits (e.g., nurturance or passivity) into his personality. Their data show that those best able to make the integration are rewarded by a more successful old age. Similarly, Neugarten, Crotty, and Tobin (1964) found older men and women who were the most satisfied with life to be those who had best achieved an integration of traits culturally defined as masculine with traits culturally defined as feminine.

While studying the structure of self-concept, Monge (1975) found certain continuities as well as discontinuities across the life cycle. Over 4,000 male and female subjects, age 9 to 89 and recruited from diverse sources, rated the concept "My Characteristic Self" on 21 polar adjective pairs (e.g., leader/follower or strong/weak). Four factors emerged for all age groups: (1) achievement/leadership, (2) congeniality/sociability, (3) adjustment (the self-perception of health and energy), and (4) masculinity/femininity. Figure 9.1 shows the mean component scores for these four factors by age group and sex. Monge's results suggest that as men and women become older, they become more *androgynous*—that is, more alike and perhaps more accepting of traits of the opposite sex in themselves.

For example, as Figure 9.1b depicts, congeniality/sociability is higher at all points in the life span for women than for men, although both show a decrease at midlife and a subsequent increase in later adulthood. Importantly, men and women are most alike in terms of mean scores on this factor (and all others) in old age. The increase in late adulthood, steeper in men, may reflect the lifting of

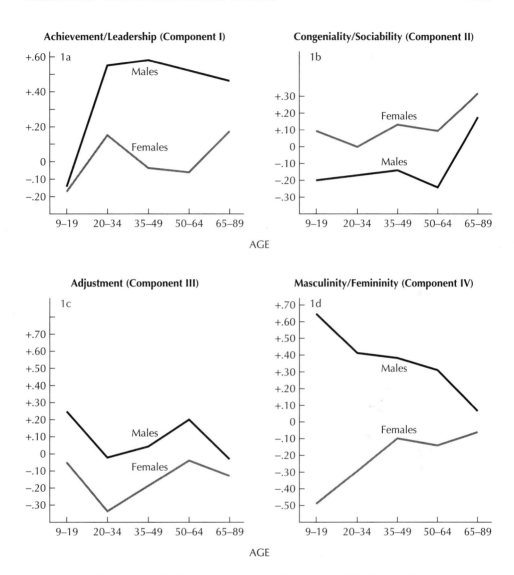

FIGURE 9.1   Factors of Self-Concept across the Adult Life Span: Mean Component Scores on Four Components by Age Group and Sex

Source: R. H. Monge, "Structure of the Self-Concept from Adolescence through Old Age," *Experimental Aging Research, 1* (2) (1975): 281–291. Copyright © Beech Hill Publishing Company (formerly EAR, Inc.). Reproduced by permission of the publisher via Copyright Clearance Center, Inc.

certain burdens of concern in the area of work responsibilities, which may allow more time for social interaction.

Clearly, more research on sex-role change across the life course needs to be carried out. In particular, more knowledge is needed about the blurring of sex roles in old age. Some of the aforementioned research suggests that certain aspects of sex-role identification may be less integral to adult personality in later life than in early adulthood.

Activity Theory

One theory of aging has appeared implicitly in much gerontological research and, in the tradition of role theory, continues to characterize aging as an individual problem. This theory, referred to here as ***activity theory*** but often called the *implicit theory of aging,* states that aging brings individual "unadjustment." Through activity, however, readjustment and life satisfaction can be achieved. The theory holds that, although aging individuals face inevitable changes related to physiology, anatomy, and health status, their psychological and social needs remain essentially the same. Those who adopt this view recognize that the social world may withdraw from older people, making it more difficult for them to fulfill these needs. Yet, the person who ages optimally is the one who stays active and manages to resist the withdrawal of the social world. According to activity theory, the individual who is able to maintain the activities of the middle years for as long as possible will be well adjusted and satisfied with life in the later years. This person will find an avocation to substitute for work and will replace the old friends and loved ones who have died with new ones.

Lemon, Bengtson, and Peterson (1972) attempted a formal and explicit test of the activity theory. Using a sample of 411 potential in-movers to a southern California retirement community, and distinguishing among informal activity (with friends, relatives, and neighbors), formal activity (participation in voluntary organizations), and solitary activity (maintenance of household), they found that only social activity with friends was significantly related to life satisfaction. Knapp's (1977) study of 51 elderly people residing in the south of England lends support to these findings. Within this sample, there was a strong positive relationship between "the number of hours spent in a typical week with friends and relatives (informal activity)" and life satisfaction. In addition, several measures of formal activity were also found to be strongly related to life satisfaction.

Longino and Kart (1982) report on the results of a formal replication of the work on activity theory carried out by Lemon and colleagues. Using probability samples from three distinct types of retirement communities (N = 1,209), they found support for the positive contribution made by informal activity to the life satisfaction of respondents. Interestingly, they observed formal activity to have a *negative* effect on life satisfaction. Longino and Kart speculate that participation in formal activities may damage self-concept and lower morale through the development of status systems that tend to emerge in formal activity settings. Invidious comparisons that can lead to dissatisfaction are less likely to operate in primary relationships with family and friends than in secondary ones limited to formal organizational settings.

Activity theory is often presented in juxtaposition with the disengagement theory of aging (which will be discussed later). Such a presentation leads to comparison of the theories and often causes students to overlook problems that may be internal to the theory. There are several theoretical problems inherent in the activity approach that deserve mention here.

First, the activity perspective assumes that individuals have a great deal of control over their social situations. It assumes that people have the capacity to construct—or, more appropriately, reconstruct—their lives by substituting new roles and activities for lost ones. Clearly, this may be the case for the upper-middle-class individual whose locus of control has always been internal and whose social and economic resources allow for such reconstruction. But the retired individual who suffers a dramatic decline in income, or the widow who faces an equally dramatic decline in her social relationships, may find it difficult, even with sufficient motivation, to substitute an avocation for work or to replace old friends and loved ones who have died. In this regard, the theory may be more about the relationships among socioeconomic status, life-style, health, and psychological well-being than about the relationship between activity and life satisfaction.

Second, the activity perspective emphasizes the stability of psychological and social needs through the adult phases of the life cycle. This makes considerable sense if one thinks about these needs developing in a stable social and physical environment. But what about the person whose environment changes at a particular age—for example, when he or she retires, is deprived of status, or is widowed? Might this individual's social and psychological needs change in the face of the substantial change in environment? Many would answer yes. A no answer smacks of a biological and/or psychological determinism, which many social scientists (including gerontologists) find unacceptable. And what of the fate of older people who cannot maintain the standards of middle age or cannot adjust to substantial changes in the environment? Activity theory offers little about what happens to these people.

Third, an important problem in activity theory is the expectation that activities *of any kind* can substitute for lost involvement in work, marriage, and parenting. In his study of the Parents Without Partners (PWP) organization, Weiss (1969) dubbed this the ***fund of sociability hypothesis.*** According to this idea, people require a certain *quantity* of interaction with others and may achieve this in a variety of ways—through one or two intense relationships or perhaps through a larger number of lesser relationships. Weiss was not able to substantiate this hypothesis. He found that the sociability that accrued to a person through participation in the PWP organization did not necessarily compensate for the marital loss. This suggests that substitutability for different losses may be governed by different considerations. Filling a particular role may not do. Fulfillment of those particular needs may be accomplished only through specific role substitution or perhaps through the alteration of a person's entire configuration of roles. Whichever is the case, the emphasis is on the quality rather than the quantity of such interaction.

Finally, although the activity theory remains an extensively used framework for thinking about the psychological well-being of older adults, empirical research has yielded inconsistent findings. In addition, there have been contradictions in the literature with regard to how researchers conceptualize and measure activity (Achenbaum & Bengtson 1994). What one critic of activity theory offered almost four decades ago may still be applicable today:

> The persistent research interest in activity as a correlate of morale among the elderly has not produced consensus about the referents of these concepts, their appropriate measurements, or a theoretical framework to account adequately for their reported association. (Maddox 1963, p. 196)

Disengagement Theory

Disengagement theory, put forth by Cumming and Henry (1961), stands in contrast to role theory and activity theory. In some respects, ***disengagement theory*** represents a transformation or new way of thinking about aging that shifted the focus away from the individual to the social system as the source of explanation (Lynott & Lynott 1996). While representing aging as an inevitable process of individual decline, Cumming and Henry asked, "How does this affect the needs of social system functioning?" Using data based on 275 respondents ranging in age from 50 to 90, all of whom resided in Kansas City and were physically and financially self-sufficient, these authors characterized the decreasing social interaction they observed to come with old age as a *mutual withdrawal* between the aging individual and others in the social system to which he or she belongs. Under the terms of the disengagement theory, the aging individual accepts—perhaps even desires— the decrease in interaction. In addition, proponents of this theory argue that gradual disengagement is functional for society, which would otherwise be faced with disruption by the sudden withdrawal of its members. Cumming (1963) states:

> The disengagement theory postulates that society withdraws from the aging person to the same extent as the person withdraws from society. This is, of course, just another way of saying that the process is normatively governed and in a sense agreed upon by all concerned.

In its original form, disengagement theory was concerned with the modal case in the United States. Important disengagements included the departure of children from families as well as retirement for men or widowhood for women. It was not concerned with nonmodal cases—early widowhood or late retirement— nor was it concerned with the special effects of poverty or illness. In 1963, Elaine Cumming, one of the originators of disengagement theory, published a paper in which she discussed the relationship between personality (or what she called *temperament*) and disengagement. She wrote that all people have a style of adaptation to the environment and went on to identify two different modes of interacting with the environment: the impinging mode and the selecting mode. The *impinger* is an activist, willing to try out his or her style of adaptation on others, whereas the *selector* is more measured in his or her ways. Each may react differently to disengagement. As Cumming (1963) describes it, the impinger's judgment may not be as good as it was, but he or she is likely to be viewed as an unusual person for his or her age: "Ultimately, as he becomes less able to control the situations he provokes, he may suffer anxiety and panic through failure both to arouse and to interpret appropriate reactions. His problem in old age will be to avoid confusion."

The selector can be expected to be more measured in his or her ways. As a youth, this individual may have appeared to others as withdrawn. With age, this style seems more appropriate: "In old-age, because of his reluctance to generate interaction, he may, like a neglected infant, develop a kind of marasmus. His foe will be apathy rather than confusion" (Cumming 1963).

Finally, in summarizing the disengagement theory, it is useful to point out that, in the initial presentation of the theory, Cumming and Henry (1961) argue that the process of disengagement was both *inevitable* and *universal.* All social systems, if they were to maintain successful equilibrium, would necessarily disengage from the elderly. Disengagement was seen as a prerequisite to social stability. Older people could be released from societal expectations that they work and be productive. Presumably, they would adapt by participating in satisfying family relationships and friendships. "When a middle-aged, fully engaged person dies, he leaves many broken ties, and disrupted situations. Disengagement thus frees the old to die without disrupting vital affairs" (Cumming 1963, pp. 384–385).

The disengagement theory has generated much critical discussion. Many have found the theory wanting and indefensible; others have defended it quite strenuously. Through the 1960s and 1970s, most research efforts were unable to offer empirical support for the theory. Youmans (1967) found that a sample of the rural elderly did not, in general, experience disengagement. Palmore (1968) interviewed 127 individuals whose average age was 78. He found little to support the notion that disengagement necessarily increases with age. Others' research has suggested possible modifications on the disengagement theme. For example, Tallmer and Kutner (1970) found that physical and social stress, rather than aging per se, often produces disengagement. Atchley's (1971) study of emeritus professors showed that individuals could disengage socially without psychological disengagement. This suggests that the extent to which a person disengages may be a function of that individual's occupation or position in the community. Thus, a retired college professor may continue to be involved in the intellectual issues in his or her field of study, while a retired construction worker may not have similar opportunities to remain professionally involved.

The controversy surrounding disengagement continues. Hochschild (1975) has examined the theory and found three problems that she believes continue to ignite the controversy. First, Hochschild argues that the disengagement theory allows no possibility for counterevidence. She points out that in their original work, entitled *Growing Old,* Cumming and Henry (1961) offered four types of "back-door" explanations to handle cases that did not fit the theory. These types included unsuccessful disengagers, those whose disengagement was "off schedule," exceptional individuals who had reengaged, and those who were offered as examples of "variation in the form" of disengagement.

Second, the major variables in the theory—age and disengagement—turn out to be "umbrella" variables, which are divisible into numerous other promising variables. Earlier, reference was made to one study that distinguished between social and psychological disengagement. Carp (1969) distinguishes among types of social disengagement, including disengagement from family, friends, social activities, and material possessions. Similarly, in discussing psychological disengagement, one could differentiate among personal adjustment, ego energy, affect intensity, mastery, and so on. As Hochschild points out, one consequence of this continual fission is that theoretical propositions that once appeared quite simple grow into something much more complex.

Third, the disengagement theory essentially ignores the aging person's own view of aging and disengagement. Behavior that looks like disengagement to the observer may have a completely different meaning for the aging person. Based on his exploratory study of retirement among 99 English couples, Crawford (1971) advances three types of meaning that men attribute to retirement: retiring *back to* something, retiring *from* something, and retiring *for* something. In the first and third types, men view their retirement in terms of continued engagement with new involvements—in the latter case, discarding past obligations to work and building a new social life outside of work; in the former, giving up work and returning to the family. Despite the objective disengagement (retirement), the men attribute different meanings to the event.

One assumption inherent in disengagement has not come under much scrutiny, perhaps because it is supportive of stereotypes about the productive capacities of older people. This assumption is that older people's withdrawal from productive roles is necessarily good for society. How can it be good for society to deprive the workplace of the skills, knowledge, and experience held by older workers? How can it be better for society to encourage people to retire early and begin collecting their pensions than to encourage people to stay in the workplace and continue paying into the Social Security Trust Fund and other public and private pensions systems?

Into the 1980s, the activity and disengagement perspectives dominated the theoretical discussion in social gerontology, but several alternative perspectives have since been put forth. Four somewhat related theories that deserve mention are the continuity theory, socioenvironmental theory, exchange theory, and symbolic interactionism. None of the four has as yet received the research attention required for determining its explanatory power.

Continuity Theory

Continuity theory holds that middle-aged and older adults make adaptive choices in an effort to preserve ties with their own past experiences (Atchley 1989). Continuity is a subjective phenomenon and can be internal, external, or both. *Internal continuity* requires memory and is tied to "a remembered inner structure, such as the persistence of a psychic structure of ideas, temperament, affect, experiences, preferences, dispositions, and skills" (Atchley 1989, p. 184). Pressures and attractions that move people toward internal continuity include the importance of cognitive continuity for maintaining mastery and competence, a sense of ego integrity, and self-esteem. Also, people can be motivated toward internal continuity as an appropriate means of meeting basic human needs for food, shelter, clothing, and social interaction with others.

External continuity involves memory of the physical and social environments of one's past, including role relationships and activities. Older people may be motivated toward external continuity by the expectations of others; the desire for predictable social support; or the need to cope with physical and mental health changes as well as changes in social roles involving the empty nest, widowhood, or retirement (Atchley 1989).

According to Atchley (1989), individuals classify the degree of continuity in their lives into three general categories: too little, optimum, and too much. When individuals perceive that life is unpredictable or discontinuous, too little continuity can be said to be present. Presumably, too little continuity leads to low satisfaction with life and difficulty in adapting to changing conditions. Change may be so severe and unpredictable that previous skills, personal strategies, and social experiences are of little use in adapting.

The older adult assumes optimum continuity when the pace of change is consistent with personal preferences and societal demands, and is in line with a person's capacity to cope with the change. In such a case, an individual's personality, prior preferences, role relationships, and social experiences serve the person well in adjusting to change.

The older adult who characterizes his or her life as having too much continuity is describing a life that is uncomfortably predictable. Previously used strategies are adequate, but life is perceived as having a sameness of quality absent new and enriching experiences.

Continuity theory has intuitive appeal. Clearly, however, additional work must be carried out to validate all or parts of the theory. Some limitations of the theory seem evident, even in advance of needed empirical research. For example, are earlier stages of development in the life course the standard for old age? Can life-styles observed in old age ever be an appropriate response to growing old, or must they always reflect continuity of lifelong patterns? As was already described in discussing the role theory of aging, some studies suggest that satisfaction in old age comes from flexibility in sex roles and being able to integrate formally unacceptable traits into personality. What about previous life-style patterns that were maladaptive? Does continuity theory require their continuation? Can people free themselves from social roles and behaviors they disliked (Fox 1981–82)? Also, continuity theory, as presented by Atchley, focuses almost uniformly on the individual and his or her social relationships with others. Are there structural factors that may constrain or prevent continuity, or even enhance it?

Socioenvironmental Theory

Socioenvironmental theory directs itself at understanding the effects of the immediate social and physical environment on the activity patterns of aged individuals. The chief proponent of this theory is Jaber Gubrium (1973, 1975). Although other gerontologists have clearly concerned themselves with the environments of old people, Gubrium concerns himself with the meaning old people place on life and with the effect different physical and social contexts may have on that meaning. This approach is based on the understanding that people respond to the social meaning of events rather than to some absolute aspect of these events. Moreover, the responses of persons to the same event might easily be different if the social meaning placed on the event by one varies from the meaning placed on that event by the other.

According to Gubrium (1973), two factors that affect the meaning old people place on events—and thus their interaction patterns—are the physical proximity of other persons and the age homogeneity of an environment. A substantial body of literature supports the importance of these two variables in affecting social interaction among both young and old. For example, Rosow's (1967) seminal work on elderly people in Cleveland shows that old people residing in apartment buildings with a high concentration of aged people were more likely to develop friendships with neighbors than was the case for old people residing in buildings with a low concentration of elderly.

A number of studies show the relationship between age homogeneity and friendship patterns. Bultena and Wood (1969) found that with a population of elderly retired males, friendships occurred primarily among persons of the same age. Messer (1967) found that elderly people in age-homogeneous public housing projects in Chicago interacted more frequently than did elderly persons living in age-heterogeneous settings.

On the basis of the possible contributions of the two variables, physical proximity and age homogeneity, Gubrium (1973) developed a typology of social contexts, each of which, he suggests, has differential impact on social interaction. The four types of social context are as follows:

Type I: *Age homogeneous, close* physical proximity
Type II: *Age heterogeneous, close* physical proximity
Type III: *Age homogeneous, distant* physical proximity
Type IV: *Age heterogenous, distant* physical proximity

Socioenvironmental theory posits that Type I social contexts have the highest degree of age concentration and are thus quite conducive to social interaction. Residential apartment buildings for the elderly are the Type I variety. Individuals living in such environments hold age-linked behavior expectations for each other. Type IV social contexts are the least age concentrated and offer reduced opportunity for initiating interaction. These social contexts include age-heterogeneous neighborhoods of single homes. Type II contexts, represented by age-heterogeneous apartment buildings, and Type III contexts, represented by retirement communities commonly found in Florida and California, fall between Types I and IV in terms of their conduciveness to social interaction.

Of utmost importance to the socioenvironmental theory is the recognition that different social contexts generate different sets of activity norms for aged people. To the extent such norms place behavioral demands on individuals, it becomes clear that different social contexts place different demands on the elderly. Gubrium suggests that individuals who have the resources (health, financial solvency, and social support) to meet the demands of the environment will show high morale and self-satisfaction. Incongruence between environmental expectations and activity resources leads to low morale and diminished life satisfaction.

Exchange Theory

An abundance of gerontological literature has consistently shown that older Americans receive regular support from family, friends, and neighbors in carrying out activities of daily living (Shanas 1979; Stoller & Earl 1983; Sussman 1976). This support may be task oriented, meaning help with housework, shopping, transportation, and the like. Support may also take the form of social or emotional assistance provided in times of stress or illness. This literature also reminds the reader that older people may themselves be support providers, helping family members or neighbors deal with instrumental or emotional problems (Riley & Foner 1968; Sussman 1976).

Informal helping or social support networks, especially those that involve a "reciprocal flow of valued behavior between the participants" (Emerson 1976), may easily be placed within an ***exchange theory*** approach to social interaction. Such an approach views social interaction as governed by rules of fairness or justice. Gouldner (1960) identified one rule of exchange as the *norm of reciprocity.* According to him, this norm establishes a set of reciprocal demands and obligations that lend stability to social systems. One component of the norm of reciprocity is that "people should help those who have helped them" (Gouldner 1960, p. 171).

Gouldner recognized that the norm of reciprocity requiring an exchange of good for good is not the only rule regulating social interaction. In fact, he proposed what could be described as a *norm of beneficence,* which requires that individuals help others as necessary without thought to what the others have done or can do in return. Gouldner is not alone in recognizing that such nonrational impulses are important components of the broader social intercourse. Almost by definition, there are groups in society who are identified by their incapacity to engage in strict exchange. The mentally disabled represent one such group. For them, beneficence supersedes reciprocity as the prevailing norm.

Dowd (1984) has suggested that in one's relations with the very old, the requirements of reciprocity may have been superseded by those of beneficence. This shift, he argues, results from a redefinition of age strata that itself has emerged from a need to reallocate scarce policy resources in the society at large. In effect, Dowd believes that the norm of reciprocity will still apply to young-old people who receive in social policy terms what is perceived to be something in balance with the value of their current social worth. Policy treatment of the very old, Dowd expects, will be regulated by a principle of beneficence—every person or household will receive as much as is needed, to a limit, regardless of the value attached to their current social worth.

Homans (1958, 1974) suggests another rule of exchange. He argues that social exchange is governed by a *rule of distributive justice*. This rule is defined in terms of the relationship between actors' rewards and costs: The greater the costs, the greater the rewards. Actors are seen as trying to strike a balance, or achieve proportionality, in social exchange. Homans indicates, "Persons that give much to others try to get much from them, and persons that get much from others are under pressure to give much to them. This process of influence tends to work out at equilibrium to balance in the exchanges." According to Homans, when individuals experience imbalance or distributive injustice, when they give more than they get (or get more than they give), they are offended and experience dissatisfaction.

Dowd (1975, 1978, 1980) attempts to place aging within an exchange framework. He believes that the problems of the aged in industrial societies today are, in reality, problems of decreasing power. Dowd argues that in social exchanges between the aged and society, the aged gradually lose power until all that is left is the capacity to comply. The shift in balance of power between the aged and society reflects the economic and social dependency of the elderly. More than any other event, the phenomenon of retirement seems to exemplify this decline in power. The worker who once exchanged his or her skill for wages must comply with retirement in exchange for pension and health care benefits.

Kart and Longino (1987) carried out what they believe to be a definitive test of distributive justice within the context of aged social exchange networks. In 1977, 1,346 persons residing in diverse settings were interviewed in the Social Security Administration's Midwestern Retirement Community Study (Longino 1980). Respondents were asked to list all the people who were important in their lives, up to as many as 15 persons. The respondents were then asked what each of these persons did on a more or less regular basis that the respondent really appreciated. Next, the relationship was reversed, and the respondents were asked what they themselves did for each person on the list, on an ongoing basis, that was important to the latter.

Students of social support research have suggested that many researchers emphasize the *amount* of support at the expense of the *types* of support being received and given (Thoits 1982). Thus, supportive activities, given and received, were coded into one of three possible categories: emotional, social, and instrumental. In addition, each individual was assigned a score based on responses to 13 items drawn from the Life Satisfaction Scale B (Neugarten, Havighurst, & Tobin 1961). Finally, each respondent was asked to summarize his or her relationships in terms of how obligated the respondent felt generally toward others.

Initially, Kart and Longino (1987) examined the amount of support given and received as they separately predicted life satisfaction and feelings of obligation. The amount of support the respondent *received*, as well as the support *given*, regardless of type, had little apparent effect on feelings of obligation to others. Correlations between the support measures and life satisfaction showed a different pattern. Low inverse correlations were present between all types of support given, emotional and social support received, and life satisfaction. Thus, the more support given *or* received, the lower the life satisfaction.

The reciprocal supportive relationship between the respondent and each primary relation was also examined. Within each support type, a ratio of support given to support received was calculated. The retirement community residents, as a whole, had a ratio above 1.0 for each type of support, indicating that they tended to receive more support than they gave. The associations between support ratios and feelings of obligation, however, were weak to nonexistent, nor did the reciprocal imbalance seem to affect the level of life satisfaction.

Kart and Longino (1987) conclude that, when actual reciprocal exchange relationships are examined, the exchange paradigm does not operate as straightforwardly between older people and those significant to them as other exchange theorists might have predicted (e.g., see Dowd, 1978). Only the support *given* by older respondents in their primary relationships seems to be systematically and inversely related to life satisfaction. Even here, the correlations were quite modest by any standard. One conclusion to draw from these empirical results is quite simply that the exchange theory fails to explain the relationship between support systems and the well-being or life satisfaction of older persons. Of course, leaping to such a conclusion may be similar to throwing out the baby with the bath water. Ward (1985) points out that the literature on the contributions of support systems to well-being in later life is equivocal. For example, Conner, Powers, and Bultena (1979) found that both the number and frequency of social ties were unrelated to life satisfaction among the elderly. Ward, Sherman, and Lagory (1984) report only a weak relationship between access to instrumental and expressive supports (through involvement with kin, friends, and neighbors) and overall morale.

When attempting to explain the contributions of social support systems to the life satisfaction of older people, the exchange theory makes good sociological as well as intuitive sense. In part, this is because it dovetails nicely with at least two other long-standing sociological traditions that address the relationship between social support and feelings of well-being. Both symbolic interactionism (to be discussed) and Durkheimian anomie theory posit that social interaction with others can provide a basis for psychological good feeling (Thoits, 1982). One advantage of formalizing theory is that it facilitates replication and reformulation by other researchers. More seems to be gained at this point by encouraging additional replications and reformulations of exchange theory in a gerontological context than by premature rejection of the theory.

Symbolic Interactionism

According to Herbert Blumer (1969), the theoretical framework known as **symbolic interactionism** is based on the premise that people behave toward objects (including other people) according to perceptions and meanings developed through social interaction. From this perspective, individuals are seen as conscious actors in the world who adapt to situations and events on the basis of the perceptions and meanings they have constructed for these situations and events. It is important to note that perceptions and meanings are not constructed in a vacuum. Rather, as Blumer points out, they arise out of social interaction with others:

> Human beings in interacting with one another have to take account of what each is doing or is about to do; they are forced to direct their own conduct or handle their situations in terms of what they take into account. Thus, the activities of others enter as positive factors in the formation of their own conduct; in the face of actions of others one may abandon an intention or purpose, revise it, check or suspend it, intensify it, or replace it. The actions of others enter to set what one plans to do, may oppose or prevent such plans, may require a revision of such plans, and may demand a very different set of such plans. One has to *fit* one's own line of activity in some manner to the actions of others. (1969, p. 8)

The importance of social interaction cannot be exaggerated for the symbolic interactionist. The emphasis in this theoretical perspective is on the human capacity for *socially* constructing reality.

Symbolic interactionism has important implications for the study of aging. Clair, Karp, and Yoels (1993) specify three important ideas that emanate from applying the symbolic interactionist perspective to age and aging: (1) like any other symbol, age has a multiplicity of meanings; (2) those meanings emerge out of interaction with others; and (3) the meanings of age may be modified and reinterpreted, depending on the definitions of the situations in which one acts. Clearly, symbolic interactionism may provide a basis for understanding how older people perceive and assign meaning to the experience of old age in U.S. society (or in any other society, for that matter). Ward (1984), for example, sees this perspective as essential to recognizing the importance of change in the social and symbolic worlds of the aging. He argues that role losses, residential mobility, health problems, and other age-related changes pull the elderly from familiar groups and situations. Thus, they may become alienated from past worlds and identities and, at the same time, be granted the potential for new worlds and new identities. This creates the possibility of satisfying personal change and growth, but also may result in stress, marginality, and unhappiness (Ward 1984, p. 360).

Spence (1986) has explored the implications of the symbolic interactionist perspective for understanding developmental issues of later life. From his view, this perspective is unique because it emphasizes the subjective and focuses on process and change in identity as one develops. Where one is going is secondary to the processes of getting there (Spence 1986). Marshall (1979) has applied the symbolic interactionist perspective to aging through his use of the concept of **status passage.** To speak of aging as a status passage is to suggest the image of an individual negotiating a passage from one age-based status to another (and perhaps to others), finally coming to the end of the passage through life, at death.

A status passage may have both an objective as well as a subjective reality. Objectively, any status passage can be defined in terms of a series of dimensions, including physical or social time and space; duration; and the extent to which it is desirable or undesirable, inevitable or optional, voluntary or involuntary. Subjectively, as Marshall indicates, awareness of any of these properties of the passage may vary. Thus, people may differ in their degree of awareness that they are even undergoing a passage. For the symbolic interactionist, the objective and subjective dimensions of the status passage set the parameters within which the lives of individuals (in this context, aging individuals) will be shaped by themselves. The degree of control over the passage becomes of central importance for aging persons. This is particularly true for this status passage because, unlike others, it offers no exit from the passage except through death. Other passages in life involve preparation for something to come. Here, however, the passage is all there is. As Marshall (1979) indicates, "No future lies beyond the passage, only the passage and its termination become relevant."

One theme of this status passage, according to Marshall, is that preparation for death involves the attempt to make sense of death itself and to make sense of one's life. This theme appears in psychoanalytic theory and in Butler's (1963) concept of *life review*. An important difference for symbolic interactionists is their recognition that control over one's own biography involves reconstruction of the past through reminiscence. Marshall (1979) argues that this process is most successful when it is conducted socially. Unfortunately, as Marshall sees it, socializing agents, such as institutional settings (including hospitals, nursing homes, retirement communities), may severely threaten an aged person's ability to maintain control of the status passage. Too often, status passage control becomes a dilemma for the aging individual who must choose between allowing others to shape his or her passage, on the one hand, and isolation on the other. This decision is most obvious in cases where others employ criteria for desired behavior that contradict the attempts of the aging person to maintain personal control (Marshall 1979).

Much more empirical research must be done to determine fully the utility of the symbolic interactionist paradigm in social gerontology. A major limitation of this approach is that it focuses on the individual and fails to account fully for the structural component of social behavior (Passuth & Bengtson, 1988). Still, one can be optimistic about any framework that suggests that older people retain the human capacity to construct and share meanings and the human tendency to attempt to maintain control over their own lives.

AGING AND SOCIETY

The Subculture of the Aging

In an attempt to clarify the nature of relations between older persons and the rest of society, Rose (1965) offers the concept of an *aged subculture*. A subculture may develop when particular members of a society interact with each other significantly more than they do with others in the society. This pattern of interaction develops when group members have common backgrounds and interests and/or are excluded from interaction with other population groups in the society. Rose believes that both circumstances exist for the large proportion of older people in U.S. society.

In addition, Rose outlines a variety of demographic, ecological, and social organizational trends that contribute to the development of an aged subculture. These include the growing number and proportion of persons who live beyond the age of 65; the self-segregation of older persons in inner cities and rural areas (caused by migration patterns of the young); the decline in employment of older people; and the development of social services designed to assist older people. Each of these trends either improves the opportunities for older people to identify with each other or separates them from the rest of society.

Rose recognizes that not all the distinctive behavior of the elderly can be attributed to the aged subculture. Biological changes, society's expectations for the elderly, and generational differences in socialization all contribute to making the elderly more segregated from other age categories than is true for the rest of society.

What about the content of this aged subculture? According to Rose, the status system among the elderly is only partially a carryover from that of the general society. Wealth carries over from the general culture, as do occupational prestige, achievement, and education, although with some lessening in importance. Physical and mental health and social activity, usually accepted as a given by younger people, have special value in conferring status among the elderly.

What are the consequences of the development of an aged subculture? Rose discusses two areas: aging self-conception and aging group consciousness. Rose argues that many Americans suffer a change in self-conception as they grow older, largely as a consequence of the negative evaluation of old age in U.S. culture. Unfortunately, the development of an aged subculture does not necessarily combat this negative evaluation. Rather, it may simply facilitate identification as old. This is a negative consequence of the development of an aged subculture. On the positive side, development of an aged subculture may stimulate a group identification and consciousness, with potential for social action. Rose envisioned older people becoming a voting bloc that exerts political power either within the existing political party structures or on its own.

Despite some debate in the gerontological literature about whether the elderly fit a traditional definition of a subculture (Streib 1965), the notion of an aged subculture has served as a useful descriptive guide to the relationship between older persons and U.S. society. Nevertheless, its predictive power generally has been found wanting (Hendricks & Hendricks 1986). However, one research team has attempted to test Rose's aged subculture hypothesis. Longino, McClelland, and Peterson (1980) compared elderly residents of eight midwestern retirement communities (five age-segregated residential settings and three age-concentrated neighborhoods) with a shadow sample of elderly respondents drawn from a national survey of public attitudes toward older Americans (National Council on Aging 1976). The shadow sample involved a random selection of older people in such a way as to replicate or shadow the characteristics of residents of the retirement communities. For example, for every widowed African American woman over age 75 with an elementary school education and living on less than

$2,000 a year in a retirement community, a person with the same profile was placed in the shadow sample. Comparisons were made using measures of social participation, preferences for age-based interaction, general perceptions of elders, and self-conception.

The study provided partial support for Rose's subculture of aging theory. On the whole, residents of the retirement communities showed a distinctive pattern of responses to the measures of comparison employed. In matters of social participation, differences showed up more in quality than quantity. The social life of retirement community residents appears no more strenuous than elsewhere, but residents find this level of activity more satisfying. Problems of feeling lonely and bored and not feeling needed seem easier to avoid in retirement communities than in more age-integrated settings. The self-conceptions of retirement community residents are mixed. Although the residents in the study tended to have significantly greater self-regard than did their shadow samples in judging their own characteristics, they did not surpass shadow sample respondents in judging themselves as useful members of their communities. Community residents are also significantly more likely to say that older people get just the right amount of respect, or even too much. In effect, this suggests that retirement community residents see themselves in less positive terms than they think society sees them. Finally, according to the authors of this study, evidence for the development of an aging group political consciousness, at least as Rose envisioned it, was nowhere to be found.

Although Longino, McClelland, and Peterson (1980) admit that aging group consciousness exists in some local settings among the elderly, they point out that it may not necessarily arise in response to age-segregated residence. Further, they suggest that as applied to retirement communities, aged subculture theory may need modification to take account of this essentially retreatist phenomenon.

Modernization Theory

In their book, *Aging and Modernization,* Cowgill and Holmes (1972) developed a theory of aging in cross-cultural perspective. As the theory emerged, and was subsequently revised (Cowgill 1974), it described the relationship between modernization and the changes in role and status of older people. The theory was originally expressed in 22 propositions. Stated tersely, however, ***modernization theory*** held that with increasing modernization, the status of older people declines. This declining status is reflected in reduced leadership roles, power, and influence, as well as increased disengagement of older people from community life.

In the initial presentation of the theory, the definition of modernization was somewhat elusive. Later, Cowgill put forth an explicit definition of the concept:

> Modernization is the transformation of a total society from a relatively rural way of life based on animate power, limited technology, relatively undifferentiated institutions, parochial and traditional outlook and values, toward a predominantly urban way of life based on inanimate sources of power, highly developed scientific technology, highly differentiated institutions matched by segmented individual

In some societies, elders are accorded prestige based on a recognition of their contributions to the group.

roles, and a cosmopolitan outlook which emphasizes efficiency and progress. (1974, p. 127)

In addition, Cowgill argued that no part of the society is left untouched, and that all change, although not uniform, is unidirectional (i.e., it always moves from the rural form to the urban form).

Four subsidiary aspects of modernization were identified as salient to the conditions of older people in a society: (1) scientific technology as applied in economic production and distribution, (2) urbanization, (3) literacy and mass education, and (4) health technology. Each of these aspects of modernization helps produce the lower status of older people in society (Cowgill 1974).

Figure 9.2 presents, in schematic form, the modernization theory as revised by Cowgill. Briefly, the causal sequences depicted in the figure can be described as follows:

1. The application of health technology—including public health measures, nutrition, and all aspects of curative and surgical medicine—dramatically affects the age structure of a society so that there is an aging of the population. This comes about through a prolongation of adult life as well as a decline in the birthrate. The theory argues that within the context of an industrialized society with emphasis on youth and new occupations, the extension of adult life leads to an intergenerational competition for jobs. Therefore, older people are forced out of the labor market; they retire. Because they are denied participation in the work

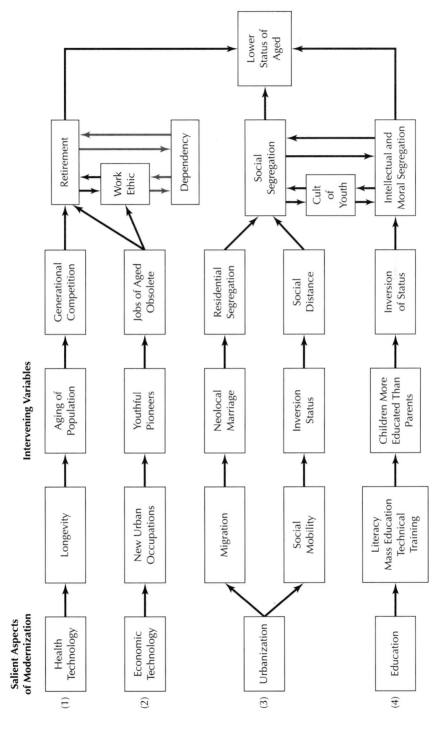

Salient Aspects of Modernization

Intervening Variables

(1) Health Technology → Longevity → Aging of Population → Generational Competition → Retirement

(2) Economic Technology → New Urban Occupations → Youthful Pioneers → Jobs of Aged Obsolete

Work Ethic ↔ Dependency

(3) Urbanization → Migration → Neolocal Marriage → Residential Segregation → Social Segregation

Urbanization → Social Mobility → Inversion Status → Social Distance

Cult of Youth

(4) Education → Literacy Mass Education Technical Training → Children More Educated Than Parents → Inversion of Status → Intellectual and Moral Segregation

Lower Status of Aged

FIGURE 9.2 Aging and Modernization

Source: D. Cowgill, "Aging and Modernization: A Revision of the Theory," in J. Gubrium (Ed.), *Late Life: Communities and Environmental Policies* (Springfield, IL: Charles C Thomas, 1974). Reproduced by permission of the publisher via the Copyright Clearance Center, Inc.

227

ethic, the elderly experience reductions in monetary income, prestige, and honor, and thus decrement in status.

2. The application of economic and industrial technology leads to new occupations located increasingly in an urban setting. Geographically and socially mobile youth migrate to these jobs, while older people are left in positions that are less prestigious and often obsolete. The lack of opportunities for retraining (especially in rural areas) leads to early retirement. This retirement, accompanied by loss of income, may also bring a reversal of traditional family and community roles. Formerly, the young were dependent on the old; now, the old suffer dependency.

3. Urbanization, including the separation of work from home and the geographical separation of youthful urban migrants from their parental homes, profoundly changes the nature of intergenerational relations. Residential segregation of the generations changes the bonds of familial association, increases social distance between generations, and—with upward mobility among the young—leads to a reduced status of the aged. This effect is compounded by retirement and dependency.

4. Promoting literacy and education (almost always targeted at the young in modernization efforts) generates a situation in which children are more literate and have greater skill than their parents do. This imbalance has the effect of inverting roles in the traditional society: The child's generation has higher status than that of the parents, and children occupy positions in the community formerly held by their parents. The increasing social change brought by that modernization widens the gap between the generations, thus causing an intellectual and moral separation or segregation of the generations. Youth comes to symbolize progress, and the society directs its resources toward the young and away from the old, accentuating the decline in status of the aged.

The work of Erdman Palmore has generally supported the modernization theory. Palmore and Whittington (1971) found that the status of the aged was lower than that of the younger population on a series of socioeconomic measures and had declined significantly from 1940 to 1969. Palmore and Manton (1974) explored the relationship between modernization and the economic status of the aged in 31 countries. Indicators of modernization included the gross national product (GNP) per capita, the percentage of the labor force engaged in agriculture, the change in the proportion of the labor force engaged in agriculture, the percentage of literate adults, the percentage of people age 5 to 19 in schools, and the percentage of the population in higher education. The relative status of the aged was measured by indexes that compared the differences in employment and occupation of the older population (age 65 and over) with those age 25 through 64. In general, correlation between the indicators of modernization and measures of the status of the aged demonstrated the theory. The relative status of older people was lower in the more modernized nations. Interestingly, Palmore and Manton discovered some patterns within their data that imply that the status of the aged decreases in the early stages of modernization (exemplified by nations such as Iran, El Salvador, and the Philippines), but, after a period of modernization, status may level off and even rise somewhat (exemplified by New Zealand, Canada, and the United States).

Finally, Palmore (1975) has used the case of Japan to show how culture may mitigate the impact of modernization on the status of the aged. According to Palmore, the social and ethnic homogeneity of the Japanese population, the attitude of the Japanese toward time, the tradition of respect for the aged reflected in filial piety, and the prominence of ancestor worship have all helped maintain the relatively high status and integration of older Japanese. Palmore quotes from Japan's 1963 National Law for the Welfare of the Elders, a law comparable in the United States to the Older Americans Act of 1965: "The elders shall be loved and respected as those who have for many years contributed toward the development of society, and a wholesome and peaceful life shall be guaranteed to them." The Older Americans Act of 1965 makes no mention of love and respect for the aged, nor does it *guarantee* a wholesome and peaceful life.

After a return to Japan, Palmore and Maeda (1985) point out that the status and integration of Japanese elderly have declined from a peak when Japan was an agricultural society. Still, they argue that even after this decline, there are large differences between the situations of Japanese elderly and those in the United States and other countries. And, importantly, in their view, these trends are likely to continue into the foreseeable future, even as Japan undergoes a westernization.

Although Cowgill's theory of the effects of modernization employs society as the unit of analysis, Hong and Keith (1992) were interested in the extent to which individual modernity and the modern circumstances of the family affected the status of the elderly within the family in Korea. They hypothesized that (1) the more modern the family environment, the less power the elderly have in family decision making; and (2) the greater the individual modernity of the elderly, the less power they have in family decision making.

Face-to-face interviews were carried out with 252 Korean men and women 60 years or older in Seoul, Korea. All sample members were living with one of their married children and other relatives. Key indicators of modern family circumstances included urban residence and high educational attainment of the children. The measure of individual modernity was an index of 13 items assessing attitudes toward different areas of Korean life. For example, respondents were asked to give their opinions about equal education opportunities for both daughters and sons. Family decisions were divided into four dimensions and respondents were asked who made the final decision in each of 13 different family matters.

Having highly educated children and living in rural areas significantly affected the decision-making power of the aged in the hypothesized direction. Contrary to what was hypothesized, however, individual modernity among the elderly was found to be positively related to decision-making power in the family. Young-old married men with modern attitudes and highly educated children had the most power in decision making. Hong and Keith speculate that individual modernity is a resource that aids the elderly in negotiating with the younger generation to gain more involvement in decision making within the family. It also may be the case that the children, especially those with higher levels of education, find these modern attitudes supportive and of value in contemporary Korean life. These data from Korea suggest that older people can protect themselves from the ravages of modernization by becoming modern themselves, even if only in attitude. Being young-old, having good health, and having a higher education were predictive of individual modernity among these Korean aged.

The modernization theory is not without its critics. A number of researchers point out how often the term *modernization* is used as synonym for *development, change, progress,* and *westernization*—suggesting that the concept is often used because of its vagueness. Achenbaum and Stearns (1978), who have written on old age in historical perspective, believe the concept of modernization is worth pursuing in gerontology only with the following stipulations:

1. There should be clear agreement on when the modernization process began. For example, David Hacket Fischer, author of *Growing Old in America* (1977), believes that America's shift from a gerontophilic to a gerontophobic society took place between 1770 and 1820. These dates precede the beginning of the fundamental aspects of modernization Cowgill finds so salient for influencing the status of older people.

2. Modernization is not necessarily a linear process. It may proceed in stages, some of which are protracted. Each stage may have a different impact on the status of the elderly.

3. The elderly in preindustrial society demonstrated great diversity of situation. Some owned property and wielded considerable power; others suffered severe degradation. Inevitably, the situation for some improved with modernization as it deteriorated for others.

4. The process of modernization has affected different age groups in different ways. This is particularly interesting in light of societal transformations that necessitated the invention of "adolescence" and redefined childhood. Today, distinctions are made among young-old and old-old. Each may modernize in a different way, with different degrees of success.

Age Stratification

Age stratification is less a formal theory than a conceptual framework for viewing societal processes and changes that affect aging and the state of being old. Matilda White Riley (1971, 1976; Riley, Johnson, & Foner 1972) and Anne Foner (1975) are the architects of this conceptual framework.

According to the theory, society is divided into strata not only by social class but by age as well. Members of the age strata differ in the social roles they are expected to play and in the rights and privileges accorded them by society. This is similarly the case for members of different social classes, who also have different societal expectations for behavior and differential access to rewards granted by society. Age stratification and class stratification approaches have much in common. In fact, Riley (1971) argues that two concepts central to class stratification theory, *social class* and *social mobility,* are analogous to two concepts central to age stratification, *age strata* and *aging.* She suggests that sociologists of age stratification use those questions that are important to class stratification theorists to stimulate thinking about age strata and aging. The four basic questions are:

1. How does an individual's location in the class structure channel that person's attitudes and the way he or she behaves?
2. How do individuals relate to one another within and between classes?
3. What difficulties beset the upwardly (or downwardly) mobile individual, and what strains does the person's mobility impose on the group (e.g., his or her parents of one class) left behind as well as on the new group (e.g., the spouse's parents of a different class) who must now absorb him or her?
4. To the extent that answers can be found to these three sets of questions, what is the impact of the observed findings on society as a whole?

In age stratification terms, the first question becomes: How does an individual's location within the age structure of a society influence his or her behavior and attitudes? Chapters 4 through 7 have already discussed the fact that age strata differ in physical and sensory capabilities, psychomotor performance, and probabilities of death. Psychologists of the life cycle often describe age strata in terms of their involvement in different developmental tasks. In addition, research shows that age strata differ in political and social attitudes, world outlook, style of life, organizational attachments, happiness, and so on (Riley & Foner 1968). How do age stratification theorists explain these differences in behavior and attitudes among people of different age strata and the similarities among people within a stratum?

Riley (1971) suggests that two coordinates or dimensions useful for locating an individual in the age structure of a society are the *life-course dimension* and the *historical dimension.* The first of these reflects chronological age, itself a rough indicator of biological, psychological, and social experience. This is only to say that individuals of the same age have much in common. They are alike in biological development as well as in the kinds of social roles they have experienced (worker, spouse, parent). The second dimension refers to the period of history in which a person lives. People born at the same time (a cohort) share a common history. Those born at different times have lived through a different historical period. Even when people born at different times share an historical event, they are likely to experience it differently. For example, persons born in 1920 and 1950, respectively, were likely to experience the Vietnam War quite differently. Riley uses the term **cohort-centric** to describe the view of the world (i.e., the behavior and attitudes) that develops from a particular intersection of the life-course and historical dimensions. People in the same place on the life-course dimension (in the same age stratum) experience historical events similarly and, as a result, may come to see the world in a like fashion. The cohort-centricity of different age strata explains the different behaviors and attitudes associated with those age strata. Riley (1985) describes the *fallacy of cohort-centrism*—that is, the erroneous assumption that members of all cohorts will age in exactly the same fashion as members of one's own cohort.

The second question becomes: How do individuals relate to one another within and between age strata? This question stimulates thinking about the nature of social relationships within age strata and the nature of intergenerational relations. From the age stratification perspective, within-age stratum solidarity and consciousness are predictable. People's similarity in age and cohort membership often signals mutuality of experiences, perceptions, and interests that may lead to integration or even to age-based groups and collective movements (Riley 1985). Yet, the continuous flow of cohorts in and out of an age stratum weakens identification with a particular stratum. As Foner (1975) points out, this is quite different from class strata, members of which share common experiences and often have a lifetime to reinforce identification with the group.

Relations among age strata reflect many factors, not the least of which is the distribution of power and wealth in a society. What about intergenerational relations within the family? Are they sequential or reciprocal? Foner (1969, cited in Riley 1971) asked parents of high school students what they would do with money unexpectedly received. Only 2 percent said they would use it to help their aged parents; most indicated a willingness to use the money to help the children get started in life. Furthermore, she reports that the aged generation concurs with this decision. This suggests agreement among generations about the flow of material support—sequential, not reciprocal, with each generation attempting to aid the younger generation.

The third set of questions asks about age mobility. When aging is viewed as mobility through the age strata, it is revealed as a process that brings many of the same strains and stresses as does class mobility. Still, age mobility is different. Whereas social mobility affects only a few, age mobility affects everyone. Although individuals age in different ways and at different rates, no one can achieve downward age mobility. As Mannheim wrote, the "sociological phenomenon of generations is ultimately based on the biological rhythm of birth and death" (1952, p. 290). Over time, a succession of waves of new individuals reach adulthood. Each wave, or cohort, is changed by *and* changes the prevailing culture. Mannheim described this as "fresh contact" (Kertzer 1983). In addition, each cohort, because of its special relationship to historical events, experiences age mobility differently. For example, successive cohorts in society in the twentieth century have increased longevity and formal education. Both these facts have dramatically changed how successive cohorts have aged.

Finally, the fourth set of questions reminds one that age stratification cannot be viewed in isolation. The system of age stratification in society influences and is influenced by the changing social-political-economic fabric of society. Sometimes, social changes may directly reflect "innovations" that emanate from one or more cohorts (Riley 1971). Thus, for example, the large proportion of "early" retirements from the labor force in recent cohorts of those age 55 to 65 has already had enormous impact throughout the society—for example, on the financing of Social Security and other pension plans, on housing, and on leisure—and will continue to do so in the future. However, when many individuals in the same cohort are affected by social change in similar ways, the change in their collective lives can, in turn, produce further social change. That is, new patterns of aging are not only caused by social change but they also contribute to it (Riley 1985).

In Maoist China (1949–1976), three policies were implemented that are repeatedly cited as evidence for a decline in the status of older people in that country. First, a new marriage law, enacted in 1950, replaced absolute parental authority with reciprocity between parents and children. Second, the elimination of private property removed the parental control of family wealth as a power resource. Third, the state emphasized patriotism over filial piety; children were encouraged to expose family members who were ideologically against the state. In the 1970s, with the death of Mao, economic development was emphasized in earnest. Although research on the impact on the aged is still ongoing, application of the modernization theory would seem to predict a further decline in the status of old people.

Yin and Lai (1983) have attempted to understand the changes in status experienced by the elderly in Maoist China within the context of the age stratification theory. In effect they ask: Did the aged lose status because they were old (*age effect*) or because of their life experiences (*cohort effect*)? Yin and Lai argue for an explanation of the status of older people in China based on cohort effects. Their position is that older age groups suffered diminished status in Maoist China mainly because of their life experience in the prerevolutionary era, when the previous government advocated capitalism and communists were in the role of revolutionaries. When the communists came to power, they feared that older adults could provide a major impetus to a revival of capitalism. In sum, these authors suggest that the position of the aged was diminished in Maoist China not as a function of their old age but, rather, as a result of generational conflict based on different life experiences.

The age stratification approach suggests a new way of viewing an increasing body of information on growing old and being old. The research literature on age stratification is still relatively scarce. Yet, it is clear the approach raises interesting and important questions. Only additional research efforts will determine its viability.

Political Economy of Aging

The *political economy perspective* on aging requires that the problems of aging be viewed in social structure rather than in individual terms. According to Estes, Swan, and Gerard, this perspective "starts with the proposition that the status and resources of the elderly and even the trajectory of the aging process itself are conditioned by one's location in the social structure and the economic and social factors that affect it" (1984, p. 28). Clearly, the political economy perspective is not concerned with old age as a biological or psychological adjustment problem but, rather, as a problem for societies characterized by major inequalities in the distribution of power, income, and property. The political economists argue that the experience of the aged in society cannot be understood separate from their relation to the mode of production (Estes 1979). Implicit in this approach is the question of whether the logic of capitalism as a productive social system is reconcilable with the needs of elderly people.

Radical political economists of aging answer that capitalism is irreconcilable with meeting the needs of the elderly. Phillipson (1982) offers four arguments:

1. Whenever capitalism is in crisis—as in the 1930s and in the early 1980s—it attempts to solve its problems through cuts in the living standards of working people.
2. Capitalism has a distinct set of priorities, which almost always subordinates social and individual needs to the search for profits.
3. Because of the cyclical nature of the capitalist economies, elderly people often find themselves caught between their own need for better services and the steady decline of facilities within their neighborhood.
4. In capitalist economies, a ruling class still appropriates and controls the wealth produced by the working class.

Political economists offer an explanation for the helplessness of the position of the elderly that is rooted in social class position. They address the troubles of old age in terms of the political and economic conditions of an impoverished collectivity of elders (Lynott & Lynott 1996). Using a political economy approach, Navarro (1984) analyzed the health care problems of older Americans. He concluded that the misery and impoverishment many elderly suffer today is a function of the dominance of the capitalist class over U.S. political, economic, and social institutions. From his view, defense of capitalist class interests has required shifting government resources from social and health expenditures, which benefit the majority of the U.S. population, to military expenditures, which benefit the few. Interestingly, Navarro remains optimistic enough to suggest that the interest-group mentality prevalent in the United States be replaced by an appreciation among the majority of Americans (whites, blacks, Latinos, females, young and old people) for their shared working-class status and hence for their collective power.

Others are not so sanguine. Estes and Binney (1991) use the concept of the *biomedicalization of aging* to describe the overdevelopment of a geriatric medical industrial complex based on the social construction of aging as a medical problem. The social construction of aging as a medical problem equates aging with illness and disease. Thus, despite increasing evidence of the importance of social and behavioral factors in the relationship between health and aging, the elements of the medical model—with its emphasis on objectivity in diagnosis and treatment of disease, concern solely for matters of physiological functioning, and evaluation solely in the domain of physicians—define the basic processes and problems of aging. As a result, viewpoints on aging emphasize more sophisticated diagnosis, therapeutic intervention or prevention, and identification of modifiable biological markers of aging (Adelman 1988).

From this perspective, aging is considered an undesirable pathological condition, rather than a phase or stage in the life cycle that brings new risks but also opportunities. Aging is equated with reduced activity, disengagement from social life, an exchange of independence for dependency, and a general loss of personal control and self-esteem (Rodin & Langer 1980). As Estes and colleagues (1984) note, all this places social control of the elderly in the hands of physicians who medically define, manage, and treat them.

Political economy of aging is not a theory in the strictest sense. It is not presented in the form of a set of systematically organized statements. Rather, political economy is an orientation or perspective that, at this relatively early stage in its development, may provide a useful guide for aging policy and research. Estes, Gerard, and Minkler (1984) employ the perspective to frame four important questions about aging policy. They believe that the answers to these questions speak to the heart of the relationship between this society and its aged constituents:

1. To what extent will aging interest groups ally themselves with a broader base and expand their concerns to encompass generic issues rather than those identified as aging issues only?
2. To what extent will state and local officials continue to accept the federal retrenchment and shift of governmental responsibility to state and local government?
3. Will the interests of the wealthy and the middle class continue to dominate public policy for the aging?
4. To what extent will the organizations serving the aging, as well as professionals and individuals, involve themselves in attempting to set the agenda for future public policy?

EMERGENT THEORIES

In the past decade or so, gerontologists have continued their efforts to bring new theoretical perspectives to the study of aging. Two approaches in relatively early stages of development deserve mention here: Critical gerontology and feminist gerontology.

Critical Gerontology

The U.S. philosopher Harry Moody (1988, 1992, 1993) has described a critical approach to gerontology that relies on the work of a German, Jurgen Habermas (1971). This approach to gerontology is not a theory, per se. Rather, it attempts to move beyond the traditional boundaries of gerontology to explore theory development from self-reflective modes of thought more characteristic of the disciplines of the humanities. Habermas (1971) distinguishes the empirical-analytic sciences, with their technical interest in prediction and control, from the historical-hermeneutic sciences, which have a practical interest in promoting interaction, communication, and understanding. He argues that neither the technical interests of the empirical-analytic sciences, nor the practical interests of the humanities, alone can lead to the knowledge that is desired and needed. Presumably, this is why it is possible to have advancements in biomedical knowledge that prolong life in old age, yet, at the same time, experience the dissatisfaction of an absence of appropriate language that would allow for serious discussion about the meaning of old age itself (Moody 1988).

How will the knowledge that is desired and needed be achieved? Borrowing from Habermas, the critical gerontologist could ask: For what (and whose) purpose is this knowledge? Habermas offers three answers.

1. *Control:* From the perspective of the empirical-analytic sciences, variables such as retirement status, widowhood, and health, on the one hand, and life satisfaction, social support, and caregiver burden, on the other hand, are assumed to describe objective states of human aging. It is assumed that knowledge developed about the relationships between and among these variables would allow for introducing desirable changes (control), through policymaking.

2. *Understanding:* From the historical-hermeneutic view, age-related concepts, such as those identified in item 1, are considered not as representing objects or objective conditions but as producing them. For example, it is virtually impossible to study the concept of an age cohort without assuming its existence. But it is exactly this assumption that is of interest here. According to Lynott and Lynott (1996), there is a double meaning of "understanding" at work in this matter. One refers to the investigator's discovery of his or her understanding; the second refers to what respondents (those being studied) offer up as their own understanding.

3. *Emancipation:* The interest in emancipation arises from the realization that the language of age-related concepts and theories of aging reifies experience as something separate from those doing the experiencing. The aim of emancipatory knowledge is to reveal to individuals that the objects of experience are the products of their own labor. The research task for this answer is systematic critique, and thus theory becomes critical. It is not research procedure that is critiqued, but rather the alienation between the aging individual and his or her experience.

What does this imply for theory in gerontology? Moody offers the following:

> Theories of aging cannot be constructed with moral indifference toward the practical horizon of their validation and application in human affairs.... Any theory of aging that settles for less than a form of emancipatory knowledge runs the risk that knowledge gained, whether technical or hermeneutic, will be used for purposes that lead not to freedom but to new domination. (1988, p. 26)

For Moody (1993, p. xvii), concern with "emancipatory knowledge" lies in creating "a positive vision of how things might be different or what a rationally defensible vision of a 'good old age' might be." This quote belies an important distinction between conventional gerontology and critical gerontology. As Tornstam (1992, 1996) has argued, conventional gerontology is based on limited positivist notions of knowledge and science, producing a model of aging based only on social problems. A critical gerontology would allow the aged, themselves, to define the research questions. Such an approach might create more positive models of aging, emphasizing strengths and variability of age.

Feminist Gerontology

Although there are many different feminist perspectives, the common focus of *feminist gerontology* is the critique of the "androcentric" (male-centered) view inherent in theorizing about aging. Calasanti (1993) argues that "gerontological theories are based on the experiences of white, middle-class men" (p. 108). A result of such theories is select "male facts" about aging which deny women centrality in the aging experience (Lynott & Lynott 1996).

A number of feminist scholars have argued that in capitalist and patriarchal societies (e.g., the United States), women occupy an inferior status in old age. Presumably this is a continuation of a lifetime of being disadvantaged, especially in a labor market segregated by gender and race. As a result of women's labor throughout their lives—in child rearing, unpaid housework, low wages in the work force, and care giving to aged and infirmed family members—they have little in the way of economic resources (including pension benefits) or necessary social supports to provide for themselves in later life (Stoller 1993). Rather than a symptomatic "problems of women in later life" approach, what Stoller suggests is needed is a major "restructuring of the economic relations between men and women and increased societal recognition and support for the unpaid work women perform throughout their caring careers" (1993, p. 165).

Betty Friedan (1993) believes that gerontologists have, wittingly or not, contributed to the "problems approach" to old age by emphasizing disease and disability over more positive portraits of aging. She seeks examples of older people who rise above the stereotypes and enjoy vital, productive, and fulfilling lives in their later years. From Friedan's view, greater awareness of such positive depictions will provide new meaning to the aging experience and enrich the quality of life of older men and women alike.

Bengtson, Burgess, and Parrott (1997) specify four contributions made by feminist theories of aging:

1. Feminist perspectives focus on the needs of the majority of the aging population: women.
2. Feminist research is linked to practice, because it focuses on issues relevant to the life worlds of women.
3. Feminist theory is diverse, addressing both individual and structural levels of theory.
4. Feminist gerontologists critique the ageist biases in mainstream feminism, which traditionally ignore issues of age.

These same authors offer three criticisms of this approach:

1. Feminist theories of aging are too broad and unfocused to represent a single theoretical tradition.
2. Feminist theories are often viewed as partisan and value-laden.
3. For the most part, feminist research in aging ignores the gendered component of aging for men.

SUMMARY

The theories in social gerontology reviewed in this chapter were divided into two broad categories. One group of theories attempts to conceptualize the adjustment of individuals to their own aging, while other theories deal with societal change and aging. Theories in the first category include the role, activity, disengagement, continuity, socioenvironmental, exchange, and symbolic interactionist theories. Those in the latter category include the subcultural, modernization, and age stratification theories, as well as the political economy perspective. None of the theories has been sufficiently tested to be completely rejected. Each acts as a guide to further research.

The earliest theory in social gerontology concentrated on adjustments to role change among the elderly. In general, this approach pointed out that role loss led to maladjustment. The activity theory states a positive relationship between activity and life satisfaction. Activity theorists argue that, although aging individuals face inevitable changes, many psychosocial needs remain the same. Thus, individuals able to maintain the activities of the middle years will be well satisfied with life in the later years. Several empirical tests of the theory show only social activity with friends to be related to life satisfaction in later life.

Standing in some contrast to these approaches, disengagement theory characterizes old age as a time of mutual withdrawal between the aging individual and society. This mutual withdrawal is seen as functional for and desired by both aging individuals and the social system. Much critical discussion still surrounds the theory, although most research efforts are unable to provide empirical support for it.

Continuity theory argues that people make adaptive choices in old age that involve applying familiar strategies in familiar arenas of life. Thus, the elderly attempt to preserve and maintain inner psychological continuity as well as outward continuity of social behavior and circumstances.

Socioenvironmental theory is directed at acknowledging the effects of the social and physical environment on the activity patterns of aged individuals. Exchange theory attempts to explain the interaction patterns of the old in terms of the relationship between support given and received. When these are out of balance, injustice is experienced and life satisfaction declines. Symbolic interactionism emphasizes the power of aged individuals to socially construct their reality.

Rose (1965) offers the concept of an aged subculture to explain the impact of trends promoting the segregation of the old from the rest of society. The development of an aged subculture has both negative and positive consequences. The most positive of these includes the potential for the elderly to form a social action group.

Modernization theory describes the relationship between modernization and the changes in role and status of older people. Stated briefly, the theory holds that increasing modernization brings a decline in the status of the aged. Riley proposes an age stratification approach to understanding the aging process and old age. She advises that an approach similar to that used in the analysis of class stratification would be useful for shedding light on problems of growing old and being old.

Political economy is a new perspective that sees the aged and the aging process as conditioned by location in the social structure. The perspective questions whether the logic of the U.S. economic system is reconcilable with the needs of older people.

In recent years, critical gerontology and feminist gerontology have emerged as new theoretical perspectives on aging. Although in many respects these approaches are still in an early development stage, it is clear that they are evolving out of dissatisfaction with the traditional theories of aging.

STUDY QUESTIONS

1. Discuss the role theory in relation to adjustment in old age. What are the major role changes individuals experience during the aging process according to this theory? What happens to sex-role differentiation with aging?

2. Compare and contrast disengagement and activity theories. Are there commonalities between the activity and continuity theories? Explain your answer.

3. Explain how Gubrium integrates the concepts of physical proximity and age homogeneity into the socioenvironmental theory of aging. List and describe the elements of his resulting typology of social contexts.

4. Discuss exchange theory and explain how it can be applied to understand the support networks of older people.

5. Explain how the theory of symbolic interactionism can be used to provide a basis for understanding how older people perceive and assign meaning to things, events, and people in their lives.

6. Discuss the positive and negative consequences of development of an aged subculture.

7. Four aspects of modernization have been identified as salient to the conditions of older people in a society. List them and explain how each affects the status of the elderly.

8. Explain how questions of social stratification can be adapted to a conceptual framework of age stratification.

9. According to radical political economists of aging, is capitalism reconcilable with meeting the needs of the elderly? Why or why not? How may the political economy perspective help frame future policy and research questions?

10. Explain the potential contributions of emergent theories of aging. Identify the similarities/dissimilarities in the approaches of critical gerontology and feminist gerontology.

REFERENCES

Achenbaum, A., & Bengtson, V. L. (1994). Reengaging the disengagement theory of aging: On the history and assessment of theory development in gerontology. *The Gerontologist,* 34 (6), 756–763.

Achenbaum, A., & Stearns, P. (1978). Old age and modernization. *Gerontologist, 18* (3), 307–312.

Adelman, R. (1988). The importance of basic biological science to gerontology. *Journal of Gerontology, 43* (1), B1–B2.

Amoss, P. T. (1981). Coastal Salish elders. In P. T. Amoss & S. Harrell (Eds.), *Other ways of growing old.* Stanford, CA: Stanford University Press.

Atchley, R. (1971). Disengagement among profes-sors. *Journal of Gerontology, 26,* 476–480.

Atchley, R. (1989). A continuity theory of normal aging. *The Gerontologist, 29* (2), 183–190.

Bengtson, V. L., Burgess, E. O., & Parrott, T. M. (1997). Theory, explanation, and a third generation of theoretical development in social gerontology. *Journal of Gerontology: Social Sciences, 52B* (2), S72–S88.

Bengtson, V. L, Rice, C. J., & Johnson, M. L. (1999). Are theories of aging important? Models and explanations in gerontology at the turn of the century. In V. L. Bengtson & K. W. Schaie (Eds.), *Handbook of theories of aging.* New York: Springer.

Blumer, H. (1969). *Symbolic interactionism.* Engle-wood Cliffs, NJ: Prentice-Hall.

Bultena, G., & Wood, V. (1969). The American re-tirement community: Bane or blessing? *Jour-nal of Gerontology, 24 ,* 209–217.

Butler, R. (1963). The life review: An interpretation of reminiscence in the aged. *Psychiatry, 26,* 65–76.

Calasanti, T. M. (1993). Introduction: A socialist-feminist approach to aging. *Journal of Aging Studies, 7,* 107–109.

Carp, F. (1969). Compound criteria in gerontological research. *Journal of Gerontology, 24,* 341–347.

Cavan, R., Burgess, E., Havighurst, R., & Goldham-mer, H. (1949). *Personal adjustment in old age.* Chicago: Science Research Associates.

Clair, J. M., Karp, D. A., & Yoels, W. C. (1993). *Expe-riencing the life cycle: A social psychology of aging* (2nd ed.). Springfield, IL: Charles C. Thomas.

Conner, K., Powers, E., & Bultena, G. (1979). Social interaction and life satisfaction: An empirical assessment of late-life patterns. *Journal of Ger-ontology, 34,* 116–121.

Cottrell, L. (1942). The adjustment of the individual to his age and sex roles. *American Sociological Review, 7,* 617–620.

Cowgill, D. (1974). Aging and modernization: A re-vision of the theory. In J. Gubrium (Ed.), *Late life: Communities and environmental policies.* Springfield, IL: Charles C Thomas.

Cowgill, D., & Holmes, L. (1972). *Aging and modern-ization .* New York: Appleton-Century-Crofts.

Crawford, M. P. (1971). Retirement and disengage-ment. *Human Relations, 24,* 255–278.

Cumming, E. (1963). Further thoughts on the theory of disengagement. *International Social Science Journal, 15* (3), 377–393.

Cumming, E., & Henry, W. (1961). *Growing old: The process of disengagement.* New York: Basic Books.

Dowd, J. (1975, September). Aging as exchange: A preface to theory. *Journal of Gerontology, 30,* 584–594.

Dowd, J. (1978). Aging as exchange: A test of the distributive justice proposition. *Pacific Socio-logical Review, 21,* 351–375.

Dowd, J. (1980). *Stratification among the aged: An analysis of power and dependence.* Monterey, CA: Brooks-Cole.

Dowd, J. (1984). Beneficence and the aged. *Journal of Gerontology, 39* (1), 102–108.

Emerson, R. M. (1976). Social exchange theory. In A. Inkeles, J. Coleman, & N. Smelser (Eds.), *Annual review of sociology* (Vol. 2). Palo Alto, CA: Annual Reviews.

Estes, C. L. (1979). *The aging enterprise.* San Fran-cisco: Jossey-Bass.

Estes, C. L., & Binney, A. A. (1991). The biomedi-calization of aging: Dangers and dilemmas. In M. Minkler & C. L. Estes (Eds.), *Critical per-spectives on aging.* Amityville, NY: Baywood.

Estes, C. L., Gerard, L. E., & Minkler, M. (1984). Re-assessing the future of aging policy and poli-tics. In M. Minkler & C. L. Estes (Eds.), *Readings in the political economy of aging.* Farm-ingdale, NY: Baywood.

Estes, C. L., Gerard, L. E., Zones, J. S., & Swan, J. H. (1984). *Political economy, health and aging.* Bos-ton: Little, Brown.

Estes, C. L., Swan, J. H., & Gerard, L. E. (1984). Dominant and competing paradigms in ger-ontology: Towards a political economy of aging. In M. Minkler & C. L. Estes (Eds.), *Readings in the political economy of aging.* Farm-ingdale, NY: Baywood.

Fischer, D. (1977). *Growing old in America.* New York: Oxford University Press.

Foner, A. (1975). Age in society: Structures and change. *American Behavioral Scientist, 19* (2), 289–312.

Fox, J. H. (1981–82). Perspectives on the continuity perspective. *International Journal of Aging and Human Development, 14,* 97–115.

Friedan, B. (1993). *The fountain of age.* New York: Simon & Schuster.

Gouldner, A. W. (1960, April). The norm of reciproc-ity. *American Sociological Review, 25,* 161–178.

Gubrium, J. (1973). *The myth of the golden years: A so-cial- environmental theory of aging.* Springfield, IL: Charles C. Thomas.

Gubrium, J. (1975). *Living and dying at Murray Manor.* New York: St. Martin's.

Habermas, J. (1971). *Knowledge and human interests.* Boston: Beacon.

Havighurst, R. (1968). Personality and patterns of aging. *Gerontologist, 8,* 20–23.

Hendricks, J., & Hendricks, C. D. (1986). *Aging in mass society: Myths and realities* (3rd ed.). Boston: Little, Brown.

Hochschild, A. (1975). Disengagement theory: A critique and proposal. *American Sociological Review, 40,* 553–569.

Homans, G. (1958, May). Social behavior as exchange. *American Journal of Sociology, 63,* 597–606.

Homans, G. (1974). *Social behavior: Its elementary forms* (rev. ed.). New York: Harcourt, Brace & World.

Hong, S. M. H., & Keith, P. M. (1992). The status of the aged in Korea: Are the modern more advantaged? *The Gerontologist, 32* (2), 197–202.

Kart, C. S., & Longino, C. F. (1987). The support systems of older people: A test of the exchange paradigm. *Journal of Aging Studies, 1* (3), 239–251.

Kertzer, D. I. (1983). Generation as a sociological problem. *Annual Review of Sociology, 9,* 125–149.

Knapp, M. (1977). The activity theory of aging: An examination in the English context. *Gerontologist, 17* (6), 553–559.

Lemon, B., Bengtson, V., & Peterson, J. (1972). Activity types and life satisfaction in a retirement community. *Journal of Gerontology, 27,* 511–523.

Longino, C. F. (1980). The retirement community. In F. Berghorn & D. Schafer (Eds.), *Dynamics of aging: Original essays on the experience and process of growing old.* Boulder, CO: Westview.

Longino, C. F., & Kart, C. S. (1982). Explicating activity theory: A formal replication. *Journal of Gerontology, 17* (6), 713–722.

Longino, C. F., McClelland, K. A., & Peterson, W. A. (1980). The aged subculture hypothesis: Social integration, gerontophilia and self-conception. *Journal of Gerontology, 35* (5), 758–767.

Lynott, R. J., & Lynott, P. P. (1996). Tracing the course of theoretical development in the sociology of aging. *The Gerontologist, 36* (6), 749–760.

Maddox, G. (1963). Activity and morale: A longitudinal study of selected elderly subjects. *Social Forces, 42,* 195–204.

Mannheim, K. (1952). The problem of generations. In *Essays on the sociology of knowledge.* New York: Oxford University Press.

Marshall, V. (1979). No exit: A symbolic interactionist perspective on aging. *International Journal of Aging and Human Development, 9,* 345–358.

Messer, M. (1967). The possibility of an age-concentrated environment becoming a normative system. *Gerontologist, 7,* 247–250.

Monge, R. H. (1975). Structure of the self-concept from adolescence through old age. *Experimental Aging Research, 1* (2), 281–291.

Moody, H. R. (1988). Toward a critical gerontology: The contributions of the humanities to theories of aging. In J. E. Birren & V. L. Bengtson (Eds.), *Emergent theories of aging.* New York: Springer.

Moody, H. R. (1992). Gerontology and critical theory. *The Gerontologist, 32,* 294–295.

Moody, H. R. (1993). Overview: What is critical gerontology and why is it important? In T. R. Cole and others (Eds.), *Voices and visions of aging: Toward a critical gerontology.* New York: Springer.

National Council on the Aging. (1976). *The myth and reality of aging in America.* Washington, DC: Author.

Navarro, V. (1984). The political economy of government cuts for the elderly. In M. Minkler & C. L. Estes (Eds.), *Readings in the political economy of aging.* Farmingdale, NY: Baywood.

Neugarten, B., Crotty, W., & Tobin, S. (1964). Personality types in an aged population. In B. Neugarten et al. (Eds.), *Personality in middle and late life.* New York: Atherton Press.

Neugarten, B., Havighurst, R., & Tobin, S. (1961). The measurement of life satisfaction. *Journal of Gerontology, 16,* 134–143.

Palmore, E. (1968). The effects of aging on activities and attitudes. *Gerontologist, 8,* 259–263.

Palmore, E. (1975). *The honorable elders: A cross-cultural analysis of aging in Japan.* Durham, NC: Duke University Press.

Palmore, E., & Maeda, D. (1985). *The honorable elders revisited: A revised cross-cultural analysis of aging in Japan.* Durham, NC: Duke University Press.

Palmore, E., & Manton, K. (1974). Modernization and status of the aged. *Journal of Gerontology, 29* (2), 205–210.

Palmore, E., & Whittington, F. (1971). Trends in the relative status of the aged. *Social Forces, 50,* 84–90.

Passuth, P. M., & Bengtson, V. L. (1988). Sociological theories of aging: Current perspectives and future directions. In J. E. Birren & V. L. Bengtson (Eds.), *Emergent theories of aging.* New York: Springer.

Phillips, B. (1957). A role theory approach to adjustment in old age. *American Sociological Review, 22,* 212–217.

Phillipson, C. (1982). *Capitalism and the construction of old age*. London: Macmillan.

Reichard, S., Livson, F., & Peterson, P. (1962). *Aging and personality*. New York: Wiley.

Riley, M. W. (1971). Social gerontology and the age stratification of society. *Gerontologist, 11*, 79–87.

Riley, M. W. (1976). Age strata in social systems. In R. Binstock & E. Shanas (Eds.), *Handbook of aging and the social sciences*. New York: Van Nostrand Reinhold.

Riley, M. W. (1985). Age strata in social systems. In R. Binstock & E. Shanas (Eds.), *Handbook of aging and the social sciences* (2nd ed.). New York: Van Nostrand Reinhold.

Riley, M. W., & Foner, A. (1968). *Aging and society: An inventory of research findings*. New York: Russell Sage Foundation.

Riley, M. W., Johnson, M., & Foner, A. (1972). *Aging and society: A sociology of age stratification*. New York: Russell Sage Foundation.

Rodin, J., & Langer, E. (1980). Aging labels: The decline of control and the fall of self-esteem. *Journal of Social Issues, 36* (2), 12–29.

Rose, A. (1965). The subculture of the aging: A framework in social gerontology. In A. M. Rose & W. A. Peterson (Eds.), *Older people and their social worlds*. Philadelphia: F. A. Davis.

Rosow, I. (1967). *Social integration of the aged*. New York: Free Press.

Rosow, I. (1985). Status and role change through the life cycle. In R. H. Binstock & E. Shanas (Eds.), *Handbook of aging and the social sciences* (2nd ed.). New York: Van Nostrand Reinhold.

Shanas, E. (1979). The family as a social support system in old age. *Gerontologist, 19*, 169–174.

Sinnott, J. D. (1977). Sex-role inconstancy, biology, and successful aging: A dialectical model. *Gerontologist, 17* (5), 459–463.

Spence, D. L. (1986). Some contributions of symbolic interaction to the study of growing old. In V. W. Marshall (Ed.), *Later life: The social psychology of aging*. Beverly Hills: Sage.

Stoller, E. P. (1993). Gender and the organization of lay health care: A socialist-feminist perspective. *Journal of Aging Studies, 7*, 151–170.

Stoller, E. P., & Earl, L. L. (1983). Help with activities of everyday life: Sources of support for the noninstitutionalized elderly. *Gerontologist, 23* (1), 64–70.

Streib, G. (1965). Are the aged a minority group? In A. Gouldner & S. M. Miller (Eds.), *Applied sociology*. New York: Free Press.

Sussman, M. (1976). The family life of old people. In R. Binstock & E. Shanas (Eds.), *Handbook of aging and the social sciences* . New York: Van Nostrand Reinhold.

Tallmer, M., & Kutner, B. (1970, Winter). Disengagement and morale. *Gerontologist, 10*, 317–320.

Thoits, P. (1982). Conceptual, methodological, and theoretical problems in studying social support as a buffer against life stress. *Journal of Health and Social Behavior, 23*, 145–159.

Tornstam, L. (1992). The quo vadis of gerontology: On the scientific paradigm of gerontology. *The Gerontologist, 32* , 318–326.

Tornstam, L. (1996). Gerotranscendence—A theory about maturing in old age. *Journal of Aging and Identity, 1*, 37–50.

Ward, R. A. (1984). *The aging experience* (2nd ed.). New York: Harper & Row.

Ward, R. A. (1985). Informal networks and well-being in later life: A research agenda. *Gerontologist, 25*, 55–61.

Ward, R. A., Sherman, S., & Lagory, M. (1984). Subjective network assessments and subjective well being. *Journal of Gerontology, 39*, 93–101.

Weiss, R. (1969). The fund of sociability. *Transaction, 6*, 26–43.

Yin, P., & Lai, K. H. (1983). A reconceptualization of age stratification in China. *Journal of Gerontology, 38* (5), 608–613.

Youmans, E. G. (1967). Disengagement among older rural and urban men. In E. G. Youmans (Ed.), *Older rural Americans*. Lexington: University of Kentucky Press.

CHAPTER TEN

AGING AND FAMILY LIFE

The institution of the family is one that is best known and that affects most people. The effects of other institutions—political, educational, and economic—are felt, but it is the family that touches people more deeply and continuously than any other. Families help regulate sexual activity and provide a context within which children are conceived and raised. Families afford individuals protection, affection, intimacy, and social identity.

Among social scientists, there is greater consensus about the functions of the family than about its form or structure. For example, anthropologists have largely been unable to agree on a common definition of a family. This should not be surprising, since much of the literature of anthropology and family sociology highlights the wide variety of forms families can take. This becomes especially clear in comparing different cultures in terms of their mate-selection procedures, child-rearing practices, and the degree of interaction allowed among family members. Variation in family structure exists within societies as well. Although most Americans today live in some form of *nuclear family* (husband/wife couple with children living in a common household), there is a wide array of family types in the United States. In fact, Bengtson, Rosenthal and Burton (1990) suggest that today's elderly are participants in a "quiet revolution" that is changing family structure, roles, and relationships. For example, Winsborough, Bumpass, and Aguilino (1991) estimate that approximately one-third of people between the ages of 45 and 64 are members of four-generation families, and Hagestad (1988) reports that 20 percent of women who died after the age of 80 were members of five-generation families.

Much discussion has focused on the relationship between family structure and the role and status of aged people in a society. One form of family structure is often considered advantageous for the aged—the extended family. The term *extended family* is conventionally used to describe all those individuals one is related to through blood and marriage, but the term is also used to characterize three or more generations who share living arrangements. Premodern, or preindustrial, societies, which are generally believed to have been organized around the extended family, are often offered as evidence of the favored status of older people in extended family settings. In such societies, the aged are thought to be well integrated into family life, with family members living and working together harmoniously. This view is most likely an overly simplistic one; neither the contemporary nor the premodern family should be seen as a monolithic entity. First, consideration of the data on longevity in premodern societies reveal that too few older people survived for three or more generation families to be universal. Also, preindustrial societies evinced a wide variation in family organization; many, even those in which the extended family was evident, treated old people quite poorly. Sieroshevski (1901) has written of the Yakuts of Siberia as follows:

> The Yakuts treat their old relatives, who have grown stupid, very badly. Usually they try to take from them the remains of their property, if they have any; then constantly, in measure, as they become unprotected they treat them worse and worse. Even in houses relatively self-sufficient, I found such living skeletons, wrinkled, half-naked, or even entirely naked, hiding in corners, from where they crept out only when no strangers were present, to get warm by the fire, to pick up together with children bits of food thrown away, or to quarrel with them over the licking of the dish emptied of food. (quoted in Simmons 1945, p. 197)

Simmons (1945, 1960), a student of aging in many different societies, argues that throughout human history, the family has been the safest haven for the aged, even though the condition of the Yakut elderly shows otherwise. Simmons studied the position of the aged among 71 different premodern societies, and his data reveal that it was the organization of kinship relationships that primarily determined the destiny of aged people. In particular, opportunities for the aged to remain effective participants in society seemed to be related to their opportunities to (1) marry younger mates, (2) exercise managerial roles in the family, (3) rely on family care and support, and (4) rely on the support of their sons-in-law. Important as kinship relationships were, however, they were not the only determinants of the position of the aged in these societies. Also included were the climate and physical environment, as well as cultural factors, including the principal means of economy, the permanency of residence, the constancy of food supply, the nature of the political system, and the establishment of property rights in land, crops, herds, and other goods.

What about the relationship between family structure and the position of aged people in modern societies such as the United States?

OLD AGE AND THE U.S. FAMILY: A LOOK BACK

In the United States, the past—that is, the preindustrial and early industrial period from the country's beginnings up to the turn of the twentieth century—is often characterized as an idyllic time during which three or more generations of relatives lived harmoniously together on the family farm. Such extended families were thought to be led by the elders, those respected members of the family and community. As the reader will see, however, this respect, along with the obligation to care for elders, often was based on their control of resources, reinforced by religious tradition and normative sanction.

This picture of family life in an earlier time is often contrasted with that of contemporary family life, involving nuclear family units composed of husband/wife couples and their children. Conventional wisdom says that these nuclear family units live apart from one another and that bureaucratic institutions perform many of the functions once fulfilled by the family, including care of dependent elderly. Moreover, younger people are said to no longer give the parental generation the love and respect that traditionally has been its due.

The major cause of this shift in family organization from the extended to the nuclear family is thought to be industrialization. Advocates of this view argue that extended families are advantageous in agrarian societies because all family members (including children and the elderly) contribute economically to the family. This is not the case in an industrial society, where children and the elderly are largely unemployable. Moreover, because they consume at a high rate, these dependent relatives are a burden rather than an advantage.

This unemployability of dependent relatives is seen as only one cause of the transformation of the extended family into the nuclear family in industrialized societies. With industrialization, the location of work shifted away from the home. Workers migrated to places where job opportunities existed. This geographical mobility strained kinship bonds and decreased the frequency and intimacy of contact among family members. In addition, some have argued that industrialization opened up opportunities for women to participate in work activities outside the home, thus diminishing the importance of some extended family functions.

With the passing of the extended family, it is believed that older people lost their economic role and became isolated from their children and relatives. Even the most noted sociologist adopted this view: Almost 60 years ago, Talcott Parsons (1942) wrote that with marriage and occupational independence of children comes "the depletion of [the] family until the older couple is finally left alone." Parsons contrasted this situation with that of other kinship systems (e.g., extended families) "in which membership in a kinship unit is continuous throughout the life cycle."

Although the position of the aged in the family in the United States certainly has undergone some historical change, not all share the perspective that a change in family structure from extended to nuclear is associated with loss of status/respect and isolation for the elderly. For example, historical demographers now argue that the nuclear family has been viable throughout history and probably was the dominant type of family structure during the American colonial period.

It is not at all likely that the family evolved from an extended to a nuclear form. Rather, it has probably remained much the same. Gerontologist Clark Tibbitts (1968, p. 132) has written that "it is now clear that the nuclear parent-child family has always been the modal family type in the United States and three-generation families have always been relatively rare."

Many family sociologists today have come to use the notion of a *modified extended family structure* to describe the interchange of visits and help between older parents and their children, which they believe to be more the rule than the exception. From this view, they argue that the family—far from being irrelevant, as some contend—is becoming increasingly important as a place where older people can find support and interpersonal warmth as society becomes more bureaucratic and impersonal.

How does one account for the fictionalized (some would say idealized) version of the U.S. extended family of the past? This is a difficult question. While arguing that this idealization of the past obscures its real character, Goode (1963, p. 7) points out that "in each generation people write of a period still more remote, their grandparents' generation, when things really were much better." Perhaps, then, the answer lies in some universal belief that things were better in the past.

The general view in sociology has been that the nuclear family was founded in western Europe and the United States and is a result of the urban-industrial revolution. As already indicated, the extended family is the form thought to have been prevalent prior to the urban-industrial revolution. This view has come into question, however, as much evidence suggests that the nuclear family was the dominant form of family organization in Europe during the preindustrial period as well.

Greenfield (1967, p. 322) argues that the "small nuclear family was brought to the United States and Great Britain by its earliest settlers" and even suggests that the nuclear family helped produce the industrial revolution. Laslett and Harrison (1963, p. 167), in their study of two seventeenth-century English counties, Clayworth and Cogenhoe, found that the family was not extended; the "household did not ordinarily contain more generations than two.... Living with in-laws or relatives was on the whole not to be expected."

Back (1974) examined census records in England from 1574 to 1821 and found that only 6 percent of households contained three or more generations of family members. It is interesting that these extended households appeared to result almost always from a family tragedy of some sort, such as widowhood. Back concluded that there is no evidence that three-generation households were the preferred family pattern during the preindustrial period. Given the low percentage of extended families to begin with (6 percent), one would be hard pressed to argue that industrialization caused a decline in multigenerational households.

What about the United States? Were extended families indigenous to this country? A number of studies of the American colonial family conclude that the extended structure was the exception rather than the rule. Using family wills as a source, Demos observed of the Plymouth colony that "there was not extended families at all in the sense of 'under the same roof'...married brothers and sisters never lived together in the same house," and "as soon as a man becomes betrothed, plans were made for the building, or purchase, of his own house...and it was most unusual for married fathers with married sons to live together in an extended family group" (1965, p. 279).

In describing the family structure in seventeenth-century Andover, Massachusetts, Greven (1966) distinguishes between the family of residence, which is nuclear, and the family of interaction or obligation, which he terms *modified extended*. Greven defines the **modified extended family** as a kinship group of two or more generations living within a single community in which the children continue to depend on their parents after they have married and are no longer living under the same roof.

Has this revised picture of the early U.S. family altered the view gerontologists have of the elderly during this period? Remember, it is generally believed that in early America, the elderly were in a more favorable position vis-à-vis family and society than they are today. Many associate this historically favorable position with the extended family and the subsequent loss of status and prestige with the change in family structure. The change in family structure (from extended to nuclear) appears to be more fiction than fact, but the change in the way Americans view the elderly is not.

Historian David H. Fischer has written about this changing disposition toward the elderly in the United States. In the following summary of his writing, notice that Fischer does not associate the historical decline in the status of older people with a change in family structure. Rather, he associates it with the kinds of cultural, demographic, and technological changes often associated with the modernization theory (discussed in Chapter 9).

Fischer (1977) lends support to the positive characterization of the position of the elderly in families of bygone days. At least, he argues, through its colonial phase, the United States was a *gerontophilic* place where being old conferred power and prestige: As Cotton Mather wrote in 1726, "the two qualities together, the ancient and the honorable." Seating arrangements in Massachusetts meeting-houses were determined by age rather than by wealth or status. Elders ran the churches. The aged occupied positions of community leadership; "grey champions" were turned to in crucial times. Names for persons in authority, such as *senator* and *alderman,* were derived from words meaning old. Men tended to overstate rather than understate their age, and powdered wigs and long coats were used to give an older appearance.

Fischer believes that between 1770 and 1820, a revolution in age relations took place in the United States. This revolution, fueled by the ideology of liberty and equality, had the effect of dissolving the authority formerly vested in age. Fischer offers numerous manifestations of this revolution in age relations. By the later part of the eighteenth century, most New England town meetings had abandoned the practice of seating members on the basis of age. Northampton, Massachusetts, sold seats at auction rather than assigning them on the basis of age. Thus, the best seats went to the highest bidder, and rank and status in the meetinghouse thereafter rested on wealth, without regard to age.

Mandatory retirement for public officials first appeared in the United States at the end of the eighteenth century. In 1777, the state of New York introduced compulsory retirement at age 70 for judges. New Hampshire followed suit in 1792, as did Connecticut in 1818. New York reduced the retirement age to 60 in 1821. These statutes angered former President John Adams, who wrote to Thomas Jefferson of his indignation: "I can never forgive New York, Connecticut, or Maine for turning out venerable men of sixty or seventy, when their judgment is often the best." Jefferson later responded, "It is reasonable we should drop off, and make room for another growth. When we have lived our generation out, we should not wish to encroach upon another" (Fischer 1977, p. 77). Jefferson, it seems, shared the revolutionary spirit in a way Adams could not.

What caused this revolution in age relations? Fischer suggests that one key factor was the changing age composition of society. The number of aged was increasing, partly because more people were surviving to old age. Perhaps more important, however, is the fact that birthrates began to fall in the decade from 1800 to 1810, and continued to do so for about 150 years. The aged became a slowly increasing proportion of the population. At the same time that old age became more common, it also became more contemptible: "Where the Puritans had made a cult of age, their posterity made a cult of youth instead" (Fischer 1977, p. 114). In 1847, Henry David Thoreau wrote:

> Age is no better, hardly so well, qualified for an instructor as youth, for it has not profited so much as it has lost.... Practically, the old have no very important advice to give the young, their experience has been so partial, and their lives have been such miserable failures, for private reasons, as they must believe; and it may be that they have some faith left which belies that experience, and they are only less young than they were. (quoted in Fischer 1977, pp. 115–116)

The developing urbanization and industrialization of U.S. society accompanied demographic changes. The young, instead of waiting to inherit the family land, could move to the city and find work. Through the nineteenth and into the twentieth centuries, moving to the city became a strategy for leaving farming and parental control alike. Industrialization and urbanization contributed to changes in the character of generational relations. The young were no longer captive to a parental generation that controlled the family property and other economic resources.

THE STRUCTURE OF FAMILY IN CONTEMPORARY SOCIETY

Families today are more heterogeneous and more complex than ever before. Longino and Earle (1996) trace this heterogeneity and complexity to various social, economic, cultural, and demographic factors. They maintain that social movements of the 1960s and 1970s encouraged women in the Baby Boom cohort to pursue educational and employment opportunities. As a result, many career women postponed marriage and childbearing. When these women did marry and/or have children, they did so at a later age, and had fewer numbers of children, than did women in earlier cohorts.

During the 1970s, the growth of the economy slowed as increasing numbers of women were attempting to enter the professional work force. Many men and women found themselves underemployed and facing slow growth in earnings. As a result, many college-educated individuals were denied the upward mobility that their parents experienced when they entered the work force following World War II. Dual-income families became the norm among middle-class families who sought to maintain and improve their socioeconomic status. Many of these same families also tended to have children at later ages and to have fewer children. Thus, within the middle class, social, economic, and demographic trends have resulted in relatively wide age gaps between the generations. This type of family structure has been referred to as an *age-gapped family structure* (Bengtson, Rosenthal, & Burton 1990).

In distinct contrast to the age-gapped family structure, there has also been an increase in age-condensed family structures among certain members of society (Bengtson, Rosenthal, & Burton 1990). The *age-condensed family structure* refers to a pattern in which teenage pregnancies within the same family over a number of generations results in age differences of fewer than 20 years between generations. This pattern, more common among ethnic minorities than among the majority population, can relatively quickly result in four- and five-generation families. Among these families, there are narrow age gaps (as few as 15 years) between each successive generation.

Regardless of socioeconomic class, the rates of divorce are higher among Baby Boomers than among earlier cohorts. As a result, the number of traditional nuclear families among Baby Boomers is declining, whereas the number of cohabitating couples and single-parent and blended families are increasing. Thus, at the same time there are increasing numbers of professional, dual-income families, there are also increasing numbers of single-parent families, age-condensed family patterns, and low-income families.

The contemporary family has been characterized as having a vertical, or "bean-pole," structure (Bengtson, Rosenthal, & Burton 1990). Contemporary families tend to have living members in a greater number of generations, but fewer members in each generation, than in the past. This structure has been attributed to two factors: decreased fertility rates and increased longevity. To illustrate, in 1900, the average number of children born per woman was 3.7; today, an average of 2.0 children are born per woman (U.S. Bureau of the Census 1999, Table 96). With respect to longevity, in 1900, the average life expectancy for men was 46.4 years and 49 years for women; the average life expectancy expected in 2000 is 73 years for men and 79.7 years for women (U.S. Bureau of the Census 1999, Table 127). Nonetheless, the commonly used bean-pole analogy should not be allowed to mask the heterogeneity in the contemporary family.

Factors that contribute to the diversity in contemporary families include gender, race and ethnicity, and family form.

Diversity by Gender

Women have long been identified as "keepers of the kin." Because of the major role that women have traditionally played, family life has long been characterized as having a matrilineal tone (Longino & Earle 1996). The matrilineal tone of contemporary families has been reinforced by a number of factors. The role of women within the family has been strengthened by the rise in teenage pregnancies and out-of-marriage births as well as growth in ethnic and racial minority populations—specifically, the African American population, where a matrilineal structure is especially strong (Bengtson, Rosenthal, & Burton 1990).

Increasing divorce rates have especially strengthened the role that women play within the family. Women are typically awarded custody in divorce cases, and many divorced men have limited access to their children. Further, 9 out of 10 single-parent households are headed by women, either because they never married or have divorced (Longino & Earle 1996). As a result, among contemporary families, the bonds between children and mothers are often stronger than are the bonds between children and their fathers.

Because of the greater longevity of women, the ***verticalization*** of the family structure has been more pronounced for women than for men. This results from changes in the amount of time that women spend in family roles, such as adult daughter to aging parents, grandmother, and widow (Bengtson & Silverstein 1993). After examining three simulated cohorts of older adults born in 1800, 1900, and 1980, Watkins, Menken, and Bongaarts (1987) conclude that women in 1980, compared to their peers in 1800, spent four times the number of years as a daughter with both parents alive. It has also been predicted that the typical woman today can expect to spend as many years of her life helping an older parent who suffers from some type of health impairment as she spends raising her children (U.S. House of Representatives 1987). Women can also expect to spend more time in the role of widow than their male counterparts.

Diversity by Race and Ethnicity

In a discussion on paradoxes in the study of families and aging, Bengtson, Rosenthal, and Burton (1996) identify two related assumptions about racial and/or ethnic minorities such as African Americans, Native Americans, Asian Americans, and Mexican Americans/Hispanics. One assumption is that higher fertility rates, extended family living arrangements, and the inclusion of fictive kin, or nonblood relatives, in the definition of family have resulted in more sources of support within the family. The second assumption is that members of these groups have stronger family networks than do whites.

Bengtson, Rosenthal, and Burton (1996) are quick to point out that the first assumption overlooks the possibility that the financial and emotional costs associated with being a member of a larger extended family very well might outweigh any potential benefits. As such, it cannot be assumed that there are greater sources of support in minority than majority families. Further, research that compares the strength of the support provided by minority and majority families does not find significant differences (Eggebeen & Hogan 1990). Still, both the sources of support and strength of family ties in minority families is more heterogeneous than previously thought (Silverstein & Waite 1993). Growing evidence shows that comparisons between minority and majority families are often too simplistic and mask differences between families from various ethnic and/or minority groups (Bengtson & Silverstein 1993; Stanford & Torres-Gil 1992). Also, discussions of the double-, triple-, and quadruple-jeopardy faced by older minorities ignores evidence that there are potential benefits of ethnicity in old age.[1]

Diversity in Family Form

Demographic and social factors together have resulted in family forms that are distinct from the traditional intact U.S. family (nuclear family living with children). Among these alternative family forms are *truncated families, reconstituted families, gay and lesbian couples,* and *sibling-based families.*

Truncated Families.   Families become truncated when members of the youngest generation fail to have children. There is debate about the extent to which truncated families will become more common in the future. On the one hand, George and Gold (1991) cite U.S. Census data to argue that there will be increasing numbers of childless older adults in the next 30 to 40 years. However, Uhlenberg (1993) maintains that although the rates of childlessness are higher among Baby Boomers than among earlier cohorts, the rates are not unprecedented; fewer than 20 percent of older adults will be childless until at least the year 2050. Regardless of which projections prove to be true, two patterns are likely for older members of truncated family structures. First, for older members of a truncated family, relationships with siblings (Gold 1987) and nonkin friends (George & Gold 1991) are likely to become especially important. Second, by necessity, intergenerational relationships will more likely occur with extended kin, such as nieces and nephews, or with fictive kin.

Reconstituted Families.   Reconstituted families are formed when people divorce and remarry. The U.S. Bureau of the Census (1999, Tables 161, 162) reports that, for 1990, the divorce rate was 48 percent of the rate of marriage and, among women aged 50 to 54, 29.5 percent were divorced after a first marriage, 63 percent were remarried after divorce, and 34.5 percent had redivorced after remarriage. Divorce itself is a challenge for families; grandparents, parents, and children must redefine their relationships with one another. The creation of a reconstituted family presents additional challenges as members of the blended family strive to establish relationships with new family members as well as redefine and maintain relationships with existing and former family members. A major challenge for older members of reconstituted families is negotiating and maintaining the types of relationships that they desire with their various family members.

Gay and Lesbian Couples.   It is estimated that approximately 10 percent of adults over age 65 are homosexual (Schlesinger 1996). Peplau (1991) reports that

---

[1]*Double jeopardy* describes a compounding of the negative effects of aging for minority group members. *Triple jeopardy* describes this compounding of effects for those who are old, female, and minority group members. *Quadruple jeopardy* describes this compounding of effects for those who are old, female, poor, and minority group members.

long-term relationships among older homosexual couples are frequent occurrences. This might be surprising because, historically, both professionals and the general public have assumed that older gays and lesbians typically do not engage in long-term relationships and are more isolated and depressed than their heterosexual counterparts (Walters & Simoni 1993). However, research suggests that isolation and depression are not particularly characteristic of older homosexuals. Dorfman and colleagues (1995) compared older homosexual and heterosexual men and women in terms of depression and social support and found no differences, after controlling for participants' gender, level of education, and whether they had a live-in partner. However, heterosexuals tended to receive more social support from family members, whereas homosexuals tended to receive more social support from friends.

Many of today's older homosexuals grew up in a time when it was necessary for them to conceal their sexual orientation. Kimmel (1978) and McDougall (1993) suggest that although the need for such concealment reflects negatively on society, it may actually facilitate successful aging. Because of the social climate in which they grew up, many of today's older gays and lesbians developed a strong sense of personal autonomy and independence, learned at a young age to fend for themselves, adopted more flexible gender roles throughout their lives, and cultivated multiple interests outside of their careers.

Homosexuals have the option of growing old in as many as three types of families: their families of origin, the family of their spouse and children (if applicable), and a created family (Kimmel 1992). The created families of older homosexuals might include selected members of the first two types of families as well as friends and significant others. Regardless of their composition, Kimmel maintains that created families provide mutual support and function like traditional families. Within the created family, older homosexuals often are viewed as role models/mentors to younger homosexuals. Kimmel also indicates that some older gay men and lesbian women occupy special roles within their family of origin. Because older homosexuals often have more disposable income, they may be called on to assist family members with financial as well as emotional support. Similar to older members of reconstituted families, a major challenge for older members of homosexual couples is negotiating and maintaining the types of relationships that they desire with their various family members.

Sibling-Based Families. In part because of a decrease in birthrates and an increase in rates of divorce, sibling relationships are expected to gain in importance to older adults (Bengtson & Silverstein 1993; Gold 1987). Sibling relationships are among the longest-lasting relationships that people sustain. Because of the length of these relationships, which often last a lifetime, relationships with siblings can help keep family experiences and memories alive. In general, adults indicate that their relationships with siblings are positive, with women reporting more positive relationships than men, and African Americans reporting more positive relationships than Whites (Bedford 1995; Brubaker 1990b).

Research by Gold (1989) elaborates on the types of relationships that older siblings have with one another. Using qualitative interviews, five types of sibling relationships are identified:

1. *Intimate:* Characterized by devotion and psychological closeness
2. *Congenial:* Characterized by friendship and caring
3. *Loyal:* Characterized by an allegiance based on shared family background
4. *Apathetic:* Characterized by indifference
5. *Indifferent:* Characterized by resentment and anger

Gold reported that 78 percent of her interviewees reported relationships with their siblings that she would consider to be at least moderately strong and positive; 34 percent were reported as intimate, 30 percent as congenial, and 14 percent as loyal. The remaining 22 percent of interviewees reported either apathetic or indifferent relationships with their siblings. A separate investigation of African Americans indicated that 95 percent of sibling relationships were classified as either intimate, congenial, or loyal (Gold 1990; Gold, Woodbury, & George 1990).

Sibling relationships appear to vary over the life course, with increased involvement in later life. In later life, siblings can serve as sources of both instrumental and emotional support. Probably the greatest challenge facing sibling-based families in later life concerns the loss of a sibling as a source of support, whether it be due to declining health or eroding functional abilities.

Researchers do not yet know as much about how these alternative families function as they would like. However, those researchers who are involved in studying alternative forms of family are quick to point out that "alternative" does not necessarily mean "lesser." What remains to be seen is how potential strengths for older members of these and all families can be maximized.

THE FUNCTION OF FAMILY IN CONTEMPORARY SOCIETY

Much of what is known about intergenerational family relationships over time derives from the Longitudinal Study of Generations (LSG). Begun by Vern Bengtson and his colleagues at the University of Southern California in 1971, researchers have studied a group of approximately 300 three- and four-generation families (consisting of more than 2,000 grandparents, parents, grandchildren, and great-grandchildren) for almost 30 years. The purpose of the LGS is to learn about long-term, intergenerational family relationships. Participants were recruited from randomly selected members of a health maintenance organization (HMO) in southern California. Initial interviews were conducted in 1971, and subsequent interviews were conducted in 1985, 1988, 1991, 1994, and 1997.

Bengtson and Schmeeckle (1995) report that, in general, intergenerational relationships have been examined along two axes: solidarity and conflict. Based on data from the LGS, among most members of contemporary families, intergenerational bonds are reported to be strong. Bengtson (1996) estimates that only 12 percent of intergenerational family relationships might be considered "long-term lousy relationships" (p. 281). Bengtson and Roberts (1991) define *intergenerational solidarity* as positive interactions, cohesion, and sentiments between parents and their adult children, and between grandparents and adult grandchildren. They identify six interrelated dimensions of intergenerational solidarity, presented in Table 10.1.

TABLE 10.1   Six Elements of Intergenerational Solidarity, with Nominal Definitions and Examples of Empirical Indicators

CONSTRUCT	NOMINAL DEFINITION	EMPIRICAL INDICATORS
Associational Solidarity	Frequency and patterns of interaction in various types of activities in which family members engage	1. Frequency of intergenerational interaction (i.e., face-to-face, telephone, mail) 2. Types of common activities shared (i.e., recreation, special occasions, etc.)
Affectual Solidarity	Type and degree of positive sentiments held about family members, and the degree of reciprocity of these sentiments	1. Ratings of affection, warmth, closeness, understanding, trust, and respect for family members 2. Ratings of perceived reciprocity in positive sentiments among family members
Consensual Solidarity	Degree of agreement on values, attitudes, and beliefs among family members	1. Intrafamilial concordance among individual measures of specific values, attitudes, and beliefs. 2. Ratings of perceived similarity with other family members in values, attitudes, and beliefs
Functional Solidarity	Degree of helping and exchanges	1. Frequency of intergenerational exchanges of resources of assistance (e.g., financial, physical, emotional) 2. Ratings of reciprocity in the intergenerational exchanges of resources
Normative Solidarity	Strength of commitment to performance of familial roles and to meeting familial obligations	1. Ratings of importance of family and intergenerational roles 2. Ratings of strength of filial obligations (familism)
Structural Solidarity	Opportunity structure for intergenerational relationships reflected in number, type, and geographic proximity of family member	1. Residential propinquity of family members 2. Number of family members 3. Health of family members

Source: V. L. Bengtson and E. L. Roberts, "Intergenerational Solidarity in Aging Families: An Example of Formal Theory Construction. *Journal of Marriage and the Family,* 53 (November 1991): 856–870. Copyrighted 1991 by the National Council on Family Relations, 3989 Central Ave. NE, Suite 550, Minneapolis, MN 55421. Reprinted by permission. (Adapted from V. L. Bengtson and S. Schrader [1982]. "Parent-Child Relations" in D. Mangen and W. Peterson [Eds.], *Handbook of Research Instruments in Social Gerontology* [Vol. 2, pp. 115–185]. Minneapolis: University of Minnesota Press; and K. Y. McChesney and V. L. Bengtson [1988]. "Solidarity, Integration, and Cohesion in Families: Concepts and Theories" in D. Mangen, V. L. Bengtson, and P. H. Landry [Eds.], *Measurement of Intergenerational Relations* [pp. 15–30]. Newbury Park, CA: Sage.)

For each of the six dimensions, the table includes a definition and at least two examples of how the dimension might be measured.

The first five dimensions of intergenerational solidarity differ from structural solidarity in an important manner. They are concerned with behaviors that occur between family members (associational and functional solidarity), emotions that family members have toward one another (affectual solidarity), and/or beliefs that family members hold about their family (consensual and normative solidarity). In contrast, structural solidarity addresses whether family members are available for intergenerational family interactions.

Of the six dimensions of intergenerational solidarity, gerontological researchers have devoted the most attention to structural, associational, and functional solidarity (i.e., the opportunity structures within families and the actual behaviors that occur among family members). Less attention has been dedicated to affectual, normative, and consensual solidarity, or those dimensions that deal with people's beliefs about, or emotions toward, their families. Nonetheless, the six dimensions of intergenerational solidarity provide a useful framework for organizing what is known about intergenerational relationships in contemporary families.

Structural Solidarity

Structural solidarity deals with opportunities for intergenerational relationships within the family. One indicator of structural solidarity is whether there are sufficient numbers of adult children who are available to interact with their aging parents. With recent demographic changes, including the decrease in birthrates, some researchers have suggested that there will not be enough family members in the future to care for older relatives. To determine the extent to which this is a legitimate concern, Himes (1992) analyzed U.S. Census data and concluded that the majority of older adults will have opportunities for intergenerational relationships with younger family members, at least until the year 2020. In fact, between now and the year 2020, the proportion of older adults who are unmarried and who do not have children is projected to decline from current rates.

A strong predictor of whether there is contact between intergenerational members of families is how close to one another the family members live (Rossi & Rossi 1990; Spitze & Logan 1991). Geographic proximity is also a strong predictor of how much intergenerational assistance is provided within a family. Almost all studies show that older people prefer to live near, but not with, their children. Analyzing data from the 1987 National Survey of Families and Households, Lin and Rogerson (1995) report that the majority of older adults have at least one adult child who lives within 10 miles. Reasons usually cited for preferring separate households include the desire to preserve independence and privacy as well as avoid interference and potential conflict with children.

Using data from nationwide surveys of the adult noninstitutionalized population of the United States, Okraku (1987) offers evidence that, since 1973, attitudes toward multigenerational residence have become more positive. The relationship between age and level of approval is inverse, however. Younger cohorts expressed more unconditional support for coresidence, whereas older cohorts expressed more conditional approval. Situations that include poor health or inadequate finances most often seem to necessitate that an older parent live with an adult child.

Approximately 20 percent of older adults who have a living child share a residence with that child (Clarke & Neidert 1992). Figure 10.1 shows the percentages of elderly (60 years of age and over) whites and blacks actually residing with adult children in each available census year from 1900 to 1980. At the turn of the twentieth century, more than 55 percent of whites age 60 years or older resided with adult children. The proportion of elderly blacks with such living arrangements was about 40 percent. By 1980, the situation had changed dramatically. Only about 15 percent of elderly whites resided with adult children, whereas about 25 percent of elderly blacks did so.

According to Ruggles and Goeken (1992), the decline in coresidence among whites came in the category of elderly persons residing with their never-married children. These researchers argue that it became socially acceptable for unmarried women to live on their own and, at the same time, obligations for caring for elderly parents declined. Also, in the years since the end of World War II, increasing

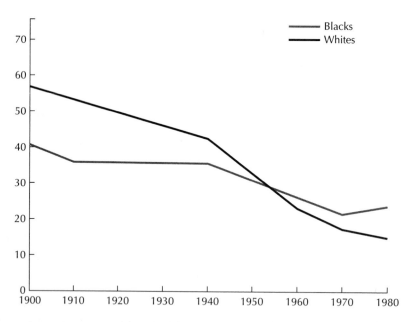

FIGURE 10.1   Percentage of Persons Age 60 and Over Residing with Adult Children Controlling for Age, Sex, Marital Status, Presence of Spouse, Metropolitan Residence, and Farm Residence by Race and Census Year

Source: S. Ruggles and R. Goeken, "Race and Multigenerational Family Structure, 1900–1980," in S. J. South and S. E. Tolnay (Eds.), *The Changing American Family: Sociological and Demographic Perspectives*, 1992, Figure 2.3b, p. 24. Reprinted by permission.

income among the elderly has allowed a greater proportion to reside independently. For African Americans, changes in population composition and improved income, especially since 1960, explain the more modest decline in coresidence.

In summary, although the popular media has claimed that contemporary families are geographically dispersed, this claim is not supported by data. The data suggest that structural intergenerational solidarity is high among members of contemporary families, and that it should remain so into at least the first quarter of this century.

Associational Solidarity

Associational solidarity deals with the frequency and patterns of intergenerational interactions among family members. Most older parents and their adult children see each other quite often. The Harris Poll (National Council on the Aging 1976) found that 55 percent of those surveyed who were age 65 and over had seen one of their children within the last day or so; an additional 26 percent had seen one of their children within the last week or two. Still, much evidence exists for the considerable and growing diversity in older parent/adult child relations among contemporary families. Researchers have concentrated on several specific factors of social differentiation, including ethnic and racial differences, proximity, urban/rural differences, and gender.

A study of aged ethnics in Washington, DC, and Baltimore, Maryland, revealed that 91 percent of the respondents had frequent to almost daily contact with their children (Gutman et al. 1979). There was some variation in contact with children among the ethnic groups: Greeks had the most frequent contact— almost twice as much as did aged Estonians. The nature of the contact was also different among ethnic groups. Hungarians had the highest percentage of those who had face-to-face contact with children, whereas the Lithuanians had the highest amount of phone contact with their children.

Geographic proximity, an indicator of structural solidarity, may also be a strong determinant of frequency of contact with family for older people. In their study of elderly black residents of Cleveland, Ohio, Wolf and colleagues (1983) report that those who had adult children in the neighborhood had contact with them daily. Those whose children lived an hour away reported significantly less contact. Conventional wisdom supports an expectation of greater kinship ties and associational solidarity across the generations in rural areas. Krout (1988) interviewed 600 individuals age 65 and over residing in a continuum of community settings from farm areas to the central city of a large metropolis in western New York. His findings suggest that the impact of rurality on the elderly person's in-person contact with children has been overstated. Proximity was a far stronger predictor of in-person contact between elderly parents and their children. Krout concludes that "people in rural areas do not have especially strong family ties or at least they are not evidenced by greater frequency of in-person contact nor are urban areas characterized by a lower level of intergenerational contact" (1988, p. 202).

There appears to be some truth to the maxim that "a son is a son until he gets a wife, and a daughter is a daughter all her life." Research does show visitation to be more frequent along the female line. Husbands are more likely to be in touch with the wives' parents than their own, unless the wife mediates contact with the husband's parents. According to Atkinson, Kivett, and Campbell (1986), familial linkages between generations that are female based are predictive of greater exchange of help. These researchers lend support to the role of women as the keepers of kin.

In a study of three-generation Mexican American families in San Antonio, Texas, respondents were asked how often they engaged in certain activities (e.g., recreation outside the home, religious activities, telephone conversation) with each of their family members in the other two generations. All-female dyads showed higher levels of association than all-male and cross-sex dyads (Markides, Boldt, & Ray 1986).

Functional Solidarity

Many people believe that as parents age, the parent/child relationship undergoes a role reversal, with the parent assuming the role of dependent and the child taking on the supportive role of the parent. This is simply not the case. ***Functional solidarity,*** or the extent to which resources are exchanged between and among the generations within a family, is a "two-way street" (Zarit & Eggebeen 1995). In general, assistance flows both from adult children to their parents as well as from parents to their children. In many transactions, adult children derive more benefit from the support of their older parents. For example, Eggebeen (1992) estimates that older parents are 1.7 times more likely to give than to get help from their adult children. However, as parents enter old-old age, parental help to children does decline over time, although children's help to parents typically continues at the same level.

Families exchange a number of resources, including assistance with finances, shared housing, and providing instrumental and emotional support. With respect to financial resources, the direction of the exchange is typically from older parents to their adult children (Cooney & Uhlenberg 1992). It is only when parents enter their 80s that this pattern reverses, and adult children provide financial support to their parents (Hill, Morgan, & Herzog 1993).

Shared housing appears to benefit older parents and their adult children equally. Coresidence affords members of both generations ready access to multiple types of support. Clarke and Neidert (1992) find that coresidence is most prevalent among families who have limited incomes, are from minority groups, or are limited in terms of their activities of daily living. Ruggles and Goeken (1992) use this rationale to explain why the decline in coresidence with adult children (shown in Figure 10.1) is more modest among elderly African Americans. They suggest that the African American extended family is more instrumental, as elderly kin help the younger generations deal with single parenthood and poverty. Ruggles and Goeken conclude: "Multigenerational families among blacks have served the needs of the younger generation as much as the needs of the older, and this may have helped the survival of this family type into the late twentieth century" (1992, p. 33).

Instrumental assistance can take many forms. It may involve carrying out nonessential, informal services that people often perform for each other when they live nearby, such as occasional shopping, carrying packages, or helping with household maintenance. Or it may involve providing highly organized, essential assistance such as regular babysitting. Spitze and Logan (1991) examined the pattern of instrumental assistance between adult children and their parents among 1,200 residents of the greater Albany (New York) area. Respondents provided information on the amount and type of instrumental aid (e.g., housekeeping, shopping/errands, repairs/yard work, babysitting) that they provided and that they received. Results indicated that, among parents age 65 and older, parents provided more instrumental aid to their children than vice versa. Among shared residence households, older parents performed an average of 100 tasks during the past month, whereas adult children performed an average of 20 similar tasks (Ward, Logan, & Spitze 1992).

It is difficult to quantify the amount of social support exchanged between generations within a family. Based on data from the 1988 National Survey of Families and Households, Eggebeen (1992) reports that almost one-half of older parents give emotional support/advice to their adult children, whereas 28 percent of older adults receive emotional support/advice from their adult children. According to Greenberg and Becker (1988), aging parents become an important source of both instrumental and emotional support when their adult children experience major life changes, most notably in coping with divorce or chemical dependency. Bankoff (1983) reports that supportive elderly parents play a crucial role for their widowed daughters. In fact, her analysis of questionnaire data from a nationwide sample of widows indicates that parents are the single-most important source of social support for still-grieving widows and that such support is strongly related to the psychological well-being of recently widowed women.

The type of assistance offered (and received) varies by the gender of the parents and the children, the life-cycle stage of the family, and social class. Older men are more likely to assist their children financially and with household maintenance and repairs, whereas elderly women help with child rearing and domestic functions (Eggebeen 1992). According to Harris and Cole (1980), adult male children are likely to receive monetary aid from parents, whereas daughters are likely to receive services. Adult children with preschool-age children typically receive the most help from their older parents (Eggebeen & Hogan 1990; Rossi & Rossi 1990). Mutual aid in lower-class families usually involves exchanges of services and shared living arrangements; the middle classes are more likely to provide direct financial assistance. Because of anecdotal evidence of involvement in mutual support activities, it is often assumed that minorities have stronger kin networks than do whites. However, several more recent studies have not shown this to be the case (Eggebeen 1992; Eggebeen & Hogan 1990).

A legitimate question is whether the mutual assistance that appears to characterize intergenerational relations in contemporary U.S. families (i.e., functional solidarity) reflects that older parents and their adult children really like each other (i.e., affectual solidarity) or that they feel a sense of obligation or duty (i.e., consensual and/or normative solidarity).

Affectual Solidarity

Affectual solidarity deals with the type and degree of positive sentiments that family members hold toward one another. In general, research indicates that most family members report relatively high levels of affectual solidarity within the family. What is especially interesting, however, is a consistent generational bias in perceptions. Across a range of studies, members of older generations rate their relationships with younger generations more positively than members of the younger generations rate their relationships with members of the older generations. Bengtson and Kuypers (1971) propose the developmental stake hypothesis to explain these findings.

The ***developmental stake hypothesis*** proposes that older and younger generations have different developmental concerns and, as a result, have different levels of investment in, and evaluations of, the relationship. Thus, for example, because continuity is a salient issue for members of older generations, parents very well might minimize reports of conflict in their relationships with their children. On the other hand, because issues of independence and autonomy are salient for members of younger generations, these individuals might tend to overestimate reports of conflict in their relationships with their parents (Giarrusso 1995). Bengtson and Kuypers (1971) believe that these competing tendencies are responsible for the systematic differences in generations' perceptions of their relationships with one another.

Using data from the Longitudinal Study of Generations, Bengtson and colleagues examined the stability of the generational bias in affectual solidarity (Bengtson 1996; Giarrusso, Stallings, & Bengtson 1995). At four points in time (i.e., 1971, 1985, 1988, 1991), members of the grandparent, parent, and grandchild generation rated their relationship with one another, so that relationships between various dyads (i.e., parent/child, grandparent/grandchild) could be examined separately. Results indicated that, on average, affectual solidarity scores were high. In addition, the scores were consistent across the 20-year period. Finally, the results confirmed the developmental stake hypothesis. Not only did parents report higher affect than did their children, but grandparents also reported higher affect than did their grandchildren.

In summary, researchers' reports show remarkable consistency in the positive feelings older parents and their adult children have for one another, with greater levels of affectual solidarity reported by members of the older generations. Perhaps this should not be surprising. Similar findings are reported in studies of parent/child relationships across the life cycle (e.g., of high school students and their parents).

Consensual Solidarity

Consensual solidarity concerns the extent to which family members agree on values, attitudes, and beliefs. Bengtson (1996) used data from the Longitudinal

Study of Generations to examine the stability of consensual solidarity across three generations within families. The results indicated high levels of intergenerational agreement and stability in the scores over time. In addition, consistent with the developmental stake hypothesis, parents reported higher perceptions of consensus than did their children at each of four assessments over a 20-year period. And why not? After all, Troll and Bengtson (1978) call attention to the high degree of intergenerational continuity there is within the family. Reviewing the available literature on generations in the family, they find parent/child similarity strongest in religious and political affiliations, but important also in sex roles and personality. Although social and historical forces affect people of different ages in different ways, there appears to be great similarity in values within families. These similarities may help explain why aged parents and adult children like each other—although not entirely. As studies seem to indicate, even when aged parents and their adult children disagree, they continue to see each other.

Normative Solidarity

Relatively little research has directly examined individuals' commitment to meeting their family obligations (i.e., *normative solidarity*). The research that is available suggests that most people believe in filial obligation—that is, that adult children should provide assistance to their older parents when assistance is needed. Unfortunately, most of this research does not examine normative solidarity among different generations of the same families.

In one of several noteworthy exceptions, Hamon and Blieszner (1990) examined filial responsibility among 144 adult child–older parent pairs. Adult children and their parents rated the extent to which they thought adult children were responsible for helping their older parents with 16 categories of assistance (e.g., providing emotional support, being together on special occasions, living in close proximity, caring for parents when they are sick, etc.). These authors found that both adult children and their parents thought it was most important that children help their parents understand available resources, provide emotional support to their parents, and talk over matters of importance with their parents. However, statistical analyses revealed that, across the 16 categories of assistance, there was only moderate agreement between adult children and their parents with respect to filial norms.

The Complexity of Family Functioning: Focus on Care Giving

Although it is possible to isolate and discuss specific domains of family functioning, in reality, the manner in which families function is quite complex. A good illustration of this complexity can be found among families in which an older adult becomes dependent on others. Almost one-half of adults over age 85 need assistance with one or more activities of daily living (U.S. Bureau of the Census 1992). Despite the myth of family abandonment when older adults become dependent, estimates from the 1982 National Long-Term Survey and Informal Caregivers Survey indicate that in the United States, approximately 2.2 million caregivers were providing unpaid assistance to 1.6 million noninstitutionalized adults with disabilities (Stone, Cafferata, & Sangl 1987). In these instances, families act as case managers, facilitating contact between the elderly individual and the bureaucracy, and provide between 80 and 90 percent of medically related care, home nursing, personal care, household maintenance, transportation, and shopping. In contrast, the formal system of government and community agency programs plays only a minor role in providing for the elderly and is viewed by caregivers as a last resort when the responsibilities become too complex to handle even with assistance (Stone, Cafferata, & Sangl 1987).

When an older adult does require assistance, typically one family member assumes the role of *primary caregiver*—the person who is most responsible, on a day-to-day basis, for assisting the dependent older adult. Primary caregivers are most likely to be spouses (if available), followed by adult children. Primary caregivers are often assisted in their efforts by *secondary caregivers*—those who provide supplemental support. There appears to be a **principle of substitution** (Shanas 1979), whereby older adults in need of assistance are likely to receive it in serial order, depending on availability, from a spouse, then an adult child, and then from siblings, other relatives, and friends and neighbors.

From the national sample they studied, Stone, Cafferata, and Sangl (1987) found that approximately 74 percent of all caregivers (i.e., primary and secondary caregivers) were family members. The majority were women, with adult daughters comprising 29 percent of all caregivers and wives constituting 23 percent of this population; husbands comprised 13 percent of caregivers and 9 percent were sons. The average age of the caregiver population was 57 years; 36 percent were 65 years or older.

According to a life-course perspective, caring for an older parent can be thought of as a continuation of a lifetime of interaction among family members that occurs in a particular social and historical context. Consistent with this perspective, Pyke and Bengtson (1996) were interested in exploring variability in family orientation toward caring for older, dependent family members. They conducted interviews with members of 20 three-generation families who were participants in the Longitudinal Study of Generations. The interviews focused on three sets of traits:

1. Beliefs about the amount of interaction and interdependence that they should engage in
2. The actual amount of contact, closeness, and interaction that occurred among the family members
3. The specific ways that families responded to an older member's need for care

Based on these three sets of traits, two distinct family orientations emerged: individualistic and collective. Families that were classified as *individualistic* reported relatively loose family ties; they valued independence, self-sufficiency, and voluntary association with one another. In contrast, families that were classified as *collectivist* reported close family ties, and valued interdependence, commitment, and contact with one another. Perhaps it is not surprising that these two orientations were associated with very different care-giving strategies.

On the one hand, the care-giving strategies demonstrated by families who adopted an individualistic orientation might best be described as *circumscribed.* Pyke and Bengtson report that adult children in these families minimized their care-giving involvement with their parents, and functioned more as "managers" rather than full-time providers of direct care. These family members were frequently motivated to provide care by a sense of obligation. In contrast, adult children of collectivist families enmeshed themselves in caring for their older parents regardless of how demanding it was, and were motivated to do so out of a sense of affection.

Pyke and Bengtson (1996) point out that for adult children from both individualist and collectivist families, it appears that "what goes around, comes around" (p. 385). Both groups of adult children justified their involvement in care giving in terms of the long-standing patterns and traditions within their family. Interestingly, third-generation members of these families (i.e., adult grandchildren of the older adult receiving care) sometimes appeared to discourage their parents from maintaining the family's orientation. For example, adult grandchildren from individualistic families might complain that their parents were not more involved in the care of a grandparent who required assistance. Nonetheless, these grandchildren rarely became involved in care giving for their grandparents themselves. Similarly, although adult grandchildren from collectivist families often encouraged their parents to minimize their role as caregivers, these grandchildren typically found themselves assisting their parents with care-giving tasks. Thus, it appears that although grandchildren might attempt to buffer their parents' care-giving involvement, their own behavior typically reflects the general family orientation.

Supporting the notion that there is a "culture for care giving" within families, Hareven (1994) found that life-course antecedents were crucial determinants of whether an individual was cast in the role of "parent keeper." For the most part, children who took on care-giving responsibilities evolved into this role over the life course. Before World War II, among many ethnic groups, the expectation was for the youngest daughter to remain at home and to postpone or give up marriage in order to ensure support for parents into old age. Even among those care-giving daughters who married, researchers have identified care giving as disruptive to one's work career, a stressor in marriage, and an extra hurdle to overcome in preparing for her own and spouse's retirement (Hareven & Adams 1994).

Despite these negative aspects of care giving, it is important to point out that a growing number of researchers are documenting positive aspects of caring for a dependent older family member (e.g., Kinney & Stephens 1989; Kinney et al. 1995). Further, there is growing evidence that caregivers who occupy multiple roles (e.g., caregiver, wife, mother, employee) experience both positive and negative "spillover" from one role to the other, and that the complexity of involvement in multiple roles should not be underestimated (e.g., Stephens, Franks, & Townsend 1994).

THE FAMILY LIFE CYCLE

Families change with time. The structure and patterns of interrelationships change, just as the functions that the family fulfills shift in importance. Some family sociologists use the notion of the *family life cycle* to characterize the changes families undergo. A well-known and frequently adopted staging of the family life cycle has been put forth by Duvall (1977):

Stage 1: Establishment (newly married, childless)

Stage 2: New parents (infant to age 3)

Stage 3: Preschool family (child age 3 to 6, possibly younger siblings)

Stage 4: School-age family (oldest child age 6 to 12, possibly younger siblings)

Stage 5: Family with adolescent (oldest child age 13 to 19, possibly younger siblings)

Stage 6: Family with young adult (oldest child age 20, until first child leaves home)

Stage 7: Family as launching center (from departure of first child to that of last child)

Stage 8: Postparental family (after all children have left home)

Families in the postparental stage, for whom child rearing is complete, can be thought of as *later-life families.* These families are characterized by contracting rather than expanding size and structure. As a result of their changing structure, the primary unit among these families typically is the original marital dyad.

It is important to recognize that any proposed sequence of stages, including those proposed by Duvall, is an ideal representation of what one might consider to be a "traditional" family, reflecting the life of a couple that marries, has children, and stays together through the course of the life cycle. Obviously, this sequence of stages might be less relevant for truncated, reconstituted, and other alternative forms of families. Furthermore, any sequencing of stages downplays the variation in family life that can be produced by differences in the earlier life experiences of family members and by changing historical conditions. In other words, it is important to keep in mind that the stages that a particular family goes through take place within a social and historical context; as such, the life-course perspective of development can be applied to families as well as individuals.

In addition, family life cycles can overlap, and, as a result, a family chain may go on. Children born into a family (sometimes referred to as their *family of orientation*) may later marry and begin their own families (their *family of procreation*). It is the adult child's family of procreation that produces the role of grandparent for the older parent.

Although this chapter especially focuses on the postparental/later-life stage of the family life cycle, it should be understood that the stages themselves are not stagnant: Within each stage, significant changes in family structure and relationships may take place. In addition, as will be seen shortly, events that occur during the last stage—death of a spouse, remarriage, or birth of a grandchild—may clearly change the character of the older person's family life.

The Traditional, Postparental/ Later-Life Family

Marital status is an obvious, albeit not the only, criterion for distinguishing older people who are in families from those who are not. Table 10.2 shows the marital status distribution of older males and females in 1996. The marital distribution of men differs sharply from that of women in the three age groupings shown. In 1996, almost 4 out of 5 men age 65 to 74 years (79.1 percent) were married; only about 1 of 10 (9.6 percent) was widowed. Women, especially those 75 years and over, are much more likely to be widowed than married. In 1996, 54.8 percent of women age 65 to 74 years and 27.4 percent of women age 75 and over were married; about one-half of all women 65 years of age and older were widowed (63.6 percent among those age 75 and over). The changes in marital status since the end of World War II have been quite substantial, especially for men. The proportion of elderly men who are married has increased, and the proportions of single and widowed men have fallen significantly.

Two important factors contribute to the sharply different marital distributions of men and women. The first is the much higher mortality rates of married men compared to married women. For example, using U.S. Census data, Himes (1992) projected an average life expectancy of 21.9 years for married white women age 65 in the year 2000, compared to an average life expectancy of 16.1 years for married white men that same year. The corresponding life expectancies were 19.6 years for black women, and 15.4 years for black men. In addition, husbands are typically

TABLE 10.2   Marital Status of Older Adults Stratified by Sex and Age: 1996

	PERCENTAGE OF OLDER ADULTS				
	Never Married	*Married*	*Widowed*	*Divorced*	*Total*
Male					
55–64 years	5.0	82.4	3.0	9.7	100.0
65–74 years	4.4	79.1	9.6	7.0	100.0
75 years +	3.3	69.8	22.9	4.0	100.0
Female					
55–64 years	4.7	69.3	12.6	13.4	100.0
65–74 years	3.8	54.8	32.8	8.5	100.0
75 years +	4.4	27.4	63.6	4.5	100.0

Source: U.S. Bureau of the Census 1997, Table 59.

older than their wives by a few years. Thus, not only do most married women outlive their husbands but they tend to do so by many years.

A second factor accounting for the significantly higher proportion of widows than widowers is the higher remarriage rate of widowers. The marriage rate of elderly men is approximately seven times that of elderly women, and the vast majority of these are remarriages. Societal norms are much more supportive of an elderly man marrying a younger woman than vice versa. Men also have a demographic advantage in the marriage market. As Table 10.2 shows, in each age group, the proportion of older women who are unmarried is more than twice as great as the proportion of unmarried men (45.1 versus 21 percent among those 65 to 74 years, for example).

Marital Satisfaction among Postparental/ Later-Life Families

Most elderly couples today have grown old together. The average couple has launched a family and can expect approximately 20 years of living together after the departure of the last child. At the turn of the twentieth century, more than half of all marriages were interrupted by the death of one spouse, usually the husband, before the last child left home. The increase in these postparental/later-life years, sometimes referred to as the *empty-nest period*, is due to increased life expectancies as well as more closely spaced and smaller families.

Rollins (1989) reports that cross-sectional studies of marital satisfaction typically reveal one of two patterns. The first pattern is a decrease in marital satisfaction from the establishment stage through the parenting years. The second pattern is curvilinear, with the highest levels of satisfaction reported by couples in the establishment and postparental stages, and the lowest levels of marital satisfaction among couples in the parenting stages. However, it is a mistake to rely on cross-sectional studies of marital satisfaction to make inferences about marital satisfaction over time. It is quite possible that unhappy or financially unstable marriages have previously ended in divorce, and that the higher levels of marital satisfaction reported by later-life families in cross-sectional studies are the result of a survivor effect. Support for this supposition derives from longitudinal studies with large samples of participants that control for attrition due to divorce. Results from these more methodologically rigorous studies do not reveal predictable relationships between marital satisfaction and stages in the family life cycle (Huyck 1996).

Summarizing the results of longitudinal investigations of marital satisfaction among couples who are in the early phases of a later-life family (i.e, they have recently launched their children), Huyck (1996) identifies three consistent findings:

1. There is diversity in marital styles (i.e., whether spouses' primary focus is the marital relationship, the general family relationship, or outside interests) across later-life families.
2. Marital styles are relatively stable over time.

3. Personality characteristics in early adulthood are associated with marital styles in later life.

Interestingly, the marital style adopted by spouses in later-life families are not associated with their reports of marital satisfaction, even when members of a couple embrace different styles. There is evidence that certain personality characteristics in early adulthood differentiate subsequent marital styles and levels of satisfaction. For example, spouses who demonstrated comparable levels of neuroticism in the early phases of their courtship were less likely to divorce in later life than were couples who differed in levels of neuroticism (Kelly & Conley 1987).

Field and Weishaus (1992) examined the stability of marital satisfaction among 17 later-life families who were participants in the Berkeley Older Generation Study and had been married for at least 50 years. Using data from interviews that were conducted across a 15-year interval, these researchers looked for changes in couples' relationships. They found that ratings of marital adjustment were relatively stable over the 15-year interval. In addition, almost one-half (47 percent) of the wives and almost two-fifths (37 percent) of the husbands reported greater feelings of closeness to their spouse and satisfaction with their marriage at the time of the second interview.

The marital relationship may not be a blessing for all older people, however. Marital disenchantment may surface during the latter stages of the family life cycle, resulting in reduced satisfaction with the relationship, loss of intimacy, and less sharing of activities. For many couples, the marital relationship becomes subordinate during the child-rearing years and remains so after the children leave home. Divorce among older people has more than doubled since 1960, although it is estimated that only 3 percent of older adults have been divorced. Because many older adults today view being divorced as a stigma, there is reason to believe that they actually underreport their current marital status as divorced. However, divorce rates are currently higher among younger cohorts of adults. Table 10.2 provides data to suggest that divorce is inclined to be more prevalent among future cohorts of older people; in 1996, men and women ages 55 to 64 years reported being currently divorced at a rate higher than that for men and women ages 65 to 74 years. What the table does not show is that men and women ages 45 to 54 years already show higher rates of divorce than those 55 to 64 years old. Uhlenberg (1993) projects that more than 20 percent of women between the ages of 65 and 69 will be divorced by the year 2025.

The effects of divorce in later life have a number of implications. Although divorce in later life can have financial implications for both men and women, the effects on women are much more devastating (Cooney 1995). In contrast, the effects of divorce on family relationships are more devastating for men than for women (Cooney & Uhlenberg 1990). In later life, divorced men have less face-to-face contact with their adult children, and they are less likely to consider their adult children to be sources of support.

Widowhood

It is estimated that one-half of all marriages in the United States will end with the death of the husband, and one-fifth will end with the death of the wife (Martin-Matthews 1996). The U.S. Bureau of the Census estimates that almost 70 percent of all women age 65 and older are widows, and 22 percent of men age 65 and older are widowers. Also, women typically enter the role at a younger age than men (66 years for women, compared to 69 years for men). In addition, women spend an average of 15 years in the role of widow, whereas men spend an average of 6 years in the role of widower. The demographic factors underlying these patterns are the greater life expectancy of women and the fact that women typically are married to men who are at least several years older. Finally, widows are less likely to remarry than are widowers; it is estimated that fewer than 10 percent of widows and 20 percent of widowers remarry (Martin-Matthews 1996; O'Bryant & Hansson 1996).

For many of today's older adults, widowhood rates as being among the most stressful role transitions confronting older adults (Lund, Caserta, & Dimond 1993). Evidence from clinicians and researchers suggests that *grief work*—the process of bereavement and mourning—often takes up to two years to complete. For example, Lund and colleagues estimated that by two years following the death of a spouse, 80 percent of widows and widowers had recovered satisfactorily. Nonetheless, small percentages of widows and widowers continue to have difficulty dealing with their loss for extended periods of time.

The short-term effects of widowhood typically include emotional and physical distress. For example, Thompson and associates (1991) found that two months following the death of the spouse, older adults reported significantly elevated levels of emotional distress, depression, and physical health symptoms. At the two-year follow-up, these indices were no longer elevated.

In general, widows and widowers are relatively resilient in terms of long-term adjustment to widowhood. For example, in the year following widowhood, when grief work is often still in progress, Smith and Zick (1996) documented lower levels of mortality among older widows and widowers than among a comparison sample of married older adults. However, widows and widowers continued to report loneliness and other grief emotions. McCrae and Costa (1988) found no difference between widowed and married older adults in terms of well-being or self-rated physical health over a 10-year period.

Among the factors that contribute to how widowhood is experienced are the extent to which the loss is "on time" versus "off time," multiple stresses surrounding the widowhood, and gender. People who enter widowhood on time (i.e., later in life) are often able to prepare psychologically for the loss, engage in anticipatory socialization, and mobilize the formal and informal supports that are available to them (Martin-Matthews 1996). A number of studies have documented that older adults have less difficulty adjusting to widowhood than do younger adults, lending support to the idea that widowhood is more difficult for those who experience it as an off-time (i.e., at a younger age) event (Martin-

Matthews 1996; Smith & Zick 1996; Stroebe & Stroebe 1987). The experience of an anticipated, rather than an unanticipated, loss appears to facilitate adjustment.

Rather than occurring as an isolated life event, widowhood is often part of a series of life events (Blieszner 1993; O'Bryant & Hansson 1996). For example, many people enter widowhood following a spouse's serious illness and/or after a period of care giving. Further, upon entering widowhood, many older adults find themselves grieving not only the loss of a spouse but also grieving the loss of a major source of social and/or financial support. Because widowhood is often accompanied by other stressful life events, identifying the specific emotional and physical consequences of widowhood is difficult.

Widows and widowers frequently are differentially challenged by widowhood (Martin-Matthews 1996). Whereas loneliness is reported by both, widows tend to report concerns regarding finances, and widowers tend to report concerns completing household tasks. This statement might lead one to conclude that widows have a more difficult time adjusting to their situation than do widowers. However, it is important to consider the different resources that men and women bring into widowhood. With respect to loneliness, widows typically have an advantage over widowers. Women tend to have much larger and more diverse social support networks than do men. As a result, widows are relatively better able to deal with their loneliness than are widowers (Martin-Matthews 1996).

Given the tasks of having to learn how to manage finances versus household tasks in widowhood, it might appear that widowers face an easier challenge. However, Blieszner (1993) points out that widowers find themselves in a position of learning tasks that their cohort has never valued as being particularly meaningful. In fact, many men in today's cohort of older adults perceive household tasks as menial and even demeaning. In contrast, widows find themselves learning tasks that require independent decision making. As a result, today's cohort of older women have the potential to develop a sense of autonomy and heightened self-esteem during widowhood.

Because of the large percentage of older adults who experience widowhood, widowhood is often thought of as a normative life event, especially for older women. In fact, Helena Lopata (1980), perhaps the foremost student of widowhood, has spent more than a quarter of a century documenting the unique cultural contexts that women have faced in the United States. She identifies three factors that appear to contribute to this uniqueness, relative both to the historical past and to some other parts of the contemporary world:

1. The modern nuclear family in the United States is expected to be socially and economically independent. Ties to the broader kinship network are there, but they are loose. In particular, ties to the male family line are weak.
2. Although the situation is beginning to change in the United States, it is still clearly the case that wives are economically dependent on their husbands' sources of income.
3. U.S. society places extremely high importance on the marital relationship and on the development of strong mutual dependence between marital partners.

More recently, Martin-Matthews (1996) has suggested that changes in the structure of families—including increasing numbers of never married, separated, and divorced older adults—should decrease the probability of being widowed in later life. She goes so far as to say that widowhood might become a non-normative life event for future cohorts. Regardless of whether widowhood becomes a non-normative event, in light of the changing roles of women in society, there is no question that future cohorts of older adults will have very different experiences with widowhood than do older women and men today.

Remarriage

Remarriage may be a desirable alternative for elderly divorced or widowed people. Whether it is a realistic alternative is another matter. In 1990, only 1 percent of all the brides and 1.9 percent of the all grooms in the United States were 65 years old and over. However, in the same year, women age 65 years and older accounted for 2.7 percent of all remarriages among women, whereas men in this age group accounted for 5.1 percent of all remarriages among men (U.S. Bureau of the Census 1999, Table 157). Brubaker (1985) reports that men are more likely to remarry than are women, that divorced older adults are more likely to remarry than are widows and widowers, and that whites are more likely to remarry than are African Americans. For those age 35 years and older, remarriage rates among men and women, divorced and widowed, have increased somewhat since 1980. Still, the great majority of these remarriages occur among those age 35 to 55 years. Society offers little impetus to marry in the later years. The reasons for marriage in the United States today are not pertinent to the single aged: premarital pregnancy or the desire for children, escape from parental domination, social validation of adult heterosexuality, and pressure for conformity.

Because there are far more single older women than single older men, older men date more often and have more dating partners (O'Bryant & Hansson 1996). Also, the motivations for dating differ. Women tend to date for prestige and the status of courtship, whereas men tend to date for emotional reasons (Bulcroft & O'Connor 1986).

Not all older adults necessarily want to remarry following divorce or the death of a spouse. The reasons underlying some older adults' reluctance to remarry include not wanting to give up new-found independence, social disapproval, the disapproval of family members, and concerns over finances. In contrast, the perceived benefits of remarriage in later life include companionship, sexual intimacy, and financial security (Moss & Moss 1980).

Bengtson, Rosenthal, and Burton (1990) report that later-life remarriages have the greatest probability for success when:

1. Both partners are in good health.
2. The couple has an adequate income.
3. Family and friends approve of the marriage.
4. The first marriages were successful.

By the year 2000, the boy in this picture, who was born in 1941, had known members of six generations of his family.

Remarriage in later life is clearly an option for certain older adults, and there is indication that these marriages can be satisfying and successful.

Grandparenthood

At the turn of the twentieth century, if an older adult lived long enough to became a grandparent, that role typically came to him or her near the end of the life span. Today, grandparenthood is a far more common experience. Most adults in the United States become grandparents in middle age, and because of increases in life expectancy, can spend more than four decades in the role of grandparent (Kivnick & Sinclair 1996). However, because of increases in life expectancy, far more people are experiencing the grandparent role, and experiencing it for longer periods of time. In 1990, 94 percent of all older adults with children were also grandparents, and almost 50 percent were great-grandparents (Kivnick & Sinclair 1996). Today, it is quite possible for people to spend more than one-half of their lives in the role of grandparent.

Even though the role of grandparent is more common today than in the past, there is great diversity in how people occupy the role. One source for this diversity is age. Schwartz and Waldrop (1992) estimate that one-third of grandparents are younger than 60 years old, and only one-fifth are 70 or older. As such, grandparents are not necessarily "old." It is just as possible to become a grandparent at age 30 in an age-condensed family as it is to become a grandparent at age 80 in an age-gapped family!

Age is not the only demographic factor that contributes to diversity in grandparenthood. The high rates of divorce and reconstituted families in the United States have provided dramatic changes in the kinship networks of grandparents. Divorce can result in strengthened grandparent/grandchild relationships for the custodial family, and weakened grandparent/grandchild relationships for the noncustodial family. Given that mothers are typically awarded custody of their children, it is often the maternal side of the family for whom ties are strengthened, and the paternal side of the family for whom ties are weakened. Further, among reconstituted families, expanding networks are more common among paternal grandmothers, who are much more likely to retain relationships with former daughters-in-law (and children-in-law, their parents and children, and even their new spouses and their relatives) than are maternal grandmothers with former sons-in-law (Johnson & Barer 1987).

Especially among low-income and age-condensed families, increasing numbers of grandparents are finding themselves either partially or fully responsible for raising their grandchildren (Minkler & Roe 1993). The U.S. Bureau of the Census (1991) estimates that at least 5 percent of children under the age of 18 live with grandparents. The Census Bureau further estimates that neither parent is present in at least one-third of these households. Grandparents often assume responsibility for raising their grandchildren when the parents are unable and/or unwilling to do so, whatever the reason (e.g., financial difficulties, drug dependence, serious illness). Yet, even when grandparents willingly accept this responsibility, health problems, financial difficulties, and social isolation can result.

It is not only members of the grandparent generation who sometimes find themselves as surrogate parents. Burton (1996) compared the roles of great-grandparents among 18 age-condensed African American families and 23 African American families whose family structures were more typical. Burton found that in age-condensed families, responsibilities for family care giving were largely assumed by the young great-grandparent generation.

Although most grandparents and grandchildren are in regular contact with one another, grandparenthood means different things to different people. For example, based on data collected from 286 grandparents, Kivnick (1982) identified five dimensions that together define the meaning that individuals derive from their role as grandparents:

1. *Centrality:* The extent to which the role of grandparent is an individual's primary role
2. *Value as an elder:* The extent to which the grandparent perceives himself or herself to be a "sage" or wise elder
3. *Indulgence:* The extent to which the grandparent obtains satisfaction from interacting with his or her grandchildren
4. *Immortality through clan:* The legacy of leaving behind multiple generations
5. *Reinvolvement with one's personal past:* The recollection, and possible continuation, of previous relationships with one's own grandparents

Often, the meaning that someone ascribes to the role of grandparenthood is reflected in the style of grandparenting that they adopt. Neugarten and Weinstein (1964) classified the different styles of grandparenting into five categories:

1. The *formal* grandparent likes to provide special treats and indulgences for the grandchild but maintains clearly demarcated lines between parenting and grandparenting. This grandparent leaves parenting strictly to the parents, maintaining constant interest in the grandchild but offering no advice.
2. The *fun seeker* maintains a playful and informal relationship with the grandchild, with the emphasis on mutual satisfaction.
3. The *surrogate parent* role is played by grandmothers whose daughters work and who assume responsibility for taking care of the child during the day.
4. The *reservoir of family wisdom* refers mainly to grandparents who possess special skills or resources and who expect young parents to maintain a subordinate position.
5. The *distant figure* is the grandparent who has contact with the grandchildren only on holidays and special occasions but otherwise remains distant and remote from the grandchild's life.

Styles of grandparenting are related to age. *Fun seekers* and *distant figures* are usually younger, whereas *formal* grandparents are more typically older.

McCready (1985) has used national survey data to determine whether ethnicity can usefully explain variation in the styles of grandparenting that are adopted. Although not every older person in these national surveys is an actual grandparent, the respondents represent a "grandparent cohort" of people of like age and experience. The ethnic groups represented were English, Scandinavian, German, Irish, Italian, and Polish. Characteristics of children were grouped in a fashion that approximated the five styles of grandparenting described here, though the *formal* and *distant* styles were combined because there was no measure of contact frequency upon which to base distance (McCready 1985).

Generally, males were more likely to exhibit attitudes and responses linked to the formal/distant style of grandparenting, whereas the women emphasized the more informal and affect-oriented styles of behavior (McCready 1985). Scandinavians, Irish, and Italians (grandmothers and grandfathers alike) were above the mean on scores of the formal/distant and surrogate styles; English and Italian grandmothers were the only groups to score above the mean on measures representing the reservoir-of-wisdom style of grandparenting. German grandfathers scored high on the formal/distant and surrogate styles, though German grandmothers only scored positively on the latter. Almost uniformly, representatives of the ethnic groups in this study scored low or negative on indicators of the fun-seeking style.

McCready suggests that "the affective dimensions of the grandparent-grandchild relationship are not as prized by these respondents as the more behavioral and 'correct' dimensions of childrens' behavior" (1985, p. 57). Clearly, the cultural diversity that exists within grandparent populations in the United States reveals itself in diverse styles of grandparent/grandchild interaction.

Some attention has begun to focus on the growing number of great-grandparents in the United States. For example, Roberto and Skoglund (1996) compared 52 college students' reports of their relationships with their grandparents and great-grandparents. Students reported that they had more interaction with their grandparents than with their great-grandparents. In addition, students perceived that their grandparents had more clearly defined roles than did their great-grandparents and were more influential in their lives.

Employing data from a small sample, Doka and Mertz (1988) identify two basic styles of grandparenting: remote and close. In the *remote* style, great-grandparents had limited and ritualistic contact with their great-grandchildren. Typically, this occurred on family and holiday occasions. Those who adopted a *close* style had frequent and regular contact with their great-grandchildren, often babysat for them, and took them on trips or shopping. As Doka and Mertz conclude, there are many similarities between grandparenthood and great-grandparenthood, but clearly more research is needed to gain a fuller perspective on the dynamics of four- or five-generation families.

FRIENDSHIP: QUASI-FAMILIAL RELATIONS?

Much gerontological research focuses on marriage and parental status. Yet, more than 20 percent of older adults in the United States have no children and approximately 5 percent have never married. As Table 10.2 shows, in 1996, among those 65 to 75 years of age, 21 percent of males and 45.1 percent of females report being unmarried; for those 75 years of age and older, 30.2 percent of males and 72.5 percent of females similarly report being unmarried.

Friendships are particularly important in later life, and especially so for elderly people who are unmarried, lack close family nearby, and have lost the social contacts of work. For those who live alone, friends may be the main, even the sole, source of emotional support. They offer protection from a hostile society, yet also provide a context within which new roles can be developed. According to Adams (1995), later-life friendships provide companionship and serve as a source of affection, and friends often provide both emotional and instrumental support.

A number of researchers report that life satisfaction among older adults is positively related to the quantity and quality of contacts with friends (Antonucci 1985; Essex & Nam 1987), and this relationship appears to cut across gender and ethnicity. The support of close friends has been found to contribute to both psychological and physical well-being (Antonucci 1989; Bryant & Rakowski 1992; Litwak 1989) and to encourage preventive health behaviors (Abella & Heslin 1984). One explanation for these effects is that friendships develop voluntarily and are based on companionship and mutual gratification. Family relationships are often sustained through prescribed norms and formal obligations; they are not always positive. Older adults are especially concerned that they not become burdens to their families.

Although friendships are generally voluntary rather than obligatory (Adams 1995), Arber and Ginn (1991) point out that opportunities for friendships may be structured by material and social circumstances—employment, social class position, health, marital status, and even gender all have an impact on friendship patterns. As Allan describes, adult men and women "occupy separate spheres [and] have different demands made of them, and consequently...develop different skills and abilities [and] different friendship patterns" (1989, p. 66). Men, especially among the working and lower middle classes, often develop work-based friendships that are weakened at retirement.

Women, on the other hand, may also lose daily contact with workmates, but, more importantly, as they age, women experience greater freedom from demands of children and extra time for existing and new friends. They are also more likely than men to replace lost friends with new ones (Wright 1989). Older women typically have more friends, on average, than do older men (Fischer & Oliker 1983). Also, the quality of their friendships appears to differ from those of men. Women's friends are more likely to be close confidants who share the ups and downs of emotional life, whereas elderly men are thought to rely on their spouses to fulfill this function.

Rubinstein and associates (1991) used extensive interviews to explore the important relationships of never married, childless older women. They identify six types of key personal relationships, including two based on blood ties, three types of "constructed" relationships, and friendship. Blood ties included the coresident daughter role (living with one or both parents until their deaths) and collateral ties based on the aunt role (involvement in the life of a sibling's family). Constructed ties included (1) affiliation with non-kin families (being "adopted" into a family to which they are not biologically related), (2) development of quasi-parental relations with younger nonrelatives to whom they acted like parents, and (3) sometimes coresidential, same-generation, same-gender companionate relations that often resemble extended family.

Although friendships were very significant in the lives of almost all the women interviewed, they were distinguishable from companionate relations by the absence of a feeling of certain and secure care if the need arose. In fact, the women typically did not desire that their friendships be sources of care, "fearing the change of voluntary mutuality into dependency" (Allan 1989, p. S275). Still, enduringness was a characteristic of these friendships. As Allan describes (p. S275), "You understand each other better if you know each other for fifty years or seventy years or whatever it is. And complete trust of course. You trust them with decisions, they trust you with decisions. You understand each other without talking. After all, seventy years is older than most married couples."

Antonucci (1985) does report that there is an age-related decline in friends and acquaintances that presumably has consequences for women as well as men, regardless of marital status. Reasons for this decline include:

1. Movement from the relatively age-segregated environments of youth (high school and college) into age-integrated work settings and neighborhoods makes friendships more difficult to establish.

2. Geographic mobility during middle and later adulthood makes long-term friendships difficult to maintain.

3. Focus on development of family and career (and often two careers) reduces the size of friendship networks.

4. The likelihood that members of one's friendship network will die increases with age.

Will the differentials observed in patterns of friendship between current cohorts of older women and men hold up in future cohorts of aged? One view is that as young women are more involved in careers and workplaces, their future friendship patterns may more resemble those of men. Arber and Ginn (1991) suggest that this is likely only if men also change in the future, being more equally involved in child care and other domestic tasks.

SUMMARY

The common perspective that family structure has changed in the United States from the extended to the nuclear type has come under serious question. Historical demographers now argue that the nuclear family probably was the dominant type of family structure during the American colonial period and has since been the modal family type in the United States.

In its colonial phase, the United States was a gerontophilic society, where being old conferred power and prestige. Cultural, demographic, and technological changes have brought a loss of status to older people. Family sociologists and gerontologists use the notion of a modified extended family to describe the place of the elderly in the contemporary U.S. kin network.

Great diversity exists in the structure of families today. A number of factors contribute to this diversity, including demographic trends and changes in the ethnic/racial composition of U.S. society. For example, there are growing numbers of both age-gapped and age-condensed families, and increasing numbers of people reside in alternative forms of families.

With respect to family functioning, Bengtson and colleagues identify six dimensions of intergenerational solidarity that family members provide to one another: structural, associational, functional, affectual, consensual, and normative. Although there is great diversity in patterns of family functioning, there is little evidence that older people are isolated from their families. Most older people live near, but not with, their children and interact with them frequently. Assistance in the form of goods, services, and financial aid flows both from adult children to their parents, and from the parents to their children.

Just as individuals change over time, so too do families. Later-life families are those in which child rearing is complete and in which new challenges appear. Among these challenges are adjusting to the empty-nest period, the possibility of divorce/widowhood, and grandparent- or even great-grandparenthood.

The marital distribution of elderly men differs sharply from that of elderly women. Most elderly men are married, whereas about one-half of all elderly women are widowed. Although there is not a single pattern of marriage in later life, most older couples are satisfied with their marriages. However, divorce does occur among later-life families, and when it does occur, men and women are differentially affected.

Approximately one-half of all marriages end with the death of the husband, and one-fifth end with the death of the wife. For many older adults, widowhood is one of the most stressful role transitions that they face, although men and women confront different challenges as a result of becoming widowed. Few elderly get the opportunity to remarry, although there is a demographic advantage to men, who are a relatively scarce resource. When marriages occur in later life, they typically are successful.

Many older adults experience the role of grandparent for a significant portion of their lives, and more people than ever before are experiencing the role of great-grandparent. Most grandchildren and grandparents are in regular contact with one another. Grandparents play a variety of roles, ranging from those who maintain a distant relationship with their grandchildren to those who are either partially or fully responsible for raising their grandchildren.

Some older people have never married; a sizable percentage of those who have married have no children. Friendships are particularly important for those who are unmarried, or have no children, or lack close family nearby. Friends provide practical assistance as well as affect and affirmation. Opportunities for friendships may differ as a function of health and gender, among other factors. There does appear to be an age-related decline in friendships experienced by both men and women.

STUDY QUESTIONS

1. Discuss the contrasting views social historians have of the U.S. family of bygone days.

2. Define *modified extended family.* How does such a family differ from extended and nuclear families?

3. Discuss Fischer's notion of a "revolution in age relations" that occurred in the United States between 1770 and 1820. What are its implications for the position of the elderly in families?

4. Describe the factors that contribute to the difficulty in identifying a "typical" family.

5. Uhlenberg (1993) projects that the age-condensed family structure will become increasingly common between 1990 and 2010, but that the age-gapped and trun-

cated family patterns will be decreasingly common. What are the implications of these projections?

6. Compare the potential strengths and weaknesses for an older member of an alternative family form relative to a "traditional" family form.

7. Using the six elements of intergenerational solidarity proposed by Bengtson and colleagues, describe what you believe to be an optimally functional family.

8. Would your own family be best described as individualistic or collective? Provide a rationale and examples as part of your response.

9. Discuss the factors that are associated with marital satisfaction in later life.

10. Compare and contrast the experiences of widowhood for men and women in the current cohort of older adults.

11. Discuss the factors that contribute to diversity in the grandparenthood role.

12. Why are friendships viewed as so important for the aged? How do friendships differ from family relationships? How would you explain different friendship patterns between men and women?

REFERENCES

Abella, R., & Heslin, R. (1984). Health, locus of control, values, and the behavior of family and friends: An integrated approach to understanding health behavior. *Basic and Applied Social Psychology, 5,* 283–293.

Adams, R. G. (1995). Friendship. In G. L. Maddox (Ed.), *The encyclopedia of aging* (2nd. ed., pp. 383–384). New York: Springer.

Allan, G. (1989). *Friendship: Developing a sociological perspective.* Boulder, CO: Westview.

Antonucci, T. (1985). Personal characteristics, social support, and social behavior. In R. H. Binstock & E. Shanas (Eds.), *Handbook of aging and the social sciences* (2nd ed.). New York: Van Nostrand Reinhold.

Antonucci, T. (1989). Understanding adult social relationships. In K. Kreppner & R. M. Lerner (Eds.), *Family systems and life-span development* (pp. 303–318). Hillsdale, NJ: Erlbaum.

Arber, S., & Ginn, J. (1991). *Gender and later life: A sociological analysis of resources and constraints.* London: Sage.

Atkinson, M. P., Kivett, V. R., & Campbell, R. T. (1986). Intergenerational solidarity: An examination of a theoretical model. *Journal of Gerontology, 41* (3), 408–416.

Back, K. (1974). *The three-generation household in pre-industrial society: Norm or expedient.* Paper presented at the meeting of the Gerontological Society, Portland, OR.

Bankoff, E. A. (1983). Aged parents and their widowed daughters: A support relationship. *Journal of Gerontology, 38,* 226–230.

Bedford, V. H. (1995). Sibling relationships in middle and old age. In R. Blieszner & V. H. Bedford (Eds.), *Handbook of aging and the family* (pp. 201–222). Westport, CT: Greenwood.

Bentgson, V. (1996). Continuities and discontinuities in inter-generational relationships over time. In V. L. Bengtson (Ed.), *Adulthood and aging: Research on continuities and discontinuities* (pp. 271–303). New York: Springer.

Bengtson, V., & Allen, K. R. (1993). The life course perspective applied to families over time. In P. G. Boss, W. J. Doherty, R. LaRossa, W. R. Schumm, & S. K. Steinmetz (Eds.), *Sourcebook of family theories and methods: A contextual approach* (pp. 469–499). New York: Plenum.

Bengtson, V., & Kuypers, J. A. (1971). Generational differences and the "developmental stake." *Aging and Human Development, 2* (1), 249–260.

Bengtson, V., & Roberts, E. L. (1991). Intergenerational solidarity in aging families: An example of formal theory construction. *Journal of Marriage and the Family, 53,* 856–870.

Bengtson, V., Rosenthal, C., & Burton, L. (1990). Families and aging: Diversity and heterogeneity. In R. H. Binstock & L. K. George (Eds.), *Handbook of aging and the social sciences* (3rd ed., pp. 263–287). San Diego: Academic.

Bengtson, V., Rosenthal, C., & Burton, L. (1996). Paradoxes of families and aging. In R. H. Binstock & L. K. George (Eds.), *Handbook of aging and the social sciences* (4th ed., pp. 253–282). San Diego: Academic.

Bengtson, V., & Schmeeckle, M. (1995). Intergenerational relationships. In G. L. Maddox (Ed.), *The encyclopedia of aging* (2nd ed., pp. 516–527). New York: Springer.

Bengtson, V., & Silverstein, M. (1993). Families, aging, and social change: Seven agendas for 21st-century researchers. In G. L. Maddox & M. P. Lawton (Eds.), *Annual review of gerontology and geriatrics: Focus on kinship, aging, and social change* (Vol. 13, pp. 15–38). New York: Springer.

Blieszner, R. (1993). A socialist-feminist perspective on widowhood. *Journal of Aging Studies, 7,* 171–182.

Brubaker, T. (1985). *Later life families.* Beverly Hills: Sage.

Brubaker, T. H. (1990a). A contextual approach to the development of stress associated with caregiving in later-life families. In M. A. P.

Stephens, J. H. Crowther, S. E. Hobfoll, & D. L. Tennenbaum (Eds.) *Stress and coping in later-life families* (pp. 29–47). New York: Hemisphere.

Brubaker, T. H. (1990b). Families in later life: A burgeoning research area. *Journal of Marriage and the Family, 52,* 959–981.

Bryant, S., & Rakowski, W. (1992). Predictors of morality among elder African-Americans. *Research on Aging, 14,* 50–67.

Bulcroft, K., & O'Connor, M. (1986). The importance of dating relationships on the quality of life for older persons. *Family Relations, 35,* 397–401.

Burton, L. M. (1996). Age norms, the timing of family role transitions, and intergenerational caregiving among aging African American women. *Gerontologist, 36,* 199–208.

Clarke, C. J., & Neidert, L. S. (1992). Living arrangements of the elderly: An examination of differences according to ancestry and generation. *Gerontologist, 32,* 796–804.

Cooney, T. (1995). Divorce. In G. L. Maddox (Ed.), *The encyclopedia of aging* (2nd ed., pp. 286–287). New York: Springer.

Cooney, T., & Uhlenberg, P. (1990). The role of divorce in men's relation with their adult children after mid-life. *Journal of Marriage and the Family, 52,* 677–688.

Cooney, T., & Uhlenberg, P. (1992). Support from parents over the life course: The adult child's perspective. *Social Forces, 71,* 63–84.

Demos, J. (1965). Notes on life in Plymouth Colony. *William and Mary Quarterly* (Third Series), *22,* 264–286.

Doka, K. J., & Mertz, M. E. (1988). The meaning and significance of great-grandparenthood. *Gerontologist, 28* (2), 192–197.

Dorfman, R., Walters, K., Burke, P., Hardin, L., & Karanik, T. (1995). Old, sad and alone: The myth of the aging homosexual. *Journal of Gerontological Social Work, 24,* 29–44.

Duvall, E. M. (1977). *Family development* (5th ed.). Philadelphia: Lippincott.

Eggebeen, D. (1992). Family structure and intergenerational exchanges. *Research on Aging, 14,* 427–447.

Eggebeen, D., & Hogan, D. (1990). Giving between the generations in American families. *Human Nature, 1,* 211–232.

Essex, M. J., & Nam, S. (1987). Marital status and loneliness among older women. *Journal of Marriage and the Family, 49,* 93–106.

Field, D., & Weishaus, S. (1992). Marriage over half a century: A longitudinal study. In M. Bloom (Ed.), *Changing lives* (pp. 269–273). Columbia: University of South Caroline Press.

Fischer, C., & Oliker, S. (1983). A research note on friendship, gender, and the life cycle. *Social Forces, 62,* 124–133.

Fischer, D. (1977). *Growing old in America.* New York: Oxford University Press.

George, L. K., & Gold, D. T. (1991). Life course perspectives on intergenerational and generational connections. *Marriage and Family Review, 16,* 67–88.

Giarrusso, R. (1995). Intergenerational stake hypothesis. In G. L. Maddox (Ed.), *The encyclopedia of aging* (2nd ed., pp. 517–518). New York: Springer.

Giarrusso, R., Stallings, M., & Bengtson, V. L. (1995). The "intergenerational stake" hypothesis revisited: Parent-child differences in perceptions of relationships 20 years later. In V. L. Bengtson, K. W. Schaie, & L. M. Burton (Eds.), *Intergenerational issues in aging: Effects of societal change* (pp. 227–263). New York: Springer.

Gold, D. T. (1987). Siblings in old age: Something special. *Canadian Journal on Aging, 6,* 199–215.

Gold, D. T. (1989). Sibling relationships in old age: A typology. *International Journal of Aging and Human Development, 28,* 37–50.

Gold, D. T. (1990). Late-life sibling relationships: Does race affect typology distribution? *Gerontologist, 30,* 741–748.

Gold, D. T., Woodbury, M. A., & George, L. K. (1990). Relationship classification using grade of membership analysis: A typology of sibling relationship in later life. *Journal of Gerontology, 45,* S43–S51.

Goode, W. (1963). *World revolution and family patterns.* New York: Free Press.

Greenberg, J. S., & Becker, M. (1988). Aging parents as family resources. *Gerontologist, 28* (6), 786–791.

Greenfield, S. (1967). Industrialization and the family in sociological theory. *American Journal of Sociology, 67,* 312–322.

Greven, P. (1966). Family structure in seventeenth century Andover, Mass. *William and Mary Quarterly* (Third Series), *23,* 234–356.

Gutman, D., Kolm, R., Mostwin, D., & associates (1979). *Informal and formal support systems and their effect on the lives of the elderly in selected ethnic groups.* Washington, DC: The Catholic University of America.

Hagestad, G. O. (1988). Demographic change and the life course: Some emerging trends in the family realm. *Family Relations, 37,* 405–410.

Hamon, R. R., & Blieszner, R. (1990). Filial responsibility expectations among adultchild–older parent pairs. *Journal of Gerontology: Psychological Science, 45,* P110–P112.

Hareven, T. (1994). Aging and generational relations: A historical and life course perspective. In J. Hagan & K. S. Cook (Eds.), *Annual review of sociology, Volume 20, 1994.* Palo Alto, CA: Annual Reviews.

Hareven, T. (1996). Life course. In J. E. Birren (Ed.), *Encyclopedia of gerontology: Age, aging, and the aged* (Vol. 2, pp. 31–40). New York: Academic.

Hareven, T., & Adams, K. (1994). The generation in the middle: Cohort comparisons in assistance to aging parents in an American community. In T. Hareven (Ed.), *Aging and generational relations over the life course: A historical and cross-cultural perspective.* Berlin: Walter de Gruyter.

Harris, T., & Cole, W. (1980). *Sociology of aging.* Boston: Houghton Mifflin.

Hill, M. S., Morgan, J. N., & Herzog, R. (1993, April). *Intergenerational aspects of family help patterns.* Paper presented at the annual meeting of the Population Association of America, Washington, DC.

Himes, C. L. (1992). Future caregivers: Projected family structures of older persons. *Journal of Gerontology: Social Sciences, 47,* S17–S26.

Hoyert, D. L. (1991). Financial and household exchanges between generations. *Research on Aging, 13,* 205–225.

Huyck, M. H. (1996). Marriage and close relationships of the marital kind. In R. Blieszner & V. H. Bedford (Eds.), *Aging and the family: Theory and research* (pp. 181–200). Westport, CT: Praeger.

Johnson, C. L., & Barer, B. M. (1987). Marital instability and the changing kinship networks of grandparents. *Gerontologist, 17,* 90–96.

Kelly, E., & Conley, J. (1987). Personality and compatibility: A prospective analysis of marital stability and satisfaction. *Journal of Personality and Social Psychology, 52,* 27–40.

Kimmel, D. C. (1992). Families of older gay men and lesbians. *Generations, 17,* 37–38.

Kimmel, D. C. (1978). Adult development and aging: A gay perspective. *Journal of Social Issues, 34,* 113–130.

Kinney, J. M., & Stephens, M. A. P. (1989). Hassles and uplifts of giving care to a family member with dementia. *Psychology and Aging, 4,* 402–408.

Kinney, J. M., Stephens, M. A. P., Franks, M. M., & Norris, V. K. (1995). Stresses and satisfactions of family caregivers to older stroke patients. *Journal of Applied Gerontology, 14,* 3–21.

Kivnick, H. Q. (1982). *The meaning of grandparenthood.* Ann Arbor, MI: UMI Research.

Kivnick, H. Q., & Sinclair, H. M. (1996). Grandparenthood. In J. E. Birren (Ed.), *Encyclopedia of gerontology: Age, ageing, and the aged* (Vol. 1., pp. 611–623). New York: Academic.

Krout, J. (1988). Rural versus urban differences in elderly parents' contact with their children. *Gerontologist, 28* (2), 190–203.

Laslett, P., & Harrison, W. (1963). Clayworth and Cogenhoe. In H. Bell & R. Ollard (Eds.), *Historical essays, 1660–1750.* London: Adam and Charles Black.

Lin, G., & Rogerson, P. (1995). Elderly parents and the geographic availability of their adult children. *Research on Aging, 17,* 303–331.

Litwak, E. (1989). Forms of friendships among older people in an industrial society. In R. G. Adams & R. Blieszner (Eds.), *Older adult friendship* (pp. 65–88). Newbury Park, CA: Sage.

Longino, C. F., & Earle, J. R. (1996). Who are the grandparents at century's end? *Generations, 20,* 13–16.

Lopata, H. (1980). Widows and widowers. In H. Cox (Ed.), *Aging* (2nd ed.). Guilford, CT: Dushkin.

Lund, D. A., Caserta, M. S., & Dimond, M. F. (1993). The course of spousal bereavement in later life. In M. S. Stroebe, W. Stroebe, & R. O. Hansson (Eds.), *Handbook of bereavement* (pp. 240–254). New York: Cambridge University Press.

Markides, K. S., Boldt, J. S., & Ray, L. A. (1986). Sources of helping and intergenerational solidarity: A three-generations study of Mexican Americans. *Journal of Gerontology, 41* (4), 506–511.

Martin-Matthews, A. (1996). Widowhood and widowerhood. In J. E. Birren (Ed.), *Encyclopedia of gerontology: Age, ageing, and the aged* (Vol. 2, pp. 621–625). New York: Academic Press.

McCrae, R. R., & Costa, P. T. (1988). Psychological resilience among widowed men and women: A 10-year follow-up of a national sample. *Journal of Social Issues, 44,* 129–142.

McCready, W. C. (1985). Styles of grandparenting among white ethnics. In V. L. Bengtson & J. F. Robertson (Eds.), *Grandparenthood* (pp. 49–60). Beverly Hills: Sage.

McDougall, G. J. (1993). Therapeutic issues with gay and lesbian elders. *Clinical Gerontologist, 14,* 45–57.

Minkler, M., & Roe, K. M. (1993). *Grandparents as caregivers: Raising children of the crack cocaine epidemic.* Newbury Park, CA: Sage.

Moss, M. S., & Moss, S. Z. (1980). Image of the deceased spouse in remarriage of elderly widow(er)s. *Journal of Gerontological Social Work, 3,* 59–70.

National Council on the Aging. (1976). *The myth and reality of aging in America.* Washington, DC: Author.

Neugarten, B., & Weinstein, K. (1964). The changing American grandparent. *Journal of Marriage and Family, 26* (2), 199–204.

O'Bryant, S. L., & Hansson, R. O. (1996). Widowhoods. In R. Blieszner & V. H. Bedford (Eds.), *Aging and the family: Theory and research* (pp. 440–458). Westport, CT: Praeger.

Okraku, I. O. (1987). Age and attitudes toward multigenerational residence, 1973 and 1983. *Journal of Gerontology, 42* (3), 280–287.

Parsons, T. (1942). Age and sex in the social structure of the U.S. *American Sociological Review, 7,* 604–616.

Peplau, L. A. (1991). Lesbian and gay relationships. In J. C. Gonsiorek & J. D. Weinrich (Eds.), *Homosexuality: Research implications for public policy* (pp. 177–196). Newbury Park: Sage.

Pyke, K. D., & Bengtson, V. L. (1996). Caring more or less: Individualistic and collectivist systems of family elder care. *Journal of Marriage and the Family, 58,* 379–392.

Roberto, K. A., & Skoglund, R. R. (1996). Interactions with grandparents and great-grandparents: A comparison of activities, influences, and relationships. *International Journal of Aging and Human Development, 43,* 107–118.

Rollins, B. C. (1989). Marital quality at midlife. In S. Hunter & M. Sunderl (Eds.), *Midlife myths: Issues, findings and practical implications* (pp. 184–194). Newbury Park, CA: Sage.

Rossi, A. S., & Rossi, P. H. (1990). *Of human bonding: Parent-child relations across the life course.* New York: Aldine de Gruyter.

Rubinstein, R. L., Alexander, B. B., Goodman, M., & Luborsky, M. (1991). Key relationships of never married, childless older women: A cultural analysis. *Journal of Gerontology: Social Sciences, 46* (3), S270-S277.

Ruggles, S., & Goeken, R. (1992). Race and multi-generational family structure, 1900–1980. In S. J. South & S. E. Tolnay (Eds.), *The changing American family: Sociological and demographic perspectives.* Boulder, CO: Westview.

Schlesinger, B. (1996). Sexless years or sex rediscovered. *Journal of Gerontological Social Work, 26,* 117–131.

Schwartz, J., & Waldrop, J. (1992). The growing importance of grandparents. *American Demographics, 14,* 10–11.

Shanas, E. (1979). The family as a social support system in old age. *Gerontologist, 19,* 169–174.

Silverstein, M., & Waite, J. L. (1993). Are blacks more likely than whites to receive and provide social support in middle and old age? Yes, no, and maybe so. *Journal of Gerontology: Social Sciences, 48,* S212–S222.

Simmons, L. (1945). *The role of the aged in primitive society.* New Haven, CT: Yale University Press.

Simmons, L. (1960). Aging in preindustrial societies. In C. Tibbitts (Ed.), *Handbook of social gerontology.* Chicago: University of Chicago Press.

Smith, K. R., & Zick, C. D. (1996). Risk of mortality following widowhood: Age and sex differences by mode of death. *Social Biology, 43,* 59–71.

Spitze, G., & Logan, J. R. (1991). Sibling structure and intergenerational relations. *Journal of Marriage and the Family, 53,* 871–884.

Stanford, E. P., & Torres-Gil, F. M. (1992). *Diversity: New approaches to ethnic minority aging.* Amityville, NY: Baywood Publishing.

Stephens, M. A. P., Franks, M. M., & Townsend, A. L. (1994). Stress and rewards in women's multiple roles: The case of women in the middle. *Psychology & Aging, 9,* 45–52.

Stone, R., Cafferata, G. L., & Sangl, J. (1987). Caregivers of the frail elderly: A national profile. *Gerontologist, 27,* 616–626.

Stroebe, W., & Stroebe, M. S. (1987). *Bereavement and health: The psychological and physical consequences of partner loss.* London: Cambridge University Press.

Thompson, L. W., Gallagher-Thompson, D., Futterman, A., Gilewski, M. J., & Peterson, J. (1991). The effects of late-life spousal bereavement over a 30-month interval. *Psychology and Aging, 6,* 434–441.

Tibbitts, C. (1968). Some social aspects of gerontology. *Gerontologist, 8* (2), 131–133.

Troll, L., & Bengtson, V. (1978). Generations in the family. In W. Burr et al. (Eds.), *Contemporary theories about the family.* New York: Free Press.

Uhlenberg, P. (1993). Demographic change and kin relationships in later life. In G. L. Maddox & M. P. Lawton (Eds.), *Annual review of gerontology and geriatrics: Focus on kinship, aging, and social change* (Vol. 13, pp. 219–238). New York: Springer.

U.S. Bureau of the Census. (1987). Fertility of American women: June 1986. *Current population reports.* (Series P-20, No. 421). Washington, DC: U.S. Government Printing Office.

U.S. Bureau of the Census. (1991). *Current population reports: Marital status and living arrangements.* (Series P-20, No. 450). Washington, DC: U.S. Government Printing Office.

U.S. Bureau of the Census. (1992). Sixty-five plus in America. *Current population reports.* (Series P-23-178). Washington, DC: U.S. Government Printing Office.

U.S. Bureau of the Census. (1997). *Statistical abstract of the United States: 1997* (117th ed.). Washington, DC: U.S. Government Printing Office.

U.S. Bureau of the Census. (1999). *Statistical abstract of the United States: 1999* (119th ed.). Washington, DC: U.S. Government Printing Office.

U.S. House of Representatives, Select Committee on Aging, Subcommittee on Human Services. (1987). *Exploding the myths: Caregiving in America.* Washington, DC: Government Printing Office, Comm. Pub. No. 99–611.

Walters, K. L., & Simoni, J. M. (1993). Lesbian and gay male group identity attitudes and self esteem: Implications for counseling. *Journal of Counseling Psychology, 40,* 94–95.

Ward, R., Logan, J., & Spitze, G. (1992). The influence of parental and child needs on coresidence in middle and later life. *Journal of Marriage and the Family, 54,* 209–221.

Watkins, S. C., Menken, J. A., & Bongaarts, J. (1987). Demographic foundations of family change. *American Sociological Review, 52,* 346–358.

Winsborough, H. H., Bumpass, L. L., & Aguilino, W. S. (1991). *The death of parents and the transition to old age.* (National Survey of Families and Households Working Paper No. 39). Madison: University of Wisconsin.

Wolf, J. H., Breslau, N., Ford, A., Ziegler, H., & Ward, A. (1983). Distance and contacts: Interactions of Black urban elderly adults with family and friends. *Journal of Gerontology, 38* (4), 465–471.

Wright, F. (1989). Gender differences in adults' same and cross-gender friendships. In R. Adams & R. Blieszner (Eds.), *Older adult friendship.* Newbury Park, CA: Sage.

Zarit, S. H., & Eggebeen, D. J. (1995). Parent-child relationships in adulthood and old age. In M. H. Bornstein (Ed.), *Handbook of parenting: Children and parenting* (Vol. 1, pp. 119–140). Mahwah, NJ: Erlbaum.

CHAPTER ELEVEN

THE ECONOMICS OF AGING

Mrs. Mary Fremont is a 77-year-old African American woman who has lived alone for 20 years. She rents an apartment in the inner city of a major metropolitan area in Ohio. Her yearly income as of April 2000, provided from the federally administered Supplemental Security Income (SSI) program, was $6,144 (or $512 per month), the federal payment standard for all recipients of SSI. (Many states supplement this basic benefit with additional money.) The actual poverty threshold for an aged individual at the end of 1999 was $7,990.

The Evanses are recent migrants to a retirement community in the Southwest. They are white, middle class, and college educated. Mr. Evans worked in a management capacity for a large corporation in Ohio. His approximate current retirement income is $35,000 and includes income from Social Security, a private pension, and other assets. The Evans's income is approximately 3.5 times the 1999 poverty threshold level for an aged couple ($10,070).

Mrs. Fremont fits the stereotype of an aged person living on what appears to be inadequate income. Certainly, most readers must be wondering how anybody in the United States today could get by on $6,144 in yearly income. What about the Evanses? It is difficult to think of them as being disadvantaged. Which case example best represents the economic situation of the elderly? Perhaps both! In 1997, 11.9 percent of females 65 years of age and older had yearly income under $5,000, and a total of 48.4 percent had yearly income under $10,000 (including Mrs. Fremont). Yet, in the same year, 50 percent of families with a head of household age 65 years or older (including the Evanses) had income above $30,660.

Is economic deprivation among the elderly a myth or reality? Are elderly households more affluent than younger households? This chapter answers these and other important questions. The economic status of the elderly is discussed first, followed by an investigation of the adequacy of their financial resources in relation to their needs.

THE ECONOMIC STATUS OF THE ELDERLY

The importance of one's economic status in old age cannot be exaggerated. The presence or absence of financial resources will have considerable impact on an individual's capacity to adjust to aging. Income will affect whether a retiree's values

and preferences can be realized. The older person with adequate financial resources can maintain some degree of control over his or her life, including making
decisions about which leisure activities to pursue, how much to travel, what kind
of diet to maintain, and how much preventive health care to seek. Older people
without money can do none of these things.

Money Income of the Aged

Older Americans receive direct money income from a variety of sources. Some
have earnings, either salaries or wages or self-employment income; most have a
retirement pension (including Social Security) of one kind or another. Direct
money income can also come from welfare payments, dividends, interest, rents,
alimony, unemployment, veterans' and workers' compensation payments, and
gifts from others.

Figure 11.1 shows the sources of money income for the elderly. Clearly,
Social Security is the major source (40 percent), although earnings (20 percent)
and asset income (18 percent) contribute to the income position of many elderly
persons. Not all elderly individuals receive income from all the sources identified

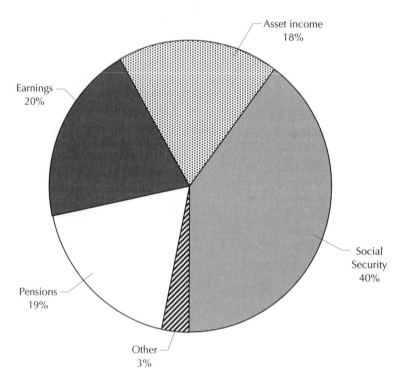

FIGURE 11.1   Share of Income by Source: 1996

Source: Social Security Administration, *Income of the Aged Chartbook, 1996* (Washington, DC: U.S. Government Printing Office, 1998).

TABLE 11.1   Percentage of Aged Persons with Income from Various Sources (1976—1996) and Percentage Share of Income by Source for the Lowest and Highest Income Quintiles (1996)

SOURCE	1976	1986	1996
Earnings	25	20	21
Social Security	89	91	91
Pensions*	31	40	41
Income from assets	56	67	63
Public Assistance	11	7	6

	LOWEST QUINTILE	HIGHEST QUINTILE
Earnings	1	31
Social Security	81	21
Pensions*	3	21
Income from Assets	3	25
Public Assistance	11	**
Other	1	2
Total	100%	100%

*Includes private pensions and annuities, government employee pensions, Railroad Retirement, and IRA, Keough, and 401(k) payments.
**Less than 0.5%.

Source: Social Security Administration, *Income of the Aged Chartbook, 1996* (Washington, DC: U.S. Government Printing Office, 1998).

in the figure. Table 11.1 describes the proportion of the elderly (combining married couples and nonmarried men and women) receiving income from a diverse list of income sources. In 1996, 91 percent of the elderly received some income from Social Security. Between 1976 and 1996, the percentage of aged with income from assets, pensions, and Social Security has increased, while those aged receiving income from public assistance has declined. Married elderly people were more likely to receive income from wages, assets, and pensions than were the single aged. A higher proportion of unmarried elderly people received income from public assistance than did the married elderly. Also, those aged households with the lowest income are most reliant on Social Security and public assistance; those aged units with the highest income are most reliant on earnings and asset income.

The accessibility of some income sources for the elderly has changed since the early 1960s as a result of broadened coverage of Social Security benefits and the rising impact of private pensions. And the accessibility of income sources for the elderly is likely to continue to change in the future. In particular, the impact of private pensions, and especially that of individual retirement accounts (IRAs) and tax-sheltered annuities, is expected to alter the configuration of sources from which the elderly derive income. In 1981, the great majority of Americans became eligible to open IRAs and to invest up to $2,000 annually on a tax-deductible basis even if covered by a qualified pension plan. According to the Internal Revenue Service <http://www.irs.gov>, almost 12 million tax returns for 1982 listed this deduction. However, the Tax Reform Act of 1986 placed significant limitations on the use of IRAs, although individuals not covered by company retirement plans remain eligible to take a tax deduction of up to $2,000 annually for a deposit in an individual retirement account.

In 2000, couples earning less than $62,000 per year and single persons earning less than $42,000 per year remain eligible to make a tax-deductible contribution to a traditional IRA. Even workers with earnings in excess of these amounts or those covered by a qualified pension plan may establish nondeductible individual retirement accounts. All IRAs, those established with nondeductible as well as deductible contributions, accumulate interest and capital gains on a tax-free basis until the withdrawal of funds. Individuals can begin withdrawing on these funds when they reach the age of 59½ or older, when their incomes are expected to be lower than during their peak working years.

In 1998, tax-free Roth IRAs were established that allow single individuals with adjusted gross income (AGI) of $95,000 or less to make a full $2,000 nondeductible contribution; couples can both make $2,000 contributions if the AGI is $150,000 or lower. These Roth IRAs not only accumulate interest and capital gains on a tax-free basis but remain tax-free upon withdrawal at age 59½ or older. Taxpayers with AGI of $100,000 or less may convert amounts to a Roth IRA from a traditional IRA during any taxable year without incurring early withdrawal penalties. However, amounts converted are included in reporting of gross income in the year in which conversion took place and are subject to taxation. After payment of taxes on the converted amount, the Roth IRA accumulates interest and capital gains on a tax-free basis and is tax-free on withdrawal.

Just how much income do the elderly have? Table 11.2 shows the money income of persons age 65 and over with earnings and without, by presence or absence of retirement benefits in 1996. Most elderly had incomes under $25,000; the median income for all aged households was $16,099. Only about 7 percent of aged households have no retirement benefits. Of these, 38 percent have earnings and their median income is $33,638; 62 percent have no earnings and their median income is only $490. In the absence of earnings, median income rises markedly with the number of retirement benefits received, from $10,054 with one retirement benefit to $23,164 with two or more. For households with both earnings and retirement benefits, median incomes are $26,982 for those with one retirement benefit and $37,996 for those with more than one.

Since 1962, the median income of the aged families has increased dramatically—even when adjusted for inflation. For example, as depicted in Figure 11.2 (in 1996 dollars), the income of married couples increased by 76 percent between 1967 and 1996, and that of nonmarried couples increased by 84 percent. There were disproportionate increases by race in this period as well. The incomes of whites increased by 90 percent between 1967 and 1996, that of African Americans increased by 53 percent.

TABLE 11.2   Money Income of Persons Age 65 and Over with Earnings and without, with Retirement Benefits and without: 1996

	MEDIAN INCOME
No Retirement Benefits	
Earnings, yes	$33,638
Earnings, no	490
One Retirement Benefit	
Earnings, yes	$26,982
Earnings, no	10,054
Two or More Retirement Benefits	
Earnings, yes	$37,996
Earnings, no	23,164

Source: Social Security Administration, *Income of the Aged Chartbook, 1996* (Washington, DC: U.S. Government Printing Office, 1998).

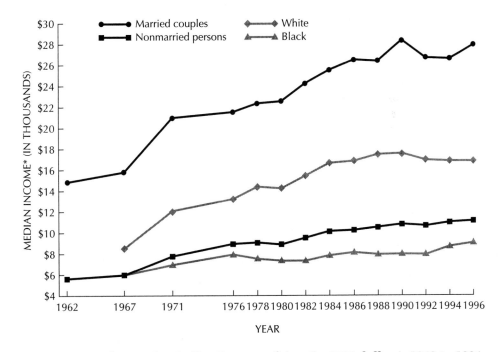

FIGURE 11.2   Changes in Median Income of Age (in 1996 dollars): 1962 to 1996

Source: Social Security Administration, *Income of the Aged Chartbook, 1996* (Washington, DC: U.S. Government Printing Office, 1998).

In describing the characteristics of an entire population, summary statistics (like those just presented) are frequently used. These measures represent statistical generalizations. It is important to recognize that the aged are a heterogeneous group, and there is wide variation in income among them. The reader has already seen how income varies along the lines of earnings and the presence of retirement benefits. Obvious other factors associated with income variation among the elderly are age, marital status, and race.

The elderly are not age homogeneous. Chapter 3 distinguished between the young- old and the very old or old-old. Although most data on the income of the aged groups all persons together, Table 11.3 disaggregates the data by age and shows the decline in median income of households with old-age members. For example, married couples with a household head aged 85 years and over have a median income of $23,373, or 71 percent of that for couples age 65 to 69 years ($32,988). Some of this decline may be a function of current work experience, with the youngest elderly more likely to be participating in the labor force, even if only part time. In addition, many of the oldest-old began their work careers before Social Security and private pension plans became commonplace. The data in Table 11.3 should not necessarily be read as indicating that the economic status of older individuals declines as they grow older. Ross, Danziger, and Smolensky (1987) show that the average income of cohorts of older persons, when controlling for retirement and marital status, did not decline over a 30-year period. Rather, incomes were found to decline with status changes such as movement into retirement and/or widowhood.

Differences in median income of the aged by race for 1996 remain quite substantial. Whites ($16,954) have a median income that is 76 percent greater than that of African Americans ($9,694) and 91 percent greater than that for Lat-

TABLE 11.3   Median Income and Percent of Units, by Age, Sex, and Marital Status: 1996

SEX AND MARITAL STATUS	MEDIAN INCOME				
	65–69	*70–74*	*75–79*	*80–84*	*85 or older*
Married couples	$32,988	$27,880	$24,655	$24,633	$23,373
Nonmarried men	15,101	14,313	14,106	13,025	10,928
Nonmarried women	11,630	11,325	10,294	10,171	9,417
	PERCENT OF UNITS				
Total number (in thousands)	6,681	6,286	5,317	3,555	2,713
Total percent	100	100	100	100	100
Married couples	51	45	36	30	17
Nonmarried men	14	15	15	16	20
Nonmarried women	35	40	49	54	63

Source: Social Security Administration, *Income of the Aged Chartbook, 1996* (Washington, DC: U.S. Government Printing Office, 1998).

inos ($8,854). Figure 11.3 shows differentials in receipt of income from major sources by race and Latino origin. White (92 percent) and African American (83 percent) aged are somewhat more likely than Latinos (73 percent) to receive Social Security. Whites are more likely than aged blacks or Latinos to receive income from assets and from pensions. Minority-aged households are much more likely to receive public assistance than are white households; 22 percent of Latino households, 14 percent of black households, and only 4 percent of white households received Supplemental Security Income in 1996. Literature summarized in Chapter 15 describes the double jeopardy or multiple hazards of being aged and of minority status in the United States. This may be especially the case with regard to income and health status (Dowd & Bengtson 1978).

Assets and In-Kind Income

Approximately 21 percent of all income to the elderly in this country comes from financial assets. These assets—sometimes referred to as *liquid assets* because of their easy conversion to goods, services, or money—generally take the form of bank deposits and corporate stocks and bonds. Typically, liquid assets are accumulated over the life course. Individuals may save for different reasons, often as a precaution against unexpected need in the future or to smooth out irregularities in the flow of income during the lifetime. As Schulz (1995) points out, however, assets

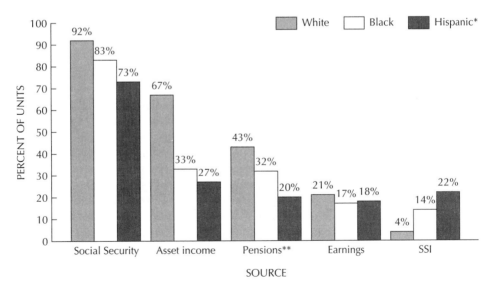

FIGURE 11.3   Receipt of Income, by Source, Race, and Hispanic Origin: 1996

*Persons of Hispanic origin may be of any race
**Includes private pensions and annuities, government employee pensions, Railroad Retirement, and IRA, Keogh, and 401(k) payments.

Source: Social Security Administration, *Income of the Aged Chartbook, 1996* (Washington, DC: U.S. Government Printing Office, 1998).

put aside as precaution against unexpected needs—medical or nursing home bills, for example—are not available for immediate needs. Accumulation of assets does not necessarily stop with old age. Inflation, increasing property taxes, or the desire to take a retirement cruise may all be appropriate reasons to continue to save during old age. There is disagreement among economists about the evidence on continued saving among the elderly. Some suggest that the elderly, as a group, continue to accumulate assets; only the old-old do not (Torrey & Taeuber 1986). Others argue that the elderly use their savings for current expenditures (Radner 1989).

Asset income is not distributed equitably across the elderly population. In fact, about 14 percent of all elderly couples and about 25 percent of unrelated individuals had no financial assets in 1984 (Schulz 1995). The concept of *net worth* is used to aggregate all the assets of a household, including financial assets, real estate (e.g., own home, rental property, etc.) and business holdings, and even the value of motor vehicles. The U.S. Bureau of the Census data for 1993 identifies 34 percent of aged household units in the lowest quintile of net worth with a median of $30,400. However, net worth minus the equity in an owned home for this group is reduced to a median of $2,993; 63 percent of aged units in the lowest two quintiles had median net worth minus home equity of less than $21,000. Even $21,000 in assets hardly constitutes a significant income supplement. Depending on the form of investment, given the relatively low interest rates prevalent in the late 1990s, even $21,000 will likely yield no more than about $1,000 per year in income. Assets tend to be correlated with income: Those families with the highest incomes are most likely to have substantial assets; those with the lowest incomes are least likely to have any assets. Aged households in the highest quintile in 1993 had a median net worth of $354,781; excluding home equity, net worth for this group was $215,335.

Some assets have less liquidity because they require more time to convert to money. These **nonliquid assets** include equity in housing or a business and possessions such as automobiles. Homes are the most common asset (liquid or nonliquid) of older people. About 80 percent of elderly households reside in an owned home; 55 percent of these homeowners owe no mortgage debt. This might suggest to some that older people need less income because they have no mortgage payments and have considerable equity tied up in a home. This may not be the case, however. Elderly households residing in mortgage-free homes are typically in older homes—homes they purchased 30 or more years ago but that were built 40 or 50 years ago. Monthly maintenance bills on such older housing stock may make up for the absence of an older low-interest mortgage payment.

Just how much equity do the elderly have in their homes? According to the U.S. Bureau of the Census (1999, Table 772), the median home equity in the United States in 1995 for families whose head is 65 to 75 years is $82,500; for those families headed by an individual 75 years or over, the median home equity is $80,000. These values are somewhat below that for all families in the United States, who report median home equity in 1995 to be $89,000. Until very recently, however, this equity was not available to aged homeowners for day-to-day living expenses. Since January 1, 1979, the Federal Home Loan Bank Board (FHLBB) <http://www.

fhlbanks.com> has allowed federally chartered savings and loan associations to offer *reverse annuity mortgages.* Under this mortgage, a homeowner may sell some equity in the house and, in turn, receive a fixed monthly sum based on a percentage of the current market value of the house (Schulz 1995). Each federal savings institution must have its reverse annuity program approved by the FHLBB, but these mortgages are not commonly employed at this time. Recently, Congress gave authority to the Federal Housing Administration <http://www.hud.gov/mortprog.html> to insure up to 25,000 reverse mortgages for homeowners 62 years of age and older over a five-year period. Such insurance, which protects both lenders and borrowers in the event of bankruptcy or takeover, may unlock some of the vast equity held by elderly homeowners. The October 1992 issue of *Consumer Reports* magazine <http://www.consumerreports.org> estimated that only about 3,000 FHA applications for reverse annuity mortgages had been processed by mid-1992.

The elderly receive indirect or in-kind income in the form of goods and services that they obtain free or at reduced cost from a wide array of federal, state, and local programs benefitting the elderly over and above those providing direct income. The largest of these federal programs, Medicare and Medicaid, provide older people with health care services. There are numerous programs aimed at providing housing to older people that are below the cost for similar housing on the open market. Under its various assistance programs, the federal government houses about 2 million older persons in as many as 1.5 million units. These programs are discussed in detail in Chapter 16. The food-stamp program is another visible source of indirect income to those elderly who are eligible to participate.

It is difficult to say how much in terms of income these programs are worth today to the aged. Information on the value of comparable services available in the marketplace is sometimes difficult to obtain. In addition, the value that recipients may place on in-kind services may differ sharply from their market value. Total social welfare expenditures for aged and nonaged persons in the United States under public programs approximated $1,505 billion in 1995; the federal share was $888 billion, or 59 percent of the total. Still, the great majority of aged people receive no federal in-kind benefits. According to the U.S. Bureau of the Census (1999, Table 612), it is difficult to discern the percentage of all U.S. households (aged and nonaged) receiving any means-tested noncash benefits. However, it is known that in 1997, 7.1 percent of U.S. households received food stamps, 4.7 percent received housing subsidies, and 13.3 percent received health care through Medicaid. (Some households receive more than one benefit.) In fact, many U.S. households with income below the poverty level do not receive any means-tested noncash benefits; in 1997, 47 percent received benefits through Medicaid, 36 percent received food stamps, and only 21 percent received public housing subsidies.

Taxes and Inflation

When we state that the median income of aged married couples in the United States in 1996 was $27,944, we are providing a pretax figure. Almost all income data, especially figures published by the Social Security Administration and the

U.S. Census Bureau, represent gross income or income before taxes. The scarcity of after-tax data makes it difficult to analyze the impact of taxation on the elderly and to determine whether, relative to other age groups, they are advantaged or disadvantaged by tax laws. After anlayzing returns filed in 1990, Gist and Mulvey (1990) used computer simulations to estimate that average federal income tax rates are about two and one-half times as great for the single population under age 65 as for the single elderly, and nearly twice as great for married persons under age 65 as for married elderly persons.

Congressional action in 1984 imposed federal income taxes on up to one-half of Social Security benefits received by taxpayers whose adjusted gross incomes exceed certain base amounts. The base amount was $25,000 for a single taxpayer, $32,000 for a married couple filing a joint return, and $0 for married persons filing separate returns. Beginning in 1994, the law was changed to increase the tax burden on higher-income Social Security beneficiaries. Initially, this 1994 increase was estimated to affect only about 20 percent of Social Security beneficiaries (Pattison & Harrington 1993). Schulz (1995) argues that eventually inflation and increases in real income will push a greater proportion of the aged into the taxable range. The standard federal income tax deduction for a single individual 65 years and older in 1999 was $5,350; an aged married couple filing a joint return in which the spousal exemption is taken has a standard deduction of $8,900. (Taxpayers under age 65 had a standard federal income tax deduction in 1999 of $4,300; for couples, this deduction was $7,200.) Beginning in 1998, individuals were permitted to exclude from federal taxation up to $250,000 ($500,000 on a joint return) resulting from the sale of a personal residence. Property tax reductions are now granted to the elderly in every state. The latter points would seem to be of more help to the higher-income elderly—those who are more likely to itemize deductions on federal income tax returns and who are more likely to be property owners.

Inflation has been called a hidden tax, one that can have a disastrous impact on the economic situation of people of all ages. Generally, the term is used to describe increases in the level of prices measured by the *Consumer Price Index (CPI)*. The CPI, a product of the Bureau of Labor Statistics, is a weighted index of the annual consumption patterns of Americans. It covers the expenditures of approximately 80 percent of the noninstitutional population, including retirees and the unemployed. A majority of workers under contract in the United States have their earnings pegged to the CPI as well. Schulz (1995) lists five principal ways older people can be affected adversely by unanticipated inflation:

1. Assets that do not adjust with inflation depreciate in value.
2. Income sources may not adjust to inflation, reducing real income.
3. For employed people, adjustments in earnings may lag behind inflation, reducing real wages.
4. The tax burden may rise because the tax brackets are defined in money rather than real terms.
5. Elderly persons may allocate their budgets differently from others (e.g., more for food, housing maintenance, and health care). Because indexes used to

measure and adjust various sources of income may not correctly reflect aged buying patterns, the elderly may not be fully compensated for increased prices.

The last two points deserve additional discussion. Many aged persons will not pay income taxes because their incomes are low. All but the highest income recipients of Social Security will be exempt from federal taxes as well. In the past, those who paid federal income taxes faced a problem. Some compensation received as protection from inflation was taxed away, at progressively higher rates (Schulz 1995). Starting in 1985, tax brackets were indexed to take inflation into account. The Tax Reform Act of 1986 simultaneously reduced the number of tax brackets and the progressivity in the federal tax structure. These actions have eliminated the problem. Unfortunately, the income exemption ceiling below which Social Security benefits are not taxed is not indexed to take inflation into account. Thus, as inflation pushes the income of Social Security beneficiaries higher, in the future more of these people will find their Social Security benefits subject to the federal income tax (Schulz 1995).

Clearly, persons living primarily on fixed incomes or pensions are hurt the most by the rising prices that accompany inflation. Historically, this has been the case for the elderly, but recent developments have changed this situation. The Social Security program, the major source of retirement income, now adjusts benefits automatically on the basis of the rate of inflation. The Social Security Amendments of 1983 have affected cost-of-living adjustments (COLA) to Social Security benefits in two ways. First, the July 1983 COLA was delayed until January 1984, with all future automatic adjustments being effective on a calendar-year basis. Second, if Social Security trust fund assets decline relative to the outflow of funds, then future automatic COLAs will be pegged to the lesser of increases in prices (measured by the CPI) or to increases in wages.

Several in-kind income sources, such as the food-stamp program, also peg their benefits to the rate of inflation. Some private pension benefits are also adjusted automatically as the cost of living increases. All this suggests that many elderly people are in an advantaged position relative to other age groups in that a major portion of their direct and indirect money income keeps pace with the rate of inflation.

THE ADEQUACY OF AGED INCOME

It is one thing to describe how much income the elderly have; it is quite another to say what they do with their income and whether it is adequate for their needs. Like Americans of all ages, the elderly are consumers of a vast array of goods and services. In 1970, older persons spent about $60 billion, or over 10 percent of the national total. This figure was consistent with the proportion of the U.S. population made up by older people in 1970, also 10 percent. It is likely that as the elderly population increases (and their incomes increase), so will the proportion of all goods and services they account for in purchases. On this basis, one would estimate personal expenditures of the aged today (2000) at about $700 billion, or about 13 percent of total personal consumption expenditures in the United States.

How do older Americans spend their income? Rubin and Koelln (1996) list the following:

1. Elderly consumers spend less than younger ones.
2. The oldest of the elderly households have the lowest average propensity to consume.
3. The elderly reduce their consumption in order to avoid spending down their wealth.

Households headed by an individual aged 65 years or over spend only 69 percent of the average annual expenditure for all consumer households in the United States (see Table 11.4). Such expenditure patterns reflect a high aversion to risk, perhaps related to the elderly's uncertainty about future health and length of life, but also likely influenced by the accumulation of goods already owned by older households (Rubin & Koelln 1996).

Table 11.4 compares the average annual out-of-pocket expenditures of households with a head 65 years of age or older with those of all household units.

TABLE 11.4   Average Annual Expenditures of All Consumer Units by Type of Expenditure: 1995

TYPE OF EXPENDITURE	AMOUNT EXPENDED			PERCENTAGE DISTRIBUTION		
	All Units	*55–64 Yrs.*	*65+ Yrs.*	*All Units*	*55–64 Yrs.*	*65+ Yrs.*
Total	$32,277	$32,604	$22,265	100.0	100.0	100.0
Food	4,505	4,539	3,388	14.2	13.9	15.2
At home	2,803	2,832	2,367	8.7	8.7	10.6
Away from home	1,702	1,707	1,021	5.3	5.2	4.6
Housing	10,465	10,291	7,590	32.4	31.6	34.1
Shelter	5,932	5,358	3,668	18.4	16.4	16.5
Utilities	2,193	2,442	1,982	6.8	7.5	8.9
Furnishings	1,403	1,603	1,051	4.3	4.9	4.7
Clothing	1,704	1,833	876	5.3	5.6	3.9
Transportation	6,016	5,726	3,377	18.6	17.6	15.2
Health Care	1,732	1,909	2,647	5.4	5.9	11.9
Entertainment	1,612	1,577	929	5.0	4.8	4.2
Personal Insurance and Pensions	2,967	3,211	802	9.2	9.8	3.6
Cash	925	1,043	1,101	2.9	3.2	4.9
Other	2,351	2,475	1,555	7.3	7.6	7.0

Source: Statistical Abstract of the United States, 1997 (Washington, DC: U.S. Bureau of the Census, 1997), Table 712.

Older household units spend proportionately more of their income on food, housing, utilities, health care, and cash contributions, and less on transportation, clothing, personal insurance and pensions, and entertainment. Interestingly, older households spend proportionately less on shelter but more on furnishings for their households than do all consumers.

The pattern of expenditures among the elderly is similar to the pattern of expenditures among lower-income groups in general. Still, one must ask: Is low income an adequate income? The most frequently used measure of income adequacy is the *poverty index* developed in the early 1960s by the Social Security Administration, based on the amount of money needed to purchase a *minimum adequate diet* as determined by the Department of Agriculture <http://www.usda.gov>. The index has been described as follows:

> The food budget is the lowest that could be devised to supply all essential nutrients using food readily purchasable in the U.S. market (with customary regional variations). The poverty line is then calculated at three times the food budget (slightly smaller proportions for one- and two-person families) on the assumption—derived from studies of consumers—that a family that has spent a larger proportion of its income on food will be living at a very inadequate level. The food budgets and the derivative poverty income cutoff points are estimated in detail for families of differing size and composition (62 separate family types) with a farm/nonfarm differential for each type. This variation of the poverty measure in relation to family size and age of members is its most important distinguishing characteristic. (U.S. House Committee on Ways and Means 1967)

In 1997, the poverty index level for a two-person family with an aged head was $9,712; the comparable level for a single person was $7,698.

Figure 11.4 shows that, in general, poverty has been declining among older people during the period 1966 to 1997, although most of the relative gains in income for the elderly were accomplished between 1966 and about 1975. As depicted in Figure 11.5, poverty varies among subgroups of the elderly. Aged whites are less likely to live in poverty than is anyone in the total U.S. population, with 9.6 percent living below the poverty level; however, 30.8 percent of aged blacks are living in poverty.

Critics of the poverty index argue that it is set too low. Remember that the index is calculated at three times the minimum adequate food budget, with different food budgets constructed for different types of families. The following characteristics are used in combination to develop indices for family units:

1. Age of head over or under 65 years
2. Size of family (two to nine or more)
3. Number of related children under age 18
4. "Unrelated" family units

The 3:1 ratio was set as a result of surveys conducted in 1955 and 1960–1961 of the ratio of food consumption to other expenditures for *all* families in the United

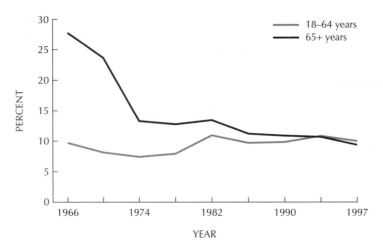

FIGURE 11.4   Poverty Rates of Elderly and Nonelderly Adults: 1966–1997

Source: J. Dalaker & M. Naifeh, *Poverty in the United States, 1997,* U.S. Bureau of the Census, Current Population Reports, Series P60-201 (Washington, DC: U.S. Government Printing Office, 1997).

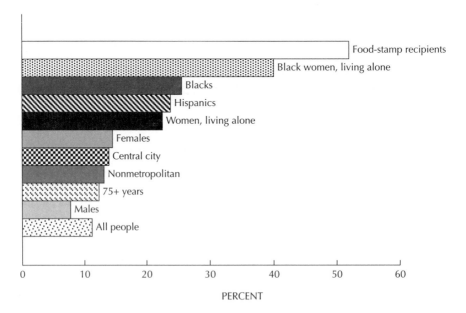

FIGURE 11.5   Percentage of Elderly below Poverty by Selected Characteristics: 1997

Source: U.S. Bureau of the Census, unpublished data from 1997 Current Population Survey.

Note: Unless otherwise noted, data are for age 65+.

States. A congressional report based on Consumer Expenditure Surveys indicated that by 1972–1973 the ratio exceeded 5:1 (Poverty Studies Task Force 1976). In testimony before the U.S. House Select Committee on Aging, one student of aging in the United States suggested that shifting to more realistic levels of what constitutes poverty would more than double the number of aged poor, so that the number of either poor or near poor would include approximately 40 percent of the aged (Orshansky 1978). Orshansky (1978) also points out that the index is not applied to the "hidden poor" (those who are institutionalized or living with relatives). Even the current figures on poverty status exclude millions of aged who are unable to live independently. In 1997, 17 percent of those 65 years and over had incomes at or below 125 percent of the poverty level measure. Had this near-poverty benchmark been employed, the number of aged persons defined as impoverished would have risen from 3.4 million to 5.4 million, an increase of almost 60 percent. Employing this benchmark for those age 75 years and over would have increased the impoverished from 1.7 million to 2.9 million, an increase of 71 percent.

Another criticism of the poverty index argues that poverty statistics are artificially high because the value of in-kind or noncash transfers is not included as income. Should government expenditures for food stamps, housing subsidies, or Medicaid be included as income for the purpose of measuring poverty? If the answer is "yes," then, by definition, many people will have additional income and the poverty rate will decline.

In 1992, a panel of the committee on National Statistics of the National Academy of Sciences (NAS) <http://www4.nationalacademies.org/nas/nashome.nsf> evaluated alternative definitions of poverty (Citro & Michael 1995). Using simulation, they showed how the numbers of impoverished people changed when tax and various transfers are subtracted or added to the definition of income. For example, the addition of nonmedical noncash benefits such as food stamps, free and reduced school lunches, and rent subsidies lowered the overall poverty rate in 1997 from 13.3 to 11.9 percent.

Where the poverty line is exactly drawn may be moot. Clearly, many elderly persons have substantial economic difficulties, which are likely to manifest themselves in poor nutrition, neglect of health and medical needs, inadequate housing, and the like.

THE SOCIAL SECURITY SYSTEM

Nine out of ten U.S. workers are covered and over 90 percent of the elderly receive some income support through a public retirement pension system administered by the federal government and colloquially referred to as *Social Security.* Despite recent public attention to the problems involved in financing this system, few people are really familiar with its principles and provisions. This section discusses Social Security, focusing primarily on pension benefits and selected special issues such as the needed reform of provisions related to women. Several related programs, including Supplemental Security Income (SSI), will be reviewed.

Background

The notion of an old-age pension received as a right by a person who had led a productive life was not seriously discussed until the end of the nineteenth century (Bromley 1974). Even then, the prevailing opinion was that an individual was solely responsible for making financial provision for himself or herself in old age. Such provision would come out of a lifetime's earnings, through either savings or insurance. Individuals unable to provide for themselves were subject to "poor laws" and the scarce resources of private charities.

By 1889, a system of social insurance had been created in Germany that included a pension scheme. For the first time, the aged were given a measure of economic security as a right rather than a charity. In Denmark, state support for needy old people was introduced in 1891. Pension rights were introduced in Great Britain in 1908 for people over the age of 70 who had been in regular employment but had little or no income.

During the early part of the twentieth century and into the 1920s, continuing attempts were made in the United States to define pensions as a right of aged Americans. These attempts met with limited success. Several states enacted old-age pension legislation, and reform groups such as the American Association of Old Age Security began to appear. The Great Depression, with its devastating economic impact on the lives of many Americans, helped create conditions that would ultimately allow the enactment of federal legislation promoting the pension rights of the aged and guaranteeing unemployment insurance.

Unemployment during the Great Depression affected more than 25 percent of the elderly. Bank failures and the declining value of estates exhausted the financial resources of millions, including even those among the more prosperous middle and upper-middle classes. In 1932, the American Federation of Labor reversed its previous position and endorsed unemployment insurance and old-age assistance at the state and federal levels.

During this period, utopian schemes were prevalent. In 1933, Upton Sinclair put forth his 12-point EPIC ("end poverty in California") plan to make people self-supporting and to grant a $50 monthly old-age pension to all needy persons who had resided in California for at least three years. Sinclair won the Democratic nomination for governor but was soundly defeated, with his opponents insisting EPIC actually meant "end property, introduce communism" in California (Fischer 1977).

The so-called ham and eggs movement, also based in California, proposed a weekly pension be given to everyone who was 50 years of age or over and out of work. The pension, initially proposed to be "twenty-five dollars every Tuesday" and later improved to "thirty dollars every Thursday," would be in the form of stamped scrip, which would expire at a given date. Not only would the economic situation of the older unemployed be enhanced by this scheme, but also the economy would be invigorated by increased circulation of money (Fischer 1977).

Perhaps the most popular of these utopian schemes was that put forth by Dr. Francis Townsend of Long Beach, California. The essence of the Townsend plan was that all Americans over age 60 receive a monthly sum of $200 on the condition that they spent their pension within 30 days; a 2 percent tax on all business transactions was to pay for the plan (Achenbaum 1978). By 1936, Townsend claimed a national following of over 5 million and at least 60 U.S. representatives sympathetic to his measure (Putnam 1970).

Clearly, the idea of an old-age pension had achieved legitimacy. The institutional structure needed to implement this idea was the Social Security Act of 1935. With its passage, the United States became one of the last industrial nations to establish a federal old-age pension program.

Principles

The influence of Social Security legislation on the whole question of retirement and pension in the United States would be difficult to overestimate. As one historian of old age in the United States has pointed out, the Social Security Act of 1935 (1) established the principle of a guaranteed "floor" income as a right bought by contributions over the course of a working life, (2) gave added impetus to demands for the extension of private pension coverage, (3) provided a standard age by which retirement could be defined, and (4) signaled a new era in financial arrangements for life after retirement (Calhoun 1978).

Still, it is important to remember that this legislation was very much a political document, reflecting divergent views prominent at the time. During the 1936 presidential campaign, President Roosevelt's Republican opponent, Alf Landon, lambasted Social Security as "unjust, unworkable, stupidly drafted and wastefully financed...a cruel hoax" (Tynes 1996, p. 4). Roosevelt won with 61 percent of the vote and many saw this as a mandate for the Social Security program. As Social Security evolved, significant questions remained: Should the program be aimed at preventing or relieving economic destitution? Should a straight government pension be provided, or a contributing insurance system for wage earners? What about England's plan, which included both insurance *and* old-age assistance? Should there be a single federal system or an aggregate of state plans? Should the plan be voluntary or compulsory, universal or selective (Achenbaum 1978)?

Schulz (1995) outlines seven principles inherent in the Social Security legislation accepted by President Roosevelt and the Congress. Some of these principles clearly reflect a consensus or compromise position on the questions raised here.

1. For the designated groups, *participation was compulsory.*
2. Social Security was set up as an *earnings-related system.*
3. *Social adequacy* was taken into account in the determination of benefits for recipients. Weighted benefits favored workers with lower earnings.
4. Social Security was not intended to be the sole means of economic protection; it was only to provide *a floor of protection.*
5. Funds for operating the program were to come from earmarked *payroll taxes* called contributions.
6. Workers were to earn their benefits through participation in the program; there was to be *no means test.*
7. A *retirement test* was established; pension benefits were withheld if an eligible person worked and earned more than a specified amount.

Pension Benefits

The Social Security Act of 1935 established a federal old-age insurance (OAI) program and a federal-state system of unemployment insurance. The original legislation, weak by comparison with other Western nations, has been strengthened and expanded since 1939, when survivors' and dependents' benefits were added (OASI). Disability insurance (OASDI) was added in 1956, Medicare (OASDHI) in 1965. Changes legislated in 1972 included the automatic adjustment of benefits for inflation (begun in 1975) and the establishment of Supplemental Security Income (SSI) to replace aid to the indigent, blind, and disabled. Important changes were made again in the Social Security Amendments of 1983.

In 1948, only 13 percent of all persons age 65 years and over were receiving Social Security payments. Since 1950, however, additional groups of workers have been brought into the system: certain farm and domestic workers (1950), the self-employed (1954), members of the uniformed services (1956), Americans employed by foreign governments (1960), physicians (1965), and ministers (1967). In 1974, the railroad retirement program was integrated into the Social Security system. Starting in January 1984, the following new groups have been covered under Social Security: (1) newly hired federal employees, including executive, legislative, and judicial branch employees; (2) current employees of the legislative branch who are not participating in the Civil Service Retirement System; (3) all members of Congress, the president, the vice president, federal judges, and most executive-level political appointees; and (4) current and future employees of private, tax-exempt nonprofit organizations. Currently, about 95 percent of all jobs in the United States are covered by Social Security.

Social Security eligibility is related to work rather than to need. An individual (and his or her dependents and survivors) is eligible if he or she has worked in employment that is covered and has worked long enough to have acquired "insured status." Most workers in jobs not covered are aware of this and are often covered by another retirement system. Insured status is acquired by earning a minimum amount during a specified number of calendar quarters in jobs covered by Social Security. In 1999, a person was credited with a quarter of coverage for each $740 earned during the year (this amount is subject to annual revision), with a maximum of four quarters of coverage in a given year. A person who reached age 62 in 1991 or later needed 10 years (or 40 quarters) of work in covered employment to achieve minimum eligibility for retirement benefits.

Benefits are financed by payroll taxes paid by both employees and employers on income up to a certain level. In 1999, this tax was 15.30 percent (7.65 percent withheld from employees; 7.65 percent withheld from employers) applied to a base level of earnings, which (since 1974) rises automatically as average earnings rise. The self-employed paid this same rate of 15.30 percent in 1999. Actually, the 1999 tax rate of 7.65 percent on employee wages represents the total of three different tax rates: (1) a rate of 5.35 percent, applied to wages (a maximum of $72,400 in 1999), which is deposited to the Old Age and Survivors Insurance (OASI) Trust Fund, the fund out of which retirement benefits are paid; (2) a rate of 0.85 percent, also applied to wages up to $72,400, which is deposited to the

Disability Insurance (DI) Trust Fund, the fund out of which workers' disability benefits are paid; and (3) a rate of 1.45 percent, applied to all wages with no upper limit, which is deposited to the Health Insurance (HI) Trust Fund, the fund out of which Medicare benefits are funded.

Some have argued that this payroll tax is regressive. That is, because only income up to a certain level is subject to taxation, those with higher incomes pay a lower proportion of their income into the Social Security tax fund. For example, an individual earning $25,000 in 1999 pays 7.65 percent, or $1,912.50, to Social Security, but someone earning $100,000 a year pays approximately $5,690.80 (6.2 percent (5.6 + 0.6) of the first $60,600 plus 1.45 percent of $100,000), or about 5.7 percent of his or her total income. Thus, the tax contribution is a heavier proportional burden for the lower-income worker, although such workers do receive proportionately higher benefits when they retire (see the discussion of pension replacement rates later in this chapter). It is also likely (perhaps even *more* likely for the lower-income worker) that the employer's share of tax contributions is actually borne by employees in lower wages and reduced benefits.

Benefits are paid to persons who have worked for a minimum period of time on a covered job. The *minimum benefit* (eliminated by 1981 legislation for workers who attained age 62 after 1982) of approximately $3,000 per year is provided to beneficiaries who reached age 62 before 1982. The *basic benefit,* applicable with retirement at age 65, is based on a worker's average indexed monthly earnings (AIME) in covered employment. It is derived from a benefit formula weighted to provide low-wage workers with a relatively greater percentage of earnings replacement than workers with higher wages. The primary insurance amount (PIA), or Social Security benefit, provided to a retired worker on a monthly basis is computed by applying a formula to the AIME. The formula consists of brackets in which three percentages are applied to amounts of AIME. The dollar amounts defining the brackets are called *bend points* and are different for each calendar year of attainment of age 62.

For retired workers who attained age 62 in 1999, the bend points are $505 and $3,043. The formula is 90 percent of the first $505 of AIME, plus 32 percent of the next $2,538 of AIME, plus 15 percent of AIME above $3,043. The following are examples of monthly PIA computations for such workers with different AIME amounts:

1. If a retired worker has an AIME of $300, the PIA is $270 per month (90 percent of $300).
2. If the AIME is $952, the monthly PIA is $597.50 (90 percent of $505 plus 32 percent of $447).
3. If the AIME is $3,300, the monthly PIA is $1,305.2 (90 percent of $505 plus 32 percent of $2,538 plus 15 percent of $257).

The average monthly benefit actually paid to a retired worker in December 1999 was $9,420 a year, or $785 a month; the average monthly benefit for a disabled worker was $736, and for a widow or widower, $757. Benefit levels vary substantially by gender and family type.

This relatively low average benefit level reflects the fact that over half of current Social Security recipients *do not* receive full benefits. This is due, in part, to the popularity of the early retirement option. Early retirement benefits may be paid to people who retire at ages 62 to 64. These benefits are reduced to take into account the longer period over which they will be paid. Benefits are actually reduced by 1/180 for each month before age 65, with a maximum reduction of 20 percent. Thus, if the full PIA amount for a worker who retired at age 63 was $1,000, the actual monthly benefit would be reduced by 13.33 percent, or 1/180, of $1,000 multiplied by 24 months. The resulting reduction, $133.33, is subtracted from $1,000 to obtain $866.67, which is rounded to $867.

Delayed benefit credits (sometimes referred to as the **delayed retirement credit** [DRC]) are also available. The DRC increases the Social Security benefit payable to workers who postpone retirement past age 65 and up to age 70. The annual rate of increase under the DRC is 6.5 percent for workers who reach age 62 in 1999 or 2000. DRCs will increase an additional 0.5 percent every other year until reaching 8 percent per year for workers aged 62 after 2004.

The Retirement Test[1]

The Social Security Administration employs a **retirement test** to determine whether a person otherwise eligible for retirement benefits is considered retired. Unless a person can be considered substantially retired, benefits are not payable. Essentially, the retirement test acts to reduce benefits paid to persons under age 70 who earn more than a certain amount. For example, a 67-year-old woman could earn up to $15,500 in 1999 ($1,292 monthly) *without* any reduction in her Social Security benefits. Benefits are reduced $1 for every $3 earned above the exempt amount. The retirement test also applies to Social Security recipients who are 62 to 64 years of age. A 63-year-old woman could earn up to $9,600 ($800 monthly) in 1999 without any reduction in her Social Security benefits. For beneficiaries in this age group, however, the retirement test "tax" is $1 for each $2 of earnings above the exempt amount.

One estimate is that 1.2 million individuals had their Social Security benefits reduced by the retirement test in 1989 (Bondar 1993). Much controversy surrounds discussion of the test, as evidenced by persistent congressional attempts to repeal or drastically modify it. Critics argue that the retirement test acts as a work-disincentive plan in that earnings above the exempt amount are, in effect, taxed at a 50 percent rate for early retirees and a 33 1/3 percent rate for retirees age 65

---

[1]On April 7, 2000, as this book was going to press, President Clinton signed into law the "Senior Citizens Freedom to Work Act of 2000." This legislation eliminates the Social Security retirement earnings test in and after the month in which a person attains full retirement age—currently age 65. Elimination of the retirement test is retroactive to December 31, 1999. In the calendar year a beneficiary attains the full retirement age (through age 69), the earnings limit ($17,000 in 2000, $25,000 in 2001 and $30,000 in 2002) and the corresponding reduction rate ($1 for $3 offset) will be applied to all months prior to attainment of the full retirement age.

and over. These critics posit that eliminating the retirement test will cause some of those no longer affected by the test to increase their work effort and thus their earnings. Others suggest that the test itself is a form of age discrimination because persons age 70 and older are not required to meet it. Proponents of the test point out that liberalization or even elimination of the retirement test would be very costly and would ultimately help only a small number of aged who are least in need.

Packard (1990) simulated the elimination of the retirement test for the 1986 population of persons age 65 to 69. He concluded that 8.1 million of the 9.7 million persons in this age group (84 percent) would not likely be affected by such a change; 600,000 persons in this age group could increase their earnings with elimination of the retirement test, but an equal number would be likely to decrease their earnings. What about tax revenues? The National Commission on Social Security (1981) estimated that complete elimination of the test would cost $6 or $7 billion in the first year. Packard's (1990) simulation suggests that changes in total tax revenue (payroll taxes plus taxation of benefits plus income taxation of earnings), though difficult to predict in advance, are likely to be quite small, especially because only a small proportion of those aged 65 to 69 are likely to change their work effort and earnings.

Responding to intense political pressure to abolish the retirement test, Congress has liberalized provisions over the past 15 years or so in three different ways:

1. It reduced the maximum age for the retirement test from age 72 to 70, effective in 1983.
2. It increased the annual exempt amount and wage-indexed the amount.
3. It changed the reduction in the "take-back" rate after age 65 from 50 to 33 1/3 percent, effective in 1990.

Social Security Replacement Rates

Social Security has had an enormous impact on the extent of poverty among the aged. In 1996, the family income of 16 percent of aged, unmarried beneficiaries fell below the poverty line. Without Social Security benefits, 61 percent of those beneficiaries would have income below the poverty line—a difference of 45 percent due to receipt of Social Security. In the same year, only 3 percent of aged beneficiaries who were members of married couples had income below the poverty line; 41 percent would have income below the poverty line, without Social Security benefits. Some 30 percent of Social Security beneficiaries in 1996 received 90 percent or more of their income from this source; 66 percent received 50 percent or more of their income from Social Security benefits. From this perspective, it is difficult to characterize Social Security as anything other than a successful antipoverty program—a "sacred entitlement." Still, many are uncomfortable with the program and especially with what is perceived to be an inadequate replacement of preretirement income. Is this perception accurate? An answer requires evaluation of Social Security replacement rates.

In 1967, a U.S. House Ways and Means Committee report specified that the retirement benefit of a man age 65 and his wife should represent at least 50 percent of his average wages under the Social Security system. Some have argued that, even assuming reduced expenses and lower taxes, 50 percent of wages is not enough. Palmer (1989) estimates that a hypothetical couple retiring in 1988 with preretirement gross earnings of $25,000 would have $4,769 less in taxes, elimination of $738 in work-related expenses, and $1,622 less in savings. Thus, $17,871, or 71 percent of gross preretirement earnings, would be required by this couple to maintain their style of living into retirement. Palmer estimates that replacement rates vary between 82 and 66 percent for couples earning $15,000 to $80,000.

How can that much income be generated in the retirement years, with people no longer working? And how much of preretirement earnings can be (or should be) replaced by Social Security alone? One must remember that Social Security is only one source of income for most of the elderly; many supplement this income. Private pensions, wages, asset income, intrafamily transfers and aid, and even welfare and SSI benefits for the poorest of the elderly all provide help to individuals attempting to maintain a preretirement standard of living.

Figure 11.6 provides a historical perspective on earnings replaced by Social Security for disabled workers and average retirees from 1947 to 1997. Clearly, the amount of preretirement income replaced by old-age insurance benefits for the average worker has changed dramatically over time. The replacement rate was at a low of 19 percent for the average retiree in 1947, and rose to a high of 44.8 per-

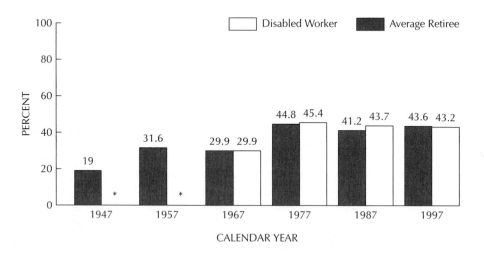

FIGURE 11.6   Percentage of Earnings Replaced (historical perspective) by Social Security

*Data not available for disability benefit payments which began in 1957.

Source: Social Security Administration, *FY1997 Accountability Report* (Washington, DC: U.S. Government Printing Office, 1998).

cent in 1977. Since 1977, the replacement rate has stayed in a narrow range, declining only slightly to 43.6 percent in 1997. According to Tynes (1996), these changes are important because they represent a "change in the deal," or a change in the nature of the social contract between generations. She argues, "These changes represent altered thinking regarding the minimum level of provision for our retirement years that should be covered by society-wide old-age benefits" (p. 2).

The replacement rate structure of Social Security benefits appears to be quite progressive: As Figure 11.7 shows, while the earnings record of a worker retiring at age 65 rises, the Social Security replacement rate falls. In January 1997, the proportion of preretirement income replaced for the worker with a history of minimum earnings ranged from 58.8 percent for an individual to 88.2 percent for a couple; for the worker with average earnings, pretirement earnings replaced ranged from 43.6 percent for an individual to 65.4 percent for a couple; and, for the maximum earner, replacement rates ranged from 25.4 percent for individuals to 38.2 percent for a couple.

Women and Social Security

In recent decades, questions have emerged about the equity of Social Security coverage for certain groups, especially women. It is generally believed that women are disadvantaged by the Social Security system. Flowers (1977), pointing out that most of the provisions of the law pertaining to women have been in effect for about 40 years, asks "why significant controversy developed only recently." In answer, she notes that the feminist movement has heightened interest

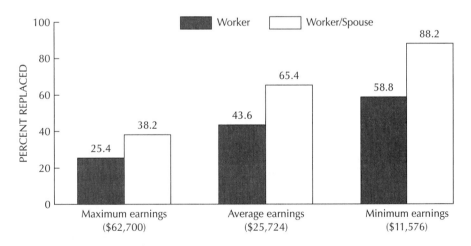

FIGURE 11.7   Percentage of Preretirement Earnings Replaced (workers age 65 entitled in January 1997) by Social Security

Source: Social Security Administration, *FY1997 Accountability Report* (Washington, DC: U.S. Government Printing Office, 1998).

in all aspects of the treatment of women in U.S. society and that the Social Security benefit structure reflects a pattern of family life that is no longer typical in the United States.

In 1939, the Social Security Act was amended to provide additional protection for spouses, widows (and widowers), and children of workers covered by the program. These amendments were based on two important presumptions generally accepted in the 1930s: First, a man is solely responsible for the support of his wife and children, and second, the overwhelming majority of married women *do not* work. Several important social trends have played havoc with these presumptions—not the least of these is the dramatic increase of women (particularly married women) in the labor force. In 1996, almost 60 percent of all women were working, and most of these women make a significant economic contribution to the standard of living of the family.

Just how are women disadvantaged by the Social Security system? Benefits tend to be lower for women than for men. The average monthly benefit for a female retiree was 77 percent of that of a retired man in December 1999 ($697 versus $905). Social Security benefits depend, to a great extent, on average earnings and length of participation in the labor force. Many women have marginal work careers with low earnings; in addition, many women earn substantially less than their equally skilled male counterparts. Finally, increasing numbers of married women divide their lives so as to spend a part as homemakers and another part in the paid labor force. This reduces their length of participation in covered employment.

Because homemaking yields no credit as work, a homemaker is fully dependent on her husband's benefits. It is generally recognized that work performed in the home by homemakers accounts for a very large amount of all unpaid work. Unfortunately, there is little consensus on an approach to placing a value on household work. One approach, the *market cost approach*, assumes that the wage rate for tasks performed in the marketplace can be applied to the same work performed *outside* the marketplace. Treating household work as covered employment would give women Social Security work credit, leave them no longer fully dependent on a husband's benefits, and increase the average monthly benefit for women. Homemaker credits are now used in several countries. In the United Kingdom, Germany, and Japan, voluntary contributions to the Social Security system are permitted by all the nonemployed, including homemakers. In Japan, 80 percent of eligible homemakers are reported to participate (Lapkoff 1981; U.S. Department of Health and Human Services 1986).

Women who are divorced before 10 years of marriage are not entitled to any of their ex-husband's benefits. Retired female workers remain at a slight benefit advantage relative to widows with survivors' benefits. The average monthly benefit for a retired woman is 111 percent of that for a woman receiving survivors' benefits in December 1999 ($697 versus $630).

The Social Security Amendments of 1983 improved the benefit status of women in the Social Security system in several important ways. Two are identified here. First, Social Security benefits are no longer terminated for surviving divorced spouses and disabled widows and widowers who remarry after entitlement to benefits. Previously, remarriage would result in termination. Second, effective January 1, 1985, a divorced spouse age 62 or over who has been divorced for at least 2 years, was married for 10 years or longer, and remains unmarried may receive benefits based on the earnings of a former spouse who is eligible for retirement benefits, regardless of whether the former spouse has applied for benefits or has benefits withheld under the earnings test. In the past, the divorced spouse could not qualify until the former spouse had filed an application.

As mentioned before, homemaker credits are not available in the Social Security system in the United States, and, over the years, little political support for reform has developed. However, an alternative reform approach—to divide the Social Security earnings credits of married couples equally between spouses—has received considerably more attention. Although *earnings sharing* is a relatively new idea for Social Security, the concept has been in use in community property states, especially in divorce settlements (Schulz 1995). The Technical Committee on Earnings Sharing, a private group seeking to improve the position of women in the Social Security system, has endorsed a proposal designed to be implemented over several decades that would result in benefit increases for women with lower benefits under current law; some decreases would be experienced by women with high benefits (Fierst & Duff 1988). To date, the Congress has not acted on this proposal. One problem is that cost estimates for the proposal vary widely. Another problem is that benefits will decline for some retirees.

The Social Security Retirement Age

The term *age*, as used by the Social Security Administration, is the age when workers can retire and receive an unreduced retirement benefit. Over the years, there has been support for raising the age. Numerous reasons have been given, including the increased longevity and health experienced by so many older Americans, future predictions of a need for additional labor, and rising pension costs resulting in part from the trend toward earlier retirement. It seems clear that this latter point was most salient for the Congress when it voted in 1983 to amend Social Security and raise the "normal" retirement age. Under the new provisions, workers starting in 2027 will have to be age 67 before receiving a full retirement benefit. Individuals will still be able to retire as early as age 62 but will suffer a 30 percent reduction in their benefit. These changes are scheduled to occur gradually, beginning in 2003 and achieving full implementation in 2027. Because the changes are not to occur for many years, the intervening period provides an opportunity for study of the consequences of the change. Already, some members of Congress have filed bills to repeal the provisions; others have suggested that the schedule to full implementation be speeded up. Congressional hearings on the matter are a certainty!

Supplementary Security Income

The Social Security Act of 1935 included a mandate for the establishment of a separate program of old-age assistance under which benefits (coming mostly

from federal funds) would be distributed to needy aged people and administered by the states. Similar programs for the blind and disabled were established
in the 1935 act and subsequent amendments. Under the Social Security Amendments of 1972, a new federal program of **Supplemental Security Income (SSI)**
<http://www.ssa.gov/pubs/englist.html#SSI> for the aged, blind, and disabled re-
placed the former state-operated welfare programs. When the SSI program began
making payments in January 1974, 3.2 million recipients were on the rolls. By
1996, this figure had increased to 6.6 million, less than 22 percent of whom were
65 years or older.

The SSI program was envisioned as a basic national income maintenance
system for the aged, blind, and disabled. It was intended to present minimal barriers to eligibility by having few requirements other than lack of income. Yet, as
its title indicates, the program was expected to supplement the Social Security
program primarily by providing income support to those not covered by Social
Security.

Because SSI is an assistance program, applicants must prove need by meeting an assets test. As of January 1, 2000, assets may not exceed $2,000 for an in-
dividual and $3,000 for a couple. Excluded from the assets test are the value of a
home (up to a certain market value), household goods, personal effects, an automobile used for essential transportation, a life insurance policy with a face value
of $1,500 or less, and burial funds not exceeding $1,500. Income must be below
$500 a month for an individual and below $751 a month for a couple, with exclu-
sions for $20 a month of most income, $65 a month of wages and one-half of
wages over $65 a month, food stamps, and home energy/home assistance. In
1999, maximum federal SSI payments were $500 monthly for an individual and
$751 monthly for a couple (if both members are eligible). Several states provide
an additional supplement to the federal benefit. Among these, in January 1999,
California provided the largest maximum supplement to an aged individual or
couple ($176 or $450); Hawaii provided the lowest maximum supplement ($4.90
or $8.80). Cost-of-living increases in SSI are based on change in the Consumer
Price Index. Depending on the state in which a person lives, being eligible for SSI
means the person will receive the following benefits and services:

- Medicaid
- Medicare premiums are paid (all states)
- Food stamps
- Other social services

Critics of SSI argue that although the program is targeted at the right population, eligibility requirements limit people's ability to lift themselves from poverty status. For example, an eligible individual working part time whose gross
income was $500 in monthly earnings would receive only $292.50 in federal SSI
payments:

$500 − (($500 − $85)/2) = $500 − $207.50 = $292.50

Meyer and Bartolomei-Hill (1994) conclude that, while benefits vary considerably across states, elderly individuals receiving SSI cannot afford a basic needs package of housing, food, and medical care. They also find that elderly couples on SSI are generally better off than elderly individuals on SSI.

Another major concern has arisen because of the low participation level of eligible persons in the SSI program. The Social Security Administration estimates that about one in three eligible aged persons do not participate in the program. Drazaga, Upp, and Reno (1982) offer two reasons for the relatively low levels of participation in SSI: lack of knowledge about the program and stigma. Their study found that 45 percent of nonparticipants had never heard of the SSI program. Even among the many who did know of SSI, some indicated a reluctance to become involved in a means-tested program.

The Future of Social Security

The most crucial questions about the future of the Social Security system concern its financial status. Current and future retirees (current contributors) want to know if the system is solvent or whether it will go bankrupt and deprive millions of a retirement pension they have counted on. The latter appears highly unlikely. As Dorcas R. Hardy, former Commissioner of Social Security, has written, "Social Security and justice are inextricably linked" (1987, p. 5). According to Hardy, the system is sound, has a significant trust fund reserve that is expected to grow significantly in this century (to be discussed), and is not likely to face another financial crisis for many years.

During the early years of Social Security, more revenue was taken in from contributions than was paid out in benefits, and a trust fund was developed. By 1975, this situation had changed. Between 1975 and 1981, the trust fund paid out $16 billion more than was taken in. At that rate, the trust fund would likely have run out during the mid-1980s. In 1977, however, significant amendments were made in the Social Security system. Many, including then President Carter, believed these changes provided a long-term financial solution for the system's problems. By 1982, economic conditions again made the financial status of the system appear vulnerable. On January 20, 1983, the National Commission on Social Security Reform (NCSSR) presented its recommendations. Passed with almost unprecedented speed after bipartisan effort, Public Law 98-21 was signed by President Reagan on April 20, 1983. This law represents the Social Security Amendments of 1983 and is substantially in line with the NCSSR recommendations. A number of the changes brought about by these amendments have already been noted in the previous discussion. In signing the bill into law, President Reagan stated:

> This bill demonstrates for all times our Nation's ironclad commitment to Social Security. It assures the elderly that America will always keep the promises made in troubled times a half a century ago. It assures those who are still working that they, too, have a pact with the future. From this day forward, they have our

pledge that they will get their fair share of benefits when they retire. Our elderly need no longer fear that the checks they depend on will be stopped or reduced. These amendments protect them. Americans of middle age need no longer worry whether their career-long investment will pay off. These amendments guarantee it. And younger people can feel confident that Social Security will still be around when they need it to cushion their retirement.

For approximately the next 15 years or so, under current economic fore-casts, the Social Security Trust Fund is expected continually to have excesses of income over outgo, creating a buildup that will peak in about 2020. For example, the 1999 excess of receipts over expenditures was estimated at $117.2 billion and increased the total in the trust fund to $799 billion. Reserves are expected to de-cline as the Baby Boom generation retires (the first Baby Boomers turned 50 years of age on January 1, 1996). The year 2015 is projected as the first in which the combined Social Security and Disability Insurance Trust Funds have "outgo" that exceeds tax income; the year 2025 is projected as the first in which these combined trust funds have outgo that exceeds tax income plus interest income. By 2037, the Social Security and Disability Trust funds are currently projected to have exhausted all their accumulated assets. At this point, payroll tax and other income will continue to flow into the fund such that, in 2037, tax income is esti-mated to be sufficient to pay about 72 percent of program costs; that ratio is pro-jected to decline to about two-thirds by 2075. Clearly, some action must be taken to ensure the long-term viability of Social Security's benefit structure, or the de-mographic imperative described here will force a reduction in benefit levels.

Could sour economic conditions place the Social Security system in earlier jeopardy? Perhaps, but Social Security is a vital program and, most important, it is guaranteed by the taxing power of the federal government of the United States of America. It is useful to remember that the federal government has the capacity to assure the long-term viability of Social Security's benefit structure by reducing benefit levels, increasing payroll taxes, bringing other assets to the trust fund, or some combination of these.

PRIVATE PENSIONS

By 1994–95, about 66 percent of all full-time employees participated in one or more retirement plans. About 96 percent of state and local government workers, 80 percent of workers in medium and large private companies (those with 100 or more workers), and 42 percent of workers in small private establishments (those with fewer than 100 workers) had retirement plan coverage in 1994–95 (Foster 1998). This represents significant growth over the last 60 years or so. In 1940, only about 12 percent of the labor force was covered by private pensions. In 1994, 91 percent of aged people with at least one member over 65 years of age received Social Security benefits, and 30 percent received income from private pensions or annuities. However, as was graphically depicted in Figure 11.1, while Social Secu-

Maintaining health and having access to medical care are important quality-of-life issues for older people.

rity benefits accounted for 40 percent of all money income for the aged, private pensions and annuities accounted for 19 percent of the total. As these data indicate, a sizable proportion of the labor force remains without pension coverage. According to Schulz (1995), the two key factors are union status and firm size: Most workers without pension coverage are nonunion and work for firms with fewer than 100 employees.

Private pensions were first introduced into U.S. industry by the railroad and express companies. The first plan, established by the American Express Company in 1875, was financed solely by the employer. The first plan supported jointly by employee and employer contributions was inaugurated by the Baltimore and Ohio Railroad Company in 1880. The railroad industry was the first to adopt pension plans rather widely; by the time of World War I, over one-half of all railroad employees were covered by such plans, and by the late 1920s, the proportion covered had risen to four-fifths (Institute of Life Insurance 1975). The first trade union plan was that of the Granite Cutters in 1905. Two years later, the first of the larger international unions, the International Typographical Union, adopted a formal pension plan for its members. By 1930, about 20 percent of all trade union members in the United States and Canada were covered by a union pension plan (Institute of Life Insurance 1975). Labor unions played an important part in the expansion of pension coverage. Many unions developed their own plans in industries that provided no company coverage.

Economic conditions during the 1930s reduced the growth of the private pension movement. The passage of the Social Security Act of 1935 did help create a climate in which the idea of pension planning would continue to flower. Schulz (1995) attributes the tremendous growth in private pension coverage since 1940 to a variety of reasons:

1. The continued industrialization of the U.S. economy
2. Wage freezes during World War II and the Korean War that encouraged fringe benefit growth in lieu of wages
3. Inducements offered by the federal government, such as the Revenue Act of 1942, which made employer contributions to qualified pension plans tax deductible
4. A favorable decision by the Supreme Court in 1949 that pensions were a proper issue for collective bargaining
5. The development of multiemployer pension plans

In 1974, Congress passed the ***Employee Retirement Income Security Act*** (ERISA) <http://www.dol.gov/dol/pwba>. This legislation established minimum standards for pension programs and strengthened the regulation and supervision of such programs. Prior to this, the policing function was left primarily in the hands of participants. Unfortunately, this had tragic consequences in many cases. Workers lost pension benefits as a result of company bankruptcies, plant closures, and unemployment. In addition, financial irregularities, including mismanagement of funds, left many new retirees with nothing despite a lifetime of paying into the company's pension fund.

The major provisions of ERISA are as follows:

1. Minimum vesting standards are established.
2. Funding standards are established and fiduciary standards are strengthened.
3. Plan termination insurance is established up to a certain level for employees whose plans terminate with insufficient funds.
4. Individual retirement accounts (IRAs) may be established by workers without private or public employee pension coverage. There are limits on the annual investment allowed.
5. Employees may transfer vested pension rights (portability) on a tax-free basis from one employer to another or to an IRA.
6. Disclosure regulations are established that permit participants to make periodic requests for statements reflecting their benefit status.
7. Employers have certain reporting and disclosure requirements through the Treasury Department to the Social Security Administration.

Amendments have been made since 1974. For example, ERISA now mandates that all pension plans subject to its provisions provide workers with a *joint and survivor option* at the time of retirement. If chosen by the worker, this option provides income to the surviving spouse in an amount equal to some percentage of the income payable during the time the employee and spouse were both alive. Under the Retirement Equity Act of 1984, employers are mandated to secure the spouse's consent in writing if the worker wishes to reject the survivor option.

ERISA has not solved all the pension problems of individuals or their employers. For example, coverage is not mandatory, state and local governmental pension plans are not covered by the law, the value of pension rights is not assured for workers who change jobs, and survivors' provisions are thought to be weak. Thousands of court cases over pension rights have been brought forth under the ERISA law. In a 1991 case involving one of the largest ERISA settlements ever, Continental Can Company agreed to pay $415 million to settle a suit in which the company was charged with deliberately firing employees before they became eligible for benefits. More than 3,000 former employees were awarded approximately $90,000 each. The case is particularly noteworthy on several counts. It dates back to a 1977 labor contract agreed upon by the company and shows how workers must be vigilant against companies that promise the pension with one hand and take it away with the other (Schulz 1995).

Special concerns remain for women in the arena of private pensions. Women are still not as likely as men to receive pension benefits; 43.8 percent of men and 39.8 percent of women have pension coverage in their current job (see Table 11.5). In part, the relatively low rates of coverage experienced by women is a function of the fact that they are more likely to be employed in low-wage jobs, small firms, and low-coverage occupations. In her review of recent trends, Korczyk

TABLE 11.5   Pension Plan Coverage of Workers, by Selected Characteristics: 1996

	PERCENT OF TOTAL WORKERS			
SEX AND AGE	*Total*	*White*	*Black*	*Hispanic*
Total	41.9%	42.3%	40.5%	28.0%
Male	43.8	44.3	40.9	27.4
15–24 years	12.0	12.0	12.6	9.8
25–44 years	48.4	49.2	43.7	30.4
45–64 years	56.5	56.9	55.9	37.9
65+ years	22.5	22.0	31.6	23.2
Female	39.8	40.0	40.1	28.9
15–24 years	10.3	10.3	10.6	8.7
25–44 years	45.0	45.4	43.5	32.1
45–64 years	50.0	49.8	56.1	39.6
65+ years	22.4	22.0	21.5	29.8

Source: Statistical Abstract of the United States, 1998, 118th ed. (Washington, DC: U.S. Bureau of the Census, 1998), Table 616.

(1993) reports that as earnings increase, the rates at which women participate in pension plans falls below those of men. As Table 11.6 shows, this pattern begins with earnings at $20,000 and above. The good news is that, among those who are pension participants, when level of earnings is controlled for, differences between men and women almost disappear.

Private pension benefits come in a variety of forms. In 1994–95, about 42 percent of all full-time workers participated in a *defined benefit pension plan,* down from 48 percent in 1990–91 (Foster 1998). Such plans generally use a pre-determined formula to calculate retirement plans. For example, benefits may be determined by multiplying a specific dollar amount by the number of years of employed service credited to an employee under the plan. Some 39 percent of full-time employees participated in a *defined contribution plan* in 1994–95, up from 34 percent in 1990–91. In defined contribution plans, the employer and often the employee make fixed (or defined) contributions to an account. Benefits at retirement are not predetermined but paid out based on accumulated funds (contributions plus investment earnings). The most prevalent form of defined contribution plan is the *savings and thrift plan* in which employees contribute a predetermined percentage of earnings, all or part of which the employer matches. In 1994–95, participation in savings and thrift plans was 41 percent among private employers with 100 workers or more and 17 percent among small private employers with fewer than 100 workers.

Deferred profit-sharing and *employee stock ownership plans (ESOPs)* are also defined contribution plans found only in the private sector and usually financed entirely by the employer. Many defined contribution plans, except ESOPs, have 401(k) type features. The term *401(k)* refers to the section of the Internal Revenue Service (IRS) Code that allows employees to choose to have a portion of their compensation (otherwise payable in cash) invested in a qualified defined contribution plan on a tax-deferred basis. Although 401(k) plans are commonly found in the private sector, cash or deferred arrangements also include

TABLE 11.6   Pension Participation Rates by Earnings and Gender

	ALL WORKERS		PENSION PARTICIPANTS	
EARNINGS	*Men*	*Women*	*Men*	*Women*
Less than $10,000	10%	23%	13%	13%
$10,000–19,999	31	46	36	46
$20,000–29,999	27	21	63	64
$30,000–49,999	23	9	74	75
$50,000 or more	8	1	79	77

Source: S. M. Korczyk, "Gender and Pension Coverage," in J. A. Turner & D. J. Beller (Eds.), *Trends in Pensions, 1992* (Washington, D.C.: U.S. Government Printing Office).

section 457 and 403(b) plans for state and local government employees. Plans with 401(k)-type arrangements typically include employer contributions as well and are most prevalent in medium and large private businesses.

Private pensions, and especially defined benefit plans, have generally been designed as supplements to Social Security. As a result, the monetary difference between public and private pension benefits tends to diminish when employee contributions and Social Security are considered (Wiatrowski 1994). Table 11.7 shows examples of income from employer pensions and Social Security for 65-year-old employees with identical salary and service histories under three circumstances:

TABLE 11.7   Retirement Income Available at Age 65 for Public- and Private-Sector Employees with Final-Year Earnings of $35,000 and $65,000

	PRIVATE SECTOR	PUBLIC SECTOR	
ITEM	*With Social Security*	*Without Social Security*	*With Social Security*
Final earnings, $35,000			
Benefit formula	1 percent of earnings up to $25,000; 1.5 percent above earnings of $25,000	2.18 percent	1.83 percent
Service	30 years	30 years	30 years
Annual pension	$12,000	$22,890	$19,215
Annual Social Security	11,244	0	11,244
Total benefit	23,244	22,890	30,459
Total benefit as a percent of final earnings	66.4	65.4	87.0
Final earnings, $65,000			
Benefit formula	1 percent of earnings up to $25,000; 1.5 percent above earnings of $25,000	2.18 percent	1.83 percent
Service	30 years	30 years	30 years
Annual pension	$25,500	$42,510	$35,685
Annual Social Security	11,976	0	11,976
Total benefit	37,476	42,510	47,661
Total benefit as a percent of final earnings	57.6	65.4	73.3

Source: Wiatrowski 1994, p. 6, Exhibit 1.

a private-sector employee with both a pension and Social Security; a public-sector employee who has a pension only; and a public-sector employee who has both a pension and Social Security. A private-sector employee with final-year earnings of $35,000 can expect retirement income to replace 66.4 percent of earnings. Approximately 52 percent of pension benefits come from the private pension and 48 percent from Social Security. At final-year earnings of $65,000, the private-sector employee can expect retirement income to replace 57.6 percent of earnings. Social Security benefits provide a proportionately lower benefit (32 percent), but is counterbalanced by higher private pension payments (68 percent).

It is important to recognize that private-sector workers covered by defined benefit pension plans and Social Security can expect their employers' pension benefits to remain unchanged during retirement (not indexed to inflation), and their Social Security benefits to increase annually as the cost of living increases. In contrast, public-sector workers are likely to have all retirement income, pension, and Social Security indexed for inflation (Wiatrowski 1994). Defined contribution plans are becoming more prevalent for private-sector employees, and can provide comfortable retirement benefits, as well.

Retirement benefits are often just one facet of an employee benefit package that can vary by establishment characteristics and/or occupation. For example, in 1997, among medium and large private businesses, the great majority of workers received paid time off for holidays, vacations, funeral leave, and jury duty leave. Lesser proportions received paid personal, military, and family leave. Among those working for the largest employers, most received paid sick leave (56 percent), and short-term disability coverage (55 percent); 43 percent received long-term disability insurance. Three of four of these workers received medical care insurance benefits (76 percent) and 59 percent received dental care benefits; only 26 percent received vision care benefits. Under the Age Discrimination in Employment Act, employers are not allowed to withhold benefits from older workers. However, because the cost of providing many benefits (e.g., life, health, and long-term disability insurance) for older employees is higher than the cost of providing the same level of coverage for their younger counterparts, employers are permitted to reduce the level of benefits to offset increased costs (Kramer 1995). Such costs are typically higher for older workers because older persons are generally in higher risk groups than younger workers based on the probability of their becoming sick or disabled, or dying.

The United States is likely to continue to have a mixture of public and private pension systems. Some of the advantages of Social Security—including almost universal coverage, cost-of-living adjustment, and financing backed by the federal government—have already been discussed. In addition, administrative costs are quite low. In 1987, administrative costs for Social Security amounted to less than 1 percent of contributions and reimbursements. Private pensions provide greater flexibility for different worker groups as well as the potential for investing pension funds in the national economy. Some disadvantages of private pensions include higher administrative costs, a general absence of indexing to protect retirees against inflation, and the difficulty involved in achieving portability, among others mentioned earlier.

SUMMARY

The major sources of income for the elderly are Social Security, earnings, pensions, and asset income. A considerable proportion of the elderly receive in-kind income in the form of goods and services they obtain free or at reduced expenditure. Examples include housing subsidies, health care, and food stamps. It is difficult to estimate how much in income these programs are worth to the aged. Since the mid-1960s, the median income of elderly has increased at a faster pace than for the population as a whole. By 1996, the median income of a couple age 70 to 74 was $27,880, about half-way between that for couples age 65 to 69 ($32,998) and those age 85 and older ($23,373). Retirement status, age, and race are factors associated with income variation among the elderly. Tax advantages received by the elderly would seem to be of more help to property owners and those with higher incomes. Inflation has adverse implications for all people, although Social Security benefits, some private pensions, SSI, and in-kind programs such as food stamps are now indexed to the rate of inflation. This gives the aged an advantage relative to other age groups.

The elderly show a pattern of expenditures quite like that of other low-income groups. Poverty has been declining among the elderly, although aged African Americans were more than three times as likely as aged whites to be deemed officially poor in the United States in 1990 (30.8 vs. 9.6 percent, respectively). Orshansky (1978) argues that the government's poverty index is set too low and is not applied to those aged who are institutionalized or living with relatives.

The Social Security Act of 1935 signaled a new era in financial arrangements for life after retirement. Nine out of ten workers are covered, and over 90 percent of the elderly receive some income from Social Security. Social Security is an earnings-based program; for the designated groups, participation is compulsory. Workers with lower earnings are favored by a weighted benefit schedule. Retirement is defined through a retirement test that withholds pension benefits if earnings are above a specified amount. Average benefits are relatively low because of the popularity of the early retirement option. Early retirement benefits (to those who retire at age 62 to 64) are reduced because of the longer period over which they will be paid. It is generally believed that women are disadvantaged by the Social Security system, although, as a proportion of the total of all benefits, the amount paid on the earnings of women is slightly greater than that paid on the earnings of men. At least for now, the Social Security Amendments of 1983 appear to have put off fears about the financial status of the Social Security system well into the twenty-first century.

The availability of private pension benefits varies by establishment size and occupation. In 1974, the Congress passed important legislation (ERISA) establishing minimum standards for these plans. Previously, the policing of private pension programs was irregular and ineffectual. Still, ERISA has not solved all the pension problems of individuals or their employers. For example, ERISA does not make private pension coverage mandatory.

Private pensions have generally been designed as supplements to Social Security. For those workers who have both Social Security and a private pension, the combined benefits do a good job of replacing preretirement earnings.

STUDY QUESTIONS

1. Discuss the economic position of U.S. elderly with regard to variation by age, race, and retirement status.

2. List and explain the various forms of indirect or in-kind income available to the elderly through federal programs.

3. Explain some of the ways in which inflation can have a detrimental impact on the economic situation of the elderly.

4. Discuss the *poverty index* and explain how it is used to determine the adequacy of elderly income. What are the problems inherent in using this measure of income adequacy?

5. With the passage of the Social Security Act of 1935, the United States became one of the last industrialized nations to execute a federal old-age pension program. Discuss the principles behind this legislation.

6. Explain why the Social Security payroll tax schedule is considered by many to be regressive.

7. Discuss the advantages and disadvantages women experience with respect to Social Security benefits.

8. Explain why ERISA was deemed a necessary piece of legislation. What are some of the major provisions of this act?

9. Identify variations in the form taken by private pension benefit plans. Why are average private pensions relatively low?

REFERENCES

Achenbaum, W. A. (1978). *Old age in the new land.* Baltimore: John Hopkins University Press.

Bondar, J. (1993). Beneficiaries affected by the annual earnings test, 1989. *Social Security Bulletin, 56,* 20–28.

Bromley, D. (1974). *The psychology of human ageing.* Middlesex, England: Penguin.

Calhoun, R. (1978). *In search of the new old.* New York: Elsevier.

Citro, C. F., & Michael, R. T. (1995). *Measuring poverty: A new approach.* Washington, DC: National Academy Press.

Dowd, J., & Bengtson, V. (1978). Aging in minority populations: An examination of the double jeopardy hypothesis. *Journal of Gerontology, 33,* 427–436.

Drazaga, L., Upp, M., & Reno, V. (1982, May). Low-income aged: Eligibility and participation in SSI. *Social Security Bulletin, 45,* 28–35.

Fierst, E. U., & Duff, N. (Eds.). (1988). *Earnings sharing in Social Security: A model for reform.* Report of the Technical Committee on Earnings Sharing. Washington, DC: Center for Women Policy Studies.

Fischer, D. (1977). *Growing Old in America.* New York: Oxford University Press.

Flowers, M. (1977). *Women and social security: An institutional dilemma.* Washington, DC: American Enterprise Institute for Public Policy Research.

Foster, A. C. (1998, Winter). Factors affecting employer-provided retirement benefits. *Compensation and Working Conditions,* pp. 10–17.

Gist, J. R., & Mulvey, J. (1990, November 5). Marginal tax rates and older taxpayers. *Tax Notes,* pp. 679–694.

Hardy, D. R. (1987). The future of Social Security. *Social Security Bulletin, 50* (8), 5–7.

Institute of Life Insurance. (1975). *Pension facts.* New York: Author.

Korczyk, S. M. (1993). Gender issues in employer pensions policy. In R. V. Burkhauser & D. L. Salisbury (Eds.), *Pensions in a changing economy.* Washington, DC: Employee Benefits Research Institute.

Kramer, N. (1995, April). Employee benefits for older workers. *Monthly Labor Review,* pp. 21–27.

Lapkoff, S. (1981). Working women, marriage and retirement. In President's Commission on Pension Policy, *Coming of age: Toward a national retirement policy.* Washington, DC: U.S. Government Printing Office.

Lawton, M. P. (1985). Housing and living environments of older people. In R. Binstock & E. Shanas (Eds.), *Handbook of aging and the social sciences* (2nd ed.). New York: Van Nostrand Reinhold.

Meyer, D. R., & Bartolomei-Hill, S. (1994). The adequacy of Supplemental Security Income benefits for aged individuals and couples. *Gerontologist, 34* (2), 161–172.

National Commission on Social Security. (1981). *Social Security in America's future.* Report of the Commission to the President. Washington, DC: Author.

Orshansky, M. (1978). Testimony in U.S. House Select Committee on Aging. *Poverty among America's aged.* Washington, DC: U.S. Government Printing Office.

Packard, M. D. (1990). The earnings test and the short-run work response to its elimination. *Social Security Bulletin, 53* (9), 2–16.

Palmer, B. A. (1989). Tax reform and retirement income replacement ratios. *Journal of Risk and Insurance, 56,* 702–725.

Pattison, D., & Harrington, D. E. (1993). Proposals to modify the taxation of Social Security benefits: Options and distributional effects. *Social Security Bulletin, 56,* 3–21.

Poverty Studies Task Force. (1976). *The measure of poverty.* Washington, DC: U.S. Department of Health, Education and Welfare.

Putnam, J. K. (1970). *Old-age politics in California: From Richardson to Reagan.* Stanford, CA: Stanford University Press.

Radner, D. B. (1989). The wealth of the aged and nonaged, 1984. In R. E. Lipsey & H. S. Tice (Eds.), *The measurement of saving, investment and wealth.* Chicago: University of Chicago Press.

Ross, C. M., Danziger, S., & Smolensky, E. (1987). Interpreting changes in the economic status of the elderly, 1949–1979. *Contemporary Policy Issues, 5,* 98–112.

Rubin, R. M., & Koelln, K. (1996, September). Elderly and nonelderly expenditures on necessities in the 1980s. *Monthly Labor Review,* pp. 24–31.

Schulz, J. (1995). *The economics of aging* (6th ed.). Westport, CT: Auburn House.

Schulz, J., Carrin, G., Krupp, H., Peschke, M., Sclar, E., & Van Steenberge, J. (1974). *Providing adequate retirement income—Pension reform in the U.S. and abroad.* Hanover, NH: New England Press.

Smeeding, T. (1982). *Alternate methods for valuing selected in-kind transfer benefits and measuring their effects on poverty.* Technical Paper No. 50. Washington, DC: U.S. Bureau of the Census.

Social Security Administration. (1986). *Income and resources of the population 65 and over.* Washington, DC: U.S. Government Printing Office.

Torrey, B. B., & Taeuber, C. M. (1986). The importance of asset income among the elderly. *The Review of Income and Wealth Series, 32,* 443–449.

Tynes, S. R. (1996). *Turning points in Social Security: From "cruel hoax" to "sacred entitlement."* Stanford, CA: Stanford University Press.

U.S. Department of Health and Human Services. (1986). *Social Security programs throughout the world—1985.* Research Report No. 60. Washington, DC: U.S. Government Printing Office.

U.S. Department of Labor. (1989). *Trends in pensions.* Washington, DC: Pension and Welfare Benefits Administration.

U.S. House Committee on Ways and Means. (1967). *President's proposals for revision in the Social Security system: Hearings Part I.* Washington, DC: U.S. Government Printing Office.

Wiatrowski, W. J. (1994, April). On the disparity between private and public pensions. *Monthly Labor Review,* pp. 3–9.

Woods, J. R. (1989). Pension coverage among private wage and salary workers: Preliminary findings from the 1988 Survey of Employee Benefits. *Social Security Benefits, 52,* 2–19.

CHAPTER TWELVE

WORK, RETIREMENT, AND LEISURE

Steven Carter (a fictitious name) had been a happy, successful man. Thirty-seven years ago, he had begun as a stock boy. Today, at age 62, he was the number-two man at a large telecommunications firm. A fine family, plenty of money, good health, and respect in the community reflected this success. Recently, Carter was given a stark choice by the board chairman: Because of a merger with a larger competitor and the cost cutting that would follow, he could retire or be transferred to a lesser position in a distant city. Carter had never given thought to retirement, because it seemed there would always be time to prepare for such a distant event. Now he was in great psychological pain. A psychiatrist, later writing Carter's case history, described him as depressed, suicidal, and a prime candidate for a debilitating physical illness such as a stroke.

Jimmy Smythe is another story. He worked in a factory in Atlanta installing engines in new Ford trucks. According to Smythe, he had been working since he was 10 years old—and it was time to rest. At age 54, he retired from the assembly line at Ford. His monthly pension is about $1,200; the mortgage payment on the house he bought 25 years ago is only $225 a month. His children are grown and self-supporting, and his wife has a part-time job at a local department store. Smythe says that if money gets a little short, "I'm not bragging, but I'm pretty good at repairing cars."

Explaining the different responses of these two individuals toward retirement is not simple. Both cases represent aspects of the American experience with retirement. Carter represents the situation of being at the top of his profession one day and then the next day, because of a corporate merger and restructuring, anticipating himself outside the arenas of achievement and competition. Smythe, on the other hand, represents what has become a significant trend in the work style of Americans—early retirement. Growing numbers of workers have an opportunity to retire early, and many are taking it.

Most Americans, men and women, who are in the labor force or about to enter it will face retirement. This itself is a radical transformation from the past. Data about changes in survivorship rates alone support this fact. Retirement requires longevity; if people do not live long enough to work and still have years left over, there can be no retirement. According to gerontologist Robert Atchley

(1976), three additional conditions are necessary for the emergence of retirement as a social institution:

1. An economy that produces enough surplus to support adults who do not hold jobs
2. The presence of mechanisms, such as pensions or Social Security, to divert part of the surplus to support retired people
3. The acceptance in a society of the idea that people can live in dignity as older adults without working at a job

Other factors have contributed to the appearance of retirement in the United States. These include the decline of agriculture as a provider of jobs to U.S. workers and the increasing importance of formal education and training as an asset valued over experience. Still, the United States has been described by many as a work-oriented society where who you are is determined by what you do. Hodson and Sullivan (1990) suggest that, in the United States (and other postindustrial societies), work has become a "master status" defining a person's overall position and sense of identity. They argue that the major change in work life that distinguishes advanced or postindustrial society from previous societal forms is the idea of commitment: "Work takes on an overriding importance in people's lives, tending to overshadow family and community attachments that prevailed in previous periods. Many factors amplify this tendency. Increased demands for geographic mobility preempt family attachments and limit the development of longstanding friendships" (p. 28). In addition, competition for the best job opportunities is intense. And employers expect a high level of commitment to work, given the rewards that workers with advanced education expect. Retirement, health care, and status in the community are all attached to one's employment position, as well.

Why is so much importance attached to work? The eminent German sociologist Max Weber offered one explanation, which is rooted in the religious ideals of John Calvin and his followers. Calvin, following Luther, believed that man (and, no doubt, woman) had a calling to God in this world, and that this calling included one's work. Whatever that work was, it was a person's duty to do the best he or she could in order to please God. Calvin added the notion of predestination to the Lutheran theology. According to Calvin, God had already decided on the future course of man- and womankind, including who would be saved and who would be damned. Thus, although one could still have a calling to God, following it no longer necessarily meant salvation.

Rather than simply accepting their fate, Calvinists sought signs of God's determination for them. Success in earthly endeavors became an indication of God's favor. Hard work (and the financial success it often brought) meant being in God's good graces. In early Christianity, by contrast, hard work reflected condemnation related to original sin.

Historically, the religious context for work eroded. Despite this secularization process, however, work still remained "the stuff of life." The Protestant ethic became the work ethic. Some argue that this work ethic became increasingly outmoded in the twentieth century. Population growth, technological progress that seemingly increases productivity while reducing reliance on labor, and increasing willingness on the part of government to influence the business cycle have caused a devaluation of the work ethic.

It may be an oversimplification to call U.S. society work oriented. Given the enormous range of jobs in the United States (from cab driver to Supreme Court justice) and the different skills required to carry out these jobs, there may not be enough equivalent meaning among jobs to speak of a common meaning attached to work. Factors that contribute to the way workers view their jobs and the degree of satisfaction taken from work include the nature of job tasks, technology, organizational characteristics, workers' participation in decision making, individual differences, and prior expectations (Hodson & Sullivan 1990). Work that is self-directed, complex, and diverse may be easy to commit to and generates the most satisfaction. Work that is closely supervised, lacking in variety, and carried out at a forced pace is perhaps the most alienating.

Much work in the United States *is* highly routinized, boring, exhausting, and without satisfaction. Mike Lefevre, a steel mill worker, talked to Studs Terkel (1972) about his "alienation" from work:

> It's hard to take pride in a bridge you're never gonna cross, in a door you're never gonna open. You're mass-producing things and you never see the end result of it.... My attitude is that I don't get excited about my job. I do my work, but I don't say whoopee-doo. The day I get excited about my job is the day I go to a head shrinker. How are you gonna get excited when you're tired and want to sit down.

Karl Marx saw the potential for *alienation* from work in industrial societies. According to Marx, work constitutes a person's most important activity—in fact, Marx called it "life activity." He said that work is "creative" and that through it people create their world and, as a consequence, create themselves. Presumably, when work is creative, it meets higher-order needs: *belongingness needs* for acceptance and friendship; *esteem needs* for recognition, attention, and appreciation; and *self-actualization needs* for developing to one's fullest potential (Steers & Porter 1983). This appears to be the case even for mature workers approaching the end of their work careers. Mutran and colleagues (1997), using data derived from interviews with men and women ages 58 to 64 years who were full-time employees, found that meaningful quality of time spent at work, job satisfaction, and an identity as a competent worker were positively associated with self-esteem.

For Marx, any other kind of work is "forced" and alienating. Alienating work produces estrangement from one's labor and, perhaps more important, from oneself and the social world: "What is true of man's relationship to his work, to the product of his work and to himself, is also true of his relationship to other men" (Marx, in Israel 1971).

One does not have to be a Marxist to recognize that many workers, old and young, are doing "forced labor." Yet, the relationship between people and their jobs is a complicated one. How people feel about their jobs (and themselves), and how central their work is to their life-styles, will strongly affect how they view the prospect of retirement. These factors may also determine how prepared a person is to deal with the demands of retirement. The following section discusses the complicated and changing relationships between aging and work, retirement and leisure. We begin by describing the status of elderly Americans in the labor force and how this status changed in the twentieth century.

THE OLDER WORKER

Although labor-force participation rates for specific groups change over time, the overall pattern is fairly consistent. Labor-force participation is generally low for young adults (because of school or child-care responsibilities), rises during the ages 25 to 44, and then declines after age 55 as workers begin to retire (Fullerton 1997b). Still, older people have always worked. In fact, it was not until sometime between 1930 and 1940 that the rate of labor-force participation by elderly American males dipped below 50 percent. This rate has continued to decline and, as Table 12.1 shows, in 1996, about one-sixth (16.9 percent) of all males age 65 and older were in the labor force. Among males ages 55 to 64 years (those approaching "normal" retirement age), labor-force participation rates declined during the twentieth century and are quite in line with overall employment trends among males. In 1976, 77.5 percent of all males 16 years old and over were in the labor force; this figure is projected to drop to 73.6 percent by 2006. The comparable figures for males ages 55 to 64 years were 74.3 percent and 70.2 percent, respectively. Interestingly, however, as Table 12.1 depicts, projections for 2006 for males ages 55 to 64 and those 65 years of age and older reflect a distinctive upturn from 1996 in labor-force participation rates.

The percentage of women 65 years of age and over employed outside the home did not exceed 11 percent in the twentieth century. Table 12.1 shows the narrow range within which the labor-force participation rate of older females has

TABLE 12.1   Civilian Labor-Force Participation Rates by Sex and Age: U.S. 1976–2006 (projected)

	MALES		FEMALES	
	55–64 Years	*65+ Years*	*55–64 Years*	*65+ Years*
1976	74.3%	20.2%	41.7%	8.3%
1986	67.3	16.0	42.3	7.4
1996	67.0	16.9	49.6	8.6
2006	70.2	17.8	55.8	8.7

Source: Fullerton 1997b, p. 348.

fluctuated since 1976. This is despite the fact that the proportion of gainfully employed women of all ages increased dramatically during the twentieth century. About 18 percent of all women were employed in 1890; this figure was 59.3 percent in 1996 and is projected to be 61.4 percent in 2006. The labor-force experience of women ages 55 to 64 also reflects this phenomenon. Since 1950, labor-force participation rates for this group increased from 27.0 to 49.6 percent in 1996, and are projected to exceed 55 percent in 2006. As a result of the continued increase in labor-force participation rates of females ages 55 to 64 years, can the labor-force participation rates of females age 65 years and older be expected ultimately to converge with the labor-force participation rates of their male counterparts?

Nonwhites (old and young) have had labor-force experiences similar to those already described here. The labor-force participation rates of all nonwhite males have declined slightly, whereas those of elderly nonwhite males fell dramatically in the twentieth century. Almost 85 percent of aged African American men were employed in 1900 (Achenbaum 1978), 40 percent in 1955, 21 percent in 1975, and 13.8 percent in 1990. Interestingly, Fullerton (1997a) reports that the actual labor-force participation rates for black men ages 65 to 69 years was 26.0 percent in 1995, an increase over the rate of 22.7 percent for 1984. At the same time, labor-force participation rates for black males age 70 years and over declined from 15.0 percent in 1984 to 9.2 percent in 1995.

Aged African American women have always had higher rates of employment than their white counterparts, although the difference in rates has narrowed. By 1990, only 9.4 percent of aged African American females were employed—a modest decline from the 10.5 percent in 1975, though a more significant decline from the employment rate of 16.5 percent in 1950. Among aged black females, the recent pattern is somewhat different than that reported for males. For black females ages 55 to 64 years, labor-force participation rates declined between 1984 and 1995 from 14.8 percent to 12.3 percent; for black females age 70 years and over, there was a modest increase in labor-force participation in this period from 5.0 percent in 1984 to 5.4 percent in 1995. Aged Latino males had a labor-force participation rate of 15.9 percent, between that for whites and African Americans in 1990; the rate for aged Latina females was 7.8 percent.

Rose C. Gibson (1987) points out that despite the formal definition of retirement employed by the U.S. Bureau of the Census and other government agencies, for many older African Americans, the line between working and being retired is not so clear. Work in low-status jobs is a necessity for many aged blacks, and this continues a disadvantaged work pattern from youth through old age. As Gibson (1987, p. 691) describes it, "This sameness of sporadic work patterns over the life course…may create for older blacks a certain ambiguity between work and retirement which, in turn, may affect the ways in which blacks define retirement."

Using data from the National Survey of Black Americans, Gibson identified four factors that, in combination, contribute to many older African Americans thinking about themselves as being in an "unretired-retired" status:

1. An indistinct line between work in youth and work in old age
2. The receipt of income from other than private pension sources
3. The knowledge that one must work during old age
4. The benefits of defining oneself as sick or disabled rather than retired

More recently, Gibson (1991) explains how the economic and psychological benefits of the disabled worker role, in combination with perceptions of a discontinuous work life, discourage a self-definition of retirement among older African Americans. Gibson's argument receives empirical support from Hayward, Friedman, and Chen (1996). As these researchers point out, when status life expectancies are compared relative to total life expectancy, blacks actually spend more—not less—of their lives in the labor force compared to whites, and a greater proportion of their lives disabled. In their words, "Retirement is more a White experience than a Black experience, while the reverse is true with regard to disability" (p. S9).

What kind of work do older workers do? Historically, farming was the occupation in which most elderly men found work; it was a lifelong occupation. Retirement on a farm was rare. An older worker physically unable to perform certain duties could assume other less demanding though equally important chores. This was especially true for white farmers. A greater proportion of African Americans than whites were in farming, but whites were much more likely to be owners or managers. Thus, they were in a position to remain in charge of planning and overseeing farm activities when they themselves were no longer able to carry out more physical farm duties.

Obviously, farming has diminished in importance as a source of jobs, not just for older men but for younger men as well. Still, older workers are more likely to be found in farming than is the total population of employed persons. Older workers are less likely than all workers to have blue-collar jobs. Many of these jobs are in industries where mandatory retirement has been the rule and where private pension plans are available. Moreover, many blue-collar jobs are physically arduous—truck driving and construction work, for example. Also, since 1970, opportunities for older workers have been undermined by economic restructuring concentrated in manufacturing industries. Between 1970 and 1987, the share of workers age 55 and over employed in goods-producing industries fell from 36 to 30 percent (Sum & Fogg 1990).

Many older workers are self-employed or work for small businesses. These include accountants, lawyers, and tavern keepers, who simply continue at the same work beyond normal retirement age. Sales and clerical work offer part-time employment and are thus amenable to elderly individuals attempting to supplement retirement income, and this is especially the case for women.

Elderly workers are more likely than all workers to be found in service jobs: gardeners, seamstresses, practical nurses, washroom attendants, night watchmen, ticket takers, and domestics, for example. A *New York Times* article (Collins 1987) reports that the child-care industry has begun to turn to older Americans to help care for the nation's preschool children. While McDonald's, the giant fast-food firm, gained attention for a television advertising campaign involving older adult employees, the largest national chain of child-care centers, Kinder-Care Inc., estimated that about 10 to 12 percent of the company's work force is over the age of 55. It has been recruiting older workers through community groups and local and national organizations for the elderly.

Through the course of the twentieth century, increased longevity and changing social and work patterns have contributed to changes in the time people devote to life activities such as education, work, and retirement. Compared to 1900, children today are spending more time in school, both males and females spend more time in work, and older people (especially males) are spending more time in retirement (U.S. Senate 1987–1988). On average, males spent almost seven more years (6.7 years) in the labor force in 1980 than in 1900. Nonetheless, a smaller proportion of their lives was spent working, 55 percent, than in 1900, when males spent 69 percent of their lives working. Since 1900, the average number of years women spent in the labor force increased from 6.3 to 29.4 years and from 13 to 38 percent of average life expectancy.

The portion of life spent in retirement also has increased substantially since the beginning of the twentieth century. In 1900, average life expectancy for males was 46 or 47 years, and only 1.2 years, or about 3 percent of that time, was spent in retirement. By 1990–95, the average male spent 17.4 years, or about 22 percent of his life, in retirement (Gendell 1998). The average female spent 21 years, or about 25 percent of her life, in retirement (Gendell 1998). Similar or larger increases in time spent in retirement have occurred in other industrial nations, including Germany, Sweden, and Japan. The gain in retirement years is a result of both a drop in the average age at retirement and a rise in longevity.

Although the twentieth century brought with it increased life expectancy, increased work life expectancy, and increased expectations of retirement, it also brought significant decline in labor-force participation rates among older men. How does one explain the declining employment level of older persons? What factors have become important in setting that employment level?

Several explanations for the decline in labor-force participation of older men have been put forth. A number of studies identify health status and the development of pension systems (including Social Security) as the most significant factors influencing the labor supply of older workers. Research also shows changes in retirement policies, changes in the occupational structure, and age discrimination in employment to be contributors to the declining employment rates of older workers. Each factor deserves some attention. (Pension systems were discussed in Chapter 11.)

Health Status

One interpretation of the decline in labor-force participation of older persons has to do with the decline in death rates during this same period. This interpretation assumes that, compared with today's elderly, those in the past were healthier and thus better able to work. This assumption is based on recognition of the increasing numbers of chronically ill and physically debilitated people who today survive well into old age. And, although the literature has shown that disability may not preclude work, people with disabilities are more likely to be unemployed, work fewer hours, or retire earlier from the work force than are people without disabilities (Wray 1996).

Unfortunately, although life expectancy has increased dramatically and mortality rates are down significantly since 1900, it is not known whether the elderly are healthier or less healthy now than in the past. The National Health Survey <http://www.cdc.gov/nchswww/about/major/nhis/nhis.htm>, which reports on the health status of Americans, was not initiated in the United States until 1956. Also, older people vary considerably in their ability to describe symptoms and in the symptoms to which they give attention. Misattribution of illness symptoms is a problem among the elderly, as is underreporting of illness. Information obtained from elderly respondents is sometimes discrepant from that obtained in clinical evaluation. Further, changes over time and differences among the elderly in the reported incidence of illness may actually reflect variations in access to medical information, health beliefs, and availability of formal health services.

Despite the methodological difficulties involved in determining whether the current elderly population is as healthy as past elderly populations, a body of literature shows poor health to be a correlate of retirement. Using data from 8,701 Americans ages 51 to 61 years with work history included in the 1992 Health and Retirement Study (HRS), Wray (1996) found the odds of being retired versus currently working to increase quite markedly by age (by 24 percent per year); for problem drinkers (by 57 percent); for individuals with circulatory conditions (by 28 percent), heart conditions (58 percent), and diabetes (56 percent); and for those experiencing great difficulty with personal care (by over 600 percent).

Santiago and Muschkin (1996) utilized data from the 1991 HRS Early Release file to examine the effects of disability status on the labor-force participation of over 3,000 Anglo, black, and Latino workers ages 50 to 64 years of age. Their results show that poor health and the presence of a work disability significantly reduced the labor-force participation and earnings of these preretirement aged men and women. Interestingly, additional "costs" were associated with some specifications of minority status. For example, being African American *and* disabled reduced the odds of being employed by 46 percent.

Parnes and colleagues (1975), reporting on results from the National Longitudinal Study (NLS) of older men, found that men who reported health problems in 1966 were twice as likely to have retired between 1966 and 1971 as men who were free of health impairments. Although dated, this study is particularly important because it reflects a *causal* sequence of events: Health problems lead to retirement. Some studies are open to the charge that respondents cite health as a reason for retirement because they deem it to be a socially acceptable response. Kingson used this data set in studying men who retired before age 62 between 1966 and 1975 (U.S. Senate 1981). He found the labor-force withdrawal of these very early retirees to be involuntary; 80 percent of the black and 66 percent of the white very early retirees did so involuntarily. Of these early withdrawees, 87 percent claimed disability or poor health.

The legitimacy of reported health problems is sometimes questioned. Reporting a health problem provides a socially acceptable reason for leaving work; thus, it was important for Kingson to determine the validity of such claims. One such test involves looking to the mortality rates of those claiming poor health as a reason for retirement and comparing the rates with those of healthy retirees. As Kingson notes, unfortunately for these early retirees, their claims of ill health were validated by their deaths. For example, by 1975, among white early retirees, the unhealthy group had died at a rate (42 percent) almost three times that of the healthy group (15 percent).

Not only do early retirees leave work involuntarily as a result of health problems, but, according to Kingson (1981), the research also shows these men to be among the most financially vulnerable retirees. One study of newly eligible beneficiaries for Social Security found that only one in four of all nonworking men entitled to Social Security benefits at age 62 retired voluntarily and had pension income in addition to Social Security; 45 percent had no pensions and did not want to retire when they had to leave their jobs. It seems that early retirees can be divided into two groups: those who leave work voluntarily (retirees in good health and with adequate pension income) and those—more numerous—with opposite characteristics.

Changing Retirement Policies

By 1990, 90 percent of all persons over the age of 65 were receiving money from one retirement program or another. This is a different picture from that in 1935, when Congress first passed the Social Security Act. The increasing number of people eligible for Social Security benefits, the rising payment level of the benefits, and the growth of other public and private pension plans not only have provided security to many people in old age but also have permitted many older people financially to afford retirement.

The availability of early retirement benefits built into Social Security and other public and private pension programs has obviously contributed to the decline in old-age work participation rates. In 1956, the Social Security Act was amended to allow female workers to receive actuarially reduced benefits for early retirement between the ages of 62 and 64. This amendment was extended to men beginning in 1962. What resulted was a major increase in the number of men accepting early retirement benefits.

Employer-sponsored pension plans have had an increasingly powerful influence on the retirement decision. As Schulz (1995) points out, it has become common practice in recent years for employers to encourage early retirement by setting a normal age for retirement in the pension plan that is below age 65. Many employers have also provided "early retirement options" to their employees. Sometimes, this takes the form of companies absorbing all the added costs of paying pensions out over a longer period of time, thus allowing workers the opportunity to retire early while at the same time assuring them of full pension benefits. For example, in 1998, the University of Toledo, a major state university in Ohio, offered immediate retirement to its eligible employees (e.g., age 55 or older with 25 or more years of service). The offer granted credit for an extra 3 years of service in calculating retirement benefits.

Kotlikoff and Wise (1989) explain that the "pension stick" has sometimes taken the "option" out of a worker's decision to retire. Using data on pension plans in 1979, they show that workers who refused the early retirement option and continued working could experience up to a 30 percent reduction in pension benefits. Rather than emphasizing sanctions, other companies have developed "incentive programs" to encourage early retirement. In this case, workers who retire early may receive either a lump-sum cash payment equal to six months, or a year's salary or additional pension credits aimed at increasing their pension benefit levels. During the 1980s and into the 1990s, many large multinational corporations—including General Motors, AT&T, and IBM—have employed these mechanisms to downsize and change the age structure of their labor force.

Changing Occupational Structure

Two theories related to changes in the composition of the labor force often surface as explanations for the changes in the work status of elderly people in the twentieth century. The first is the argument that changing technology places older persons at a disadvantage. Occupational skills may become outmoded with technological innovation, and emphasis on assembly-line production may place a greater premium on speed and physical stamina than on work experience.

At first glance, the theory may seem credible, although evidence in support of it is difficult to obtain. Technological change that makes work skills obsolescent would seem to do so for all workers in an occupational category—not just the old. Moreover, older workers may be in a stronger position to hang on in such situations through recognition of seniority. Work careers sometimes involve shifts from one occupational group to another. Managers and administrators often are recruited from clerical and sales personnel, foremen from operatives. Typically, such a career pattern might tend to favor an older worker under conditions of changing technology. Additionally, in occupations where opportunities are undergoing contraction (because of technological change or otherwise), the greatest impact often is felt by young workers attempting to enter the occupation. Frequently, this is seen in the way craft unions regulate apprenticeship when demand for a particular skill is declining.

One should not forget that although new technology makes some job skills unnecessary, it also prolongs working lives and opens up careers to some. Machines and automation often reduce the physical burdens and stress associated with industrial jobs and open the jobs to women, who were previously excluded, justly or not, on the basis of insufficient physical strength. Bowen and Finegan (1969) suggest that the reduction in the work week, itself often associated with automation in the labor force, may have *offset* the decline in elderly men's labor-force participation rates by as much as 3.5 percent between 1948 and 1965.

One place where older workers may have had special difficulty in the face of automation is in rural areas. Historically, rates of employment among older men have declined more in rural than in urban places. In rural areas, nonfarm employment opportunities for older people are minimal, and it seems likely that elderly men who followed the migration to urban areas did not do well. How much the population migration from rural to urban areas contributed to declining labor-force opportunities for older workers is difficult to discern, although it appears less than might have been expected. On the basis of his labor-force analysis, Long (1958) concludes that the effect of population migration between 1890 and 1950 on the elderly male labor-force rate was "relatively little." According to one study, rural to urban migration accounted for about a 3 percent decline in elderly male workers between 1948 and 1965 (Bowen & Finegan 1969).

A second theory regarding changes in labor-force composition is that the decline in the importance of farming as a source of jobs has had a depressing effect on the employment of older people. In 1890, almost 61 percent of all employed aged men were farmers; by 1980, this figure was only 11.3 percent. Yet, older workers were not the only ones affected by the twentieth-century revolution in agriculture. The increased technology and science involved in farming, the consolidation of small farms, and the development of multinational agribusiness had significant impact on farming employment for people of all ages. In 1900, about 36 percent of all those in the labor force were employed in agriculture, compared with about 2.6 percent in 1997.

These changes have affected younger and older men differently. Rapid expansion of the nonfarming components of the labor force has been a source of opportunities for younger workers, but no concomitant compensatory expansion of opportunities has occurred for older workers. Further, occupational longevity is greater for farmers than for other workers: "Age grading" is less relevant in agriculture. Retirement on the farm does not have the same meaning it does in other industries. The decline in the number of persons engaged in farming has been large enough to affect appreciably the labor-force participation rates of older men. In 1910, over 12 million workers were engaged in farming; by 1997, this figure had dropped to about 3.3 million.

A variation on this second theory which appears since 1970 is the effect the decline in manufacturing has had on the employment opportunities of older workers. Plant closings and layoffs resulting from corporate downsizing have disproportionately reduced opportunities for older workers in manufacturing industries. According to the U.S. Bureau of the Census (1998, Table 669), 4.2 million individuals age 20 or over with job tenure of three years or more lost or left a job between January 1993 and December 1995. Of this total, 73.6 percent were employed in February 1996. However, among those 55 to 64 years, 52.1 percent were employed, and among those age 65 and over, only 31.6 percent were employed. Of the total group, 44.0 percent reported a plant or company closing or moving as the reason for their job loss. Among those 55 to 64 years and 65 years of age and over, 45.3 percent and 50.4 percent, respectively, offered this as a reason for their job loss. Interestingly, these percentages were only exceeded by that for the youngest workers, ages 20 to 24 (52.9 percent).

Age Discrimination in Employment

No one really knows the extent of age discrimination in employment that exists in U.S. society, although it is considered pervasive and in recent years has drawn increasing attention. A 1964 Department of Labor study reported that over one million "man-years" of productive output are lost each year in the United States because of age discrimination. The Congress passed the ***Age Discrimination Employment Act (ADEA)*** <http://www.dol.gov/dol/public/regs/main.htm> in 1967 and amended it in 1974, 1978, 1986, and 1990. The federal law prohibits the following:

1. Discrimination in the hiring of an employee on the basis of age
2. Discrimination in discharging a person on the basis of age
3. Discrimination in pay and other privileges and conditions of employment because of age
4. Instructions to an employment agency not to refer a person to a job or to only certain kinds of jobs because of age
5. Placement of any advertisement that shows preferences based on age or that specifies an age bracket

All employers with more than 20 employees are subject to the provisions of ADEA, as are employment agencies, labor organizations, and states and their agencies and subdivisions. With the 1986 amendments, virtually all employees age 40 or older are protected, including firefighters, law-enforcement officers, and tenured faculty at institutions of higher learning, who, until December 31, 1993, may have been discharged on the basis of age at age 70 or older.

One study of employed aerospace workers age 45 and over reported that *one-half* of them had at least one personal experience with discrimination in employment due to their age (Kasschau 1976). Many workers suffer from age discrimination but do not identify it as such; others may be unaware of their protection under ADEA. Age discrimination may occur in different forms. Employers may offer training opportunities only to younger workers, for example. As a result, younger workers may receive salary increases and promotion at a faster pace than older workers. Older applicants may be told they are overqualified or that because they have too much experience, they would be unhappy in a position. (In this regard, ADEA has been deemed ineffectual in promoting hiring of older workers [Ventrell-Monsees 1991]). Companies may reorganize or restructure, thereby combining or consolidating functions and eliminating positions previously filled by older workers. However, 1990 amendments to ADEA, referred to as the Older Workers Benefit Protection Act, prohibit employers from treating older workers differently from younger workers during a reduction in force.

One theory of age discrimination, sometimes referred to as a *decrement theory of aging* (McEvoy & Cascio 1989), is that employers assume decrement or decline in reaction time, in sensory and cognitive processes, in physical strength, and consequently in work performance. However, a recent survey of the literature on age and job performance reported little relationship between the two. In fact, older workers tend to have lower absenteeism, accident, and turnover rates than do younger workers; in addition, their commitment to the organization and job satisfaction is often higher than that of younger workers.

Instances of age discrimination in employment can be difficult to identify. For workers not covered by federal law, states may vary in the protection they offer an older worker. According to one report, although state laws generally are not as broad as the federal ADEA, many states do offer better protection to public than private employees (Goldberg 1978). This same report found only four states having coverage equal to or better than federal laws.

Because the ADEA covers all employees age 40 or older, discrimination based on age is not as clear-cut or obvious as race or sex discrimination (where unchanging characteristics are involved). When race or sex discrimination is proven, it usually affects the protected group as a whole. Age discrimination, on the other hand, may be directed at a subgroup of the protected class. For example, in one case brought before the U.S. Court of Appeals in Denver (*Equal Employment Opportunity Commission* v. *Sandia Corporation*), the trial court found that in the company's layoff decisions, a pattern and practice of age discrimination began to appear at age 52, and the inference that age was a factor became stronger after age 55, increasing to age 58, where it remained a steady influence in decisions until age 64. In a related 1996 case, *O'Connor* v. *Consolidated Coin Caterers Corp.*, the U.S. Supreme Court ruled that an employer may be liable for age discrimination even if it replaced one older worker with another. Thus, just because the 56-year-old plaintiff in *O'Connor* was replaced with a 40-year-old does not mean that he was not a victim of age discrimination.

RETIREMENT

Retirement as a mass phenomenon is a modern industrial creation. People certainly retired in preindustrial times, but only if they could generate income by performing some productive function or if they owned enough property to provide income. People who stopped working because they were too old and/or sick led a difficult life. They were "dead weight"—often treated, at least figuratively, like the Eskimo grandmother who, when she could no longer function, was abandoned or walled up in an igloo to await death (Donahue, Orbach, & Pollak 1960).

Calhoun (1978) points out that, in the sense of giving up "business or occupation in order to enjoy more leisure or freedom," the *Oxford English Dictionary's* first example of retirement comes from a 1667 entry in Samuel Pepys's diary. The example makes clear, through reference to pensions and "competences," that retirement was a status available only to the nobility or mercantile elites. Working people of the day did not retire. Generally they did not have access to pensions. Also, "busy hands are happy hands"; retirement was not valued.

In the U.S. context, Achenbaum (1978) explains that the word *retirement,* meaning stopping work at some prescribed age, was literally absent from pre– Civil War vocabulary. People retired, but as in "retiring" from winter storms to the warmth of a family circle. Webster, in the first edition of *An America Dictionary* (1828), defined **retirement** as "1. the art of withdrawing from company or from public notice or station; 2. the state of being withdrawn; 3. private abode; 4. private way of life." Obviously, old age was no prerequisite to retirement; anyone might retire. By the 1880 edition, however, a new meaning was attributed to the verb *to retire:* "to cause to retire, specifically to designate as no longer qualified for active service, as to retire a military or naval officer."

According to Achenbaum, the first federal retirement measure became law in December 1861, when Congress passed an act requiring any naval officer below the rank of vice admiral who was age 62 or older to resign his commission; the retirement age for naval officers was raised to age 64 in 1916. Also noteworthy in the 1880 definition is the implicitly negative attitude toward old age. People were retired when they were no longer qualified for employment because of age.

From the mid-nineteenth to the mid-twentieth century, retirement policies became more prevalent in both public and private sectors. During this period, much debate surrounded issues of a standard age for defining retirement, mandatory versus voluntary retirement, and the adequacy of pension income. Debaters differed on the advantages and disadvantages of various retirement policies to older workers and to the national economy. Business, for example, regarded the issue of adequacy of pension as the price of management gaining prerogative over setting retirement age. Such power was essential for manipulating the size of the labor pool during business up- or downturns. Organized labor, on the other hand, viewed pension adequacy as a bread-and-butter issue—a right of every worker. Academicians and social reformers saw pension reform as extraneous, an issue used to exclude older workers from the labor force and deny them the freedom to work as long as they are able and desirous of doing so (Calhoun 1978).

Many older workers saw retirement as a threat. They recognized that retirement (particularly forced retirement) might create an economically disadvantaged situation. Some believed the myth that death comes at retirement. Others believed in work as the American way of life.

In 1949, novelist James Michener published a short story in *Nation's Business* that he believed reflected the attitude of Americans toward retirement. The fictitious John Bassett was the head accountant at J. C. Gower and Company. The story involved his last day of work at the firm, which was forcing Mr. Bassett into retirement. He plotted revenge, but his employer—concerned about the impact of the forced retirement on Bassett and aware of the accountant's work record— waived the company's 65-and-out rule. Bassett stayed on the job, though at half pay. Mr. Gower also gave the employee a set of woodworking tools in an effort to increase the accountant's avocations. Mr. Bassett gave the tools to his grandson and, in doing so, summed up the attitude that Michener believed to be prevalent among U.S. workers: "Such substitutions for paid employment are for kids; what a man needs is a job."

Nevertheless, by the 1960s, something had changed. Retirement was becoming an accepted part of the life cycle for a greater proportion of the population. Ash (1966), studying the attitudes toward retirement among steelworkers, found that in 1951, retirement was justified only if an individual was physically unable to continue. By 1960, however, retirement was justified as reward for a lifetime of work. Gerontologist Robert Atchley (1974) also found that retirement had become an overwhelmingly favorable concept. In his research, he discovered that people saw retirement as an active, hopeful, meaningful, healthy, relaxed, and independent time.

Even early retirement became acceptable. Apparently, when workers are provided adequate income for retirement before age 65, even to age 50, there is little resistance to retirement. Whereas in the immediate postwar environment unions debated whether to set the retirement age at 65, by the 1960s, 30-years'-service-and-out by age 55 was not atypical of union demands. The United Auto Worker's (UAW) 1965 collective bargaining agreement with the Big Three—Chrysler, Ford, and General Motors—had the effect of reducing retirement age to 60. Under the plan, an auto worker age 55 with 30 years of service retired on a monthly pension plus a supplement until such time as the worker qualified for full Social Security benefits; at age 60, with at least 10 years of service, an autoworker could retire with a reduced benefit.

In retirement, many people remain vital by taking advantage of new opportunities and activities.

Ekerdt, Vinick, and Bosse (1989) provide formal support for the view that retirement—early or otherwise—has been institutionalized as an anticipated and orderly event in the life course. These researchers found that 66 percent of workers participating in the Veteran's Administration Normative Aging Study accurately predicted their eventual date of retirement within plus or minus one year; 40 percent were exact to within three months.

Mandatory Retirement

Some attribute the choice of age 65 as the age for retirement to the Old Age and Survivors Pension Act that Otto Von Bismarck pushed through as the first chancellor of the German Empire in 1889. One unverifiable account of how this came to be suggests that Bismarck's actuaries recommended 65 as a safe age because life expectancy at birth during the 1880s was about 45 years and few people could be expected to reach age 65. The English, playing it even safer, passed similar legislation in 1908 using 70 as a retirement age; they later reduced the age to 65. The United States followed in 1935 with its own Social Security program. Wilbur Cohen (1957), former Secretary of Health, Education and Welfare and one of the staff members who helped draft the 1935 legislation, has written that the choice of age 65 as a boundary line for providing old-age assistance had no scientific, social, or gerontological basis. There was simply a general political consensus that 65 was an acceptable age.

Although the original Social Security Act of 1935 was not involved in establishing a compulsory retirement age, the choice of age 65 seems to have carried over from Social Security to mandatory retirement policies. As already pointed out, recent amendments to the Age Discrimination Employment Act (ADEA) have, for the most part, eliminated 65 as the age for mandatory retirement.

It is difficult to say who was affected by mandatory retirement policies. A 1961 Cornell University sample survey (Slavick 1966) of industrial firms in the United States with 50 or more employees found that most establishments had flexible retirement policies. Almost 95 percent of firms without pension plans, almost 70 percent of those with profit sharing, and 60 percent of those with formal pension plans had flexible retirement policies. The Brandeis economist James Schulz (1995) has pointed out the relationship between flexible retirement rules and establishment size evident in this survey. For example, 68 percent of the firms with 50 to 99 employees had flexible rules, yet only 30 percent of those with 500 or more employees had such rules. Thus, it is possible that relatively few firms have had mandatory retirement rules, while at the same time many workers have been subject to such policies.

A 1972 survey of the largest state and local government retirement systems covering about 70 percent of all employees enrolled in such systems showed that most had a mandatory retirement age; for two-thirds of the plans, retirement age was set at age 70 or later. James Schulz has developed the tabulations of responses from this survey, which shows the incidence of mandatory retirement. Although 54 percent of male retirees were subject to mandatory retirement rules, only 7 percent of the total cohort of retired workers were able and willing to work but unable to find a new job. This small proportion of workers affected by mandatory retirement policies supports data on this issue provided by some of the largest corporations in the United States.

Why the fuss over mandatory retirement practices in light of how relatively few workers were forced out of work because of them? And given that such practices are now against the law? One reason may be that although mandatory retirement practices are gone, "encouraged" or "forced" retirement practices remain quite prevalent. Quadagno and Hardy (1996) describe how defined-benefit (DB) pension plans—plans that promise workers a specified benefit that the firm is obliged to pay—discourage staying in the work force. The value of DB plans typically does not grow smoothly with gradual, regular deposits. Rather, pension wealth remains low in the early years of tenure and increases rapidly as the worker approaches the early or normal retirement age (age 55, 60, or 65). Once the worker actually exceeds the designated normal retirement age, pension accrual values decline sharply and may even turn negative. As a result, workers who remain with the firm beyond the early or normal retirement age may actually lose pension wealth.

Mandatory, forced, or encouraged retirement may have a number of similar effects on retirees. Butler (1975) describes these as a "retirement syndrome." Although not all retirees develop these characteristics, many formerly healthy workers do develop headaches, irritability, nervousness, lethargy, and the like in connection with retirement. Susan Haynes of the National Heart, Lung, and Blood Institute found that the mortality rate of workers who were in good heath when mandatorily retired at age 65 was 30 percent higher than expected three and four years following retirement.

Another reason for concern over forced or encouraged retirement may have to do with the traditional arguments made for and against mandatory retirement. These are often based on misconceptions and myths associated with the aging process and the employment of older people. Many studies indicate that older workers produce a quality of work as good as or better than that of younger workers. As has already been pointed out in Chapter 7, there is no reason to expect a decline in intellectual capacities with age and every reason to assume that older workers in good health are capable of learning new skills when circumstances require it.

The argument that forced or encouraged retirement of older workers opens needed jobs for the young may be especially appealing to some. Yet, no study can be cited that demonstrates that the termination of an older worker because of mandatory retirement directly caused the hiring of young workers. Given the high rate of early retirement and the small proportion of retirees who would have continued working without mandatory retirement, it does not appear that the elimination of mandatory retirement policies would have any substantial impact on the labor supply or the unemployment rate.

Adjustment to Retirement

Adjustment to retirement can be difficult for many people, although most studies show that a majority of people adjust reasonably well. Finances, health and physical mobility, social involvement, and the specific circumstances of the retirement appear to top the list of factors researchers have identified as affecting adjustment to retirement. For example, Beck (1982) identifies poor health, lower income, and earlier-than-expected retirement as main determinants of a negative evaluation of retirement. Boaz (1987) implies some anxiety about retirement in her study of work as a response on the part of retirees to low and decreasing real retirement income. Findings from this research suggest that work during retirement among men *and* women "is a response to low or moderate levels of nonwage income at the beginning of retirement and, for men, work is also a response to a decrease in the real value of such income during retirement" (p. 437).

Using longitudinal data from the 1984 Survey of Income and Program Participation, Mutchler and associates (1997) found that 25.1 percent of the sample of men ages 55 to 74 at first interview experienced at least one transition in labor-force status over a 28-month period. Fewer than one-half of these (10.1 percent of the total sample) could be characterized as "crisp exits" from the labor force. A crisp exit is unidirectional and, in the context of late-life work behavior, would typically describe a clean break from employment through a single, final labor force exit to retirement. The majority of those experiencing at least one transition (15 percent of the total sample) could be characterized as exhibiting "blurred transition behavior." Blurred transition patterns include repeated exits, entrances, and periods of unemployment. Interestingly, crisp exits were most commonly observed among men younger than age 65. Blurred transition patterns are not particularly unique to any group, but are uncommon beyond age 68. The mulitvariate analysis shows that blurred transition patterns seem part of a strategy to maintain economic status in late life. For example, while availability of a pension seems to precipitate a crisp exit, those without a pension or adequate nonwage resources remain attached to the work role, even on some sporadic basis.

Midanik and colleagues (1995) found that retirees have lower stress levels and engage in regular exercise more often as compared to those who did not retire during their two-year study period. Recognizing the need to assess the effects of retirement over longer periods, these researchers report no difference between retirees and the nonretired (ages 60 to 66 years) on self-reported mental health status, coping, depression, smoking, and alcohol consumption.

Evans, Ekerdt, and Bosse (1985) used data from 816 male workers participating in the Normative Aging Study of the Veterans Administration in Boston to investigate the preretirement socialization process. These researchers found a strong linear relationship between proximity to retirement and informal preretirement involvement (measured by how often the preretiree had talked with his wife, his relatives, his close friends, or people on the job, or had read articles about retirement). This finding indicates that an anticipatory self-socialization to retirement was underway at least 15 years prior to the retirement itself. In addition, other factors—such as attitudes toward retirement, job characteristics, and personal resources (especially the existence of an already-retired good friend)—were of relevance in explaining variation in preretirement involvement.

Attitudes toward retirement may directly determine adjustment. A study of college professors showed that about three-quarters of them looked forward to retirement; one-fourth did not have a positive attitude. A professor of the biological sciences held this negative view (Patton 1977, p. 350):

> The problem I see about retirement is the failure of our society to appreciate the worth of all the education…packed into an academic. One can be a professor one minute, then a park bench occupant the next…. The greatest tragedy of retirement is the lack of imagination of our institutions, including universities, to develop a plan whereby an individual's worth and self-esteem can be maintained in a meaningful way.

The feelings of worth and self-esteem referred to by this professor may be at the core of discussions about adjusting to retirement. Miller (1965) takes the position that retirement brings with it an ***identity crisis.*** He argues that retirement is basically degrading because it implies that the individual is no longer able to carry out the work role. This is especially problematic, Miller says, because occupational identity is so much a part of a person's life. It affects how all the other roles (spouse, parent, friend, etc.) are played. Leisure roles cannot replace work as a source of self-respect and identity because society does not support them in the same way it supports work roles. According to Miller, leisure is not sufficient replacement for work as a source of worth and self-esteem. The crisis comes because the individual's former claims to prestige and status are negated by retirement, and no replacement sources of prestige and status are available. This embarrasses the individual and causes withdrawal from social life.

In response to Miller's identity crisis theory, Robert Atchley (1971) puts forth an *identity continuity theory* of adjustment to retirement. Atchley points out that few people rest their entire identity on a single role. Rather, most people have several roles in which to base identity. The probability that retirement will lead to identity crisis or breakdown is slim because the roles (e.g., parent, grandparent, or spouse) are maintained well into old age. Also, retired workers will likely continue to identify with their occupation even though they no longer play the role. Thus, the retired professor will continue to see himself or herself as a professor beyond the retirement age.

Furthermore, Atchley argues that people *can* gain self-respect from leisure pursuits in retirement, especially if they have sufficient financial resources available and a cohort of retired friends who accept full-time leisure as a legitimate enterprise. A final point of identity continuity theory is that many people develop skills during the course of their occupational careers that are quite useful in retirement and do provide a degree of identity continuity. Skill in interpersonal interaction developed in careers in sales or teaching, for example, may serve a person well in leisure activities and at the same time facilitate a sense of continuity in his or her life.

Although it does not appear to be a typical pattern, some people, especially those forced to retire, do undergo the identity crisis described by Miller. The "retirement syndrome" Butler referred to may reflect this identity crisis. This crisis can be an important precipitating factor in the adoption of the sick role. Having come to define illness as a more legitimate role to occupy than being retired, retirees may become "sick" (i.e., behave as if they were ill). It may be easier in U.S. society for a person to say he or she has retired because of poor health than to explain that the employer no longer considers him or her competent to do a job.

A more typical pattern of adjustment in retirement involves those whose experiences fit the continuity perspective. Snow and Havighurst (1977) studied the careers after age 60 of administrators in U.S. higher education. Those with a life-style pattern that they identified as *maintainers* were able to hold on to their professional activities successfully, even after formal retirement, pursuing part-time assignments, and filling time with other activities. Interestingly, the maintainers were contrasted with another group, the *transformers*. The transformers changed their life-styles with retirement, reduced their professional activities (by choice), and created a new pattern of living that often emphasized a nonprofessional area of activity (hobbies, arts and crafts, or travel). As one transformer put it (Snow & Havighurst 1977, p. 548):

> At the time of my full retirement, I was confronted by a series of invitations and opportunities to engage in continued professional work in various cities and as far away as Taiwan.... My wife and I decided to reject all of them.... We wished to stay here among our good friends. This would give me opportunity to activate a long smoldering interest in painting. The painting now claims my primary interest and labor, and I have become President of our local Art League.... I have opened up a new career which beckons me on to achievement and a new kind of fulfillment.

Reitzes, Mutran, and Fernandez (1996) add to the discussion of "identity crisis" versus "identity continuity" through analysis of data from their ongoing study of transition into retirement carried out in the Raleigh-Durham-Chapel Hill area of North Carolina. They used in-depth telephone interviews with 300 retired workers to investigate whether preretirement investment in the role of worker (and spouse) has positive or negative consequences for postretirement self-esteem. Interestingly, they report no statistically significant difference between the preretirement and postretirement self-esteem scores of these retirees, and strongly suggest that there is a continuity in self-assessment that is maintained through career transitions, including retirement. This supports work by Ekerdt and DeViney (1993), who suggest that retirement is an anticipated transition for most workers and so is less likely to have impact on self-esteem.

As Reitzes and colleagues (1996) point out, however, these findings may be used to support both an "identity crisis" as well as an "identity continuity" perspective. That past identity and self-esteem provide a reference point or foundation for current self-esteem seems straightforward enough and supportive of an identity continuity theory. But, how could the same data be used to support an identity crisis theory? These authors provide an answer:

> We suggest that given the uncertainties of being retired, former workers may rely on the ways they viewed themselves in the near-past to provide an initial reference

point or benchmark in assessing themselves at a new stage in their lives. Rather than being directionless, or without a sense of self, individuals entering new situations or stages in their life cycle may use their past, in this case their past self-esteem, to guide them in the present. (p. S248)

Reitzes and his research team (1996) also suggest that there are things to be done in preretirement that work to foster self-esteem in retirement. For example, programmatically, workers can be encouraged to take advantage of new or deferred opportunities that may become available in retirement. Such preretirement programs have been around since early in the post–World War II period. In general, their appearance is evidence of the belief that the work role is central and an important source of self-identity and status. As already discussed, some believe that the notion of work as central to self-identity has been given undue consideration in research on adjustment to retirement. Almost despite this ongoing discussion in the gerontological literature, there has been a substantial growth in the prevalence of preretirement programs. Two important questions are, Do workers participate in such programs? and Do preretirement programs work?

Campione (1988) has used data from the National Longitudinal Survey of Mature Men to estimate the probability of participation in a retirement preparation program. The final sample employed in the study included 294 retired men who reported having had the opportunity to participate in a preretirement program and for whom longitudinal data were available. Most workers who do participate in such programs do so within two years of their retirement. Campione finds that those individuals who prepare for retirement during their working lives are more likely to participate in formal retirement preparation programs. In addition, those who are married and have families to plan for, those who have minimal health problems, and those of higher occupational status are more likely to plan for retirement. She concludes that program sponsors are failing to attract a broad cross-section of employees into preretirement preparation programs. Apparently, those most likely to succeed in retirement anyway are those most likely to be given an opportunity to participate in such programs (Beck 1984).

Glamser (1981) has reported on a longitudinal study to determine the longer-term impact of two different preretirement programs. Two experimental groups and one control group were used to test the merits of a "comprehensive group discussion program" and an "individual briefing program." Those male industrial workers in the group discussion program met eight times during a one-month period, with sessions lasting approximately 90 minutes each. Those assigned to the individual briefing program met with the plant personnel officer for 30 minutes and received four booklets to read dealing with retirement planning, income, health, and leisure activities.

Questionnaire data were collected prior to program initiation and again six years later. The results showed no significant effect on the retirement experience of individuals by either program. Further, no substantive differences with the control group were noted in the length of the adjustment period, accuracy of expectations, level of preparation, life satisfaction, attitude toward retirement, or job deprivation. Glamser suggests that the major impact of preretirement programs may be of considerably shorter duration than six years. Further, their primary value may actually be in the period before employees leave the work setting.

Retirement in Cross-Cultural Perspective

As already indicated, retirement is a modern industrial phenomenon, with the emphasis on *industrial.* There are numerous examples of retirement patterns in contemporary preindustrial societies that are different than those in the United States. Holmes (1972) reports that in Samoa there is the concept of retiring from the position of household head, an influential position in the village council. Sometimes this is done to allow younger men to achieve status and power, but stepping down does not mean a complete withdrawal from village council activities. Often, the former chief will become an elder statesman and function in an advisory capacity with the council.

Among the !Kung San of the Kalahari Desert in southwestern Africa, the aged are held in high esteem. They act as the following:

1. Stewards of rights to water and resources in the area
2. Storehouses of knowledge, skills, and lore
3. Teachers and minders of children
4. Spiritual specialists and healers
5. Ritually privileged figures

In this subsistence economy, these roles are based on reciprocal obligations across the life cycle, not on the accumulation of economic power and resources (Biesele & Howell 1981). Adult men are hunters, and many are healers. They do not know retirement. Aging men carry out these roles as long as they can and then replace them with less strenuous activities, such as trapping, gathering, making artifacts, telling stories, and visiting. Women are gatherers, and many of them are healers also. With age, they also continue these roles and gradually move to less physically arduous activities, including child care and handicrafts work (Biesele & Howell 1981).

In 1990, almost one in five people in the countries of the Organization for Economic Cooperation and Development (OECD) were over age 60. The OECD includes 29 nations, with the original 20 coming from western Europe and North America. By 2030, that figure is expected to have risen to over 30 percent, and the share of those over 80 years of age will likely double, from 3 to 6 percent (Beck 1996). Still, being old in the developed countries does not mean being necessarily poor. Because of state transfers and private pension supplements, most old people in the developed world receive relatively decent pensions and available medical service.

The developing world is another matter. Many nations are starting to age quickly. The 60 years of age and over population is set to double to 14 percent in

Latin America and Asia between now and 2030, and in China the percentage of elderly is expected to grow from about 10 to 22 percent in the same period (Beck 1996). Today (2000), there are approximately 400 million people over age 60 in the developing countries, about twice the number in the developed world. As Beck (1996) describes it, the world is on the verge of a historical first: countries with large populations of old people who are also poor. Other combinations are somewhat more familiar. Most of the industrial world is old and somewhat affluent; most of the developing world until now has been young and poor; less common in the contemporary world has been young and affluent, although to this point this characterizes the United States, Australia, and New Zealand.

This new combination will create many problems familiar to the industrial nations; however, fewer resources will be available to deal with these problems. In the poor countries of the developing world, old people usually work until frailty or ill health forces them to stop. Absent work, people have no means of support or care, save for their families. And many of these developing countries have no formal state-supported pensions schemes or available national medical system. Clearly, as developing countries become more affluent, more people will be covered by retirement schemes and health care insurance. But such a solution is decades away. In the interim, it is fair to say that the average "retiree" in the developing world will be thinking about more important considerations than whether identity crisis or identity continuity better describes his or her adjustment to retirement!

Women and Retirement

Most research on retirement has emphasized the experience of men, who traditionally have dominated in the labor force. The employment experience of women is changing, however, especially among younger cohorts. As these women enter old age, an increasing proportion will have participated in the labor force and will have done so for a longer period of time. This will have a positive effect on the economic position of women in old age; they will have accumulated more primary Social Security credits and more private pension benefits. Further, retirement is likely to become more salient as an experience of older women.

In the short run, employment in the labor force will not be a major activity for older women. As Table 12.1 showed, the proportion of women 65 years and over participating in the labor force has declined only modestly since 1976; in 1996, only 8.6 percent of these women were working. The table also showed a slight increase in labor-force participation rates among women ages 55 to 64 between 1976 and 1986, but a more dramatic increase to 49.6 percent by 1996. By the year 2006, 55.8 percent of women ages 55 to 64 are expected to be participating in the labor force.

In the past, data on the retirement experiences of female workers were culled from studies of male workers. Today, there is an emerging literature on women's retirement. And, there is some evidence that women have different attitudes toward retirement than men do. Calasanti (1996) suggests that this occurs in two ways, as a consequence of the intersection of gender, employment experiences, and retirement. *First,* employment influences objective aspects of retirement. As much literature describes, women, as a group, are more likely than men to be employed in sectors of the economy (by industry and occupation) that have negative effects on the stability of work and retirement income (Meyer 1990). For example, women in the service sector are most likely to be in sales or clerical positions. In manufacturing, women assemble, inspect, pack, and wrap. They also occupy a limited number of professional and technical jobs, including teacher, nurse, librarian, and array of health technician/assistant positions. Many of these occupations are in cyclical industries; when the economy is strong, work is plentiful, but when the economy is weak, layoffs are likely. Also, these are relatively low wage/benefit jobs that result in lower retirement income.

Second, how one's job is organized—level of autonomy, diversity of task, extent of hierarchy, and so on—in turn shapes an individual's view of the world and self. Thus, if "women's jobs" are less likely then men's positions to involve supervisory behavior, less likely to contain a "power" dimension over others, more likely to require social and nurturant behavior, and more restrictive in occupational mobility, then one might expect, on a subjective level, that these differences would influence how women and men think about retirement. As Calasanti (1996) describes it, "The resources available during the retirement process and the sense of self derived from work-related experiences should lead to different patterns of adjustment for women and men" (p. S20).

Campione (1987) has used data from the University of Michigan's Panel Study of Income Dynamics to study the retirement decisions of married women ages 55 to 70. She found the married woman's decision to be influenced significantly by changes in financial status, including Social Security wealth, wage wealth, pension wealth, and age. In addition, the married woman's retirement decision was significantly influenced by her spouse's labor-force status. Thus, the retirement of her husband does increase the likelihood of the wife's retirement.

Working women seem to be opposed to mandatory retirement. Many have interrupted work careers; others do not start working until age 40 or 45 and are not ready to retire by age 62 or 65 (as long as they remain healthy and capable of job performance). As described earlier, women are concentrated in occupations and industries where pensions are low or nonexistent, and receive lower wages on average than do men. The gaps in their work histories translate to low Social Security payments. Add to these conditions the probability of an older woman being widowed, divorced, or married to a man with a low income, and it becomes understandable that older women workers are willing to struggle to delay the years of reduced income that accompany retirement. Eliminating the mandatory retirement age should have the dual effect of allowing a large population of low-income older women to continue working, while reducing the strain on Social Security and pension funds by keeping this population contributing to these funds rather than withdrawing from them.

Is a woman's satisfaction with retirement different if she is married as opposed to widowed? Dorfman and Moffett (1987) addressed this question in their study of older women in two rural Iowa counties. The sample included women who reported that they had retired from a paying job in the last 10 years. Two factors, self-perceived health status and increases in social participation in voluntary associations, were predictors of retirement satisfaction for married *and* widowed rural women. Perceptions of financial status and the frequency and perceived certainty of receiving aid from friends were predictors of retirement satisfaction among married women, whereas maintenance of preretirement friendships and frequency of contacts with friends predicted retirement satisfaction for widowed women. Should one be surprised by the fact that retirement satisfaction among rural widows seemingly was not affected by concerns about financial status or whether aid from close friends could be counted on in a crisis? According to Dorfman and Moffett (1987), these findings may simply reflect rural values of independence and the acceptance of unfavorable conditions of life without complaint.

Ruhm (1996) analyzed survey data on a national cross-section of women ages 50 to 59 years and men ages 55 to 64 years. Although unmarried men and women with work experience after age 50 have identical probabilities of working or holding full-time jobs, marriage was associated with an elevated labor supply for males and reduced employment for females. Women are much more likely than men to cite family motivations, including supplying more care to relatives, as the important reason for not working. Also, there is some evidence that couples coordinate retirement decisions, although the pattern seems more complex than a tradition in which husbands "lead" and wives "follow." Two important trends in the future could depress the labor supply of married females in their middle to late 50s and propel them into "early retirement:" (1) If patterns of care giving do not change, growth of the oldest (and most frail) elderly could increase care-giving obligations among this group; and (2) given coordination of retirement decisions among couples, increased labor-force involvement of women is likely to reduce future retirement ages among married persons of both ages—particularly as two-income households accumulate greater wealth than those with only one income (Ruhm 1996).

LEISURE

The conventional wisdom was that older people spent more time in leisure activities, on the average, than people in the middle years (Riley & Foner 1968). The assumption was that old age brings retirement for men and a reduction in obligatory pursuits for women. This would leave more time free for leisure pursuits.

However, as Cutler and Hendricks (1990) point out, much cross-sectional research shows a decline in overall leisure and recreation participation with age. This is especially the case when participation is measured in terms of frequency or time spent in particular activities. Table 12.2 shows the decline in participation in various sports activities across age categories. The sports activities with the highest percentage of participants age 65 and older include exercise walking (32.7 percent), swimming (9.4 percent), and bicycle riding (7.4 percent). Still, there is

TABLE 12.2   Percentage Participating in Sports Activities by Age: 1996

| | AGE | | | |
ACTIVITY	35–44 years	45–54 years	55–64 years	65+ years
Aerobic exercising*	12.0%	9.2%	6.4%	4.7%
Bicycle riding*	19.4	13.4	11.6	7.4
Bowling	17.9	10.9	7.2	5.5
Calisthenics*	4.1	3.1	1.5	1.3
Camping	21.6	14.3	11.7	5.7
Exercise walking	34.2	38.7	39.5	32.7
Fishing—fresh water	19.0	15.9	13.3	7.0
Golf	11.6	10.7	8.7	6.4
Hunting	9.9	7.7	5.8	3.5
Running/jogging*	8.9	5.3	2.9	1.4
Swimming*	23.8	16.9	13.5	9.4
Tennis	4.4	2.6	1.5	1.0

*Participant engaged in activity at least six times in the year.

Source: Statistical Abstract of the United States, 1998, 118th ed. (Washington, DC: U.S. Bureau of the Census, 1998), Table 438.

variability across different types of activities. Gordon, Gaitz, and Scott (1976) report that activities involving high physical exertion and intensity conform to the age pattern just described, but that moderate-intensity activities, especially those that are home-based, show more consistency across the life course. Kelly (1987) reports marked decreases with age in physically active outdoor recreation but much smaller age differences for social, home-based, and family activities.

Considerable controversy exists in the gerontological literature concerning leisure-time pursuits. One argument, with which the reader is already familiar, is that leisure roles are not adequate substitutes for the work role. Presumably, this is because leisure roles are not supported by norms that would legitimate the replacement (Miller 1965). Basic to this argument is the notion that work (and not leisure) is the dominant value in the United States; thus, individuals are unable to develop self-respect from leisure-time pursuits. An opposing position is that leisure can, in fact, replace the work role and provide personal satisfaction in later life (Atchley 1971). This may be the case especially in the presence of adequate income and good health.

Thompson (1973) has tested the relative merits of these two positions. Data from personal interviews with almost 1,600 older men were analyzed in this study. The results challenged the position that argues for the centrality of work as a value in the lives of older Americans. Those retirees in the sample who were found to have low self-respect (the actual variable employed in the study was labeled "morale") were also found to be older, to have negative evaluations of their health, and to have more disability and less income. The research suggests that low self-respect is related to these factors, not to their lack of work role. As Thompson (1973) writes, "It appears that given relative youth, an optimistic view of health, a lack of functional disability, and an adequate income, the retirement years can be pleasant as the years of employment for a great many men and that leisure roles can adequately substitute for that of worker" (p. 344).

One reason that people may have difficulty occupying leisure roles is simply that they lack the practice. Television, gardening, visiting, and reading are so popular precisely because older people have had so much practice time with these activities. Many people are reluctant to engage in leisure activities because they feel incompetent at such activities. Miller (1965) argues that the prospect of embarrassment keeps many older people from participating in new leisure pursuits.

Efforts should be made to prepare people for the life of leisure, because once people are already old, it is too late for such preparation. Older people tend to retain activity patterns and preferences developed earlier in life. Leisure competence should be learned early. Doing so may be the only way to assure leisure competence in later life. In recent years, preretirement planning programs have been used to help workers identify activities and roles that may be rewarding after retirement, but such programs do little to enhance a lifelong learning approach to leisure.

Understanding the relationship between participation in leisure and recreational pursuits and aging requires placing leisure in some life-course perspective (Cutler & Hendricks 1990). In doing so, one may identify how structural factors differentially affect leisure participation levels of successive cohorts of older people. For example, Riley (1987) points out that differences in leisure-time pursuits among successive cohorts of older people may simply reflect differences in normative expectations, other social roles, occupational stages, and personal resources. Table 12.2 gives the impression that there is a negative relationship between bicycle riding and age. However, longitudinal data, not yet developed, may show that younger cohorts maintain a level of participation in this particular leisure-time pursuit that is consistent with changes in normative expectations for older people or in the social roles adopted by future cohorts of elderly.

Finally, it is useful to remind the reader that much of the research on leisure-time pursuits of older people is based on frequency counts or time-use studies. Missing from this literature are studies that take the view of the actor and attempt to specify the symbolic value of leisure. Kelly, Steinkamp, and Kelly (1987) argue, for example, that leisure, like work, is a central life focus that deserves more serious attention.

SUMMARY

Labor-force participation rates of old people declined throughout the twentieth century. Currently, about one-sixth of aged males and fewer than 9 percent of aged females are in the labor force. Factors that have contributed to this decline include the health status of older people, new pension systems, changes in retirement policies, changes in characteristics of the economy, and age discrimination in employment.

Retirement is a modern industrial creation. According to Atchley (1976), the emergence of retirement as a social institution in a society requires four factors: longevity, economic surplus, pension systems, and acceptance of the idea of retirement. Recently, early retirement has become more acceptable. This reflects a changing attitude (increasingly positive) toward retirement on the part of industrial workers. Most current retirees did not wait to be "forced" into leaving the work force.

Adjusting to retirement is seldom easy. Adequate finances, good health, and social activities may positively affect adjustment to retirement. Some gerontologists believe that retirement necessarily brings an "identity crisis." Others argue that self-respect can be gained from leisure pursuits. In the future, retirement is likely to become an issue that is salient to the experiences of older women, as well.

Finally, although older people seem to prefer solitary leisure activities, it may be that most older people simply have more practice with such activities. Americans need to be educated for leisure, and this should begin early in life. Leisure needs to be placed in a life-course perspective. Doing so may help identify structural factors useful for explaining age-based differentials in leisure and recreational participation.

STUDY QUESTIONS

1. Discuss the social conditions necessary for the emergence of retirement as a social institution.

2. In what types of jobs are older workers likely to be employed? How did the occupational distribution of the elderly work force change during the twentieth century?

3. Discuss the relationship between health status and retirement.

4. Discuss age discrimination in employment in the United States, with emphasis on the Age Discrimination Employment Act. Why are age discrimination cases sometimes more difficult to prove than race or sex discrimination?

5. Within a historical context, describe changing attitudes toward retirement in the United States.

6. Discuss the many social and psychological factors that contribute to or detract from adjustment to retirement.

7. Compare and contrast the *identity crisis* and *identity continuity* theories of adjustment to retirement.

8. Explain why leisure time can actually create problems for older people. What can older people do to prepare for more effective use of their leisure time?

REFERENCES

Achenbaum, W. A. (1978). *Old age in the new land.* Baltimore, MD: John Hopkins University Press.

Ash, P. (1966). Pre-retirement counseling. *Gerontologist, 6,* 97–99, 127–128.

Atchley, R. (1971). Retirement and leisure partici-pation: Continuity or crisis. *Gerontologist, 11,* 13–17.

Atchley, R. (1974). The meaning of retirement. *Journal of Communication, 24,* 97–100.

Atchley, R. (1976). *The sociology of retirement.* New York: Halsted.

Beck, B. (1996, January 27). The economics of age-ing. *The Economist,* pp. 2–16.

Beck, S. H. (1982). Adjustment to and satisfaction with retirement. *Journal of Gerontology, 37* (5), 616–624.

Beck, S. H. (1984). Retirement preparation pro-grams: Differentials in opportunity and use. *Journal of Gerontology, 39,* 596–602.

Biesele, M., & Howell, N. (1981). The old people give you life: Aging among !Kung hunter-gathers. In P. T. Amoss & S. Harrell (Eds.), *Other ways of growing old: Anthropological perspectives.* Stan-ford, CA: Stanford University Press.

Boaz, R. F. (1987). Work as a response to low and decreasing real income during retirement. *Re-search on Aging, 9* (3), 428–440.

Bowen, W., & Finegan, T. (1969). *The economics of labor force participation.* Princeton, NJ: Prince-ton University Press.

Butler, R. (1975). *Why survive? Being old in America.* New York: Harper & Row.

Calasanti, T. M. (1996). Gender and life satisfaction in retirement: An assessment of the male model. *Journal of Gerontology: Social Sciences, 51B* (1), S18–29.

Calhoun, R. (1978). *In search of the new old.* New York: Elsevier.

Campione, W. A. (1987). The married woman's re-tirement decision: A methodological compar-ison. *Journal of Gerontology, 42* (4), 381–386.

Campione, W. A. (1988). Predicting participation in retirement preparation programs. *Journal of Gerontology, 43* (3), S91–S95.

Cohen, W. (1957). *Retirement policies under Social Secu-rity.* Berkeley: University of California Press.

Collins, G. (1987, December 15). Wanted: Child-care workers, age 55 and up. *The New York Times,* pp. 1, 8.

Cutler, S. J., & Hendricks, J. (1990). Leisure and time use across the life course. In R. H. Bin-stock & L. K. George (Eds.), *Handbook of aging and the social sciences* (3rd ed.). San Diego, CA: Academic.

Donahue, W., Orbach, H., & Pollak, O. (1960). Re-tirement: The emerging pattern. In C. Tibbitts (Ed.), *Handbook of social gerontology.* Chicago: University of Chicago Press.

Dorfman, L. T., & Moffett, M. M. (1987). Retirement satisfaction in married and widowed rural women. *Gerontologist, 27* (2), 215–221.

Drucker, P. (1971). What can we learn from Japa-nese management? *Harvard Business Review, 49,* 110–122.

Ekerdt, D., & DeViney, S. (1993). Evidence for a preretirement process among older male workers. *Journal of Gerontology: Social Sciences, 48,* S35–S43.

Ekerdt, D. J., Vinick, B. H., & Bosse, R. (1989). Or-derly endings: Do men know when they will retire? *Journal of Gerontology, 44* (1), 528–535.

Evans, L., Ekerdt, D. J., & Bosse, R. (1985). Prox-imity to retirement and anticipatory in-volvement: Findings from the Normative Aging Study. *Journal of Gerontology, 40* (3), 368–374.

Fullerton, H. N. (1997a, September). Evaluating the 1995 labor force projections. *Monthly Labor Review,* pp. 5–9.

Fullerton, H. N. (1997b, November). Labor force 2006: Slowing down and changing composi-tion. *Monthly Labor Review,* pp. 23–38.

Gendell, M. (1998, August). Trends in retirement age in four countries, 1965–1995. *Monthly Labor Review,* pp. 20–30.

Gibson, R. C. (1987). Reconceptualizing retirement for black Americans. *Gerontologist, 27* (6), 691–698.

Gibson, R. C. (1991). The subjective retirement of black Americans. *Journal of Gerontology, 46* (4), S204–S209.

Glamser, F. D. (1981). The impact of preretirement programs on the retirement experience. *Jour-nal of Gerontology, 36* (2), 244–250.

Goldberg, D. (1978). Mandatory retirement and the older worker. *Aging and Work, 1,* 264–267.

Gordon, C., Gaitz, C. M., & Scott, J. (1976). Leisure and lives: Personal expressivity across the life span. In R. H. Binstock & E. Shanas (Eds.), *Handbook of aging and the social sciences.* New York: Van Nostrand Reinhold.

Hayward, M. D., Friedman, S., & Chen, H. (1996). Race inequities in men's retirement. *Journal of Gerontology: Social Sciences, 51B,* 1, S1–S10.

Hodson, R., & Sullivan, T. A. (1990). *The social orga-nization of work.* Belmont, CA: Wadsworth.

Holmes, L. (1972). The role and status of the aged in changing Samoa. In D. Cowgill & L. Holmes (Eds.), *Aging and modernization.* En-glewood Cliffs, NJ: Prentice-Hall.

Israel, J. (1971). *Alienation: From Marx to modern soci-ology.* Boston: Allyn and Bacon.

Kasschau, P. (1976). Perceived age discrimination in a sample of aerospace employees. *Gerontologist, 18,* 166–173.

Kelly, J. R. (1987). *Peoria winter: Styles and resources in later life.* Lexington, MA: D. C. Heath.

Kelly, J. R., Steinkamp, M. W., & Kelly, J. R. (1987). Later life satisfaction: Does leisure contribute? *Leisure Sciences, 9,* 189–200.

Kingson, E. (1981). Involuntary early retirement. *Journal of the Institute for Socioeconomic Studies, 6* (3), 27–39.

Kotlikoff, L. J., & Wise, D. A. (1989). *The wage carrot and pension stick.* Kalamazoo, MI: W. E. Upjohn Institute.

Long, C. D. (1958). *The Labor force under changing conditions of income and employment.* Princeton, NJ: Princeton University Press.

McEvoy, G. M., & Cascio, W. F. (1989). Cumulative evidence of the relationship between employee age and job performance. *Journal of Applied Psychology, 74* (1), 11–17.

Meyer, M. H. (1990). Family status and poverty among older women: The gendered distribution of retirement income in the United States. *Social Problems, 37,* 551–563.

Midanik, L. T., Soghikian, K., Ransom, L. J., & Tekawa, I. S. (1995). The effect of retirement on mental health and health behaviors: The Kaiser Permanent Retirement Study. *Journal of Gerontology: Social Sciences, 50B,* (1), S59–S61.

Miller, S. (1965). The social dilemmas of the aging leisure participant. In A. Rose & W. Peterson (Eds.), *Older people and their social world.* Philadelphia: F. A. Davis.

Mutchler, J. E., Burr, J. A., Pienta, A. M., & Massagali, M. P. (1997). Pathways to labor force exit: Work transitions and work instability. *Journal of Gerontology: Social Sciences, 52B* (1), S4–S12.

Mutran, E., Reitzes, D. C., Bratton, K. A., & Fernandez, M. E. (1997). Self-esteem and subjective responses to work among mature workers: Similarities and differences by gender. *Journal of Gerontology, 52B* (2), S89–S96.

Palmore, E. (1975). *The honorable elders.* Durham, NC: Duke University Press.

Parnes, H., Adams, A. V., Andrisani, P. J., Kohen, A. I., & Nestel, G. (1975). *The pre-retirement years. Volume 4. A longitudinal study of the labor market experience of men.* U.S. Department of Labor, Manpower Research and Development Monograph No. 15. Washington, DC: U.S. Government Printing Office.

Patton, C. (1977). Early retirement in academia: Making the decision. *Gerontologist, 17* (4), 347–354.

Quadagno, J., & Hardy, M. (1996). Work and retirement. In R. H. Binstock & L. K. George (Eds.), *Handbook of aging and the social sciences* (4th ed.). San Diego, CA: Academic.

Reitzes, D. C., Mutran, E., & Fernandez, M. E. (1996). Preretirement influences on postretirement self-esteem. *Gerontologist, 51B,* 5, S242–S249.

Riley, M. W. (1987). On the significance of age in sociology. *American Sociological Review, 52,* 1–14.

Riley, M. W., & Foner, A. (1968). *Aging and society. Volume One: An inventory of research findings.* New York: Russell Sage Foundation.

Ruhm, C. J. (1996). Gender differences in employment behavior during late middle age. *Journal of Gerontology: Social Sciences, 51B* (1), S11–S17.

Santiago, A. M., & Muschkin, C. G. (1996). Disentangling the effects of disability status and gender on the labor supply of Anglo, Black, and Latino older workers. *Gerontologist, 36* (3), 299–310.

Schnore, M. M., & Kirkland, J. B. (1981). *Sex differences in adjustment to retirement.* Paper presented at joint meetings of the Canadian Association of Gerontology and the Gerontological Society of America, Toronto, Ontario.

Schulz, J. (1995). *The economics of aging* (6th ed.). New York: Auburn House.

Slavick, F. (1966). *Compulsory and flexible retirement in the American economy.* Ithaca, NY: Cornell University Press.

Snow, R., & Havighurst, R. (1977). Life style types and patterns of retirement of educators. *Gerontologist, 17* (6), 545–552.

Steers, R. M., & Porter, L. W. (1983). *Motivation and work behavior.* New York: McGraw-Hill.

Sum, A., & Fong, W. N. (1990). Profile of the labor market for older workers. In P. Doeringer (Ed.), *Bridges to retirement: Older workers in a changing labor market.* Ithaca, NY: ILR Press.

Terkel, S. (1972). *Working: People talk about what they do all day and how they feel about what they do.* New York: Random House.

Thompson, G. (1973). Work versus leisure roles: An investigation of moral among employed and retired men. *Journal of Gerontology, 28,* 339–344.

U.S. Bureau of the Census, (1998). *Statistical abstract of the United States, 1998* (118th ed.). Washington, DC: U.S. Government Printing Office.

U.S. Senate, Select Committee on Aging. (1981). *The early retirement myth: Why men retire before age 62*. Washington, DC: U.S. Government Printing Office.

U.S. Senate, Special Committee on Aging. (1987–1988). *Aging America: Trends and projections, 1987–88 edition*. Washington, DC: U.S. Government Printing Office.

Ventrell-Monsees, C. (1991). Enforce the age discriminations laws. In A. Munnell (Ed.), *Re-tirement and public policy*. Washington, DC: National Academy of Social Insurance.

Wray, L. A. (1996). The role of ethnicity in the disability and work experience of preretire-ment-age Americans. *Gerontologist, 36* (3), 287–298.

CHAPTER THIRTEEN

THE POLITICS OF AGING

This chapter takes the view that age issues have become a substantial element in U.S. politics in recent years. Demographic trends already in place suggest that many future political issues are likely to be centered on questions of age. Do old people stick together in their voting attitudes and behavior? Will long-standing bases of political conflict, such as race and social class, be superseded by questions of age? Have old people become a favored political constituency in the United States? What is the future of the political economy of aging? These important questions have only recently become substantive concerns for gerontologists. Some of these questions have fragmentary and incomplete answers; on others, a growing body of literature is emerging.

Before beginning a discussion of these questions and of the answers emerging in the gerontological literature, it seems useful to remind readers of the discussion in Chapter 2 about the age/period/cohort problem. Interpretation of the political attitudes and behavior of older people involves the ability to understand and elicit the effects of the distinct perspectives represented by these three concepts (Hudson & Binstock 1976):

1. One must consider the possibility that the political attitudes and behavior of older persons can be explained by developmental patterns inherent in the processes of human aging. This consideration describes what could be called the *age effect*.
2. One must look at the possibility that changes in the political attitudes and behaviors of older people simply mirror the impact of historical or period effects on an entire population. If older people have become more conservative over a period of time, perhaps this tendency can be explained by showing that people in *all* age groups have become more conservative over the time period examined. This describes the *period effect*.
3. It is possible that the political attitudes and behaviors of older people result from the shared experiences and perceptions of a particular older generation. This perspective describes the *cohort effect*.

Only recently has gerontological research used quantitative techniques to distinguish among these three analytical perspectives effectively. Much of the work discussed in this chapter overlooks this important methodological and conceptual

351

problem. Nevertheless, the reader must not be insensitive to these issues, as the chapter begins with a discussion of the relationship between political participation and age.

POLITICAL PARTICIPATION AND AGE

Voting Behavior

A basic indication of participation in the political process is voting behavior. A variety of factors affect an individual's voting participation. Reviewing census data since 1980 for presidential and congressional elections, it seems that women were somewhat more likely to vote than were men, and those with more education voted more frequently than those with low levels of education.

Table 13.1 presents data on voting behavior by age, race, sex, region, employment status, and education for the United States in the 1996 presidential election. Race, employment status, education, and age seem the most important contributors to variation in voting behavior in 1996. Whites were more likely to report voting than were African Americans (56.0 vs. 50.6 percent, respectively), and more than twice as likely to vote as those of Latino origin (26.7 percent). The employed were about 50 percent more likely to vote than the unemployed (55.2 vs. 37.2 percent, respectively). Interestingly, however, the proportion of those reporting they voted among the employed was only slightly greater than the proportion voting among those who were not in the labor force (e.g., retirees, among others). College graduates report voting at a higher rate in the 1996 presidential election than any other group (73.0 percent).

The proportion of individuals reporting they voted in the 1996 presidential election is lowest in the youngest two age groups. Voter participation increases with successive age levels until old age. This pattern seems consistent with generalizations about the relationship between chronological age and voting behavior made by students of political since the 1960s.

Interest in politics seems to increase steadily with age in the United States. Jennings and Markus (1988) employ a theory of selective withdrawal and augmentation that may help explain the relationship between age and voting exhibited in Table 13.1. This theory suggests that older individuals may reduce some forms of participation while expanding others or substituting new activities for previous ones. Thus, the elderly may participate in fewer demanding, high-energy forms of political behavior, including being active in political campaigns, but actually engage in more low-intensity activity, such as voting.

Binstock and Day (1996) offer that the high level of political interest among the elderly in the United States may be a function of both life-course and cohort effects. For example, younger people are typically not as well integrated into the communities in which they reside as are mature and older adults. And the concerns of early adulthood, finishing school, raising children, and building careers may predominate. Those who own homes, have families, enroll children in the

TABLE 13.1   Voting-Age Population, and Percentage Reporting Registered and Voted, 1996 Presidential Election

CHARACTERISTIC	VOTING-AGE POPULATION (MILLION)	PERCENTAGE REPORTING THEY REGISTERED	PERCENTAGE REPORTING THEY VOTED
Total	193.7	65.9%	54.3%
18–20 years old	10.8	45.6	31.2
21–24 years old	13.9	51.2	33.4
25–34 years old	40.1	56.9	43.1
35–44 years old	43.3	66.5	54.9
45–64 years old	53.7	73.5	70.0
65 years old and over	31.9	77.0	70.1
Male	92.6	64.4	52.8
Female	101.0	67.3	55.5
White	162.8	67.7	56.0
African American	22.5	63.5	50.6
Hispanic	18.4	35.7	26.7
Northeast	38.3	64.7	54.5
Midwest	45.2	71.6	59.3
South	68.1	65.9	52.2
West	42.1	60.8	51.8
8 yrs or less of school	14.1	40.7	28.1
1–3 years high school	21.0	47.9	33.8
4 years high school	65.2	62.2	49.1
1–3 years college	50.9	72.9	60.5
4 yrs or more of college	42.5	80.4	73.0
Employed	125.6	67.0	55.2
Unemployed	6.4	52.5	37.2
Not in labor force	61.6	65.1	54.1

Source: Statistical Abstract of the United States, 1997, 117th ed. (Washington, DC: U.S. Bureau of the Census, 1997), Table 462.

local schools, and pay local taxes may be more affected by political issues (both local and national) and thus are more likely to vote. As children grow up, become more independent, and leave home, mature and older adults may have more available leisure time to become active in the political process. Finally, although most older people are in good health with little activity limitation, age does bring an increased risk of deterioration in mental and physical health. The greater likelihood of experiencing a health impairment later in the life cycle may be associated with reduced participation in a variety of forms of social behavior, including the political process. This final point makes the high rate of voting among older adults even more impressive. We have suggested in the previous chapter that older people may spend more time in leisure pursuits of a passive nature, such as reading and/or watching television, and this may help explain their attentiveness to current events and politics. This attentiveness likely promotes their high participation rates in voting.

Active Participation in Politics

Voting is a relatively passive form of political participation, occurring infrequently and requiring minimal effort on the part of an individual. It is a far cry from active involvement in the political process through community or campaign activity. Two often cited investigations of older people's political involvement have been carried out by Verba and Nie (1972) and Nie, Verba, and Kim (1974). In general, these authors find (1) that the level of older people's participation in the political process is higher than the population average and (2) that when variation in socioeconomic status is controlled for, older people show even higher participation scores. In fact, when this variation is controlled for, these authors find the peak period of political activity to occur in the sixth decade of life.

Verba and Nie (1972) created a political participation typology and looked to the distribution of those age 65 and over across the six types in this categorization schema. The six types are as follows:

1. *Inactives:* No political activity
2. *Voting specialists:* Regular voters
3. *Parochial participants:* Those who make occasional contact with a public official
4. *Communalists:* Those working actively in community organizations
5. *Campaigners:* Those working actively around campaigns, including working for a party or a candidate and contributing money
6. *Complete activists:* Those highly involved in each of the preceding activities

The aged were found to be overrepresented among the *inactives,* the *voting specialists,* and the *parochial participants.* They were moderately underrepresented among the *communalists* and the *campaigners* and highly underrepresented as *complete activists.* Data reported by Nie, Verba, and Kim (1974) provide some support in a cross-national context for the findings presented here.

Jennings and Markus (1988) examined the political involvement of middle-aged and elderly respondents in a three-wave panel with data collected in 1965, 1973, and 1982. They attributed some of the decline among older people in such political activities as campaign work and meeting attendance to period effects—a general decline in participation of adults of all ages during this time—and life-course effects—a decline in belief that one can influence the political process that appears to be a consequence of aging. Still, as Binstock and Day (1996) point out in the contemporary period, not all forms of political activity decline with age. Contacting public officials by mail and/or telephone is a demanding form of political participation engaged in by older people at the same rate as the nonelderly. These activities can be carried out within the quiet of one's own home. As it turns out, older people, who are the beneficiaries of many government programs, have valid reasons for staying in contact with their governmental representatives.

Approximately 1,500 Americans 18 years of age and older were interviewed by the National Opinion Research Center (NORC) for the 1991 General Social Survey <http://www.norc.uchicago.edu>. Respondents were asked how much confidence they had in the executive branch of the federal government and whether they believed government should do more or less. For purposes of presentation here, respondents were divided into three approximately equal-sized age groups: 18 to 34 years, 35 to 54 years, and 55 years and older. In general, older people pay more attention to government and public affairs than do the young; they are more vigorous consumers of news and current-affairs radio and TV programming, for example. Only 22.5 percent of the older respondents reported having complete or a great deal of confidence in the executive branch of the federal government, although this was the highest percentage among the three age groups; 16.9 percent of the younger adults and 13.2 percent of the middle-aged reported similarly.

Political Leadership

Perhaps the most intense form of political participation involves occupying an office or holding a position of political leadership. It is widely believed that persons in late middle age and old age disproportionately occupy positions of leadership in the United States and other advanced industrial nations. The continuing visibility of national political leaders—such as Chief Justice of the Supreme Court William Renquist (born in 1924) and North Carolina Senator Jesse Helms (born in 1921), Chair of the U.S. Senate's Foreign Relations Committee—provide support for these beliefs. In a wide variety of political contexts in the United States (e.g., presidents, senators, U.S. representatives, governors, Supreme Court justices, U.S. ambassadors, and cabinet members), positions of political leadership have been held by relatively old persons. In the 97th Congress (1981), 20 percent (20/100) of the senators and 15.4 percent (67/435) of the representatives were 60 years of age or over. Just 14 years later, the 104th Congress (1995) showed substantial increases in the number of members of the United States Senate (34/100) age 60 or over and the number of U.S. representatives (92/435) 60 years of age or older.

Lammers and Nyomarkay (1980) have shown a changing age pattern among the appointees to cabinet-level positions in five advanced industrial nations, including the United States. These authors find a growing concentration of middle-aged cabinet members, with aging populations increasingly underrepresented in the political leadership in these five nations. Through the 1950s, the general pattern was clearly toward overrepresentation. By the 1960s (and through the 1970s), a significant and uniform shift had taken place: The underrepresentation of the elderly in cabinet positions has been the case in every country.

How do Lammers and Nyomarkay (1980) explain the increasing underrepresentation of the aged in the leadership groups of these advanced industrial societies? One answer is found in greater bureaucratization, which has caused career patterns to become more routinized. This has brought a more focused age structure, resulting in the exclusion of older cabinet appointees and a greater uniformity of ages at time of appointment and departure. Also, *gerontocracy,* or rule by older people, may be more common in traditional or folk societies than in modern societies, and the research by Lammers and Nyomarkay focused on Canada, France, the United Kingdom, Germany, and the United States.

As Guttmann (1988) points out, older people are more likely to rise to top leadership positions in stable as opposed to revolutionary societies, and their attainment of leadership positions is most often related to an accumulation of experience and resources that comes with age.

Do the aged suffer as a function of underrepresentation in leadership positions? It is certainly possible that more youthful leaders will develop an identification with the problems of old age, perhaps out of a belief that they constitute a significant voting bloc. On the other hand, if it is true that "the wearer is the best judge of the shoe," then there are fewer individuals who both directly experience the vagaries of aging and are directly responsible for making public policy that affects the aged.

POLITICAL ORIENTATIONS AND ATTITUDES OF OLDER PERSONS

One indicator of political orientation is party affiliation. As Table 13.2 shows, people of all age groups report more identification with the Democratic party than with the Republican party. And, although identification as a Republican ap-

TABLE 13.2   Political Party Identification of the Adult Population by Age: 1994

AGE	TOTAL	DEMOCRAT[1]	REPUBLICAN[2]	INDEPENDENT	APOLITICAL
Under 25 yrs old	100	51	37	10	1
25–34 yrs	100	44	43	12	1
35–44 yrs	100	45	43	12	–
45–54 yrs	100	46	45	7	1
55–64 yrs	100	48	43	8	–
65–74 yrs	100	51	42	9	–
75–99 yrs	100	54	35	9	2

[1]Includes those who identify as weak Democrat, strong Democrat, and independent Democrat.
[2]Includes those who identify as weak Republican, strong Republican, and independent Republican.

Source: Statistical Abstract of the United States, 1997, 117th ed. (Washington DC: U.S. Bureau of the Census, 1997), Table 461.

pears *not* to change between 25 and 74 yeas of age, in general, the older cohorts (those 55 and over) show more identification as Democrats than do younger cohorts. Older people report less identification as Independents than do those under 44 years of age. Does this mean that aging brings with it conversion to the Democratic party? Hardly. What seems more likely is that the association between the Democratic party and aging is a function of cohort or generational differences. Thus, it is possible that early socialization experiences have made many of today's aged cohorts (those 65 years and older) Democrats.

Although a disproportionate number of older people, compared with the young, say they identify with the Democratic party, a view persists that older people are more politically conservative than are the young. Is this the case? Campbell and Strate have addressed this question while analyzing data from 14 American National Election Studies <http://www.umich.edu/~nes> collected by the Center for Political Studies at the University of Michigan from 1952 to 1980. After using a variety of measures of political attitudes available in these studies, these authors warn against facile generalizations:

> If one takes these results as a whole a general conclusion does emerge. The political orientations of older people are not peculiar. Knowing that someone is old will not help very much in predicting how conservative he or she is, in most important respects. The elderly are very much in the mainstream of American political opinions. (1981, pp. 590–591)

Cutler and colleagues (1980) have studied this issue by examining the relationship between age and attitudes about legalized abortion. They found that, if controls for cohort differences are employed, little variation exists among the different age groups. Looking at changes over time in specific cohorts, they found that people who are now old had more conservative views when they were younger than currently younger cohorts do, but that their attitudes have become more liberalized at the same rate as those of the younger group. Cross-national studies of social and political values suggest that, when generational differences in value orientation are identified, they are due to cultural and environmental conditions affecting the socialization of particular age cohorts, and not to universal life-course changes (Ingelhart 1977).

Are old people more conservative? Aging per se does not appear to bring with it a set of conservative positions on prominent political issues. Yet, a different set of self-interests may be associated with age than with youth. In this respect, the answer to the original question (Are old people more conservative?) would seem to be both yes and no!

According to Binstock and Day (1996), older voters departed from their usual pattern in the 1992 presidential election. Using data from the Portrait of the Electorate (1992), they describe that the elderly voted for Republican George Bush in the same proportion as did other age groups, but they voted for Democrat Bill Clinton at a higher rate and for Independent Ross Perot at a lower rate than did younger voters. One explanation is that older voters did not take the Perot candidacy seriously.

Another is that their greater attachment to traditional political institutions make them less supportive of independent parties, regardless of the candidate.

ARE THE AGED A FAVORED CONSTITUENCY?

The aged have been a favored social welfare constituency in the United States; that is, across the last 35 years or so, older persons have done relatively well in the arena of public policy in comparison with other population groups whose needs can be argued to be equally pressing. Binstock and Day (1996) report that over 100 national organizations, mass membership groups, as well as organizations of professionals and service providers, are focused on aging policies and concerns. Many of these groups also have local chapters. Among the largest and/or most well known are the American Association of Retired Persons (AARP) (35 million members), the National Council for Senior Citizens <http://www.ncscinc.org> (5 million members), and the Gray Panthers (40,000 members) <http://graypanthers.org/home.htm>.

Federal programs benefitting the elderly are plentiful. The program categories represented include employment and volunteer, health care, housing, income maintenance, social services, training and research, and transportation. Virtually every agency in the executive branch and many independent agencies are represented. Many of these programs involve mandatory spending at the federal level. For example, mandatory spending accounts for approximately 56 percent of net federal outlays for fiscal year 1995, including Social Security retirement benefits and Medicare. Total federal expenditures on aging comprise more than one-third of the budget and approach twice the percentage of expenditures on defense.

Robert Hudson (1978) of Brandeis University distinguishes between breakthrough and constituency-building policy enactments that may bring favored status to a special-interest group. ***Breakthrough policies*** consist of those pieces of legislation that involve the federal government in providing or guaranteeing some fundamental benefit. ***Constituency-building policies*** are those that recognize that different groups have common interests and give these interest groups a voice in the making of public policy. The aged have been the principal beneficiaries and most functional constituency in the federal government's involvement in breakthrough legislation to ensure health care financing for high-risk populations (Medicare and Medicaid) and to guarantee minimum income for the impoverished (e.g., Supplemental Security Income).

Still, several commentators have described the differential success of federal intervention on behalf of the elderly. Kutza (1981) points out that nonwhite older persons and older women have not shared in the gains experienced by other elderly in this recent period of concentrated assistance provided to older people. Hess (1983) has also identified what she describes as a gerontological "gender gap" in the application of federal programs to the elderly. Three areas where older women are especially disadvantaged are income, health, and housing. Hess argues that "public programs have been shaped by assumptions based on the life experience of men...Yet, not only are the real problems of old age disproportionately experienced by women, but it is women who are increasingly expected to bear the brunt of dealing with these problems."

Despite a recognition of the differential impact of public-policy efforts for the elderly, there is currently considerable debate about the economic costs of this favored status for the elderly. This may be part of a resistance to social welfare expenditures in general. Some writers see the costs of programs for the elderly as the dominant factor shaping federal spending and taxing decisions. In 1992, one analyst characterizing the cost of an aging America offered that "the tyranny of America's old...is one of the most crucial issues facing U.S. society" (Smith 1992, p. 68). Such characterizations deserve careful scrutiny.

Spending for Social Security and Medicare alone amounted to about one-quarter (25.5 percent) of the federal budget in 1980; by fiscal year 1995, this figure had increased to about 34 percent of outlays in the federal budget. If, as some suggest, expenditures for Social Security and Medicare represent 80 percent of all federal spending for the elderly, then the outlay of programs for the elderly represented about 42 percent of the 1995 federal budget.

There will be continued pressure on the federal budget in coming years. By 1990, federal outlays for Social Security and Medicare alone had more than doubled from 1980 (an increase of about 133 percent) and accounted for more than the entire outlay of federal spending for the elderly in that year. By 1993, these expenditures had increased another 26 percent. Although the continuing strong U.S. economy has created surpluses in the federal budget, the memory of regular annual federal deficits will not fade easily. As a result, the prevalent political scenario would seem to be one of continuing resistance to increases in federal spending and continued pressure to reduce federal taxes. A literature has evolved on issues of intergenerational equity and what exactly the generations may owe to each other (e.g., Bengtson & Achenbaum 1993). The publicity received by various organizations concerned with so-called intergenerational justice, and the work of advocacy groups for children, education, the homeless and other constituencies, suggest that any restructuring of the federal budget will likely occur through politics and not the academic literature. The specter of these needy and powerful political interest groups battling for scarce federal dollars is not inviting, but it is one that many policy analysts consider will become a reality.

The view that "greedy geezers" are busting the budget and accounting for too large a proportion of federal expenditures need not be subscribed to by all. After all, for example, the Social Security program provides income to many millions of younger men, women, and children as part of its dependents', survivors', and disability programs. Over seven million people alone received survivor benefits in 1990 under Social Security. By 1993, about 38 percent of Social Security recipients were *not* themselves retired workers, but rather included workers who are disabled, wives and husbands of retired workers or workers with disabilities, and the children of retirees and of workers who are deceased or disabled.

In addition, remember that workers "buy in" to Social Security (as do employers): To include employee contributions when computing government expenditures on behalf of the aged makes little sense. Beyond simply confusing matters, it creates the impression that Social Security is just another government welfare program, rather than a return of money put aside during the course of a person's working years. This holds true as well for the Federal Civil Service Retirement System; redistributed employee contributions should not be counted as government expenditures. Playing hocus pocus with the federal budget figures creates the impression that the elderly are receiving lavish treatment from the federal government. This is clearly not the case; as we have reported earlier, about 10 percent of the U.S. aged have incomes below the poverty level, and this percentage increases about 2.5 times for aged blacks and Latinos. The proportion in near-poverty is substantial, as well.

Butler (1978) takes a different tack. He suggests that the discussion over expenditures in the federal budget for the elderly is misdirected—a case of blaming the victims. Butler makes three important points:

1. The need for all those dollars in retirement systems might be lessened somewhat if people were not pressured to leave the work force while they are still able and willing to continue working. If people were free to continue working after age 65 or 70, as is now the case by law, they could continue to contribute to retirement systems, and the budget would become less menacing.

2. A considerable proportion of the federal budget reflects the existence of illness and disability in the aged population. What if one could identify the biomedical and socioenvironmental factors that produce illness and disability and that prompt people to retire? If these illness factors could be minimized in any way, it would reduce expenditures made through the Medicare and Medicaid programs.

3. Government expenditures for health care services have increased dramatically in recent years. Nevertheless, the elderly now pay as much out of pocket for health care as they did before Medicare. To what extent is the increasing cost of health care to be attributed to the elderly? To what extent should it be attributed to the providers of health care services?

What are the political consequences of this debate over federal expenditures for the elderly? Will proposed funding for programs for the aged face opposition in the future? Can the aged mobilize political pressure to serve their interests? Proposals such as those offered by Butler get little attention today in the popular media and press. More fashionable are proposals to ration health care for older people, most of which is financed through government programs, as a means for reducing health care costs and providing care to other groups, such as poor children (Callahan 1987; Preston 1984).

ARE THE ELDERLY A POLITICAL FORCE?

One commonly held image of the aged is as a political force capable of playing interest-group politics. Political scientist Robert Binstock, former president of the

Gerontological Society of America, believes this image to be inaccurate, though nurtured by several aging-based membership organizations:

> There is little reason to believe that a phenomenon termed "senior power" will significantly increase the proportion of the budget devoted to the aging, or redirect that portion of the budget toward solving the problems of the severely disadvantaged. Whatever senior power exists is held by organizations that cannot swing decisive voting blocs. (Binstock 1978, p. 1844)

Binstock's assessment of the senior lobby has changed only slightly in recent years. He suggests that the proliferation of old-age interest groups has mostly followed, rather than preceded and/or influenced, the creation of major governmental programs for the elderly. Further, he argues that the power of these interest groups is mostly defensive, "aimed at protecting existing programs and fighting tax hikes" (Binstock & Day 1996, p. 373).

One reason the image of senior power persists lies in the belief that the elderly are a homogeneous group and thus a homogeneous political constituency. This is simply not the case. The elderly are as heterogeneous politically as they are socially and economically. Binstock argues that most older voters do not primarily identify themselves, and hence their self-interests, in terms of aging. When a

Many older people are actively involved in the political process through community and campaign activity.

person reaches age 65, retires, or is widowed, he or she does not suddenly lose all prior self-identities; self-interest is still derived from race, education, religion, community ties, and so on.

Not everyone sees senior power as illusory, however. Pratt (1976) notes that the elderly have come to expect some degree of income security as well as adequate health care. Theirs may be a revolution of rising expectations. Pratt cites the 1971 White House Conference on Aging as the watershed for old-age political influence. Through the Conference, he argues, national groups such as the National Retired Teachers Association (NRTA) <http://www.aarp.org/nrta/nrtahome.htm>, the American Association of Retired Persons (AARP), and the National Council of Senior Citizens (NCSC) developed the political acumen necessary for effecting legislation that benefits the aged. Pratt credits the NCSC with helping to formulate and pass the Social Security Amendments of 1972. These amendments pegged increases in Social Security benefits to the rate of inflation and replaced welfare programs for the aged, blind, and disabled with SSI. Williamson and Pampel (1993) offer evidence to conclude that old-age interest groups have become important factors in the formation of aging policy in other developed industrial nations, as well.

Can an old-age political movement become institutionalized? According to Achenbaum (1983), such a "gray lobby" would differ from other interest groups in at least two important ways. First, there are ideological and political schisms within and among the organizations that purport to represent and work for the elderly. Second, the gray lobby is the only interest group to which every American can hope to aspire. Hence, it is especially important for leaders of these organizational entities to weigh the future ramifications of current policy decisions. What looks good in the short run may have devastating implications for the elderly in future decades.

Hudson (1987) sees great potential surrounding the organization of a political agenda "of and for the able elderly." Presumably, the *able elderly* are those not frail, not in poverty, and not dependent; the concept captures a growing number of older people who are integrated, vigorous, affluent, and well. They constitute a political and economic generation "caught between the demands of a frailer generation ahead of it and the pressures of a command generation behind it" (p. 406). Still, as Hudson correctly notes, formalizing the concept of the able elderly and organizing a political agenda around this group creates potential problems for the less able old as well as for those who may properly be described as able. For example, in the area of employment, the concept of an able elderly highlights the contradiction between the desire to eliminate mandatory retirement rules (and thus allow older workers to continue in place) and to take early retirement. In areas such as income support and medical care, the improved education and economic status associated with being able is likely to bring new proposals. These would include self- and private financing of pension and health benefits, as well as the imposition of more means-tested and needs-tested standards to better target services for the elderly.

How willing will current and future aged be to identify themselves as old? The development of a widespread ***aging group consciousness*** would bring recognition among the elderly of their common interests. As Hudson (1987) notes, the development of an aging group consciousness may have important consequences beyond helping to create and sustain an old-age political movement. Not the least of these would be a lessening of the stigmatization and isolation of the aged, the maintenance of self-esteem, and a viewing of intergenerational policy proposals in a more favorable light (Wisensale 1988).

THE FUTURE OF OLD-AGE POLITICS: AGE VERSUS NEED ENTITLEMENT

Much of the material contained in this book is aimed at describing a new set of realities regarding the aged and the aging. In general, it has been argued that many of the conditions prevalent in the early part of the twentieth century led one to see old age as a social problem (e.g., incapacity, isolation, and poverty). These conditions have changed dramatically as a result of collective political action that took the form of governmental legislation to create programs of income maintenance, housing, transportation, health services, social services, and tax benefits.

In creating these programs, which emanated from real concern about the welfare of older people, chronological age was used as a convenient indicator of need. Remember that older people in the United States were seen as a homogeneous population. Even through the 1950s and 1960s, they were described as poor and lacking in access to health services and the like. As Neugarten (1982) indicates, programs based on age eligibility did catch a large proportion of persons in need. Today, however, the situation is different. The elderly are a heterogeneous group, in many respects indistinguishable from the general population. For example, the proportion of those 65 years and over with incomes below the poverty line is approximately the same as the proportion of the total population with incomes below the poverty line. Further, some subpopulations of the aged that have been differentially advantaged by governmental programs remain relatively disadvantaged despite these programs.

Rather than emphasizing the special disadvantages of minority elderly and older women, Nelson (1982) examines the relationship between social class and public policy for the elderly. Essentially, he argues that government programs for the aged act to perpetuate the existence of socioeconomic differences among the elderly that existed prior to old age, and this argument appears to hold up almost 20 years after Nelson originally made it. According to Nelson, three classes of elderly beneficiaries of governmental initiatives can be identified:

1. The marginal elderly
2. The downwardly mobile elderly
3. The integrated elderly

Each class of elderly receives a different level of support that, in total, serves to sustain the social class inequalities that were present prior to the experience of old age. We will briefly describe these three classes of elderly and exemplify how government provides different levels of support for the different classes:

1. *Marginal elderly:* The marginal elderly are characterized by absolute need and poverty. For most of them, poverty in old age is a continuation of a life of poverty. They are more likely to be living alone, female, minority, and old-old. Their work careers were in unskilled, semiskilled, or domestic labor that has been transient or interrupted during the adult years. Many such jobs were not covered by Social Security or other pension programs. These individuals represent the truly needy.

2. *Downwardly mobile elderly:* This class of elderly corresponds most closely to those who were considered middle class or lower-middle class prior to old age. The downwardly mobile elderly experience need as a sense of relative deprivation. They are trying to maintain a preretirement life-style on more limited resources. Some are at risk of falling into poverty. They may prevent this by using available sources of public support.

3. *Integrated elderly:* These individuals are presumed to be continuing a middle- or upper-middle-class life-style. The integrated elderly are likely to be able to do this by marshaling personal and private resources together with public support. Because these individuals are able to maintain their socioeconomic status—including social values, roles, and group and community memberships—they are referred to as the *socially integrated elderly.*

How does this three-tiered approach to the elderly affect government support for income-transfer programs? The central income-transfer program for the marginal elderly is SSI. As already noted, eligibility is determined by meeting certain income and assets standards. The program establishes a common minimum income benefit for the approximately 2.1 million elderly receiving SSI benefits in March 1999. (An additional 4.5 million children and adults were also receiving SSI benefits in March 1999.) Some states provide an additional supplement to the federal benefit. The average monthly amount of combined federal and state SSI payments in the United States for elderly recipients was a paltry $358.57 in December 1998. The average federal payment was $243.28; the average state supplementation (only 24 states) was $115.29. Still, many who are eligible for SSI do not receive it, and many who are receiving it are clearly still living below the poverty level. It seems reasonable to conclude that the marginal elderly are guaranteed a modest subsistence, at best, under the SSI income-transfer program.

The second tier of income support for the elderly is Social Security. Most of the work force is covered by this program, which is underwritten by the collected contributions of workers and their employers. Average monthly benefit amounts payable in January 1999 were $780 for retired workers and $733 for workers who are disabled. The *downwardly mobile elderly* include most recipients of Social Security who were average wage earners. Members of this group have a special reliance on the Social Security check plus accumulated private savings. For most of them, the Social Security check is a guarantee against falling into near- or absolute poverty.

The third tier of income support programs for the elderly includes those that are directed at the integrated elderly. Many of the integrated elderly receive Social Security; they are also recipients of (1) government-supported public (railroad retirement, civil service, state and local governments) and private pensions; (2) cash benefits from government-supported private savings plans (annuities, 401(k)s, individual retirement accounts, and Keogh plans); and (3) favorable tax policies, including property tax reductions. These tax preferences, in conjunction with private and public pension supplements to Social Security, act to maintain the socioeconomic position of the higher-income elderly.

The federal government's cost of maintaining the integrated elderly at a lifestyle consistent with that prior to retirement is staggering, in comparison with the costs, for example, of maintaining the marginal elderly. By December 1998, total federal and state supplemental expenditures for all elderly on SSI amounted to approximately $2.5 billion for the year. For 1993 (the latest year for which such data were available), almost $69 billion was contributed on a pretax basis by wage earners to their qualified retirement plans (sometimes referred to as 401(k) plans). If these contributions were taxed at only a 15 percent marginal federal tax rate, the yield would be $10.35 billion, or approximately four times the cost of providing SSI to the poorest aged Americans in 1998! Many who contribute pretax dollars to their 401(k) plans are high-wage earners whose marginal federal tax rates are actually 28 or 31 percent, or higher. Comparable examples of higher government expenditures and subsidies for those least in need are also available in the areas of health care and social services.

As Nelson's (1982) use of the term *integrated elderly* implies, the higher-income elderly are more likely to be socially integrated into the broader society than are other classes of elderly. Yet, as already noted, age entitlement programs cause a considerable proportion of government resources to be directed at those elderly who are least in need. Is this fair? Shouldn't public-policy benefits be redistributed on the basis of need?

The obvious answers seem to be *no*, it is not fair, and *yes*, benefits should be redistributed on the basis of need. Still, who is to decide who is needy and how? Some readers might say to redistribute benefits only to the marginal elderly or to some combination of the marginal and downwardly mobile elderly. One problem with such a reform is that it continues to employ age as a basic organizing principle in the development of policies and programs. After all, the elderly do not have a monopoly on need in the United States. As Elizabeth Kutza (1981) describes it, "No problem occurs in old age that does not occur also in other age groups, whether it be poverty, mental or physical disability, isolation, or malnutrition." Further, she quotes from an Administration on Aging study in which researchers were struck not by the differences among the young, the middle-aged, and the old but by the similarities: "When the picture is examined as a whole, the most striking aspect is how much alike were the values placed on quality of life factors regardless of age and how relatively little people's needs seem to change over time."

Reorganizing the distribution of federal policy benefits on the basis of need rather than age is an effort fraught with political liability. Benefits to the aged have been remarkably popular, especially those aimed at the downwardly mobile and integrated elderly. In part, this may result from the high value placed on independence by the elderly and their family members. It also may result from an understanding that the aged are a unique group—the one minority group to which *all* people anticipate belonging!

It seems likely that political support for the basic needs of the elderly will continue to be strong (Crystal 1982). In the current political environment, however, federal budgets are under constant pressure. As Crystal (1982) describes it, "If human services are to be cut, it is poor policy to slash benefits for the needy aged and spare those aiding mostly the middle-class and higher-income elderly."

Binstock and Day (1996) suggest that a trend is already in place to combine age and economic need as policy criteria in old-age benefit programs. The Social Security Reform Act of 1983 made 50 percent of Social Security benefits subject to taxation for the first time; this affected individuals with incomes exceeding $25,000 and married couples with incomes exceeding $32,000. The Tax Reform Act of 1986 eliminated the extra personal exemption available to persons 65 years and older filing their federal income tax returns and provided new tax credits to low-income elderly. The Omnibus Budget Reconciliation Act of 1993 increased the proportion of Social Security benefits subject to taxation to 85 percent for individuals with incomes over $34,000 and married couples over $44,000. Most recently, President Clinton's 1994 proposal for health care reform differentiated among older people by income level; those with higher income were asked to pay more for certain services within Medicare, including long-term care. While this proposal did not pass muster with the Congress, it may foretell things to come.

SUMMARY

Age-related issues have become a substantial element in U.S. politics, and the demographics of aging suggest that this trend will continue. Understanding the relevant questions and answers emerging from research into the politics of aging requires a sensitivity to the methodological and conceptual issues inherent in the age/period/cohort problem.

In the 1996 presidential election, the percentage of people reporting they voted was lowest in the youngest age groups; the proportion of people reporting that they voted increased with age. Only 31.2 percent of voters ages 18 to 20 reported voting in 1996, whereas 70.1 percent of those 65 years of age and older reported similarly. Factors contributing to this pattern include (1) the increased social integration of mature and older adults and (2) the increased leisure time available to adults. Age does bring a greater likelihood of experiencing a health impairment, and this may be associated with reduced participation in many forms of social behavior, including political process.

The aged are actively involved in partisan politics. They seem more likely than the young to make occasional contact with a public official. Many older people are also involved in working for community organizations and in political campaigns. Some suggest that older people's involvement in politics has more to do with their attempting to remain active and fulfilled than with a desire to achieve particular political goals.

It is widely believed that persons in middle age and old age are disproportionately in positions of political leadership. The trend in advanced industrial nations seems to be away from such a pattern. This is likely a result of a greater bureaucratization of government, which causes career patterns to become more routinized.

Are the elderly politically more conservative than the young? It is difficult to say. A higher proportion of the older cohorts—those 65 to 74 years old and those 75 and older—identify with the Democratic party than is the case for the youngest cohorts (those under 34 years of age and those 34 to 49 years old). Rather than aging bringing with it a change in positions on prominent political issues, it is more likely that today's older people, when younger, had different political views than currently younger cohorts.

There is considerable debate about the impact of a growing aged population on the federal budget. Some analysts view increased outlays for the elderly as being about to bust the budget. Others believe this characterization of the budget to be inaccurate. Unfortunately, it may create the impression that the federal government gives lavish treatment to the elderly. There is considerable debate about whether the aged constitute a political force that can mobilize to serve their own interests.

Several groups of aged—including the poor, minority elderly, and older women—have not been advantaged by government initiatives on behalf of older people. Public policy appears to perpetuate the existence of social class differences among the elderly that existed prior to old age. There was a time when age entitlement programs seemed necessary to identify a large proportion of elderly persons in need. The current question, however, is whether a change to need entitlement would more effectively target government programs for the truly needy elderly. Evidence is mounting that suggests that public policy is already on a course that combines age and need as important policy criteria for old-age benefit programs.

STUDY QUESTIONS

1. With regard to the political attitudes and behaviors of older persons, how would the concepts of *age effect, period effect,* and *cohort effect* be conceptualized? Give examples of each.

2. Explain how age, employment status, education, and race influence voting behavior in the United States.

3. List the six categories described by Verba and Nie in their typology of political participation. In which categories are the elderly overrepresented, and what could explain their overrepresentation?

4. Discuss the changing trend of political participation of the elderly in leadership positions in advanced industrialized nations.

5. Explain the difference between *breakthrough* and *constituency-building* policy enactments. Give examples.

6. Distinguish among the *marginal, downwardly mobile,* and *integrated* elderly. How does the distribution of policy benefits act to perpetuate social class differences among the elderly?

7. Discuss the concept of *senior power*. How does it relate to the presence or absence of *aging group consciousness?*

8. Discuss the relative merits of providing programmatic support to older people on the basis of age and need.

REFERENCES

Achenbaum, W. A. (1983). *Shades of gray: Old age, American values, and federal policies since 1920.* Boston: Little, Brown.

Bengtson, V. L., & Achenbaum, W. A. (1993). *The changing contract across generations.* New York: de Gruyter.

Binstock, R. H. (1978, November 11). Federal policy toward the aging—Its inadequacies and its politics. *National Journal,* pp. 1838–1845.

Binstock, R. H., & Day, C. L. (1996). Aging and politics. In R. H. Binstock & L. K. George (Eds.), *Handbook of aging and the social sciences* (4th ed.). San Diego, CA: Academic.

Butler, R. (1978, November 4). The economics of aging: We are asking the wrong questions. *National Journal,* pp. 1792–1797.

Callahan, D. (1987). *Setting limits: Medical goals in an aging society.* New York: Simon & Schuster.

Campbell, J. C., & Strate, J. (1981). Are old people conservative? *Gerontologist, 21* (6), 580–591.

Crystal, S. (1982). *America's old age crisis: Public policy and the two worlds of aging.* New York: Basic Books.

Cutler, S. J., Leutz, S. A., Muha, M. J., & Riter, R. N. (1980). Aging and conservatism: Cohort changes in attitudes about legalized abortion. *Journal of Gerontology, 35,* 115–123.

Guttmann, D. (1988). Age and leadership: Cross-cultural observations. In A. McIntyre (Ed.), *Aging and political leadership.* Albany, NY: SUNY Press.

Hess, B. (1983, September). *Aging policies and old women: The hidden agenda.* Paper presented at the 78th Annual Meeting of the American Sociological Society, Detroit.

Hudson, R. (1978). The "graying" of the federal budget and its consequences for old-age policy. *Gerontologist, 18* (5), 428–439.

Hudson, R. (1987). Tomorrow's able elders: Implications for the state. *Gerontologist, 27* (4), 405–409.

Hudson, R., & Binstock, R. H. (1976). Political systems and aging. In R. H. Binstock & E. Shanas (Eds.), *Handbook of aging and the social sciences.* New York: Van Nostrand Reinhold.

Inglehart, R. (1977). *The silent revolution: Changing values and political styles among western publics.* Princeton, NJ: Princeton University Press.

Jennings, M. K., & Markus, G. B. (1988). Political involvement in the later years: A longitudinal survey. *American Journal of Political Science, 32,* 302–316.

Kutza, E. A. (1981). *The benefits of old age: Social-welfare policy for the elderly.* Chicago: University of Chicago Press.

Lammers, W. W., & Nyomarkay, J. L. (1980). The disappearing senior leaders. *Research on Aging, 2* (3), 329–349.

Nelson, G. (1982, March). Social class and public policy for the elderly. *Social Service Review,* pp. 85–107.

Neugarten, B. L. (1982). Policy for the 1980s: Age or need entitlement? In B. L. Neugarten (Ed.), *Age or need? Public policies for older people.* Beverly Hills: Sage.

Nie, N., Verba, S., & Kim, J. (1974). Political participation and the life-cycle. *Comparative Politics, 6,* 319–340.

Portrait of the Electorate. (1992, November 5). *New York Times,* p. B9.

Pratt, H. (1976). *The gray lobby.* Chicago: University of Chicago Press.

Preston, S. H. (1984). Children and the elderly in the U.S. *Scientific American, 251* (6), 44–49.

Reitzes, D. C., & Reitzes, D. C. (1991). Metro Seniors in Action: A case study of a citywide senior organization. *Gerontologist, 31* (2), 256–262.

Smith, L. (1992). The tyranny of America's old. *Fortune, 125* (1), 68–72.

Verba, S., & Nie, N. (1972). *Participation in America: Political democracy and social equality.* New York: Harper & Row.

Williamson J. B., & Pampel, F. C. (1993). *Old-age security in comparative perspective.* New York: Oxford University Press.

Wisensale, S. K. (1988). Generational equity and intergenerational policies. *Gerontologist, 28* (6), 773–783.

CHAPTER FOURTEEN

RELIGION AND AGING

Writing in 1972, Heenan described the literature on religion and aging as "empirical lacunae." Have things changed since then? Although the literature on death and dying (see Chapter 19) has grown dramatically in the last decade or so, empirical research on the religious attitudes and behavior of older people is still relatively scarce. One explanation for the scarcity is that this aspect of older life is taken for granted. Elders are consistently portrayed as both more superstitious and more religious than younger people, and the assumption is that the role of older people in religious activities remains strong and enduring (Hess & Markson 1980; Orbach 1961).

Another explanation is that the relative scarcity of research on religion and aging may have roots in methodological concerns. First, most research in social gerontology is cross-sectional in design. Thus, it is difficult to disentangle age, period, and cohort effects on a wide variety of behaviors and attitudes, including that of religion (Maddox 1979). Moberg (1965, p. 80) observes:

> Whether the differences in religious beliefs between the generations are a result of the aging process or of divergent experiences during the formative years of childhood and youth, which are linked with different social and historical circumstances, is unknown. Longitudinal research might reveal considerably different conclusions from the cross-sectional studies which provide the foundation for current generalizations about age variations in the ideological dimensions of religion.

Additionally, certain concepts are difficult to define in the area of religion. What constitutes a religious individual, anyway? And how should religiosity be measured: by church or synagogue attendance or by engagement in private devotional activities?

Also, though religious groups "differ in terms of the amount of participation and interest demanded of their adherents, the degree of organization they possess and the opportunities they offer for the individual to achieve his or her goals" (Atchley 1980, p. 331), there seems to be a general insensitivity within the field of gerontology toward the need to distinguish among religious groups. Thus, what few studies there are make no basic attempt to separate Protestants, Catholics, and Jews, and further subdivision among these groups is even more rare. One review of the measures used in studies of age and religiosity indicates that most are Christian and church oriented (Payne 1982). Insensitivity toward religious diversity among the aged may simply be an extension of the development of the broader field of social gerontology. Only recently has recognition of the ethnic and racial diversity present in the aging experience begun to infiltrate the field.

Young and Dowling (1987) suggest that a period effect accounts for a vacillating interest in religion on the part of researchers. Following World War II and peaking in 1965, considerable work focused on religiosity and old age, with particular emphasis on attendance at religious services. During the 1980s and into the 1990s, interest in religion once again increased on college campuses and among the U.S. population at large. One chronicler corroborating this perceived resurgence indicates that researchers in the field of aging have increasingly incorporated religion-related variables in their research designs (Fecher 1982). Thus, Heenan's "empirical lacunae" appear to be closing.

Coloring the execution and any interpretation of this empirical research, however, is a richness of history and myth. Many contemporary beliefs and attitudes toward older people are built on an orientation first recorded in Scripture. This chapter uses such chronicles of life and humanity to assess the relationship between religion and aging. Following Achenbaum's lead (1985), we begin with a review of perceptions of age among the ancient Hebrews and early Christians as these are reflected in the Old and New Testament. Subsequently, the functions that organized religion provides to society and to its aged constituents are identified. Literature on the relationship between age and religious commitment is reviewed, although, as already indicated, such studies generally have not distinguished among individuals of different religious affiliation. Finally, the interactions among age, religion, and health are examined.

IN THE BEGINNING...

As many commentators have pointed out, the images of old age presented in the Old Testament[1] are generally quite positive: "The hoary head is a crown of glory, it is found in the way of righteousness" (Proverbs 16:31). Longevity is presented as the reward for service to the Lord. This is especially evident in Moses' discourses on the religious foundations of the Covenant. For example, "Ye shall walk in all the way which the Lord your God hath commanded you, that ye may live, and that it may be well with you, and that ye may prolong your days in the land which ye shall possess" (Deuteronomy 5:30).

---

[1]All references to the Old Testament come from *The Holy Scriptures According to the Masoretic Text: A New Translation,* published by The Jewish Publication Society of America (Philadelphia). Copyright © 1917, by The Jewish Publication Society of America. References to the New Testament refer to *The Holy Bible, King James Version,* which may be accessed on-line through the electronic library resources of the University of Virginia, among other places. The website address is <http://etext.lib.virginia.edu/kjv.browse.html>.

In Genesis 5, the book of the generations of Adam, a list of individuals who lived abnormally long lives is provided. Adam is said to have lived 930 years, Seth 912 years, Enosh 905 years, and so on. Most biblical scholars doubt the accuracy of this chronology, however. Maimonides holds that only the distinguished individuals named in this chapter lived these long years, whereas others lived a more or less normal span (Hertz 1981).

The general respect toward and favorable position of the elderly in ancient Hebraic culture was a function of three vital roles they played (Achenbaum 1985). First, the elderly were often instruments of the Lord's will. Noah exemplifies this function. In the face of God's decision to cleanse the earth of corruption and violence, Noah is instructed to "Make thee an ark of gopher wood" (Genesis 6:14) and bring "all thy house into the ark" (Genesis 7:1). Noah was 600 years old when "the flood of waters was upon the earth" (Genesis 7:6) and 601 years when instructed to "Be fruitful, and multiply, and replenish the earth" (Genesis 9:1); he died at the age of 950 (Genesis 9:29).

The second function fulfilled by the elderly was that of wielder of political influence and power. The Book of Numbers describes the wanderings of the Israelites after their departure from Egypt. In Chapter 11, Moses complains to the Lord that he is unable to bear alone the burden of all these people. The Lord instructs Moses as follows:

> Gather unto Me seventy men of the elders of Israel, whom thou knowest to be the elders of the people, and officers over them; and bring them unto the tent of meeting, that they may stand there with thee. And I will come down and speak with thee there; and I will take of the spirit which is upon thee, and will put it upon them; and they shall bear the burden of the people with thee. (Numbers 11:16–17)

Finally, the elderly are viewed as custodians of the collective wisdom of the years. Job, who had his family and material possessions stripped from him and his body covered with boils, asks, "Is wisdom with aged men, And understanding in length of days?" (Job 12:12) One answer he receives is as follows: "Days should speak, And multitude of years should teach wisdom" (Job 32:7).

It is difficult, if not impossible, to discuss the positive themes attached to old age and aging in ancient Hebraic culture without speaking to the conception of parent-child relations presented in the Old Testament. The Fifth Commandment provides the basic guideline: "Honor thy father and thy mother, as the Lord thy God commanded thee; that thy days may be long, and that it may go well with thee, upon the land which the Lord thy God giveth thee" (Deuteronomy 5:16). As Achenbaum (1985) points out, however, the Old Testament may have been written in a time when ideals were not always realized. Thus, the Fifth Commandment can be juxtaposed with descriptions of the severe punishments assigned to children if a parental order was disobeyed or if a child cursed a parent. For example, an incorrigible son, whom milder measures failed to reclaim, might be tried by the elders at the gate of the city, and be liable to death by stoning (Deuteronomy 21:18–21).

Despite the general positive regard in which the aged are held, there was recognition of the frailty and physical decline that could accompany old age. The Book of Ecclesiastes offers a powerful description of this. Careful readers should pay special attention to the metaphors used to describe various parts of the body: "The guards of the house" could be considered the arms; "men of valor," the legs; "maids that grind," the teeth; "ladies that peer through the windows," the eyes, and so on (Shenk 1994).

> So appreciate your vigor in the days of your youth, before
> those days of sorrow come and those years arrive of
> which you will say, "I have no pleasure in them";
> before sun and light and moon and stars grow dark,
> and the clouds come back again after the rain:
> When the guards of the house become shaky,
> And the men of valor are bent,
> And the doors to the street are shut
> With the noise of the hand mill growing fainter,
> And the song of the bird growing feebler,
> And all the strains of music dying down;
> When one is afraid of heights
> And there is terror on the road....
> Before the silver cord snaps
> And the golden bowl crashes,
> The jar is shattered at spring,
> And the jug is smashed at the cistern.
> And the dust returns to the ground
> As it was,
> And the lifebreath returns to God
> Who bestowed it. (Ecclesiastes 12:1–7)

New Testament perspectives on old age and aging were built on Old Testament precedents. Honor to parents specifically and to the older generation generally is a device for expressing obedience toward God (Ephesians 6:1–4). Yet, distinctively Christian views of age and aging are put forth in the New Testament. For the most part, these are intertwined with the conception of the personhood of Christ:

> But grace was given to each of us according to the measure of Christ's gift...until we all attain to the unity of the faith and of the knowledge of the Son of God, to mature manhood, to the measure of the stature of the fulness of Christ;...speaking the truth in love, we are to grow up in every way into him who is the head, into Christ, from whom the whole body, joined with which it is supplied, when each part is working properly, makes bodily growth and upbuilds itself in love. (Ephesians 4:7, 13–16)

This image of aging posits that the goal of human development is to grow into the "mature manhood" of Christ. The theme of growth and continuity stretching through the course of human life is accentuated in the New Testament (Achenbaum 1985). Still, no Christian, no matter how old, can attain full maturity in this world. Presumably this results when one becomes fully incorporated into the Body of Christ. Achenbaum (1985) suggests that this may explain why no older person in the New Testament is portrayed as vividly or with the same stature as the patriarchs of the Old Testament; the central figure of the New Testament is a vigorous middle-aged Christ.

Another important difference between the Old and New Testament is the portrayal of the relationship between death and aging. The Old Testament offers little comfort or consolation for the reality of death. Afterlife or immortal life was not a substantive issue for the ancient Hebrews—nor is it one for contemporary Jews, for that matter. For Christians, Old Testament teaching has been transformed by the story of Christ's death, resurrection, and ascension. The New Testament proclaims victory over death, although, as Achenbaum notes, different Christian sects have come to visualize the afterlife in different ways.

FUNCTIONS OF RELIGION

As a social institution, religion fulfills several basic functions within human societies. For example, religion defines the spiritual world and provides explanation for events and occurrences that seem difficult to understand. On a more mundane level, religious institutional services provide a meeting ground for unattached and otherwise disaffiliated individuals. Three functions of religion worthy of discussion here include social integration, social control, and social support.

Social Integration

According to French sociologist Emile Durkheim (1912/1965), ideas about the ultimate meaning of life and ritual ceremonies that express these ideas arise out of the collective experience of individuals. Beliefs, including religious beliefs, depend on agreement among people for their meaning. The content of religious belief systems—ideas expressed, ritual ceremonies enacted, and values held sacred—all express the shared fate of the believers. For Durkheim, all systems of religious belief "have the same objective significance and fulfill the same function everywhere.... There are no religions that are false. All are true in their own fashion; all answer, though in different ways, to the given conditions of human existence."

The sharedness of religious bonds, the common adherence to a religious belief system, can overcome personal and divisive forces (Koenig, George, & Siegler 1988). It can act as a societal glue, holding together individuals and social groups with diverse interests and aspirations. It is exemplified in ritual ceremonies of passage, such as confirmation, bar and bas mitzvahs, weddings, and funerals. The integrative function of religion is perhaps most apparent in traditional, preindustrial societies where agricultural events—such as seeding and harvesting, kin relationships, and even the exercise of authority by leaders are governed by

Religion can be a powerful integrative force for older people in society.

religious beliefs and rituals (Schaefer 1986). But, even in modern, postindustrial societies, religious belief systems continue to foster an ethos of responsibility and care for others, as well as influence the ways in which individuals evaluate, restore, and preserve the quality of relationships (Marcoen 1994).

Religion can be a powerful integrative force for older people in a society. In their analysis of aging and modernization in 14 societies, Cowgill and Holmes (1972) listed nine universals of human aging. *Universals* represent common denominators, or constants of behavior, that are found in the same form in most societies around the world. One of these universals is as follows: *Societies rich in ceremonialism and religious ritual tend to honor the aged and accord them prestige seldom found in less formalistic societies.* Old people can be the caretakers of ritual tradition. Not only can they teach the details of the ceremonies but they also represent a liaison between the affairs of earth and the realm of the supernatural (Holmes 1983). De Beauvoir (1972, p. 83) adds:

> As the custodian of the traditions, the intercessor, and the protector against the supernatural powers, the aged man ensures the cohesion of the community throughout time and in the present.... Generally speaking, the services, taken as a whole, that the old are enabled to render because of their knowledge of the traditions, mean that they have not only respect but also material prosperity. They are rewarded with presents. The gifts that they receive from those whom they initiate

into their secrets are of particular importance—they are the surest source of private wealth, a source that exists only in societies that are insufficiently well-to-do to have an advanced culture.

Many of the ceremonial and ritual roles performed by the elderly are described by Simmons (1945, p. 164):

> They have served as guardians of temples, shrines, and sacred paraphernalia, as officers of the priesthood, and as leaders of the performance of rites associated with prayers, sacrifices, feast days, annual cycles, historic celebrations, and the initiation of important and hazardous enterprises. They also have been prominent in ceremonies with critical periods in the life cycle—such as birth, puberty, marriage and death.

Amoss (1978, 1981) has described the Coast Salish Indians of Washington State and British Columbia as a society in which the aged have continued to be valued because of their knowledge of ritual and ceremonial detail. According to Amoss, contact with the white world in the late nineteenth century was initially devastating for the Coast Salish aged. With the shift to wage labor (away from hunting and gathering), old people's knowledge and skills became outdated and irrelevant. Religious leadership passed to younger men, and the supernatural powers of the old were challenged.

Since World War II, the Coast Salish have faced economic hardship, jobs have been difficult to come by, and many individuals have been on welfare. During the 1940s and 1950s, many sought relief in revivalistic Christianity. Christian churches, however, were not able to offer them the opportunity to feel dignity as Indians, and some ministers were even antagonistic toward Indian belief systems. Traditional religious ceremonies, including the revival of traditional-type spirit dancing rituals, began to reappear. These traditional rituals emphasized solidarity with past generations as well as among present-day Coast Salish. Old men and women became the focus of this new revivalism. The young wanted to be proud of their traditional culture, and it was the elderly who had preserved traditions from the past.

Similarly, Sinclair (1985) reports that older Maori (a culture indigenous to New Zealand) women have achieved a degree of equality if not dominance in modern society through their participation in a religious movement referred to as *Maramatanga*. Affiliated with the Catholic Church in New Zealand, the ideology of this movement draws heavily on traditional Maori religion and the Maori prophetic tradition. Although men participate in the movement, it is the women who receive messages from the "spirits of the dead," who return as these spirits, and who monitor relations between humans and spirits. Middle-aged and older women, freed of the responsibilities of domestic life, participate most vigorously in the Maramatanga movement and often experience an enhancement of status within both the Maori and European communities. Some of the women become effective culture brokers, comfortable with the Maori traditions of the past but simultaneously accommodating themselves to modern directions dominated by the Europeans.

As Spencer and Jennings (1977) report, societies without a ceremonial tradition may provide little or no opportunity for the prestige or the participation of the elderly. Among the Chipewyn Indians of the western subarctic region of North America, elderly men no longer able to hunt command little respect. There is minimal interest in myth or legend about the past, and there are few, if any, remaining religious rituals. As a result, the elderly are left with almost no opportunities for participation in the society.

Social Control

Karl Marx agreed with Durkheim's view of the collective and socially shared nature of religious behavior. But Marx (1844/1963) was also concerned that religion produced an otherworldly focus that diverts attention from the circumstances and realities of life in this world. From this perspective, religion supports the status quo and helps to perpetuate patterns of social inequality. Long-held religious beliefs and practices enforce taken-for-granted beliefs that sometimes act as significant barriers to new or different ways of thinking and behaving. Traditional practices, handed down from previous generations, become defined as God-approved ways of doing things and are resistant to change. This is so even when the results of such traditional practices include inequalities and inequities.

Racism, sexism, and, to some extent, ageism have been linked to religion, and when this occurs, the social control functions of religion may be enhanced. For example, Vander Zanden (1990, p. 296) quotes Louisiana State Senator W. M. Rainach in defending racial segregation in 1954: "Segregation is a natural order—created by God, in His wisdom, who made black men black and white men white."

Marx portrayed religion as a painkiller for the suffering experienced by all oppressed peoples, including the poor and indigent of all ages. Like other painkillers, it may suppress the symptoms for a while, but the underlying condition remains. Religious suffering is at the same time an expression of real suffering and a protest against real suffering. Religion is the sigh of the oppressed creature, the sentiment of a heartless world, and the soul of soulless conditions. It is the opium of the people.

From a Marxist perspective, religion keeps people from understanding their living conditions in political terms. Marxists argue that religion induces a "false consciousness" among the disadvantaged that lessens the possibility of collective political action to change the material conditions of people's lives. Have the elderly experienced a false consciousness that hides from them the possibility of changing the material conditions of their lives? Or have they, in fact, enjoyed political and legislative successes far beyond their relative proportion in the U.S. population? These remain much-debated questions among students of aging (see Chapter 13).

Social Support

Religious institutions bring together people of all ages and help reduce the isolation of the elderly. For many elderly residing in smaller communities, religious pursuits help instigate and provide nurturance for social relationships. Friendships, opportunities for reciprocal exchanges, sympathy, empathy, encouragement, and reassurance all represent supportive aspects of religious organizational environments and may contribute to well-being in later life (Koenig, Kvale, & Ferrel 1988). Even when capacities for firsthand participation in religious services and activities diminish, the importance of continued interaction with representatives of the religious institution cannot be underestimated.

Care giving is extraordinarily stressful. Religiosity and spirituality, used interchangeably in the literature, have been shown to be a supportive resource for caregivers to the elderly, regardless of age. In the Project on Religion and Coping, Pargament and his colleagues (1990) assessed support through a spiritually based coping activities scale. Items on the scale reflected three components of spiritual support: emotional reassurance ("trusted that God would not let anything happen to me"), a close spiritual relationship ("sought God's love and care"), and guidance in problem solving ("God showed me how to deal with the situation"). Overall, people employing more spiritually based coping reported better adjustment to life crises. And, among all methods of religious coping, spiritually based coping was the best predictor of outcomes.

Picot and colleagues (1997) suggest that religiosity operates differently as a support resource for black and white caregivers. They found that black caregivers scored significantly higher on prayer and comfort from religion than their white counterparts, and black caregivers perceived higher rewards than white caregivers. It is surmised that the function of black caregivers' religiosity may be to raise the threshold for stress (as opposed to buffering the experience of stress). To illustrate this point, Picot and colleagues (1997) report that, in their study of 391 caregivers with an average age of 52 years, black caregivers prayed more frequently and obtained more comfort from their religion. Although data are not available on this point, these authors believe that such behaviors likely preceded their care giving and, as a result, they may have perceived less stress than white caregivers when confronted by the same care-giving situation. Lawton and his research team (1992) also report that white caregivers perceive higher levels of burden and strain than blacks in similar care-giving situations.

Another option for religious participation has become available in recent years—that of the electronic church. Almost one in three U.S. viewers say they watch religious programming on television. These viewers are disproportionately older, female, southern, from small towns, and are less well educated than are people who do not watch religious programs (Clymer 1987). Although most use television as a supplement to participation in local religious activities, many elderly shut-ins use it as a substitute for attendance at religious services. Television allows viewers to "privatize" religious worship, to gain a feeling of immediate and personal help in coping with their troubles, and to enjoy the illusion of a face-to-face relationship with a dynamic religious leader (Hadden & Swann 1981).

AGE AND RELIGIOUS COMMITMENT

Data from the 1998 General Social Survey (GSS) show a strong relationship between age and several different dimensions of religious commitment. Carried out by the National Opinion Research Center at the University of Chicago, the GSS is a survey taken regularly of the attitudes and opinions of a representative sample of noninstitutionalized adults 18 years of age and older in the United States. For example, survey results for 1998 show that although a majority of Americans have confidence in the existence of God, age differences do exist. Almost three-fourths (71.4 percent) of people age 65 and older have full confidence in the existence of God; at the same time, 59.5 percent of respondents ages 18 to 44 indicate a similar belief. One place where age differences do not appear is in the proportion of GSS respondents who believe in life after death. Approximately 81 percent of all Americans believe in life after death, with differences between the oldest and youngest respondent groups at less than two percentage points (82.5 versus 81.6 percent, respectively). Additional results are reported in Tables 14.1 through 14.3.

According to Table 14.1, older people are more likely than younger people to characterize themselves as being strongly religious. More than one-half (56.9 percent) of GSS respondents age 65 and over describe themselves as being strongly religious. This compares with 40.4 percent of those 18 to 44 years and 46.5 percent of those 45 to 64 years who make the same claim.

Does this relationship between age and strength of religious affiliation hold up in a review of patterns of attendance at religious services? A decline in attendance at religious services and participation in organized religious activities is sometimes associated with physical limitations or disability as well as the lack of transportation. According to Moberg (1965):

> Persons who have commuted to church for as much as half a century blame their declining participation on poor eyesight, "old age," or failing health. Driving to church, especially at night, has become an arduous task, and they do not wish to be a "bother" or to become a burden upon someone else by "begging" rides to all of the church's meetings.

Table 14.2 provides data on the variation by age in attendance at religious services among GSS respondents in 1998. Although those 65 years and over are

TABLE 14.1   Strength of Religious Affiliation, by Age: 1998

	AGE		
	18–44	*45–64*	*65+*
Strongly religious	40.4%	46.3%	56.9%
Not very strong	46.6	42.0	30.3
Somewhat strong	13.0	11.7	12.8

Source: Data from the 1998 General Social Survey by the National Opinion Research Center at the University of Chicago.

TABLE 14.2   Attendance at Religious Services, by Age: 1998

	AGE		
	18–44	*45–64*	*65+ (%)*
Once a week or more	19.8%	28.0%	39.2%
Once a month or more	23.2	21.6	24.1
Once a year or more	24.9	21.0	12.2
Less than once a year/never	32.1	29.4	24.5

Source: Data from the 1998 General Social Survey by the National Opinion Research Center at the University of Chicago.

twice as likely as those 18 to 44 years to attend religious services once a week or more frequently (39.2 versus 19.8 percent, respectively), there is a lesser, albeit still sizable, difference in patterns of attendance at religious services between the old and middle-aged. Almost one-half (49.6 percent) of those 45 to 64 years of age and 63.3 percent of those 65 years and over report attending religious services more frequently than once a month.

Table 14.3 shows that compared with young and middle-aged adults, the old pray more often. More than two-thirds (70.1 percent) of the GSS respondents age 65 and over report engaging in prayer once a day or more frequently. It is interesting to note, however, that most middle-aged respondents (55.6 percent) report praying at least once a day, whereas almost one-half (49.5 percent) of all younger respondents report doing similarly.

The sociodemographic correlates of prayer are different for the three age groupings. In 1998, among those 18 to 44 years of age, blacks, females, those who are older, those who resided in the South, and central city dwellers were most

TABLE 14.3   Frequency of Prayer, by Age: 1998

	AGE		
	18–44	*45–64*	*65+*
Several times a day	20.6%	24.8%	38.8%
Once a day	28.9	30.8	31.3
Once a week or more	24.5	21.0	13.8
Less than once a week/never	25.9	23.4	16.3

Source: Data from the 1998 General Social Survey by the National Opinion Research Center at the University of Chicago.

likely to engage in more frequent prayer. Being black, female, and a resident of the South was also associated with more frequent prayer among GSS respondents ages 45 to 64 years. Interestingly, for those GSS respondents 65 years and older, only being female was associated with more frequent prayer. Marital status, education, and family income were not associated with frequency of prayer in any of the age groupings.

There appears to be only modest evidence of age differences in the association between other measures of religiosity and frequency of prayer in the 1998 GSS data. For example, across all age groups, the more frequently one attends religious services and the greater one's belief that God watches over one, the more likely one is to engage frequently in prayer. Confidence in the existence of God was also a correlate of frequency of prayer among those 18 to 44 years and those 65 years and older. Among those 45 to 64 years, there was no statistically significant association between confidence in the existence of God and frequency of prayer.

General Social Survey data for 1998 provides a single snapshot of the relationship between age and religious commitment. Just what is really known about how age affects religious behavior and commitment? Bahr (1970) analyzed prior research in this area and suggested that the relationship between aging and church attendance be interpreted with reference to four distinct models: (1) traditional, (2) lifetime stability, (3) family life cycle, and (4) progressive disengagement. According to the **traditional model**, there is a sharp decline in religious activity during young adulthood, with the lowest point in the life cycle being between ages 30 and 35. Beyond age 35, this model posits a steady increase in church activity until old age.

The **lifetime stability model** alleges that aging and church attendance or religious activity are not related. One interpretation of this model is made by Lazerwitz (1962, p. 433): "Perhaps church attendance is based upon patterns established fairly early in life and subject to little (if any) change with aging." Wilensky's (1961) review of studies of the variations in religious participation by age supports this interpretation. He found that church membership and attendance was fairly stable in the middle years and did not drop off until after age 70 or 75.

A third model derives from the view that religious participation is related to the stage of **family life cycle**. In general, family life cycle seems to be a euphemism for presence or absence of children. According to this model, when children are young and tied to the home, parental involvement in religious services peaks; with children no longer in the home, regularity of religious participation falls off. Although this model speaks to the influence of the presence of children on parental involvement in organized religion, there is general agreement that parents' religious orientations are particularly important influences on young people's development (Hoge & Petrillo 1978). Hunsberger (1985) reports that mothers have the strongest proreligious influence.

The **progressive disengagement model** is tied to the disengagement theory of aging. From the perspective of this theory, aging is seen as "an inevitable mutual withdrawal or disengagement," resulting in decreased interaction between the aging person and others in his or her social systems (Cumming & Henry 1961).

Applied to participation in religious activities, the theory suggests a model of decline following middle age. Riley and Foner (1968, p. 489) conclude that "the evidence, though slight, suggests that more individuals decrease than increase their attendance as they reach old age."

Bahr's own interviews with more than 600 men from three distinctive socioeconomic strata (skid row, urban lower class, and urban middle class) show substantial religious disaffiliation during adult life in all three groups; the progressive disengagement model is most congruent with the pattern of church attendance reported by his respondents. With advancing age, church attendance is increasingly less important as a source of voluntary affiliation among both well-to-do and poor men (Bahr 1970). As Bahr himself suggests, however, it may be that age brings a qualitative change in the nature of religiosity such that the decline in attendance is not matched by declines in religious belief or feeling.

Wingrove and Alston (1974) have argued that support for each of Bahr's four models varies by the type of sample and methodology used and by the year of data collection. Applying cohort analysis to data collected by the Gallup Poll between 1939 and 1969, these authors found that, although church attendance appears related to age, no consistent support for any one of the four models was provided. Each cohort was found to show its own church attendance pattern. Gender and social environment seemed to have greater impact on church attendance than did age.

Blazer and Palmore (1976) report the results of a longitudinal study of the religious attitudes and activities of 272 community residents over an 18-year period. Subjects were interviewed at two- to three-year intervals beginning in 1957. Measures included church attendance and Bible reading, among others. They found that positive religious attitudes remain fairly stable over time. If individuals were religious or nonreligious when young, chances are they will continue to have the same basic religious orientation when they become old. As Figure 14.1 shows, Blazer and Palmore's findings do show a gradual decline in religious activities in the later years.

Criticism of these and other studies of the relationship between age and religious behavior often centers on the fact that researchers have too narrowly conceptualized religiosity in terms of attendance or participation in formal organizations. As Mindel and Vaughn (1978) point out, the role of "religious person" encompasses more than simple participation in a religious organization and may include private or nonorganizational religious behavior. Some even suggest that, with aging, these more private and nonorganizational religious expressions increase in importance (Moberg 1972). Stark (1968) found that greater piety among the elderly, compared with the young, was manifested in the reported frequency of praying.

Employing a small sample of elderly from Central Missouri, Mindel and Vaughn (1978) observed that, although a majority did not attend religious services frequently, a majority of sample members maintained that they were nonorganizationally religious "very often." For the purposes of this study, examples of non-organizational religious activity included engaging in individual or family prayer and listening to religious music or a religious service on the radio or television.

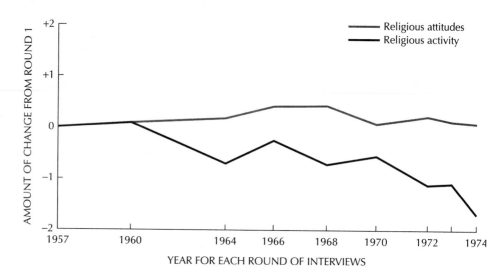

FIGURE 14.1 Religious Attitudes and Activities over Time

Source: Dan Blazer and Erdman Palmore, "Religion and Aging in a Longitudinal Panel," *The Gerontologist, 16* (1), 1976, Part 1, p. 84. Copyright © The Gerontological Society of America. Reprinted by permission of the publisher via Copyright Clearance Center, Inc.

Young and Dowling (1987) attempted to extend the work of Mindel and Vaughn by identifying factors that account for the variation in dimensions of religious participation. They sampled American Association of Retired Persons (AARP) members in El Paso, Texas, who were fairly evenly split between large "liberal" Protestant denominations (e.g., Methodist, Presbyterian, or Episcopal) and "conservative/ traditional" churches (e.g., Baptist, Mormon, or Roman Catholic). Strength of religious conviction was the strongest predictor of organized religious activity and private religious behavior. These authors hypothesized that indicators of social or personal deprivation (including poor health, low income, reduced activity, and living alone) would predict higher levels of nonorganizational or private religious behavior. The assumption is that private religious behavior *compensates* for these deprivations. The researchers were forced to reject this hypothesis. Interestingly, they did find that strong kin and friend networks predict high levels of private devotion. Young and Dowling contend that frequent interaction in an informal social network contributes to the spiritual well-being of older persons through nonorganizational religious participation.

Kart, Palmer, and Flaschner (1987) studied the relationship between age and religiosity among Jews residing in northwest Ohio. Religiosity was measured in a variety of ways under two broad categories: organizational religious commitment and nonorganizational, or individual, religious commitment. Indicators of organizational religious commitment included synagogue attendance and the number of Jewish organizational memberships reported by each respondent. Indicators of individual religious commitment included whether the respondent follows religious dietary laws and keeps a kosher home, whether the respondent recites prayers of mourning for deceased parents and other family members, whether the respondent posts mezuzahs (parchment scrolls) on the doors of the household, whether female respondents light sabbath candles, and whether male respondents ritually pray over a cup a wine to consecrate the Sabbath. Respondents were also asked a question aimed at determining the strength of their religious beliefs.

For men in this sample, no statistically significant age differences could be observed on the array of organizational and individual measures of religious commitment. This is in contrast to Orbach's (1961) report made 40 years ago from the Detroit Area Study in which Jewish men showed increased synagogue attendance with age. In northwest Ohio, only the number of Jewish organizational memberships showed age-related differences. Older men were much more likely to report holding multiple memberships in Jewish voluntary associations or organizations than were younger men.

Women in this study provide a different picture. Statistically significant age differences can be observed on a number of organizational and individual measures of religiosity, including synagogue attendance and the use of mezuzahs on the doorposts of the home. In all cases, older women evidence stronger religious commitment than do younger women. Only on a single scale made up of two items—observance of dietary laws and the lighting of Sabbath candles—did Kart and colleagues find no apparent age differences.

Analyzing data from a large sample of Washington State residents, Finney and Lee (1976) found that age had a small, positive influence on private devotional practices but no effect on four other dimensions of religious commitment: belief, ritual, knowledge, and experience. Finney and Lee suggest that older people may tend to employ religion as a means of reducing or alleviating anxieties, and the researchers point to the small effect of age on several dimensions of religious commitment as indicative of the need "to raise questions about recent thought in both social gerontology and the sociology of religion."

Age and Mystical Experience

Have you ever had a mystical experience? Thought you were somewhere you had not been before? Felt as if you were in touch with someone who had died? Are such experiences associated with aging? And, if so, how? Are people more or less likely to have such experiences as they grow older?

As Levin (1993) reports, the 1988 General Social Survey (GSS) contained five measures of mystical experience, grouped together after the question, "How often have you had any of the following experiences?" These included *deja vu* ("Thought you were somewhere you had been before, but knew that is was impossible"), *ESP, clairvoyance, spiritualism* ("Felt as though you were really in touch with someone who had died"), and *numinous experience* ("Felt as though you were very close to a powerful spiritual force that seemed to lift you out of yourself").

On average, GSS respondents reported experiencing each of the mystical phenomena roughly once or twice in their lives, with *deja vu* and *ESP* being considerably more common than the other experiences. At the high end, 67.3 percent of respondents indicated that they had experienced deja vu once or more in their lives; at the low end, 28.3 percent of respondents indicated that they had a clairvoyant experience once or more in their lives.

Levin divided GSS respondents into four roughly equal-sized age groups: 18 to 30, 31 to 40, 41 to 60, and 61 and over. Statistically significant age differences were revealed in two of the five mystical experiences. Lifetime prevalence of deja vu steadily declined across age cohorts from younger to older, as did prevalence of clairvoyance, although the decline is less steep. Also, the overall mysticism scale (a composite of the five items) was lowest in the oldest group.

Religiosity (measured in different ways) appears to exert statistically significant effects on mystical experience in each age group, although the pattern of significant effects varies across the age groups. For example, among young adults (18 to 30 years), mystical experience is more likely to occur among *subjectively* (strength of religious preference) and *nonorganizationally* religious people (those who say grace after meals or read the Bible at home) and less likely among *organizationally* religious people (those who attend religious services and take part in various religious activities). Among the oldest respondents (age 61 and over), only subjective religiosity predicted mystical experience—that is, people who defined themselves as strongly religious and feeling close to God were more likely to have mystical experiences.

The same five items were asked in the 1973 GSS. In the 15 years that passed, the percentage of respondents who reported ever having experienced mystical phenomena increased for four of the five indicators, declining only slightly for numinous experience. Thus, both aging and cohort effects could be thought to be operating: Mystical experience may decline with age but simultaneously be increasing over the years. Levin (1993, pp. 511–512) points out,

> If the past few decades represent a period of increasing secularization of culture… then perhaps an increase in certain mystical experiences with successively younger age cohorts reflects a successive substitution of engagement of the pyschic world for organized, institutional religious practice. [Or, perhaps] it may be that, among those whose religious expression is predominantly organizational, regular participation in public worship discourages paranormal involvement (or at least reports of such experiences to survey researchers).

RELIGION, AGING, AND HEALTH

Krause (1997) identifies three sources for increased interest in religion and health: (1) an increase in scholarly efforts submitted to mainstream journals and funding agencies; (2) the emergence of academic journals devoted solely to religion and aging (e.g., *Journal of Religious Gerontology*), as well creation of special issues in already-existing journals; and (3) sponsorship by major funding sources of special committees charged with promoting better understanding of religion and health (e.g., National Institute of Aging). But, why this interest now? Krause (1997) admits that specific reasons are hard to pin down. Still, he suggests three factors at play:

1. Greater willingness to consider the role played by nontraditional factors in health, especially as medical care costs continue to rise
2. Growing level of sophistication and quality in studies of religion and health
3. Continuing (if not mounting) evidence of persistent religious differences between younger and older adults

The general hypothesis that social ties may protect individuals from a variety of disease outcomes has received support from numerous researchers. The effect of marriage (e.g., Gove 1973), contacts with relatives and friends (Zuckerman, Kasl, & Ostfeld 1984), and group membership (Berkman & Syme 1979) all have been reported as significantly associated with health status; those individuals most isolated (fewest contacts with others) have an increased risk to their health and greater mortality. Greater religiousness has been associated with lower levels of functional disability and symptoms of depression (Idler 1987). Researchers have reported an association between religious involvement and lower levels of hypertension (Graham et al. 1978) and myocardial infarction (Medalie et al. 1973) as well as lower risk of mortality (Berkman & Syme 1979; House, Robbins, & Metzner 1982; Schoenbach et al. 1986; Zuckerman et al. 1984). It is unclear, however, how or why health benefits may be derived from social ties.

Idler (1987) suggests focusing on the structure and support-giving characteristics of particular unique institutions, such as the church or synagogue, in order to discover the linking mechanisms between individual health status and involvement in the social environment. Presumably, benefits from social ties are not only differentially distributed among social institutions in terms of frequency of occurrence but potential benefits may be qualitatively unique as well.

The question remains, however, as to how and why social ties generate health benefits. Classical sociological theory holds at least four explanations for the influence of religiosity or participation in religious organizational activity over health status (Idler 1987; Norgard & Kart 1989):

1. Religious organizations are comprised of distinctively normative patterns from which individuals may structure their behaviors and attitudes. Many religious traditions expressly sanction health-promoting behaviors through proscriptive and prescriptive guidelines related to smoking, drinking, and/or diet *(health behaviors hypothesis)*. As Levin and Vanderpool (1989, pp. 72–73) describe this:

> The Mosaic code prohibits the consumption of *tref* (nonkosher) products; Mormons are warned against caffeine and alcoholic beverages; Seventh-Day Adventists are directed to be vegetarian; monks fast; nuns are celibate; Jews and Muslims

require circumcision; Parsis marry late and are strictly monogamous. Each of these religiously-sanctioned behaviors is a component of a larger religious *Lebensstil,* or style of life, and each of these behaviors is generally promotive of health.

Mormons have been shown to have low cancer rates. This likely reflects adherence to their Church doctrines advocating abstention from the use of tobacco and alcohol. All Mormons do not adhere equally to the health practices of the Church, however. Gardner and Lyon (1982a) studied cancer in Utah Mormon men in relation to their adherence to Church doctrines. Cancer rates for 1966–1970 indicate that the most devout group had lung cancer rates 80 percent lower than those of the least devout group. The same was seen for all smoking- and alcohol-associated cancer sites combined. Cancer rates of the stomach and the leukemias and lymphomas also were lower in the most devout group. Mormon women classified as having the strongest adherence to Church doctrine had lung cancer rates during 1966–1970 much lower than did women with the weakest adherence (Gardner & Lyon 1982b).

2. Religious involvement may also influence health status by giving individuals an opportunity to participate in a "moral community" (Durkheim, 1897/1951), whereby religious involvement is seen as an affirmation of belonging to a group of like-minded people. Belonging may provide emotional as well as material support *(social cohesiveness hypothesis).*

Graham and colleagues (1978) examined the relationship between blood pressure levels and church attendance patterns in a group of white male heads of households in the 1967–1969 follow-up examination of the Evans County, Georgia, Cardiovascular Epidemiologic Study. A consistent pattern of lower systolic and diastolic blood pressures was found among frequent church attendees. The findings held up when controls for age, obesity, cigarette smoking, and socioeconomic status were employed.

Strawbridge and colleagues (1998) used data of over 2,500 individuals age 50 years and over from the 1994 Alameda County Study to test the extent to which religiosity buffers relationships between different stressors and depression. They found that both nonorganizational religiosity (including prayer and the importance of religious and spiritual beliefs) and organizational religiosity (including attendance at services and other activities) buffered associations with depression for nonfamily stressors, such as individual financial problems and health problems. In effect, among individuals experiencing such stressors in their life, those with higher religiosity scores were less likely to report feeling "sad, blue, or depressed."

Interestingly, these researchers found nonorganizational religiosity to exacerbate the association with depression for individuals experiencing relationship problems with children, while organizational religiosity exacerbated associations with depression for individuals with marital problems, those experiencing physical or verbal abuse, and those providing care to a spouse or other relative living with them. Why should religiosity exacerbate the effect of family stressors on depression? Ellison (1994) suggests that stressors that raise conflicts with values emphasized by religious traditions may be especially problematic for the religious to confront. As Strawbridge and associates (1998) point out, to the extent that family cohesiveness is valued and harmony expected, conflict within the family may be surprising when it occurs and more difficult to resolve:

> Faced with unruly children, difficult marriages, or problems caring for an older parent, religious persons may feel more at fault themselves, both because problems in these areas are not perceived as likely to happen to them and because the advice they receive from clergy and fellow congregation members may involve acquiescence over more active conflict resolution. (p. S124)

Individuals experiencing such problems may also feel stigmatized by others in the congregation who view such problems as a flaw in the relationship with God.

3. Another functional aspect of religion, as a "unified system of beliefs and practices relative to sacred things" (Durkheim, 1897/1951), is to define the spiritual and to give meaning to the divine. A belief system that emphasizes people's relationships to a spiritual world provides an explanation for events that may otherwise seem unexplainable. Religious involvement may therefore provide a coherent framework for interpreting uncertainties associated with day-to-day experiences, and may provide support in stressful, out-of-the-ordinary situations *(cognitive coherence hypothesis)*.

Zuckerman, Kasl, and Ostfeld (1984) reviewed mortality data during a two-year follow-up of some 400 elderly poor residents of three Connecticut cities in 1972 and 1974. Religiousness, measured by frequency of attendance at services and by two measures of religious strength and intensity, had an important protective effect among the elderly of both sexes in poorest health. This is the case when sociodemographic variables and health status measures are controlled. Among the religious, 19 percent of the males and 12 percent of the females who were ill died; the comparable mortality figures for the nonreligious in poor health were 42 percent of the males and 20 percent of the females. Virtually no differences in death rates were apparent between the religious and nonreligious elderly in good health. Borrowing from Antonovsky, the authors suggest that religiosity may provide individuals with a *sense of coherence* that events "are predictable and that there is a high probability that things will work out as well as can reasonably be expected" (Antonovsky 1979, p. 123).

More recently, Levin, Chatters, and Taylor (1995) used data from the National Survey of Black Americans, a nationally representative sample of black adults, to test the links among religiosity, health, and life satisfaction. These authors report that measures of both organizational (e.g., How often do you usually attend religious services?) and subjective (e.g., How religious would you say you are?) religiosity were found to be significantly related to life satisfaction after controlling for the effects of health. Even after controls for sociodemographic characteristics (e.g., gender, education, income, etc.) are employed, organizational religiosity still maintained a positive association with life satisfaction. This was the case across three age cohorts, those under 31 years of age, those 31 to 54 years, and those 55 years and over.

Why is organizational religiosity so strongly associated with the life satisfaction of blacks in this study, independent of health status? One answer, argued by Lincoln and Mamiya (1990), is that the basic aims and purposes of black American religious belief and expression are oriented toward buffering and/or abolishing conditions that negatively impact the well-being of blacks. As Levin, Chatters, and Taylor (1995) describe it:

> Black religious involvement, particularly that occurring within the organizational context of the church, serves to buffer and redress the deleterious social, psychological, and political-economic conditions that affect the lives of Blacks. In so doing, religious behaviors and attitudes impact on the physical and emotional well-being of Black Americans. (p. S161)

4. Finally, religious involvement may act to modify how individuals perceive particularly stressful situations, including hospitalization, disability, or other traumatic events. Typically, religious belief systems provide a variety of contexts for understanding and interpreting individual human suffering. In part, this function of religion may be an extension of the social support and cognitive coherence functions mentioned earlier *(theodicy hypothesis)*.

Idler and Kasl (1997a, 1997b) used data from the New Haven site of the Established Populations for the Epidemiologic Study of the Elderly ($N = 2,812$ in 1982) to explore the relationship between religious involvement and functional disability among elderly people. In both cross-sectional and longitudinal analysis, these authors find that the lives of religious-involved elderly persons are really quite different from those of the uninvolved. In general, they find religious involvement to be beneficial, with public religious participation (e.g., attendance at services) to be "positively associated with other types of social roles and activities as different from each other as exercising and getting together with family and friends for holidays" (1997a, p. S303).

Perhaps more importantly, these researchers discover that participation in traditional, organizational religious services presages better disability outcomes for the elderly. First, they show that, among already-disabled elderly, religious attendance has positive impact on participation in social activities and feelings of well-being. Second, they posit that religious participation may be an influential determinant of the recovery of elderly people with new disabilities. Why would such outcomes come about? Idler and Kasl (1997b) suggest an answer:

> Worshipping together with the religious congregation may offer the disabled elderly person a route, through prayer, or receiving the sacraments, or appreciation of the beauty of the place, to a transcendent state in which the body and its frailties don't matter that much. The motivation to return to this state, and to the accompanying social support and pleasant pastimes that religious groups provide, may be a strong factor influencing the recovery of elderly people with new disabilities. (p. S315)

About two-thirds of Idler and Kasl's sample of elderly people report some amount of difficulty with at least one disability item. Although this proportion may be higher than what is reported for the similarly affected elderly population at large, it does point out the scope of need for helping resources in one's community. Religious involvement can invigorate everyday life and be a source of help for troubles both in the present as well as in the future.

SUMMARY

The relative scarcity of research on religion and aging may have roots in methodological concerns. Most research is cross-sectional in nature, making it difficult for researchers to disentangle age, cohort, and period effects. Religiosity is a difficult concept to operationalize: Are organizational affiliations and attendance of more importance than measures of private devotional activity? Finally, most research simply does not distinguish between and among religious groups.

Contemporary beliefs and attitudes toward older people have roots in Scripture. Images of aging presented in the Old Testament are quite positive. Longevity is often presented as a reward for service to the Lord. The elderly often played vital roles as instruments of God, wielders of political power and influence, and custodians of the collective wisdom of the years. The Fifth Commandment offers the basic guideline in parent-child relationships. New Testament perspectives on old age and aging built on the Old Testament precedents. Distinctively Christian views of age and aging are intertwined with the conception of the personhood of Christ. Another important difference between the Old and New Testament is the portrayal of the relationship between death and aging.

Major societal functions of religion include social integration, social control, and social support. Religion can be a powerful integrative force for older people in society. Societies rich in ceremonialism and religious ritual tend to honor the aged and accord them prestige seldom found in less formalistic societies. Religion can also be a powerful force for social control. It can provide barriers to new ways of thinking and behaving. It can also force people to focus on otherworldly issues rather than the material conditions of their lives.

Data from the 1998 General Social Survey show a strong relationship between age and religious commitment. Older people are more likely than young adults to describe themselves as being strongly religious. There is difference between the old and middle-aged when it comes to attendance at religious services; also, the elderly report praying more often than the young or middle aged.

Early research on age and religious commitment provided four distinct models: traditional, lifetime stability, family life cycle, and progressive disengagement. Criticism of the early work centered on the narrow conceptualization of religiosity strictly in terms of attendance at religious services. The distinction between organizational religious commitment and private or individual religious commitment has become relevant. In addition, various researchers have identified different dimensions of organizational commitment.

Religiosity may influence the health status of older people in at least four ways: health behaviors hypothesis, social cohesiveness hypothesis, cognitive coherence hypothesis, and theodicy hypothesis. Empirical support exists for each hypothesis.

STUDY QUESTIONS

1. What methodological issues help explain the relative scarcity of research on religion and aging?

2. What is the general position of the elderly in ancient Hebraic culture as reflected in the Old Testament? How do the Old Testament and New Testament differ in their conception of the aging process and the elderly?

3. Describe three major functions of religion. Give examples.

4. Distinguish the old from young and middle-aged adults with regard to strength of religiousness, attendance at religious services, and frequency of prayer.

5. Describe Bahr's four models of the relationship between aging and church attendance. Which model does Bahr's own data support?

6. List some measures or dimensions of religiosity that are alternatives to attendance at religious services. What is the importance of being able to identify these alternative measures?

7. How may religion affect the health status of older people?

REFERENCES

Achenbaum, W. A. (1985). Societal perceptions of the aging and the aged. In R. H. Binstock & E. Shanas (Eds.), *Handbook of aging and the social sciences* (2nd ed.). New York: Van Nostrand Reinhold.

Amoss, P. (1978). *Coast Salish spirit dancing*. Seattle: University of Washington Press.

Amoss, P. (1981). Coast Salish elders. In P. Amoss & S. Harrell (Eds.), *Other ways of growing old*. Stanford, CA: Stanford University Press.

Antonovsky, A. (1979). *Health, stress, and coping*. San Francisco: Jossey-Bass.

Atchley, R. (1980). *Social forces in later life* (3rd ed.) Belmont, CA: Wadsworth.

Bahr, H. (1970). Aging and religious disaffiliation. *Social Forces, 49*, 59–71.

de Beauvoir, S. (1972). *Coming of age*. New York: G. P. Putnam's Sons.

Berkman, L. F., & Syme, S. L. (1979). Social networks, host resistance, and mortality: A nine-year follow-up study of Alameda County residents. *American Journal of Epidemiology, 109*, 186–204.

Blazer, D., & Palmore, E. (1976). Religion and aging in a longitudinal panel. *Gerontologist, 16* (1), 82–85.

Clymer, A. (1987, March 31). Survey finds many skeptics among evangelists' viewers. *New York Times*, pp. 1, 14.

Cowgill, D., & Holmes, L. 1972. *Aging and modernization*. New York: Appleton-Century-Crofts.

Cumming, E., & Henry, W. (1961). *Growing old: The process of disengagement*. New York: Basic Books.

Durkheim, E. (1897/1951). *Suicide*. New York: Free Press.

Durkheim, E. (1912/1965). *The elementary forms of religious life*. New York: Free Press.

Ellison, C. G. (1994). Religion, the life stress paradigm, and the study of depression. In J. S. Levin (Ed.), *Religion in aging and health*. Thousand Oaks, CA: Sage.

Fecher, V. (1982). *Religion and aging: An annotated bibliography*. San Antonio, TX: Trinity University Press.

Field, M. (1968). *Aging with honor and dignity*. Springfield, IL: Charles C. Thomas.

Finney, J. M., & Lee, G. R. (1976). Age differences on five dimensions of religious involvement. *Review of Religious Research, 18* (2), 173–179.

Gardner, J. W., & Lyon, J. L. (1982a). Cancer in Utah Mormon men by lay priesthood level. *American Journal of Epidemiology, 116,* 243–257.

Gardner, J. W., & Lyon, J. L. (1982b). Cancer in Utah Mormon women by church activity level. *American Journal of Epidemiology, 116,* 258–265.

Gove, W. (1973). Sex, marital status and mortality. *American Journal of Sociology, 79,* 45–67.

Graham, T. W., Kaplan, B., Cornoni-Huntley, J., James, S., Becker, C., Hadden, J. K., & Swann, C. E. (1978). Frequency of church attendance and blood pressure elevation. *Journal of Behavioral Medicine, 1,* 37–43.

Hadden, J. K., & Swann, C. E. (1981). *Prime time preachers: The rising power of televangelism.* Reading, MA: Addison-Wesley.

Heenan, E. F. (1972). Sociology of religion and aged. *Journal of Scientific Study of Religion, 11,* 171–176.

Hertz, J. H. (Ed.). (1981). *Pentateuch and haftorahs: Hebrew text, English translation and commentary.* London: Soncino Press.

Hess, B., & Markson, E. (1980). *Aging and old age.* New York: Macmillan.

Hoge, D. R., & Petrillo, G. H. (1978). Development of religious thinking in adolescence: A test of Goldman's theories. *Journal for the Scientific Study of Religion, 17,* 359–379.

Holmes, L. D. (1983). *Other cultures, elder years: An introduction to cultural gerontology.* Minneapolis: Burgess.

House, J. S., Robbins, C., & Metzner, H. L. (1982). The association of social relationships and activities with mortality: Prospective evidence from the Tecumseh community health study. *American Journal of Epidemiology, 116,* 123–140.

Hunsberger, B. (1985). Religion, age, life satisfaction, and perceived sources of religiousness: A study of older persons. *Journal of Gerontology, 40* (5), 615–620.

Idler, E. L. (1987). Religious involvement and the health of the elderly: Some hypotheses and an initial test. *Social Forces, 66* (1), 226–238.

Idler, E. L., & Kasl, S. V. (1997a). Religion among disabled and nondisabled persons I: Cross-sectional patterns in health practices, social activities, and well-being. *Journal of Gerontology: Social Sciences, 52B* (6), S294–S305.

Idler, E. L., & Kasl, S. V. (1997b). Religion among disabled and nondisabled persons II: Attendance at religious services as a predictor of the course of disability. *Journal of Gerontology: Social Sciences, 52B* (6), S306–S316.

Kart, C. S., Palmer, N. P., & Flaschner, A. B. (1987). Aging and religious commitment in a midwestern Jewish community. *Journal of Religion and Aging, 3* (¾), 49–60.

Koenig, H. G., George, L. K., & Siegler, I. C. (1988). The use of religion and other emotion-regulating coping strategies among older adults. *Gerontologist, 28* (3), 303–310.

Koenig, H. G., Kvale, J. N., & Ferrel, C. (1988). Religion and well-being in later life. *Gerontologist, 28* (1), 18–28.

Krause, N. (1997). Religion, aging, and health: Current status and future prospects. *Journal of Gerontology, 52* (6), S291–S293.

Lazerwitz, B. (1962). Membership in voluntary associations and frequency of church attendance. *Journal of Scientific Study of Religion, 2,* 74–84.

Lawton, M. P., Rajagopal, D., Brody, E., & Kleban, M. H. (1992). The dynamics of caregiving for a demented elder among Black American and white families. *Journal of Gerontology, 47,* S156–S164.

Levin, J. S. (1993). Age differences in mystical experience. *Gerontologist, 33* (4), 507–513.

Levin, J. S., Chatters, L. M., & Taylor, R. J. (1995). Religious effects on health status and life satisfaction among Black Americans. *Journal of Gerontology: Social Sciences, 50B* (3), S154–S163.

Levin, J. S., & Vanderpool, H. Y. (1989). Is religion therapeutically significant for hypertension? *Social Science and Medicine, 29* (1), 69–78.

Lincoln, C. E., & Mamiya, L. H. (1990). *The Black church in the African American experience.* Durham, NC: Duke University Press.

Maddox, G. (1979). Sociology of later life. *Annual Review of Sociology, 5,* 113–135.

Marcoen, A. (1994). Spirituality and personal well-being in old age. *Aging and Society, 14,* 521–536.

Marx, K. (1844/1963). Estranged labour—Economic and philosophic manuscripts of 1844. In C. W. Mills (Ed.), *Images of man.* New York: George Brazilier.

Medalie, J. H., Kahn, H. A., Neufeld, H. N., Riss, E., & Goldbourt, U. (1973). Five year myocardial infarction incidence II: Association of single variables to age and birthplace. *Journal of Chronic Disease, 26,* 329–349.

Mindel, C. H., & Vaughn, C. V. (1978). A multidimensional approach to religiosity and disengagement. *Journal of Gerontology, 33,* 103–108.

Moberg, D. O. (1965). Religiosity in old age. *Gerontologist, 5* (2), 80–85.

Moberg, D. O. (1972, January). Religion and the aging family. *The Family Coordinator*, pp. 47–60.

Norgard, T., & Kart, C. S. (1989, April). *Religiosity and health status among the elderly: Replication with national samples.* Paper presented at the annual meeting of the North Central Sociological Association, Akron, OH.

Orbach, H. (1961). Aging and religion. *Geriatrics, 16,* 534–540.

Pargament, K. I., Ensing, D. S., Falgout, K., Olsen, H., Reilly, B., Van Haitsma, K., & Warren, R. (1990). God help me: I. Religious coping efforts as predictors of the outcomes to significant negative life events. *American Journal of Community Psychology, 18,* 793–824.

Payne, B. (1982). Religiosity. In D. J. Mangen & W. A. Peterson (Eds.), *Research instruments in social gerontology: Vol. 2. Social roles and social participation.* Minneapolis: University of Minnesota Press.

Picot, S. J., Debanne, S. M., Namazi, K. H., & Wykle, M. L. (1997). Religiosity and perceived rewards of Black and White caregivers. *Gerontologist, 37* (1), 89–101.

Riley, M., & Foner, A. (1968). *Aging and society: Vol. 1. An inventory of research findings.* New York: Russell Sage Foundation.

Schaefer, R. T. (1986). *Sociology* (2nd ed.). New York: McGraw-Hill.

Schoenbach, V., Kaplan, B., Fredman, L., & Kleinbaum, D. G. (1986). Social ties and mortality in Evans County, Georgia. *American Journal of Epidemiology, 123,* 329–349.

Shenk, D. (1994). Honor thy mother: Aging women in Jewish tradition. In L. E. Thomas & S. A. Eisenhandler (Eds.), *Aging and the religious dimension.* Westport, CT: Auburn House.

Simmons, L. (1945). *The role of the aged in primitive society.* New Haven, CT: Yale University Press.

Sinclair, K. P. (1985). Koro and Kuia: Aging and gender among the Maori of New Zealand. In D. A. Counts & D. R. Counts (Eds.), *Aging and its tranformations: Moving toward death in Pacific societies.* Pittsburgh, PA: University of Pittsburgh Press.

Spencer, R., & Jennings, J. D. (1977). *The native Americans.* New York: Harper & Row.

Stark, R. (1968). Age and faith: A changing outlook as an old process. *Sociological Analysis, 29,* 1–10.

Strawbridge, W. J., Shema, S. J., Cohen, R. D., Roberts, R. E., & Kaplan, G. A. (1998). Religiosity buffers effects of some stressors on depression but exacerbates others. *Journal of Gerontology: Social Sciences, 53B* (3), S118–S126.

Vander Zanden, J. W. (1990). *Sociology: The core* (2nd ed.). New York: McGraw-Hill.

Wilensky, H. L. (1961). Life style, work situation, and participation in formal associations. In R. W. Kleemeier (Ed.), *Aging and leisure.* New York: Oxford University Press.

Wingrove, C. R., & Alston, J. (1974). Age, aging and church attendance. *Gerontologist, 11* (4), 356–358.

Young, G., & Dowling, W. (1987). Dimensions of religiosity in old age: Accounting for variation in types of participation. *Journal of Gerontology, 42* (4), 376–380.

Zuckerman, D., Kasl, S., & Ostfeld, A. M. (1984). Psychosocial predictors of mortality among the elderly poor: The role of religion, well-being, and social contacts. *American Journal of Epidemiology, 119,* 410–423.

CHAPTER FIFTEEN

RACIAL AND ETHNIC AGING

The United States has been described as a **melting pot** in which ethnic minorities lose their distinctive character and become assimilated into the broader culture. Healey (1998) suggests that contrary to the melting-pot image, assimilation in the United States has been a one-sided process better described by the terms *Americanization* and *Anglo-conformity*. These terms, he believes, more clearly highlight the fact that immigrant and minority groups are expected to adapt to Anglo-American culture as fast as possible.

The ideology of the melting pot has been challenged by those who emphasize the pluralism and diversity of U.S. society. Interest in pluralism and diversity in the United States may simply be a function of the fact that full assimilation has not materialized. Racial minorities in the United States continue to increase in number, and members of different ethnic and racial groups question whether full assimilation is a desirable outcome.

According to Healey (1998), pluralism comes in at least three forms. *Cultural pluralism* exists in a society when ethnic and racial groups are able to retain their unique character and when they are also able to participate equally in key roles in the society. *Structural pluralism* exists when a group has adopted the broader culture but does not have full and equal access to the institutions of the larger society. A third type of pluralism is exemplified by immigrant groups who prosper economically but who do not become Americanized. The "Chinatowns" found in many larger U.S. cities are *ethnic enclaves* in which individuals achieve some material success but do not necessarily learn English or adopt American values and norms.

Whether the United States is a melting pot or a pluralistic society may be an academic question. Clearly, as much as any society in the world, the United States has retained enormous ethnic and racial diversity. Andrew Greeley (1974) uses the notion of ethnogenesis to explain this diversity. **Ethnogenesis** describes a model of ethnic relations in which pressures to assimilate exist alongside pressures to maintain ethnic identification. In this model, maintaining an ethnic identity becomes a device for expressing group interests and maintaining group identity. Glazer and Moynihan (1970), in their classic work *Beyond the Melting Pot,* anticipated the ethnogenesis perspective. They recognized, for example, that European immigrants often lost original customs and ways by the third generation yet still voted differently, had different ideas about sex and the value of education, and were still, in many ways, as different from one another as their grandfathers had been. Glazer and Moynihan concluded, "The point about the melting pot is that it did not happen" (p. 290).

Ethnogenesis may be useful for explaining the experience of white ethnic groups; racial minority groups are a different matter. Perhaps the persistence of racial minority groups is easier to explain as a function of their identifying physical characteristics and their respective histories of exploitation, prejudice, and discrimination. Still, Torres-Gil (1992) predicts that early in this century, the aggregation of racial minorities—Asian and Pacific Islanders, Latinos, African Americans, and American Indians—will compose a new majority. By the end of this century, whites in the United States are likely to be a minority group. Among those 65 years of age and older, nonwhites (especially Latinos and Asian Americans) are among the fastest-growing groups.

Recognition of the ethnic and racial diversity present in the U.S. experience has only recently begun to have an impact on the field of social gerontology. Clearly, much of what has been learned about aging stems from studies of working- and middle-class whites. Unfortunately, from this point of view, minority aging has been defined as "deviance" and racial and ethnic aging has focused on differences from "white standards." Is there really anything to learn from studying the aging experiences of U.S. minorities? After all, there are many commonalities among the elderly that appear to cut across racial and ethnic lines. The greater number of older women and the higher remarriage rates of males, to cite two examples, appear in all elderly groups in the United States, regardless of racial and ethnic identification.

Kent (1971a, 1971b) believed that the study of minority patterns of aging was important for practical as well as theoretical reasons. From a practical point of view, it is important to remember that the aggregate number of minority aged is substantial, and these individuals are underrepresented among the prosperous and healthy. Thus, for those making social policy as well as those in practice in health care and social service, the study of minority aging is useful. From a theoretical point of view, it is important that ideas about the aging process be generalizable across cultural groups. There is no way to accomplish this without studying a variety of aged groups. Researchers often learn most about how their ideas work when they observe them in "extreme" situations, and the position of many minority aged in the United States makes it possible to test principles of aging in just such extreme situations. Finally, older people in minority racial/ethnic communities are significant in their own right. Their presence in the United States illustrates the role of race, ethnicity, and culture in shaping later life. As we shall see from the data presented next, their presence points to a future of increasing racial/ethnic diversity in old age and to multicultural lifestyles and preferences among the older population.

MINORITY AGING: A CASE
OF DOUBLE JEOPARDY?

Minority aging has been characterized by many as a case of *double jeopardy* (Jackson 1970, 1971; U.S. Senate 1971).[1] This term is used to reflect the idea that the negative effects of aging are compounded among minority group members. The suggestion is that aged minority group members suffer the double disadvantage of aged *and* race discrimination. Inherent in the concept of double jeopardy is the idea of comparison. Generally, researchers and policymakers have employed the concept to determine whether minority group members are more disadvantaged than are whites in the same age groupings. For example, 30 years ago, the U.S. Senate Special Committee on Aging (1971) reported that, compared to the white aged, minority aged were less well educated, had less income, suffered more illnesses and earlier death, had poorer quality housing and less choice as to where they live and where they work, and, in general, had a less satisfying quality of life. The Senate Committee followed this up by suggesting that social policy be generated to reflect these differences.

Dowd and Bengtson (1978) were among the first to empirically test the hypothesis of minority aging as a double jeopardy. To support the double jeopardy hypothesis, it should be demonstrated that differentials between adult whites and blacks *increase* with age. These authors analyzed data collected as part of a larger survey of adult (ages 45 to 74) African American, Mexican American, and Anglo residents of Los Angeles County. The researchers divided each group into three age strata—45 to 54, 55 to 64, and 65 to 74 years old—and compared them on a series of variables that included (1) total family income, (2) self-assessed health, (3) two measures of life satisfaction, and (4) a series of social interaction items. In general, the data on income and self-assessment of health from this study supported the double-jeopardy hypothesis.

For example, whereas the data gathered by Dowd and Bengtson showed that the incomes of all groups decline with age, the mean income reported by the oldest (ages 65 to 74) African American and Mexican American respondents was considerably lower than any other group. The relative decline in income from ages 45 to 74 was also substantially greater for minority respondents (55 percent for African Americans and 62 percent for Mexican Americans) than it was for whites (36 percent). Older minority respondents also reported poorer subjective health status than white respondents. The average health scores of African Americans and Mexican Americans declined 13 percent and 19 percent, respectively, across the age strata represented in the sample. The decline for whites was only 9 percent.

Two measures of life satisfaction were analyzed in this study: *optimism* and *tranquility.* A typical item related to optimism was: "As you get older, do you feel

---

[1]Some social scientists have used the term *triple jeopardy* to represent the position of minority aged. The reference is to being old, poor, and a member of a minority group. Jackson (1971) has used the designation *quadruple jeopardy* to represent those who are black, female, old, and poor.

less useful?" A negative response indicated life satisfaction. An item related to tranquility was: "Do you worry so much that you can't sleep?" Presumably, a negative response here would indicate life satisfaction.

The tranquility scores of Mexican Americans aged 65 to 74 were significantly lower than those of whites and African Americans. The decline in scores across the three age strata for Mexican Americans was so slight, however, that the impact of age on tranquility scores is questionable. The pattern is different for the second measure of life satisfaction, optimism, and clearly supports the double-jeopardy hypothesis. Mexican Americans showed a significant decline in optimism with age; their optimism scores were significantly lower than the scores of whites; and the differences in scores when compared to whites increases with age. Whites show a 2 percent decline in average optimism scores between those ages 45 to 54 and those ages 65 to 74, whereas the decline for Mexican Americans is 23 percent. In contrast, when African Americans and whites are compared on the two measures of life satisfaction, the differences present between younger respondents *narrow* and almost disappear entirely with age. This is sometimes referred to as the *leveling* function of age.

One measure of social interaction involved asking respondents the frequency with which they had contact with children and grandchildren. Mexican Americans at every age reported the most frequent contact with their children and grandchildren. Relative to whites, African Americans maintain an advantageous position on this measure in all but the oldest age stratum. A similar pattern exists on a second measure of social interaction, which asked respondents about their contacts with other relatives. Younger whites had fewer contacts with relatives than either African Americans or Mexican Americans, although the differences become smaller in the older age groups. The result is a *leveling of differences* across the ethnic groups.

In summary, Dowd and Bengtson's (1978) study found the notion of double jeopardy to characterize accurately the situation of minority aged (African Americans and Mexican Americans) on selected variables (especially income and self-assessment of health). Interestingly, the data also suggest that aging influences some variables in ways that *reduce* racial/ethnic differences that existed in midlife. Kent (1971a, 1971b; Kent & Hirsch 1969) has written of age as a *mediator* of racial and social differences. From this perspective, the problems faced by old people are seen as very similar regardless of ethnic or racial background.

More recently, Ferraro and Farmer (1996) tested the relative merits of the double jeopardy and age as leveler hypotheses. Using three waves of longitudinal data from a 15-year national survey of adults, they sought to determine if the health disadvantage experienced by young and middle-aged black Americans increases, decreases, or stays about the same in the later years. At baseline and for each subsequent wave of data collection, blacks showed health disadvantage relative to whites on all the measures of chronic and serious illness, disability, and subjective health. In addition, African Americans were found to be less likely to survive into older ages. Evidence that health problems may have worse effects on African Americans was also demonstrated in this research. For example, the data

Family members can be an important social support for people as they age.

show that once black people have heart problems, the condition is more likely to lead to disability than is the case among whites.

When analysis was confined to the survivors of the 15-year study, there was no evidence for the double-jeopardy hypothesis. Ferraro and Farmer (1996) also suggest that the age as leveler hypothesis may simply reflect "selective survival" among different populations. In summary, these authors offer that health inequities between older blacks and whites have likely been present since early in life and have persisted throughout the life course.

Some believe that too much attention continues to be focused on the concept of double jeopardy. They argue that, at best, the concept may be period bound and unable to capture the most recent social and political changes in the status of minority group members. At worst, investigators who have used the concept can be accused of providing very little useful information about age changes "in the statuses, roles, interpersonal relationships, attitudes, and values of adult minority individuals or populations as they age in their later years" (Jackson 1985, p. 284).

Data on the comparative average disadvantage of minority aged may not be particularly useful for recognizing diversity in the total minority aged population or within a specific subgroup, such as aged African American males (Kart 1990). The concept of double jeopardy has been employed in many studies in a fashion that suggests insensitivity to issues of aging and social change. Most researchers interested in measuring double jeopardy have used cross-sectional data that confound age and cohort effects. For example, income differences between young-old and old-old African American males are not a function of age alone, but also of differences in educational achievement as well as occupational and wage histories of males in different birth cohorts. Further, although there is abundant literature on racial differences in patterns of aging, very little attention has been paid to the issue of how social change differentially affects racial groups.

Schaie, Orchowsky, and Parham (1982) have used data on the life satisfaction of white and African American respondents to show "the interacting effect of race not only with age, but also with cohort and period effects" (p. 229). They determined that there were significant cohort effects in life satisfaction favoring earlier-born cohorts, regardless of race (even while controlling for health and income). Nevertheless, there were race differences across the period studied, with life satisfaction increasing for African Americans and remaining stable for whites. The authors speculate that this finding may result from African American respondents, on average, "beginning to perceive positive societal changes, which affect their overall levels of life satisfaction" (p. 229). This work may provide a model for moving beyond the double-jeopardy concept.

Manuel (1982) argues that people need to move beyond the assumption that application of a minority group label can be used as an indication that an individual has experienced the sociocultural events generally thought to be associated with the label. Given the complexity of racial and ethnic identity, the experience of some individuals may more closely resemble that of members of the majority than it will the experience of other members of what is only a nominal reference group. Clearly, there may be diversity within a minority group with regard to the extent and manner in which group members have been victimized by their minority group status. To paraphrase a question asked by Manuel, Can one assume that all aged African American males, for example, have had significantly less of a chance than their white counterparts to participate fully in U.S. institutions? To the contrary, he answers. It can be expected that there will be differential circumstances of aging within minority groups (Manuel 1982).

AGING AND THE MINORITY EXPERIENCE

This section describes the situation of aged members of selected racial and ethnic minority groups. In each case, demographic statistics are presented, followed by a discussion of some special aspects of the aging minority experience.

The African American Aged

The diversity of experience represented in the population of older African Americans cannot be overstated. Each cohort of African Americans in the United States has been exposed to different cultural practices as well as different social and political conditions. African Americans in the United States have experienced three major historical stages (Wilson 1978). The first stage includes slavery and the post–Civil War period. The second stage is the period of industrial expansion beginning in the last quarter of the nineteenth century and continuing through

World War II. The third stage comprises the contemporary era since the end of World War II.

During the first two stages, racial barriers were explicit and designed to systematically deny African Americans access to economic, political, and social resources. Efforts to minimize, neutralize, and even negate the voting privileges of African Americans exemplify these barriers (Simon & Eitzen 1982). Very few African Americans were employed in industrial plants prior to World War I. Most blacks resided in the South (perhaps as many as 90 percent) and most industrial plants were located in the North. African American labor in the South was restricted largely to agricultural work and domestic services. There was no major land reform after the Civil War, so former slaves often sold their labor to those controlling the agricultural system—their former slave masters (Feagin & Feagin 1999). Black sharecroppers and tenant farmers were tied to one farm or one rural area by mounting debts owed to whites who controlled the lending system.

The emergence of Jim Crow segregation[2] effectively prevented the employment of African Americans in industry. "King Cotton" declined in significance in the South and mechanization reduced the need for farm labor during the 1920s and 1930s, thereby increasing unemployment among African Americans. Anti-immigration legislation in the 1920s and subsequent decline in foreign immigration increased demand for black laborers in the industries of the North. World War II instigated a wave of African American migrants to the industrial cities of the North. Following the war, this concentration of African Americans in cities increased the likelihood of group actions in response to oppressive conditions in housing, employment, and the like. Increased educational opportunities allowed for the development of a cadre of African American leaders. The economic expansion in the United States between 1955 and 1972 and the civil rights movement of the 1950s and 1960s helped reduce overt discrimination in employment, housing, education, and transportation, and provided African Americans with access to economic and social resources (Eitzen 1986).

As Greene and Siegler (1984) point out, gains that occurred during the post–World War II period came too late to make appreciable impact on the educational level or economic condition of the oldest cohorts of African American elderly. Old-old African Americans today were in their mid-50s and perhaps the latter phases of their work careers by the time of the passage of the Civil Rights Act of 1964. Many in the younger cohorts of African American aged have benefitted, however, so that social and economic differentiation is greater among the young-old than the old-old.

---

[2]Named for an antebellum minstrel show character, the system of Jim Crow segregation included late nineteenth- and early twentieth-century statutes passed by the legislatures of the southern states that created a racial caste system in the American South. "Jim Crow" laws barred African Americans from access to employment and to public places such as restaurants, streetcars, hotel, and cemeteries, among other facilities. By 1914, every southern state had passed laws that created two separate societies—one black, the other white. This artificial structure was maintained by denying the voting franchise to blacks through the use of devices such as poll taxes and literacy tests.

Recent African American experience in the United States contains an important immigrant component. About 5 percent of the African American population, perhaps as many as 1.6 million people, is made up of immigrants from Africa and the Caribbean. Most of these individuals have come to the United States since 1970. The 1990 census reported about 200,000 African-born individuals living in the United States, with large concentrations in New York, California, Massachusetts, and Texas. The census also reported about 1.1 million black Americans of Caribbean ancestry. This does not include Latino groups, such as Puerto Ricans. Rather, it includes a number of different national-origin groups, including Jamaicans, Trinidadians, and Haitians, among others. Most live in New York or Florida, and each group has its own history, language, and culture.

Today, African American elderly make up about 8 percent of the total elderly population; about 12 percent of the total U.S. population is African American. In general, the U.S. African American population is younger than the population of whites. As Table 15.1 shows, at the end of the 20th century, the median age for whites was 36.5 years, whereas that for African Americans was 30.1 years. U.S. populations of Latinos and American Indians are even younger than African Americans. The proportion of the African American population that is old is considerably smaller than that of the white population; 14.1 percent of whites are 65 years or older today, but only 7.8 percent of African Americans are similarly aged. Disparities in the respective proportions of the population made up by those 55 to 64 years (9.1 vs. 6.4 percent, respectively) suggest that the differences in "agedness" between whites and African Americans is likely to persist.

Most people attribute the relative youthfulness of African Americans to lower life expectancy. Although the differential in life expectancy between the two races contributes moderately to the relative youthfulness of the African

TABLE 15.1   Age Distribution by Race, 55 Years of Age and Over: 1997–1999[1]

	ALL RACES	WHITE	BLACK	LATINO[2]	ASIAN & PACIFIC ISLANDER	AMER. INDIAN, ESKIMO, & ALEUT
Total (in 1,000s)	269,094	192,178	34,598	29,703	10,071	2,029
Percent	100%	100%	100%	100%	100%	100%
Ages 55 to 64	8.3%	9.1%	6.4%	5.5%	6.9%	6.5%
65 to 74	6.6	7.7	4.7	3.3	3.6	4.0
75+	5.3	6.4	3.1	1.8	2.8	3.2
Median age (in years)	35.4	36.5	30.1	26.4	31.6	27.6

[1]Estimates taken from different sources ranging from 1997 to 1999.
[2]Latinos may be of all races.

Source: U.S. Bureau of the Census website <www.census.gov>.

American population, the key factor is the higher fertility rate among African Americans. Based on fertility during 1997, the number of births a woman could be expected to have in a lifetime was 1.99 for whites and 2.43 for blacks. A total fertility rate of 2.11 represents "replacement level" fertility for the total population. This disparity in fertility rates contributes to the fact that approximately 45 percent of all African Americans are under the age of 25, whereas only about 35 percent of all whites are in this age grouping.

As an aside, it is useful to note that the phrase *racial crossover in mortality* describes the fact that the death rate for African Americans in virtually all age groups, except the very aged, is significantly higher than the rate for whites. In the older years, the racial differential declines and, among people in their 80s, a crossover occurs in which the reported death rates of African Americans of both sexes fall below those of whites (Zopf 1986). Several hypotheses for this crossover effect have been put forth, although hard data are scarce. Some suggest that the effect is an artifact of age misreporting in older African American cohorts, while others argue that genetic and environmental factors combine to produce hardier older African Americans (Jackson 1988).

Readers should be reminded that the size and age composition of the African American population show wide geographical variation. For example, 26 percent of the total Atlanta metropolitan statistical area (MSA) population was made up of African Americans in 1996; the San Diego MSA was composed of only 6.4 percent African Americans in 1996. These differences reflect the residential patterns of African Americans. Approximately 53 percent of all African Americans live in the South; only 9.4 percent live in the West. Most aged African Americans residing in the North and West have their roots in the South. Moreover, these southern roots have greatly affected African American cultural patterns, including religion, culinary habits, language, and life-style.

Despite the historical situation, African Americans have become urbanites. By 1990, 68 percent of all African Americans in the United States resided in the 51 metropolitan areas with the largest African American population. African American urbanization has come about at the same time as white suburbanization, leaving many areas in central cities without a sufficient tax base to support programs for the less affluent minority aged.

Aged African Americans fare worse than aged whites across a variety of socioeconomic indicators. Elderly blacks have fewer years of education, lower incomes, and lower occupational status. Census data comparisons for the older population in 1993 show that 46.3 percent of African Americans completed less than nine years of formal education, as compared with 24.1 percent of people of all races. Black aged are only about one-half as likely to have a high school diploma or higher than is the case for white aged (33.0 vs. 63.3 percent, respectively, in 1993).

The median income of aged black males in 1992 was $8,031, or about 53 percent of that received by aged white males ($15,276); aged black females had median income that was 73 percent that of their aged White female counterparts in 1992 ($6,220 vs. $8,579, respectively). Nearly two-thirds (65.8 percent) of White married couples with a householder aged 65 or older in 1992 had incomes of at least

$20,000. Only about 43 percent of elderly Black married couples had incomes greater than $20,000 in the same year.

Older African Americans are found in the labor force in about the same proportion as older whites; as with African Americans at all other ages, however, their work brings them less income. The work histories of many African Americans have clearly had an impact on their retirement income. African American unemployment has been significantly higher than that of whites. African Americans have also been overrepresented in jobs (e.g., domestic service) and industries (nonunionized) that do not afford protection from the whims of the marketplace. Interestingly, Belgrave (1988), using data gathered from African American and white women ages 62 through 66 in Cleveland, Ohio, found that African American women were more likely than whites to have worked steadily most of their adult lives, more likely to be eligible for pensions, but less likely to have retired. Gender is probably the most widely studied predictor of socioeconomic status among aged African Americans. In summarizing this body of work, Taylor and Chatters report that "elderly black women tend to have more years of education than older black men" (1988, p. 436). Despite this educational advantage, however, older African American women have lower levels of occupational prestige, lower incomes, and higher incidences of poverty.

The health status of older African Americans is generally thought to be poorer than that of older whites (Ferraro 1987). Krause (1987) made a similar finding, although he identified different stress-related correlates of health status for whites and African Americans. Chronic financial strain was found to be associated with ill health among older whites, whereas crisis events in the social support network were related to poor health among older African Americans. Krause argues that older African Americans may be more integrated into their communities than are older whites. This social involvement often occurs within the context of family ties and church-related social networks. Still, as Krause points out, social support entails reciprocity and greater involvement in the lives of others. Such involvement in the lives of others can be stressful and detrimental to health, especially when network members experience stressful events.

The disadvantaged health status of older African Americans also is displayed in reduced life expectancy, particularly among males. As a result, many African Americans do not live long enough to collect the benefits of Social Security and other programs for the elderly—even those to which they have contributed through many years of taxation.

Income—or more accurately, the lack of it—is probably the most serious problem faced by aged African Americans in the United States. The high rate of poverty among aged African Americans (26.0 percent in 1997 vs. 9.0 percent for aged whites) reduces their capacity to deal effectively with other major concerns, including health, crime, transportation, housing, and nutrition. We can put a human face on such dry assertion:

> Mrs. Mary C. was a widow. She eked out her existence on a tiny allotment from Social Security....Mrs. C. had suffered chronic health problems for ten years...

regular check-ups by the doctor were important.... On one occasion, after Mrs. C had left the doctor's office and returned to the car, she remarked that the doctor...had written a prescription for her. Mrs. C.'s friend immediately turned her car in the direction of the drugstore. Seeing where her friend was headed, Mrs. C. said, "Oh, no, I'm not going to get the prescription filled now.... I'm going to wait until the first of the month." (Dancy 1977, pp. 12–13)

An unfilled prescription can do nothing to keep Mrs. C. healthy. Lacking resources, however, she must wait until the first of the month when the Social Security check arrives before filling the physician's prescription.

Income is not the only factor affecting the health status of elderly African Americans. Even if health services are readily available (and this is not always the case if one is poor or African American or both), many factors may affect the likelihood of accessing those services, including fear of illness and its consequences, questions about the efficacy of modern medicine, mistrust of physicians and hospitals, education and language barriers, and transportation, among other factors.

Fear of crime is a problem for elderly people of all races. In the 1995 National Criminal Victimization Survey (NCVS), 2.5 times as many black as white households indicated that crime was a problem in their neighborhood. Interestingly, actual victimization data reflected only modest differences between blacks and whites. While 27 percent of black households experienced at least one criminal victimization in the past 12 months, only 23 percent of white households had similar experiences.

Compared to other age groups, victimization rates are lowest among the aged. For example, the victimization rate for the total population for all crimes of violence in 1996 was 42 per 1,000 persons. All groupings of persons under 35 years of age had victimization rates higher than this total rate. The rate for those 65 years of age was 4.9/1,000. In general, blacks had a victimization rate from all violent crimes that was 27.9 percent higher than that for whites (52.3/1,000 vs. 40.9/1,000, respectively). Compared to whites, blacks were 270 percent more likely to be victimized by robbery and 63 percent more likely to have experienced an aggravated assault.

Many African American elderly reside in poorer inner-city neighborhoods. Often, the official crime statistics simply do not reflect all the victimization of the elderly in such neighborhoods. Old people fear attacks and robberies but also may feel that going to the police is useless. Many remember a time when they were accorded less than first-class citizenship by police and the courts. The U.S. Bureau of Justice reports that in 1996, 22.1 percent of the white population 12 years of age or older had contact with the police for any reason; this compared with 15.6 percent for similarly aged blacks. Whites were almost 60 percent more likely to report a crime and 76 percent more likely to ask the police for help (U.S. Bureau of the Census 1998, Table 360).

About 44 percent of all African American households in the United States were owner occupied in 1995; this compares with 69 percent for whites. While home ownership generally increases with age, rates actually peak in the 55 to 64 age category. In 1997, 79.1 percent of the aged reported living in owner-occupied households. Thus, it seems a reasonable assumption that more than 44 percent of the African American elderly own their homes.

Many elderly homeowners reside in housing units with internal deficiencies. Such deficiencies include leaking water (6.5 percent), exposed electrical wiring (1.6 percent), and broken plaster or peeling paint (2.3 percent), among others. African American owners (regardless of age) have higher rates of internal deficiencies (e.g., leaking water, 12.5 percent; broken plaster or peeling paint, 5.3 percent).

Housing costs constitute a substantial portion of regular income. According to the Department of Housing and Urban Development (HUD), renters who spend more than 30 percent of before-tax income on housing and homeowners with housing expenditures in excess of 40 percent of income have *excessive housing costs*. Estimates for 1995 from the American Housing Survey are that 15.4 percent of elderly homeowners and 40.2 percent of elderly renters have monthly housing costs at 40 percent or more of their income. The median percent of monthly income spent on housing in 1995 by elderly homeowners was 18 percent; for elderly renters, the median amount is 38 percent. For all African Americans who own a home, the median amount of monthly income spent on housing was 20 percent; 18.8 percent of all African American homeowners spent 40 percent or more of monthly income on housing costs. Many low-income elderly are simply unable to keep up with the rising housing costs, whether for rent or for home mortgage and related maintenance costs.

The 1968 Civil Rights Act officially banned most housing discrimination in the United States. The conventional wisdom is, however, that this and subsequent housing laws are generally unenforced and that discriminatory practices in housing persist at some level in all areas of the nation. According to Feagin and Feagin (1999), housing audit studies for the 1995–97 period in New Orleans, Montgomery (Alabama), Fresno (California), and San Antonio found discrimination rates against perspective black renters from 61 to 77 percent. Massey and Denton (1993) describe such efforts at residential segregation as "the institutional apparatus that supports other racially discriminatory processes" (p. 8).

African American aged are residentially concentrated in central cities and low-income areas; thus, they are somewhat more likely to reside in older housing. Many of the homes owned by the elderly were built before World War II. In fact, 20.2 percent of all housing units in the United States were built before 1940. Many of these units are of high quality, but some are substandard. The pace of housing construction in the 1990s means that many physically substandard units have been removed from the housing inventory, but many substandard units remain and are necessary to provide some degree of shelter for individuals. An undersupply of housing, especially in the inner city, also means that those with low income are often crowding two or three generations together in their homes or apartments and are at great risk for homelessness.

Although, in general, many of the problems of aged African Americans are related to income deprivation, two areas of strength emerge in which participation is not affected by income status: family and religion. These deserve special mention.

African American Family Ties. It has become part of the conventional wisdom that family ties are a source of strength among African Americans. Much evidence suggests that in the African American experience, the notion of family extends beyond the immediate household. Over a generation ago, Stack (1970) showed how family functions were carried out for urban African Americans by clusters of kin who may or may not reside together. She offered the example of Viola Jackson's brother, who, after his wife died, "decided to raise his two sons himself. He kept the two boys and never remarried. His residence has been consistently close to one or another of his sisters who have fed and cared for his two sons" (p. 309).

Groger (1992) identified six major strategies for coping, based on her interviews with 35 black informants aged 59 to 90 residing in the rural Piedmont region of North Carolina. Among these strategies was the pooling of resources by living together in an extended household. This provided an opportunity to share limited resources. Mr. and Mrs. F, retired sharecroppers, exemplified this strategy:

> They have 12 children: three sons and three daughters within six miles, one son and one daughter 25 miles away, one daughter in New Jersey, and three adult daughters who, with two of their own children, live with them.... Mrs. F cooks, sews, and mends for all but the daughter in New Jersey. They all share food, household items, and clothing, and whoever has money pays the bills. (p. 213)

Elderly African American women continue to play an important role in this extended kin network that so well characterizes the family life of many urban African Americans. The proportion of black households headed by women increased from 18 percent in 1950 to almost 49 percent in 1998 (about two-thirds of these are single women heading family households with no spouse present); only 26.9 percent of white households were headed by women in 1998 and two-thirds of these (67.5 percent) were single females living alone or heading nonfamily households. In 1998, 78 percent of all black female-headed households without a spouse present contained their own and/or related children under 18 years of age.

Is this matriarchal structure of the African American family a cause or a result of income deprivation so prevalent in the black community? One argument, consistent with a *culture of poverty* theory, is that poverty is perpetuated by the characteristics of the poor. From this perspective, the female-headed family structures of the black community and other cultural characteristics correlated with poverty are defined as part of the problem and must be fixed. The assumption is that if only the poor could be assimilated to "good," white, middle-class values, the "problem" of a matriarchal family structure would be solved.

An opposing view is that the matriarchal structure of the African American family is a consequence of urban poverty rather than a cause. From this view, this family structure is an adaptive mechanism, reflective of racial discrimination and the scarcity of jobs for urban black males (Healey 1998). In poor black neighborhoods, the supply of men available to support a family is reduced by unemployment, violence, and incarceration. These conditions are themselves creations of urban poverty and the development of the underclass (Wilson 1996). As a result, child rearing falls disproportionately on females, and female-headed households are more common than in advantaged neighborhoods. Aged black females carry more than their share of this child-rearing burden.

The importance of aged females as a resource for the African American family structure cannot be exaggerated. In part, this is a result of the poverty of such families, which sits at the intersection of racism and sexism. Farley (1995, p. 80) offers:

> Black…female-householder families experience a double disadvantage in income—the low wages and high unemployment rates associated with minority group status *and* the low wages of women. Significantly, neither of these has anything to do with the effects of one-parent, female-headed families per se.

From this vantage point, the family structure is anything but weak or pathological. What needs "fixing" is not the African American family. Rather, the solution to urban black poverty will require fundamental changes in the urban-industrial economy and substantial changes in the distribution of resources and opportunities in U.S. society (Healey 1998).

African Americans are more likely than whites to rely on family members because many believe that they have little expectation of receiving effective service from social service agencies. This may especially be the case for older African Americans, who have a painful history of inequality, rejection, and ejection when it comes to dealing with such agencies.

Family members often value their aged relations because they serve as important role models. Dancy (1977) listed four strengths of the African American elderly that continue to be relevant today:

1. The accumulation of wisdom, knowledge, and common sense about life comes not only from age but from the experience of hardship and suffering.
2. A creative genius allows African Americans to do much with little.
3. The ability to accept aging results from their belief that old age is a reward in itself. Many elderly African Americans voice this sentiment: "I thank the Lord that He spared me!"
4. African Americans maintain a sense of hope and optimism for a better day.

The African American Church.   In general, religion is a source of strength to African American elderly. Historically, the church has been a frame of reference for African Americans in coping with racial discrimination, and it has played a role in their survival and advancement. The church is one institution that African Americans control locally; it has remained relatively free from white authority. The role of the church in the African American community became especially important after the Civil War. Churches were mutual-aid societies, ministering to those who were ill, and they functioned as centers for the pooling of economic, social, and political resources (Feagin & Feagin 1999). Many churches established schools and functioned as community schooling centers well into the twentieth century. Beginning in the 1950s, the nonviolent civil rights movement had significant support in the black churches. Minister-leaders such as Dr. Martin Luther King, Jr., and, more recently, the Reverend Jesse Jackson, have been able to harness the religious sentiments of African Americans to mobilize support for political action (Feagin & Feagin 1999).

The African American church is really many churches, including traditional Protestant denominations, such as Baptists and Methodists, as well as fundamentalist groups. Religious behavior within these churches often differs from that in comparable white churches. The African American church is a place of expression, and worship frequently takes the form of celebration. More recently, new urban religious groups have become forces in the black community. For example, the Nation of Islam broke with the Christian background of many African Americans, and has pressed for a more black-oriented theology with strong messages of pride and self-help inherent in the orthodoxy.

Religion is a main involvement of many African American elderly. For most, this simply reflects the continuation of a lifelong trend. Church attendance and participation in church activities were important early in life and continue to be so in later life. Participation in church activities provides an opportunity for many to "be somebody." African American elderly receive high status and respectability in the community as a function of such participation.

> Mr. John Jordon worked as a baggage handler.... He was in his late fifties and had worked for twenty-five years for the same company.... He had been passed over...for promotion to a job with more pay and responsibility.... He was told that he was "not ready" or lacked the skills or was given other excuses. Yet he saw whites with the same education as his—tenth grade—get better opportunities. What kept Mr. Jordon from becoming demoralized and bitter was his church.... Now he was also treasurer of the church—a job of enormous responsibility.... Mr. Jordon's church appreciated his talents, and Mr. Jordon was a faithful man and loved his church. There he was somebody. (Dancy 1977)

Finally, considering the influential position of the church in the African American community, it is essential that service providers understand the roles the church plays in the lives of African American elderly. The church is not only a place where large numbers of elderly can be reached but it is also a place where needs can be assessed and services delivered.

The Latino Aged[3]

In 1997, Latinos constituted 11.1 percent of the U.S. population, or over 29 million people. Next to African Americans, they make up the largest minority in the

---

[3]Following Murguia (1991), we use the term *Latino* because it suggests cultural pluralism and cultural maintenance, including continued use of the Spanish language. An alternative designation, *Hispanic,* is an English-language word that suggests assimilation or aspirations to assimilation.

United States. The Latino population is fast growing, with relatively high birthrates and immigration rates. Officially, this population has about doubled in size since 1980. Few doubt that the actual rate of growth has been higher as a function of illegal immigration. Current U.S. Census Bureau projections show the Latino population exceeding the African American population in the United States by the year 2010, making it the nation's largest minority group.

The Latino population is a heterogeneous group. About 63 percent of all Latinos are Mexican, 11 percent are Puerto Rican, and 25 percent are of other Latino heritage, including Cubans and those from Central and South America. The diversity of the population has created real problems for researchers and helps explain why so little systematic research is carried out on Latinos. Latinos are not easily categorized; attempts to generalize from Cubans in Florida to Puerto Ricans in New York and Mexican Americans in California is likely to bear little fruit. In addition, Latinos are one of the youngest ethnic groups in the United States; as seen in Table 15.1, the median age in 1999 was 26.4 years, the youngest of all groups represented in the table and 10 years more youthful than the white population.

The elderly account for only 5.1 percent of the total Latino population. In light of the major problems faced by the population in general, the special concerns of the elderly have not emerged with a visibility in any way comparable to the situation among Anglos. Until this changes, gerontologists are forced to rely on widely and varied sources for relevant materials. Because much of this available (although scarce) literature concerns itself with Mexican Americans, they dominate the discussion here. This is the case, despite the fact that the proportion of Mexican Americans who are 65 years or older is lower than for Cubans, Puerto Ricans, and other Latinos (see Table 15.2).

Before the 1830s, Mexicans had established numerous communities in what is now the southwestern United States. The annexation of Texas in 1845 precipitated a war with Mexico. By 1848, Mexico was forced to cede most of the Southwest to the United States for a $15 million settlement. Mexican residents had the choice of remaining there or moving south, and most stayed on, believing

TABLE 15.2   Age Distribution of the Latino Population: 1997

AGE	LATINO TOTAL	MEXICAN	PUERTO RICAN	CUBAN	CENTRAL AND SOUTH AMERICAN	OTHER LATINOS
Under 5 years	11.6%	12.8%	9.9%	6.1%	9.6%	10.3%
5 to 14 years	18.7	20.1	20.3	10.0	14.7	17.2
15 to 44 years	50.9	51.0	48.7	40.4	56.8	50.0
45 to 64 years	13.8	12.1	15.8	22.8	15.8	15.5
65 years +	5.1	4.1	5.3	20.7	4.2	7.0

Source: Statistical Abstract of the United States, 1998, 118th ed. (Washington, DC: U.S. Bureau of the Census, 1998), Table 55.

that their legal rights would be protected by treaty. By the late 1850s, new settlers came to Texas to ranch and farm. Eventually, land owned by Mexicans was lost to these new immigrants, most of whom were white.

At least three peak immigration periods during the twentieth century can be identified. According to Feagin and Feagin (1999), Mexican migration increased during the 1920s, with approximately 500,000 workers and their families entering the United States. New markets were opening for agricultural produce, and business interests opposed restrictions on Mexican immigration. World War II brought a more substantial migration of Mexican workers. A 1942 Emergency Farm Labor (*Bracero*) agreement between the United States and Mexico again provided needed Mexican workers for U.S. agriculture. Feagin and Feagin (1999) estimate that between 1942 and 1962, about five million braceros entered the United States. While many of these were seasonal workers with temporary permits, many were undocumented. Many employers were eager to employ these low-wage workers.

The mid-1960s brought an abrupt change in attitude toward Mexican immigrants amid efforts to protect employment for nativist whites. The 1965 Immigration Act set an annual limit of 120,000 immigrants into the United States from the Western Hemisphere. This limit was later lowered to 20,000 per year for Mexican immigrants. Despite efforts to restrict legal immigration, what became clearer was the extent to which the U.S. economy was dependent on undocumented immigrants. Urrea (1996), who grew up on the Texas-Mexico border, has written of how these immigrants are the

> financial backbone of Dole, Green Giant, McDonald's, Stouffers, Burger King, the Octopus car wash chain, Del Monte, Chicken of the Sea, Heinz, Hunt's, Rosarito, Campbell's m-m-m good, Wendy's, Taco Bell, Lean Cuisine, Dinty Moore, Hormel, midnight shifts, front lawn raking, pool scrubbing, gas station back rooms, blue-jean stitching, TV assembly, [and] athletic-shoe sole gluing [and many other such jobs]. (p. 18)

Nevertheless, concerns about undocumented immigrants have remained in the public eye. Passed in 1986, the Immigration Reform and Control Act (IRCA) contained the following provisions:

1. Legalization of undocumented immigrants resident continuously since 1982
2. Sanctions for employers who hire undocumented aliens
3. Reimbursement of governments for the added costs of legalization
4. Screening of welfare applicants for immigration status
5. Special programs to bring in agricultural laborers

The general consensus is that a clear majority of those granted IRCA legalization were Mexican immigrants. Anti-immigrant sentiment and rhetoric have increased over the past decade, most especially in California, where ballot initiatives have been employed in an effort to restrict access of undocumented immigrants to an array of public services. Motivated in part by concern that immigrants would become dependent on public welfare programs, in 1996, the Congress passed the Illegal Immigration Reform and Immigrant Responsibility Act (IIRIRA). This legislation imposed new restrictions on legal immigrants, increased the number of border control agents, and imposed income requirements for families seeking to sponsor immigrant relatives. Interestingly, as Feagin and Feagin (1999) point out, Latino immigrants are employed at higher levels and use welfare programs less often than other racial/ethnic groups in the United States.

The Latino population is concentrated largely in the southwestern states of California and Texas, where 53 percent of all Latinos are projected to be living today. Most of these people are of Mexican descent. A majority of Puerto Ricans live in New York and New Jersey; in 1996, 15.5 percent of the residents of New York State were of Latino origin and almost 17 percent of the New York City metropolitan area were Latinos. Cubans have settled primarily in Florida; in 1996, 36.6 percent of the 3.5 million residents of the Miami–Fort Lauderdale metropolitan area were of Latino origin. A majority of the Latino population resides in urban areas, with most living in central cities.

About half of the Latino elderly are foreign born. Cubans and Puerto Ricans are more recent migrants than Mexican Americans, many of whom are descendants of original settlers of territories annexed by the United States in the Mexican-American War. The Latino population is an even younger population than African Americans (30.3 percent under 15 years of age vs. 28 percent for African Americans in 1997). High fertility and large family size, in addition to immigration of the young and repatriation of the middle-aged, contribute to the youthfulness of this group.

Overall, a lower proportion of Latinos than African Americans had a Bachelor's degree or higher by 1997 (10.3 vs. 13.3 percent, respectively). However, a higher proportion of Latinos than African Americans are employed (63 vs. 58.2 percent, respectively, in 1997); there is negligible difference between Latino and black families in 1997 median income ($26,179 vs. $26,522, respectively) (U.S. Bureau of the Census 1998, Tables 51 and 55). One in four (24.4 percent) Latino elderly persons lived below the poverty level in 1996 (vs. 25.3 percent for black elderly), although there are substantial differences by ancestry. On family income and poverty measures, Puerto Ricans ranked low, whereas Cuban Americans were closer to the European American population than they were to Mexican Americans or Puerto Ricans.

The proportion of Latinos holding managerial and/or professional jobs is only a small fraction of that for whites. However, there are marked differences between Cubans, who more frequently hold high-paying positions, and Mexican Americans and Puerto Ricans who are more likely to be found in lower-income occupations. For example, in 1997, median income among Cubans was $35,616 and among Puerto Ricans was $23,646. Many elderly Latinos work in unskilled labor or as farm workers, and likely stay in the labor force longer than white elderly. Few have had lengthy work careers in settings that provide retirement preparation. Others either entered the country illegally or have failed to maintain certification of their residential status as aliens. In either case, they forfeit benefits and services for which they might otherwise be eligible.

Often, the special needs of Latino elderly are understated because of the popular assumption that they are properly cared for within the context of the extended family. Aged Latinos are seen as receiving positive emotional and social support because of their unique position as older family members. Historically, this popular view of Latinos may have been correct; today, however, it is incomplete and misleading. For example, many widowed women over age 75 do live in an extended family household. Those who live alone, however, are often found in inadequate housing, with the incidence of substandard housing greater among Latinos than among whites (Cuellar 1990).

The traditional Mexican American family has been described as a supportive and flexible structure that assumes a variety of functions in dealing with the environment and with the emotional and psychological aspects of the family unit and individuals (Sotomayor 1971). Such a family pattern maintains the elderly within the physical and social life of the family, thus reducing the likelihood of isolation. In general, the aged person holds high status and has considerable influence in the family's social life. Maldonado (1975) argues that this division of labor in the Mexican American family often changes as family members grow older. Close observation, he says, reveals that the woman plays an increasingly more active role as she grows older, to the point that the grandmother may be dominant in the extended family. In part, this may reflect the higher early death rate among Mexican American males.

To a great extent, the foregoing describes a picture of the Mexican American family that may not take into account the rapidly changing situation in the Mexican American community. These changes, which may have a negative impact on the elderly, include the increased urbanization of Mexican Americans (*barrioization*) and a gradual movement toward a stronger nuclear family. Still, there is no easy characterization of Latino communities. In discussing Mexican American communities in Los Angeles, Moore and Vigil (1993) find widespread poverty, continuing immigration, and strained social institutions together with a strong enclave economy, many extended families, growing political power, and vital religious organizations.

However, many elderly find themselves either in a small town or rural community isolated from their adult children, or in a barrio where, because of the social and educational mobility of the young, their status and influence have declined significantly. Language facility creates another barrier to social integration. Using data from the 1990 Census, Mutchler and Brallier (1999) report that about one-third of the older Latino population in the United States speaks English poorly or not at all. A sizable number of these individuals are "linguistically isolated" in that they live either alone or with other nonproficient speakers of English.

This generation gap leaves elderly Latinos misunderstood by the society at large and by younger members of their own families. In addition, the general society, with its failure to recognize the diversity of Latino culture and its misunderstanding of the issues confronting Latino families, believes that the Latino family will provide for its older members. Although patterns of intergenerational assistance remain strong, especially in comparison to white populations, more older Mexican Americans are reporting unfulfilled expectations of filial responsibility by their adult children (Markides, Boldt, & Ray 1986; Markides, Liang, & Jackson 1990).

The American Indian Aged[4]

The aged American Indian population is small and relatively invisible. Despite the enormous diversity among American Indian cultures (500 federally recognized tribes and nearly 200 native languages spoken), they suffer deprivation by any social or economic indicator employed. To a great extent, this reflects the special history of American Indians and their relationship with the U.S. government. Certainly, no other minority group has been as physically and socially isolated from the mainstream of U.S. life.

The total population of American Indians in 1999 (including Eskimos and Aleuts) was approximately 2.4 million. A century or so ago, anthropologists estimated that the aboriginal population of North America before contact with the Europeans (circa 1600) was between 500,000 and 1.5 million persons. Some critics have suggested that these figures are too low and were generated for the purpose of legitimating European conquest of an allegedly unoccupied land (Feagin & Feagin 1999). A considered estimate by Dobyns (1966) puts the number of Americans Indians in North America at near 10 million at the time of the initial European contact. European diseases and firepower sharply reduced the number to a low point of about 200,000 in 1850.

This decrease may be a unique occurrence in United States history. Presumably, other minority groups have experienced involuntary relocation and social and economic discrimination, but none has been subjected to a comparable assault on life itself. Despite general agreement that high fertility and reduced mortality have contributed to an increase in the American Indian population, even current estimates should be regarded as crude. The Bureau of Indian Affairs (BIA) and the U.S. Census Bureau often disagree on their respective estimates.

Almost 45 percent of the American Indian population resides in the western United States, although the largest concentrations of Native people are found in California, Oklahoma, Arizona, and New Mexico, in that order. Oklahoma, California, and Arizona all had in excess of 200,000 American Indians in 1997. Almost two-thirds of the native population resides on or near a reservation; the remainder are urbanized. This is the only minority group that is less urbanized than the U.S. population as a whole. Los Angeles has the most American Indians

---

[4]The term *Indian*, as well as names of major Native American tribes, were generally applied as a matter of convenience by European settlers. In part, this renaming is a result of subordination reflecting a process whereby the colonized lost control even over their own names. We use the term *American Indian* throughout this chapter not because we endorse this process but simply to reflect the reality of the status of Native Americans in the western Hemisphere.

of any urban area, approximately 113,000. Phoenix-Mesa, New York, Tulsa, Oklahoma City, San Francisco, and Seattle all had over 45,000 American Indians in 1996. The urbanization of this population is a relatively recent phenomenon. The migration of American Indians to the cities was likely triggered by the push factors of poverty and unemployment on reservations, and the pull factor of expanding economic opportunities.

The population is quite young. The median age in 1980 was 23; by 1998, it was 27.6 years. Women live longer than men. About 5.9 percent of this population is 65 years or older. However, the U.S. Census Bureau reports differences by tribal affiliation. For example, in 1990, the Navajo were relatively young, with 13.6 percent of their population under 5 years of age, 4.6 percent age 65 or older, and a median age of 22.0 years. On the other hand, the Cherokee had a higher proportion of elderly (7.2 percent) than children under 5 years of age (6.3 percent), and a median age of 31.6 years.

The fertility rate for 1997 was 2.15, higher than that of either whites (1.99) or Asian and Pacific Islanders (1.95), but lower than that of African Americans (2.43) and Latinos (2.98). Life expectancy among American Indians has increased to above 71 years, according to the Indian Health Services (1990). If this is true, it is a remarkable improvement likely resulting from control of infectious diseases and making acute medical care available (John 1991). Several researchers have pointed out that American Indians exhibit a mortality crossover with the white population at about age 65, much earlier than that for African Americans (John 1991). High mortality rates at younger ages may be associated with selective survival of healthier elderly American Indians (Kunitz & Levy 1989; Markides & Machelek 1984).

The contemporary American Indian experience is characterized by poverty; the official poverty rate among this group in 1990 was 27.2 percent for families and 31.2 percent for individuals. Typically, Americans Indians are concentrated in unskilled, semiskilled, and low-wage service jobs. In 1990, among the 25 largest tribes, American Indians were more likely than the U.S. population at large to be employed in service occupations (15.5 vs. 11 percent, respectively), craft and repair occupations (13.8 vs. 11.3 percent, respectively), and as laborers (5.7 vs. 3.9 percent, respectively). They were less likely than the total population to be employed in executive positions (8.6 vs. 12.3 percent, respectively) and the professions (9.7 vs. 14.1 percent, respectively). Work in the job categories in which they are likely to be employed is often seasonal. Unemployment is considerably higher than the national average. Historically, the unemployment rate among American Indians was more than double that of whites—and these rates did not include the large numbers who gave up looking for work. Retirement is both a luxury and a hardship for this population. For many, there has been no work from which to retire; old age is simply a continuation of a state of economic deprivation to which American Indians have had ample time to accustom themselves.

Formal educational attainment levels for American Indians of all ages lag behind those of the total U.S. population. In 1990, 65.6 percent of American Indians aged 25 years or older were high school graduates or higher, compared with

75.2 percent for the population at large. Remember, however, that the oldest American Indians were of school age at a time when only a small percentage attended any type of formal school. Schooling took place within informal tribal circles. The few boarding schools (run by the BIA) and mission schools were often oppressive environments that attempted to enforce acculturation. Students were punished for speaking Native languages, and American Indian values were denigrated. Until very recently, this remained an accurate characterization of the educational environments in which American Indians found themselves. By 1990, 38.6 percent of American Indians 5 years of age or over were identified as not speaking English "very well" compared with 43.9 percent for the total U.S. population.

Although the diversity of tribal cultures makes generalization difficult, it is fair to say that the status of elderly American Indians has undergone enormous change in the last 100 years or so. According to Simmons (1945), most North American Indian societies ensured respect for the aged—at least until they were obviously powerless and incompetent. Close inspection, however, shows that respect was given not simply as a function of age but rather on the basis of some particular asset that an older person possessed. The range of avenues that afforded access to homage was great. An individual might be respected for extensive knowledge, seasoned experience, expert skill, power to work magic, control of property rights, or skill in games, dances, songs, and storytelling. The Iroquois associated long life with wisdom. A common prayer began, "Preserve our old men among us." Among the Chippewa, the elderly men held the central positions in council gatherings where the young were expected to sit in silence. Aged Navaho women were custodians of much property and highly regarded in both family and public life.

Hudson and colleagues (1998) offer contemporary evidence that the historical norm of respect for elders continues to hold true among different groups of American Indians. Still, much has changed. Today, elderly American Indians are, for the most part, ministered to by government bureaucracies. Social and financial services are provided by the Bureau of Indian Affairs; health needs are provided by the Public Health Service. (Even as we enter the twenty-first century, American Indian health conditions remain among the worst in the United States.) The way these programs are operated often denies the old their traditional position in tribal society. According to Native American advocates, the Bureau of Indian Affairs expends 90 percent of its annual $3 billion budget on maintaining and supporting the bureaucracy, with only 10 percent going to services for Native American people (Cook 1990).

No program can immunize the American Indian elderly from a lifetime of inadequate nutrition, housing, and health services. These deprivations usually take their toll long before old age. Clearly, many changes must be made before future generations of elderly Native Americans can expect a significantly better day.

The Asian-Pacific Aged

Over 10 million Asian-Pacific Americans (APA) were estimated from current population reports by the U.S. Census Bureau in 1997; this is equivalent to less than

4 percent of the total population and about 20 percent of the nonwhite population in the United States. Only 6.4 percent of the total APA population was 65 years or older in 1997, although Tanjasiri and colleagues (1995) assert that Asian-Pacific elderly have been the fastest-growing racial group aged 65 years and older in the United States between 1980 and 1990.

Asian-Pacific Americans are a mosaic of at least 26 Census-defined Asian and Pacific Islander ethnic groups. Among the largest of these groups in the United States are the Chinese, Filipinos, Japanese, Asian Indians, and Koreans. All of these groups have shown substantial increase since 1980. In particular, the Chinese (+103 percent), Korean (+123 percent), and Asian Indian (+103 percent) populations have more than doubled in size in the United States since the 1980 Census. Most APAs are urbanites, residing in ethnic enclaves in cities such as Los Angeles, San Francisco, New York, and Honolulu. Each of these metropolitan areas is home to over 500,000 people of Asian or Pacific Islander descent. About 15 percent of the San Francisco metropolitan area population is composed of Asian and Pacific Islanders.

The median family income of Asian-Pacific Americans was $49,105 in 1997—higher than for all other racial groups, including whites. Further, 1990 Census data on APA elderly show higher proportions completing "some college or more" (24.5 percent), compared to whites (23.1 percent) and blacks (12.2 percent). Compared to whites and blacks, higher proportions of APA elderly householders in families with married couples report incomes of $50,000 or more, and higher proportions of APA elderly who live alone have incomes of $35,000 or more. Also, aggregated data from National Health Interview Surveys show a lower proportion of APA elderly reporting fair or poor health status compared to Latinos, blacks, and non-Hispanic whites (Tanjasiri, Wallace, & Shibata 1995).

Such evidence is often used to characterize Asian-Pacific Americans as being a successful model minority. This concept of *model minority* describes the general belief that Asian-Pacific families—and communities, for that matter—are stable and in full command of their social and economic concerns. Perceptions that those of Asian-Pacific heritage and their elderly have succeeded in the United States (and other countries outside their homelands) stem from continued belief that success beyond that achieved by other minorities is due to cultural factors that emphasize education, family, and hard work (Kim 1990).

Over a generation ago, Kim (1973) argued that this view of APAs as a model minority supports a myth and is a convenient device for excluding them from programs related to education, health, housing, and employment. He suspects that behind the prosperous shops of the Chinatowns and Little Tokyos are thousands of disaffiliated old people waiting out their remaining years in poverty and ill health. This view was supported by a White House Conference on Aging (1972) report:

> The Asian American elderly are severely handicapped by the myth that pervades society at large and permeates the policy decisions of agencies and governmental entities…that Asian American aged do not have any problems, that Asian Americans

are able to take care of their own, and that Asian American aged do not need or desire aid in any form. (p. 2)

The report went on to characterize older Asian Americans as:

1. Having problems that are, in many respects, more intensive and complex than the problems of the general senior citizen population
2. Being excluded by cultural barriers from receiving their rightful benefits
3. Committing suicide at a rate three times the national average
4. Being among the people most neglected by programs presumably serving all elderly

Since that White House Conference report, the existence of a bifurcation or bimodal distribution has been recognized in measures of socioeconomic status and health (among other indicators) for Asian-Pacific Americans generally and for APA elderly specifically.

Contemporary data on those with incomes below the poverty level support this view of a bimodal distribution. In 1996, about 15 percent of the Asian-Pacific American population had incomes below the poverty level. This number was consistent with the population as a whole but above that of whites (9.5 percent). Among those 65 years of age and older, Asian-Pacific Americans actually have a higher rate of poverty (10.6 percent) than does the population as a whole (8.7 percent). Based on 1990 Census data, elderly APAs (12.7 percent) are 9 times more likely than elderly whites (1.4 percent) and more than 2 times as likely as elderly blacks (5.7 percent) to possess no education. Consistent with relatively high rates of poverty and absence of formal education, many APA elderly are at risk for infectious diseases. For example, rates of tuberculosis among Asian elderly is 12 times higher than among whites (Kitano 1994). Also, many APA elderly are foreign born and speak no English. According to the 1990 Census, 30.6 percent of APA elderly live in households in which no one speaks English. Presumably, only elderly Latinos are more linguistically isolated. Poverty, no formal education, and no facility with the English language creates a special challenge for health and social service practitioners.

Generally, when data are collected on Asian-Pacific Islanders, the statistics are often not broken down for ethnic groups. For example, the Current Population Survey of the U.S. Census collects important social and economic information annually, but only has a single Asian-Pacific islander category (Tanjasiri, Wallace, & Shibata 1995). In addition, many datasets do not have a sufficiently meaningful representation of Asian-Pacific Americans as a whole to allow for racial or ethnic group comparison. One exception is the annual health survey carried out by the National Center for Health Statistics, which began collecting data on 10 different Asian-Pacific groups in 1992.

The situation of older Asian-Pacific Americans cannot really be grasped without an understanding of their cultural origins and their history in the United States. These factors are integrated with brief discussions of two of the largest elderly Asian American populations: the Japanese and the Chinese.

Japanese Americans.   Japanese Americans are one of the oldest Asian American groups. The significant migration of Japanese to the United States mainland occurred after 1880. Many came to this country as sojourners with an intent to stay a while, establish themselves financially, and then return home. Migrants were young, uneducated, and unskilled. Hostility against the Japanese was great. Racist attitudes were prevalent: The Japanese were said to be wily, lacking in morals, and inassimilable. In 1905, California newspapers began a campaign against the so-called yellow peril, which they saw as a threat to public schools. Discriminatory laws and local nuisance ordinances were used to limit the activities of the Japanese. Unions were successful in excluding Japanese, and city governments were pressured into refusing permits to Japanese businesses.

In 1913, California passed an Alien Land Law, which disallowed land purchase or lease on the part of Japanese Americans. The Immigration Act of 1924 placed severe restrictions on Japanese immigration to this country. This hostility culminated during World War II, when all people of Japanese ancestry were evacuated from their homes along the West Coast and placed in "relocation camps." Approximately two-thirds of those evacuated were U.S. citizens. At the time, the U.S. Supreme Court upheld this evacuation without investigation. To many, this seemed a blatant violation of the civil rights guaranteed all citizens by the U.S. Constitution. It is useful to remember that no people of Italian or German ancestry were similarly imprisoned or evacuated to relocation camps.

After the war, the camps were closed, and treatment of Japanese Americans improved. In 1987, the U.S. House of Representatives passed a law, including formal apology to Japanese Americans for the internment and providing monies for reparations. In general, the group has made enormous progress since 1950; they are upwardly mobile. This success has been attributed to Japanese American family life and support of education provided by parents.

In traditional Japan, families occupied a central position. The extended family was an associational and supportive institution and most important for early socialization and upbringing. Marriage was often arranged by a father intent on maintaining family solidarity. The father/son relationship was preeminent in the family; women were dutiful and deferred to men. Caring for aged parents was the responsibility of the eldest son in particular, although clearly all adult children were expected to bear some responsibility in this area.

Among the first-generation Japanese American families (called *Issei*), this traditional family picture survived in some modified form. As Kitano and Kikumura (1976) point out, there were no grandparents to serve as reminders of old traditions, and many immigrants felt free to Americanize. One powerful constraint on assimilation was the norm of *enryo* brought from Japan and still in existence in the United States. This norm is related to power and regulates how those who have power are to behave toward those without it (and vice versa). In the Japanese family and community, power and privilege were associated with the father.

In the U.S. context, the norm *enryo* helped reinforce this association, even when the Japanese father was subject to the humiliation and abuse of whites outside the family. Montero (1979) has described the continued importance of the family to *Issei* elderly. He points to data showing the disengagement of elderly Japanese Americans from many social and organizational ties, but the continued existence of a strong family support system. It is the adult children with whom *Issei* visit regularly and who form the foundation of this family support system.

Pressures to assimilate increased for subsequent generations of Japanese (*Nisei* and *Sansei*). Data presented earlier on the income status of Japanese Americans reflects their successful economic assimilation. For example, according to the U.S. Census, by 1960 there were approximately 7,000 Japanese-owned businesses in the Los Angeles metropolitan area. Many were in gardening, groceries, laundries, and hotels. Success in the niche economy of small business was appropriate to *Issei* and *Nisei*. Subsequent generations used the education provided by their parents to move into professional and other white-collar jobs. Cultural assimilation, particularly in regard to language and religion, also advanced among younger Japanese Americans.

Kalish and Moriwaki (1973) write of the problems created as different generations of Japanese reflect different degrees of assimilation to the U.S. context. As an example, they use the theme of **filial piety**—"honor thy father and thy mother"—which is common in Western as well as East Asian literature. Kalish and Moriwaki argue that the theme of filial piety is undermined by other themes in U.S. culture—independence, self-reliance, and mastery over one's own fate. This creates a situation whereby first-generation elderly retain expectations consistent with the theme of filial piety, while the second- and third-generation members become assimilated into a society "where future potential is more important than past accomplishments in evaluating the worth of a person, [and] the wisdom and the accomplishments of the elderly were often perceived as irrelevant or were forgotten and ignored" (p. 201).

As *Nisei* and *Sansei* move into old age, these intergenerational incongruities should lessen. Increased interracial marriage and upward social mobility are also likely to reduce the relevance of traditional values among Japanese Americans. The Japanese American elderly in the future are likely to be more diversified in terms of social class and geographical distribution (Osako & Liu 1986).

Chinese Americans.   The Chinese began to arrive in California during the middle of the nineteenth century. Railroad and mining agents often went to China to recruit laborers with promises of work, higher wages, and free passage. Racism was rampant against the highly identifiable Chinese. Violence and murder were not uncommon and rarely punished by the authorities. Efforts to expel Chinese from California and other western states began almost with their arrival. California passed exclusion laws in 1852, 1855, and 1858; each was declared unconstitutional by the U.S. Supreme Court. Taxes and other discriminatory devices were used against the Chinese. Article XIX of the California State Constitution, initiated in 1879, prohibited corporations from directly or indirectly employing Chinese. Chinese were considered sinister and inassimilable. A mixture of racism and concerns about the Chinese as an economic threat is inherent in this 1877 manifesto of an anti-Chinese group based in San Francisco (quoted in Kitano & Daniels 1988, 22–23):

> Before the world we declare that the Chinaman must leave our shores. We declare that white men, and women, and boys and girls, cannot live as the people of the great republic should live and compete with the single Chinese coolie in the labor market. We declare that we cannot hope to drive the Chinaman away by working cheaper than he does. None but an enemy would expect it of us; none but an idiot would hope for success; none but the degraded coward and slave would make the effort. To an American, death is preferable to life on a par with the Chinaman.

Federal laws eventually passed in 1882, 1888, 1902, and 1904 severely limited Chinese immigration into this country until World War II. During this period, the Chinese retreated into invisibility. Chinese Americans benefitted somewhat from the war, however, because China was an ally of the United States. In 1943, as a token gesture, China was awarded a yearly quota of 105 immigrants. Large-scale immigration from China did not resume until federal policy was revised in the 1960s.

Many Chinese immigrants who arrived in the United States were young adults, mostly male, who had no intention of staying. They expected to work hard, save their money, and return to family and community in China to enjoy the fruits of their labors. Perhaps this explains why they were able to withstand the racism and hostility encountered in the United States. Before 1949, when the People's Republic of China assumed control of the mainland, it was still the practice of many older immigrants to return to China after they retired.

By 1990, there were approximately 1.6 million Chinese in the United States, with about 52 percent residing on the West Coast. The Chinese are the largest of the major Asian and Pacific Islander groups in this country. The group has increased by 103 percent between 1980 and 1990, and currently makes up almost 15 percent of all Asian and Pacific Islanders in the United States.

The early immigrants were mostly males who married before they left for the United States. The wives lived with the husbands' families and were supported by money sent home from the United States. The scarcity of Chinese women in the United States is an important phenomenon, because it essentially delayed the appearance of a second generation of more acculturated Chinese (Wong 1995). Typically, second-generation children of immigrants have greater facility with language and greater familiarity with the society at large. Also, as a function of their birth in the United States, these second-generation children of immigrants are citizens with all the attached legal and political rights not available to their parents. As Healey (1998, p. 421) suggests, "The decades-long absence of a generation of more Americanized, English-speaking children may have reinforced the exclusion and isolation of the Chinese-American community that resulted from the overt discrimination of the dominant group."

With the ebb and flow of anti-Chinese sentiment and discrimination, Chinese became increasingly urbanized in larger cities (e.g., San Francisco), which offered the safety of ethnic neighborhoods where traditions could be followed while contact with the hostile society at large could be minimized. These neighborhoods were places in which the earliest waves of immigrants, experienced in commerce, could establish small businesses and retail outlets. As the numbers of urban Chinese increased, cheap labor was available to provide the additional services required.

Whether by self-selection or the hostility from the outside society, the segregation of these Chinatowns helped preserve traditions of the homeland and resist pressures to assimilate. Social structure in these ethnic enclaves was organized around family, clan, and region in China from which the immigrant had come. *Huiguan* were the most prominent of the regional associations, controlled by the merchants. Like benevolent associations, they aided new arrivals and performed a variety of social and welfare services (Lai 1980). Clan groups, based on family and lineage, overlapped and supplemented the *huiguan*. As associational life evolved, these Chinese enclaves became highly organized, self-contained communities with their own leadership structure. As such, they were hidden from general societal view; discriminatory barriers remained, job opportunities were limited, and housing was often substandard and overpopulated.

Second-generation Chinese were another matter. They were much more influenced by the culture at large. They came in contact with the broader culture through school, religious institutions, voluntary organizations, and popular media. They were less interested in clan and regional associations and more willing to abandon traditional customs and adopt an American lifestyle. They were more mobile and, with greater language facility and educational credentials, sought success outside of Chinatown. This was the case for men and women alike.

In the contemporary period, a number of researchers describe the bipolar nature of the Chinese American community: educational and occupational success and affluence on the one hand, poverty and unemployment on the other hand. As Kitano and Daniels (1995) point out, however, even those near the top of the American occupational structure still do not find themselves in positions that require direct supervision of whites. As Barringer and associates (1995) conclude, Chinese immigrants as well as less affluent Chinese Americans rely for survival on low-wage jobs in the garment and service industries in a fashion comparable to other groups who have experienced exploitation and exclusion in the United States.

No doubt, the mix of social class and generational differences between young and old Chinese and Chinese Americans in the United States continues to create tensions within families and communities. Presumably, as is the case for Japanese Americans, educational and occupational success, assimilation reflected in intermarriage, and geographic mobility within the country will reduce the relevance of traditional Chinese values and narrow differences in experience between the generations.

SUMMARY

Recognition of the ethnic and social diversity present in the U.S. experience has only recently begun to be presented in social gerontology. Much of what has been learned about aging stems from studies of working- and middle-class whites. Unfortunately, minority aging has been defined as "deviance" and racial and ethnic aging has focused on differences from "white standards." The study of minority patterns of aging is important for practical as well as theoretical reasons.

Many have characterized minority aging as a case of double jeopardy. This term is used to reflect the idea that the negative effects of aging are compounded among minority group members. Although, in general, research supports the notion of double jeopardy among African American and Mexican American aged, some data suggest that aging may reduce ethnic differences that existed in middle life. Recently, some have contested the importance of a double-jeopardy concept of minority aging.

By 1999, African American elderly made up about 8 percent of the total elderly population; about 12 percent of the total U.S. population is African American. In general, the U.S. black population is younger than the population of whites. Aged African Americans fare worse than aged whites across a variety of socioeconomic indicators. Elderly blacks have fewer years of education, lower incomes, and lower occupational status. This has major impact on the health status of elderly African Americans and underscores problems related to transportation and housing, among others. Two areas of strength that have emerged for African American elderly that are not related to income deprivation are family and religion.

Next to African Americans, Latinos make up the largest minority in the United States. In 1997, Latinos constituted 11.1 percent of the country's population, or over 29 million people. This population is quite heterogeneous, although about 63 percent of all Latinos are of Mexican heritage. The elderly only account for about 5.1 percent of the total Latino population. As with African American elderly, the problems of Latino elderly emanate primarily from a disadvantaged socioeconomic status. About 25 percent of Latino elderly lived below the poverty level in 1996. However, a generation gap between old and young leave many elderly Latinos misunderstood by the society at large and by the young in their own families. In addition, the general society, with its failure to recognize the diversity of Latino culture and its misunderstanding of the issues confronting Latino families, believes that the Latino family will provide for its older members.

The aged American Indian population is quite small and relatively invisible. Their special history has clearly contributed to their deprived situation. The official poverty rate for American Indians in 1990 was 27.2 percent for families and over 30 percent for individuals; there is every reason to believe that the rates for the aged are higher. No simple social program can immunize the American Indian elderly from a lifetime of inadequate nutrition, housing, and health service.

Asian-Pacific Americans have been described as a model minority. This may be myth. Despite the successful economic assimilation of many Asian-Pacific Americans, the accommodation of younger generations to U.S. values has left many aged Asian Americans isolated from family and community. In addition, a bimodal or bipolar distribution has become evident in this group with data available to show both the success of the group as well as its relative disadvantage. Perhaps future generations of elderly Asian Americans will have expectations and experiences more like those of elderly whites than is currently the case.

STUDY QUESTIONS

1. Is the United States a melting pot or a pluralistic society? How does the concept of *ethnogenesis* speak to this question? How would you characterize the visibility of minority aged in the United States? Explain this characterization.

2. Define *double jeopardy* as it relates to the minority aged. According to the study by Dowd and Bengtson (1978), how accurately does this term describe the social situation of the U.S. minority aged? Briefly critique the double-jeopardy concept.

3. Identify three major stages of experience for African Americans in the United States. Why are these stages so central to any discussion of the African American elderly in the United States?

4. Despite the socioeconomic problems that still confront African American elderly, two major strengths of African American culture should not be ignored. Identify and discuss the importance of these strengths.

5. The special needs of Latino elderly are often understated because of the belief that this group takes care of its own. Give a more realistic picture of the modern Latino (Mexican American) family.

6. How has the status of elderly American Indians changed over the last 100 years?

7. Explain what is meant by the concept of *model minority* in referring to Asian-Pacific Americans. In what way has this view of Asian Americans likely been detrimental to the social conditions of their elderly?

REFERENCES

Barringer, H., Takeuchi, D., & Levin, M. (1995). *Asians and Pacific Islanders in the United States.* New York: Russell Sage Foundation.

Belgrave, L. L. (1988). The effects of race differences in work history, work attitudes, economic resources, and health on women's retirement. *Research on Aging, 10* (3), 383–398.

Cattell, S. (1962). *Health, welfare and social organization in Chinatown.* New York: Community Service Society of New York.

Chen, Y. P. (1985). The economic status of the aging. In R. H. Binstock & E. Shanas (Eds.), *Handbook of aging and the social sciences* (2nd ed.). New York: Van Nostrand Reinhold.

Cook, C. D. (1990). American Indian elderly and public policy issues. In M. S. Harper (Ed.), *Minority aging*. DHHS Pub. #HRS (P-DV-90-4). Washington, DC: U.S. Government Printing Office.

Cuellar, J. (1990). Hispanic American aging: Geriatric educational curriculum development for selected health professions. In M. S. Harper (Ed.), *Minority aging*. DHHS Pub. #HRS (P-DV-90-4). Washington, DC: U.S. Government Printing Office.

Dancy, J. (1977). *The black elderly: A guide for practitioners.* Ann Arbor: Institute of Gerontology, University of Michigan–Wayne State University.

Dobyns, H. (1966). Estimating aboriginal American populations. *Current Anthropology, 7,* 395–416.

Dowd, J., & Bengtson, V. (1978). Aging in minority populations: An examination of the double jeopardy hypothesis. *Journal of Gerontology, 33,* 427–436.

Eitzen, D. S. (1986). *Social problems* (3rd ed.). Boston: Allyn and Bacon.

Farley, J. (1995). *Majority-minority relations* (3rd ed.). Englewood Cliffs, NJ: Prentice-Hall.

Feagin, J., & Feagin, C. B. (1999). *Racial and ethnic relations* (6th ed.). Upper Saddle River, NJ: Prentice-Hall.

Ferraro, K. F. (1987). Double jeopardy to health for black older adults? *Journal of Gerontology, 42* (5), 528–533.

Ferraro, K. F., & Farmer, M. M. (1996). Double jeopardy, aging as leveler, or persistent health inequality? A longitudinal analysis of white and black Americans. *Journal of Gerontology: Social Sciences, 51B* (6), S319–S328.

Glazer, N., & Moynihan, D. P. (1970). *Beyond the melting pot* (2nd ed.). Cambridge, MA: MIT Press.

Greeley, A. (1974). *Ethnicity in the United States.* New York: Wiley.

Greene, R. L., & Siegler, I. C. (1984). Blacks. In E. B. Palmore (Ed.), *Handbook on the aged in the United States.* Westport, CT: Greenwood.

Groger, L. (1992). Tied to each other through ties to the land: Informal support of black elders in a southern U.S. community. *Journal of Cross-Cultural Gerontology, 7,* 205–220.

Healey, J. F. (1998). *Race, ethnicity, gender and class: The sociology of group conflict and change* (2nd ed.). Thousand Oaks, CA: Pine Forge Press.

Hudson, M. F., Armachain, W. D., Beasley, C. M., & Carlson, J. R. (1998). Elder abuse: Two Native American views. *Gerontologist, 38* (5), 538–548.

Indian Health Services. (1990). *Trends in Indian health—1990.* Washington, DC: U.S. Government Printing Office.

Jackson, J. J. (1970). Aged negroes: Their cultural departures from statistical stereotypes and rural-urban differences. *Gerontologist, 10,* 140–145.

Jackson, J. J. (1971). Negro aged: Toward needed research in social gerontology. *Gerontologist, 11,* 52–57.

Jackson, J. J (1985). Race, national, origin, ethnicity, and aging. In R. H. Binstock & E. Shanas (Eds.), *Handbook of aging and the social sciences* (2nd ed.). New York: Van Nostrand Reinhold.

Jackson, J. S. (1988). Growing old in black america: Research on aging black populations. In J. S. Jackson & others (Eds.), *The black American elderly: Research on physical and psychological health.* New York: Springer.

John, R. (1991). The state of research on American Indian elders' health, income security, and social support networks. In *Minority elders: Longevity, economics, and health.* Washington, DC: Gerontological Society of America.

Kalish, R., & Moriwaki, S. (1973). The world of the elderly Asian American. *Journal of Social Issues, 29* (2), 187–209.

Kart, C. S. (1990). Diversity among aged black males. In Z. Harel, E. A. McKinney, & M. Williams (Eds.), *Black aged: Understanding diversity and service needs.* Newbury Park, CA: Sage.

Kent, D. (1971a). Changing welfare to serve minority. In *Minority aged in America.* Ann Arbor: Institute of Gerontology, University of Michigan–Wayne State University.

Kent, D. (1971b). The elderly in minority groups: Variant patterns of aging. *Gerontologist, 11,* 26–29.

Kent, D., & Hirsch, C. (1969). *Differentials in need and problem solving techniques among low income Negro and White elderly.* Paper presented at the International Congress on Gerontology, Washington, DC.

Kim, B. (1973, May). Asian Americans: No model minority. *Social Work, 18,* 44–53.

Kim, P. K. (1990). Asian-American families and the elderly. In M. S. Harper (Ed.), *Minority aging: Essential curricula content for selected health and allied health professions* (DHHS Pub. No. HRS-P-DV90-4). Washington, DC: U.S. Government Printing Office.

Kitano, H. (1994). Health and Asian American elderly: Research and policy issues. In C. M. Baressi (Ed.), *Health and minority elders: An analysis of applied literature.* Washington, DC: AARP.

Kitano, H., & Daniels, R. (1988). *Asian Americans: Emerging minorities.* Englewood Cliffs, NJ: Prentice-Hall.

Kitano, H., & Kikumura, A. (1976). The Japanese American family. In C. Mindel & R. Habenstein (Eds.), *Ethnic families in America.* New York: Elsevier.

Krause, N. (1987). Stress in racial differences in self-reported health among the elderly. *Gerontologist, 27* (1), 72–76.

Kunitz, S. J., & Levy, J. E. (1989). Aging and health among Navajo Indians. In K. S. Markides (Ed.), *Aging and health: Perspectives on gender, race, ethnicity and class.* Newbury Park, CA: Sage.

Lai, H. M. (1980). Chinese. In S. Thornstrom (Ed.), *Harvard encyclopedia of ethnic groups.* Cambridge, MA: Harvard University Press.

Maldonado, D. (1975, May). The Chicano aged. *Social Work,* pp. 213–216.

Manuel, R. C. (1982). The dimensions of ethnic minority identification: An exploratory analysis among elderly black Americans. In R. C. Manuel (Ed.), *Minority aging: Sociological and social psychological issues.* Westport, CT: Greenwood.

Markides, K., Boldt, J. S., & Ray, L. A. (1986). Sources of helping and intergenerational solidarity of Mexican-Americans. *Journal of Gerontology, 41,* 506–511.

Markides, K., Liang, J., & Jackson, J. (1990). Race, ethnicity and aging: Conceptual and methodological issues. In R. Binstock & L. K. George (Eds.), *Handbook of aging and the social sciences* (3rd ed.). New York: Academic.

Markides, K. S., & Machelek, R. (1984). Selective survival, aging, and society. *Archives of Gerontology and Geriatrics, 3,* 207–229.

Massey, D. S., & Denton, N. A. (1993). *American apartheid: Segregation and the making of the underclass.* Cambridge, MA: Harvard University Press.

Montero, D. (1979). Disengagement and aging among the Issei. In D. E. Gelfand & A. J. Kutzik (Eds.), *Ethnicity and aging: Theory, research, and policy.* New York: Springer.

Moore, J., & Vigil, J. D. (1993). Barrios in transition. In J. Moore & R. Pinderhughes (Eds.), *In the barrios: Latinos and the underclass.* New York: Sage.

Murguia, E. (1991). On Latino/Hispanic ethnic identity. *Latino Studies Journal, 2* (3), 8–18.

Mutchler, J. E., & Brallier, S. (1999). English language proficiency among older Hispanics in the United States. *Gerontologist, 39* (3), 310–319.

Osako, M. M., & Liu, W. T. (1986). Intergenerational relations and the aged among Japanese Americans. *Research on Aging, 8* (1), 128–155.

Schaie, K. W., Orchowsky, S., & Parham, I. A. (1982). Measuring age and sociocultural change: The case of race and life satisfaction. In R. C. Manuel (Ed.), *Minority aging: Sociological and social psychological issues.* Westport, CT: Greenwood.

Simmons, L. (1945). *The role of the aged in primitive society.* New Haven, CT: Yale University Press.

Simon, D. R., & Eitzen, D. S. (1982). *Elite deviance.* Boston: Allyn and Bacon.

Sotomayor, M. (1971, May). Mexican-American interaction with social systems. *Social Casework, 5,* 321.

Stack, C. (1970). The kindred of Viola Jackson: Residence and family organization of an urban black American family. In N. Whitten & J. Szwed (Eds.), *Afro-American anthropology.* New York: Free Press.

Tanjasiri, S. P., Wallace, S. P., & Shibata, K. (1995). Picture imperfect: Hidden problems among Asian Pacific Islander elderly. *Gerontologist, 35* (6), 753–760.

Taylor, R. J., & Chatters, L. M. (1988). Correlates of education, income, and poverty among aged blacks. *Gerontologist, 28* (4), 435–441.

Torres-Gil, F. (1992). *The new aging: Politics and change in America.* New York: Auburn House.

U.S. Bureau of the Census. (1994). *Statistical abstract of the United States, 1994.* Washington, DC: U.S. Government Printing Office.

U.S. Bureau of the Census. (1998). *Statistical abstract of the United States, 1998* (118th ed.). Washington, DC: U.S. Government Printing Office.

U.S. Senate Special Committee on Aging. (1971). *The multiple hazards of age and race.* Washington, DC: U.S. Government Printing Office.

Urrea, L. A. (1996). *By the lake of sleeping children: Secret life of the Mexican border.* New York: Anchor Books.

White House Conference on Aging. (1972). *The Asian American elderly.* Washington, DC: U.S. Government Printing Office.

Wilson, W. J. (1978). *The declining significance of race: Blacks and changing American institutions.* Chicago: University of Chicago Press.

Wilson, W. J. (1996). *When work disappears.* New York: Knopf.

Wong, M. (1995). Chinese Americans. In P. G. Min (Ed.), *Asian Americans: Contemporary trends and issues.* Thousand Oaks, CA: Sage.

Zopf, P. (1986). *America's older population.* Houston, TX: Cap and Gown.

CHAPTER SIXTEEN

LIVING ENVIRONMENTS
OF THE ELDERLY

Elderly Americans, like people of all ages, reside in a variety of settings—from single-room-occupancy hotels to Palm Springs condominiums, from urban homes and apartments to isolated rural farmhouses. Although the first public housing units designated explicitly for the elderly were mandated in the 1959 Housing Act, not until the mid-1960s did gerontologists begin to focus on the special problems of the elderly in securing physically adequate housing at a reasonable cost. Most recently, gerontologists have addressed themselves to broader questions about the relationship between behavior and living environments. In particular, some have asked: How and to what extent is the physical, social, and psychological functioning of an elderly individual influenced by the kind of environment in which he or she lives? This chapter summarizes some of the growing body of literature that has appeared in response to this question. It begins by addressing some general issues important to understanding the impact of the environment on older people.

THE IMPACT OF ENVIRONMENT
ON OLDER PEOPLE

Housing may be the single-most important element in the life of an older person, aside from his or her spouse or significant other. Still, one sign of the growing maturity of this subfield of gerontology is recognition of the limited utility of considering housing out of context. Gerontologists have come to understand that, although number of rooms, square footage, and closet space are important, so is the broader living environment in which the housing unit is located.

The main elements of this living environment include characteristics of the neighborhood and community, such as (1) the age and ownership of the housing stock; (2) the physical condition and availability of funds for maintenance and repair; (3) the location of specific support services needed by older people; (4) the proximity to commercial activities (e.g., banking, shopping, etc.); (5) the proximity to recreational activities; (6) the proximity to informal supports, including family and friends and age peers; (7) the accessibility and usability of transportation; and (8) the congeniality or threat in the surrounding environment, such as landscaping, street lighting, and crime rate.

What kind of neighborhood environment is most supportive for older persons? Chapman and Beaudet (1983) explored the relationship between the neighborhood as a physical and social context and the well-being of a sample of relatively frail elderly persons living independently in a variety of community settings within Multnomah County (Portland), Oregon. Measures of the physical and social environments of the sample groups, the personal characteristics of the respondents, and their well-being were developed out of personal interviews. Environmental variables used in the analysis were house type, neighborhood quality, crime rate, age concentration of the neighborhood, distance to services, the social status of the neighborhood area, and distance to the city center.

The important part of this analysis involved determining whether, when personal characteristics are controlled for, environmental variables are useful predictors of the well-being of frail elderly people. Using a measure of life satisfaction as a global indicator of well-being, Chapman and Beaudet (1983) found that people living in higher-quality neighborhoods were significantly more satisfied with their lives. How satisfied were people with their neighborhoods? Living in a higher-quality neighborhood and living relatively far from downtown were two factors that significantly increased satisfaction with the neighborhood.

Three additional indicators of well-being were employed. Each provides a measure of social interaction with others. Interaction with neighbors was highest among those individuals residing in good-quality neighborhoods, relatively far from the center of the city, and with a low percentage of older people in the area. Frequent social contact with friends and relatives was associated with the environmental variables of good neighborhood quality, relatively low social status of the neighborhood, a low crime rate in the area, and relatively greater distance from the city center. No environmental variables were predictive of a general activity level, measured by the frequency of visits to the bank, grocer, and other families.

The environmental variables most consistently associated with well-being were increased distance from the center of the city and the quality of the neighborhood. Quality of the neighborhood is a composite measure reflecting a residential area that is quiet, has little traffic, and is well maintained and landscaped. Such attributes suggest a neighborhood that is especially well suited to the competence levels of the frail elderly. One surprising finding is the failure of distance to services to show any value in predicting well-being. As Chapman and Beaudet (1983) point out, however, this may simply result from members of the study population having available social contacts and supports on whom they can rely to provide transportation.

Some living environments make greater physical, social, and psychological demands on people than do others. As a result, it is possible to place living environments on a hypothetical continuum from "very demanding" to "not demanding at all." Following the terminology of noted psychologist Henry Murray

(1938), Lawton and Nahemow (1973) use the term *environmental press* to describe this continuum. They posit that when a person of a given level of competence behaves in an environment of a given press level, the outcome can be placed on a scale from positive to negative (Lawton 1980a, p. 15). Another way of describing this is to talk of the *fit* between an individual's competence and the environment in which that individual resides. When the fit is good, the competence of an individual will be consistent with the demands of the environment, and adaptation is positive. This may be the case for the great majority of older people. When environmental demands are too great, adaptation is poor and the outcome is negative. An example may be useful:

> Mrs. L. is 74 years old and resides with her never-married brother. She has been a diabetic for 30 years and suffers from heart disease, as well. Therefore, she requires frequent medical care, including in-home personal care. When Mrs. L. began to show signs of mild confusion and forgetfulness, she was no longer able to meet the demands of the living environment. She was less able to participate in her own care and often found it difficult to navigate her way through the small house in which she and her brother lived. Her brother tried to find some home assistance, but this was scarce and expensive. Because he feared for his sister's safety, the brother reluctantly sought a nursing home.

A small change in the environment, such as the presence of a homemaker, might have reduced the environmental press and made it compatible with Mrs. L.'s competence. She might have been able to defer entrance to the long-term care facility. Lawton and Simon (1968) stated this relationship between environmental press and individual competence in the form of a principle referred to as the **environmental docility hypothesis:** The less competent the individual, the greater the impact of environmental factors on that individual.

This principle is particularly relevant to older people because of the broad way in which competence may be viewed. Competence not only is reflective of characteristics within the person—such as biological health, sensorimotor coordination, and cognitive skills—but also reflective of external processes, including the availability (or lack) of informal social supports in the form of family and friends, needed formal support services (e.g., shopping, housekeeping), and economic resources (e.g., retirement income). Deprivations or setbacks may be suffered by any person at any time in the life course, although the elderly seem particularly vulnerable to them. The occurrence of one or more of these phenomena, regardless of age, may say nothing about the basic competence of the individual who experiences them. Yet, an individual often experiences these occurrences as threats to or reductions in competence. Although the deprivation occurs outside the person, it may significantly affect his or her ability to deal with the demands of the environment (Lawton 1980a).

The environmental docility hypothesis has a positive side. If features of the broader living environment can deprive individuals of competence, then perhaps

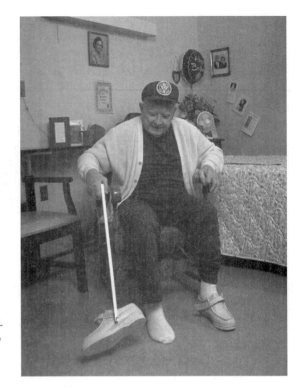

Small accommodations in a living environment allow an elderly individual to maintain competence and elevate the quality of life.

there are features of the living environment that can increase competence and elevate the quality of life. Lawton (1980a, p. 15) states, "If we could design housing with fewer barriers, neighborhoods with more enriching resources, or institutions with higher stimulating qualities, we could improve the level of functioning of many older people more than proportionately."

Achieving the ideal fit between the individual and the living environment may be difficult in the real world. This is reflected in Lawton's (1980c) discussion of two contrasting developmental models of independent living environments: the constant model and the accommodating model. The *constant environment model* attempts to maintain the essential character of the environment and assumes that the needs of residents remain relatively stable over time. The *accommodating environment model* assumes that all aspects of the environment (including the resident) change over time.

According to Lawton (1980c), characteristics of the **constant environment** are:

1. Admission criteria for replacement tenants are the same as those for original tenants.
2. Criteria for continued residence are established so that administrators may initiate termination of residence when a tenant's physical or mental condition declines below a specific level.

3. Termination of residence because of reduced independence leads to transfer to either the home of a family member, congregate housing, or an institution. Some individuals will experience multiple transfers—to the home of a family member and then again to an institution. Much research demonstrates that such late-life relocations are undesirable.
4. The community continues to regard the housing environment as a place for independent living; thus, there is a continuation of the effort to recruit replacement tenants who are fully independent.

In some contrast, a typical *accommodating environment* might be characterized as follows:

1. Criteria for continued residence in the environment are considerably less stringent than those applied to the original applicants.
2. Changes in tenants' physical and mental conditions require the addition of a variety of services, including on-site health services.
3. The provision of such services requires alteration in the physical environment to provide for the delivery of such services.
4. The needs of tenants do not change at an equal rate; thus, at first, new services provided are not cost effective. Moreover, there will be a mix of independent and less independent residents.
5. Admission criteria for replacement tenants may be relaxed as the service environment changes to be able to provide for less independent tenants.
6. The community image of the housing changes such that more marginally independent people apply in greater numbers. Over an extended period of time, such an accommodating environment could evolve into a long-term care institution.

As Lawton (1980c) points out, most housing environments are not as extreme as the two types characterized here. Still, housing that attempts to become accommodating certainly may face difficulty in remaining financially viable while attempting to provide services in physical settings not originally planned to function in this way. At the same time, those environments that attempt to remain constant and resist accommodation face the unpleasant task of terminating residents because of lack of services or of maintaining marginal tenants without being able to provide them with needed services.

Ehrlich, Ehrlich, and Woehlke (1982) completed a needs assessment that examined the tenant population of the Delcrest Apartments for the Elderly in St. Louis, Missouri. Essentially, they asked, "Can a congregate housing program remain constant over a long period of time (13 years) without making some attempt to accommodate to an aging population?" Their findings failed to support an accommodating environment concept. Yet, the constant model embodied in the original program was not sufficient to take into account the diverse needs represented in a population of young-old and old-old residents.

These same authors put forth what is described as a balanced environmental model that would allow for the maintenance of the traditional mobile–well independent environment at the same time still guaranteeing some support for those with need. In many respects, this balanced model sits midway between the constant and the accommodating models described by Lawton. In particular, these authors emphasize the importance of strengthening informal support networks, as evidence suggests the feasibility of elderly people assisting each other in all basic supportive tasks, such as crisis intervention, activities of daily living, and advice giving.

Although most older persons, even those with health problems, mobility limitations, and/or dependency in one or more ADL, live in housing units without special features, some are able to move to more accommodating housing or alter their housing units to better fit their needs. Most common housing adaptations or alterations include handrails, raised toilet seats, ramps, and extra-wide doors (LaPlante, Hendershot, & Moss 1992). Other adaptations made by older persons include modifications in kitchens and bathrooms that facilitate access to the sink, faucet, and cabinets. Changing placement of wall sockets and light switches is also a desirable accommodation for older persons with mobility limitations. Still, such modifications to a residence represent only one possible coping strategy for aging in place. Other possible coping strategies may require increased financial assistance, a more helpful set of household/housekeeping arrangements, and greater availability of responsive home and community services (Pynoos & Golant 1996).

Assisted-living facilities, a relatively new class of housing that sits on the housing continuum between independent living and institutional care, often gives the impression of being accommodative. Although they generally cater to older people with physical and/or mental impairments, assisted-living facilities are not necessarily more accommodating. According to Mollica and colleagues (1992), although such facilities are capable of housing older people with impairments comparable to those in nursing homes, many maintain inflexible upper thresholds of care. Persons who exceed the fixed threshold may be required to move to a nursing home.

Interestingly, some of the most accommodating settings have been board-and-care homes, foster-care living situations, and shared group-living arrangements. Because they are less regulated, operators have greater discretion to allow residents to remain in their facilities. Thus, even residents who require "heavy" care loads may be allowed to stay (Baggett 1989). Also, in such facilities, the informal consensus of other residents may be important. If a resident with a heavy care burden is disruptive and uncooperative, he or she may be asked to leave. On the other hand, a similarly impaired resident who is likable and cooperative may be viewed as being less burdensome and allowed to stay (Streib, Folts, & Hilker 1984).

So-called life-care or *continuum-of-care retirement communities (CCRCs)* are generally classified as the most accommodating. Although the definition of such facilities is inconsistent because of the wide range of contractual agreements, they usually provide housing, personal and supportive care, congregate meals, social and recreational activities, and nursing care if needed. The key feature is that residents may pay an entrance fee and monthly fees that will provide for their care for the rest of their lives. Most CCRCs are sponsored by nonprofit organizations and require long-term contracts. Upon entering such a facility, an older person or couple may reside in independent living, then, as needed, progress to supportive care or assisted living, and on to nursing home care, all within the same retirement community complex. Such arrangements are not cheap; perhaps only about 1 percent of the elderly population currently reside in such living arrangements.

WHERE DO THE ELDERLY LIVE?

This section describes the living arrangements of older people, the characteristics of their housing, and their degree of satisfaction with their housing situations. Earlier, Chapter 3 discussed the geographical distribution of the elderly in the United States, including their residential mobility and concentration.

Living Arrangements

Nearly all elderly live in independent households. In 1995, approximately two-thirds of the elderly were living with family, with the great majority of these married and residing with a spouse (54.1 percent). Figure 16.1 presents data on the living arrangements of the elderly, by gender, for 1995. In 1995, approximately 5.3 percent of the elderly were in institutions on any given day. Chapter 17 discusses the elderly in old-age institutions.

There is a striking difference in the household composition of elderly men and women, reflecting differences in marital status between the sexes. In 1995, elderly women were more than twice as likely as men to live alone or with non-relatives (43 vs. 20 percent, respectively), whereas almost three-quarters (72 percent) of all aged men were married and living with their wives. Only about 40

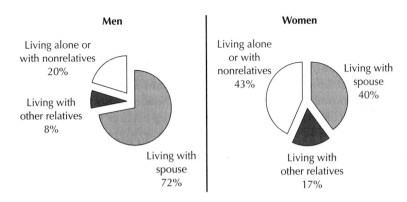

FIGURE 16.1   Living Arrangements of Persons Age 65 and Older: 1995

Source: Based on data from U.S. Bureau of the Census. See "Household and Family Characteristics: March 1997," *Current Population Reports,* P20–509.

percent of elderly women were married and living with a spouse. (The proportions are even lower for African American and Latino women).

The proportion of the elderly living alone appears to be increasing. In 1965, for example, 30 percent of aged women lived alone, as compared with 43 percent in 1995. In addition, the proportion of older men and women who live alone increases with age. This seems to be chiefly the result of the increasing number of widows among the elderly and the fact that more elderly persons today can afford to live alone than in the past. Among men, for example, those living alone increases from about 13 percent at ages 65 to 74 to over 28 percent among those 85 years and over. Among women, the percentage living alone increases from 33 percent at ages 65 to 74 to almost 57 percent at ages 85 and over. The high proportion of the very-old living alone does not portend well for them. A study conducted on behalf of the Commonwealth Fund Commission on Elderly People Living Alone concluded:

> The elderly person living alone is often a widowed woman in her eighties who struggles alone to make ends meet on a meager income. Being older, she is more likely to be in fair or poor health. She is frequently childless or does not have a son or daughter nearby to provide assistance when needed. Lacking social support, she is at high risk for institutionalization and for losing her independent life style. Finally, like one-half of all elderly people living alone, she may have lived alone for ten years or more. Many elderly people living alone are poor; one-quarter have income below the federal poverty level. The elderly living alone are likely to be dependent on Social Security; are overburdened with health care bills; lack pensions; are less likely to own their own home; and are unlikely to be receiving Supplemental Security Income assistance and Medicaid. (Louis Harris & Associates 1987, p. i)

In 1995, 17 percent of aged women and 8 percent of aged men lived with a relative other than a spouse only. The incidence of such living arrangements has declined steadily since the end of World War II. Still, such data must be viewed cautiously. Percentages reflecting a single point in time typically understate the likelihood of the arrangement occurring over the lifetime of the older person. Also, data describing those 65 years and over may mask substantial differences among the subgroups. For example, older African Americans and Latinos (and especially women) are more likely than older whites to live with a relative other than a spouse (U.S. Senate Special Committee on Aging 1991).

Serious physical illness or disability that make remaining alone safely without supervision impossible is the most important factor that may determine the choice of a shared household, even one with nonfamily members (Horowitz 1985). Other important influences include poverty, widowhood, or loneliness. Soldo (1979) found that older people living with relatives were twice as likely to have low incomes as older people living independently. When the low income of the elderly person is pooled with that of the household in which he or she resides, a higher quality of living may be afforded to all. Figure 16.2 shows the relationship between living alone and poverty status in 1990. Some 24 percent of the elderly living alone were poor, compared with 14 percent of those who live with others. An additional 27 percent of elderly people living alone have incomes between 100 and 149 percent of the poverty level.

Living in the household of a nonrelative or a relative other than one's spouse sometimes implies greater limitations in mobility and activity than living with a spouse or alone. Although differences are not extraordinarily large, data from the National Health Interview Surveys do suggest that a shared household may act as protection when circumstances preclude maintaining an independent household.

Housing Characteristics

Most Americans, including the elderly, live in single-family owner-occupied homes. Of the almost 21 million households headed by older persons in 1997, 79 percent were owner occupied and 21 percent were rental units. Among the elderly, however, there are wide variations in patterns of home ownership by age, sex, race, and living arrangements. Householders 75 years old and over are more likely to rent than those 65 to 69 years old, as are elderly persons living alone when compared with those living with a spouse. Elderly men are more likely than women to own their own homes. Only 68 percent of African American elderly households and 59 percent of Latino elderly households were homeowners.

Homes owned by the elderly are older than those owned by younger people, in part because the elderly are less likely to have moved after age 45. According to the 1997 American Housing Survey <http://www.census.gov/hhes/www/housing/ahs/ahs97/tab79.html>, 36.3 percent of elderly homeowners and 15.6 percent all

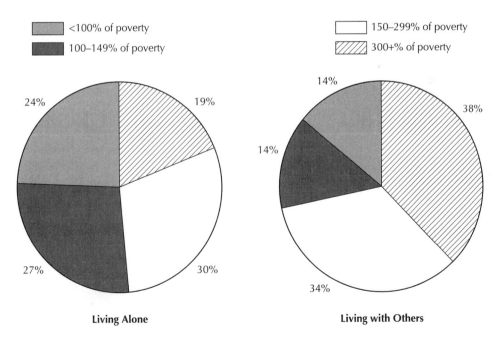

FIGURE 16.2   Economic Status of People Age 65 and Older Living Alone or with Others: 1990

Source: U.S. Special Committee on Aging, *Aging America: Trends and Projections* (Washington, DC: U.S. Government Printing Office, 1991).

homeowners in the United States moved into their current home before 1970; 50 percent of elderly homeowners, compared with 24.2 percent of all homeowners, lived in housing built before 1960. Approximately 22 percent of elderly renters had lived in their current dwellings since before 1980, compared to 5.2 percent of all renters.

Housing Quality.   There has been poignant evidence of elderly persons living in dirty, unsafe, and thoroughly wretched conditions. Although, in general, there is no consensus on what measures should be included in efforts to assess housing, the U.S. government employs three indicators: (1) presence of physical defects, (2) overcrowded living situations, and (3) excessive costs of housing.

The 1997 American Housing Survey (AHS) employed "selected deficiences" as an indicator of the quality of housing. Specified housing flaws falling under the definition of selected deficiencies included those related to plumbing, heating, electric systems, water leakage, and signs of rodents, among others. According to this survey, only 1.6 percent of elderly households were in dwellings with severe physical problems, and another 4.1 percent were in dwellings with moderate physical problems. While only 1.4 percent of older households reported a moderate or severe plumbing problem, 2.5 percent reported a moderate or severe heating problem, 5.7 percent reported seeing signs of rodents in the last three months, and 15.3 percent reported some form of interior or exterior water leak. The 1997 AHS asked elderly households to provide an overall rating from 1 (worst) to 10 (best) of the structure in which they resided. Most elderly households had a very high rating of their building. Almost 41 percent rated their structure a 10, with 78 percent rating the structure an 8, 9, or 10. Only 1.1 percent of elderly households rated the structure in which they lived as a 1, 2, or 3. The upgrading of the housing stock over time, the improved economic circumstances of older people, and the availability of government assistance programs has led a number of analysts to argue that the elderly are less likely than ever before to be found living in physically defective housing (Kingsley & Struyk 1991; Redfoot & Gaberlarage 1991).

Older households are rarely "overcrowded"; more likely, older people are "overhoused." The 1997 AHS reported a median of 1.6 persons in each elderly household residing in a median of 5.3 rooms, including 2.6 bedrooms. Elderly single-person households report a median of 4.7 rooms; elderly two-person households report a median of 5.3 rooms. Thus, it seems clear that a sizable proportion of elderly households in the United States had at least one extra bedroom and more than two extra nonsleeping rooms, given the size of the household. Older widows living alone are perhaps predictably the most likely to occupy overhoused accommodations. The disadvantages of overhoused situations include the extra physical maintenance that may be required to keep the home fit and clean, and the higher dollar costs of maintenance and utilities. Advantages include the ability to accommodate return visits by adult children and their families or a home office/storage area. Also, the costs of maintaining these dwellings (with low rent or paid-up mortgage) may still be less than if the household relocated to smaller accommodations.

With defective and/or overcrowded housing receding as problems for elderly homeowners and renters, an emerging problem is that many elderly have to pay too large a portion of their incomes to meet housing expenses. Clearly, if expenses are too high for rent and/or mortgage, basic utility costs, and real estate taxes and insurance for homeowners, older persons may be prevented from maintaining their homes and/or providing other basic necessities such as food, health care, and transportation. Using data from the 1997 American Housing Survey, the median percent of income spent on housing costs by elderly households (homeowners as well as renters) was approximately 21 percent. Among those elderly households residing in units with only one or two rooms, most of whom are likely single-person household residing in rental units, 50 percent of them paid more than 35 percent of their income for housing.

Estimates of those elderly experiencing financial burden related to housing may be both understated and overstated. Those understating the size of the elderly population experiencing financial burdens may be excluding large one-time maintenance expenditures such as a new roof or heating system. Estimators may also have no way of factoring in how many older people reduce food consumption or use of utilities to the detriment of their health in order to cope with overly costly housing. At the same time, estimates of the financial burden of housing may be overstated if estimators fail to include the value of wealth assets of elderly people as well as benefit assistance from governmental programs such as food stamps, Medicare, and Medicaid.

Three important points on the housing costs of the elderly are evident from review of additional data on housing costs (U.S. Senate Special Committee on Aging 1985, 1991):

1. Lower-income households pay a higher proportion of their income for housing, regardless of age, sex, or home ownership status.
2. At more advanced ages, males and females pay a higher proportion of their income for housing in all home ownership categories.
3. Female householders pay proportionately more for their housing than do male householders, at all ages and in all home ownership categories.

High-quality living environments can show up in the most unlikely places. Eckert (1980) has studied the "unseen elderly" who reside in single-room-occupancy (SRO) hotels in San Diego. A distinguishing feature of these living environments for older people is that men outnumber women. In virtually every other residential setting for older persons, older women predominate.

In one SRO, the Ballentine Hotel, 10 women reside on a permanent basis; 4 of the women have lived in the hotel for more than 10 years. They are old and retired. As a group, the women view the hotel as home and prefer it to other living arrangements they have experienced. Why would the SRO be preferable to an apartment? One woman answers:

> The advantages are that you have a lot of people. If you get tired of staying in your room, you can go to the lobby, then back to your room. I don't like apartments because here if you get sick or anything happens you get help right away. If you live in an apartment by yourself, you can drop dead and no one will know the difference. That's what I like about living here. I can get help right away if something happens, which is good health-wise. (p. 118)

The availability of social supports in the SRO is a theme expressed by both older men and women. As Eckert (1980) points out, living in the hotel gives these elders instant access to a helping network. Women seem more likely than men to be involved in social networks and to have worked out supportive arrangements with others. Such arrangements are more likely worked out with other women, although, because the SRO is a predominantly male environment, the women do have a large pool of older men from which to choose relationships. For many of these older women, living in a hotel is an adaptive strategy that provides benefits over and above those of other living environments.

Satisfaction with Housing. The American Association of Retired Persons (AARP 1990) commissioned nationwide surveys relating to housing arrangements and housing concerns of older adults. The findings emphasize that the majority of older people are satisfied with their housing arrangements. Over 70 percent of older respondents indicated being "very satisfied" with neighborhood or location of home (75 percent), physical condition of the home (71 percent), personal safety in the home (74 percent), type of home (76 percent), and general comfort of home (80 percent). Small minorities expressed that they were "very dissatisfied" with the cost of utilities (11 percent), cost of property taxes (8 percent), and lack of public transportation (7 percent).

The most significant housing concerns included failing health (61 percent were "very concerned"), losing independence (56 percent), and keeping the home in good condition (59 percent). One explanation for the generally high satisfaction with housing expressed by older people may be the strong attachment they have to their homes and neighborhood. After all, a great proportion of the elderly have spent the better part of their adult lives in their present homes and neighborhoods.

O'Bryant (1982) investigated the housing satisfaction of elderly people living in a large midwestern metropolitan area. She was particularly interested in whether subjective or objective factors better explained satisfaction with housing. She found that subjective factors (e.g., feelings of competence and emotional security that can be derived from a home) explained more of the variation in housing satisfaction than did demographic characteristics of residents or objective housing characteristics.

While controlling for individual differences, Golant (1985) identified six social and physical environmental experiences that helped influence life satisfaction within a sample of aged respondents in Evanston, Illinois. The careful reader of these experiences listed below will recognize the multidisciplinary content of the environment that impinges on the lives of older people.

1. Feeling bored in the dwelling
2. Thinking about memories of personal things
3. Having a good time in the community or neighborhood
4. Feeling satisfaction with stores and shopping in the community
5. Feeling lonely
6. Feeling annoyed because appliances have broken down

In an overall assessment of the neighborhood, Struyk and Soldo (1980) report that the distinction between homeowners and renters appears to be more salient than that between elderly and nonelderly; 25 to 30 percent of renters rate their neighborhood as "fair" or "poor," but only 12 to 13 percent of homeowners give such ratings. Interestingly, the elderly and nonelderly both viewed the lack of adequate public transportation as the greatest service inadequacy in their neighborhoods. In general, the elderly found fewer bothersome conditions in their neighborhoods than did the nonelderly. Street noise and neighborhood crime led the list of complaints for both groups.

Homelessness. Estimates of the number of homeless people in the United States are numerous; advocacy groups identify between one and three million. The U.S. Department of Housing and Urban Development (HUD) estimates between 250,00 and 350,00 homeless on any given night in the United States. The Urban Institute estimates as many as 600,000 homeless Americans, whereas the United States Census Bureau counted 250,000 in the 1990 census.

What proportion of the homeless population is made up of elderly people? Buss (1991) reviewed almost 100 studies and found between 1 and 7 percent of the homeless population is elderly. Why does this proportion seem so low when, after all, many homeless people on the streets of the nation's cities appear to be elderly? One explanation is that with age, survivorship becomes difficult. Many homeless may die prematurely; others may find their way into public or Veterans' Administration nursing homes or other long-term care facilities.

Another explanation for the low proportion of homeless who are elderly is that the safety net works more efficiently for older people than it does for other age groups. The health and human service delivery system program environment is relatively rich for older people and these programs may do a better job of preventing homelessness among the elderly than programs for younger and middle-aged adults. Also, as Buss (1991) states, the homeless come from a variety of backgrounds and are exposed to extremely hostile environments. As a result, they may give the appearance of premature aging. This may especially be the case for long-term substance abusers, alcoholics, and the chronically mentally ill. Problems of illiteracy, lifelong chronic health problems, and the absence of social support also confound the lack of housing among those old and young (Weiss 1992).

Homelessness is not confined to bag ladies and skid-row bums. Buss offers the example of "Blondie" to put a personal face on homelessness:

> They call her "Blondie" on the streets, but she says her real name is Nancy. She hangs out at a downtown street she calls "Main Street." Nearby is a soup kitchen that serves a meal every day except Wednesdays, Saturdays, and Sundays. On Sundays, Blondie goes to another place that serves meals only on that day. She does not eat on Wednesdays and Saturdays.
>
> Blondie is 52 years old but looks older. She is very thin, her remaining teeth are rotten, and her straight blond hair touches her shoulders.... Blondie says she was 28 when her "nerves let go." At the time, she spent about six weeks in a state mental hospital.... She had no income, no family, and lost the house she occupied before her breakdown. She has not been hospitalized in recent years. Usually when it gets cold, Blondie rents a room above a downtown tavern for $91 a month. She receives a General Assistance check for $117 a month and $78 in food stamps. But when the

weather turns warm, she is on the streets again. Her checks stop coming because, she says, she can never get a check when she does not have a residence. During the warm months, she carries a bag containing her belongings. (1991, pp. 13–14)

Fear of Crime.   Researchers have generally failed to achieve consensus on the reality and pervasiveness of fear of crime among the elderly (Akers et al. 1987). Some describe the elderly as living under "house arrest"; others point out that such fear is out of proportion to the actual probability of an elderly person being a victim of crime. In the 1997 American Housing Survey, approximately 13 percent of elderly households report the presence of crime as characteristic of their neighborhood, and 54 percent of those so reporting describe the condition as bothersome.

Generally, older people are victimized least often relative to other age groups. For example, in 1997, the rate of victimization for personal theft among individuals 65 years of age and over was approximately 75 percent of that for the total population. Also, the rate of violent crime against the total population was approximately nine times the rate against the elderly (U.S. Bureau of the Census 1999, Table 354). Although they are victimized less than the young, at least one researcher argues that crimes against the elderly are more serious, result in larger losses, are more likely committed by strangers who are armed, and occur close to their homes (Whitaker 1989).

The relationship between age and fear of crime continues to be a subject of scrutiny as a result of two different motivations. On the one hand, researchers have sought to distinguish segments of the elderly population that are more or less fearful of crime. On the other hand, investigators have employed a variety of test factors, including residential location and income, to explain the relationship between age and fear of crime. For example, Braungart, Braungart, and Hoyer (1980), using a nationwide sample, found that the elderly were only somewhat more fearful of crime than their younger and middle-aged counterparts. These researchers identified gender as more strongly related to fear of crime than either age or community size. Using Washington State residents, Lee (1982) reports that elderly urban dwellers showed more fear of walking alone in their own neighborhoods than did elderly residents of rural areas, although they did not estimate their chances of being victimized much differently. Interestingly, when the actual incidence of recalled victimization was introduced into the analysis, the statistical significance of residential location disappeared.

FEDERAL SUPPORT OF HOUSING FOR THE ELDERLY

In 1908, a presidential housing commission examined the problem of slums in U.S. cities. Appointed by President Theodore Roosevelt, the commission was particularly interested in those eastern seaboard cities that had become the entry point for masses of new immigrants (Jacobs et al. 1986). Federal intervention in housing in the country's major cities was recommended. But not until 1918, after World War I, did Congress intervene by authorizing a loan program for housing construction for shipyard workers. In 1918, Congress also created the U.S. Housing Commission and authorized the development of 25 community housing projects for defense workers.

The Great Depression of 1932 marked the beginning of large-scale federal intervention in housing. Between 1932 and 1937, several important government initiatives were begun. For example, direct funding of low-income housing and slum clearance was provided under the Emergency Relief and Construction Act of 1932. The National Housing Act of 1934 created the Federal Housing Administration (FHA) to provide government insurance for mortgages made by private lenders.

Jacobs and colleagues describe the Housing Act of 1949 as the beginning of the modern era in federal housing and development programs. This act declared that the quality of life of the nation's people required "housing production and related community development sufficient to remedy the serious housing shortage, the elimination of substandard and other inadequate housing through the clearance of slums and blighted areas, and the realization as soon as feasible of the goal of a decent home and a suitable living environment for every American family" (1986, p. 12).

The Housing Act of 1959 provided public housing specifically for the elderly, with the creation of two new programs. Section 231 of the National Housing Act provided Federal Housing Administration mortgage insurance for rental projects for the elderly, and Section 202 created a direct-loan program for elderly rental housing developed by private nonprofit corporations. Since that time, a considerable amount of construction has taken place. At the end of the 1980s, more than 1.9 million elderly were living in housing subsidized in some manner by the federal government. This represented about 9.6 percent of the nation's older households. To the uninformed, these numbers seem impressive. Yet, the 1971 White House Conference on Aging called for the annual production of 120,000 units of new housing for the elderly. By 1983, one estimate was that a minimum of 136,000 replacement units (new and rehabilitated) would be needed annually to supply the elderly in the United States over the next 20 years (Handler 1983). The need certainly exists, but these goals were unrealistically high. One problem is that, as Lawton (1980a) points out, most federal housing programs lead a precarious existence. They may be initiated and terminated within the time of one or two national political administrations. The Reagan-Bush years (1981 through 1992) were noteworthy for the absence of a federal housing policy, with no new initiatives for the low income and elderly. In the current budget-cutting environment of Washington, DC, the likelihood of new initiatives for subsidized housing for the poor and elderly is small.

Another kind of barrier to the development of housing for the elderly can be called *community resistance* (Mangum 1985). Lawton and Hoffman have observed that "community response to the announcement of plans to construct elderly housing in a neighborhood is frequently hostile, sometimes to the point of a local group taking legal action to bar the construction" (1984, p. 42). Community resistance may result from (1) threats associated with perceived change in the characteristics of people in the area, (2) concern about the development of stigmatizing service facilities, (3) concern that the neighborhood may be disturbed by a secondary set of resource users, and (4) the fact that any increase in density is threatening (Winkel, cited in Lawton & Hoffman 1984).

Mangum (1985) makes four recommendations for sponsors of housing for the elderly to help overcome possible community resistance:

1. If possible, build in a "nice" semicommercial area.
2. If housing can be built only in a residential area of predominantly single-family homes, obtain community input.
3. If there is opposition from the community, make efforts to reach a compromise with opposing residents.
4. If a compromise cannot be reached, look for an alternative site.

Most public housing construction has involved low-cost, high-rise apartment buildings. To be eligible for public housing designed specifically for the elderly, a person must be 60 years or over, the spouse of a person 62 years or over, or disabled (without age restrictions). Restrictions on income and assets are usually set at the local level. Almost uniformly, tenants pay rent on a sliding scale up to a maximum of 30 or 35 percent of total income. According to the U.S. Senate Special Committee on Aging (1991), 1.9 percent of families with any member age 65 years or over and 11.9 percent of single-person households lived in publicly supported rental housing in 1988. Almost one-quarter (23.3 percent) of single-person households with incomes below the poverty level lived in publicly subsidized housing in 1988.

Federal programs responsible for rent-subsidized apartment units occupied by the elderly (age 62 and over) are briefly described here. These include the Low-Rent Public Housing Program, Section 202, Section 8, and several programs of the Farmers Home Administration.

Low-Rent Public Housing

The federal Public Housing Program was established through the Housing Act of 1937. It was the first public agency to finance construction of apartment units for low-income elderly and nonelderly persons. Today, eligible tenants must have an income that is 50 percent or less of their locality's median income and pay 30 percent of their net income on rent and utilities. There are approximately 1.2 million units in the current inventory, located in low-rent projects. About 480,000 of these apartments were occupied by the elderly in 1990. The low-rent projects are owned, operated, and maintained by nonprofit housing authorities in localities throughout the United States. Most units were produced prior to the 1980s, although the housing authorities can finance additional construction or modernization of units on their own. Thus, in most cases, apartment units become available as a result of vacancies.

Section 202

This program, enacted as part of the Housing Act of 1959, was designed to provide independent living for the elderly as well as the nonelderly disabled. Suspended because of criticism in 1969, the program was revived in 1974 under an amendment to the Housing and Community Development Act of that year.

The program authorizes direct loans to nonprofit organizations so that they can develop and operate multifamily housing projects. The program provides capital advances to finance property acquisition, site improvement, conversion, demolition, relocation, and other expenses associated with supportive housing for the elderly. These housing projects are aimed at low-income persons age 62 and older. The number of annual units produced under Section 202 seems to have peaked at about 20,000 in the late 1970s and has declined steadily to under 10,000 in 1990. By 1990, about 3,200 projects had been funded with approximately 230,000 units; 95 percent of these units are occupied by the elderly. Each year, a Notice of Fund Availability (NOFA) is published in the *Federal Register.* The 1995 NOFA provided $510 million in capital advances for 7,409 units; the 1997 NOFA was $390 million in capital advances for 5,554 units.

Most Section 202 projects are located within cities and in predominantly residential neighborhoods that offer little or no other public or subsidized housing. A 20-year-old U.S. Department of Housing and Urban Development (1979) report has been critical of the program for several reasons: The program appears to have served primarily white, elderly females of middle socioeconomic status and current incomes that, though low in absolute terms, are above the poverty level. Also, males, African Americans and other minorities, the disabled, and persons with the lowest incomes were not as well served by the program (U.S. Department of Housing and Urban Development 1979). More recently, Section 202 has been identified to be among the more successful housing programs for the low-income elderly (U.S. House of Representatives 1989).

Since 1978, Section 202 housing has been involved in a project that attempts a marriage between housing and services to meet the needs of frail elderly persons in subsidized housing. It is a direct effort to put off premature institutionalization. In the Congregate Housing Services Program (CHSP), federal funds were given directly to the managers and administrators of public housing and Section 202 projects, who had to deal with the problem of "aging in place" (Nachison 1985). In 1990, the demonstration covered 59 projects in 33 states and served about 1,500 people. Eligible elderly needed help with three or more activities of daily living (ADLs) and were an average age of 77. Recipient projects were to provide at least one hot meal per day in a group setting, seven days a week. Other services offered must be necessary for independent living. According to Nachison (1985), costs are less than the delivery of services through agencies in the general community and there seems a real and measurable impact on unnecessary institutionalization.

Although the CHSP is generally thought to be a success, perhaps in part because it is such a small program, HUD has neither solicited nor funded applications for new grants under CHSP since 1994. Congress has provided funds to extend expiring grants; in fiscal year 1998, about $3.5 million was available for this purpose.

Section 8

The Section 8 program was created by the Housing and Community Development Act of 1974. This program has been the principal federal means of providing housing assistance to the elderly. It offers rental assistance through several different mechanisms, including (1) construction or rehabilitation/relocation of public housing units, (2) support of already-built rental units funded through other federal programs, (3) support of already-built private-sector rental units with Section 8 certificates, and (4) support of already-built rental units with Section 8 vouchers.

Section 8 subsidies are designed to compensate a household for the difference between the cost of housing it can afford (some percentage of adjusted household income) and the cost of comparable housing in the local area where it resides. To be eligible for Section 8 housing subsidies, families and single persons must have incomes well below the area median (classified as lower-income households). The federal government pays the difference between the contract rent (an approximation of fair market rent) and the rent paid by the tenant, usually 30 percent of adjusted family income.

There are many Section 8 programs and all cannot be described here. Two important ones, providing assistance for approximately 1.4 million households in the United States, are the Rental Voucher Program and the Rental Certificate Program.

Authorized under the U.S. Housing Act of 1937, the Section 8 Rental Voucher Program attempts to increase affordable housing choices for very low-income households by allowing families to choose privately owned rental housing. The public housing authority (PHA) generally pays the landlord the difference between 30 percent of household income and the PHA-determined payment standard, about 80 to 100 percent of the fair market rent (FMR). The rent must be reasonable compared with similar unassisted units. The household may choose a unit with a higher rent than the FMR and pay the landlord the difference or choose a lower cost unit and keep the difference. According to the U.S. Department of Housing and Urban Development, about 400,000 families were using the vouchers in September 1996. Unfortunately, the proportion of vouchers being used by elderly households is not available. Currently, HUD is not accepting new applications; it is only extending expiring commitments and vouchers dedicated for special purposes.

The Section 8 Rental Certificate Program issues certificates to income-qualified households. The PHA then pays the landlord the amount equal to the difference between the tenant portion of the rent (30 percent of adjusted income, 10 percent of gross income, or the portion of welfare assistance designated for housing) and the contract rent, which must not exceed the HUD-established fair market rent for the area. The administering PHA inspects the housing units to make sure they comply with HUD quality standards. Landlords must agree to accept no more than fair market rent. HUD pays the PHA an administration fee to cover costs of running the program, including accepting and reviewing applications, recertifying eligibility, and inspecting the rental units.

A system of "portability" allows families to use the assistance outside the boundaries of a particular housing authority's jurisdiction. If a PHA chooses, up to 15 percent of assistance under the Section 8 Rental Certificate Program may be used in specific buildings or units developed for the program. Families receiving such assistance have no right to continued assistance if they leave the assisted rental unit. However, tenant-based certificates may be used in any qualifying housing unit where the landlord agrees to participate in the program. In theory, certificates could be used for home ownership, but this has not yet been implemented. HUD spent an estimated $15.5 billion for all Section 8 programs in fiscal year 1996 and $16.7 billion in fiscal year 1997. However, current funding is only for renewals and families in assisted housing.

Farmers Home Administration

Assistance to the elderly can be provided under both of the Farmers Home Administration's (FmHA) programs: the Section 502 single-family and the Section 515 rural rental housing assistance programs. Section 502 provides subsidized and unsubsidized direct loans and unsubsidized guaranteed loans. An unsubsidized Section 502 loan can be used to finance the construction or acquisition of a new, substantially rehabilitated, or existing home. Homes are limited to those that are modest in size, design, and cost. The maximum loan term is 33 years, and interest rates are adjusted periodically according to market changes.

In 1962, Congress added Section 515 in recognition of the need for rental housing in rural areas and small towns. This section authorizes loans to finance cooperative and rental housing projects. Nonprofit, limited-dividend, and profit-motivated sponsors may participate in the rental housing program. The 515 program is open to low- and moderate-income families and to those 62 years or older (Jacobs et al. 1986). Congregate housing services have been available under Section 515 programming. Assistance takes the form of grants to provide at least one hot meal per day in a group setting, seven days per week, plus other supportive services necessary for independent living. Projects may not duplicate services that are already available at affordable rates. HUD administers this program in coordination with the Rural Housing Service of the U.S. Department of Agriculture. As indicated earlier, CHSP funding appears to be drying up.

In recent years, there have been a number of important state housing initiatives for the elderly (Council of State Housing Agencies et al. 1986). In part, these resulted from the abdication of federal responsibility in this area that characterized the 1980s. These state initiatives occur in the areas of leadership and planning, technical assistance, service development, and financial support. Programs and projects may be categorized as those that help older people remain in their own homes (including home equity conversion, home repair and improvements, property tax relief, rental assistance, and condominium conversion protection programs); those that help older people continue living near familiar supports and institutions (e.g., shared housing programs); and those that provide specific services along with shelter. Examples abound. Those presented here are taken from a publication of the Council of State Housing Agencies and the National Association of State Units on Aging (1986):

1. The state of Maryland awards grants to local entities—such as development corporations, local governments, and Area Agencies on Aging—for programs to provide minor repairs and maintenance of properties occupied by low-income elderly homeowners and homeowners who are disabled. These programs are administered by the Department of Economic and Community Development Office of Housing Assistance, part of the Division of Local Government Assistance.

2. The Senior Citizen Shared Housing Program is a project of the California Department of Aging and the California Department of Housing and Community Development. California has a critical shortage of senior housing. More than one-quarter of older renters pay more than 50 percent of their limited income for housing, and two-thirds of all elderly renters pay more than 25 percent of their income for housing. State general funds and local matching resources are used to provide information and referral about housing issues and to help older persons find a home-sharing partner. Funds are distributed primarily to nonprofit agencies to operate the services. Some government agencies and cities are also sponsors. Since 1981, when the program began, over 3,700 persons over age 60 have been matched with housemates.

3. Through a program started in 1983, the Ohio Housing Finance Agency (OHFA) has financed 19 congregate facilities. Mortgage funds come from tax-exempt bonds and HUD mortgage insurance. Tenant services include one or two meals a day, maid and linen service, transportation, and social services. Services are provided by the management company itself or in conjunction with a nearby nursing facility, using that facility's caterers and nursing staff. A minimum of 20 percent of the units must be occupied by low-income residents. Suggested rent levels are 30 to 80 percent of the area median income.

RETIREMENT COMMUNITIES

Increasingly, gerontologists have given attention to supportive housing arrangements for older persons that include special design features and the presence of services. Pynoos and Golant (1996) identify five forces that have promoted supportive housing options to both older persons and public-policy experts:

1. There has been rapid growth in the number of older persons who require supportive services not readily available in conventional housing arrangements.

2. Older people have a strong preference for residential over institutional settings.
3. Because facilities vary greatly in design, services available, populations being served, and quality, evaluation and oversight have become necessary.
4. Over time, a substantial amount of age-specific housing in the United States has been developed. Originally built without links to services, this housing has the potential to accommodate service-needy elderly.
5. At all levels, government continues to look for appropriate and cost-efficient alternatives to institutional and/or nursing home care.

Retirement communities represent one form of supportive housing for the elderly. The term **retirement community** evokes an image of wealthy older people residing in a country-club setting. This is one type of retirement community, but a retirement community may also look like an urban ethnic neighborhood, a suburban town, or a single apartment building. Hunt and Gunter-Hunt (1985) describe naturally occurring retirement communities (NORCs) as housing developments that are not planned or designed for older people but that, over time, come to house primarily older people.

Retirement communities may be defined more by their membership than by their geographic boundaries. Longino (1980) defines a *retirement community* as any living environment most of whose residents have relocated there since they retired. The essential elements of the definition are *retirement* and *relocation*. Although many residents of retirement communities still work, almost all who have worked have also retired from full-time employment at least once. In addition, the definition excludes communities of retirement-aged people who have aged in place; only the settings to which retired people *move* may be defined as retirement communities.

Retirement communities can be distinguished by the amount of conscious planning that goes into developing and operating them. Some are designed specifically for individuals of a certain chronological age. These *de jure* retirement communities are designed to take into account the more common needs of retirees. Planned communities may be separated into two types: subsidized and unsubsidized (Longino 1980). A housing project built under the auspices of any of the federal programs described in the previous section can be classified as a *subsidized* retirement community. *Unsubsidized* planned communities for retirees range along a continuum from housing alone to life-care communities that attempt to provide a full range of services.

Some retirement communities place no age restrictions on new residents but nonetheless attract people who are retired. These *de facto* retirement communities are not designed as such, but in them a series of organizations and services arise that cater to older people (Longino 1980).

Why do people move to retirement communities? According to Longino (1981), there are positive (pulls) and negative (pushes) triggering mechanisms in the relocation decision process. Residents of three different retirement communities in the Ozark region connecting the states of Missouri, Arkansas, and Oklahoma were all asked for the single-most important reason for their move. In general, Longino reports a congruence between personal needs and community selection.

Residents of the Ozark Lakes County, a de jure retirement community that attracts relatively younger couples who are in better physical and financial health to the existing towns of the region, report the outstanding natural beauty of the region as primary justification for relocating there. Some 54 percent of residents gave this as the most important reason for their relocation. Another 21 percent reported social needs as the most important reason for their move.

Horizon Heights is a de facto subsidized retirement community, part of a public housing facilities network in a midwestern city with a population of almost 200,000. It is exclusively for less affluent people of retirement age, who pay 25 percent of their adjusted income toward the rent. Almost one in four (23 percent) gave financial reasons as the most important reason for the move. Another 25 percent offered the push factor of wanting to leave an unhappy neighborhood situation.

Finally, over half (51 percent) of the residents of Carefree Village, a nonsubsidized life-care retirement community inhabited by upper-middle-class migrants, cited health needs as the major reason for selecting this community. Another 19 percent indicated the availability of other services as the primary reason for the move.

Planned communities specialize in providing services and meeting special needs of older people. They make their advantages known to prospective residents and they attract people who, because of unhappy events in their lives or changing circumstances, feel they must move. Such people generally show a higher push level of explanation for their relocation. People who reside in unplanned, or de facto, communities generally have more positive or pull factors as explanation for their move (Longino 1981).

Although the literature on retirement communities is not large, several interesting ethnographic studies have been carried out. *Ethnography* is a branch of anthropology that studies and reports on everyday lives of particular cultural groups. Two of these studies are worth noting, for they help highlight a question of practical and theoretical importance to gerontologists today: Are older people better served by age-integrated or age-segregated environments?

Merrill Court

Merrill Court is an apartment building that houses 43 retired individuals. Most of the residents are women who are widowed, fundamentalist Christians, and of working-class background. Hochschild (1973) worked at Merrill Court in a variety of jobs, including recreation director. When she began, Hochschild expected to find a disengaged, lonely group of individuals. Instead, she found an "unexpected community" of active and engaged older people who appeared to be quite satisfied with their lives. Residents have a great deal of interaction, much of which began with the installation of a coffee machine in the recreation room. Visitation among residents and between residents and their families occurs frequently. Having frequent contact with their neighbors provides these elders with the gratification of friendship, as well as an opportunity for relaying information about other people. Although the status equality among residents led Hochschild to characterize their relationships as a sibling bond, informal status distinctions are made among the residents.

According to Hochschild, within Merrill Court there is a status system based on a distribution of honor accumulated through holding offices in the service club. A parallel hierarchy existed based on the distribution of "luck": Being young-old, having good health, and living close to one's children were defined as having luck. Those who fall short on the criteria for luck are called "poor dears." This hierarchy ran in one direction. Someone who was a "poor dear" in the eyes of another seldom called that other person a "poor dear" in return. Many residents applied the term to those in nursing homes they visited. Hochschild explained the "poor dear" hierarchy as follows:

> The way the old look for luck differences among themselves reflects the pattern found at the bottom of other social, racial and gender hierarchies. To find oneself lucky within an ill-fated category is to gain the semblance of high status when society withholds it from others in the category. The way old people feel above and condescend to other old people may be linked to the fact that the young feel above and condescend to them. The luck hierarchy does not stop with the old. (1973)

Despite these informal status differences among the residents of Merrill Court, no one is isolated. The widows of Merrill Court are independent. They do not use "poor dear" when referring to themselves. They take care of themselves, fix their own meals, pay their own rent, shop for their own food, and make their own beds. And, when it is necessary, they do these things for others.

Fun City

Jacobs (1974, 1975) has written about Fun City, a pseudonym for a retirement community of about 6,000 residents located 90 miles from a large western metropolitan area. Fun City is a planned community of single-level, ranch-style tract homes. A nearby shopping center caters to the needs of residents. An on-site activity center houses 92 clubs and organizations available to residents. Fun City residents are predominantly white and middle to upper class; the average age is 71 years.

Fun City bills itself as promoting "an active way of life." From Jacobs's reports, however, it seems clear that Fun City is a false paradise. The retirement community exhibits many of the negative aspects residents associate with life on the "outside." Fun City has no public transportation, no police department, and no adequate health care facilities. It is geographically isolated. Despite all the scheduled activities, fewer than 10 percent of the residents participated in any activity on a given day, and generally the same individuals participated in different activities on different days. Thus, inactivity is the norm for Fun City residents.

Jacobs concludes that many residents were withdrawing from society when they moved to Fun City and simply continued this withdrawal after arrival. Despite the promise of an active way of life, the environment was organized in a way that promoted disengagement. No transportation, geographical isolation, and a lack of ties among the residents led to dissatisfaction with life on the part of many in Fun City. Those in the retirement community expressing the highest degree of satisfaction with Fun City were those whose financial situations allowed for travel, vacations, and visits with family.

Age Integration versus Age Segregation

Merrill Court and Fun City are both age-segregated living environments; nearly all the residents of both retirement communities are older people. Both are planned retirement communities. Merrill Court represents public housing for the elderly, whereas Fun City is an unsubsidized retirement community. In contrast, there are the Ozark lakes region retirement communities that developed on a de facto basis and remain age integrated.

Much discussion in the gerontological literature has evaluated the relative merits for older people of age-segregated and age-integrated housing. Very influential in this discussion has been the research of Rosow (1967), who examined the social behavior of older people living in apartment buildings in Cleveland (privately developed and public housing). In particular, he was interested in how social behavior was affected by the concentration of age peers in the buildings. Rosow classified apartment buildings into three categories of age density: those buildings in which the elderly represented 1 to 15 percent of the residents, those in which 33 to 49 percent were elderly, and those in which 50 percent or more of the residents were elderly. For both working-class and middle-class aged, Rosow found that the presence of more age peers was positively associated with social interaction with neighbors. In addition, he demonstrated that this relationship was even more advantageous for those with lower status.

Generalizing from Rosow's evidence is difficult. For example, both Merrill Court and Fun City have age densities that are higher (almost 100 percent) than Rosow's highest category (50 percent plus). Yet, Merrill Court shows high sociability among its residents, whereas social interaction among Fun City residents is minimal. Accounting for this difference is no easy task. Carp (1976) cites five reasons that she believes generalizing from Rosow's work is so difficult. These reasons point to differences between Merrill Court and Fun City and may help explain why social interaction among residents was high in one and low in the other:

1. Rosow's work was not conducted in new housing for the elderly, but in older apartment buildings.
2. In the highest age density of Rosow's apartment buildings, only about half of the residents were elderly. In public housing for the elderly and other planned retirement communities such as Fun City, the percentage of elderly in the environment approached 100 percent.
3. Rosow studied long-time residents of apartment buildings, whereas tenants in newly constructed public housing or newly developed tract housing for the elderly are often the first in-movers.

4. Rosow studied people in old housing located in older established neighborhoods. In-movers to retirement communities have left accustomed living environments and have relocated, often in new housing in newer neighborhoods.

5. Rosow's respondents may have been a special population, and no one knows how it differs from the population of other age-segregated environments or from the general population of older people.

Certainly one important difference between Merrill Court and Fun City that affected the potential for social interaction is the physical layout. For example, it would be considerably easier for interaction to occur among the 43 residents of a five-story building at Merrill Court than among 6,000 residents distributed one or two to each home in the sprawling tract home community of Fun City (Jacobs 1975). Hochschild makes this clear in her description of the design of the building:

> There was an elevator midway between the apartments, and a long porch extended the length of all the apartments. It was nearly impossible to walk from any apartment to the elevator without being watched from a series of living room windows that looked out into the porch.... A woman who was sewing or watching television in her apartment could easily glance up through the window or wave to the passerby. (1973, p. 4)

No such arrangement existed at Fun City. Other factors that likely contributed to the generation of an "unexpected community" at Merrill Court included the greater status similarity and "good health" that existed among Merrill Court residents compared to residents of Fun City.

Fun City notwithstanding, the evidence from most studies of age-segregated living situations show them to be satisfactory environments for aging. Generally, the studies show higher rates of activity and social interaction in age-segregated housing. Research on morale or life satisfaction in age-segregated versus age-integrated housing is less clear. Messer (1967) measured morale and social interaction of elderly living in two public housing projects. One was age segregated; the other was a mixture of older and younger families. In the age-integrated setting, there was an association between the morale of older tenants and the amount of social interaction they engaged in; no such association appeared in the age-segregated project. Messer believes morale was linked to activity in the age-integrated environment because the norms of that environment were based on standards of youth; the older person who did not succeed in becoming active would feel deficient in light of these standards. The age-segregated environment fostered social norms appropriate to the ages of its residents; lack of activity did not reflect a deficiency; and it was commonly recognized that some individuals preferred to be active, whereas others did not.

Data from two large-scale research studies (reported in Lawton 1980a) show that older people *themselves* approve of age-segregated living arrangements. Still, there is great danger in concluding that achieving the ideal social situation for older persons is contingent on their residing in age-segregated housing. Although such environments do meet friendship and social needs for many elderly, others' needs may not be filled by such arrangements. Apparently, age segregation in Fun City did little to enhance the social relationships of many of the residents.

One special problem with much of the research on age-segregated versus age-integrated housing for the elderly is that it is virtually impossible to isolate the age composition of an environment from other variables that may be operating in that environment. As Carp (1976) points out, it is very difficult to locate sites for research that are otherwise equivalent and whose tenants are similar. Thus, it is possible (perhaps even likely) that reports of high satisfaction on the part of the elderly tenants of age-segregated housing have more to do with the *fit* of the physical and social environment than with age segregation in itself.

SUMMARY

Housing is an important element in the life of an older person. Yet, gerontologists have come to understand that the physical characteristics of housing represents only one part of the broader living environment in which an older person resides.

Lawton and colleagues have been particularly interested in the relationship between an older person's competence and the demands the living environment places on that individual. This relationship is stated in the form of a hypothesis: The less competent the individual, the greater the impact of environmental factors on that individual. Lawton sees competence in the broadest possible terms. It may be affected not only by internal biological or physiological factors but also by external social processes, such as age discrimination and social isolation.

Nearly all elderly Americans live in independent households; the majority live with a spouse or other relatives, but women are more than twice as likely as men to live alone. Physical disability, poverty, widowhood, and loneliness have an important impact on the choice of living arrangements.

Most elderly Americans live in single-family, owner-occupied homes. Homes owned by the elderly are older than those owned by younger people. The upgrading of the housing stock over time has led a number of analysts to argue that the elderly are less likely than ever before to be found living in physically defective housing

Determining how many elderly persons live in inadequate housing is problematic, primarily because there is no consensus on what measures should be included in efforts to assess housing. Although few elderly households are overcrowded, many are "overhoused." A principal problem for the elderly is that a large proportion of their income is used to meet housing expenses; this is especially the case for elderly renters. Housing costs, as a percentage of income, increase with age. Lower-income households pay a higher proportion of their income for housing.

In general, the elderly are quite satisfied with their housing arrangements. Over 70 percent of older respondents indicated being "very satisfied" with neighborhood locations of their homes, physical condition of their homes, personal safety in their homes, type of homes, and the general comfort of their homes. Small minorities expressed that they were "very dissatisfied" with the cost of utilities and property taxes as well as the lack of public transportation. Housing concerns that topped the list included failing health, loss of independence, and keeping the home in good condition. The high level of satisfaction with housing accommodations is thought to reflect a strong attachment of older people to their homes and neighborhoods.

Although federal involvement in housing began with the Great Depression, the Housing Act of 1959 first provided public housing specifically for the elderly. By 1990, almost two million elderly households, or 10 percent of the nation's older households, lived in housing subsidized by the federal government. In 1983, estimates were that 136,000 replacement units would be needed annually to supply the elderly in the United States over the next 20 years. That goal appears unrealistically high.

The principal federal housing programs for the elderly have been the Low-Rent Public Housing Program, Sections 202 and 8 of the National Housing Act, and several programs of the Farmers Home Administration. In recent years, the states have taken diverse initiatives in creating housing programs for the elderly.

Gerontologists have given increasing attention to supportive housing alternatives such as retirement communities—living environments defined by the retirement and relocation experiences of the residents. Retirement communities may be planned or not, and planned communities may be subsidized or unsubsidized. There is considerable discussion in the gerontological literature about whether age-segregated or age- integrated housing is more advantageous for older people. Although the evidence from most studies of age-segregated environments show them to be satisfactory for aging, it is still too early to conclude that achieving the ideal social situation for older persons is contingent on their residing in age-segregated housing.

STUDY QUESTIONS

1. List the major neighborhood and community characteristics that influence the study of housing for the aged. How do these relate to the concept of *environmental press?*

2. Define and discuss the accommodative model of independent living environments. How does it differ from the constant model?

3. Discuss the living arrangements of the elderly in contemporary society. What is the impact of sex and marital status on those arrangements?

4. How do elderly homeowners and renters assess their living accommodations? With which factors do they express the most satisfaction? The least satisfaction? What are their greatest concerns about housing?

5. Discuss the federal housing programs aimed at helping to provide for housing needs of the elderly.

6. Define *retirement community*. Distinguish between *de facto* and *de jure* communities. Describe the elderly who reside in this type of housing and reflect on the selection processes that operate to get them there.

7. Identify the relative merits of age-segregated and age-integrated housing for the elderly. Which is more advantageous? Why do you think so?

REFERENCES

Akers, R. L., LaGreca, A. J., Sellers, C., & Cochran, J. (1987). Fear of crime and victimization among the elderly in different types of communities. *Criminology, 25,* 487–505.

American Association of Retired Persons. (1990). *Understanding senior housing for the 1990s.* Washington, DC: Author.

Baggett, S. A. (1989). *Residential care for the elderly: Critical issues in public policy.* New York: Greenwood.

Braungart, M., Braungart, R., & Hoyer, W. (1980). Age, sex, and social factors in fear of crime. *Sociological Focus, 13* (1), 55–66.

Buss, T. F. (1991). *Meeting the health care needs of the homeless elderly.* Cleveland, OH: Western Reserve Geriatric Education Center.

Carp, F. (1976). Housing and living environments of older people. In R. Binstock & E. Shanas (Eds.), *The handbook of aging and the social sciences.* New York: Van Nostrand Reinhold.

Chapman, N. J., & Beaudet, M. (1983). Environmental predictors of well-being for at-risk older adults in a mid-sized city. *Journal of Gerontology, 38* (2), 237–244.

Council of State Housing Agencies et al. (1986). *State initiatives in elderly housing.* Washington, DC: Author.

Eckert, J. K. (1980). *The unseen elderly: A study of marginally subsistent hotel dwellers.* San Diego, CA: Campanile Press.

Ehrlich, P., Ehrlich, I., & Woehlke, P. (1982). Congregate housing for the elderly: Thirteen years later. *The Gerontologist, 22* (4), 399–403.

Golant, S. M. (1985). The influence of the experienced residential environment on old people's life satisfaction. *Journal of Housing for the Elderly, 3* (3/4), 23–49.

Handler, B. (1983). *Housing needs of the elderly: A quantitative analysis.* Ann Arbor: University of Michigan, National Policy Center on Housing and Living Arrangements for Older Americans.

Hochschild, A. (1973). *The unexpected community.* Englewood Cliffs, NJ: Prentice-Hall.

Horowitz, A. (1985). Family caregiving to the frail elderly. *Annual Review of Gerontoloy and Geriatrics, 5,* 194–246.

Hunt, M. E., & Gunter-Hunt, G. (1985). Naturally occurring retirement communities. *Journal of Housing for the Elderly, 3* (3/4), 3–21.

Jacobs, B. G., Harney, K. R., Edson, C. L., & Lane, B. S. (1986). *Guide to federal housing programs* (2nd ed.). Washington, DC: Bureau of National Affairs.

Jacobs, J. (1974). *Fun city: An ethnographic study of retirement community.* New York: Holt, Rinehart and Winston.

Jacobs, J. (1975). *Older persons and retirement communities.* Springfield, IL: Charles C. Thomas.

Kingsley, G. T., & Struyk, R. J. (1991). Housing policy in the United States: Trends, future needs, and implications for congregate housing. In L. W. Kaye & A. Monk (Eds.), *Congregate housing for the elderly: Theoretical, policy, and programmatic perspectives.* New York: Haworth.

LaPlante, M. P., Hendershot, G. E., & Moss, A. J. (1992). *Assistive technology devices and home accessibility features: Prevalence, payment, need and trends.* Advance Data, No. 217. Hyattsville, MD: National Center for Health Statistics.

Lawton, M. P. (1980a). *Environment and aging.* Monterey, CA: Brooks-Cole.

Lawton, M. P. (1980b). Housing the elderly: Residential quality and residential satisfaction. *Research on Aging, 2* (3), 309–328.

Lawton, M. P. (1980c). *Social and medical services in housing for the aged.* Rockville, MD: U.S. Department of Health and Human Services.

Lawton, M. P., & Hoffman, C. (1984). Neighborhood reactions to elderly housing. *Journal of Housing for the Elderly, 2* (2), 41–53.

Lawton, M. P., & Hoover, S. (1979). *Housing and neighborhood: Objective and subjective quality.* Philadelphia: Philadelphia Geriatric Center.

Lawton, M. P., & Nahemow, L. (1973). Ecology and the aging process. In C. Eisdorfer & M. P. Lawton (Eds.), *Psychology of adult development and aging.* Washington, DC: American Psychological Association.

Lawton, M. P., & Simon, B. (1968). The ecology of social relationships in housing for the elderly. *Gerontologist, 8,* 108–115.

Lee, G. (1982). Residential location and fear of crime among the elderly. *Rural Sociology, 47* (4), 655–669.

Longino, C. (1980). The retirement community. In F. Berghorn & D. Schafer (Eds.), *Dimensions of aging.* Boulder, CO: Westview.

Longino, C. (1981). The retirement community. In C. Kart & B. Manard (Eds.), *Aging in America: Readings in social gerontology* (2nd ed.). Sherman Oaks, CA: Alfred.

Louis Harris & Associates. (1987). *Problems facing elderly Americans living alone.* New York: Author.

Mangum, W. P. (1985). But not in my neighborhood: Community resistance to housing for the elderly. *Journal of Housing for the Elderly, 3* (3/4), 101–119.

Messer, M. (1967). The possibility of an age-concentrated environment becoming a normative system. *Gerontologist, 7,* 247–251.

Mollica, R. L., Ladd, R. C., Dietsche, D., Wilson, K. B., & Ryther, B. S. (1992). *Building assisted living for the elderly into long term care policy: A guide for states.* Portland, ME: National Academy for State Health Policy

Murray, H. (1938). *Explorations in personality.* New York: Oxford University Press.

Nachison, J. S. (1985). Congregate housing for the low and moderate income elderly—A needed federal state partnership. *Journal of Housing for the Elderly, 3* (3/4), 65–80.

O'Bryant, S. L. (1982). The value of home to older persons: Relationship to housing satisfaction. *Research on Aging, 4* (3), 349–363.

Pynoos, J., & Golant, S. (1996). Housing and living arrangements for the elderly. In R. H. Binstock & L. K. George (Eds.), *Handbook of aging and the social sciences* (4th ed.). San Diego, CA: Academic.

Redfoot, D., & Gaberlavage, G. (1991). Housing for older Americans: Sustaining the dream. *Generations, 15* (3), 35–46.

Rosow, I. (1967). *Social integration of the aged.* New York: Free Press.

Soldo, B. (1979). The housing characteristics of independent elderly: A demographic overview. *Occasional papers in housing and urban development,* No. 1. Washington, DC: U.S. Department of Housing and Urban Development.

Streib, G., Folts, E., & Hilker, M. A. (1984). *Old homes—New families: Shared living for the elderly.* New York: Columbia University.

Struyk, R., & Soldo, B. (1980). *Improving the elderly's housing.* Cambridge, MA: Ballinger.

U.S. Bureau of the Census. (1991). *Statistical Abstract of the United States, 1991* (111th ed.). Washington, DC: U.S. Government Printing Office.

U.S. Bureau of the Census. (1999). *Statistical Abstract of the United States, 1999* (119th ed.). Washington, DC: U.S. Government Printing Office.

U.S. Department of Housing and Urban Development. (1979). *Housing for the elderly and handicapped.* Washington, DC: Office of Policy Development and Research, U.S. Department of Housing and Urban Development.

U.S. House of Representatives, Select Committee on Aging. (1989). *The 1988 national survey of Section 202 housing for the elderly and handicapped.* Washington, DC: U.S. Government Printing Office.

U.S. Senate, Special Committee on Aging. (1985). *How older Americans live: An analysis of census data.* Washington, DC: U.S. Government Printing Office.

U.S. Senate, Special Committee on Aging. (1990). *Developments in aging, 1989* (Vol. 1 & 2). Washington, DC: U.S. Government Printing Office.

U.S. Senate, Special Committee on Aging. (1991). *Developments in aging, 1990* (Vol. 1 & 2). Washington, DC: U.S. Government Printing Office.

U.S. Senate, Special Committee on Aging, American Association of Retired Persons, Federal Council on Aging, & U.S. Administration on Aging. (1991). *Aging America: Trends and projections.* Washington, DC: U.S. Government Printing Office.

Weiss, L. M. (1992). *There's no place like...no place: Confronting the problems of the aging homeless and marginally housed.* Washington, DC: AARP.

Whitaker, C. J. (1989). Elderly victims. In U.S. Senate, Special Committee on Aging, *Developments in aging, 1988: Volume 2—Appendixes.* Washington, DC: U.S. Government Printing Office.

CHAPTER SEVENTEEN

LONG-TERM CARE

RUTH E. DUNKLE
CARY S. KART
VAN H. LUONG

In the minds of many Americans, the phrase *long-term care* is synonymous with *old age* or *nursing home*. In part, this is because it is not so long ago when such facilities were the primary place for the provision of long-term care. Today, long-term care is a hybrid of health and health-related support services provided in informal or formal settings to people who have functional limitations with the goal of maximizing their independence. Nursing homes are now viewed as just one point or place on a continuum of long-term care service options in the community. Also, they are shifting from a social service model of providing personal care toward a health care model that manages illness and dysfunction. At the same time, social service and home health care agencies are extending community services to include respite care and hospice programs, mental health counseling, visiting nurses and in-home care, as well as case management. The encompassing modes of services inherent in the long-term care sector make it challenging to develop a concise, theoretically and operationally meaningful definition of *long-term care*. These changes are a reflection of a growing frail elderly population and the changing attitudes of patients' rights and care (Gelfand 1994). In this chapter, the concept of long-term care is used to describe a continuum of services from those delivered at home or in community settings to those delivered within institutional facilities. In addition, this chapter shows increasing awareness that the boundaries between and among various long-term care services (e.g., home care, institutional care, and other services) is increasingly blurred (Kane 1995).

Long-term care involves the provision of a wide variety of health, social, and personal care services, provided either formally or informally, to people who are functionally compromised so that they can maintain their maximum levels of psychological, physical, emotional, and social well-being (Barresi & Stull 1993). However, individual family members provide the major portion of long-term care, perhaps as much as 80 to 90 percent, and they also finance the bulk of long-term care services (Congressional Budget Office 1991; Stone, Cafferata, & Cohn

1987). Typically, long-term care is evoked when an individual is functionally disabled enough to require assistance in two or more activities of daily living (Kane & Kane 1989).

Evashwick (1987) identifies over 60 distinct types of services that are available to long-term care recipients, and groups them into seven categories. Together, these services constitute the continuum of care for the elderly:

1. Extended inpatient care is provided by a formal health care institution for a prolonged period to individuals who are sick or functionally disabled and need ongoing nursing and support services (e.g., nursing facilities, step-down units, swing beds, and nursing home follow-up).
2. Acute inpatient care constitutes services provided by hospitals on a short-term basis for those who have major and acute health care problems (e.g., medical inpatient unit, psychiatric inpatient unit, rehabilitation inpatient unit, and consultation service).
3. Ambulatory care provides a variety of preventive, maintenance, diagnostic, and recuperative care in a formal setting (e.g., physicians' offices, outpatient offices, day hospitals, and alcohol and substance abuse care).
4. Home care includes a combination of services—such as nursing, therapy and support services—to people who are homebound with illnesses (e.g., hospice, home visitors, home-delivered meals, and respite care).
5. Outreach programs help ensure continuity and access to needed services by linking healthy or mildly ill individuals to health and social services available in the community (e.g., transportation, meals on wheels, information and referrals, and senior membership programs).
6. Wellness programs allow those who are healthy or want to maintain a healthy life-style to actively engage in health promotion and prevention programs (e.g., health educational programs, exercise programs, recreational and social groups, and senior volunteers).
7. Housing services provide both health and support services in a home setting (e.g., continuing care retirement communities, independent senior housing, assisted living facilities, and adult family homes).

Long-term care services can be continuous or intermittent, and delivered over an extended period of time. According to the U.S. Senate Special Committee on Aging (1982), the goals of long-term care involve a three-part strategy: (1) to delay the onset of preventable disease in healthy adults, (2) to lengthen the period of functional independence in those elderly with chronic disease, and (3) to improve the quality of one's later life.

This chapter begins with a review of the long-term care needs and patterns of service utilization in the elderly population. Selected types of noninstitutional services are then described. The actual risks of an older person being institutionalized are discussed, as is the logic of institutional care in the United States, and the effects that institutionalization may have on the aged individual. Policy issues related to long-term care are explored in Chapter 18.

LONG-TERM CARE NEEDS AND PATTERNS OF UTILIZATION

Data from the 1997 National Nursing Home Survey (NNHS) estimate 1.47 million elderly in nursing homes on an average day in the United States (Gabrel 2000). This represents less than 5 percent of the elderly population. Both the absolute number of nursing home residents and the proportion of the elderly population to be residing in a nursing home have declined in recent years. The desire to shift from institutional care to use of community support services and the need to control health care costs have no doubt contributed to this slight decline in the number of elderly living in nursing homes.

It is generally believed that an additional 10 percent of elderly living in the community are homebound and as functionally impaired as those in institutions (Kemper, Applebaum, & Harrigan 1987). Although the help needed by older people living in the community varies greatly, anywhere from 12 to 40 percent may require some kind of supportive services (Manton 1989). The Pepper Commission (1990) estimates that between 9 and 11 million additional Americans of all ages are at risk for needing long-term care services.

Who are those most likely to need long-term care assistance? The type of person who receives services at various stages of the life course in various places on the long-term care service continuum is not understood very well. This is particularly the case for those using community services. It is known, however, that people with limitations in activities of daily living are likely to use long-term care services (OMB Watch 1990).

Currently, about 7 million elderly are limited in activities of daily living or instrumental activities of daily living. A little more than 3 million of these older people are severely disabled (in need of assistance in three or more activities of daily living), with approximately 4 million suffering from significant mental health problems as well (Pepper Commission Hearing 1990). According to the 1997 NNHS, those elderly most likely to reside in a nursing home are described as predominantly female (75 percent), 85 years of age and over (50 percent), white (88 percent), non-Hispanic (92 percent), widowed (63 percent), and about 57 percent were admitted directly from a hospital (45 percent) or another nursing home (12 percent) (Gabrel 2000).

Not every individual who needs long-term care assistance receives it. Service delivery barriers for older persons are numerous, such as lack of transportation, ability to pay for services, and lack of services in the neighborhood (Congressional Budget Office 1991). In addition, lack of knowledge of services as well as language and cultural differences also prevent some minority elders from utilizing formal long-term care services and agencies (Tsai & Lopez 1997). To complicate the situation, the elderly sometimes are reluctant to admit need or accept help; many even deny using services.

Simply creating services and making them available is not enough to ensure that they are utilized. Information about available services distributed through the media, service providers, and informal sources are important determinants of service utilization (Silverstein 1984). Ward indicates, "Making services objectively available to older people is not sufficient—they must perceive a need, know about the service, view it as appropriate, etc." (1977, p. 66). Generally, those services they do use are perceived by them as being earned (Moen 1978). Who delivers the service, where and when, and what type of service is delivered are also important dimensions of the service utilization issue (Little 1982).

How older people choose the long-term care services they will use is determined by a complex set of interacting personal and environmental factors, especially for minority elderly (McAuley & Blieszner 1985). Personal factors include demographic, psychological, economic, and health-related characteristics. Environmental factors relate to the availability of informal support and of community and institutional services (Branch & Jette 1982; Deimling & Poulshock 1985; Soldo 1981).

In a study of long-term care use (Mui & Burnette 1994), race/ethnicity was found to be a significant predictor of service use. Whites reported more use of professional in-home services and nursing-home services, and racial/ethnic minority groups reported more care provided by informal helpers (i.e., family members, friends, neighbors, and religious organizations) (Gibson & Jackson 1987; Soldo & Manton 1985; Taylor & Chatters 1986). In addition, elderly women and elderly minority persons are more likely to receive long-term care assistance. Generally, elderly women and elderly minority persons have poorer health, both self-rated and on functional indicators (Barresi & Stull 1993).

Although researchers have identified predictors of use of institutional versus noninstitutional long-term care services (e.g., Branch & Jette 1982), few have examined how older people might select among various types of long-term care services. This is especially the case among the African American and Latino elderly (Kart 1991; McAuley & Blieszner 1985). Stoller (1982) asked elderly people living in the community what they would do if they were ill and needed constant care. Most frequently mentioned was the nursing home; 30 percent could offer no strategy for obtaining care. Dunkle and colleagues (1982) found that a majority of hospitalized elderly persons with long-term care needs had no idea what services were available in their own communities. Lack of knowledge about resources and services appears to reduce the search for information about what services do exist (Silverstein 1984). In addition, knowledge about services does not mean that people are able to see the connection to their own needs. Older people may not know how to negotiate receiving services from agencies.

McAuley and Blieszner (1985) surveyed over 1,200 elderly Virginians on their attitudes toward different long-term care arrangements. Respondents favored paid in-home care, care from a relative in one's own home, and adult day care over nursing home care. When arrangements require a change of residence, however, people identify a nursing home as the residence of preference more often than moving into a relative's home. The nursing home was the long-term care arrangement of choice for nonwhites, single persons, and those with higher incomes who felt they did not have anyone to care for them for an extended period (McAuley & Blieszner 1985). Adult day care was the choice of younger persons and nonwhites in better health; paid home care seemed more appealing for whites and those with emotional problems. Schoenberg, Coward, and Dougherty (1998) found that African American elders expressed more enthusiasm toward community-based services than their white counterparts and were more likely to access community-based services (i.e., senior citizen centers).

Despite the apparent contradictory evidence in the foregoing paragraph, the conventional wisdom in the minority aging literature has it that blacks are less likely than whites to use nursing homes. However, Groger and Mehdizadeh (1998) argue that studies of racial differences in nursing home utilization are often based on national data sets that ignore state-by-state variation. This is noteworthy because racial differences in utilization may be influenced by state-level variables such as the number of nursing home beds and the availability of in-home services. Analyzing 1995 U.S. Bureau of the Census projections and 1995 survey data on long-term care facilities in Ohio, Groger and Mehdizadeh conclude that African American elders are more likely than whites to use nursing homes. From additional data on occupants of Medicaid-certified beds, they found African American nursing home residents to be younger, disabled at an earlier age, and more functionally impaired than their white counterparts.

A body of research suggests that presence of family is an important factor in delaying, if not preventing, the institutionalization of a chronically ill elderly person (McAuley & Prohaska 1982). Still, not enough is actually known about the views toward various long-term care arrangements held by family members of elderly who are prospective consumers of such services. It is not known if the views of the elderly and their family members differ with regard to the perceived efficacy of these various arrangements (Neu 1982) or even if congruence of view is related in any way to successful outcomes for the elderly person.

The risks of needing long-term care are high for elderly Americans, particularly for women and minority elders (Kart 1997; Logue 1990). The growth in the elderly population, coupled with longer age-specific life expectancy among the aged, will increase demand for long-term care services in the coming decades. Some argue that access to these needed services is already compromised for many elderly, especially as state and federal cost containment efforts increase. Some subpopulations of elderly, the poor, those with cognitive and/or neurological impairment, and those who generally have heavy care requirements, may be at greatest risk to be denied access to needed long-term care.

THE DUALITY OF INFORMAL AND FORMAL SUPPORTS

Many gerontological researchers and practitioners recognize the duality of informal and formal supports to the elderly (Cantor & Little 1985). Litwak (1985), among others, argues that the needs of the frail and vulnerable elderly are best met if there is a proper balance between formal and informal support, with each system performing the tasks for which it is best suited.

The main source of informal support for older persons is the family. Yet, research findings indicate that residing with other relatives is not the living arrangement of choice for most elderly (Kobrin 1981; Troll, Miller, & Atchley 1979). Living with relatives is typically a result of impaired health or low income. Certain living

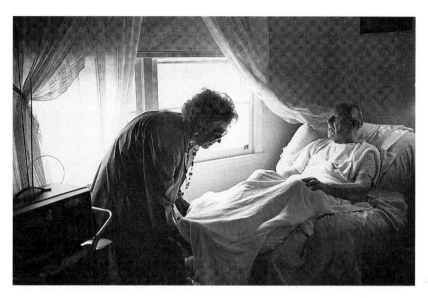

The likelihood is greatest that the caregiver will be a spouse, although various family members may be available to provide support for older people.

arrangements are more satisfying than others. Johnson (1983) found that dissatisfaction with care-giving arrangements is more likely when the caregiver is a child rather than a spouse. She suggests that dissatisfaction may result from the change in the relationship between child and parent when the parent becomes ill.

Various family members seem to be used for care giving, depending on the type of help required. The likelihood is greater that the caregiver will be a spouse before an adult child (Hanson & Sauer 1985), especially for the bedfast and homebound. When children are available, they provide a second important source of help. Childless elders rely on other sources of informal support. A third tier of helpers includes siblings. This three-tiered preferential list of helpers has been termed the ***hierarchical compensatory model*** (Cantor 1979).

It is generally recognized that family and other informal supports frequently have difficulty providing help on a long-term basis to elders who are impaired and disabled (Brody et al. 1987). Emotional, physical, and financial strains appear to be associated with personal and situational characteristics of the caregiver, with emotional strain seemingly the hardest to bear (Cantor 1981; Cicirelli 1988; George 1987). Caregivers frequently experience declines in emotional resilience and morale, and often turn to formal service providers to supplement their efforts (Zarit, Pearlin, & Schaie 1993).

The array of services available to older people outside of institutions covers a broad range, including health, housing, and nutrition. Services have been designed to aid the informal care-giving structure, and it has actually been demonstrated that the provision of formal services can prolong the duration and effectiveness of informal care (Chappell 1990). The organization and delivery of these services are the result of complex policy and financial issues. Estes and Wood (1986) demonstrate that economic constraints, as well as hospital reimbursement policies primarily guided by Medicare and Medicaid regulations for community care, have begun both to medicalize services and to raise the possibility of limiting reimbursable services.

Measurable outcome benefits appear to be minimal for in-home care services and may cost more than is saved by prolonging time to institutionalization. Even in the face of these facts, however, home care has the promise of breaking even financially, while benefiting more people, if appropriate subgroups are served and outcomes are measured appropriately (Weissert 1991).

In order to help define the range of services available, some existing formal services are identified here. This listing is not all-inclusive. Many communities have a substantial number of these services, but only a limited number of communities are providing a complete set of services.

Adult Day Care

The term *day care* applies virtually to any service provided during the day. Such services range from social to health-related care, from home care to hospital care, and include rehabilitation as well as physical and mental health care (Harder, Gornick, & Burt 1986). Weiler and Rathbone-McCuan (1978) define *day care* as a unique service modality because it meets people's long-term care needs yet allows for individual differences. These tailor-made services can have a therapeutic objective of prevention, rehabilitation, or maintenance. Length of hospital stays may also be shortened when elderly adults can be discharged to take advantage of adult day-care centers (Chappell & Blandford 1983). Table 17.1 depicts the services available under the rubric of day care. Four different service modalities are presented: day hospitals, social/health centers, psychosocial centers, and social centers. A wide range of services is offered to various types of clients in many different service settings. Geriatric day services help the older person placed in day care and can be used to provide respite care for caregivers as well.

The National Adult Day Center's (NADC) survey found that over one-third of adult day-care centers are located in small metropolitan or large rural areas, and about one-fifth are located in large urban centers (National Institute on Adult Daycare 1989). Most of the adult day-care programs are nonprofit, but an increasing number of new programs are for-profit organizations. Most participants of adult day care have physical or mental conditions and cannot remain at home alone during the day, but have caregivers who can take care of them when they are not in the adult day care.

Home Health Care

Home health care entails the provision of coordinated multidisciplinary services including skilled nursing; therapeutic services; social casework; mental health; legal, financial, and personal care; and household management assistance (Applebaum & Phillips 1990). Noelker and Harel state, "Its purpose is to aid the elderly

TABLE 17.1   Geriatric Day Services

MODALITY	MAJOR SERVICE OBJECTIVE	TYPE OF CLIENT	SERVICE SETTING
Day hospital	To provide daily medical care and supervision to help the individual regain an optimal level of health following an acute illness	Individual is in active phase of recovering from an acute illness, no longer requiring intense medical intervention on a periodic basis	Extended care facility or hospital
Social/health center	To provide health care resources when required to chronically impaired individuals	Individual has chronic physical illness or disabilities; condition does not require daily medical intervention but does require nursing and other health supports	Long-term care institution or free-standing center
Psychosocial center	To provide a protective or transitional environment that assists the individual in dealing with multiple problems of daily coping	Individual has a history of psychiatric disorder; could reactivate and/or suffer from mental deterioration (organic or functional) that places him or her in danger if not closely supervised	Psychiatric institution or free-standing center
Social center	To provide appropriate socialization services	Individual's social functioning has regressed to the point where, without formal, organized social stimuli, overall capacity for independent functioning would not be possible	Specialized senior citizen center

Source: P. Weiler & E. Rathbone-McCuan, *Adult Day Care: Community Work with the Elderly.* Copyright © 1978 by Springer Publishing Company, Inc. New York 10012. Reprinted by permission of the publisher via Copyright Clearance Center, Inc.

person in the performance of activities of daily living which are essential for continued independence yet are problematic for many aged given their health problems and functional impairments" (1978, p. 37). Home health services include the in-home services of a homemaker, home health aid, or home aide assistant (Surpin 1988). According to Benjamin, however, the term *home* includes any residential setting in which formal medical services are not provided as part of the housing component. Thus, *home* may "mean a detached home, an apartment in a family member's home, or a large complex, or a unit in a congregate housing arrangement with supportive services" (1992, p. 13).

Home health care expenditures have been the fastest-growing component of health care expenditures over several decades, from $0.6 billion in 1960 to

$38.5 billion in 1990. The number of home care agencies has also grown from 1,100 in 1963 to 12,000 in 1993, with half of the agencies being Medicare-certified home health care agencies (Hughes 1996). In 1991, 38 percent of the home health care agencies reported proprietary ownership.

Historically, home health services were available only under voluntary or public auspices. Usually, this involved a visiting nurse service, the public health or welfare department, and, on rare occasions, an extension of hospital services. With the increased profitability of this sector of the health care market, there has been increased development of profit-making agencies that function as local franchises of national organizations.

Home health services are available from proprietary and private service organizations, although use of such organizations may be limited by availability and cost. The National Medical Expenditures Survey revealed in 1987 that Medicare was the largest single payer of home health care services. It accounted for roughly 19 percent of all home health care expenditures in 1987.

The increasing costs and expenditures on home health care has forced the federal government to change eligibility requirements for Medicare coverage to limit access to this type of service. At the same time, the prospective payment plan (diagnostic-related groups, or DRGs) under Medicare also shortened hospital stays of patients (Seifer 1987). Medicare requires the beneficiary of services to be homebound, to have rehabilitation potential, and to have a medically identified need for skilled care on an intermittent basis. Medicaid programs in most states mimic this model (Kane 1995). About 80 percent of home care patients are posthospital referrals; the others are referred by a physician after an outpatient episode of illness or by family or friends who need help in providing care. Data from the National Medical Expenditure Survey indicate that, in 1987, about 5.9 million Americans used an average of 44 home care visits, such as home care aide and nurse visits (Halamandaris 1992).

Utilization of home health care increases sharply with age, with persons over age 75 constituting over 60 percent of aged patients (Ruther & Helbing 1988). The National Health Interview Survey Supplement on Aging found that home health care users had significantly more ADL and IADL limitations than nonhome health care users (Fredman, Droge, & Rabin 1992). On average, home health care users are 70 years old, have 1.7 ADL impairments, receive 94 days of service, and experience improved or stabilized conditions when services are terminated (U.S. Department of Health and Human Services 1993).

Foster Care

Foster family care approximates the normal living environment, with the added dimension of supervision. It allows the older person an element of privacy as well as freedom not possible in the larger protected environment of the nursing home. *Adult foster care* is considered among the least restrictive housing options available to help older persons remain in the community. It utilizes private residences for the care of a nonrelated elderly person who is in need of supervision and/or assistance with activities of daily living. Definitions of foster care vary from state to state. In Ohio, only homes that have Supplemental Security Income recipients are subject to licensing regulations that control foster care, whereas in Oregon, for example, adult foster care has gained respectability and is frequently used as an alternative to nursing homes (Ladd 1986).

Certain problems are inherent in the provision of adult foster care. For example, unlike foster care for children, where the child moves toward independence and gains the capacity to contribute to the foster family, the elderly person is often viewed as only moving toward greater dependence. As a result, many potential care providers are reluctant to offer their foster homes to the elderly.

Hospice

Hospice is a concept of care for the terminally ill that is gaining popularity in the United States. It is a model of care that is more than a program of medical health care for the terminally ill. Hospice services are often directed by a physician with an interdisciplinary team to provide psychological, social, and spiritual services when needed by the patient and/or family members on a 24-hour, seven-day-a-week basis. These services can continue for family and friends after the patient's death.

Hospice care continues to grow as part of the mainstream health care and social service system for many U.S. families. According to the National Hospice and Palliative Care Organization <http://www.nhpco.org/general.htm>, there are currently over 2,400 hospice programs in the United States. Data from the 1996 National Home and Hospice Care Survey show that, among current patients, 77.7 percent are 65 years of age or over. (53.1 percent are 75 years of age or over) and 55.1 percent are female. Most hospice patients are white (83.7 percent), followed by African Americans (8.3 percent), and other races (8 percent). Over 40 percent (43.7 percent) of hospice patients are married, 32.2 percent are widowed, and 9.3 percent are divorced or separated. The majority of hospice patients have a disease diagnosis of cancer (59.6 percent), followed by diseases of the circulatory system (12.3 percent) and diseases of the nervous system and related organs (8.1 percent) (U.S. Bureau of the Census 1998, Table 215). Much hospice care is delivered in the patient's home, but it can also be delivered in virtually any homelike or institutional setting. Additional material on hospice is located in Chapter 19.

Protective Services

Protective or surrogate services describe visits by a social worker with supplemental community services such as visiting nurses, homemakers, clinical services, meals, telephone checks, and transportation. The myriad of needs addressed under **protective services** include daily living, physical health, psychosocial problems, household management, housing, economic management, and legal protection. These services are similar to those delivered through the social service delivery system, although their effects may vary because of the potential for legal intervention in the form of guardianship, placement, and commitment and emergency services.

Every older person who is incapacitated is not necessarily a candidate for protective services. The decisive factor appears to be the availability of a reliable person to help the needy individual. Thus, protective services encompass a wider range of considerations than just the condition of the individual alone.

Three dimensions of protective services are provided to older persons (Hall & Mathiasen 1968): prevention, support, and surrogate service. *Preventive services* strive to maintain the well-being of the older person through reducing or remedying conditions that place the older person at risk, thereby preventing unnecessary institutionalization. *Support services* provide the aid necessary for the impaired older person to maintain independence and self-direction to the maximum level possible. In providing *surrogate services,* the service provider is required to act on behalf of or assist someone to act on behalf of the impaired older person. The task is to provide the necessary supportive services, with or without the client's approval.

Respite Care

Respite care offers support to family caregivers so that they can continue to provide care for the frail elderly (General Accounting Office 1989). This service aims to support the entire family by providing a break for the caregiver and a safe place for the care receiver. Coming in several forms, these programs can be delivered to the home or they can be temporary beds in the hospital or nursing home where the person in need of care can stay for a few days. There is clear evidence that families express a need for respite care (Miller & Goldman 1989) and that it may prevent or delay institutionalization by sustaining informal care by nonspouse caregivers (Doty et al. 1996; Townsend & Flanagan 1976). Paradoxically, evaluations of home and community-based care programs find that as many as 30 to 50 percent of participating families do not use respite services even when respite is made available free of charge or at greatly reduced cost (Kosloski & Montgomery 1993). These authors also find that caregivers' perceptions of the convenience, quality, and usefulness of respite services had significant effects on service use.

The four models of respite care are (1) home-based respite care, (2) group day care, (3) group residential care, and (4) residential programs providing respite care as an adjunct service (Upshur 1983). *Home-based respite care* uses trained sitters who provide the service in the client's home or other homelike space and who are matched with appropriate families. *Group day care* involves provision of daytime activities for brief time periods during the week so that family caregivers may shop or attend meetings. *Residential care* involves a residential facility that is established to provide overnight respite care to small groups of disabled persons (Upshur 1983). More intensive care can be given in this setting to medically and behaviorally difficult clients. These services, offered in a facility designed and staffed for short stays, can also be given on an adjunct basis.

Board and Care Homes

Board and care facilities provide shelter, food, and protection to frail and disabled individuals (Subcommittee on Health and Long Term Care 1989). The U.S. Bureau of the Census reports 18,000 licensed board and care homes accommodating approximately 360,000 residents (U.S. Bureau of the Census 1995, Table 201). Most of these facilities have fewer than 10 beds. However, estimates run as high as one million Americans living in 68,000 licensed and unlicensed board and care homes, with an additional 3.2 million at risk for placement in such facilities. Two-thirds of all residents are old and female, with the majority coming to board and care facilities from mental institutions.

Case Management

Case management is an administrative service that coordinates the delivery of multiple services to frail elders. The Omnibus Budget Reconciliation Act (OBRA) of 1981 introduced case management as a service package under Medicaid waivers. This service package is a combination of formal long-term care services and informal services provided by friends and family (Capitman, MacAdam, & Abrahams 1991). Case management is recommended for clients with multiple problems that cut across traditional service delivery systems (Kane et al. 1991) and provides a channel for clients to gain access to other services, as well (U.S. Health Care Financing Administration 1984). It is the case manager's job to coordinate formal and informal, as well as traditional and nontraditional, services for a holistic approach.

The initial step involves assessing information from the clients and caregivers to develop an individualized care plan for the clients. Next, a care plan is developed to address the needs of the clients as well as involve family members and caregivers in achieving goals and priorities. The case manager then arranges and coordinates services delivery for clients and their families. Finally, the case manager conducts follow-up visits with the clients and their families to ensure quality and continuity of services.

Policymakers and practitioners alike have feared that the programs offered through case management would be overwhelmed by elders and families requesting service. This has not been the case. In the actual running of these programs, there are staffing and service delivery problems. Recruitment and retention problems plague the staffing of case management programs. In part, lack of professional social work or nursing training may contribute to the retention problem. Under such circumstances, case managers do not have the skilled personnel available to them to do the job in an effective manner.

Unfortunately, given the differences among elderly clients in impairment level, living arrangements, and access to informal supports, the development of tailor-made service plans is difficult. If anything, case management can be accused of suffering from a "cookie-cutter" approach, which frequently results in some elders receiving too much service while others receive too little (Capitman, Mac-Adam, & Abrahams 1991).

There are numerous models of care that combine various types of case management care. The identification of benefits and disadvantages of these various models has begun to emerge. For instance, there is doubt that case management reduces inpatient hospitalization or costs (Capitman, Haskins, & Bernstein 1986; Kemper, Applebaum, & Harrigan 1987; Franklin et al. 1987). Targeting is the key to understanding which type of client will benefit from which type of service. For instance, in some cases, only information and referral are offered, thus leaving the individuals themselves to coordinate these services. Case management can also be offered for limited periods of time or over an extended time period. Unfortunately, there is no evidence, as yet, for the effectiveness of case managers in improving access to care, limiting costs, and coordinating services (Estes, Swan et al. 1993).

THE LOGIC OF FORMAL CARE

Formal supports consist of open and closed care (Little 1979, 1982). *Open care* is provided in the community and encompasses all the formal social services aimed at allowing the individual to maintain life at home and avoid premature or unnecessary institutionalization. *Closed care* describes formal care in institutions such as acute care hospitals. Hospitals service more elderly than any other community agency. Approximately 20 percent of all older people use inpatient facilities at least once a year. Based on discharge data for 1996 from the National Discharge Survey, discharge rates (per 1,000 persons) are 122 percent higher for patients 65 to 74 years of age and 292 percent higher for patients 75 years and older than they are for patients of all ages. Also, the average length of a hospital stay in days is 19 percent longer (6.2 vs. 5.2) for patients 65 to 74 years of age and 31 percent longer (6.8 vs. 5.2) for patients 75 years of age and older than it is for the total population. Patients 65 years of age and older consumed 48 percent of all hospital bed days in the U.S. health care system in 1996 (U.S. Bureau of the Census 1998, Table 205). It is in the hospital setting that many older people make decisions about long-term care services. When the hospitalization is associated with physical or mental impairment, plans must often be made for nursing home care.

A sense of urgency typically accompanies discharge from the hospital, and this may interfere with usual patterns of problem solving. Moreover, the extent to which the elderly patient participates in arriving at a decision may be limited by the circumstances under which the plans are made (Brody 1984).

The Risks of Institutionalization

As indicated earlier, approximately 1.47 million elderly, or about 5 percent of those 65 years and older, are found in nursing homes at any one time. Estimates are that 3 million elderly (over 7 percent of those 65 years and over) will be in nursing homes by 2010 (Zedlewski et al. 1990). Disagreement exists over whether these figures represent overuse of nursing homes.

Kastenbaum and Candy (1973) were the first to point out the fallacy of assuming that the number or proportion of elderly in nursing homes could be used as an estimate of their cumulative chances for institutionalization. They reviewed 20,234 death certificates for those age 65 and over filed in the metropolitan Detroit area during the 1971 calendar year. They found that 20 percent of all these deaths were reported in nursing homes, and approximately 24 percent were reported occurring in a larger category of institutions that included all identifiable extended-care facilities. Others were able to substantiate these findings, with a consensus opinion emerging by the mid-1970s that "the total chance of institutionalization before death among normal aged persons living in the community would be about one in four" (Palmore 1976).

More recently, it seems that the actual chance of residing in a nursing home at some point in old age has increased to almost one in three for men and about one in two for the women who turned age 65 in 1990 (Kemper & Murtaugh 1991). For example, people 85 years of age and older represent only about 11 percent of the total elderly population in the United States but about 45 percent of the population of nursing home residents.

Incarceration is another form of institutionalization that is on the rise among the elderly. In fact, the risks of incarceration also increase with age. The overall national incarceration rate per 100,000 residents over age 55 rose 39 percent in a four-year period between 1990 and 1994 (U.S. Government Printing Office 1995). From 1995 through 1998, almost 280,000 persons 65 years of age and older were arrested, an average of 69,797 arrests per year (Uniform Crime Reports <http://www.fbi.gov>). Prisoners over the age of 50 made up 6.6 percent of the total inmate population in the United States, a population that exceeded the total number of female inmates in the U.S. penal system (Camp & Camp 1996). Generally, the elderly do not commit violent crimes. Almost one-third (32 percent) of all arrests of elderly citizens in 1998 involved alcohol (e.g., drunkenness, driving under the influence); another 11 percent of arrests involved property crimes (e.g., larceny-theft, burglary) and 4 percent of arrests were for disorderly conduct (no doubt, some of these arrests also involved alcohol). The change in sentencing patterns since the 1980s, coupled with increasing numbers of older persons committing offenses in this period, has resulted in an increasing number of older inmates in federal and states prisons (Long 1994).

Such information reveals an increasing chance for the elderly to be institutionalized as they age, either in a nursing home or prison. Furthermore, it helps to clarify why many older persons experience a major fear that they will become dependent and have to face institutionalization. Also, the high rates of institutionalization among the elderly make it easier to understand the potentially high financial and human costs of institutionalization and the tremendous strain this phenomenon may place on public and private resources.

Who Gets Institutionalized

A complex array of factors seems to influence who among the elderly gets institutionalized. Confusing matters is the fact that studies differ in focus, with some emphasizing new admissions, others characterizing residents currently in nursing homes, and still others focusing on discharges. Further, most research on institutionalization limits variables to characteristics of individuals and neglects health care system and community characteristics. According to the 1997 National Nursing Home Survey (NNHS), 75 percent of residents are female and 63 percent are widowed; 30 percent have no living children (National Center for Health Statistics 1989); 50 percent are 85 years of age or older; 71 percent are dependent in three or four IADLs; and 40 percent are dependent in four or five ADLs (Gabrel 2000). Although 16 percent of nursing home residents carry a primary diagnosis of "mental disorder" at admission, estimates are that more than 60 percent of residents have some sort of cognitive, mental, or behavioral disorder (Lair & Lafkowitz 1990). Data from the 1997 NNHS show the average length of time since admission for current elderly nursing home residents to be 870 days, with considerable variation in average length of stay by age and marital status.

The picture of the typical nursing home resident has been changing. Increasingly, the nursing home is shaped by regulatory and financial pressures, which encourage the admission of patients who are more incapacitated and have more complex medical problems (Karuza & Katz 1994). There is also a prevalence of mental health problems among these residents (Rovner, Burton, & German 1992), including chronic behavioral problems as well as acute problems of adjustment and coping (Karuza & Katz 1994). Services need to be provided to meet these mental health needs.

Research results have reported characteristics of persons who are more likely to be discharged from nursing homes. This reality has been largely ignored until recently. Previously, it was believed that all those admitted to a nursing home would die there. Greene and Ondrich (1990) found the following characteristics to predict greater likelihood of being discharged alive from a nursing home: not being African American; owning a home; being younger; and having better health, cognitive capacities, and mental acuity.

Elderly inmates in both the U.S. state and federal prisons are mostly men and nonwhite, with African Americans making up about one-half of the nonwhite elderly inmate population (Goetting 1984). In addition, elderly whites generally have lower educational attainment than elderly persons in the free community. On average, Goetting (1984) found that elderly inmates had an eighth-grade education. However, Fry (1987) and Kratcoski and Pownall (1989) separately noted that educational attainment among elderly inmates varied considerably according to the inmate's race, class, and commission of the first crime.

Compared to elderly persons in the free community, few elderly inmates were living with their spouses prior to the arrest, and only a third of the elderly men in state and federal prisons remain married (Beck 1996). However, most of the elderly inmates who were still married are first-time offenders. Also, elderly

inmates came from poor families who were living at poverty level prior to entering the prison system (73 percent) (Merianos et al. 1997). As for minority elderly
inmates, approximately 85 percent of them came from a low socioeconomic background. Furthermore, almost all of the "old-timers," those who were arrested at a
young age and then grew old in prison, came from impoverished environments.

Characteristics of Nursing Homes

According to the National Center for Health Statistics, there were 14,744 freestanding nursing homes in the United States in 1991, with 1,559,394 beds and an
average occupancy rate of 91.5 percent. The data do not include step-down units
of hospitals, intermediate care facilities for the mentally retarded, board and care
facilities, or supportive living residences licensed by some states (NCHS 1994).
This is a 43 percent increase from 1980. Some (44.6 percent) of these facilities are
nursing homes; the rest are board and care homes. The great majority of nursing
homes (71.4 percent) are run for profit. Although nonprofit and government
nursing homes make up only 28 percent of the facilities, their greater capacity (an
average of 112 beds versus 103 beds for proprietary facilities) enables them to
serve 30 percent of all nursing-home residents.

   Nursing homes may also be classified according to their certification status.
About two-thirds of all nursing homes (65.9 percent) in 1991 were certified as
Skilled Nursing Facilities (SNFs). Certified for participation under Medicare, SNFs
typically have transfer agreements with hospitals and provide skilled nursing care
services for rehabilitation of people who are injured, disabled, or sick.

   Over the past three decades, medical care prices rose much faster than costs in
general. Nursing-home costs have been no exception. According to *Consumer Reports*
(1995), a long stay in a nursing home can consign a resident's family to financial
hardship, even poverty. Through the 1980s to date, nursing-home charges have
continued to rise at a faster pace than the Consumer Price Index (CPI). According to
NursingHomeReports.com <http://NursingHomeReports.com>, an independent
website that does not own or hold interests in nursing homes or other eldercare
service providers, the cost of nursing home care in the United States averages
about $115.00 per day, or approximately $42,000 per year. There is considerable
variation around this figure, with some homes costing less than $100 per day and
others charging over $300 per day. Quality of care seems less dependent on cost
than on human interaction, attention to detail, hard work, and compassion. The
cost of care will vary from facility to facility, depending on various factors such as
the level of care being provided and the cost of labor in a geographic area.

THE DECISION TO INSTITUTIONALIZE
AN OLDER PERSON

   Old-age institutions have been described as dehumanizing and depersonalizing
(Townsend 1962). Nursing-home critics describe many facilities as human junkyards

and warehouses (Butler 1975). Studies of old persons residing in a variety of institutional settings have shown them to be more maladjusted, depressed, and unhappy; to have a lower range of interests and activity; and to be more likely to die sooner than aged persons living in the community (Mendelson 1974).

Despite the unfavorable reputation of old-age institutions and the negative attitudes of elderly citizens toward them, many elderly individuals need and seek out institutional care. Usually, this need is apparent to family members or is based on a physician's recommendation. In fact, in cases involving physical illness or debility, the need may be apparent to the elderly person, as well.

As already mentioned, the availability of adequate and applicable home care and community services can prevent the institutionalization of many elderly people. Family members are often very much involved in decisions concerning the institutionalization of an elderly person. When an aged family member is placed into a nursing home, many of the responsibilities for caring for that individual shift from the family to the institution. Still, many families continue to remain involved with that family member.

What is the most effective way for a family to remain involved with an institutionalized relative so as to promote higher-quality nursing-home care? What responsibilities do institutions have to provide support to families that want to stay involved? A first step in answering these questions and ultimately in providing optimal care is for both parties—families and nursing-home staff—to understand and accept their respective responsibilities in providing services to the institutionalized individual.

Shuttlesworth, Rubin, and Duffy (1982) have assessed the extent to which Texas nursing-home administrators and relatives of institutional residents have congruous attitudes about whether the nursing home or the family is responsible for performing an inventory of tasks that are essential in nursing-home care. Two findings are worthy of mention. First, administrators as well as relatives assigned responsibility to the nursing home for the majority of tasks that they see as vital to care. These include technical tasks involving medical care, security, housekeeping, cooking, and the like. Second, in most cases of discrepancies, relatives were more likely than administrators to assign responsibility to families. For the most part, these discrepancies involved nontechnical tasks, such as room furnishings, leisure-time activities, clothing, and special foods.

This study suggests that a problem in engaging families in the care of institutionalized relatives is not the willingness of families to claim responsibility for nontechnical aspects of care, but rather the administrators' insufficient recognition of family responsibility for nontechnical tasks. As a result, administrators may fail to communicate sufficient support for family involvement in such tasks. They may overlook possible policy or procedural changes in institutional arrangements that could better facilitate family involvement in overseeing the nontechnical aspects of care.

Lack of congruence of view between relatives of the institutionalized individual and nursing-home staff may result in aggressive behavior directed at nursing-home personnel by residents' family members. In a survey of 70 Florida nursing homes over a six-month period, administrators reported 1,193 cases of verbal aggression and 13 acts of physical aggression (Vinton & Mazza 1994). Dissatisfaction over how the care needs of residents were being met was most frequently cited as the contributing factor. Social workers were often called on to help resolve conflicts, and discussing the incident with either the staff person or family member alone was the most frequently reported conflict resolution strategy.

INSTITUTIONAL EFFECTS: REAL OR IMAGINARY?

The gerontological literature is filled with descriptions of the institutionalized elderly as disorganized, disoriented, and depressed. Tobin and Lieberman (1976) offer three explanations for this portrait: (1) relocation and environmental change, (2) preadmission and selection effects, and (3) the totality of institutions.

Relocation and Environmental Change

Relocating to a nursing home is a major disruption of a person's social life, alters relationships with family and friends, and shifts control of life from the individual to the institution (Kane & Caplan 1990). Often, the additional burdens of physical and/or chemical restraint are imposed (Foldes 1990; Shield 1988). According to Mor and colleagues (1995, p. 1), "Nursing home residents are also often obligated to accept a 'sick role' that relieves them of their usual social obligations while requiring compliance with the regimen of professionals and other caretakers."

The relationship of environmental change to mortality and morbidity has been investigated in nursing homes and other facilities for the aged. Some disagreement exists about the effects of relocation on mortality and other health status outcomes (Horowitz & Schulz 1983). Researchers generally agree, however, that moving an older person from a familiar setting into an institution leads to psychologic disorganization and distress, especially when the move is involuntary (Schulz & Brenner 1977). Having a sense of choice over the relocation and receiving visits from preferred visitors may predict a smoother transition to the nursing home setting (Harel & Noelker 1982).

Some investigators argue that the disruption of life caused by relocating an elderly individual into new surroundings may create many of the effects attributed to living in that new setting (Lieberman & Tobin 1983). Others argue that it is not simply the stress of relocation, but rather environmental discontinuity— the degree of change between a new and an old environment—that explains the effects observed after placement into a nursing home (Lawton 1974). Interestingly, some evidence suggests that environmental change can elicit desirable behavior and increase the competence of the older individual. Important in such settings are the physical proximity of age peers and the development of behavioral expectations appropriate to the level of competence of the average resident (Lawton 1974).

Preadmission and Selection Effects

Anticipating and preparing for the move into an institution can be very stressful. The effects of this stress on the older person before admission are often very similar to what are described as institutional effects. Tobin and Lieberman (1976) found old people who were awaiting placement into a nursing home to be markedly different from others living in the community in cognitive functioning, affective response, emotional state, and self-perceptions. What is even more interesting is that the psychological status of the study sample awaiting institutionalization was not unlike the psychological status generally descriptive of aged persons in institutions: slight cognitive disorganization, constriction in affective response, less than optimal feelings of well-being, diminished self-esteem, and depression (Tobin & Lieberman 1976, pp. 55–56).

Jette, Tennstedt, and Crawford (1995) report that many elderly are sufficiently impaired cognitively and physically and that efforts by families to supplement informal care with formal nursing services actually increase the risk of placement into a nursing home. This suggests that many in the community are already as impaired as those within nursing homes before they enter the nursing home. Deficits in hearing, vision, and communicative abilities make it difficult to develop relationships, participate in activities, and maintain a sense of well-being (Resnick, Fries, & Verbrugge 1997). This is the case, whether residing in the community or in a nursing home. In fact, sensory deficits among community residents may be risk factors to nursing-home placement. As Resnick, Fries, and Verbrugge (1997) report with regard to visual impairment, both community-dwelling elders and those in the nursing-home setting show associations between visual impairment and ADL disability. If selection is playing a role in nursing-home placement, then, in Tobin and Lieberman's (1976) words, "The institutionalized aged share some characteristics because of who they are and not where they are" (p. 17).

The Total Institution

A compelling answer to the question, What do institutions do to the old? has been offered by Goffman (1961) in his characterization of the total institution. According to Goffman, a basic social arrangement in contemporary society is that the individual tends to sleep, play, and work in different settings with different coparticipants. A central feature of total institutions is the breakdown of the barriers that ordinarily separate these activities, so that all three activities take place in the same setting with the same people. One category of total institution includes those places that take care of persons who are perceived to be generally incapable of caring for themselves and harmless to themselves and others. Included in this category are nursing homes, homes for the aged, and homes for the poor and indigent.

Goffman argues that common to all total institutions is the fact that individuals in such institutions undergo a process of *self-mortification*. This process, which involves interacting with others in the institutional setting, makes it difficult for the resident to maintain his or her identity and reduces the control individuals perceive they have over events of daily life. Goffman (1961, pp. 14–43) identifies the features of an institutional environment that he suggests contribute to the *mortification* process. These features are discussed here with particular emphasis on nursing-home residents.

Admission Procedures.   The individual, often deprived of personal possessions and clothing, is detached from the social system at large. Sometimes a person even loses his or her name, being addressed as "you" instead of as "Mrs. Jones" (Henry 1973).

Barriers.   The total institution places barriers between the resident and the outside world that result in a loss of the roles that are a part of the resident's self. Most nursing home residents simply are not able to play the roles of mother and father, grandmother and grandfather, aunt and uncle, and friend in the way they played these roles on the outside. A familiar way of living is lost. Most describe it simply in terms of losing others and leaving their families' possessions at home.

Deference Obligations.   Because total institutions deal with almost all aspects of a resident's life, there is a special need to obtain the resident's cooperation. A resident required to show deference to the staff members may be humiliated and lose self-esteem. The individual may be asked to engage in activities with symbolic implications that are incompatible with conceptions of self. Sharon Curtin (1972) describes the case of Miss Larson, at shower time, in the Montcliffe Convalescent Hospital:

> I could hear Miss Larson. "No, no, I can bathe myself, just let me alone, I can do it."... Two aides, one on each side, would pick up the old carcasses, place them in a molded plastic shower chair, deftly remove the blanket, push them under the shower and rather haphazardly soap them down.... The aides were quick, efficient, not at all brutal; they kept up a running conversation between themselves about food prices, the new shoes one had bought, California divorce laws. They might have been two sisters doing dishes. Lift, scrub, rinse, dry, put away. And did you hear the one about.... (pp. 145–146)

Verbal or Physical Humiliation.   Residents may have to ask for little things, such as a glass of water or permission to use the telephone. Staff or fellow residents may humiliate residents or talk about them as if they were not there. At the extreme, residents may feel a loss of a sense of personal security.

Contaminative Exposure.   Outside of the nursing home, an individual can withhold his or her feelings, actions, thoughts, and possessions clear from others. Inside the nursing home, this is more difficult. Facts about the residents' health and social status are collected upon admission, regularly recorded, and monitored by staff. Privacy may be difficult to achieve and some social relationships may be forced (e.g., sharing a room or dining with others).

Admission procedures, barriers, deference obligations, verbal and/or physical humiliation, and contaminative exposure represent the mortifying processes that residents experience in old-age institutions (and other institutions). The resident must adapt to these processes. Goffman (1961) identifies four modes of adaptation to the processes of mortification that take place in an institution. The first, *situational withdrawal,* occurs most frequently in old-age institutions and can be described in terms previously used to describe institutional effects. The resident withdraws attention from everything around him or her, and there is a drastic curtailment of involvement in interaction. Regression can occur and may be irreversible. A second mode of adaptation is what Goffman calls the *intransigent line:* The resident intentionally challenges the institution by flagrantly refusing to cooperate with staff members. This mode of adaptation can lead to resident abuse.

Two other modes of adaptation to the total institution are *colonization* and *conversion.* Residents who take a colonization tack accept the sampling of the outside world provided by the institution and build a stable, contented existence by attempting to procure the maximum satisfaction available in the home. Such residents turn the institution into a home away from home and may find it difficult to leave. As Goffman (1961, p. 63) points out, the staff who try to make life in total institutions more bearable must face the possibility that doing so may increase the likelihood of colonization. Residents who convert take on the staff view and often attempt to act out the role of perfect resident. A resident employing this mode of adaptation might adopt the manner and dress of the attendants while helping them manage other residents.

THE QUALITY OF LONG-TERM CARE

Goffman (1961) implies that mortification of the self is characteristic of all total institutions (no matter how therapeutic the environment). It makes intuitive sense, however, that some institutional settings are less mortifying than others and provide higher-quality care. One recent example of a trend away from the total institution is the Eden Alternative (Thomas 1996). The basic principle underlying the Eden Alternative is that it is possible to create a caring environment within a nursing home. This is accomplished in part by creating a habitat that incorporates animals, children, and plants within the nursing home. Proponents maintain that the creation of such a habitat leads to improved quality of life for all participants—residents, staff, and visitors—alike.

Health care practitioners and researchers find the issue of evaluating institutional care to be extraordinarily complex. What is a good nursing home? Should quality be measured in terms of resident satisfaction or professional nursing care? Given limited resources, is it more important to spend money on gardeners, interior design, janitorial services, food quality, or an abundance of aides, orderlies, and health professionals?

Over the past three decades, a number of researchers have looked to the relationship between institutional characteristics and quality of care (see Kart & Manard 1976; Lemke & Moos 1986; and Castle, Fogel, & Mor 1996 for detailed reviews of this literature). Characteristics of institutions thought to be related to quality of care include ownership status, size, socioeconomic status, social integration, and staff professionalism.

Can high-quality care be assured in nursing homes? Some cynics argue that even the inspectors and regulators themselves admit regulation is a poor tool for assuring high-quality institutional care. Approaches suggesting administrative change and accountability through greater community involvement have been offered in the past. In recent years, government efforts to control abuse have been aimed primarily at reducing costs rather than improving quality of care. Still, cost containment efforts by the federal government could force better compatibility of resident needs and long-term care services. One approach involves some efficient substitution of long-term care services for acute services (Vladeck 1985). Another is the single or channeling agency, an organizational reform intended to provide opportunities for better matching resources in the community with the needs of the area's elderly population (Brecher & Knickman 1985).

Little is known about the best ways to deliver long-term care services. For the most part, the lack of homogeneity within the nursing-home population requires flexibility in service delivery. For example, the needs of the short-stay rehabilitation patient differs from the needs of short-stay terminally ill person or the long-term cognitively ill patient. Many times, the patient's needs are not primarily medical. The interdisciplinary nature of service delivery personnel allows for these diverse needs to be potentially met within one setting. Still, variability in the course of long-term care makes it problematic to determine which long-term care services can be delivered most effectively to which residents and where.

Within the long-term care service delivery system, certain measures are commonly identified as appropriate criteria to study service efficacy. These include mortality, morbidity, functional deficits of residents, overall health condition, appropriateness of use of health facilities (e.g., emergency rooms and acute care hospitals), and resident complaints (Mezey & Knapp 1993).

The lack of firm consensus on an outcome measure for long-term care has resulted in staffing being used as a measure of quality of care in nursing facilities (Mezey & Scanlon 1988). Staffing personnel characteristics alone do not ensure high quality of care, but without good professional and paraprofessional staff, the quality of care provided to residents does suffer (Institute of Medicine 1986; Mohler & Lessard 1991).

One complex aspect of viewing staffing as an indicator of quality of care is that organizational, managerial, and professional staffing characteristics that may influence quality of care in nursing homes are mediated through nursing aides and assistants. These are the staff members who provide the greatest amount of direct care to residents (Bowers & Becker, 1992).

Nursing aides and assistants are often described as poorly trained, with high turnover and low job satisfaction (Chartock et al. 1988). This is particularly problematic in the case of mentally ill elders. Estimates of mental illness among residents of nursing homes run in excess of 50 percent. Nursing aides and assistants constitute most of the primary caregivers for mentally ill elderly. Since nursing assistants have become de facto mental health technicians, additional training in mental health and aging is clearly required to maintain some semblance of quality of care (Spore, Smyer, & Cohn 1991). Almost by definition, without such training, most nursing-home residents could be defined as inappropriately placed relative to the resources available in that nursing home.

In response to the problems with quality of care in nursing homes in the United States, the federal government initiated reforms in the Omnibus Budget Reconciliation Act of 1987 to improve care planning. One aspect of this involves a commitment to a uniform assessment of all nursing-home residents. It was believed that improved assessment would lead to improved care planning and thus to improved quality of care. Toward this end, in 1989, a group of researchers developed the National Nursing Home Resident Assessment Instrument (Morris et al. 1996). The instrument attempts to provide accurate and reproducible data on a broad range of domains of care (Hawes, Mor, & Phillips 1997). Guidelines for care planning were also developed to help staff in these homes take the next steps in providing improved care that meets the residents' needs (Resident Assessment Protocols, RAPs). Some 18 problem areas facing most nursing-home residents are covered in the RAP, including falls, incontinence, and mood problems.

Some evaluative work has been conducted on the RAP. Comparing a nationally representative sample of nursing-home residents prior to the existence of the RAP (1991) with one post-RAP (1993) showed that assessments were more accurate and complete, care plans addressed problems that the residents had, and conditions that the RAP addressed decreased in prevalence and incidence (Fries 1998).

If specifying precisely what constitutes quality of care in nursing homes is difficult for researchers and professionals, what are families to do when pressed to make a decision when a sudden illness or disability requires a nursing-home stay? Sometimes, the government's patchwork payment system dictates the choice of facility, or a hospital discharge planner forces a quick decision in an effort to move patient's out of expensive hospital beds as quickly as is possible.

Consumer Reports (1995) offers that there is no substitute for a personal first-hand investigation in selecting a nursing home. Where to start?

1. Federal law requires that nursing homes make their latest inspection report (conducted every 12 to 15 months) available and readily accessible to residents and the public. It is essential to read these reports. They detail deficiencies and violations of federal law. Included with the report is the facility's Plan of Correction, which details how noted deficiencies will be addressed.

2. No matter how good the inspection report, it is necessary to personally inspect the facility. Visit unannounced at different times of the day and week. Talk with staff and residents, where possible.

3. Decor counts for little. Appearance of residents' rooms is more important. Does the facility allow residents to personalize their rooms? Furniture? Photos? Books? Curtains? Plants?

4. The best facilities have no lingering stench. Accidents will happen, but generally, smells should be confined to certain rooms. "If intense odors waft from several rooms at, say 10 A.M., it could mean that staff hasn't changed residents' clothing since the night before" (*Consumer Reports* 1995, p. 523).

5. Assess safety hazards. Are mops and brooms propped about in the hallways? Are spills and wet towels on the floors ignored?

6. Is staff turnover high? Many facilities are understaffed, so job stress is high. Are staff responsive to residents? Do you observe interaction between staff and residents? And, if so, what is the quality of this interaction? Is it rude and unpleasant or warm and abundant?

7. Are residents well groomed? According to *Consumer Reports,* a sure-fire sign of neglect is the failure to keep residents clean, well dressed, and well groomed. Are residents wearing soiled clothing? Are they appropriately dressed for the season? Do they have on shoes?

8. Visit at mealtime and taste the food. Is it attractively served? Tasty? Served at the proper temperature? Dining rooms should be pleasant and attractive. Menus should be posted and followed. Are between-meal and bedtime snacks available?

9. Is there an activities calendar that is followed? Are residents actively engaged? Is socialization encouraged? Do residents have reason to come out of their rooms?

10. Federal law prohibits nursing homes from using restraints, unless there is medical justification or the order of a physician. "If you see a high proportion of residents in a sitting room or at an activity who are restrained, alarms should go off" (*Consumer Reports* 1995, p. 524). Freedom to move about is central to quality of life in a nursing home. If a facility is free of restraints, it is likely a good one.

11. *Consumer Reports'* review of inspection reports found that 25 percent of facilities were cited for deficiencies for allowing the development of bed sores. Almost one-third failed to give appropriate treatment for bed sores that had developed. A family cannot observe the development of bed sores and may have no way of knowing whether a facility is moving residents frequently enough to prevent sores from forming. If the inspection report notes a problem with bed sores, however, this should certainly be a red flag. Ask questions.

12. Are residents with cognitive deficits (e.g., demented or with Alzheimer's) separated from or mixed with other residents? According to *Consumer Reports* (1995), many nursing homes are pushing special-care units for demented patients at extra cost. The magazine cites the Alzheimer's Association, indicating that these special-care units "may too often be an expensive marketing technique" (p. 526). Is controlled space available for residents to wander outdoors? Is there a special place for those residents who are agitated? Those with sleep disturbances?

13. Finally, nursing homes are required to complete an assessment of each resident who enters. This should include physical, mental, and social abilities. This assessment is the basis of a care plan. Are care plans written and carried out? Is there a care plan conference? Follow-up conferences? Are family members encouraged to attend? If the care plan requires particular behavior or activities (e.g., walking twice a day), it may be necessary for family members to assume the role of advocate to be sure the activity is done.

No clear consensus exists on what exactly contributes to or reflects quality of care in a nursing home. There is no substitution for visiting, observing, and speaking up. If a family member believes care is poor, it probably is. Confirm perceptions with reports from the local ombudsman or citizens advocacy group, where these are available.

SUMMARY

Assessing the long-term care needs of the elderly and matching services to those needs can be difficult. There are many service delivery barriers for older people. Sometimes, the elderly are reluctant to admit that they have needs, and many even deny using services. The mere fact that services are created and made available to the elderly does not mean that those services will be utilized. How older people choose the long-term care services they will use is determined by a complex set of interacting personal and environmental factors.

The main source of support for older persons is the family. A body of research suggests that the presence of family is an important factor in delaying, if not preventing, the institutionalization of a chronically ill elderly person. Still, some argue that the needs of the frail and vulnerable elderly are best met if there is a proper balance between formal and informal support. A broad array of services is available to older people in the community, including health, housing, and nutrition services. A limited number of these noninstitutional services are discussed in this chapter. These include adult day care, home care, foster care, hospice, protective services, board and care homes, and respite care.

Currently, about 1.47 million elderly individuals (5 percent of the aged population) reside in nursing homes in the United States. The risk of an elderly person in the United States being institutionalized is currently about one in three for men and one in two for women. Typically, the nursing-home population is white, female, widowed, age 80 or over, and poor, and has lived in an institutional facility for about two years. Over 80 percent of nursing-home residents were admitted primarily for physical reasons. There are more than 33,000 nursing and board and care homes in the United States today. The great majority of these are run for profit.

Nursing homes have an unfavorable reputation, and elderly individuals often have strong negative feelings toward being institutionalized, even when institutional care is absolutely necessary. In part, this may result from the portrait the gerontological literature paints of the institutionalized elderly. This population is overwhelmingly characterized as disorganized, disoriented, and depressed. Three explanations for this negative portrait are discussed. These include problems of relocation, preadmission and selection effects, and the totality of institutions.

Quality nursing-home care is difficult to define and assess. Some characteristics of nursing homes—such as nonprofit status, wealth of resources, and staff with positive attitudes toward the residents—are thought to be related to quality of care. In recent years, government has emphasized cost containment. A better approach might emphasize compatibility between resources and the needs of the elderly population. In the nursing home, such compatibility would require additional training for nursing aides and assistants—those staff persons who have the most direct contact with residents.

Strategies are available to determine whether a particular facility provides an acceptable level of care.

STUDY QUESTIONS

1. Identify the goals of long-term care.

2. Profile the long-term care service user. Does every individual who needs long-term care assistance receive it? Why or why not? Explain what the service delivery barriers are.

3. What is known about how older people select from among long-term care alternatives?

4. What role does the family play in providing long-term care assistance?

5. Identify the following:
   a. Adult day care
   b. Home care
   c. Foster care
   d. Hospice
   e. Protective services
   f. Respite care
   g. Board and care homes
   h. Case management

6. Why can't the institutionalization rate for the elderly be used as an estimation of their cumulative chances for institutionalization?

7. Describe the so-called typical nursing-home resident. Explain the disproportionate number of women and the underrepresentation of nonwhites in nursing homes.

8. List some major organizational dimensions along which nursing homes vary. How have nursing-home costs increased in relation to costs in general? Why might one expect significant variation in charges among nursing and board and care homes?

9. What is the process of "self-mortification" as defined by Goffman? List and explain the features of institutional environments that Goffman suggests contribute to the mortification process.

10. Why is it so difficult to get a handle on the concept of quality of care in nursing homes? Is staff a measure of a quality-of-care indicator? If so, how do many U.S. nursing homes shape up on this dimension?

REFERENCES

Applebaum, R., & Phillips, P. (1990). Assuring the quality of in-home care: The "other" challenge for long-term care. *Gerontologist, 30* (4), 444–450.

Barresi, C. M., & Stull, D. E. (1993). Ethnicity and long-term care: An overview. In C. M. Barresi & D. E. Stull (Eds.), *Ethnic elderly & long-term care.* New York: Springer.

Beck, A. (1996). Growth, change, and stability in the U.S. prison population, 1980–1995. *Corrections Management Quarterly, 1,* 1–14.

Benjamin, A. E. (1992). In-home health and supportive services. In M. G. Ory & A. P. Duncker (Eds.), *In-home care for older people: Health and supportive services.* Newbury Park, CA: Sage.

Bowers, B., & Becker, M. (1992). Nurse's aides in nursing homes: The relationship between organization and quality. *Gerontologist, 32* (3), 360–366.

Branch, L. G., & Jette, A. M. (1982). A prospective study of long-term care institutionalization among the aged. *American Journal of Public Health, 72,* 1373–1379.

Brecher, C., & Knickman, J. (1985). A reconsideration of long-term care. *Journal of Health Politics, Policy and Law, 10,* 245–273.

Brody, E. M., Kleban, M. H., Johnson, P. T., Hoffman, C., & Schoonover, C. B. (1987). Work status and parent care: A comparison of four groups of women. *Gerontologist, 27* (2), 201–208.

Brody, S. J. (1984). Goals of geriatric care. In S. Brody & N. Persily (Eds.), *Hospitals and the aged: The new old market.* Rockville, MD: Aspen.

Butler, R. N. (1975). *Why survive? Being old in America.* New York: Harper & Row.

Camp, C. G., & Camp, G. M. (1996). *The corrections yearbook, 1996.* South Salem, NY: Criminal Justice Institute.

Cantor, M. (1979). Neighbors and friends: An overlooked resource in the informal support system. *Research on Aging, 1,* 434–463.

Cantor, M. (1981). *Factors associated with strain among family, friends and neighbors caring for the frail elderly.* Paper presented at the Annual Scientific Meeting of the Gerontological Society of America, Toronto, Canada.

Cantor, M., & Little, V. (1985). Aging and social care. In R. Binstock & E. Shanas (Eds.), *Handbook of aging and the social sciences* (2nd ed.). New York: Van Nostrand Reinhold.

Capitman, J., Haskins, B., & Bernstein, J. (1986). Case management approaches in community oriented long term care demonstrations. *Gerontologist, 26* (4), 398–404.

Capitman, J., MacAdam, M., & Abrahams, R. (1991). Case management roles in emergent approaches to long-term care. In P. Katz, R. Kane, & L. Mezey (Eds.), *Advances in long-term care.* New York: Springer.

Castle, N. G., Fogel, B. S., & Mor, V. (1996). Study shows higher quality of care in facilities administered by ACHCA members. *The Journal of Long-Term Care Administration, 23,* 11–16.

Chappell, N. (1990). Aging and social care. In R. Binstock & L. George (Eds.), *Handbook of aging and the social sciences* (3rd ed.). San Diego, CA: Academic.

Chappell, N. L., & Blandford, A. A. (1983). *Adult day care: Its impact on the utilization of other health care services and on quality of life.* Ottawa, Ontario: NHRDP, Health and Welfare Canada.

Chartock, P., Nevins, A., Rzetelny, H., & Gilberto, P. (1988). A mental health training program in nursing homes. *Gerontologist, 28,* 503–507.

Cicirelli, V. G. (1988). A measure of filial anxiety regarding anticipated care of elderly parents. *The Gerontologist, 28* (4), 478–482.

Congressional Budget Office. (1991). *Policy choices for long-term care: A CBO study.* Washington, DC: Congress of the United States.

Consumer Reports. (1995). Nursing homes: When a loved one needs care. *Consumer Reports, 60* (80), 518–528.

Curtin, S. (1972). *Nobody ever died of old age.* Boston: Little, Brown.

Deimling, G. T., & Poulshock, S. W. (1985). The transition from family in-home care to institutional care. *Research on Aging, 7* (4), 563–576.

Doty, R., Stone, R., Jackson, M. E., & Alder, M. (1996). Informal caregiving. In C. J. Evanshwick (Ed.), *The continuum of long-term care: An integrated systems approach.* New York: Delmar.

Dunkle, R., Coulton, C., Mackintosh, J., & Goode, R. (1982). The decision making process among the hospitalized elderly. *Journal of Gerontological Social Work, 4* (3), 95–106.

Estes, C. L., Swan, J. H., & associates. (1993). *The long term care crisis: Elders trapped in the no-care zone.* Newbury Park, CA: Sage.

Estes, C. L., & Wood, J. B. (1986). The non-profit sector and community based care for the elderly in the U.S.: A disappearing resource? *Social Science and Medicine, 23,* 175–184.

Evashwick, C. (1987). Definition of the continuum of care. In C. Evashwick & L. Weiss (Eds), *Managing the continuum of care: A practical guide to organization and operation* (pp. 23–43). Rockville, MD: Aspen.

Foldes, S. F. (1990). Life in an institution: A sociological and anthropological view. In R. A. Kane & A. L. Caplan (Eds.), *Everyday ethics: Resolving dilemmas in nursing home life.* New York: Springer.

Franklin, J., Solovitz, B., Mason, M., Clemons, J., & Miller, G. (1987). An evaluation of case management. *American Journal of Public Health, 77,* 674–678.

Fredman, L., Droge, J. A., & Rabin, D. L. (1992). Functional limitations among home health care users in the national health interview survey supplement on aging. *Gerontologist, 32,* 641–646.

Fries, B. E. (1998, March 23). *The national Nursing Home Resident Assessment Instrument or what do you do with 6 million assessments?* Presented at the Eighteenth Annual Leon and Josephine Winkelman Lecture.

Fry, L. J. (1987). Older prison inmate: A profile. *Justice Professional, 2,* 1–12.

Gabrel, C. S. (2000). Characteristics of elderly nursing home current admissions and discharges: Data from the 1997 National Nursing Home Survey. *Advance Data from Vital and Health Statistics, 312.* Hyattsville, MD: National Center for Health Statistics.

Gelfand, D. E. (1994). *Aging and ethnicity: Knowledge & services.* New York: Springer.

General Accounting Office. (1989, April 6). *Respite care insights on federal, state and private sector involvement.* GAO/HRD-89-12.

George, L. K. (1987). Easing caregiver burden: The role of internal and formal supports. In R. A. Ward & S. S. Tobin (Eds.), *Health in aging: Sociological issues and policy directories.* New York: Springer.

Gibson, R. C., & Jackson, J. S. (1987). The health, physical functioning, and informal supports of the Black elderly. *Milbank Quarterly, 65* (Suppl. 2), 421–454.

Goetting, A. (1984). Elderly in prison: A profile. *Criminal Justice Review, 9,* 14–24.

Goffman, E. (1961). *Asylums.* New York: Doubleday.

Greene, V., & Ondrich, J. (1990). Risk factors for nursing home admissions and exits: A discrete-time hazard function approach. *Journal of Gerontology, 45,* S250–S258.

Groger, L., Mehdizadeh, S. (1998). Scrutinizing accepted wisdom: A racial comparison of utilization rates and selected characteristics of Ohio's older nursing home population. *Journal of Aging and Ethnicity, 1* (3), 131–148.

Halamandaris, J. V. (1992). How rapidly has the home care field grown? *Basic statistics about home care, 1992.* Washington, DC: National Association for Home Care.

Hall, G., & Mathiasen, G. (1968). *Overcoming barriers to protective services for the aged: Report of the National Institute on Protective Services.* New York: National Council on Aging.

Hanson, S. M., & Sauer, W. J. (1985). Children and their elderly parents. In W. J. Sauer & R. T. Coward (Eds.), *Social support networks and the care of the elderly.* New York: Springer.

Harder, W. P., Gornick, J. C., & Burt, M. R. (1986). Adult day care: Substitute or supplement? *The Milbank Quarterly, 64* (3), 414–441.

Harel, Z., & Noelker L., (1982). Social integration, health and choice: Their impact on the well-being of institutionalized aged. *Research on Aging, 4,* 97–111.

Hawes, C., Mor, V., Phillips, C. D., et al. (1997). The OBRA-87 Nursing Home Regulations and Implementation of the Resident Assessment Instrument: Effects on process quality. *Journal of the American Geriatrics Society, 45,* (8), 977–985.

Henry, J. (1973). Personality and aging—With special reference to hospitals for the aged poor. In J. Henry (Ed.), *On sham, vulnerability and other forms of self-destruction.* New York: Random House.

Horowitz, M. J., & Schulz, R. (1983). The relocation controversy: Criticism and commentary in five recent studies. *Gerontologist, 23,* 229–234.

Hughes, S. (1996). Home health. In C. Evashwick (Ed.), *The continuum of long-term care: An integrated systems approach.* New York: Delmar.

Institute of Medicine. (1986). *Improving the quality of care in nursing homes.* Washington, DC: National Academy Press.

Jette, A. M., Tennstedt, S., & Crawford, S. (1995). How does formal and informal community care affect nursing home use? *Journal of Gerontology, 50B* (1), S4–S12.

Johnson, C. (1983). Dyadic family relations and social supports. *Gerontologist, 23* (4), 377–383.

Kane, R. A. (1995). Expanding the home care concept: Blurring distinctions among home care, institutional care, and other long-term care services. *The Milbank Quarterly, 73* (2), 161–186.

Kane, R. L., & Caplan, A. L. (1990). *Everyday ethics: Resolving dilemmas in nursing home life.* New York: Springer.

Kane, R. L., & Kane, R. A. (1982). Long term care: A field in search of values. In R. L. Kane & R. A. Kane (Eds.), *Values and long term care.* Lexington, MA: Lexington Books.

Kane, R. L., & Kane, R. A. (1989). Transitions in long term care. In M. Ory & K. Bond (Eds.), *Aging and health care: Social science and policy perspectives.* New York: Routledge.

Kane, R., Pernod, J., Davidson, G., Moscovice, I., & Rich, E. (1991, June). What cost case management in long-term care? *Social Service Review,* pp. 281–303.

Kart, C. S. (1991). Variation in long-term care service use by aged Blacks. *Journal of Aging and Health, 3,* 511–526.

Kart, C., & Beckham, B. (1976). Black-white differences in the institutionalization of the elderly: A temporal analysis. *Social Forces, 54,* 901–910.

Kart, C., & Manard, B. (1976). Quality of care in old-age institutions. *Gerontologist, 16* (3), 250–256.

Karuza, J., & Katz, P. (1994). Physician staffing patterns correlates of nursing home care: An initial inquiry and consideration of policy implications. *Journal of the American Geriatrics Society, 42,* 787–793.

Kastenbaum, R., & Candy, S. (1973). The 4 percent fallacy: A methodological and empirical critique of extended care facility population statistics. *International Journal of Aging and Human Development, 4,* 15–21.

Kemper, P., Applebaum, R., & Harrigan, M. (1987). Community care demonstration: What have we learned? *Health Care Financing Review, 8* (4), 87–100.

Kemper, P., & Murtaugh, C. M. (1991). Lifetime use of nursing home care. *New England Journal of Medicine, 324,* 595–600.

Kobrin, F. (1981). Family extension and the elderly: Economic, demographic and family cycle factors. *Journal of Gerontology, 36,* 370–377.

Kosloski, K., & Montgomery, R. J. (1993). Perceptions of respite services as predictors of utilization. *Research on Aging, 15,* 399–413.

Kratcoski, P. C., & Pownall, G. A. (1989). Federal bureau of prisons programming for older inmates. *Federal Probation,* pp. 28–32.

Ladd, R. C. (1986). Oregon's long-term system for the elderly and disabled. In R. A. Kane & R. L. Kane (Eds.), *Long-term care: Principles, programs, and policies.* New York: Springer.

Lair, T., & Lefkowitz, D. (1990). *Mental health and functional status of residents of nursing and personal care homes* (DHHS Pub. No. (PHS) 90–3470). Agency for Health Care Policy and Research. Rockville, MD: Public Health Service.

Lawton, M. P. (1974). Social ecology and the health of older people. *American Journal of Public Health, 64,* 257–260.

Lemke, S., & Moos, R. H. (1986). Quality of residential settings for elderly adults. *Journal of Gerontology, 41* (2), 268–276.

Levenson, S. A. (1993). The changing role of the nursing home medical director. In P. R. Katz, R. L. Kane, & M. D. Mezey (Eds.), *Advances in long term care* (Vol. 2). New York: Springer.

Lieberman, M., & Tobin, S. S. (1983). *The experience of old age: Stress, coping, and survival.* New York: Basic Books.

Little, V. (1979). For the elderly: An overview of services in industrially developed and developing countries. In M. Teicher, D. Thursz, & J. Vigilante (Eds.), *Reaching the aged: Social services in forty-four countries: Vol. 4. Social service delivery systems: An international annual.* Beverly Hills, CA: Sage.

Little, V. (1982). *Open care for the aging.* New York: Springer.

Litwak, E. (1985). *Helping the elderly.* New York: Guilford.

Logue, B. J. (1990). Race differences in long-term disability: Middle-aged and older American Indians, Blacks, and Whites in Oklahoma. *The Social Science Journal, 27,* 253–272.

Long, T. A. (1994). The federal sentencing guidelines and elderly offenders: A tightrope between uniformity and discretion (and slipping). *Elder Law Journal, 2,* 69–95.

Manton, K. G. (1989). Epidemiological demographic, and social correlates of disability among the elderly. *The Milbank Quarterly, 67* (2–1), 13–58.

McAuley, W., & Blieszner, R. (1985). Selection of long-term care arrangements by older community residents. *Gerontologist, 25* (2), 188–193.

McAuley, W., & Prohaska, T. (1982). Professional recommendations for long-term placement: A comparison of two groups of institutionally vulnerable elderly. *Home Health Care Services Quarterly, 2,* 44–57.

Mendelson, M. A. (1974). *Tender loving greed.* New York: Random House.

Merianos, D. E., Marquart, J. W., Damphousse, K., & Herbert, J. L. (1997). From the outside in: Using public health data to make inferences about older inmates. *Crime and Delinquency, 43,* 298–313.

Mezey, M., & Knapp, M. (1993). Nursing staffing in nursing facilities: Implications for achieving quality of care. In P. R. Kane, R. L. Kane, & M. D. Mezey (Eds.), *Advances in long term care* (Vol. 2). New York: Springer.

Mezey, M., & Scanlon, W. (1988). *Registered nurses in nursing homes: Secretary's Commission on nursing.* Washington, DC: Department of Health and Human Services.

Miller, D. B., & Goldman, L. (1989). Perceptions of caregivers about special respite services for the elderly. *Gerontologist, 29* (3), 408–410.

Miller, G. (1993). Hospice. In C. J. Evashwick (Ed.), *The continuum of long-term care: An integrated systems approach.* Boston: Delmar.

Moen, E. (1978). The reluctance of the elderly to accept help. *Social Problems, 25,* 293–303.

Mohler, M., & Lessard, W. (1991). *Nursing staff in nursing homes: Additional staff needed and cost to meet requirements and intent of OBRA'87.* Washington, DC: National Committee to Preserve Social Security and Medicare.

Mor, V., Branco, K., Fleishman, J., Hawes, C., Phillips, C., Morris, J., & Fries, B. (1995). The structure of social engagement among nursing home residents. *Journal of Gerontology, 50B* (1), P1–P8.

Morris, J. N., Murphy, K., Nonemaker, S., Fries, B. E., et al. (1996). *Resident Assessment Instrument Version 2.0.* Washington, DC: Government Printing Office.

Mui, A., & Burnette, D. (1994). Long term care service used by frail elders: Is ethnicity a factor? *Gerontologist, 34* (2), 190–198.

National Center for Health Statistics. (1989). *The national nursing home survey: 1985 summary for the United States* (Vital and Health Statistics, Series 13, No. 97, DHHS Pub. No. [PHS] 89–1758). Public Health Service. Washington, DC: U.S. Government Printing Office.

National Center for Health Statistics. (1994). Nursing homes and board and care homes. Data from the 1991 National Health Provider Inventory. *Advance Data From Vital and Health Statistics, 244.*

National Institute on Adult Daycare. (1989). *National Adult Day Center (NADC) Census.* Washington, DC: National Council on the Aging.

Neu, C. R. (1982). Individual preferences for life and health: Misuses and possible uses. In R. L. Kane & R. A. Kane (Eds.), *Values and long term care.* Lexington, MA: D. C. Heath.

Noelker, L., & Harel, Z. (1978). Aged excluded from home health care: An interorganizational solution. *Gerontologist, 18,* 37–41.

OMB Watch. (1990). *Long-term care policy: Where are we going?* Boston: The Gerontology Institute, University of Massachusetts at Boston.

Palmore, E. (1976). Total chance of institutionalization among the elderly. *Gerontologist, 16,* 504–507.

Pepper Commission Hearing. (1990). Washington, DC: U.S. Government Printing Office.

Resnick, H. E., Fries, B. E., & Verbrugge, L. M. (1997). Windows to their world: The effect of sensory impairments on social engagement and activity time in nursing home residents. *Journal of Gerontology, 52B* (3), S135–S144.

Rovner, B., Burton, L., & German, P. (1992). The role of mental morbidity in the nursing home experience. *Gerontologist, 32,* 152–158.

Ruther, M., & Helbing, C. (1988). Health care financing trends: Use and cost of home health agency services under Medicare. *Health Care Financing Review, 10,* 105–108.

Schoenberg, N. E., Coward, R. T., & Dougherty, M. C. (1998). Perceptions of community-based services among African American and White elders. *The Journal of Applied Gerontology, 17,* 67–78.

Schulz, R., & Brenner, G. (1977). Relocation of the aged: A review and theoretical analysis. *Journal of Gerontology, 32,* 323–333.

Seifer, S. (1987). The impact of PPS on home health care: A survey of thirty-five health agencies. *Caring, 6* (4), 1–12.

Shuttlesworth, G. E., Rubin, A., & Duffy, M. (1982). Families versus institutions: Incongruent role expectations in the nursing home. *Gerontologist, 22* (2), 200–208.

Shield, R. R. (1988). *Uneasy endings: Daily life in an American nursing home.* Ithaca, NY: Cornell University Press.

Silverstein, N. M. (1984). Informing the elderly about public services: The relationship between sources of knowledge and service utilization. *Gerontologist, 24,* 37–40.

Silverstone, B. (1985). Informal social support systems for the frail elderly. In Institute of Medicine/National Research Council (Ed.), *America's aging: Health in an older society.* Washington, DC: National Academy Press.

Soldo, B. J. (1981). The living arrangements of the elderly in the near future. In S. B. Kiesler, J. N. Morgan, & V. K. Oppenheimer (Eds.), *Aging: Social change.* New York: Academic Press.

Soldo, B., & Manton, K. (1985). Changes in the health status and service needs of the oldest old. *Milbank Memorial Fund Quarterly, 63,* 266–323.

Spore, D. L., Smyer, M. A., & Cohn, M. D. (1991). Assessing nursing assistants' knowledge of behavioral approaches to mental health problems. *Gerontologist, 31,* 309–317.

Stone, R. I., Cafferata, G., & Sangl, J. (1987). Caregivers of the frail elderly: A national profile *Gerontologist, 31,* 724–725.

Stoller, E. P. (1982). Sources of support for the elderly during illness. *Health and Social Work, 7,* 111–122.

Subcommittee on Health and Long Term Care, Select Committee on Aging, United States House of Representatives. (1989, March). *Board and care homes in America: A national tragedy.* Washington, DC: Government Printing Office.

Surpin, R. (1988). The current status of the paraprofessional in home care. *Caring, 4* (1), 4–9.

Taylor, R. J., & Chatters, L. M. (1986). Patterns of informal support to elderly Black adults: Family, friends, and church members. *Social Work, 31,* 432–438.

Thomas, W. H. (1996). *Life worth living: The Eden alternative in action.* Acton, MA: Vander Wyk & Burnham.

Tobin, S., & Lieberman, M. (1976). *The last home for the aged.* San Francisco: Jossey-Bass.

Townsend, P. (1962). *The last refuge.* London: Routledge & Kegan Paul.

Townsend, P. W., & Flanagan, J. J. (1976). Experimental pre-admission program to encourage home care for severely and profoundly retarded children. *American Journal of Mental Deficiency, 180,* 562–569.

Troll, L., Miller, S., & Atchley, R. (1979). *Families in later life.* Belmont, CA: Wadsworth.

Tsai, D. T., & Lopez, R. A. (1997). The use of social supports by elderly Chinese immigrants. *Journal of Gerontological Social Work, 29,* 77–94.

U.S. Bureau of the Census. (1995). *Statistical abstract of the United States, 1995* (115th ed.). Washington, DC: U.S. Government Printing Office.

U.S. Bureau of the Census. (1997). *Statistical abstract of the United States, 1997* (117 ed.). Washington, DC: U.S. Government Printing Office.

U.S. Bureau of the Census. (1998). *Statistical abstract of the United States, 1998* (118th ed.). Washington, DC: U.S. Government Printing Office.

U.S. Department of Health, Education and Welfare. (1977). *Characteristics, social contacts, and activities of nursing home residents, U.S. 1973 National Nursing Home Survey* (DHEW Publication. No. [HRA] 77-1778). Public Health Service. Hyattsville, MD: U.S. Government Printing Office.

U.S. Department of Health and Human Services. (1993). *Morbidity and Mortality Weekly Report, 42,* 42.

U.S. Government Printing Office. (1995). *Bureau of Justice Statistics: Sourcebook of criminal justice statistics—1994.* Washington, DC: U.S. Government Printing Office.

U.S. Health Care Financing Administration. (1984). *Report to Congress: Studies evaluating Medicaid home and community based waivers.* Baltimore, MD: Department of Health and Human Services.

U.S. Senate Special Committee on Aging. (1982). *Developments in aging* (Vol. 1). Report 97-314, 97th Congress, Second Session. Washington, DC: U.S. Government Printing Office.

Upshur, C. (1983). Developing respite care: A support service for families with disabled members. *Family Relations, 31,* 13–20.

Vinton, L., & Mazza, N. (1994). Aggressive behavior directed at nursing home personnel by residents' family members. *Gerontologist, 34,* 528–533.

Vladeck, B. (1985). Reforming Medicare provider payment. *Journal of Health Politics, Policy and Law, 10,* 513–532.

Ward, R. (1977). Services for older people: An integrated framework for research. *Journal of Health and Social Behavior, 18,* 61–70.

Weiler, P., & Rathbone-McCuan, E. (1978). *Adult day care: Community work with the elderly.* New York: Springer.

Weissert, W. G. (1991). A new policy agenda for home care. *Health Affairs, 10* (2), 67–77.

Zarit, S. H., Pearlin, L. I., & Schaie, K. W. (Eds.). (1993). *Caregiving systems: Formal and informal helpers.* Hillsdale, NJ: Erlbaum.

Zedlewski, S. R., Barnes, R. O., Burt, M. R., McBride, T. D., & Meyer, J. A. (1990). *The needs of the elderly in the 21st century.* Washington, DC: Urban Institute Press.

CHAPTER EIGHTEEN

HEALTH POLICY AND AGING

This chapter begins by identifying the patterns of health and medical service utilization among the elderly. Of particular interest are physician visits and the use of nonphysician professional and hospital inpatient services. In addition, policies, programs, and funding mechanisms available for the health and medical care of the elderly are assessed. The chapter concludes by placing health care in a broader political economy of aging perspective.

USE OF SERVICES

Table 18.1 presents data on physician contacts per person per year by sex and age for 1995. The average number of physician contacts by persons 65 years and over was 11.1, compared with 5.9 contacts for persons of all ages. As the table depicts, with the exception of males under 18 years old, the average number of physician contacts per person generally increases with age. The likelihood of seeing a doctor at least once during a given year also increases with age. About 73 percent of people 25 to 44 years of age reported seeing a doctor in the last year, compared to 80 percent of those 45 to 64 years of age and 92.1 percent of those 75 years of age and older. The elderly account for a disproportionate amount of the physician utilization in the United States. In 1995, they represented between 12 and 13 percent of the nation's noninstitutionalized population and accounted for 22 percent of the office visits and 22.6 percent of all contacts (including all places) with physicians.

The average number of physician contacts per person 65 years of age in a year are up over 25 percent since 1987, and 66 percent since 1964. In 1987, the average number of physician contacts among those 65 years and over was 8.9; in 1964, it was 6.7. The change in this indicator for the entire elderly population masks changes that have taken place within the population. According to the U.S. Department of Health and Human Services, the number of physician contacts per person per year has *increased* for the elderly poor and *decreased* for the nonpoor. This finding suggests that differences in the rate of physician utilization by the poor and nonpoor elderly have been narrowed in recent years. Data for the whole population from the 1995 National Health Interview Survey (NHIS) show that aged individuals with family income of less than $10,000 had, on average, 13.9 physician contacts (including telephone contacts and office visits); those with

TABLE 18.1   Physician Contacts per Person, United States: 1995

	AVERAGE
ALL PERSONS	5.9
Age	
Under 5 years	6.5
5–17 years	3.4
18–24 years	3.9
25–44 years	5.2
45–64 years	7.1
65–74 years	9.8
75 years and over	12.9
SEX AND AGE	
Males	4.9
Under 18 years	4.4
18–44 years	3.3
45–64 years	6.0
65 years and over	10.4
Females	6.9
Under 18 years	4.2
18–44 years	6.4
45–64 years	8.1
65 years and over	11.6

Note: A physician contact may occur at a hospital, the physician's office, at some other place (e.g., ambulatory clinic), or on the telephone.

Source: Centers for Disease Control and Prevention, National Center for Health Statistics. Data from the 1995 National Health Interview Survey.

family income of $35,000 or more had, on average, 10.3 physician contacts for the year. One problem with this suggestion is that it fails to distinguish the differential need for health and medical services in various income groups.

The inference here is that 10 physician contacts a year may be sufficient, given the need for services of an average elderly individual with income at or above the median for the total population. Nevertheless, 13 or 14 physician contacts may not meet the needs of the average elderly individual with income at or below the poverty level.

Physician visits also vary by race and sex. In 1995, elderly whites reported more physician contacts per person than did elderly African Americans (11.2 vs. 10.4, respectively, among those 65 years and over); elderly women also reported more physician visits than did elderly men (11.6 vs. 10.4, respectively, among those 65 years and over). Differences in health and medical service use by race are generally explained by racial differences in socioeconomic status. The gender differential in utilization of physician services exists in all age groups except for those ages at which a mother usually makes the health care decisions. The largest differential occurs between the ages of 18 and 44, when women are most likely to be making use of obstetrical and gynecological services (6.4 vs. 3.3 physician contacts, on average, in 1995).

Explanations for these sex differences in utilization of medical services (and in morbidity rates) have focused primarily on the social situation of women. Nathanson (1975) groups these explanations into three categories:

1. Women report more illness than men and utilize medical services more frequently than men because it is culturally more acceptable for women to be ill.
2. Reporting illness and visiting the doctor is more compatible with a woman's other role responsibilities than is the case for men.
3. Women's assigned social roles are, in fact, more stressful than those of men—consequently, they have more real illness and need more care.

As Nathanson points out, insufficient data are available to evaluate the merits of these explanations.

The elderly have higher rates of usage than people under age 65 for a whole array of health services, including prescription drugs, vision aids, medical supplies and equipment, and nonphysician health care providers (including optometrists, podiatrists, psychologists, chiropractors, and physical therapists, among others). For example, according to the National Center on Health Statistics, in 1991, elderly people were more likely to receive a drug prescription during an office visit with a physician than is the case for any other age group. In 68.2 percent of their office contacts with physicians, older people were given a drug prescription; 58.9 percent of physician contacts made by those ages 15 to 44 similarly yielded a drug prescription. In 1988, the elderly accounted for 34 percent of all outpatient prescription drugs used in the United States.

Dental problems increase with age. More than one-fourth of persons 45 to 64 years old have lost all their teeth; almost 90 percent have diseases of the tissues supporting or surrounding remaining teeth (Shanas & Maddox 1977). Yet, in 1993, only about 52 percent of those 65 years and over visited a dentist in the past year, according to National Health Interview Survey data; this compares with about 62 percent of people 45 to 64 years who visited the dentist in the past year.

Unlike medical care, dental care is rarely financed by public programs or private health insurance. Thus, financial barriers to dental care are still substantial.

On average, elderly women report more physician contacts than do elderly men. What factors might explain this?

Data from the National Health Interview Surveys suggest that those with higher income make substantially more dental visits per year, on average, than do those at or below the poverty level. In 1993, individuals in families with income below the poverty level were only about one-half as likely as those at or above poverty to have visited a dentist in the past year (35.9 vs. 64.3 percent, respectively).

The lack of dental care among the elderly is serious. Fully 50 percent of the elderly have no natural teeth. Of those, 10 percent have no false teeth or have an incomplete set. Even those with false teeth do not use them all the time; many report that their dentures do not fit properly. Increasing availability of dental services could improve the quality of life of many older people. Fear and embarrassment about socializing because of oral health problems has led many old people to isolation. This could be overcome if dental care services were made available to more elderly people. Nutritional status could also be improved by making it possible for those people who are edentulous or who have periodontal disease (and thus are restricted in diet) to eat a wider variety of foods.

The elderly are the heaviest utilizers of hospital care; in 1995, they accounted for 35 percent of all hospital discharges (excluding deliveries). Discharge rates for those 65 to 74 years of age (23.5 per 100 persons) were about twice as high as those for individuals 45 to 64 years (12.2 per 100) and almost four times those for individuals 25 to 44 years of age (6.4 per 100). Hospital utilization rates vary by age and other demographic variables. As shown in Table 18.2, starting at age 5, both the discharge rate and the average length of stay increase with age for both males and females. Discharged patients ages 45 to 64 years spent 5.6 days in the hospital, on average, per episode of hospitalization; for patients age 75 and over, the average length of hospital stay was 7.7 days.

In 1983, Medicare introduced a prospective payment system (PPS) that was expected to produce shorter lengths of stay and greater admission rates. Discussed in more detail later, this new system paid hospitals a fixed amount per admission according to the diagnostic-related group (DRG) the patient was assigned to on the basis of an admitting diagnosis. As expected, the length of hospital stays decreased; since 1983, the trend has been to shorter hospital stays. In 1983, patients

TABLE 18.2   Utilization of Short-Stay Hospitals by Sex and Age: 1995

	HOSPITAL DISCHARGES* (PER 100 PERSONS)	HOSPITAL DAYS (AVG. LENGTH OF STAY)
ALL PERSONS	9.2	5.7
Age		
Under 5 years	7.2	5.2
5–17 years	2.8	4.7
18–24 years	4.3	3.7
25–44 years	6.4	4.5
45–64 years	12.2	5.6
65–74 years	23.5	6.5
75 years and over	31.2	7.7
SEX AND AGE		
Males		
All ages	9.0	6.0
Under 18 years	4.3	5.7
18–44 years	5.1	4.8
45–64 years	12.6	5.7
65 years and over	30.5	7.1
Females		
All ages	9.4	5.5
Under 18 years	3.8	4.0
18–44 years	6.8	4.1
45–64 years	11.9	5.6
65 years and over	24.0	7.1

*Excluding deliveries.

Source: Centers for Disease Control and Prevention, National Center for Health Statistics. Data from the 1995 National Health Interview Survey.

75 years or older averaged 10.2 days per stay; this indicator fell to 9.1 days in 1987, then fell again to 7.7 days by 1995.

The elderly have lower rates of admission to inpatient psychiatric facilities than all other age groups, including those under 18 years of age. Data from 1975 to 1986 (National Center for Health Statistics 1997) show lower rates of admission for the aged for all diagnoses in state and county mental hospitals and private psychiatric hospitals. These diagnoses include schizophrenia, affective disorders, and drug- and alcohol-related diagnoses. Only for organic disorders do those 65 years and older have higher rates of admission to psychiatric facilities than is the case for the total population.

In 1996, the elderly accounted for 34 percent of all ambulatory (outpatient) surgery procedures. Such procedures are generally carried out in hospitals or freestanding ambulatory surgery centers. Included in these figures are 84 percent of the almost 2.4 million lens extractions and 83 percent of the 1.8 million prosthetic lens that were surgically inserted in 1996. Persons 65 years of age and over also accounted for almost 43 percent of the 4.0 million endoscopies of the large and small intestine in the single year in question. Many of these examinations were accompanied by biopsies and/or removal of polyps.

As Table 18.3 shows, persons 65 years of age and older are the dominant consumers of home health care and hospice care. They represent 72.2 percent of all home health care patients and 77.7 percent of all hospice patients in 1996. Among the aged, home health care use appears to peak in the ages 75 years and over; the oldest-old (those 85 years of age and older) are the largest consumers of hospice care. Although most elderly home health patients require some help with

TABLE 18.3   Current Home Health and Hospice Care Patients, by Age: 1996

	TOTAL	HOME HEALTH CARE	HOSPICE CARE
TOTAL (1,000)	2,486.8	2,427.5	59.4
Percent Distribution			
AGE			
Under 45 years old	14.1	14.3	7.3
55–64 years old	5.3	5.4	4.5
65 years and over	72.4	72.2	77.7
65–69 years	8.8	8.8	8.4
70–74 years	13.0	12.9	16.2
75–79 years	17.1	17.1	16.6
80–84 years	16.6	16.7	15.2
85 years and over	16.8	16.7	21.3

Source: U.S. Bureau of the Census, *Statistical Abstract of the United States: 1998* (Washington, DC: U.S. Government Printing Office, 1998), Table 215.

basic activities of daily living, services being billed for suggest that the greatest needs for nursing services, physical therapy, and homemaker-household services.

EXPLAINING USE OF HEALTH AND MEDICAL SERVICES

Although the focus thus far has been on the impact of age on utilization of various health and medical services, clearly other variables affect the utilization of such services, as well. Certainly, health beliefs or values and knowledge about health and the health care system are related to use of health services (Andersen & Newman 1973). What Ward (1977) calls *community variables* also affect utilization. These include location of residence, density of age peers, availability of local transportation, and availability of neighborhood-based services and social supports.

Writers and researchers have looked at how the health care delivery system itself affects patterns of utilization. Many criticize the current system of service delivery as being too fragmented and disorganized. Such critics emphasize the extent to which financing programs are predisposed to fund inpatient care at the expense of community-based or home care and the way public funding mechanisms discourage preventive care and mental health services.

Determining the conditions under which people use health care services is a difficult enterprise. The presence of an impairment or a self-assessment of poor health does not necessarily indicate a need for medical care. Even an objective indication of need for medical care may not be a foolproof predictor of whether an individual will use available health services.

Studies have implicated structural, social, and psychological factors in utilization behavior. The costs of medical care, the level of psychological distress, and the availability of social support are among those variables that apparently have an effect on the utilization of health services among the population at large.

Andersen (1968) and colleagues (Aday, Andersen, & Fleming 1980; Aday, Fleming, & Andersen 1984; Andersen & Newman 1973) have generated a conceptual framework within which to sort factors that contribute to the use of health services. Referred to as the *health behavior model,* this framework is arguably the most widely used for studying health services utilization. Basically, the health behavior model views the use of health services as a function of the predisposing, enabling, and need characteristics of the individual.

The predisposing element of the model reflects the idea that some individuals have a greater propensity for using health services than do others. Presumably, these propensities can be predicted prior to an illness episode from knowledge of the personal characteristics of elderly individuals. *Predisposing factors* include three dimensions that represent the sociocultural component of the model: demographics, social structure, and health beliefs. Indicators of demographics usually include age, sex, marital status, and other life-cycle indicators. Social-structural measures more typically reflect life-styles and routinely include education, employment, and ethnicity, among other such indicators. Health beliefs are assessments of attitudes about medical care, physicians, and disease.

The enabling element of the model comes from the idea that even if an individual is predisposed to employ health services, he or she must have some means for doing so. Thus, this element contains factors that make health services available to individuals. *Enabling factors* include two dimensions that represent the economic component of the model: familial resources and community resources. Familial resources are measured by income, the availability of health insurance, and the availability of sources of health care. Indicators of community resources typically include physician and hospital service-to-population ratios, geographic location, and population density indices.

The need element of the model is the most immediate cause of health service use. It assumes that, even in the presence of predisposing and enabling factors, individuals will not use health services unless they have or perceive themselves to have some illness. *Need factors* tap the individual's recognition of a present health problem or one in the making and consist of two dimensions. The first includes subjective perceptions of overall health status; the second includes professional evaluations of illness symptoms and need for service.

Using this categorization schema in an early study in Sweden, Andersen, Anderson, and Smedby (1968) found that the social class (a predisposing factor) and income (an enabling factor) of an individual were important predictors of the use of health services. More recently, Wolinsky and Johnson (1991) carried out what is arguably the most complete test of the health behavior model. Including a broad array of predisposing, enabling, and need factors, 29 in all with interaction between race and need, they used the first wave of the National Center for Health Statistics' Longitudinal Study on Aging ($N = 5$, 151 people age 70 and over) to test the health behavior model. Nine different measures of health services utilization were employed, tapping formal as well as informal services. Examples include measures of physician and hospital use, as well as bed disability and home health service use, among other factors. Three important themes emerged from this analysis.

First, in Wolinsky and Johnson's (1991) analyses, the health behavior model typically explains between 10 and 25 percent of the variation in health service utilization by a population of elderly people. This is consistent with other studies in the literature. These authors suggest a number of ideas for future research that may increase the robustness of the findings. For example, some research shows that older people are relatively consistent users of health care services (Mossey, Havens, & Wolinsky 1989), thus it would seem advantageous to incorporate some measure of prior use patterns into the model. Some insist that the consistent pattern of health care service use is physician driven. The argument here is that elderly patients are particularly compliant with physician insistence on regular visits and referral to other services. Others argue that a core group of elderly are reliant on informal or lay networks of friends, relatives, or indigenous leaders and that these networks are particularly resistant to the use of professional health services (Freidson 1989). Measures that tap compliance with physician instruction for subsequent visits as well as reliance on informal networks for service referrals also might increase the power of the health behavior model in future research. Along these same lines, it is useful to recall that Wolinsky and Johnson's test of the model was on a cross-sectional data set. Use of longitudinal data are necessary to test whether the model is sensitive to changes in health services utilization over time.

A second theme to emerge from these analyses involves the dominance of need factors in explaining variation in use of health services. Andersen and colleagues (Aday, Andersen, & Fleming 1980; Aday, Fleming, & Andersen 1984) have used the model to assess the equitable nature of the health delivery system. They employ evidence that utilization appears to be primarily a function of need to conclude that equitable access to health care has been achieved in the United States. Wolinsky and Johnson (1991), among others, urge caution in arriving at such a conclusion. They point out that most of the variation in health services utilization remains unexplained. As a result, researchers still do not know what accounts for most of the health service use by older people. Another concern of these researchers has to do with the differential effects of need characteristics for white versus minority older adults. A number of reports, for example, document the fact that, compared to whites, minority elderly are far more constrained by and sensitive to the need characteristics in their use of health services (Blendon et al. 1989; Freeman et al. 1987). Such findings are not consistent with conclusions of equity. Kart (1993) adds that until more is known about how and why older people employ community and home-based long-term care services, it is premature to declare the health delivery system to be equitable.

A third theme from this research involves the identification of important effects from previously absent or improperly measured factors. Several of these are worthy of mention. Wolinsky and Johnson found that worrying about one's health resulted in greater levels of health services utilization. This suggests that among both well and ill elderly, worrying about health places greater demands on the health delivery system than need characteristics alone would indicate.

Contrary to expectations from previous research (e.g., Brody 1985), non-kin rather than kin supports appear to substitute for the use of formal health care services. Interestingly, however, both kin and non-kin supports were found to have positive effects on rates of physician contact. Wolinsky and Johnson suggested that in the course of discussions with friends and family about health matters, older people receive encouragement for going to see the doctor.

Finally, in operationalizing need characteristics, Wolinsky and Johnson distinguished between basic activities of daily living (the need for help with bathing, dressing, getting out of bed, walking, and toileting) and those IADLs that required more precise cognitive capacities (needing help with managing money, using the telephone, and eating). Only the IADLs had consistent effects on health services outcomes, predicting the number of bed disability days, hospital use, and mortality. These results highlight the importance of identifying cognitive deficits in assessing functional status, prognosis, and placement of older adults.

Roos and Shapiro (1981), using data from a sample of Manitoba (Canada) elderly, suggest that relatively few elderly account for a disproportionate share of health service utilization. The majority of older people in their study use services at approximately the same rate as younger people. Having advanced age, low self-perceived health status, and several self-reported health problems seem to place individuals at a higher risk for the use of hospital services. Still, although the very old were at greater risk to be hospitalized, they used only marginally more physician services than their younger counterparts. This finding is in opposition to a widely held belief that advancing age significantly increases the consumption of *all* types of health care. Stoller, Kart, and Portugal (1997) asked almost 700 aged residents of upstate New York to keep a three-week-long health diary in which they recorded symptoms they were experiencing and their response or treatment strategy. Only 30.7 percent of the symptoms resulted in a consultation with a health care professional. Clearly, the majority of symptoms experienced by these aged respondents were manged without a physician or contact with the formal health care system.

Several studies have tried to identify additional sociodemographic determinants of medical care use among the elderly. Haug (1981) finds that older persons in general are more likely to get physical checkups and more likely to overutilize the health care system for minor complaints than younger persons. Yet, they are little different from younger persons in underutilization for conditions that should receive a doctor's attention. Interestingly, currently married elderly are more likely than younger married persons to overutilize the health care system. As Haug points out, this may be due to what Eliot Freidson (1961) has described as the *lay-referral system:* A person who is ill turns first to a spouse for advice; it appears that spouses are more likely to recommend contacting a physician when an older husband or wife has a complaint. Stoller, Kart, and Portugal (1997) also reported that married respondents were more likely than single respondents to self-treat or consult a relative or friend before seeing a health care professional.

Wan (1982) has studied the use of health services among almost 2,000 elderly individuals residing in low-income areas of Atlanta, Kansas City, and Boston, among other selected cities. He describes the regular user of neighborhood health centers as being African American, having low income, being relatively uneducated, and on some form of public assistance. Persons using a hospital ambulatory clinic as a regular source of health care have a similar profile, although they seem more likely to be younger (65 to 69 years), male, and suffering from acute episodes of illness and a chronic disability.

In a multivariate analysis of his data, Wan (1982) finds that health status (as measured by the number of acute illnesses experienced by an individual and the level of chronic disability) accounts for more variation in physician contacts than does access to a regular source of medical care. Access to medical care (as measured by the availability of a usual source of care and insurance coverage) correlates with more frequent visits to physicians. Those with a regular source of care are three times more frequent users of ambulatory care as those with no regular source.

Interestingly, Wan's (1982) analysis shows Medicaid recipients and those with access to neighborhood health centers to be the most frequent users of physician care. African Americans also have a greater number of physician contacts than whites. Previously, a number of studies had indicated that the poor have less access to health care services. At least in the United States, this was the case prior to the implementation of Medicare and Medicaid, when, for example, the lowest socioeconomic groups had fewer physician visits than those with more income. According to Wan, poor elderly African Americans appear to have benefited significantly from the advent of Medicaid and other forms of public assistance. They have also taken advantage of various services provided by neighborhood health centers. Wan concludes, "One inference that can be drawn is that the removal of financial barriers, coupled with a concerted effort toward making health services readily available to the medically needy, has greatly facilitated the use of ambulatory physician care" (1982, p. 104). This does not necessarily mean, however, that equity or parity in the use of health care services in the United States has been achieved.

PAYING FOR MEDICAL CARE

During the fiscal year 1980, the total cost of health care in the United States reached over $247 billion, for an average of $1,002 per person. By 1996, these numbers had increased quite dramatically. National health care expenditures were in excess of $1,035 billion, with per-capita expenditures reaching approximately $3,645. National health expenditures increased at a rate of 4.4 percent in 1996, the lowest annual rate of increase in the 1990s, and personal consumption expenditures for medical care accounted for approximately 11.3 percent of the gross domestic product (GDP). This is a substantially different picture from that of 1965, the year Congress passed the Medicare and Medicaid legislation. In 1965, total health care expenditures amounted to $42 billion, 6.1 percent of the GDP, or $207 person.

Health costs for the elderly have increased as rapidly, if not more so. The amount of money expended on Medicare alone increased more than five times between 1980 and 1996 ($37.5 vs. $203.1 billion). The source of funds to pay for health care of the elderly has also changed dramatically. During 1966, the year Medicare and Medicaid were implemented, only 30 percent of these funds were public; since then, the percentage of expenditures from public funds has increased by more than one-half again, to 46.7 percent.

The largest single item on the health care bill of elderly individuals is hospital care. In 1981, this item cost $36.6 billion and accounted for 44 percent of all personal health care expenditures for the aged. By 1996, Medicare expenditures for hospital insurance alone exceeded $129 billion.

Hospital care, nursing-home care, and physicians' services together account for most of the dollars spent on health care for the elderly. Items such as drugs, dental services, eyeglasses, and medical appliances constitute a very small part of the total bill and are mostly funded by the elderly out of pocket. Generally, expenditures for these latter items are thought to be low because many elderly people are going without them. As costs continue to rise and such services continue to remain outside the scope of most public funding mechanisms for health care of the elderly, one can expect continued low utilization. About 10 percent of all health care expenditures in 1996 went to drugs and related medical supplies. How many older people go without needed drugs because public funding mechanisms typically do not underwrite the costs of drugs and personal funds are unavailable?

Payments for health care are made under a variety of public and private programs designed to provide care or access to care for specified population groups. The two largest programs are Medicare and Medicaid. They are the principal public funding mechanisms for health care of the elderly.

Medicare

In 1965, the *Social Security Act of 1935* was amended to provide health insurance for the elderly. This amendment, which became effective July 1, 1966, is known as *Title XVIII* or *Medicare*. It marked the inauguration in the United States of a national system of financing individual health services on a social insurance basis. It was not, however, the country's first attempt at establishing national health insurance. Such attempts and their failures date back to the beginning of the century. The historical record is worthy of a brief review.[1]

Between 1915 and 1918, a group of academics, lawyers, and other professionals who were organized under the American Association for Labor Legislation attempted to push a model medical care insurance bill through several state legislatures. They had no success. The American Medical Association (AMA) <http://www.ama-assn.org> opposed the bills, as did the American Federation of Labor (AFL) <http://www.aflcio.org/front/unionand.htm>. The AFL feared that any form of compulsory social insurance might lead to further government control of working people. Not until the Great Depression did interest in governmental health insurance reappear on a sustained basis.

In 1934, President Roosevelt created an advisory Committee on Economic Security. In the climate of destitution and poverty that accompanied the Great Depression, this committee was charged with drafting a Social Security bill providing a minimum income for the aged, the unemployed, the blind, and the widowed and their children. The result was the Social Security Act of 1935. The Social Security Act was originally intended to include health insurance provisions also. Nevertheless, as Feingold (1966) points out, the extent of this intention was little more than one line in the original bill that suggested that the Social Security Board study the problem and report to Congress. When opposition to this line became so strong that it appeared to jeopardize the Social Security bill itself, the line was dropped.

Although advocates of compulsory health insurance proposed congressional bills from 1939 on, it was not until Truman's "Fair Deal" that the possibility of passing such a bill became strong. In the interim (1939 to 1949), private health insurance—through Blue Shield—was endorsed by the AMA and commercial insurance carriers became firmly established in the United States as a way of paying for medical expenses.

In 1949, President Truman requested congressional action on medical care insurance. In order to placate the AMA and its allies, it was specified that doctors

---

[1]Historical material on Medicare comes primarily from Marmor (1973) and Feingold (1966).

and hospitals would not have to join the plan. In addition, doctors would retain the right to refuse to serve patients whom they did not want. This was not enough. The American Medical Association was adamantly opposed to so-called socialized medicine, and despite Truman's characterization of the AMA as "the public's worst enemy in the efforts to redistribute medical care more equitably," efforts at passing a national health insurance bill were defeated.

What were the major objections to these early national health insurance proposals? According to Marmor (1973), they were as follows:

1. Medical insurance was a "giveaway" program that made no distinction between the deserving and undeserving poor.
2. Too many well-off Americans who did not need financial assistance in meeting their health needs would be helped.
3. Utilization of health care services would increase dramatically and beyond capacity.
4. There would be excessive control of physicians, establishing a precedent for socialism in the United States.

Clearly, another strategy was necessary. The one that developed shifted attention away from the health problems of the general population to those of the aged. There was great appeal in focusing on the aged, for, as a group, they were needy yet deserving. Most had made a contribution to the nation; yet through no fault of their own, many suffered reduced earning capacity and higher medical expenses. Proponents of this new strategy waged a public war of sympathy for the aged and a private war of pressure politics from 1952 until 1965. Not until then was the political climate ripe for amending the original Social Security Act to provide health insurance (Medicare) for the U.S. aged.

Medicare consists of two basic components. Part A is a compulsory hospital insurance (HI) plan that covers a bed patient in a hospital and, under certain conditions, in a skilled nursing facility or at home after having left the hospital. It is financed by employer/employee contributions and a tax on the self-employed. Most of the elderly are automatically eligible as a result of their own or a spouse's entitlement to Social Security. Currently, over 30 million persons age 65 years and over are covered by Medicare. If for any reason a person is not eligible for HI at age 65, it can be purchased on a voluntary basis. The monthly premium was $301 in 2000.

Part B represents a voluntary program of supplemental medical insurance (SMI) that helps pay doctor bills, outpatient hospital benefits, home health services, and certain other medical services and supplies. Financing is achieved through monthly premiums paid by enrollees and matching funds by the federal government. As of January 1, 2000, the monthly premium was $45.50, or $546 for the year.

Hospital insurance (Part A) benefits are measured by periods of time known as *benefit periods.* Benefit periods begin when a patient enters the hospital and end when he or she has not been a hospital bed patient for 60 consecutive days. This concept is important because it determines the amount of care to which a Medicare beneficiary is entitled at any particular point in time. Medicare will help pay covered services for a patient for up to 90 days of in-hospital care, for up to 100 days of extended care in a skilled nursing facility, for posthospital home health care in each benefit period, and for hospice care for terminally ill beneficiaries who have a life expectancy of less than six months. If an individual runs out of covered days within a benefit period, he or she may draw on a lifetime reserve of 60 additional hospital days. Use of these days within the lifetime reserve, however, permanently reduces the total number of reserve days left. For example, if a patient has been in the hospital for 90 days and needs 10 more days of hospital care, he or she may draw 10 days from the reserve of 60, leaving a reserve of 50 days.

Part A Medicare benefits will pay for such services as semiprivate accommodations, including meals and special diets, regular nursing services, laboratory tests, drugs furnished by the hospital, and medical supplies and appliances furnished by the hospital. It will not pay for convenience items, such as a private room or private-duty nurses.

A Medicare patient is financially responsible, through copayments and deductibles, for various components of his or her hospital insurance plan. As a bed patient in a participating hospital, he or she is responsible for the first $776 of costs in each benefit period (the 2000 figure). After this, Part A pays for covered services for the first 60 days of hospital care. From day 61 through day 91 in a benefit period, hospital insurance pays for all covered service except for $194 per day (in 2000). If more than 90 days of inpatient care are required, reserve days may be used. The copayment after 90 days of care is $388 a day in 2000. Beyond 150 days in a hospital, Medicare pays nothing.

Extended-care benefits provide for covered services for the first 20 days in a benefit period. After the first 20 days in a skilled nursing facility (SNF), the recipient must pay $97 (2000 figure) per day for up to an additional 80 days in a benefit period. Home health care, from a home health agency participating in Medicare, covers part-time nursing care by a registered nurse or under her or his supervision, physical or speech therapy, and medical supplies and appliances. It does not cover services of part-time health aides at home. Currently, 210 or more days of hospice care are available to beneficiaries certified as terminally ill.

The medical insurance program (Part B) of Medicare is a voluntary one; an individual must pay a monthly premium in order to be eligible for coverage. In addition, the subscriber pays a deductible each year (currently $100) and 20 percent of the remainder. Although Part B pays for a broad array of outpatient hospital services, doctors' services, home health benefits, and other medical supplies, it does *not* routinely cover such things as regular physical examinations, eye and/ or hearing examinations, eyeglasses or hearing aids, prescription drugs, false teeth, or full-time nursing care. However, such coverage may be provided to Medicare beneficiaries who opt to participate in special coordinated care plans, such as health maintenance organizations (HMOs).

Medicaid

Medicaid, or *Title XIX* of the Social Security Act, also passed in 1965 and became effective July 1, 1966. According to Stevens and Stevens (1974), some observers of the time saw Title XIX as the "sleeper" of the 1965 legislation. After all, Medicare is limited in terms of who is covered (primarily the aged), the types of services covered (described previously), and the presence of deductibles and copayments. Medicaid was intended as a catchall program to handle the medical expenses not covered by Medicare as well as to provide medical assistance to needy groups other than the aged. The program is jointly funded by federal and state governments, with the federal government contributing in excess of 50 percent in poorer states. Eligibility varies from one state to another, as states have broad discretion in determining which groups their Medicaid programs will cover. The federal government does mandate certain Medicaid eligibility groups, including recipients of Aid to Families with Dependent Children (AFDC), Supplementary Security Income (SSI) recipients, children in poor families, pregnant women in families with income below 133 percent of the poverty level, and certain other protected groups.

Financial criteria for Medicaid eligibility is also somewhat variable, although one requirement seems to be almost universal. Wherever an individual qualifies for Medicaid, "pauperization" has preceded qualification. All persons, including the elderly, may find themselves eligible for Medicaid only after they have drained their resources and qualified as a member of the poor. Effective September 30, 1989, Medicaid eligibility was accelerated for some nursing-home residents by protecting more income and assets for the institutionalized person's spouse living at home. Also, new limits were placed on the amount of assets and income of a married couple that must be "spent down" before Medicaid will pay for nursing-home care.

Although Medicaid is often perceived as a health insurance program for low-income mothers and children, long-term care absorbs a sizable and disproportionate share of the program's spending. Received by fewer than 10 percent of all recipients, over one-third of Medicaid's dollars go to long-term care, and the elderly account for almost 60 percent of total expenditures on long-term care services (Kaiser Commission on the Future of Medicaid 1996).

HEALTH POLICY: IS THERE A CRISIS IN MEDICAL CARE FINANCING?

The Medicare program has made and continues to make various medical services available to many persons who would not receive them otherwise. Older people living on low, relatively fixed incomes might not be able to secure the services of a physician, a hospital, a skilled nursing home, or a home health care program without Medicare. Nevertheless, the Medicare program is riddled with various out-of-pocket deductibles and copayments for its beneficiaries, not to mention limitations in services provided. Many elderly Americans supplement their Medicare with some private health insurance plan. The Omnibus Budget Reconciliation Act of

1990 directed that standards be set for Medicare supplemental insurance (*Medigap*) policies. Further, Medigap policies may not be canceled or a renewal refused by an insurer solely on the basis of the health of the policyholder.

In 1988, Congress passed the largest expansion of Medicare benefits since the program's inception in 1965. Elderly and disabled beneficiaries were to be protected from the costs of catastrophic medical bills. Also provided was the program's first coverage of outpatient prescription drugs. The new benefits were to be paid for with two premiums. First, all beneficiaries would pay for increases in Medicare Part B premiums. Second, all Part A enrollees would be assessed a "supplemental" premium based on their amount of federal income tax liability, subject to an annual limit.

This supplemental premium for Part A enrollees broke new ground. All other Part A benefits are funded from payroll taxes, as described in Chapter 11. For the first time, older people alone (and really only those with annual income tax liability) were being asked to underwrite an expansion in the Medicare benefits. Faced with pressure from politically active older adults and their organizational representatives, who were upset about the funding mechanisms for these expanded benefits, Congress passed the Medicare Catastrophic Coverage Repeal Act of 1989 and repealed the Medicare catastrophic benefits legislated in 1988. Also repealed were the proposed premium increases.

In addition to limits in coverage, Medicare focuses too narrowly on providing acute care. The maintenance of chronic health conditions and quality-of-life issues do not receive appropriate attention. Eye examinations for eyeglasses, hearing examinations for hearing aids, orthopedic shoes, and false teeth are all excluded from coverage. Under this system, Medicare patients could not take advantage of geriatric consultation clinics that are concerned with the prevention of illness and the maintenance of chronic conditions. Such clinics could exist only for private, paying patients.

The language employed throughout the Medicare regulations refers to medical need, medical care, and medical necessity. Health teaching, health maintenance, prevention of illness, aspects of rehabilitation, and personal care are related to health care but not necessarily to medical care. The elderly often need health care services in far greater proportion than medical care services. If the health needs of the elderly population are to be served and if suitable health maintenance programs are to be developed, then a financing system must be initiated that allows for funding of services that prevent illness and maintain health.

Because Medicare and Medicaid result from legal entitlements to services, there has been some concern that expenditures from these programs are uncontrollable. The costs of providing medical care under these programs has increased at a rate exceeding the growth of the federal economy and the Consumer Price Index. Medicaid may be more problematic in this respect than Medicare. In 1997, nursing facility services for the elderly accounted for 24.7 percent of all Medicaid payments; the average annual payment for nursing-home care for the elderly was $19,029 per person. The outlay for Medicaid has increased from $23.3 billion in

1980 to $123.5 billion in 1997. The compound rate of growth for Medicaid was 12.9 percent per year between 1990 and 1997.

Frustration over apparently uncontrollable costs has led to major reform in Medicare and Medicaid. Starting in October 1983, a new system began that fixed Medicare hospital payment rates in advance. Under this *prospective payment system (PPS)*, hospitals know in advance what Medicare will pay them for treating a patient with a particular ailment. A fee is set for the treatment of illnesses and injuries categorized into **diagnosis-related groups (DRGs)**. Fees vary by region, according to whether the hospital is in an urban or a rural setting and according to the prevailing wage rate in the area. Rates are adjusted annually. Psychiatric care, long-term care, rehabilitation, and children's hospitals were initially excluded from this prospective payment system.

The fixed fee will have to be accepted as payment in full for treatment of a Medicare patient who has been hospitalized, although hospital administrators may be able to choose the best paying DRG justified by the clinical picture presented by the patient. Those hospitals that can provide the care for less than the fixed payment rate will be allowed to keep the extra money. Hospitals unable to provide the care for the fixed payment rate may charge patients only for the deductibles and copayments that already are part of the Medicare payment system. Some argue that this PPS provides incentives to hospitals to admit patients at a later stage in the progress of illness and discharge them at an earlier stage of illness recovery (Blumenthal, Schlesinger, & Brown Drumheller 1988). Kane and Kane argue that the DRG system runs directly contrary to the goals of geriatrics: "Whereas geriatrics addresses the functional result of multiple interacting problems, DRGs encourage concentration on a single problem. Extra time required to make an appropriate discharge plan is discouraged. Use of ancillary personnel, such as social workers, is similarly discouraged, except to expedite discharges from the hospital" (1990, p. 420).

In 1994, Congress revised the Medicare physician payment system. Begun in 1999, and phased in over a four-year period, the new schedule is based on a scale of resource-based relative value units (RVUs) that measures the time, training, and skill required to perform a given service. The new schedule allows adjustments for overhead costs and geographical differences, and limits what doctors may charge beneficiaries over and above the Medicare allowed fee.

Medicaid has also experienced reform. States have been given greater program autonomy over which services to provide. They may employ managed care options to limit the freedom to select a medical care provider, develop new formulas for hospital reimbursement, and emphasize community-based alternatives to institutional care. With a focus on introducing managed care and reducing costs, states are in a position to negotiate with providers about the organization and price of health and medical care delivery. However, the Maryland experience with Medicaid managed care has met with two important constraints: (1) the concern for quality and appropriateness of care and (2) the motivation of providers to conserve their professional and economic status in the health care system (Oliver 1998). According to Oliver (1998), Medicaid-managed care is by necessity a work in progress. Some studies continue to find evidence that managed care, with its concern for "cost effectiveness," produces worse outcomes than fee-for-service medicine for vulnerable groups—the chronically ill, elderly, and the poor (Schlesinger & Mechanic 1993; Ware et al. 1996).

Despite these reform efforts, Medicare and Medicaid still represent legal entitlement to medical care. Although the price of medical care is more regulated than in the past, costs continue to rise. Combined payments for Medicare (HI and SMI) and Medicaid (federal and state contributions) are projected to be $440.9 billion in 2000. The actuarial status of the Hospital Insurance (HI) and Supplementary Medical Insurance (SMI) Trust Funds suggests that in the absence of additional asset funds, services and costs will need to be cut. The Social Security Administration reports $141.4 billion in trust funds available for the HI program at the end of 1999, an increase of 43 percent since the end of 1990. However, since 1990, benefit payments have increased about 97 percent, suggesting that the present financing schedule for the HI program is sufficient to ensure the payment of benefits into this century. Over the long term (after about 2010), the HI Trust Fund is expected to be out of balance, with benefits paid out exceeding income. The SMI program is actually more problematic. Trust fund assets had declined between 1992 ($24.2 billion) and 1995 ($13.1 billion), but increased dramatically by the end of 1999 (to $44.8 billion). At the same time, benefits increased by 67 percent between 1992 and the end of 1999, and benefit payments during 1999 were approximately two times the funds remaining in the SMI Trust Fund at the end of 1999.

Argument can be made to expand eligibility and enduring services for both Medicaid and Medicare. However, there is also great pressure to keep the federal budget in balance and to limit state budget expenditures for Medicaid, as well. As of this writing, the possibility for changes in federal laws is difficult to assess. One political position being staked out involves using any surplus appearing in the federal budget to support Social Security and Medicare (including expanding services to include prescription drug coverage). Another position involves returning any federal surplus to taxpayers in the form of tax cuts and letting private market mechanisms determine the characteristics of medical care in the United States. Thus, one could more easily predict programmatic and/or financial changes in Medicaid and Medicare than one could predict the direction of such changes.

HEALTH POLICY: LONG-TERM CARE ISSUES

Services that are delivered across the continuum of long-term care (LTC) are fragmented. Community-based LTC programs, including those described in this chapter, comprise a heterogeneous collection of agencies, institutions, and programs dominated by public funding. In particular, Medicaid, which accounts for about 37 percent of all nursing care facilities expenditures in the United States, does attempt to meet the acute and LTC needs of the elderly poor. As Kane and colleagues (1998) point out, however, to a great extent, this occurred by happenstance and

not design. Medicaid was an unplanned vehicle for many long-term care developments and, in the case of older persons, is still very much shaped by Medicare. As
these researchers note, "Medicaid fills the gaps left by Medicare. One of the largest such gaps is long-term care" (Kane et al. 1998, p. 366).

In addition to home health care and nursing-home care, chore services,
homemaker aid, and other types of social services are now covered by Medicaid
under a waiver provision if a state can demonstrate that total expenditures are not
increased by the use of this type of service. States, the key governmental players in
LTC, vary widely in the funding mechanisms they employ for LTC (including the
regular Medicaid program, waiver programs, Social Services block grant programs,
Older Americans Act programs, and state appropriations) and in their approaches
to determining eligibility for LTC services. Some states (e.g., Oregon, New Jersey,
and Washington) have well-developed efforts, including administrative infrastructure, to create coordinated, managed programs. Others make do with disjointed
efforts. Virtually everywhere in the country, public spending has, for the most
part, favored the use of nursing homes for providing LTC.

According to Kane and colleagues (1998), arguments for shifting the emphasis of LTC from nursing homes to home and community-based services
(HCBS) are based on beliefs about social values and economics. Not all needed
LTC can be provided at home, but most surveys show that older people and their
families have a sizable preference for receiving LTC at home. Sentiment aside,
what is required to make this happens is (1) the availability of a home,
(2) adequate support (informal or formal or both), and (3) the capacity to provide
home- and/or community-based services.

Considerable disagreement exists about whether money could be saved by
shifting the provision of care from nursing homes to the home and community.
One argument is that, at the very least, the amount of money now being spent on
nursing-home care could be spent on a much larger number of equally disabled
and frail individuals, if they were cared for at home. A counterargument is that
money is unlikely to be saved because of increased demand for HCBS. The
modest literature suggests that the cost issue is likely to be a wash, especially with
active case management (Kemper 1988; Greene, Lovely, & Ondrich 1993).

Medicare accounted for about 28 percent of all nursing-home and home care
expenditures in the United States in 1997. Home health care benefits under Medicare have been liberalized to cover some part-time health care and/or physical therapy on an intermittent basis if the beneficiary is housebound and under a
physician's care. Coverage also includes home health aid services and durable medical equipment (such as wheelchairs, hospital beds, oxygen, and walkers). Recent
amendments to Medicare have shown increased sensitivity to connecting acute
care services to long-term care services. It is not unusual for long-term care patients
to be frequently moved back and forth between hospital and nursing home. In fact,
Kane and Kane suggest that "hospitalizations might be more accurately viewed as
phases of acute care within the long-term care episode" (1990, p. 235).

Anticipating relationships between acute care and long-term care service
use should help meet needs and control costs. Improved patient assessment can

identify high-risk cases, reduce subsequent long-term care utilization and mortality, and improve function (Rubenstein et al. 1984). Providing postacute care is an area of service need that requires greater recognition. How this care will be provided in local communities is a frequent problem.

Short-term long-term care is considered care that is offered for a period less than 90 days. *Step-down* services, which range from outpatient rehabilitation to community outreach services, can be used. Brody and Magel (1986) recommend the use of step-down services to cross traditional service lines where settings are organized to respond to a hierarchy of patient care needs. When short-term care is used, case management is frequently called into play: It is a "method of providing comprehensive, unified, coordinated, and timely services to people in need of them through the efforts of a primary agent who, together with the client (and the client's family), takes responsibility for providing or procuring the services needed" (Kemp 1981, p. 213).

Posthospital care is often provided by long-term care service agencies. Although Medicare usually pays for these services, there has been discussion to explore ways to tie these costs to the prospective payment system now used in reimbursing hospitals (Kane & Kane 1989). A total capitation system may be a device for recognizing episodes of care in payment policies. Within such a system, a single payment would cover all care, including long-term care (Kane & Kane 1989).

Medicaid and Medicare are *not* the only public payers for long-term care for the elderly. At the federal level, the Social Services Block Grant, Title III of the Older Americans Act, and the Department of Veterans' Affairs <http://www.va.gov> accounted for about 3 percent of all long-term funding for the elderly in the United States in the mid-1990s (Wiener, Hanley, & Illston 1994). The largest of these public programs is the Veterans Administration, which maintains nursing homes, domiciliary care facilities, and hospital-based home health care programs for low-income veterans.

According to the Health Insurance Association of America <http://www.hiaa.org>, about 5 million private long-term care insurance policies had been sold by 1996, many to nonelderly, with sales running at about 500,000 new LTC insurance policies per year starting in 1991 (Cohen & Weinrobe 1999). Thus, while approximately 97 percent of those 65 years and older had Medicare coverage, and over 60 percent had supplementary insurance to Medicare, about 5 percent of the aged had private insurance to cover the catastrophic costs of long-term care.

In addition to the public programs and private insurance, long-term care recipients have considerable out-of-pocket costs, perhaps as much as 38 percent of all expenditures in the United States in 1997. Still, Hanley, Wiener, and Harris (1994) estimate that fewer than 10 percent of elderly nursing-home users are able to pay for a year of nursing-home care out of income. Average out-of-pocket cost for nursing-home care in 1997 was over $40,000 annually; and one estimate is that about one-third of all nursing-home admissions spend more than 40 percent of their income and assets for long-term care in a year.

Policy proposals and initiatives for reforming the system abound. Until relatively recently, these proposals were for expanded or additional services, including additional homemaking and other community-based services to reduce the rate of institutionalization, providing transportation to or centralizing the location of needed services, or even providing direct payment or tax incentives to family caregivers for their services (Benjamin 1985; Doty 1986).

Some policy suggestions contain latent functions that may be difficult to anticipate. One special concern involves the possibility that a new program or a program change might act as a disincentive to continuation of family care or that a newly developed service would simply act as a substitute for family care. Although there is no research to support this concern, no family policy for older people has been developed in the United States. The future trend in family support of older people is somewhat unpredictable as a result of declining fertility rates, continuing changes in the status of women in U.S. society, and normative changes related to family elder care. Changes in family composition and/or dependency ratios may cause changes in the quantity and types of care families can offer their elders. Nevertheless, commitment to the ideal of individuals taking responsibility for themselves and their family members is likely to remain strong.

Most people agree that reform is needed in the current system for financing health and long-term care services for the elderly, as this current system appears to satisfy no one. Clearly, there is some conflict between the need for acute and chronic health services, long-term care, and budgetary constraints. Other flaws include a lack of public and private insurance, high catastrophic out-of-pocket costs, an institutional bias, lack of services in many communities, and a finance system oriented toward welfare rather than the assumption that the need and use of long-term care services is a normal life risk (Wiener & Illston 1996).

Tapping home equity and employing private insurance are two private-sector approaches to financing long-term care. Money accumulated in home equity could be released to older people through reverse annuity mortgages and other sale-leaseback arrangements. According to *Consumer Reports,* however, by mid-1992, only about 3,000 individuals nationwide had taken advantage of an FHA program to promote reverse annuity mortgages.

Private insurance is being marketed to enable people who can afford to pay for services to have access to some sort of saving insurance mechanism (Brody & Magel 1986). Tax-deductible or tax-deferred medical or long-term care retirement accounts, medical or long-term care versions of IRAs, are also being promoted, especially for those upper-middle and upper-income individuals with discretionary incomes. This assumes that working-age adults will prepare for the risk of needing long-term care. Many have competing demands, deny the risk, or mistakenly believe that Medicare will cover these costs (Wiener & Illston 1996). Even if private insurance and/or LTC IRAs are available and grow in the near future, they are unlikely to have impact on Medicaid spending (Wiener, Hanley, & Illston 1994).

Unfortunately, in the current political environment, *reform* is often simply a euphemism for *reducing costs.* As of this writing, Democrat and Republican leaders in Congress, and President Clinton, seem in agreement about the value of moving elderly individuals into managed-care arrangements. Such options could become widely available under both Medicare and Medicaid. According to the U.S. Bureau of the Census (1999, Table 181), approximately 40 percent of Medicaid beneficiaries are currently enrolled in managed care, although most are mothers and children (Riley 1995); only 18 states are currently enrolling noninstitutionalized people in risk-based managed care. About 2.3 million Medicare beneficiaries (7 percent) were enrolled in managed-care programs in 1994, and most of these were in California, Oregon, Arizona, New Mexico, Nevada, and Florida. This figure has no doubt increased dramatically in the interim, as has the geographic availability of managed-care options inside of Medicare.

Arizona may have the longest experience enrolling older people in managed care. According to Riley (1995), over the past nine years, Arizona found costs to increase at a slower pace in their managed-care program than was the case in the fee-for-service Medicaid program. Minnesota has most currently received the first waiver to operate a managed-care demonstration for elders dually enrolled in Medicare and Medicaid. Conflicts in the rules that govern the two programs remain. Also, as other states proceed with applications for the waiver, it is not clear whether they will be held accountable for providing certain mandatory services. And, if not, which critical services are most likely to be jeopardized by cost controls?

TOWARD A POLITICAL ECONOMY OF HEALTH AND AGING

In attempting to understand the relationships among aging, health, and health services utilization, students of aging in the United States have directed their analyses primarily at the individual older person. Resultant research has been concerned with biomedical, psychological, and social-psychological models of aging. Much of the material presented in this book can be located in one or more of these models. Thus, one might ask, How do individuals adjust to the aging process? Why are certain aged persons healthier than others? Why do some elderly people avail themselves of health services and others do not?

As Estes and colleagues point out, questions like these make the economic and political structure of the society residual in explaining old age. These authors offer an alternative approach that "starts with the proposition that the status and resources of the elderly, and even the trajectory of the aging process itself, are conditioned by one's location in the social structure and the economic and political factors that affect it" (Estes, Swan, & Gerard 1984, p. 28).

From this *political economy* perspective, the structure and operation of the major societal institutions (including the family, the workplace, the medical and welfare institutions) shape both the subjective experience and objective condition of the individual's aging. In the area of health and aging, Estes, Swan, and Gerard (1984) note that the political economy perspective emphasizes the following:

1. The social determinants of health and illness
2. The social creation of dependency and the management of that dependency status through public policy and health services

3. Medical care as an ideology and as an industry in the control and management of the aging
4. The consequences of public policies for the elderly as a group and as individuals
5. The role and function of the state vis-à-vis aging and health
6. The social construction of reality about old age and health that reinforces both the institutional arrangements and public policies concerning health and aging in the society

Political economy provides a critical approach to the study of aging that does *not* attempt to individualize or psychologize the health problems of the aging. An analysis of health and aging from a political economy perspective emphasizes the broad implications of economic life for the aged and for society's treatment of the aged and their health. This view also examines the special circumstances of different classes and subgroups of older persons. It is a systematic view based on the assumption that old age cannot be understood in isolation from other problems or issues raised by the larger social order.

From this perspective, the future seems grim for positive health policy initiatives for the elderly. Minkler (1984), for example, sees a continuation of victim blaming and scapegoating of the elderly for economic problems and fiscal crises projected in Medicare and Social Security, although the character of victim blaming is changing. She describes how earlier efforts at victim blaming defined the elderly as a social problem and, as a consequence, solutions were devised for dealing with that problem. Medicare and Medicaid represent but two highly visible programs generated to deal with the health problems of the aged. Victim blaming in the 1980s began to define these solutions as part of the problem. Thus, not only are the elderly themselves seen as a problem but also programmatic efforts to address their needs are characterized as "budget busting" and in need of being cut, dismantled entirely, or privatized.

The terms of discussion have shifted to proposals for allocation of health care. For example, Longman (1987) argues that each new generation inherits valuable new medical technologies without the dedicated capital to pay for their use. The result is accumulating debt that can be discharged only by younger, coming generations. The pattern is exacerbated by efforts to prolong life to an advanced age. Implicit is the suggestion that those who benefit from such advances (the aged) are not those who will have to pay (the young).

Blank (1988) identifies three obstacles that stand in the way of traditional reform of U.S. medical care system: (1) the belief that individuals have the right to unlimited medical care should they choose it, (2) the traditional acceptance of this maximalist approach by the medical community, and (3) the insulation of the individual from feeling the cost of treatment. He asks not whether we must ration health care, but how.

Callahan (1988) similarly argues that the "happy days" strategies are no longer working. The nation can no longer maintain the illusion of a health care system that will be all things to all people. Presumably, rationing will help restore the balance. And *age* may be the first standard that is employed for the rationing or limiting of medical care.

The political economy perspective raises a whole new set of questions that need to be asked *and* answered as the country proceeds into the future. These questions and their answers will provide a significant opportunity for students of aging to rethink the relationship between society and its elderly constituents.

SUMMARY

The average number of physician visits per person generally increases with age. Although differences in the rate of physician utilization by the poor and nonpoor elderly have been narrowed or eliminated in recent years, the poor likely continue to use fewer services relative to their needs than do those in higher socioeconomic circumstances.

There is a gender differential in the utilization of physician services in all adult age groups. Explanations have focused primarily on the social situation of women. In general, the utilization of dental services by older people is lower than among younger groups, despite the fact that dental problems increase with age. Few third-party reimbursement plans for health care include dental services; thus, financial barriers to dental care are still substantial. The elderly are the heaviest utilizers of hospital care; they accounted for 35 percent of all hospital discharges in 1995. In 1996, the elderly accounted for 34 percent of all ambulatory (outpatient) surgery procedures.

The elderly have lower rates of admission to inpatient psychiatric facilities than all other age groups, including those under 18 years of age. Data from 1975 to 1986 show lower rates of admission for the aged for all diagnoses in state and county mental hospitals and private psychiatric hospitals. Only for organic disorders do those 65 years and older have higher rates of admission to psychiatric facilities than is the case for the total population.

Andersen and colleagues have generated a conceptual framework within which to sort factors that explain variation in the use of health services. Referred to as the *health behavior model,* this framework is arguably the most widely used for studying health services utilization. Basically, the health behavior model views the use of health services as a function of the predisposing, enabling, and need characteristics of the individual. Generally, researchers employing the model have been able to explain between 10 and 25 percent of variation in health services utilization among the elderly at any one point in time.

Health care expenditures have increased rapidly in recent years. The amount of money expended on Medicare alone has increased more than five times between 1980 and 1996. The source of funds to pay for health care for the elderly has also changed. Increasingly, more of the health care dollars expended are public monies—about 47 percent today. The largest single item on the health care bill of elderly people is hospital care. Public funds, including Medicare and Medicaid, pay for most of this service.

The Medicare program for the elderly contains many out-of-pocket deductibles and copayments, as well as limitations in services, and focuses too narrowly on acute care problems. The language employed throughout the Medicare regulations refers to medical need, medical care, and medical necessity. The elderly are often in greater need of health promotion and illness prevention services than they are in need of medical care services. Some reforms of Medicare have recently been made. Arguably, the most notable among these are the institution of a prospective payment system for hospitals and the payment for hospice care for the dying. Despite reforms, Medicare and Medicaid still represent legal entitlement to medical care and costs continue to rise. Pressures to rein in costs are likely to result in congressional revision of federal law regulating these programs.

Medicaid, which accounts for about 37 percent of all nursing care facilities expenditures in the United States, does attempt to meet the acute and long-term care needs of the elderly poor. To a great extent, however, this occurred by happenstance and not design. Medicaid was an unplanned vehicle for many long-term care developments and, in the case of older persons, is still very much shaped by Medicare.

The political economy perspective is a newer critical approach to understanding the relationships among aging, health, and health services utilization. Rather than "biologizing" or "psychologizing" the problems of health and aging, this perspective tries to place problems of health and aging in the broader context of the economic and political life of the society. Whereas earlier victim-blaming efforts identified the elderly as a social problem, current victim blaming defines programmatic efforts to address the health care needs of the elderly as part of the problem. Consequently, suggestions to ration health care by age are seen somewhat favorably.

STUDY QUESTIONS

1. How does use of physician services vary by sex? What are some possible explanations for this difference in utilization of medical services between men and women?

2. What is the apparent relationship between age and dental problems? Dental visits? How can the low rates of utilization of dental services among the aged be explained?

3. Identify the three factors in Andersen's categorization schema that contribute to the use of health services. Give an example of each of these factors. How do the three factors rank in their ability to account for variation in health care utilization by the elderly?

4. Distinguish between Medicare and Medicaid. What are the major gaps in these programs? How have programs such as Medicare and Medicaid influenced the amount of physician contact among poor elderly?

5. Is there a crisis in medical care financing? Explain your answer. What reforms have been instituted in the past to ensure the financial integrity of Medicare?

6. What reforms are needed in the current system of long-term care services for the elderly?

7. What is the value of the political economy perspective in understanding the relationships among aging, health, and health services utilization? Why do you think that the allocation of health care resources continues to be an issue today?

REFERENCES

Aday, L. (1975). Economic and non-economic barriers to the use of needed medical services. *Medical Care, 13*, 447–456.

Aday, L., Andersen, R. M., & Fleming, G. V. (1980). *Health care in the U.S.: Equitable for whom?* Beverly Hills: Sage.

Aday, L., Fleming, G. V., & Andersen, R. M. (1984). *Access to health care in the U.S.: Who has it, who doesn't?* Chicago: Pluribus Press.

Andersen, R. M. (1968). *A behavioral model of families' use of health services.* Research Series 25. Chicago: Center for Health Administration Studies.

Andersen, R. M., Anderson, O., & Smedby, B. (1968). Perceptions of and response to symptoms of illness in Sweden and the U.S. *Medical Care, 6*, 18–30.

Andersen, R. M., & Newman, J. (1973). Societal and individual determinants of medical care utilization in the U.S. *Milbank Memorial Fund Quarterly, 51*, 95–124.

Benjamin, A. (1985). Community based long-term care. In C. Harrington, R. Newcomer, C. Estes, & associates (Eds.), *Long term care of the elderly: Public policy issues.* Beverly Hills: Sage.

Blank, R. H. (1988). *Rationing medicine.* New York: Columbia University Press.

Blendon, R. J., Aiken, L. H., Freeman, H. E., & Corey, C. (1989). Access to medical care for black and white Americans. *Journal of the American Medical Association, 261*, 278–281.

Blumenthal, D., Schlesinger, M., & Brown Drumheller, P. (1988). *Renewing the promise: Medicare and its reform.* New York: Oxford University Press.

Brody, E. M. (1985). Parent care as normative family stress. *Gerontologist, 25*, 19–29.

Brody, S. J., & Magel, J. (1986). Long term care: The long and short of it. In C. Eisdorfer (Ed.), *Reforming health care for the elderly: Recommendations for national policy.* Baltimore: Johns Hopkins University Press.

Callahan, D. (1988). Allocating health resources. *Hasting Center Report, 18* (2), 14–20.

Cohen, M. A., Kumar, N., McGuire, T., & Wallack, S. S. (1992). Financing long-term care: A practical mix of public and private. *Journal of Health Politics, Policy and Law, 17* (3), 403–424.

Cohen, M. A., & Weinrobe, M. (1999). *Tax deductibility of long-term care insurance premiums: Implications for market growth and public long-term care expenditures.* Washington, DC: Health Insurance Association of America.

Coronel, S. (1994). *Long-term care insurance in 1992.* Washington, DC: Health Insurance Association of America.

Doty, P. (1986). Family care of the elderly: The role of public policy. *The Milbank Quarterly, 64* (1), 34–75.

Estes, C. L., Gerard, L. E., Zones, J. S., & Swan, J. H. (1984). *Political economy, health, and aging.* Boston: Little, Brown.

Estes, C. L., Swan, J. H., & Gerard, L. E. (1984). Dominant and competing paradigms in gerontology: Towards a political economy of aging. In M. Minkler & C. L. Estes (Eds.), *Readings in the political economy of aging.* Farmingdale, NY: Baywood.

Feingold, E. (1966). *Medicare: Policy and politics.* San Francisco: Chandler.

Freeman, H. E., Blendon, R. J., Aiken, L. H., Sudman, S., Mullinix, C. F., & Corey, C. (1987). Americans report on their access to health care. *Health Affairs, 6*, 6–18.

Freidson, E. (1961). *Patient views of medical practice.* New York: Russell Sage Foundation.

Freidson, E. (1989). Client control and medical practice. In E. Freidson (Ed.), *Medical work in America: Essays on health care.* New Haven, CT: Yale University Press.

Greene, V. L., Lovely, M. E., & Ondrich, J. I. (1993). The cost effectiveness of community services in a frail elderly population. *Gerontologist, 33* (2), 177–189.

Hanley, R. J., Wiener, J. M., & Harris, K. M. (1994). *The economic status of nursing home users.* Washington, DC: Brookings Institute.

Haug, M. (1981). Age and medical care utilization patterns. *Journal of Gerontology, 33*, 103–111.

Kaiser Commission on the Future of Medicaid. (1996). *Medicaid and long-term care.* Washington, DC: Kaiser Family Foundation.

Kane, R. L., & Kane, R. A. (1989). Transitions in long term care. In M. Ory & K. Bond (Eds.), *Aging and health care: Social science and policy perspectives.* New York: Routledge.

Kane, R. L., & Kane, R. A. (1990). Health care for older people: Organizational and policy issues. In R. H. Binstock & L. K. George (Eds.), *Handbook of aging and the social sciences* (3rd ed.). San Diego, CA: Academic.

Kane, R. L., Kane, R. A., Ladd, R. C., & Veazie, W. N. (1998). Variation in state spending for long-term care: Factors associated with more balanced systems. *Journal of Health Politics, Policy and Law, 23* (2), 363–390.

Kart, C. S. (1993). Community-based, noninstitutional long-term care service utilization by aged blacks: Facts and issues. In C. M. Barresi & D. E. Stull (Eds.), *Ethnic elderly and long-term care*. New York: Springer.

Kemp, B. (1981). The case management model of human service delivery. In E. Pan, T. Barker, & C. Vash (Eds.), *Annual Review of Rehabilitation* (Vol. 2). New York: Springer.

Kemper, P. (1988). Evaluation of the National Channeling Demonstration: Overview of the findings. *Health Services Research, 23* (1), 161–174.

Longman, P. (1987). *Born to pay: The new politics of aging in America*. Boston: Houghton Mifflin.

Marmor, T. (1973). *The politics of medicare*. Chicago: Aldine.

Minkler, M. (1984). Blaming the aged victim: The politics of retrenchment in times of fiscal conservatism. In M. Minkler & C. L. Estes (Eds.), *Readings in the political economy of aging*. Farmingdale, NY: Baywood.

Mossey, J. M., Havens, B., & Wolinsky, F. D. (1989). The consistency of formal health care utilization. In M. Ory & K. Bond (Eds.), *Aging and the use of formal health services*. New York: Routledge.

Nathanson, C. (1975). Illness and the feminine role: A theoretical review. *Social Science and Medicine, 9*, 57–62.

National Center for Health Statistics. (1997). *Health, United States, 1996–97 and injury chartbook*. Hyattsville, MD: National Center for Health Statistics.

Oliver, T. (1998). The collision of economics and politics in Medicaid managed care: Reflections on the course of reform in Maryland. *The Milbank Quarterly, 76* (1), 59–101.

Riley, P. (1995). Long-term care: The silent target of the federal and state budget debate. *The Public Policy and Aging Report, 7* (1), 4–5, 7.

Roos, N., & Shapiro, E. (1981). The Manitoba longitudinal study on aging: Preliminary findings on health care utilization by the elderly. *Medical Care, 19*, 644–657.

Rubenstein, L. Z., Josephson, K. R., Wieland, G. D., English, R. A., Sayre, J. A., & Kane, R. L. (1984). Effectiveness of a geriatric evaluation unit: A randomized clinical trial. *New England Journal of Medicine, 311*, 1664–1670.

Schlesinger, M., & Mechanic, D. (1993). Challenges for managed competiton from chronic illness. *Health Affairs, 12* (suppl.), 123–137.

Shanas, E., & Maddox, G. (1977). Aging, health, and the organization of health resources. In R. Binstock & E. Shanas (Eds.), *Handbook of aging and the social sciences*. New York: Van Nostrand Reinhold.

Stevens, R., & Stevens, R. (1974). *Welfare medicine in America: A case study of Medicaid*. New York: Free Press.

Stoller, E. P., Kart, C. S., & Portugal, S. S. (1997). Explaining pathways of care taken by elderly people: An analysis of responses to illness symptoms. *Sociological Focus, 30* (2), 147–165.

Trager, B. (1981). *In place of policy: Public adventures in non-institutional long-term care*. Unpublished paper presented at the American Public Health Association Annual Meeting, Los Angeles.

U.S. Bureau of the Census. (1999). *Statistical abstract of the United States* (119th ed.). Washington, DC: U.S. Government Printing Office.

U.S. General Accounting Office. (1982). *The elderly should benefit from expanded home health care but increasing these services will not insure cost reductions*. Public No. GAO/ IDE-83-1. Washington, DC: U.S. Government Printing Office.

U.S. Senate Special Committee on Aging et al. (1991). *Aging America: Trends and projections*. Washington, DC: U.S. Government Printing Office.

Van Gelder, S., & Johnson, D. (1991). *Long-term care insurance: A market update*. Washington, DC: Health Insurance Association of America.

Wan, T. (1982). Use of health service by the elderly in low income communities. *Milbank Memorial Fund Quarterly, 60*, 82–107.

Ward, R. (1977). Services for older people: An integrated framework for research. *Journal of Health and Social Behavior, 18*, 61–70.

Ware, J. E., Bayliss, M. S., Rogers, W. H., Kosinski, M., & Tarlov, A. R. (1996). Differences in 4-year health outcomes for elderly and poor, chronically ill patients treated in HMO and fee-for-service systems: Results from the Medical Outcomes Study. *Journal of the American Medical Association, 276*, 1039–1047.

Wiener, J. M., Hanley, R. J., & Illston, L. H. (1992). Financing long-term care: How much public? How much private? *Journal of Health Politics, Policy and Law, 17* (3), 425–434.

Wiener, J. M., & Illston, L. H. (1996). The financing and organization of health care for older Americans. In R. H. Binstock & L. K. George (Eds.), *Handbook of aging and the social sciences* (4th ed.). San Diego: Academic.

Wiener, J. M., Illston, L. H., & Hanley, R. J. (1994). *Sharing the burden: Strategies for public and private long-term care insurance*. Washington, DC: Brookings Institute.

Wolinsky, F. D., & Johnson, R. J. (1991). The use of health services by older adults. *Journal of Gerontology, 46* (6), S345–S357.

▪ ▪ ▪ ▪ ▪ ▬▬▬▬▬▬▬▬▬▬▬▬▬▬▬▬▬▬▬▬▬▬▬▬▬▬▬▬▬▬▬

CHAPTER NINETEEN

DEATH AND DYING

CARY S. KART
EILEEN S. METRESS

Age is an important variable in the study of a wide array of issues relating to death and dying. These issues include the relationship between age and the meaning of death, study of the grief and bereavement process, characterizations of the dying process, and decisions about where death should take place and who should decide about the access of older people to life-sustaining medical treatments. This chapter presents an overview of a selection of such issues as they pertain to the older adult.

AGING AND THE MEANING OF DEATH

The meanings that individuals give to death vary as a function of age. Nagy (1959) studied postwar Hungarian children and argued that children's ideas of death develop in three stages, each marked by a different view of death. She found that children under age 5 did not recognize death as irreversible; they viewed it as a temporary departure or sleep, or as a type of separation. Between the ages of 5 and 9, death was often personified and seen as a contingency. Although viewed as irreversible, it was not necessarily inevitable, at least as far as the child was concerned. Death existed but was remote. By age 9 or 10, the children understood death to be inevitable, final, and less remote, and as a part of the life cycle of all living organisms.

Some have questioned the universal application of Nagy's findings. McIntire, Angle, and Struempl (1972) found that, unlike Hungarian children, U.S. children are able to conceptualize "organic decomposition" as early as age 5 and in some cases as early as age 3. The tendency to personify death noted by Nagy during stage 2 is not a common finding in more recent studies (Kastenbaum 1991). Kastenbaum considers that, since Nagy's research, children may have developed a fashionably scientific outlook in response to death. He notes one 7-year-old who likened death to "when the computer is down." Perhaps the children's tendency to personify is masked by contemporary images and terms. In addition, such work demonstrates the need to examine variations within cultural groups.

Likewise, the work of anthropologist Bluebond-Langner (1974, 1989) illustrates the need to consider children's personal experiences in relation to their understanding of death. Her work with hospitalized, terminally ill children showed them capable of a more sophisticated death awareness at a younger age than early researchers thought possible. Such awareness included the perception that death is final, inevitable, and happens to everyone—including them!

Bluebond-Langner (1977) summarizes research on the relationship between social class and children's views of death as follows: Children from lower socioeconomic groups are more likely to cite violence as the general and specific cause of death, whereas middle-class children are more likely to cite disease and old age as the general cause and the arrest of vital functions as the specific cause of death. These variations seem to reflect differences in the life experiences of the children.

Two meanings of death with particular significance for the elderly are suggested by a large body of literature: death as an organizer of time and death as loss. To the elderly and the terminal patient, death is a clearly perceived constraint that limits the future (Kalish 1976). Anticipating the end of one's life may bring a reorganization of time and priorities. Kastenbaum (1991) found that older persons projected themselves into a much more limited time frame than did younger persons when asked to report coming important events in their lives and the timing of these events.

Death also makes all possessions and experiences transient. For many elderly persons, the anticipation of death may generate feelings of meaninglessness. There is nothing meaningful to do because whatever is attempted will be short lived or unfinished (Kalish 1976). Back (1965) asked residents of rural communities in the West what they would do if they knew they were to die in 30 days. The elderly were less likely than younger respondents to indicate that their activities would change at all. Kalish and Reynolds (1976) provide support for Back's findings. Using respondents in three age groups and extending the duration to the time of death to six months instead of 30 days, more of the older group were found unwilling to change their life-styles. Nearly three times as many older persons as younger reported they would spend their remaining time in prayer, reading, contemplation, or other activities that reflected inner life, spiritual needs, or withdrawal.

Perception by the elderly of the finitude of life comes not only from within. Older persons receive many reminders of their impending death from other individuals and from social institutions. Society tends to perceive the older person as not having sufficient futurity to deserve a major investment of the resources of others.

Among the Managalase of Papua New Guinea in the South Pacific, death is central to cultural ideology and key concepts of power and exchange (McKellin 1985). Managalase dead continue to participate in the life of the society. Because so few people achieve old age, longevity requires explanation. Why does a person outlive his or her contemporaries? The answer lies in the strength of one's soul. A strong soul may avoid or withstand attacks by sorcerers or bush spirits, the main explanations of death among the young. Responsibility for a younger person's death also rests with family and community. In part, death reflects failed obligations to protect the victim from assault. It suggests unsatisfactory exchanges and offerings to ancestral ghosts.

Death in youth and adulthood can be enormously disruptive to social life. Exchange relations are interrupted and alliances may end. The death of a man may be less problematic than that of a woman, as his siblings assume his responsibilities. Multiple deaths in a village threaten the life of the village itself. Note one case described by McKellin:

> After the death of…the village councilor and area bigman, the whole web of political alliances in Siribu and surrounding villages began to unravel. After two or three more deaths, the village was pronounced *derahar* "dead," and over the course of several years the people dismantled their houses and established three new villages at different sites. (1985, p. 193)

Death from old age is described as "passing away." It reflects the end of participation in village life and is explained as a failure of the soul to return to the body after long and distant travels. Ultimately, the strength and magic of soul which contributed to longevity fail the older person and cause his or her death.

Death of the old is much more conclusive for village life than death of a younger person. The old have lost power by outliving their contemporaries; they come to rely on younger relatives for food and sustenance. Surviving kin have already developed exchange relations with ghosts and others in the village and are not dependent on ties with the recently deceased. In fact, by the end, the reverse has occurred. Prior to passing away, the position of the old has typically come to mirror that of a dependent child.

GRIEF AND BEREAVEMENT

Bereavement refers to the state of having sustained a loss. For the elderly, losses accumulate and become very much a part of life. *Grief* is the reaction to loss. It is a painful yet necessary process that facilitates adjustment to the loss. Its course is quite variable; it may be short or long, taking months to a few years for the loss to be resolved and a normal life to resume. It may vary in its intensity. In addition to depression, reactions may include anger, guilt, anxiety, and preoccupation with thoughts of the deceased.

In his pioneering work, Lindemann (1944) described the physical symptoms of grief, which may include sensations of somatic distress lasting from 20 minutes to an hour. Stomach upset, shortness of breath, tightness in the throat, frequent sighing, an empty feeling in the abdomen, lack of muscular power, and "subjective distress" were found to be common among the grieving. Confusion, disorganization, absentmindedness, and insomnia were also expressed.

In part, the loss reaction is shaped by cultural norms and experiences. In less-developed societies with extended families, the trauma of death is only minimally disruptive. In preliterate families, the primary relationships involving parents, children, and spouses may be extended to other relatives. In this way, others may serve to compensate for a loss. For instance, among the Trobrianders, the role of the father is assumed by the mother's brother. Such is *not* the case in the smaller nuclear family units that characterize industrialized societies. Nuclear family members are customarily left to their own resources to adjust to the psychological and social impact of loss.

In many societies, including that of the United States, established rituals determine how life crises, such as death, are to be managed. Rituals have important social functions as well as utilitarian value to those who are grieving. They serve to channel and legitimize the normal expression of grief, as well as to rally emotional support for the bereaved through the participation of friends and relatives. *Mourning,* the culturally patterned manner by which grief is managed, is quite variable from one society to another and among subcultures within U.S. society, as well.

Many believe that among African Americans, funerals provide a number of psychological mechanisms that facilitate the grief process (Masamba & Kalish 1976). One factor that permits emotional expression at funerals in African American churches is the visual confrontation with the deceased. This is carried out in at least two ways. First, the picture of the deceased uniformly appears on the program of the order of the service. According to a member of one deceased person's family, printing the picture in this fashion helped him accept the reality of the loss and generated a feeling of the spiritual presence of the deceased in the church (Masamba & Kalish 1976).

Second, the visual confrontation with the deceased is especially vivid when the remains are viewed by the living. In almost all the African American funerals attended by Masamba and Kalish (1976), caskets were closed at the beginning of the service and opened at the end of the concluding sermon. Those present were asked to view the body. Responses varied: Some walked by silently; others touched and even talked to the deceased. Members of the family were always last to view the body, although this is usually done by bringing the body closer to where they are seated so that they can see the body without standing up. Overt expression can be quite strong, including vehement physical motion.

According to Masamba and Kalish (1976), emotion may not be expressed when (1) there is a feeling that such expression may be seen as masculine inadequacy, (2) there is belief that such expressions should not be made in front of people who are not family members or friends of the family, and (3) the minister expresses a belief that such behavior implies a lack of acceptance of resurrection and hope in Christ.

Expression takes a different form in the funeral rites of American Jews. For example, the service begins with the cutting of a garment or a black ribbon. As Cytron (1993) describes it, this rite symbolizes the individual being "cut away" from loved ones. Children make the cut in a garment above the heart; others do it on the right side of the garment. At the grave site, many family members choose to participate personally in placing some earth on the lowered coffin. It symbolizes both acceptance of the finality of death and assurance of a proper burial (Cytron 1993). Typically, the Jewish service ends with a recitation of the "homecoming" prayer called *kaddish*. This prayer makes no overt reference to death, yet offers an affirmation of life through "an ancient formula praising God as the author of life and its wonderous ways" (Cytron 1993, p. 119).

The elderly in U.S. society are not always provided an outlet for the expression of grief. Goodstein (1984) asserts that because of their own significant longevity, the elderly may be expected to grin and bear their losses rather than to grieve. Loss is expected with old age. When held by family, friends, and practitioners, such an attitude may compel older persons to act strong out of fear that doing otherwise might label them as weak.

Various types of losses accumulate with age, underscoring the possibility of severe grief reactions after the loss of a spouse, relative, friend, home, employment, financial security, or health, as well as the loss of personal belongings such as a domestic pet (Keddie 1977). All of these losses can be accompanied by grief. As a result, attachments to remaining people and objects may take on increasing value. Their loss may generate an intense response.

Symptoms of grief in the elderly may be mistaken for other conditions in what is referred to as a *devious pattern of grief* (Goodstein 1984). The clinician may attribute the symptoms to another physical illness or to dementia. As the grief remains ignored, episodic exacerbation of symptoms may result. Unresolved grief is one of the most frequently misdiagnosed illnesses in the elderly. Continued physical and emotional pain, if verbalized by the victim, may be dismissed as hypochondriasis.

Physical and emotional symptoms of grief usually subside in time, but some bereaved individuals are at increased risk for illness and possibly death (Osterweis 1985). Existing illness may worsen, and new illnesses may be precipitated. Frederick (1976, 1982–83) has suggested a pathway by which illnesses might be triggered. He has proposed that a chain of hormonal responses to the stress of loss leads to depression of the body's immune system; if the response pattern continues, the immune suppression can lead to the development of infection and even cancer. Until about age 75, widowed men are one and one-half times more likely to die than are married men (Helsing & Szklo 1981). Morbidity, hospitalization, and mortality exceed expected rates in the two-year period following a loss of spouse (Greenblatt 1978; Rowland 1977).

A number of factors appear to exert significant influence on the resolution of grief (Lieberman 1978; Osterweis 1985; Osterweis, Solomon, & Green 1984). The nature of the lost relationship is important. Loss of spouse has received considerable attention. More research needs to be directed at the loss of friends, siblings, and adult children. Gorer (1965) posits that the loss of an adult child would seem to be the most distressing and long lasting of all griefs. Besides exerting emotional trauma, the death of an adult child might leave the older person without a caregiver. Yet, research focusing on such a loss is extremely limited (Levav 1982). How the death occurred, the availability of a social support system, experiencing several deaths within a short period of time, the existence of illness prior

Losses accumulate with age, making remaining attachments to people, pets, and objects especially valuable.

to or at the time of the loss, and life changes necessitated by the loss can all influence the intensity, duration, and consequences of the grieving process.

Although it is almost always best to allow the bereaved to experience the grieving process, problems may arise if the grieving appears interminable and treatment may be necessary. Care may involve simple encouragement, personal warmth, understanding, and compassion; or it may require antidepressant drug therapy and psychiatric management. Life decisions related to finances, living arrangements, and personal care may have to be made. Counsel should be given carefully, lawfully, and together with the physician and family members. No irrevocable decisions involving such important matters should be made until the main period of grieving has passed.

Bereavement is a significant contributing factor to suicide. Suicide is more frequent among the widowed. The resolution of grief goes hand in hand with the resumption of existing and the development of new interpersonal relationships. The psychosocial environment of the aged widow or widower may not furnish the opportunity for reestablishing relationships or building important new links (Bromberg & Cassel 1983). Older persons who are married and who maintain contact with their children and other relatives are less likely to commit suicide (Robbins, West, & Murphy 1977).

The elderly are more likely than the young to complete a suicide effort (Maris 1981). Perhaps the older person who attempts suicide is less ambivalent about doing so and more likely to use a more lethal technique. Chapter 6 includes additional material on suicide and the mental health of the elderly.

THE DYING PROCESS

Death and the dying process itself are being seen more and more as the terminal phase of the life cycle. Professionals who work with the dying and those who study death and dying have made attempts to understand this final stage. It is hoped that such understanding will help health care professionals to enrich the lives of the dying and their families and to provide personalized care for those who have been defined as terminally ill.

The Dying Trajectory

The Glaser-Strauss research team was the first to study and clarify the various sequences and distinctive characteristic of the terminal course. They observed the social process of dying in six medical facilities in the San Francisco area. The majority of their findings are published in two books: *Awareness of Dying* (1966) and *Time for Dying* (1968). Although their research was not limited to older patients, the results of their work are relevant to the elderly dying patient.

According to Glaser and Strauss (1968), staff members working with the ill must answer two questions for themselves about every patient: Will he or she die? And, if so, when? These questions are important because the staff generates expectations about a patient's death and takes its treatment and other attitudinal cues from the answers that are developed.

Perceptions about the course of dying are referred to as *dying trajectories.* The nature of staff interaction with the patients is closely related to the particular expectations the staff has formed about the patient's dying. This is the case regardless of whether the staff members happen to be correct in their expectations. Patients' expectations about their own dying trajectories are greatly affected by staff expectations, as well.

Two important cues that contribute to the perception of the dying trajectory are the patient's physical condition and the temporal references made by medical staff members. Physical cues are easiest to read and help establish some degree of certainty about the outcome. Temporal cues are more difficult to read, in part because they have many reference points. Doctors' expectations about the progression of a disease ("It's going fast," "He's lingering"); length of hospital stay; and even the work schedule (e.g., whether the patient continues to be bathed, turned, and/or fed) are temporal cues that contribute to expectations about how much longer the patient will live (Glaser & Strauss 1968, p. 10).

In perceptions of a lingering trajectory, custodial care predominates. Aggressive treatment is rare. Health care professionals tend not to find the support of such patients challenging or rewarding. Lower-paid staff may provide the majority of care for such patients (Friedman & DiMatteo 1982).

When the staff perceives patients as being in a lingering death trajectory, these patients may suffer a loss in their own perceived social worth and relinquish control over their care (Kastenbaum 1991). Staff members may feel that they have done everything that is possible to care for the patient, and they may view a downhill course as inevitable. Death of one who has been on a lingering trajectory may seem appropriate to the staff, who rationalize that the patient's life held limited value. Intense emotional reactions at the death of such a patient may serve to confuse those who have made assumptions about the patient's present limited social worth. Or stress may result when the lingering patient does not die on schedule.

In contrast, the expected quick trajectory typically involves acute life-or-death crises. The patient's perceived social worth can influence the type of care delivered. The unexpected quick trajectory involves an unanticipated crisis that may challenge the professional caregiver's defenses regarding anxiety about death.

Dying: The Career Perspective

"When people go through the same series of events, we speak of this as a career and of the sequence and timing of events as their career timetable" (Roth 1963, p. 93). Roth used the institutionalized tuberculosis patient as his career model. He argued that individuals involved in a career try to define when certain salient things will happen to them, developing time norms against which to measure their individual progress. The benchmarks on this timetable are the significant events that occur in the average career (Gustafson 1972).

Gustafson (1972) applied Roth's notion of career timetables to the nursing-home setting. She views the last phase of life as a career that moves in a series of related and regressive stages toward death. These stages, she argues, are defined by a series of benchmarks, which, for elderly patients, consist of the degree of deterioration indicated by their social activity, mobility, and physical and mental functioning. A successful career, in this sense, consists of the slowest possible regression from one stage to another.

Bargaining is an important aspect of the career timetable, according to Gustafson (1972), although she identifies it in a way that contrasts with Roth's original model. Roth depicts the tubercular patient as bargaining with medical and hospital authorities to move as quickly as possible toward the goal of restored health. Gustafson sees the elderly nursing-home patient as bargaining with God, the disease, and the nursing-home staff in an attempt to slow down the movement toward death.

By use of this perspective, the dying process is not conceptualized as an undifferentiated, unbroken decline toward death. Rather, the *dying career* is viewed as comprising a social stage and a terminal stage. In the social stage, the elderly patient is fighting against the tendency of society (as represented by relatives, staff, visitors, and peers) to impose a premature social death. Bargaining may involve holding on to status symbols that indicate the possibility of a future. An elderly woman may never read, but she indignantly demands a new pair of eyeglasses, for example, or an elderly man may not be able to walk, yet he demands a new walker or cane. In the terminal phase, when the signs of death are more dependable and its imminence cannot be avoided, the patient may begin bargaining directly with God or the disease in an effort to secure additional time.

According to Gustafson (1972), a nursing-home patient's dying career can be made less difficult if the staff adopts a view of the dying process as consisting of a social stage and a terminal stage. A nursing staff with this view might try to extend the social stage as long as possible and be supportive during the terminal stage. Later in this chapter, we discuss some ways in which health professionals, family members, and others can help ease the dying process for terminal patients.

The Stages of Dying

The best-known conceptualization of the dying process is that proposed by Kübler-Ross (1969) in her landmark best-seller, *On Death and Dying*. In her view, various stages or emotional reactions mark an awareness of dying. The patient may experience denial, anger, bargaining, depression, and acceptance. The applicability and universality of these five **stages of dying** are still empirical questions. Kübler-Ross (1974, pp. 25–26) points out that patients may skip a stage, exhibit two or three simultaneously, or experience them out of order. Kalish contends that Kübler-Ross's stages are in danger of becoming self-fulfilling prophecies: "Some health caretakers have been observed trying to encourage, or even manipulate, their dying patients through Kübler-Ross's stages; patients occasionally become concerned if they are not progressing adequately" (1976, p. 38).

The first stage, *denial*, is most evident during the early period of awareness of impending death. It may be viewed as a coping mechanism to buffer the shock of such news ("No, not me; it can't be true"). Kübler-Ross offers the case of a patient who went through a long and expensive ritual to support her denial:

> She was convinced that the x-rays were "mixed up." She asked for reassurance that her pathology report could not possibly be back so soon and that another patient's report must be marked with her name. When none of this could be confirmed, she quickly asked to leave the hospital, looking for another physician in the vain hope "to get a better explanation for my troubles...." She asked for examination and re-examination, partially knowing that the original diagnosis was correct, but also seeking further evaluations in the hope that the first conclusion was indeed in error. (1969, p. 38)

When the first stage of denial cannot be maintained any longer, it is often replaced by feelings of *anger* or *rage*. The patient finally realizes that denial is fruitless ("It is me; it was not a mistake"). The next question becomes, Why me? This stage is perhaps the most difficult for staff and family members to deal with. Anger may be displaced and projected on anyone and everyone who comes into contact with the patient. Much of this anger is rational and should be expected.

Place yourself in the terminal patient's position. You, too, would be angry if your life's activities had been interrupted and you could no longer enjoy life, especially if you had been kept too long in a hospital, had been subjected to unpleasant tests and treatments, and were constantly being reminded that you could no longer carry out your own affairs.

The third stage, *bargaining,* is really an attempt on the part of the patient to postpone the inevitable. As Kübler-Ross indicates, the terminal patient in this stage uses the same maneuvers as a child; he or she asks to be rewarded "for good behavior" (1969, p. 82). Most bargains are made with God and almost always include wishes for the removal of pain or discomfort and for life extension. Kübler-Ross presents the case of a woman quite dependent on injections for painkillers. The woman had a son who was to be married, and she was sad at the prospect of being unable to attend the wedding. With great effort, she was taught self-hypnosis and was able to be comfortable for several hours at a time. She had made all sorts of promises if she could only live long enough to attend this marriage. The day preceding the wedding she left the hospital as an elegant lady. Nobody would have believed her real condition. She was "the happiest person in the whole world" and looked radiant. Patients rarely hold up their end of the bargain. This same woman returned to the hospital and remarked, "Now don't forget, I have another son" (1969, p. 83).

When the terminally ill person is unable to continue to deny the illness, when the rage and anger are dissipated, and when bargaining efforts are seen as hopeless, *depression* may begin. This fourth stage is characterized by feelings of loss, and two types of depression may be evident. **Reactive depression** is a result of the various other losses that accompany illness and dying. For instance, the patient may mourn the loss of a limb that has been amputated, or the cancer patient may mourn the loss of her beautiful hair to radiation therapy. The second type of depression, **preparatory depression,** takes impending losses into account; that is, it prepares the individual for loss of all love objects. It facilitates the final stage of acceptance.

Acceptance should not be mistaken for happiness or capitulation. The dying patient can accept his or her imminent death without joy and without giving up the life that remains. According to Kübler-Ross, this is often a time when the dying individual will "contemplate his coming end with a certain degree of quiet expectation." This stage may represent "the final rest before the long journey" (1969, pp. 112–113).

Although many researchers and practitioners find Kübler-Ross's conceptualization of the dying process extremely valuable, others are critical (Corr 1992, 1993; Feigenberg 1977; Kastenbaum 1991; Metzger 1979; Schulz & Aderman 1974; Shneidman 1980; Weisman 1992). Weisman (1972), for example, rather than using the notion of *acceptance of death,* encourages the concept of **appropriate death.** Such a death means that the person has died in a fashion that resembles as much as possible the way that he or she wished to die. To date, the effects of age, gender, ethnic background, and one's life experience have not been studied as they apply to Kübler-Ross's stage theory (Kastenbaum 1991). Remember as well that the process of dying may be very strongly influenced by the behavior and attitudes of those persons in the dying individual's social milieu.

Consider the inhabitants of the Etal Island in the Caroline Islands (Micronesia). They have no formal theory of dying, yet it is important to them that some resolution be achieved. "Dying is the last important social act an old person can perform. Past conflicts must be resolved. Also, this is the time for the old person to make a final decision about the disposition of property" (Nason 1981, p. 170).

Islanders believe that the dying should pass on in an atmosphere of peace and solitude. A new ancestor, pleased with attention and respect provided by kin while he or she was alive, is likely to aid and protect islanders. On the other hand, a person who dies angry or dissatisfied with the inattention of relatives might take revenge on them. Actually, an older person might be driven to suicide to make a public protest against ill treatment by relatives. To prevent this, relatives may stay constantly with the dying person. Such a suicide would bring public shame on the relatives and would cause trouble with the final settling of the estate, because suicides often make no final distribution of their property (Nason 1981). Just the threat of suicide by a dying person (or any elder, for that matter) can quickly bring about a change in relations with extended kin members.

Kübler-Ross's work has been of tremendous value in sensitizing people to the needs and rights of the dying. Shortcomings in the application of her work or its uncritical acceptance by some should not lead to a dismissal of her many useful insights or of the need for further research in this area (Kastenbaum 1991). Kübler-Ross argues that the physician can help the patient reach a calm acceptance of death. Schulz (1978) summarizes a body of literature that finds that physicians avoid patients once they begin to die. The nature and impact of the doctor/dying patient relationship on the dying process would seem an area ripe for additional research.

THE WHERE OF DYING

Today, most people die in health care institutions of one kind or another. In hospitals, rest homes, and nursing homes, the dying process has become bureaucratized and, to a great extent, depersonalized. Such institutions, while treating the terminally ill, also isolate them from the rest of society. These institutions have routinized the handling of death for their own benefit. This may reduce disturbance and disruption for the institution. Standardized procedures render death nearly invisible. To protect relatives and other visitors, bodies may not be removed during visiting hours. When death appears imminent, the patient may be moved to a private room to protect other residents.

Many people, health professionals and laypeople alike, are aware of the depersonalized treatment provided to the terminally ill in many health facilities. On the basis of their study of individuals in four ethnoracial communities in Los Angeles, Kalish and Reynolds (1976) report that most people of all ages would prefer to die at home, particularly those under age 40 and those over age 59. A recent Gallup

Poll (1996) found that 88 percent of adults surveyed would prefer to die in their own home or that of a family member if they were faced with a terminal illness.

Although many dying patients and their families wish for death in the home, the wish is not often realized. Even when plans for home death have been made, they may be precluded by many factors, the most prominent of which appears to be the emotional and physical exhaustion of the family (Groth-Junker & McCusker 1983).

Options for caring for the dying are now available. One such option, called *hospice,* combines the technical expertise for caring for the ill that is available in health care bureaucracies with the personalized attention of home care. The most widely known is St. Christopher's Hospice in London, founded by Dr. Cicily Saunders.

A hospice is not a place; rather, it is a concept of care that combines various elements. It emphasizes *palliative care* rather than cure. Control of pain and distressing symptoms is viewed as a treatment goal in its own right. If a patient's preoccupation with suffering is of such intensity that everything else in life is excluded, then self-control, independence, human dignity, and interpersonal relations are sacrificed. Each dying individual is seen as a part of a family whose total well-being and life-style may be affected by the circumstance of having a terminally ill member. Caring does not stop when the individual dies, but the hospice continues to help the family during bereavement. The hospice concept also views the home as a suitable domain for providing care. An interdisciplinary team of professionals from the fields of medicine, nursing, social work, and counseling assist hospice workers in the provision of care.

The first hospice in the United States became operative in 1974. Known as the Connecticut Hospice (originally Hospice, Inc.), it provides both inpatient and home care services. Since its inception, hospice programs have developed in every state in the nation. They now take several forms in their organization. Home care programs have been preferred in the United States. The Connecticut Hospice began as a home care program and later added an "inpatient" facility. Some hospitals are developing hospice care units within their walls; others seek to deliver hospice care in separate freestanding facilities. Recently, some nursing homes have begun to contract with hospice programs to provide services for eligible terminally ill residents (Keay & Schonwetter 1998; Knight 1998).

In the United States, hospice has evolved from a fringe alternative led by a group of idealistic professionals and volunteers to an accepted mainstream approach to terminal care (Tehan 1985). Much of this change was precipitated by the National Hospice Study (NHS) and legislation that allows terminally ill adults over the age of 65 to receive Medicare reimbursable services from certified hospice programs.

Conducted between 1980 and 1984, the NHS was spawned by a concern for the feasibility of a hospice Medicare benefit (Greer & Mor 1985). In general, results of the study demonstrate that hospice care tends to be less expensive than traditional hospital care and that hospice patients spend more time at home during the course of their terminal illness.

Medical anthropologist Robert Buckingham and colleagues (1976) have, through participant observation, compared the relative merits of standard hospital versus hospice care for the dying. Using an elaborate and deceptive scheme that was aided by physicians, Buckingham played the role of a cancer patient. He prepared himself in a number of ways before entering the hospital. He went on a severe six-month diet and lost 22 pounds from his already spare frame. Exposure to ultraviolet rays made it appear that he had undergone cancer radiation therapy. Puncture marks from intravenous needles on his hands and arms indicated that he had also had chemotherapy cancer treatment. A cooperative surgeon performed minor surgery on him in order to produce biopsy scars, indicating that exploratory surgery had been performed. Buckingham reviewed medical charts and maintained close contact with patients dying of cancer of the pancreas. He was thus able to observe and imitate suitable behavior. A patchy beard and the results of several days of not washing or shaving completed the picture. He spent two days in the holding unit, four days on a surgical care ward, and four days on the hospice or palliative care ward of Royal Victoria Hospital in Montreal.

Buckingham's findings lend empirical support to the assumption that the hospice system of care for the terminally ill is effective. He lists certain hospital staff practices that were observed in the surgical care ward that should be sources of concern in attempting to develop an optimal environment for the dying. These practices are as follows:

1. The tradition of physicians making their patient rounds in groups (This fostered social and medical discussion between the doctors but completely prevented doctor/patient communication on any but the most superficial level.)
2. The lack of eye contact between staff members and patient (Patients walked in the halls close to the walls, greetings were rare, and staff frequently crossed to the other side of the hall and walked by with heads averted.)
3. The reference to a patient by the name of his or her disease rather than by the name of the person
4. The accentuation of negative aspects of a patient's condition
5. The lack of affection given to the complacent patient
6. The discontinuity of communication among medical and nursing staff

Staff/patient and staff/family relationships were qualitatively different on the hospice care ward. Buckingham and associates (1976) describe Buckingham's arrival on this ward as follows:

> The initial nursing interview was conducted by a nurse who introduced herself by name, sat down so that her eyes were on a level with [the patient's] and proceeded to listen. There was no hurry, her questions flowed from [the patient's] previous answers, and there was acceptance of the expression of his concerns. She asked questions such as "What do you like to eat?" and "Is there anything special you like to do?"
>
> In the hospice care unit Buckingham observed relatives inquiring for the doctor five times. On each occasion the doctor was reached and either came or

spoke to the family on the phone…families also spent much time at the bedside participating in the care of the patient. They changed the bed linen, washed and fed the patient, brought the urinal and plumped the pillows frequently. The staff encouraged the family to experience the meaning of death by allowing them to help in the care of the dying. (pp. 1213–1214)

A greater effort is necessary to accomplish total care of the terminally ill. Four observations made by Buckingham (Buckingham et al. 1976) that are often overlooked by health care professionals may facilitate consummating the total care effort:

1. The sharing and help provided by other terminally ill adults form a powerful social support system for patients with terminal disease.
2. The need for the terminally ill person to give and thus retain his or her individuality should be recognized.
3. The care given by families is a source of support for dying individuals that must be recognized and emphasized.
4. The interest and care given by student nurses and volunteers is important, particularly in bringing the person out of the patient.

TERMINATION OF TREATMENT

Who Decides?

Central issues concerning who decides or exerts control in matters related to death and dying are exemplified in a series of recent court cases about the access of older people to life-prolonging medical treatments. One such case worthy of attention here is that of Earle Spring (Kart 1981).

Earle Spring was born in 1901. In his working years, he was a chemist and metallurgist at a tool-and-die plant in Greenfield, Massachusetts. He was an avid outdoorsman who retired in 1966. In November 1977, Spring hurt his foot, developed an infection, and was hospitalized. He subsequently suffered pneumonia and then developed kidney failure and nearly died. Early in 1978, he was transferred to a hospital closer to his home, where hemodialysis treatments began. Within several weeks, Spring was returned to his home, where he received dialysis treatments three times a week, on an outpatient basis, at a private facility in the community.

According to the court record, Spring began showing signs of mental deterioration in conjunction with his progressive kidney failure. At home, he became destructive and was unable to care for himself. After being diagnosed as having chronic organic brain syndrome, he was admitted to a nursing home. By early 1979, his mental deterioration had continued to the point that he failed to recognize his wife and son. Yet he was ambulatory and, except for his kidney failure, in good physical condition.

On January 25, 1979, Spring's son and wife petitioned a local probate court for an order that hemodialysis treatments be terminated. The medical consensus was that Spring might live for four or five weeks following the termination of these treatments. The probate judge appointed a guardian for Spring in this case, who opposed the petition. Yet, in May 1979, the judge ordered the temporary guardian to "refrain from authorizing any further life-prolonging medical treatment." The guardian appealed; but after a stay of the order, the judge ruled that the attending physician, together with the wife and son, were to make the decision to continue or terminate the dialysis treatments.

The guardian appealed this decision to the Appeals Court of Massachusetts, where it was affirmed. A further appeal was made to the Massachusetts Supreme Judicial Court, where, on May 13, 1980 (approximately one month after Earle Spring's death), it was reversed and remanded to the lower court. The Massachusetts Supreme Judicial Court acknowledged the substance of the lower court's decision, yet opined that the ultimate decision-making responsibility should not have been shifted away from the probate court by delegating the decision to continue or terminate care to the physician and Spring's wife and son.

Who should decide in this matter? The court itself? The physicians? Spring's family members? What about Earle Spring himself? A close examination of some underlying issues in this case is noteworthy. A careful reading of the transcript of the probate court's hearing in the matter of Earle Spring shows that the court found that Spring would "if competent, choose not to receive the life-prolonging treatment." In so finding, the court followed a standard applied in another Massachusetts case, *Superintendent of Belchertown State School* v. *Saikewicz* (370 N.E. 2d 417, 1977), and invoked the principle of **substitute judgment.**

Joseph Saikewicz was 67 years old, had a mental age of approximately 3 years, and had been a resident of the Belchertown State School for 48 years. He was well nourished and ambulatory, could make his wishes known through gestures and grunts, but was suffering from leukemia. In April 1976, the superintendent of the school filed a petition in local probate court asking for the appointment of a guardian for purposes of making a decision about Saikewicz's care and treatment for the leukemia. The judge did so, and the guardian filed a report with the court stating that the illness was incurable, that the indicated treatment would cause adverse side effects and discomfort, and that Saikewicz was incapable of understanding the treatment. In sum, it was the view of the guardian that the negative aspects of the treatment situation outweighed the uncertain and clearly limited extension of life the treatment could bring; in the guardian's opinion, treating Saikewicz would not be in his best interests.

In May 1976, the probate judge entered an order agreeing with the guardian; the Massachusetts Supreme Judicial Court concurred, and later that summer, Joseph Saikewicz died without pain. It is noteworthy that in November of that year, the Supreme Judicial Court handed down a written decision in the Saikewicz case. In this written opinion, the court argued that, like competent persons, incompetents must also have the right to refuse medical treatment. In making this argument, the court recognized what may currently be a widely held view—that medical treatment does not always further the best interests of the patient. The central problem the court faced, however, was in deciding how to determine what is in the best interest of an incompetent person (Glantz & Swazey 1979). The standard adopted was the substitute judgment test, which, according to the court, seeks "to determine with as much accuracy as possible the wants and needs of the individual involved."

In the case of Joseph Saikewicz, the use of the substitute judgment test would seem a "legal fiction" (Glantz & Swazey 1979). How is it possible to know the wishes of a 67-year-old man who has been severely retarded all his life? In effect, the court substituted its own judgment for that of the incompetent person. Earle Spring's case, however, is another matter. He was competent for the greater part of his adult life. Nevertheless, how did the *Spring* court ascertain that "if competent, Spring would choose not to receive the life-sustaining treatment"? Mr. Spring had never stated his preference regarding continuing or terminating life-sustaining medical treatment.

The probate court substituted the judgment of Earle Spring's wife, who indicated that, on the basis of their long years of marriage, she believed "he wouldn't want to live." In doing so, the court employed a variant of the substitute judgment standard used by the Supreme Court of New Jersey *In re Quinlan* (355 A. 2d 647, 1976). Karen Quinlan was an adult woman in a persistent vegetative state from which her physicians felt she could not recover. Her father sought to be appointed her guardian so that he could have the power to authorize the discontinuance of all extraordinary medical procedures for sustaining his daughter's vital processes. The *Quinlan* court assumed that, if Karen were competent and perceptive of her irreversible condition, "she could effectively decide upon discontinuance of the life-sustaining apparatus, even if it meant the prospect of natural death." Because the patient was not competent, the court concluded that her father and other family members, with the concurrence of a hospital ethics committee, could assert this decision for her.

This variant of the substitute judgment test was applied by the probate court in the *Spring* case, even though Spring's wife could offer no evidence in support of her conclusion about his wishes. No evidence was put forth that might provide a basis for believing that Earle Spring would reject life-sustaining medical treatment. Nothing was made of the fact that when Spring first began hemodialysis treatments, before he was believed to be incompetent, he cooperated in taking these treatments. In fact, the court took testimony from family members that Earle Spring's activity level had fallen off considerably before the diagnosis of organic brain syndrome. He was no longer able to hunt and fish, as was the case in his younger years. This is precisely what some gerontologists argue is supposed to happen in old age. From this view, activity reduction in the later years is natural, expected, and even looked forward to by the aging.

The Massachusetts Supreme Judicial Court rejected the lower court's delegation of authority to withhold life-sustaining medical treatment to Earle Spring's wife, family, and physicians. In effect, the higher court rejected the approach employed in the *Quinlan* case and reasserted the standard employed in the *Saikewicz* case: "When a court is properly presented with the legal question, whether treatment may be withheld, it must decide the question and not delegate it to some private person or group" (Mass., 405 N.E. 2d 115, 122).

Is there basis in relevant literature for rejecting the substitute judgment of family members for that of an incompetent organic brain syndrome patient? Some would say yes. Several papers suggest that great stress is felt by family members of organic brain syndrome patients (Mace, Rabins, & Lucas 1980; Schneider & Garron 1980). Mace and colleagues report that more than 90 percent of the families they studied showed anger—at the situation, the patient, other family members, or professionals—as a response to the presence of a dementia patient in the family. Other stress responses include depression, grief, conflict with family members, withdrawal from social activity, and the like. Such research suggests that family members may not be in the best position to substitute their judgment for that of an incompetent in the question of whether to continue life-sustaining medical treatment.

Some would argue that the decision about whether to continue medical treatment in cases like Spring, Saikewicz, and Quinlan should be based on quality-of-life issues. Defining the issue in these terms may serve to exclude physicians, given that there is nothing inherently medical about a quality-of-life decision. Rather, it seems, as some have indicated, cases that raise quality-of-life questions are the ones that need to be resolved by a court of law.

Traditionally, decisions about how long to maintain a hopeless patient have been made by the physician, sometimes in concert with family members, and less frequently with input from the dying person. Many dying patients, particularly those who are very old and extremely deteriorated, have no input whatsoever into decisions about their own death. There have been several recent attempts to better represent the patient's wishes in such a decision through the use of **advanced directives (AD)**.

Living wills, sometimes referred to as *instructional advance directives,* are being used by some to specify the conditions under which they would prefer not to be subjected to extraordinary measures to keep them alive. In all 50 states and the District of Columbia, living wills have legal standing. With them, a competent person can instruct a physician not to use heroic measures to prolong life when "there is no reasonable expectation of recovery from physical or mental disability."

Still, controversy exists over the meaning and application of the document. In particular, some argue, difficulties may arise out of uncertainties of clinical prognosis that allow for misinterpretation of the living will. Two safeguards are in order. First, the details of the living will should be discussed with the personal physician at the time it is completed. This may lessen the chances of misinterpretation. If the physician refuses to carry out the wishes expressed in the will, the individual who wrote the will should consider finding another doctor. Second, the will should name someone who can interpret the exact wishes of the writer should he or she ever be unable to express them. This provision, more commonly known as a *Durable Power of Attorney for Health Care (DPAHC),* is afforded in the proxy advance directive. It is especially important should the writer become incompetent. Such a person can then make decisions as to specific measures to be taken or not taken on the writer's behalf. Presently, over 30 states recognize the DPAHC.

The major purpose of the Patient Self-Determination Act (PSDA) is to inform patients of their right to participate in decisions about the use of life-sustaining medical treatment and to execute advance directives. Under this federal law, implemented in 1991, designated health care institutions receiving Medicare and/or Medicaid funding must inform their adult patients in writing about:

1. Their right under state law to take part in medical decisions including accepting or rejecting medical and surgical treatment;
2. Their right under state law to execute advance directives such as a living will or durable power of attorney for health care; and
3. The policies and procedures the institution has formulated to honor these rights. (Fulton & Metress 1995)

The law requires the institutions (which include hospitals, skilled nursing facilities, home health agencies, and health maintenance organizations) to provide this information to patients upon admission to their programs. Additionally, they must document in the medical record whether a patient has an AD. In the case of a hospital or skilled nursing facility, an existing AD must be made part of the patient's medical record.

Removal of Food and Fluids

As Steinbock (1983) indicates, a substantial body of legal opinion views the disconnection of all life-support apparatus from irreversibly comatose patients as morally and legally permissible. Nevertheless, many fear that such permissiveness leads to the "slippery slope" whereby the lives of all individuals who are terminally ill and disabled are endangered. Steinbock (1983) asks, for example, "If it is permissible to remove a feeding tube from a permanently comatose patient, why not from a barely conscious, senile and terminal patient?"

In January 1985, the Supreme Court of New Jersey ruled that artificial feeding, like other life-sustaining treatment, may be withheld or withdrawn from an incompetent patient if it represents a disproportionate burden and would have been refused by the patient under the circumstances. This decision was made in the case of Claire Conroy, an 84-year-old nursing-home resident who had suffered irreversible physical and mental impairments. She could move to a minor extent, she did groan, and she sometimes smiled in response to certain physical stimuli. She had no cognitive ability and was unaware of her surroundings.

She had been placed in a nursing home after having been declared incompetent. Eventually, she was transferred to a hospital for treatment of a gangrenous leg (a complication of her diabetes). Amputation was recommended, but Ms. Conroy's nephew, who was her legal guardian, refused consent. He maintained that she would have refused treatment. Surgery was not performed, but while she was in the hospital, a nasogastric tube was inserted. Her nephew requested that its use be discontinued in the hospital and, likewise, in the nursing home where she eventually returned. On both requests, permission was denied by her attending physician.

Conroy's nephew filed suit to obtain court permission to remove her feeding tube. A lower court granted permission. The decision was appealed and reversed by the appellate court in a declaration that termination of feeding constituted homicide. Conroy died during the appeal with the nasogastric tube still in place. Her guardian carried the case to the state supreme court.

The New Jersey Supreme Court ruling is consistent with that of the *Barber* case decided by the California Court of Appeals in 1983. In this case, the cessation of intravenous feeding was equated with the removal of a respirator. The *Conroy* case represents the first time that a state supreme court eliminated a distinction between artificial feeding and other artificial life supports (Nevins 1986). Four years later, in the now well-known and much discussed *Cruzan* case, the United States Supreme Court agreed that artificial feeding and hydration constituted medical treatment that could be refused.

Nancy Cruzan, a young woman grievously injured in an automobile accident, had been unconscious and in a persistent vegetative state for more than four years when her parents requested that her feeding tube be removed. The Missouri Supreme Court had denied this request, emphasizing the lack of clear and convincing evidence of Cruzan's own wishes in this matter. At the same time, the court also stated that artificial feeding or hydration could not be refused in Missouri. The importance of advance directives was seemingly underscored by the United States Supreme Court's upholding of the state of Missouri's right to demand evidence that treatment cessation is what the patient would choose for herself or himself. Nancy Cruzan had never executed an advance directive. Her parents ultimately prevailed when they returned to the Missouri court with several new witnesses who testified that conversations with the young woman convinced them that, under the circumstances, she would not want treatment of any kind, including feeding or hydration. Her feeding tube was removed, and Cruzan died, after having been unconscious for almost eight years.

While recognizing the legal rights of all patients to self-determination, the New Jersey court, in the *Conroy* case, also imposed very strict requirements in providing previously competent patients the right to exercise treatment refusal by proxy. Through the application of a "best-interest test," the court must ascertain the patient's known or suspected personal attitude toward life-sustaining treatment and the burden of pain.

The New Jersey court apparently felt a special duty to protect the rights of the now-incompetent nursing-home resident. It maintains that the resident's guardian, next of kin, the attending physician, two consulting physicians (unaffiliated with the nursing home) and the state Office of the Ombudsman for the Institutionalized Elderly must all concur in the decision to remove life-sustaining treatment. The procedural portion of the New Jersey court decision has received considerable criticism on the basis that it fosters a climate of distrust, is difficult to implement, and artificially distinguishes between nursing-home residents and hospital patients (Annas 1985a, 1985b; Nevins 1985, 1986; Olins 1986).

The court does heavily involve the state ombudsman, an office charged with guarding against and investigating allegations of elder abuse in conjunction with the state's Elder Abuse Statute. The ombudsman must be notified before any such decision to terminate treatment is rendered and must consider every such decision as a possible case of abuse.

The court asserts that special precautions are necessary because elderly nursing-home residents present special problems. Indeed, the court's holding is restricted to nursing-home residents. Reasons cited are the residents' average age, their general lack of next of kin, the limited role of physicians in nursing homes, reports of inhuman treatment and understaffing in nursing homes, and the less urgent decision making that occurs within these facilities allowing for more time to review options.

It has been held by others that nursing-home–based decisions can confound ethical considerations in a number of ways (Besdine 1983):

1. Personal autonomy may be lost because nursing-home admission might result in a new physician providing care rather than one who has previously treated the resident and is familiar with the resident's wishes.
2. The resident may view that life is diminished by virtue of entry into the nursing home.
3. The possibility of dementing illness does not allow for informed consent.
4. The typical advanced age of the residents may influence decisions concerning treatment limitations.

Annas (1985b) charges that the court's strict differentiation between nursing-home residents and hospital patients regarding life-sustaining treatment decisions is artificial. He states that almost all nursing-home residents will be transferred to hospitals when invasive treatment is required. He adds that if ombudsman intervention is appropriate, it should apply in both settings. More appropriately, the ombudsman should be available to investigate cases of suspected abuse. Otherwise, the Conroy approach requires that time be wasted on cases that do not need investigation. Annas also posits that the court decision may create confusion in its applicability to nursing-home residents who are temporarily hospitalized.

Changes in Medicare funding are moving patients from hospitals to nursing homes "sooner and sicker." Although differences exist, problems of the two populations promise to become more similar. Nevins concludes, "So although their rhythms may differ, the two populations and their problems are becoming more homogeneous. No doubt differences exist, but to devise a totally new mechanism to resolve the same clinical issues depending on the locus of decision-making is unnecessary and unwise" (1986, p. 143).

The court's ruling is binding only in New Jersey, and how it influences decision making there rests largely with how the ombudsman's office interprets and applies the court's rulings in the Conroy case. Although the mechanism set forth to allow incompetent patients to exercise the right to refuse treatment is cumbersome and restrictive, it stands as testimony to a sensitive concern for human dignity and autonomy for people of all ages.

Physician-Assisted Suicide

The United States Supreme Court in 1997 ruled that there is no constitutional right to physician-assisted suicide (PAS) whereby a physician intentionally acts to help a terminally ill person die. In so ruling, the Court did not deny individual states the right to legislate the controversial practice. As evidenced by the passage of Oregon's Death with Dignity Act, states clearly are in a position to permit PAS. Under Oregon's Act, a physician may write a terminally ill person a prescription for a lethal dosage of medication.

While the Supreme Court also ruled that a state can ban PAS, it withheld from states the right to ban the heavy sedation of a terminally ill person even if it hastens that person's death. Known as *terminal sedation,* the deliverance of certain medications to patients with intolerable symptoms, such as intractable pain, may induce a coma. The unconscious person cannot eat and thus dies from a lack of food and water. Terminal sedation can shorten a person's life by hours, days, or weeks. Some view this practice as "slow euthanasia" or covert physician-assisted suicide (Orentlicher 1997). Proponents of terminal sedation argue that the intent is not to cause the person's death; rather, it is to relieve suffering.

SUMMARY

Death is something that must inevitably be faced by everyone. The deaths of friends, relatives, and others are more frequent occurrences for older adults. Yet, death may have different meanings for people of different ages. Two meanings of death with particular significance for the elderly include death as an organizer of time and death as loss.

Bereavement refers to the state of having sustained a loss, whereas *grief* is a term that describes the reaction to loss. In part, this reaction is shaped by cultural norms and experiences. *Mourning,* the culturally prescribed manner in which grief is managed, varies from group to group within a society as well as between societies. A wide variety of factors appear to exert influence on the resolution of grief.

A number of conceptualizations of the dying process have been offered as attempts to understand this final stage of life. Dying has been described as a *trajectory,* a *career,* and a *five-stage process.* It is hoped that added understanding of the dying process will allow health care professionals and family members to provide for personalized care to the dying.

Today, most people die in health care institutions. One response to this practice is the development of hospice—a new caring community that provides medical and psychosocial care to the dying and their bereaved family members. The Earle Spring case involves the question of whether the decision to continue life-

UCC Health Sciences Brookfield

Customer name: Hennessy, Kathleen Ag

Title: The realities of aging : an introduction
gerontology / Cary S. Kart, Jennifer M. Kinne
ID: 0009357150
Due: 21-11-08

Total items: 1
07/11/2008 14:20

Please retain this receipt

prolonging medical treatments should be in the hands of the individual, the family, the physicians, or the courts. This is especially problematic in cases involving incompetent persons. Advance directives, such as a living will, represent a possible solution to such dilemmas in the future.

Recently, the morality of withholding food and hydration in the case of severely demented or comatose elderly has emerged. Do such provisions constitute life-sustaining medical treatment? In the case of Claire Conroy, the Supreme Court of New Jersey ruled that artificial feeding, like other life-sustaining medical treatment, may be withheld from an incompetent person if it represents a disproportionate burden. In 1997, The U.S. Supreme Court ruled that there is no constitutional right to physician-assisted suicide (PAS), while at the same time it allowed states the right to permit the practice. The Court also ruled that states cannot ban the heavy sedation of a terminally ill person even if it hastens that person's death.

STUDY QUESTIONS

1. Explain how the meanings individuals give to death vary as a function of age. Describe the two meanings of death found to have particular significance for the elderly.

2. Note some symptoms associated with the grieving process. Differentiate *bereavement, grief,* and *mourning.*

3. What factors might influence the expression of grief among the elderly? What is meant by a *devious pattern of grief?* Note various factors that might influence the resolution of grief.

4. Define the *dying trajectory.* What role does perception play in staff and patient definitions of the dying trajectory? What cues contribute to the perception of the dying trajectory?

5. Discuss Gustafson's concept of dying as a career timetable. How is bargaining used to manipulate the timetable?

6. List and explain the five stages of the dying process as conceptualized by Elisabeth Kübler-Ross. What has been the reaction to the stage theory of dying?

7. Define *hospice,* tracing its development in the United States. Explain how hospice provides care for the terminally ill person and his or her family.

8. Discuss the conflicting private and public interests involved in decisions about the continuance of life-prolonging medical treatments. Use the *Spring* and *Saikewicz* cases in your answer.

9. Explain the purpose of advance directives such as the living will. What are the arguments against the use of these instruments?

10. Present an overview of the *Conroy* case. What has been the reaction to the Supreme Court of New Jersey's ruling in this case?

REFERENCES

Annas, G. (1985a). Fashion and freedom: When artificial feeding should be withdrawn. *American Journal of Public Health, 75,* 685.

Annas, G. (1985b). When procedures limit rights: From Quinlan to Conroy. *Hastings Center Report, 15,* 24–26.

Back, K. (1965). Meaning of time in later life. *Journal of Genetic Psychology, 109*, 9–25.

Besdine, R. (1983). Decisions to withhold treatment from nursing home residents. *Journal of the American Geriatrics Society, 31*, 602.

Bluebond-Langner, M. (1974). I know, do you? Awareness and communication in terminally ill children. In B. Schoenberg & associates (Eds.), *Anticipated grief.* New York: Columbia University Press.

Bluebond-Langner, M. (1977). Meanings of death to children. In H. Feifel (Ed.), *New meanings of death.* New York: McGraw-Hill.

Bluebond-Langner, M. (1989). World's of dying children and their well siblings. *Death Studies, 13*, 1–6.

Bromberg, S., & Cassel, C. (1983). Suicide in the elderly: The limits of paternalism. *Journal of the American Geriatrics Society, 31*, 698–703.

Buckingham, R., Lack, S., Mount, B., MacLean, L., & Collins, J. (1976). Living with the dying. *Canadian Medical Association Journal, 115*, 1211–1215.

Corr, C. (1992). A task-based approach to coping with dying. *Omega, 24*, 81–94.

Corr, C. (1993). Coping with dying: Lessons that we should learn and should not learn from the work of Elisabeth Kübler-Ross. *Death Studies, 17*, 69–83.

Cytron, B. D. (1993). To honor the dead and comfort the mourners: Traditions in Judaism. In D. P. Irish, K. F. Lundquist, & V. J. Nelsen (Eds.), *Ethnic variations in dying, death and grief: Diversity in universality.* Washington, DC: Taylor & Francis.

Feigenberg, L. (1977). *Terminalvard.* Lund: Liber Laromedel.

Frederick, J. (1976). Grief as a disease process. *Omega, 7*, 297–306.

Frederick, J. (1982–83). The biochemistry of bereavement: Possible basis for chemotherapy. *Omega, 13*, 295–304.

Friedman, H., & DiMatteo, M. (1982). Interpersonal issues in health care: Healing as an interpersonal process. In H. Friedman & M. DiMatteo (Eds.), *Interpersonal issues in health care.* New York: Academic.

Fulton, G., & Metress, E. (1995). *Perspectives on death and dying.* Boston: Jones & Bartlett.

Gallup Poll. (1996). *Knowledge and attitudes related to hospice care: Conducted for the National Hospice Organization.* Princeton, NJ: Gallup.

Glantz, L., & Swazey, J. (1979, January). Decisions not to treat: The Saikewicz case and its aftermath. *Forum on Medicine*, pp. 22–32.

Glaser, B., & Strauss, A. (1966). *Awareness of dying.* Chicago: Aldine.

Glaser, B., & Strauss, A. (1968). *Time for dying.* Chicago: Aldine.

Goodstein, R. (1984). Grief reactions and the elderly. *Carrier Letter, 99*, 1–5.

Gorer, G. (1965). *Death, grief and mourning.* New York: Doubleday.

Greenblatt, J. (1978). The grieving spouse. *American Journal of Psychiatry, 135*, 43–47.

Greer, D., & Mor, V. (1985). How Medicare is altering the hospice movement. *Hastings Center Report, 15*, 5–9.

Groth-Junker, A., & McCusker, J. (1983). Where do elderly patients prefer to die? Place of death and patient characteristics of 100 elderly patients under the care of a home health care team. *Journal of the American Geriatrics Society, 31*, 457–461.

Gustafson, E. (1972). Dying: The career of the nursing home patient. *Journal of Health and Social Behavior, 13*, 226–235.

Helsing, G., & Szklo, M. (1981). Mortality after bereavement. *American Journal of Epidemiology, 114*, 41–52.

Kalish, R. (1976). Death and dying in a social context. In R. Binstock & E. Shanas (Eds.), *Handbook of aging and the social sciences.* New York: Van Nostrand Reinhold.

Kalish, R., & Reynolds, D. (1976). *Death and ethnicity: A psychocultural study.* Los Angeles: University of Southern California Press.

Kart, C. (1981). In the matter of Earle Spring: Some thought on one court's approach to senility. *Gerontologist, 21*, 417–423.

Kastenbaum, R. (1991). *Death, society and human experience.* Columbus, OH: Charles E. Merrill.

Keay, T., & Schonwetter, R. (1998). Hospice care in the nursing home. *American Family Physician, 57*, 491–494.

Keddie, K. (1977). Pathological mourning after the death of a domestic pet. *British Journal of Psychiatry, 139*, 21–25.

Knight, A. (1998). The integration of hospice programs in nursing homes. *American Family Physician, 57*, 424–425.

Kübler-Ross, E. (1969). *On death and dying.* New York: Macmillan.

Kübler-Ross, E. (1974). *Questions and answers on death and dying.* New York: Macmillan.

Levav, I. (1982). Mortality and psychopathology following the death of an adult child: An epidemiological review. *Israel Journal of Psychiatry and Related Sciences, 19*, 23–38.

Lieberman, S. (1978). Nineteen cases of morbid grief. *British Journal of Psychiatry, 132,* 159–163.

Lindemann, E. (1944). Symptomatology and management of acute grief. *American Journal of Psychiatry, 101,* 141–148.

Mace, N., Rabins, P., & Lucas, M. (1980). *Areas of stress on families of dementia patients.* Paper presented at the annual meeting of the Gerontological Society of America, San Diego, CA.

Maris, R. (1981). *Pathways to suicide.* Baltimore: Johns Hopkins University Press.

Masamba, J., & Kalish, R. (1976). Death and bereavement: The role of the Black church. *Omega, 7* (1), 23–34.

McIntire, M., Angle, C., & Struempl, L. (1972). The concept of death in Midwestern children and youth. *American Journal of Diseases of Children, 123,* 527–532.

McKellin, W. H. (1985). Passing away and loss of life: Aging and death among the Managalase of Papua New Guinea. In D. A. Counts & D. R. Counts (Eds.), *Aging and its transformations: Moving toward death in pacific societies.* Pittsburgh, PA: University of Pittsburgh Press.

Metzger, A. (1979). A Q-methodological study of the Kubler-Ross stage theory. *Omega, 10,* 291–302.

Nagy, M. (1959). The child's theories concerning death. In H. Feifel (Ed.), *The meaning of death.* New York: McGraw-Hill.

Nason, J. D. (1981). Respected elder or old person: Aging in a micronesian community. In P. T. Amoss & S. Harrell (Eds.), *Other ways of growing old: Anthropological perspectives.* Stanford, CA: Stanford University Press.

Nevins, M. (1985). Big brother at the bedside. *New Jersey Medicine, 82,* 950.

Nevins, M. (1986). Analysis of the Supreme Court of New Jersey's decision in the Claire Conroy case. *Journal of the American Geriatrics Society, 34,* 140–143.

Olins, N. (1986). Feeding decisions for incompetent patients. *Journal of the American Geriatrics Society, 34,* 313–317.

Orentlicher, D. (1997). The Supreme Court and physician assisted suicide. *New England Journal of Medicine, 337,* 1236–1239.

Osgood, N. (1995). Assisted suicide and older people—a deadly combination: Ethical problems in permitting assisted suicide. *Issues in Law and Medicine, 10,* 415–435.

Osterweis, M. (1985). Bereavement and the elderly. *Aging, 348,* 8–13.

Osterweis, M., Solomon, F., & Green, M. (1984). *Bereavement: Reactions, consequences and care: A report of the Institute of Medicine.* Washington, DC: National Academy Press.

Robbins, L., West, P., & Murphy, G. (1977). The high rate of suicide in older white men: A study testing ten hypotheses. *Social Psychiatry, 12,* 1–20.

Roth, J. (1963). *Timetables.* Indianapolis, IN: Bobbs-Merrill.

Rowland, K. (1977). Environmental events predicting death for the elderly. *Psychological Bulletin, 84,* 349–372.

Schneider, A., & Garron, D. (1980). *Problems of families in recognizing and coping with dementing disease.* Paper presented at the annual meeting of the Gerontological Society of America, San Diego, CA.

Schulz, R. (1978). *The psychology of death, dying and bereavement.* Reading, MA: Addison-Wesley.

Schulz, R., & Aderman, D. (1974). Clinical research and the stages of dying. *Omega, 5,* 137–144.

Shneidman, E. (1980). *Voices of death.* New York: Harper & Row.

Steinbock, B. (1983). The removal of Mr. Herbert's feeding tube. *Hastings Center Report, 13,* 13–16.

Tehan, C. (1985). Has success spoiled hospice? *Hastings Center Report, 15,* 10–13.

Weisman, A. (1972). *On dying and denying.* New York: Behavioral Publications.

Weisman, A. (1992). Commentary on Corr's "A task-based approach to coping with dying." *Omega, 24,* 95–96.

EPILOGUE

Education and Careers
in the Field of Gerontology

It is an exciting time to be a student of gerontology. Whether reading this book because of personal interest, as part of a course for a discipline-specific degree (e.g., nursing, psychology, sociology, social work), or to obtain a degree or other credential in aging, the readers of this book are among an increasing number of students who are learning about the challenges of an aging society. Many of the challenges confronting older adults and U.S. society have been discussed in the previous chapters. What has not been discussed are the educational choices and subsequent career opportunities that are available for students who are interested in, and knowledgeable about, older adults.

Peterson (1990) defined *educational gerontology* as "an attempt to apply what is currently known about aging and education in order to extend the healthy and productive years and improve the quality of life for older people" (p. 3). Included in educational gerontology are efforts to instruct older adults themselves, efforts to instruct other audiences about older adults, and instruction for professionals and practitioners who will work with and on behalf of older adults. Peterson's definition illustrates the richness of educational gerontology. It does not, however, give any hint of a number of educational and training issues that remain controversial within the field. The purpose of this epilogue is to provide an overview of the diverse educational and employment opportunities that exist for students of gerontology. Students who plan to pursue careers in the field will be able to gain a better understanding of the options that are available to them. Students who are not actively pursuing careers in gerontology might become aware of some of the ways in which knowledge of aging and gerontology could result in increased opportunities within their chosen discipline or profession.

EDUCATIONAL OPPORTUNITIES: GERONTOLOGICAL SPECIALISTS VERSUS GERONTOLOGISTS

More opportunities exist today than ever before to obtain formal training in gerontology. Friedsam (1995) reports that a national survey conducted in 1957 found that 52 colleges and universities offered a total of 75 courses in social geron-tology (White House Conference on Aging 1960). Although these researchers did not include community colleges in their sample, thereby underestimating the total number of courses that were available, the increase in educational opportunities since that time is nonetheless remarkable. Data collected by the Association for Ger-ontology in Higher Education (AGHE) in 1992 revealed that more than 50 percent of colleges, universities, and community colleges offered gerontology courses for credit, and almost one-fourth offered classes that result in some type of formal aca-demic recognition (Peterson, Wendt, & Douglass 1994). When compared to similar data collected by AGHE in 1985, the 1992 data revealed a 23 percent increase in the number of institutions that offered courses in gerontology, geriatrics, or aging stud-ies, and a 69 percent increase in the number of institutions that offered some type of formal academic recognition (Douglass 1995a).

The needs of older adults are best served when the individuals who provide services have aging-specific knowledge and skills (Wendt & Peterson 1992). Indi-viduals who wish to pursue formal training to become professionals in the field of aging have two options (Peterson 1995): to become *aging/gerontological specialists* or to become *gerontologists*. Actually, Peterson originally used the term *aging spe-cialist;* shortly thereafter, AGHE began using the term *gerontological specialist* (e.g., Peterson, Douglass, & Lobenstine 1996). For the purposes of this chapter, the more recent "gerontological specialist" will be used.

Gerontological specialists are individuals who obtain a degree in a traditional discipline (e.g., psychology, sociology, social work) and supplement their disci-pline specific education, experience, and skills with additional training or experi-ence (e.g., concentration, minor, certificate) in aging studies or gerontology. Upon completion of their training, gerontological specialists emphasize service to older adults within their profession (e.g., geriatric nurse specialists, gerontological social workers). In contrast, **gerontologists** are an emerging group of professionals who have formal training that is separate from traditional disciplines/professions and that results in a degree in gerontology. The advent of degree programs in geron-tology is relatively recent. Only 30 years ago, it was not possible to earn a four-year degree in gerontology; in 1999, 203 colleges and universities identified themselves as offering a bachelor's-level program in gerontology (Stepp 2000). Postbaccalaureate degrees in gerontology are an even more recent phenomenon.

The discussion of gerontological specialists and gerontologists is not meant to suggest that gerontological education should be reserved only for individuals who desire a career in the aging network. All individuals can benefit from an in-creased understanding of aging and gerontology. However, different levels of in-terest in as well as career aspirations involving gerontology require different instructional orientations. The instructional orientations proposed by Peterson and Wendt (1990) include a liberal arts model, a professional model for geronto-logical specialists and gerontologists, and a scientific model for future gerontolog-ical researchers and educators.

Peterson and Wendt believe that the *liberal arts orientation* to gerontology is best suited for students who are not interested in pursuing formal training in ger-ontology but who plan to be general practitioners in an existing profession. This orientation focuses on personal development, and the purpose is to help students acquire a philosophical understanding of their own aging as well as the aging of others.

A *professional orientation* for aspiring gerontological specialists and gerontologists has also been proposed by Peterson and Wendt. Both gerontological specialists and gerontologists are concerned with knowledge and skills that will enable them to increase the quality of life for older adults. However, the primary knowledge base for gerontological specialists derives from their specific discipline or profession, whereas gerontologists require greater breadth and depth of knowledge than do gerontological specialists. As such, gerontologists are expected to supplement their knowledge of facts and concepts regarding aging with knowledge about the mechanisms that underlie normal and pathological aging, program design, administration and evaluation, organizational behavior, and networking. In addition, they must be knowledgeable about service operations, client assessment, intervention, and professional conduct.

Finally, the *scientific orientation* to gerontology is best suited for those who aspire to be employed as gerontological researchers and educators. This orientation stresses the importance of description, prediction, and control, and emphasizes generation and replication of knowledge. This model of instruction emphasizes conceptual frameworks, hypotheses, and research techniques rather than applied issues.

SELECTING AN EDUCATIONAL PROGRAM IN GERONTOLOGY

Individuals who decide to pursue formal education in gerontology have several decisions to make. The first decision is whether to become a gerontological specialist or a gerontologist. Often, this decision is made on practical grounds. That is, far more universities and colleges offer degrees in the traditional disciplines, and some courses in aging/gerontology, than offer degrees in gerontology. However, if an individual is in a position to choose between the two options, the Association for Gerontology in Education (AGHE) has several recommendations (Peterson, Douglass, & Lobenstine 1996).

One important consideration identified by AGHE is the specific role an individual ultimately hopes to play in the aging network. Individuals who want to serve older adults as social service or health professionals, or as scientists or researchers in a traditional discipline, should probably pursue that specific discipline, and supplement their training with gerontological information (i.e., become gerontological specialists). In contrast, it is sensible for individuals who want to work with older adults, but not necessarily in a traditional discipline or in a discipline that requires some type of licensure or certification, to pursue degrees in gerontology (i.e., become gerontologists).

According to AGHE, there are several attributes that all gerontology programs should have, regardless of whether they are training gerontological specialists or gerontologists (Peterson, Douglass, & Lobenstine 1996). First, the program

In the twenty-first century, interests and opportunities in gerontology avail themselves to students young and old.

should be formalized within the institution, with a description of the curriculum appearing in the college/university catalog, and a process whereby students apply and are admitted to the program. Second, there should be a defined curriculum, and the courses comprising the curriculum should be offered for credit. The content of the courses should be multidisciplinary, and at least one of the courses should integrate the various multidisciplinary perspectives that are represented across the various courses. Specific courses that are believed to be essential for all individuals pursuing gerontological education include introduction to social gerontology, biology/physiology of aging, psychology of aging, sociology of aging, and a practicum or field placement. Finally, completion of the program should be officially recognized by the college/university, and result in the receipt of a certificate or degree, and a transcript notation.

Probably the most helpful resource for individuals who are interested in exploring educational opportunities in gerontology is AGHE's *Directory of Educational Programs in Gerontology and Geriatrics* (Stepp 2000). This directory contains information on approximately 775 programs from more than 350 colleges and universities that offer some type of program (i.e., degree, credit certificate, minor, concentration, specialization, emphasis and/or track, and postbaccalaureate opportunities) in gerontology, geriatrics, or aging studies. For each listed institution of higher education, it is possible to identify what specific educational opportunities are available, the number of courses that are offered, the number of faculty who teach aging-related courses, and other useful information.

Currently, there is no accreditation for gerontology programs. There are, however, several resources that can help individuals evaluate the relative strengths of a specific gerontology curriculum. AGHE's *Standards and Guidelines for Gerontology Programs* (Rich, Connelly, & Douglass 1990) provides specific curriculum and policy recommendations for a variety of gerontology programs ranging from associate-level certificates in gerontology through doctoral degrees in gerontology. The topics that are addressed for each educational opportunity include an overview of the credential; a list of the required courses, elective courses, and a practicum that comprises the curriculum; and relevant administrative issues. Individuals can use this document to determine whether a specific program in which they are interested includes the courses that are identified as necessary for that program in the standards and guidelines document.

A second valuable resource is the *Core Principles and Outcomes of Gerontology, Geriatrics and Aging Studies Instruction* (Wendt, Peterson, & Douglass 1993). This resource does not provide a list of course titles that are appropriate for the different types of gerontology programs. Rather, it identifies six core principles that they believe underlie all types of gerontological education:

- Structure/contexts/heterogeneity
- Conceptualizations and theories
- Stability and directions of change
- Ethical issues
- Scholarship and research
- Application/practice

Wendt, Peterson, and Douglass maintain that the specific knowledge and skills that are important within each principle depend on individuals' reasons for pursuing gerontological education. For each of the six core principles (listed above), the *Core Principles and Outcomes of Gerontology, Geriatrics and Aging Studies Instruction* makes recommendations as to the specific knowledge and skills outcomes that students should acquire. The value of this document for individuals who are interested in pursuing gerontological education is that it provides a conceptual framework for understanding the various educational orientations and a comprehensive overview of the knowledge and skills that should be included in gerontological education.

CONTROVERSIAL ISSUES IN GERONTOLOGICAL EDUCATION

In 1995, an entire issue of *Generations*, the journal of the American Society on Aging, was devoted to the topic of what it means to be a professional in the field of aging (Seltzer & Kunkel 1995). A major theme of the issue was that, despite tremendous growth in the field of gerontology over the past several decades, members of the gerontological community are not necessarily in agreement as to the directions that future development of the field should take. In the years since that issue of *Generations* appeared, many of the featured issues continue to be debated, but it does not appear that the gerontological community is prepared to reach consensus about four key issues:

1. Whether gerontological education functions best as a supplement to traditional, established disciplines or as a freestanding discipline (i.e., whether colleges and universities should be preparing gerontological specialists or gerontologists)
2. The appropriateness of accrediting gerontology programs
3. The appropriateness of credentialling individuals based on their training in gerontology
4. Whether gerontology is a discipline and/or a profession

In an effort to develop better-informed consumers of gerontological education and practice, the major arguments for and against each of these issues are outlined here. Although these issues are discussed separately, in actuality they are inextricably linked.

Issue #1: *Does gerontological education function best as a supplement to traditional, established disciplines or as a freestanding discipline (i.e., Should colleges and universities be preparing gerontological specialists or gerontologists)?*

It is universally acknowledged that gerontology is multidisciplinary in nature. And, although the differences in the formal education received by gerontological specialists and gerontologists might appear to be minor, there is substantial debate about the relative merits of each approach among members of the gerontological community.

Proponents of gerontological education as a supplement to traditional, established disciplines maintain that this approach results in graduates with a clear professional identity (e.g., nurse, social worker, speech language pathologist) who have a defined knowledge base and set of skills, and who oftentimes are eligible for licensure or certification through their primary discipline. For students with this type of background, education and credentials in aging are viewed as a bonus (Maddox 1995). Advocates of this approach to gerontological education question whether there is an accepted base of common knowledge and set of skills for gerontological specialists, whether they have a common professional identity, and, finally, whether there is an employment market for individuals with gerontology degrees (Friedsam 1995).

Proponents of gerontology as a freestanding discipline maintain that there is a labor demand that cannot be met through gerontological specialists alone, and that there is a market for individuals who have a more in-depth understanding of aging than is obtainable through a certificate, minor, or specialization (Connelly

1995). Proponents of this educational approach believe that professionals within the field need to identify the jobs that people who earn degrees in gerontology are uniquely qualified to hold, establish limited entry to these jobs, and explore possibilities for accrediting gerontology degree programs and/or credentialling the graduates of these programs.

Issue #2: *Should gerontology programs be accredited?*

Despite ongoing efforts of AGHE to establish guidelines, standards, and core principles for gerontological education (e.g., Lobenstine, Wendt, & Peterson 1994; Rich, Connelly, & Douglass 1990), the issue of whether gerontology programs should be accredited has been a topic of debate (e.g., Seltzer & Kunkel 1995). On the one hand, Connelly (1995) argues in favor of accreditation on the grounds that it should result in an increase in the overall quality of gerontological education. Specifically, he believes that accreditation will lead to the recruitment of better faculty and students, facilitate the employment of graduates within the aging network, and contribute to development of the profession of gerontology. On the other hand, Connelly identifies several disadvantages surrounding accreditation, including concern about the possibility of overly rigid criteria and the amount of time, effort, and money that might be involved in the accreditation process.

Johnson (1995) shares Connelly's concerns and argues that as society changes, gerontology programs will need maximal flexibility to meet emerging needs and opportunities. Accreditation might limit that flexibility. Further, Johnson questions Connelly's claim that accreditation necessarily results in a higher quality product.

Despite ongoing debate regarding the accreditation of gerontology programs, in 1999 AGHE initiated a program of merit for gerontology programs. The Program of Merit designation can be applied for by programs that offer academic degrees, minors, or certificates in gerontology. Gerontology programs whose extensive self-study is reviewed favorably by a group of AGHE-trained reviewers are awarded the designation. The Program of Merit designation provides an AGHE "stamp of approval" that can be used to verify program quality, to lobby for additional resources, to market the program, and to recruit prospective students into the program. The designation is awarded for a five-year period.

Issue #3: *Should individuals be credentialled based on their training in gerontology?*

In contrast to accreditation, which deals with the overall quality of a program (including the curriculum, course content, faculty competence, etc.), credentialling addresses the issue of a particular individual's level of competence in a given area. Peterson (1995) identifies at least three arguments for credentialling individuals as gerontologists/gerontological specialists, and three arguments against such credentialling. Peterson (1995) first points out that most health and human service providers have some type of credentialling. For example, nurses, psychologists, nursing-home administrators, social workers, and other professionals are eligible for state licensure. State licensure typically is awarded to individuals who achieve a certain educational attainment, a specified number of supervised hours in the field, and pass a standardized test. Second, Peterson maintains that the establishment of credentialling for gerontologists would help them to gain acceptance as professionals. Peterson's remaining argument in support of credentialling for gerontologists is to protect older adults who are served by members of the professional aging network by assuring they have adequate preparation for their jobs and that they follow an appropriate code of ethics.

A major reason against credentialling is that gerontology degrees do not provide the skills that are necessary for practice. In addition, gerontological specialists would be subjected to credentialling in both gerontology and their specific discipline. Finally, the risks of noncredentialled gerontologists/gerontological specialists is minor, because most professionals employed in the field of aging already adhere to a code of ethics (Peterson 1995).

Results from two surveys suggest that, among the professional community, there is a fair amount of support for the credentialling of gerontologists. As part of their larger research on the status of gerontology, geriatrics, and aging studies programs in institutions of higher education, Peterson, Wendt, and Douglass (1994) reported that 52 percent of faculty respondents believe that credentialling of graduates would promote gerontology. In a survey of 150 randomly selected members of the American Society on Aging, 72 percent of respondents reported that credentialling was at least important (if not very important), and 54 percent of respondents indicated that they personally would apply for credentialling were it available (Dupont 1994).

The issues of accrediting gerontology programs and credentialling professionals in gerontology might appear to be one and the same, but there is a fundamental difference underlying the two (Lubben 1995). The motivation underlying the accreditation of gerontology programs is to legitimize the discipline of gerontology, whereas the motivation underlying the credentialling of professionals in gerontology is to legitimize the profession of gerontology. Consistent with Maddox's (1995) claim that the fundamental goal for all professionals in gerontology is to empower older adults to make the most of their lives, Lubben (1995) suggests that decisions regarding accreditation and credentialling should be based on the extent to which they enhance the status of older adults, rather than either the discipline or the profession of gerontology.

Issue #4: *Is gerontology a discipline and/or a profession?*

Gerontology is widely acknowledged as a field of study—specifically, the study of the biological, psychological, and social processes of aging. In addition, there is consensus that gerontology is a field of practice, in that professionals and paraprofessionals strive to apply knowledge from the study of aging to meet the needs of older adults. However, in order to be characterized as a discipline, a field of study must have its own body of knowledge and methods of inquiry, emphasize the acquisition of new knowledge, and have access to professional networks through which new knowledge can be disseminated (Peterson, undated).

Many members of the gerontological community argue that because gerontology is multidisciplinary, by definition it will never be able to attain the status of a discipline (e.g., Jarvis 1990). Opponents of this perspective point out that despite gerontology's recent beginnings, the field has generated a tremendous amount of knowledge, that methods of inquiry and analysis have been developed to address some of the fundamental questions asked by researchers in the field, and that many professionals choose to disseminate new knowledge through gerontological rather than discipline-specific conferences and scholarly journals. Perhaps anticipating these developments, some 15 years ago, Seltzer (1985) expressed the opinion that gerontology was moving toward becoming a discipline. She did not, however, express an opinion as to whether gerontology would ultimately achieve this status.

Peterson (undated) makes the distinction between disciplines from professions. He maintains that the function of a discipline is to create knowledge for its own sake, whereas the function of a profession is to provide services and to solve "individual, social, and community problems" (p. 1). As part of his discussion, Peterson presents eight criteria of professions and their members:

1. Members of a profession have full-time occupations that provide them with a primary income.
2. Members of a profession have a strong motivation that results in long-term dedication to, and strong identification with, the field.
3. Members of a profession have a specialized body of knowledge and a set of skills that are acquired during a lengthy period of education and training.
4. Members of a profession have a clear service orientation that requires practitioners to use their experiences of behalf of their clients.
5. Members of a profession have autonomy of performance. That is, they are in a position to use their judgment, based on their specialized knowledge and skills, to assess and facilitate clients' best interests.
6. Members of a profession rely on organizations that establish admission to the profession and monitor the standards of performance within the profession.
7. Members of a profession have a monopoly on the delivery of certain services that can only be provided by credentialled personnel.
8. Members of a profession have a code of ethics that provides guidance on moral questions that they confront during the conduct of their practice.

When these eight criteria are applied to the field of gerontology, Peterson concludes that gerontology has acquired some of the attributes of a profession, but that it has not reached full professional status. With respect to specific criteria, clearly there are professionals who are full-time employees in the aging network who manage to support themselves. And gerontological specialists and gerontologists alike typically are quite committed to the field of gerontology. However, with respect to the remaining criteria, the status of gerontology as a profession is more debatable. Whether gerontology will ever reach full professional status remains to be seen.

Before leaving the topic of controversial issues in gerontological education, a few concluding comments are in order. First, it is quite likely that the range of educational opportunities that are available for individuals who are interested in the field of gerontology today developed as a direct result of these controversies. Second, it would be enlightening to know the extent to which opinions regarding these issues derive from concerns for academic and professional "turf" rather than concerns for the development of the field of study and practice of gerontology. Finally, it is quite possible that the discussions that surround these controversial issues are far more interesting than the "answers" to the issues will prove to be.

CAREERS IN AND BEYOND THE AGING NETWORK

To talk about careers "in the aging network" is probably somewhat limiting. Given the demographic changes in the population, most notably the aging of Baby Boomers, many traditional jobs will increasingly involve interaction with older adults. As such, many more service-oriented jobs in the future than today will include a gerontological component.

Individuals with gerontological education perform a variety of functions in a wide range of settings (Williams 1995). For example, Peterson, Douglass, and Lobenstine (1996) identify seven categories of jobs for individuals with gerontological expertise:

1. Direct service provision
2. Program planning and evaluation
3. Administration and policy
4. Education and training
5. Research
6. Advocacy
7. Marketing and product development

Figure E.1 presents examples of specific tasks that fall under five of the seven job categories (the categories of advocacy and marketing and product development are not included). Many of these categories of jobs can be carried out

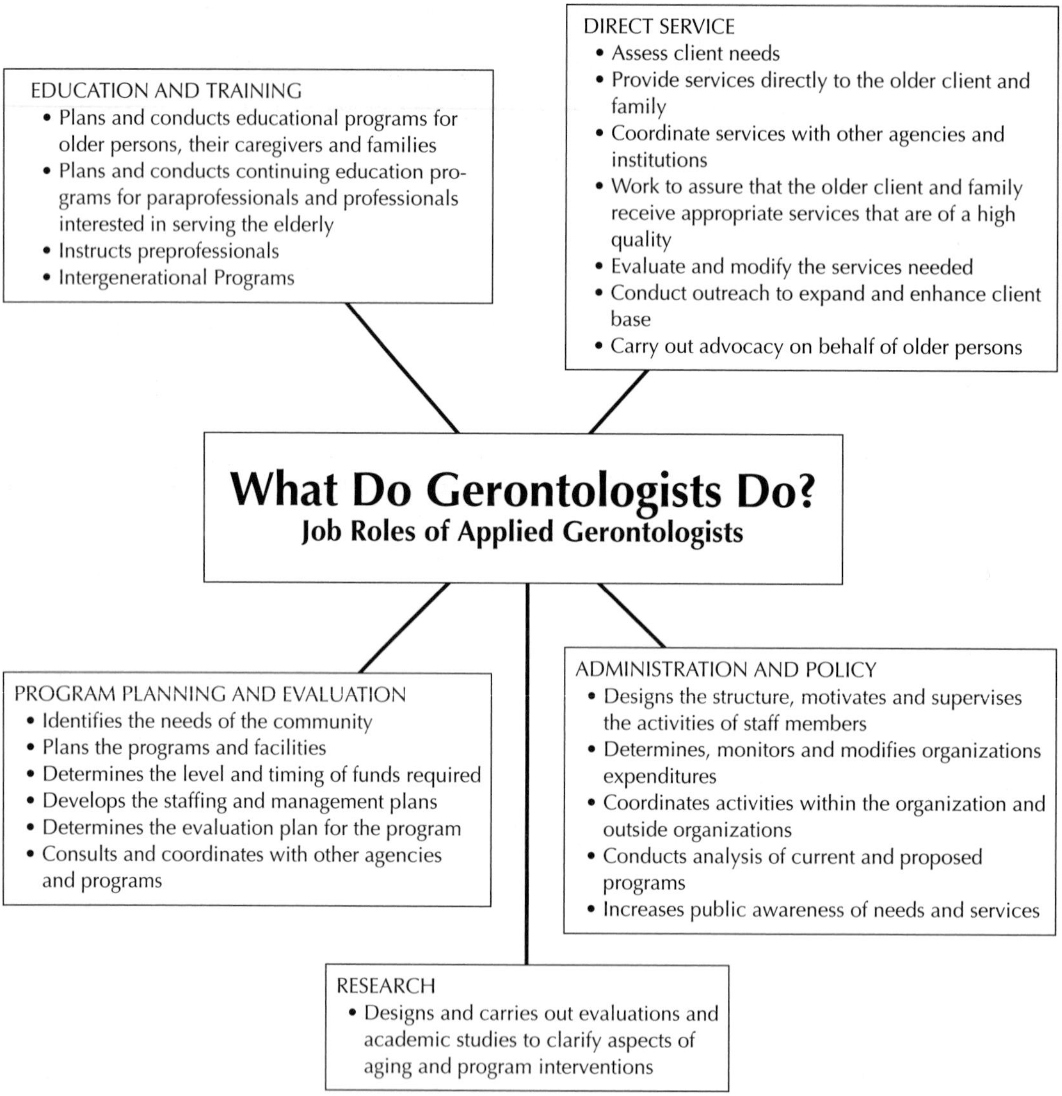

DIRECT SERVICE
- Assess client needs
- Provide services directly to the older client and family
- Coordinate services with other agencies and institutions
- Work to assure that the older client and family receive appropriate services that are of a high quality
- Evaluate and modify the services needed
- Conduct outreach to expand and enhance client base
- Carry out advocacy on behalf of older persons

EDUCATION AND TRAINING
- Plans and conducts educational programs for older persons, their caregivers and families
- Plans and conducts continuing education programs for paraprofessionals and professionals interested in serving the elderly
- Instructs preprofessionals
- Intergenerational Programs

What Do Gerontologists Do?
Job Roles of Applied Gerontologists

PROGRAM PLANNING AND EVALUATION
- Identifies the needs of the community
- Plans the programs and facilities
- Determines the level and timing of funds required
- Develops the staffing and management plans
- Determines the evaluation plan for the program
- Consults and coordinates with other agencies and programs

ADMINISTRATION AND POLICY
- Designs the structure, motivates and supervises the activities of staff members
- Determines, monitors and modifies organizations expenditures
- Coordinates activities within the organization and outside organizations
- Conducts analysis of current and proposed programs
- Increases public awareness of needs and services

RESEARCH
- Designs and carries out evaluations and academic studies to clarify aspects of aging and program interventions

FIGURE E.1   What Do Gerontologists Do?

Source: Marti Klein and David A. Peterson, University of Southern California. Reprinted by permission.

in a variety of employment settings. Figure E.2 provides an overview of some of the settings where gerontological specialists and gerontologists can put their education to use. (It should be pointed out that the figure also lists some services

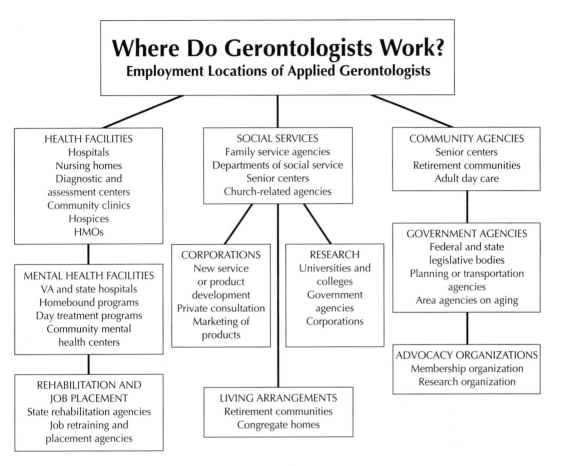

FIGURE E.2   Information on Applied Gerontologists

Source: Marti Klein and David A. Peterson, University of Southern California. Reprinted by permission.

within particular settings.) Whereas many of the settings included in the figure clearly fall within the aging network (e.g., nursing homes, senior centers, Area Agencies on Aging), other settings (e.g., corporations) lie outside what is traditionally thought of as the aging network. The multitude of employment possibilities becomes evident when one considers that almost all the settings that are included in the figure have positions for each of the seven job categories, as do many settings that are not included in the figure. It should be noted that there is overlap in the job categories and settings depicted in Figures E.1 and E.2. It is also important to note that gerontologists and gerontological specialists are not restricted to these roles and settings.

Who Chooses a Career with a Gerontological Focus?

When members of the general population learn that someone is interested in working with older people, a common response, usually said in a rather nasty tone, is "Why would you want to work with *old* people?" Students of gerontology quickly learn to use this question as an opportunity to dispel negative attitudes by explaining the exciting challenges and benefits that can result from working with older adults. But the question of what motivates individuals to study gerontology is an interesting one.

Carpenter (1996) surveyed 108 undergraduate and graduate students who were interested in gerontology and geriatrics to determine which of seven factors most motivated their interest. Carpenter found that the most influential motives (in order of importance) were a desire to serve an undervalued group, a desire to understand their own aging, and a desire to better understand the aging of their family and friends. In addition, previous experience with older adults was rated as relatively important. In contrast, encouragement from others and potential financial, employment, and research opportunities were less important motivators. These results suggest that, among this group of students, humanistic motives for studying gerontology were more important than were tangible motives.

Preparing for a Career That Has a Gerontological Focus

Because there are so many employment opportunities for individuals with gerontological training, the challenge of choosing a specific career can be daunting. However, there are several reasons why it is beneficial for students to identify an initial career goal early in their educational careers. The primary reason is that certain professions require specific educational curricula and/or some type of credentialling. Thus, it is in students' best interest to identify their "niches" as early as possible so that they can complete an academic curriculum that will enable them to fill those niches.

For example (and not surprisingly), anyone who wishes to work as a geriatric nurse or geriatric nurse practitioner must have a degree in nursing. Thus, individuals with this career aspiration should pursue a degree in nursing, supplementing their standard curriculum with as many gerontology and aging courses as possible. Upon obtaining the degree and passing certifying examination, these individuals will be eligible to fill their niche in the aging network. In contrast to nursing, prior to 1993, anyone with a bachelor's degree in social work or a related discipline, such as gerontology, was permitted to sit for the social work licensing exam. Individuals who passed the exam were licensed social workers. Beginning in 1993, in order to sit for licensure as a social worker, individuals are required to have a bachelor's degree in social work.

Even if particular career options do not require specific curricula, it is still a good idea for students to identify an initial career goal while they are pursuing their formal training. This will enable them to select elective courses, practica, and volunteer experiences that will maximize the probability that they will be employed in their preferred position. The AGHE guidelines recommend that both gerontological specialists and gerontologists complete a practicum in the aging network. Careful selection of a practicum site will result in a supervised opportunity to apply knowledge acquired in the classroom in a specific environment that serves older adults. An added benefit of practica and volunteer experiences is that they give students an opportunity to confirm that the career toward which they are working will meet their expectations.

Marketing Oneself for a Career That Has a Gerontological Focus

A common lament of recent graduates who are educated as gerontological specialists or gerontologists is, "What now?" In part because of the variety of employment opportunities that have a gerontological focus, the task of finding suitable employment can appear to be overwhelming. As students are quick to point out, it is not possible to look in the employment notices under *G* for *gerontologist* and find the job of one's dreams. In some ways, the task is probably more difficult for gerontologists than for gerontological specialists who have some form of credentialling (AGHE Task Force in Education-Employment Linkages 1998). For example, gerontological nurse practitioners and gerontological social workers can explore job postings under the headings of "nursing" and "social work." But for gerontologists and gerontological specialists who do not have professional credentials, the search for a position in the aging network requires a bit more creativity. But this is no different from the prospects facing majors of many different disciplines, such as English, history, or political science. Actually, the employment prospects for gerontology graduates are quite good. Peterson, Douglass, and Lobenstine (1996) report that within six months of graduation, 70 percent of gerontology/geriatrics graduates are employed full-time within the aging network. They indicate that this employment rate is higher than the rate for graduates of liberal arts programs, but comparable to the rates reported for graduates of human services programs.

Several strategies will facilitate a search for employment in the aging network or in an aging-related setting. Obviously, formal training (i.e., academic coursework, practica) is important. But it is also important for individuals to take advantage of opportunities to network with other professionals in the gerontological community. These opportunities exist at all levels, ranging from local to national.

Involvement in local professional gerontological associations enables participants to be current on happenings in their communities (e.g., changes in agency policies, the implementation of new services) and can serve as a source of information about potential employment opportunities.

At a national level, there are three categories of professional associations involved in what Douglass (1995b) calls "the aging business." These categories include organizations whose membership primarily consists of older adults (e.g., American Association of Retired Persons [AARP]), organizations whose members are professionals and/or service providers in the aging network (e.g., American Association of Homes and Services for the Aging [AAHSA] <http://www.aahsa.org>, National Council on the Aging [NCOA]), and organizations whose members are faculty, administrators, and students in the education and research communities (e.g., Association for Gerontology in Higher Education [AGHE], Gerontological Society of America [GSA]). Participation in these types of organizations can facilitate involvement in advocacy efforts, continued professional development, and a greater sense of professional identity with the field of gerontology.

Probably the biggest challenge facing individuals who wish to pursue a career with a gerontological focus is that many potential employers do not recognize the value of education in gerontology and/or they are not certain what it is that gerontologists "do" (Coyle 1985; AGHE Task Force in Education-Employment Linkages 1998). Rather than viewing this as a liability, gerontologists and gerontological specialists are encouraged to embrace this state of affairs as an asset. In the absence of clear-cut responsibilities and expectations, well-educated gerontologists and gerontological specialists have the opportunity to create their own niches within the rapidly expanding field of gerontology.

SUMMARY

Educational gerontology includes efforts to instruct older adults themselves, efforts to instruct other audiences about older adults, and instruction for professionals and practitioners who will work with and on behalf of older adults. Because educational gerontology is a diverse field, there are a number of educational and career opportunities for students who are interested in gerontology.

Individuals who wish to pursue formal training and become professionals in the field of aging have two options: *Gerontological specialists* obtain a degree in a traditional discipline and supplement their discipline specific education, experience, and skills with additional training or experience in aging studies or gerontology. In contrast, *gerontologists* have formal training that results in a degree in gerontology.

Individuals who want to serve older adults as social service or health professionals, or as scientists or researchers in a traditional discipline, should probably pursue a traditional discipline, and supplement that training with gerontological information (i.e., become gerontological specialists). Those who want to work directly with older adults, but not necessarily in a traditional discipline or in a discipline that requires some type of licensure or certification, should probably pursue a degree in gerontology (i.e., become gerontologists). The Association for Gerontology in Higher Education (AGHE) has developed a number of resources that assist individuals in the evaluation of specific educational offerings in gerontology.

Despite tremendous growth in the field of gerontology over the past several decades, members of the gerontological community are not necessarily in agreement regarding four key issues: (1) whether gerontological education functions best as a supplement to traditional, established disciplines or as a freestanding discipline; (2) the appropriateness of accrediting gerontology programs; (3) the appropriateness of credentialling individuals; and (4) whether gerontology is a discipline and/or a profession.

Given the demographic changes in the population, many traditional jobs will increasingly involve interaction with older adults. Still, the challenge of choosing a specific career can be daunting. It is beneficial for students to identify an initial career goal early in their educational careers so that they can complete academic curricula that will enable them to achieve their career goals. Being able to select particular courses, practica, and volunteer experiences will maximize the probability that they will be employed in their preferred positions. An added benefit of practica and volunteer experiences is that they give students an opportunity to confirm that the career toward which they are working will meet their expectations.

The employment prospects for gerontology graduates are quite good, especially for individuals who have obtained appropriate formal education and who take advantage of opportunities to network with other professionals in the gerontological community. Probably the biggest challenge facing individuals who wish to pursue a career with a gerontological focus is that many potential employers do not recognize the value of education in gerontology. Gerontologists and gerontological specialists are encouraged to embrace this state of affairs as an asset. Well-educated gerontologists or gerontological specialists have the opportunity to create their own niches within the rapidly expanding field of gerontology.

STUDY QUESTIONS

1. Using Peterson's (1990) definition of *educational gerontology,* describe at least one role within the field that you would feel comfortable occupying.

2. Discuss the major factors that should be taken into account when deciding between pursuing a career as a gerontological specialist or a gerontologist.

3. Why is it important to have different orientations of gerontological education as a function of students' professional aspirations? Given your own professional and personal aspirations, which orientations to gerontological instruction would be most useful to you? Within that orientation, what type of information is most important, and why?

4. Evaluate the extent to which each of the four controversial issues in gerontology actually affect professionals in the field and older adults who seek the services of professionals in the field.

5. Using Peterson's characteristics of a profession, what changes would be required

in order for gerontology to achieve the status of a fully developed profession?

6. What are some of the barriers to gerontology achieving the status of a fully developed profession?

7. Is a lack of consensus among professionals in an emerging field such as gerontology an advantage or a disadvantage?

8. Given the range of jobs and employment settings for individuals with gerontological expertise, design a job for yourself as a gerontological specialist/gerontologist.

REFERENCES

AGHE Task Force in Education-Employment Linkages. (1998, June). *Gerontological education and job opportunities in aging*. Washington, DC: Association for Gerontology in Higher Education.

Carpenter, B. D. (1996). Why students are interested in the elderly: An analysis of motives. *Gerontology and Geriatrics Education, 16,* 41–51.

Connelly, R. C. (1995). Claiming boundaries: The time for accreditation has come. *Generations, 19,* 25–27.

Coyle, J. M. (1985). Entrepreneurial gerontology: Creative marketing of gerontological skills. *Educational Gerontology, 11,* 161–167.

Douglass, E. B. (1995a). Gerontological education and training. In G. Maddox (Ed.), *The encyclopedia of aging* (2nd ed.). New York: Springer.

Douglass, E. B. (1995b). Professional organizations in aging: Too many doing too few for too little. *Generations, 19,* 35–36.

Dupont, J. L. (1994). *The viability of certification of gerontologists.* Unpublished manuscript. Los Angeles: University of Southern California.

Friedsam, H. (1995). The imperatives of societal aging remain. *Generations, 19,* 46–50.

Jarvis, P. (1990). Trends in education and gerontology. *Educational Gerontology, 16,* 401–409.

Johnson, H. R. (1995). Claiming boundaries: The foibles and follies of gerontological imperialists. *Generations, 19,* 23–24.

Lobenstine, J. C., Wendt, P. F., & Peterson, D. A. (1994). *National directory of educational programs in gerontology and geriatrics* (6th ed.). Washington, DC: Association for Gerontology in Higher Education.

Lubben, J. (1995). Claiming boundaries: A reaction to the debate. *Generations, 19,* 31–32.

Maddox, G. L. (1995). Marking a career in aging: Past and future. *Generations, 19,* 54–55.

Peterson, D. A. (undated). *The professional field of gerontology.* Unpublished manuscript. Los Angeles: University of California.

Peterson, D. A. (1990). A history of the education of older learners. In R. H. Sherron & D. B. Lumsden (Eds.), *Introduction to educational gerontology* (3rd ed.). New York: Hemisphere.

Peterson, D. A. (1995). Claiming boundaries: Professionals in the field of aging should be credentialed. *Generations, 19,* 28–30.

Peterson, D. A., Douglass, E. B., & Lobenstine, J. C. (1996). *Careers in aging: Opportunities and options.* Washington, DC: Association for Gerontology in Higher Education.

Peterson, D. W., & Wendt, P. F. (1990). Gerontology instruction: Different models for different results. *Educational Gerontology, 16,* 359–372.

Peterson, D. A., Wendt, P. F., & Douglass, E. B. (1994). *Development of gerontology, geriatrics, and aging studies programs in institutions of higher education.* Washington, DC: Association for Gerontology in Higher Education.

Rich, T. A., Connelly, J. R., & Douglass, E. B. (1990). *Standards and guidelines for gerontology programs* (2nd ed.). Washington, DC: Association for Gerontology in Higher Education.

Seltzer, M. M. (1985). Issues of accreditation of academic gerontology programs and credentialling of workers in the field of aging. *Gerontology and Geriatrics Education, 5,* 7–18.

Seltzer, M. M., & Kunkel, S. R. (Eds.). (1995). *Generations: What it means to be a professional in the field of aging.* San Francisco: American Society on Aging.

Stepp, D. D. (Ed.). (2000). *Directory of educational programs in gerontology and geriatrics* (7th ed.). Washington, DC: Association for Gerontology in Higher Education.

Wendt, P. F., & Peterson, D. A. (1992). Transition in the use of human resources in the field of aging. *Journal of Aging and Social Policy, 4,* 107–123.

Wendt, P. F., Peterson, D. A., & Douglass, E. B. (1993). *Core principles and outcomes of gerontol-ogy, geriatrics and aging studies instruction.* Washington, DC: Association for Gerontology in Higher Education.

White House Conference on Aging. (1960). *Background paper on role and training of professional personnel.* Washington, DC: Author.

Williams, E. (1995). *Opportunities in gerontology and aging services careers.* Lincolnwood, IL: VGM Career Horizons.

Abkhasians The long-lived people of the Soviet state of Georgia; they attribute their longevity to practices in sex, work, and diet.

accommodating environment A model that assumes that all aspects of the environment (including the resident) will change over time.

active life expectancy (ALE) Operationally defined as the period of life free from limitations in activities of daily living.

activities of daily living (ADLs) Basic self-care or activities of daily living include bathing, dressing, going to the bathroom, getting into or out of a bed or a chair, walking, getting outside the house or apartment, and feeding. In the elderly, ability to carry out these tasks without assistance is used as a measure of functional health.

activity theory Often referred to as the *implicit theory of aging,* this theory states that there is a positive relationship between activity and life satisfaction. The individual who is able to maintain the activities of the middle years for as long as possible will be well adjusted and satisfied with life in the later years.

acute illness A condition, disease, or disorder that is temporary.

adult foster care The least restrictive housing option that utilizes private residences for the care of a nonrelated elderly person who is in need of supervision and/or assistance with activities of daily living.

advanced directives A legal document, such as a living will or a durable power of attorney, in which people provide others with instructions about their preferences for health care should they not be able to act on their own behalf.

affectual solidarity The type and degree of positive sentiments family members hold toward one another.

age composition Involves a quantitative description of the proportions of young and old people in a society. A population's age composition depends first on its level of fertility and only secondarily on mortality.

age-condensed families Families in which there are fewer than 20 years between generations.

Age Discrimination Employment Act A federal law passed in 1967 and amended several times since. The law prohibits discrimination in hiring, firing, and conditions of employment on the basis of age.

age-gapped families Families in which there are relatively wide gaps (e.g., 30 years or more) between generations.

age/period/cohort problem The importance of distinguishing among changes in individuals that are a function of maturation (aging), biographical factors (cohort), and those that result from environmental and/or historical factors (period).

age-related macular degeneration Visual impairment that results from damage to the macular area of the retina; the leading cause of blindness among older adults in the United States.

age-specific life expectancy The average duration of life expected for an individual of a given age.

age stratification A concept that perceives society as divided on the basis of age with each age stratum having its own set of rights, obligations, and opportunities.

aged subculture A concept based on the premise that because of changes in the aged population and in U.S. society, the aged have developed their own norms, system of stratification, and consciousness.

ageism A term coined by Robert Butler to describe negative attitudes toward aging and the aged.

aging group consciousness The belief that the development of an aged subculture would stimulate a group identification and consciousness among older people with the potential for social action.

ancestry group Defined by individuals in terms of the nation or nations of family origin.

angle-closure glaucoma   An acute form of primary glaucoma; it appears suddenly and runs a short course.

antediluvian theme   Involves the belief that people lived much longer in the past.

antioxidants   Chemicals used to combine with and disarm free radicals. A common one is the food preservative BHT.

aphasia   A term used to denote impaired ability to comprehend or express verbal language, and a clinical feature of stroke in many elderly victims.

appropriate death   A concept meant to describe that the person has died in a fashion that resembles as much as possible the way that he or she wished to die.

arteriosclerosis   A hardening of, or loss of elasticity in, the arteries.

arthritis   Inflammation or degenerative joint change often characterized by stiffness, swelling, and joint pain. Some forms of arthritis are believed to be autoimmune diseases.

assisted-living facilities   A housing facility that sits on the housing continuum between independent living and institutional care and provides some supportive services.

associational solidarity   Frequency and patterns of intergenerational interaction among family members.

atherosclerosis   A condition whereby the inner wall of an artery becomes thickened by plaque formation.

autoimmune theory   This theory maintains that because of copying errors in repeated cell divisions, protein enzymes produced by newer cells are literally not recognized by the body. This brings the body's immunologic system into play, forcing it to work against itself.

average life expectancy at birth   Defined as the average number of years a person born today can expect to live under the current mortality conditions.

Baby Boomers   Persons born after World War II, typically between 1946 and 1964.

bereavement   The experience of getting over another person's death. In part, the character that bereavement takes is shaped by society. Physical symptoms, such as shortness of breath and psychological distress, may accompany bereavement.

biological aging   A term often used to describe the postmaturational changes in physical appearance and capability.

breakthrough policy   A piece of governmental legislation that involves the federal government in providing or guaranteeing some fundamental benefit.

cataracts   The most common disability of the aged eye. The normally transparent lens of the eye becomes opaque and interferes with the passage of rays of light to the retina.

centenarians   Those who live 100 years or more.

cerebrovascular disease   A term used to describe impaired brain cell circulation. When a portion of the brain is completely denied blood, a cerebrovascular accident or stroke occurs.

chronic illness   A condition, disease, or disorder that is permanent or that will incapacitate an individual for a long period of time.

chronic strains   Recurrent, enduring problems, including ambient, role, and quotidian strains.

cognitive coherence hypothesis   A coherent, supportive framework, provided by religious involvement, for interpreting uncertainties associated with day-to-day stresses and out-of-the-ordinary situations.

cohort   The term used for a group of persons born at approximately the same time. Although defined broadly, no two birth cohorts can be expected to age in the same way; each has a particular history and arrives at old age with unique experiences.

cohort-centric   Describes the fact that people in the same place on the life-course dimension experience historical events similarly and, as a result, may come to see the world in a like fashion.

collagen   A protein fiber distributed in and around the walls of blood vessels and in connective tissue; it has been implicated in age-related changes in physiological functions.

compression of morbidity   According to Fries, a compression of morbidity occurs if the length of time between onset of disease and death is shortened.

conductive hearing loss   Results from changes in the outer and middle ear that interrupt the conduction of sound waves.

consensual solidarity The extent to which family members agree on values, attitudes, and beliefs.

constant environment A model of the physical and social environment that assumes that the needs of residents remain relatively stable over time.

constituency-building policy A governmental policy that recognizes that different groups can have a common interest and that allows "space" for these interest groups in the making of policy.

content analysis A research technique that involves analyzing the content of records or documents.

continuity theory Put forth by Robert Atchley, this theory argues that few people rest their entire self-identities on the work role. Most people have several roles in which identity is based; thus, they are able to adjust to retirement and gain self-respect and self-esteem from leisure-time pursuits.

continuum-of-care retirement communities (CCRCs) The most accommodating housing option that usually provides housing, personal and supportive care, congregate meals, social and recreational activities, and nursing care if needed.

coping Behavioral strategies designed to modify a stressful situation (i.e., problem-focused coping) and cognitive/emotional strategies designed to manage negative emotions that result from the stressful situation (i.e., emotion-focused coping).

coronary thrombosis A coronary artery suddenly blocked by a blood clot.

cross-linkage A process whereby proteins in the body bind to each other.

cross-sectional study A study based on observations representing a single point in time. Studies employing this research design are useful for emphasizing differences.

crystallized pragmatics (intelligence) The knowledge that an individual acquires as a result of socialization into, and experiences as part of, a given culture.

cultural age deadlines The age by which people think certain family transitions ought to occur in men's and women's lives.

day care Includes a wide range of services for older people who have some mental or physical impairments but can remain in the community if supportive services are provided.

deductive logic Reasoning from the general to the specific or from certain premises to a logically valid conclusion.

defined benefit pension plan Pension plans in which benefits are determined by multiplying a specific dollar amount by the number of years of employed service credited to an employee under the plan.

defined contribution plan Pension plans in which the employer and often the employee make fixed (or defined) contributions to an account.

delayed retirement credit (delayed benefit credit) Increase in Social Security benefits payable to workers who postpone retirement past age 65 up to age 70.

delirium A major mental disorder that is a direct physiological consequence of a medical condition. Usually characterized by disruptions in consciousness and change in cognitive abilities or perceptual difficulties that are not due to a dementia. Delirium develops over a short period of time (usually within hours or a day) and fluctuates over the course of a day.

dementia A major mental disorder characterized by memory impairment (which can include either difficulty learning new material or recalling previously learned material) and difficulty with at least one of the following cognitive capacities: language, recognition, and organization and/or performance of motor activities.

demographic transition A three-stage conceptual model of population growth and change.

demography The study of the size, territorial distribution, and composition of population and the changes therein.

dependency ratio The ratio of the population of ages too young or too old to work to the population of working age.

depression The most common psychiatric disorder among older people; it can vary in duration and degree and show psychological as well as physiological manifestations.

desexualization One stereotype of ageism: If someone is old (or getting old), he or she is finished with sex.

developmental stake hypothesis Perspective that argues that the older generation is more invested in the parent/child relationships than are the young.

diabetic retinopathy Vascular changes in the retina that may result in diminished vision or blindness.

diagnosis-related groups (DRGs) Under this *prospective payment system,* hospitals know in advance what Medicare will pay them for treating a patient with a particular ailment. A fee is set for the treatment of illnesses and injuries categorized into different groupings. Fees vary by region, according to whether the hospital is in an urban or a rural setting and according to the prevailing wage rate in the area. Rates are adjusted annually.

disengagement theory This theory postulates that aging involves a mutual withdrawal between the older person and society.

DNA (deoxyribonucleic acid) The molecule of heredity in nearly all organisms.

double jeopardy A term used to reflect the idea that the negative effects of aging are compounded among minority group members.

DSM-IV The criteria currently used to diagnose mental disorders for people of all ages are contained in the fourth edition of the American Psychiatric Association's *Diagnostic and Statistical Manual of Mental Disorders.*

dying career This concept views the last phase of life as a career that moves in a series of related and regressive stages toward death.

dying trajectory A term used to describe the dying process. All dying processes take time and can be visualized as having a certain shape through time. The combination of duration and shape can be charted as a trajectory.

educational gerontology An application of what is known about aging and education to extend the number of healthy and productive years and to improve the quality of life of older adults.

empirical method A broad category that includes quantitative and qualitative research techniques that can be replicated by many.

Employee Retirement Income Security Act (ERISA) An act, passed by Congress in 1974, to establish minimum standards for private pension programs.

employee stock ownership plans (ESOPs) A type of defined contribution plan found only in the private sector and usually financed entirely by the employer.

empty-nest period The period of time after grown children have left home, sometimes referred to as *postparental period.*

environmental docility hypothesis The less competent the individual, the greater the impact of environmental factors on the individual.

episodic memory A process whereby individuals encode, store, and retrieve information about events that are personally experienced.

ERISA The Employee Retirement Income Security Act, passed by Congress in 1974, to establish minimum standards for private pension programs.

error cascade A catastrophe of random errors in the synthesizing of information-carrying proteins that results in cell deterioration.

ethnogenesis Describes a model of ethnic relations in which pressures to assimilate exist alongside pressures to maintain ethnic identification.

exchange theory A social-psychological theory recently applied to the situation of the aged. The basic assumption of the theory is that people will attempt to maximize benefits from an interaction while incurring the least costs.

extended family Three or more generations living together in one household.

familial old-age dependency ratio Defined in simple demographic terms (e.g., population 65–79 years/population 45–49 years, etc.), this concept can be used to crudely illustrate the shifts in the ratio of elderly parents to the children who would support them.

family life cycle A concept used by family sociologists to characterize the changes that families undergo from their establishment through the postparental stage.

family life cycle model According to this model, parental involvement in religious services peaks when children are young; when children are no longer in the home, regularity of religious participation falls off.

feminist gerontology A critique of the "androcentric" (male-centered) view inherent in theorizing about aging.

fertility rate   The total number of births in society in a year per 1,000 individuals in the society.

fibroblasts   Embryonic cells that give rise to connective tissue.

filial piety   Reflects the respect and deference owed to one's elders, perhaps especially to a father. Filial piety is most often present in traditional societies dominated by a patriarchal social order.

fluid mechanics (intelligence)   A person's ability to solve novel problems that is determined by biological-genetic factors, including health.

fountain theme   Involves the idea that there is some unusual substance that has the property of greatly increasing the length of life.

401(K)   The section of the Internal Revenue Service (IRS) code that allows employees to choose to have a portion of their compensation (otherwise payable in cash) invested in a qualified defined contribution plan on a tax-deferred basis.

free radicals   Highly unstable molecules that contain an unpaired electron. Their presence reduces cellular efficiency and causes an accumulation of cellular waste that may lead to cell aging.

functional solidarity   Extent to which resources are exchanged among generations within a family.

fund of sociability hypothesis   According to this idea, there is a certain quantity of interaction with others that people require and that they may achieve in a variety of ways—either through one or two intense relationships or through a larger number of less intense relationships.

generativity   The desire to become a productive and caring member of society.

geriatrics   A subfield of gerontological practice; the medical care of the aging.

gerontocracy   Rule by older people.

gerontological specialist   An individual who supplements discipline-specific education, experience, and skills with additional training or experience in aging studies or gerontology.

gerontologist   An individual who has formal training that results in a degree in gerontology.

gerontology   The systematic study of the aging process.

gerontophilia   Respect and reverence for the aged.

gerontophobia   A fear of and negative attitude toward the aged.

gerotranscendence   A shift in overall perspective from a rational and maternalistic vision of the world to a more transcendent one.

glaucoma   The most serious eye disease affecting the aged. It results from an increase in pressure within the eyeball.

Gompertz's law   The suggestion that human mortality is governed by an equation with two terms. The first accounts for chance deaths that would occur at any age; the second, characteristic of the species, represents the exponential increase with time.

grief   The reaction to loss.

health behavior hypothesis   The notion that individuals may structure their behaviors and attitudes consistent with religious guidelines related to smoking, drinking, and/or diet.

health behavior model   Conceptual framework within which to identify predisposing, enabling, and need factors that contribute to the use of health services.

hierarchical compensatory model   Various family members are used for care giving, depending on the type of help required. The likelihood is greater that the caregiver will be a spouse before an adult child; when children are available, they provide a second important source of help.

home health care   The provision of coordinated multidisciplinary services, including skilled nursing and therapeutic services as well as social casework; mental health; legal, financial, and personal care; and household management assistance.

hospice   A concept of care for the terminally ill that provides psychological, social, and spiritual services when needed by the patient and/or family members on a 24-hour, seven-day-a-week basis.

Hunza   A group of allegedly long-lived people in the mountains of Kashmir, Pakistan.

hyperborean theme   Involves the idea that in some remote part of the world, there are people who enjoy remarkably long lives.

identity crisis theory   Because occupational identity is so much a part of a person's life, this theory argues that retirement necessarily brings an identity crisis. Accordingly, leisure roles cannot be expected to replace work as a source of self-respect and identity.

instrumental activities of daily living (IADLs) Includes both the personal self-care reflected in the ADL measures and more complex activities, such as going shopping or doing housework. Because the IADL tasks are more complicated and multifaceted, functional health decrements are expected to show up first in these items.

intergenerational solidarity Positive interactions, cohesion, and sentiments between parents and adult children and between grandparents and adult grandchildren in a family.

interiority The process whereby people, as they age, move from active to passive mastery; a greater orientation toward introspection and self-reflection.

intuition The direct perception of truth apart from any reasoning process or logic.

ischemic heart disease A term for coronary artery disease. Tissue that is denied adequate blood supply is called *ischemic.*

later-life families Families for whom child rearing is complete and, as such, are characterized by contracting, rather than expanding, size and structure; typically the original marital dyad.

life-course perspective of development Conceptualization of development in terms of aging-related transitions that are socially created, socially recognized, and socially shared.

life review Used to describe an almost universal tendency of older persons toward self-reflection and reminiscence.

life span The extreme limit of human longevity; the age beyond which no one can expect to live.

life-span construct A person's unified sense of the past, the present, and the future.

life-span perspective of development Conceptualization of development as a multidirectional process that extends from birth to death and is characterized by both gains and losses, and by inter- and intraindividual variability.

life-stage perspective of development Conceptualization of development as an ongoing process that proceeds through a set pattern of sequential stages that most individuals experience.

life story A personal narrative history that organizes past events into a coherent sequence. Each life story includes features such as tone, imagery, characters, and an ending.

life table A mathematical model, based on age-specific death rates, that estimates an average number of years remaining to persons at birth and at each subsequent age. The life table is sometimes called a *mortality table.*

lifetime stability model According to this model, aging and church attendance/religious activity are not related.

liquid assets Financial assets (e.g., stocks or bonds) easily convertible to goods, services, or money.

living will A legal document in which a competent person can instruct a physician not to use heroic measures to prolong life when there is no reasonable expectation of recovery from physical or mental disability.

locus of control The extent to which a person believes that he or she can influence the outcomes in his or her life.

longitudinal study A study designed to collect data at different points in time. This research design emphasizes the study of change.

mania Characterized by an abnormally and consistently elevated, expansive, or irritable mood that lasts for at least one week.

mastery The extent to which people believe that they can control what happens to them in the world.

medical model Describes the basic paradigm that rules medical practice. Patients are viewed as having transitory technical problems that can be overcome by some physical or biochemical intervention that only the physician is qualified to perform. The assumption is that the patient can be cured and discharged.

melting pot A term often applied to the United States to describe a situation in which ethnic minorities lose their distinctive character and become assimilated into the broader culture.

metamemory An individual's perceptions, knowledge, and beliefs about how information is stored and retrieved.

micturition reflex The onset of the desire to urinate.

migration Refers to the movement of populations from one geographical region to another.

minimum adequate diet Lowest-cost food budget that could be devised to supply all essential nutrients using food readily available in the U.S. market.

modernization theory Attempts to describe the relationship between societal modernization and the changes in role and status of older people. It holds that with increasing modernization, the status of older people declines.

modified extended family A term used to describe several related nuclear families who do not share the same household but who do maintain strong kinship ties and have frequent social interaction and helping patterns.

mortality rate The total number of deaths in society in a year per 1,000 individuals in the society.

mortification A process, associated with institutional settings, by which an individual is stripped of his or her identity.

mourning Culturally patterned process by which grief is managed or resolved.

myocardial infarction A common form of ischemic heart disease. In time, if a deficient blood supply to the heart persists, heart tissue will die, resulting in an infarct or a "heart attack."

nonliquid assets Assets that are not easily convertible into cash.

normative solidarity Commitment of individuals to perform family roles and obligations.

nuclear family A family unit composed of husband, wife, and children.

old-age dependency ratio Ratio of the population of those too old to work to the population of working age.

old-old Those 75 years of age and older.

open-angle glaucoma The chronic form of glaucoma; it accounts for 80 percent of primary glaucomas.

osteoarthritis Degenerative joint change that takes place with aging. It is often referred to as *wear and tear arthritis.*

osteopenia A gradual loss of bone that reduces skeletal mass and is associated with the aging process.

osteoporosis A demineralization of bone, often associated with aging.

palliative care Care directed at symptom control rather than cure. The term is often used synonymously with *hospice care.*

panel study A form of longitudinal study in which the same set of people is studied over time.

participant observation A type of field research that includes observing and participating in events in a group.

pathological aging Changes that occur as a result of disease processes may be categorized as relating to pathological aging.

perception Processes that enable an individual to acquire and interpret information from the environment.

political economy perspective A critical approach that allows for broadly viewing old age and the aging process within the economic and political context of the society.

population pyramid A technique used to graphically depict the age and sex composition of a societal population.

possible selves An individual's ideas of what he or she might become, both positive (hoped-for selves) and negative (feared selves).

poverty index An index developed by the Social Security Administration and based on the amount of money needed to purchase a minimum adequate diet as determined by the Department of Agriculture; it is the most frequently used measure of income adequacy.

preindustrial society A premodern society characterized by a lack of technological sophistication.

preparatory depression A type of depression, associated with the stages of dying, that takes impending losses into account. This depression prepares the individual for loss of all love objects.

presbyalgos Age-related changes in sensitivity, perception, and affect regarding pain.

presbycusis Normal, age-related change that occurs in the aging auditory system; results in impaired hearing.

presbyopia A normal age-related change that occurs in the aging eye.

principle of substitution The notion that elderly who need support typically receive it in serial order, depending on availability, from a spouse, then a child, followed by siblings, other relatives, and friends and neighbors.

proactive aging Preventive and corrective adaptations that older adults make as they anticipate or confront normative stresses of aging.

progressive disengagement model According to this model, religious activity declines following middle age.

prolongevity The significant extension of the length of life by human action.

protective services Visits by the social worker with supplemental community services, such as visiting nurses, homemakers, clinical services, meals, telephone checks, and transportation.

psychological aging A term often used to describe all the developmental processes, such as intellectual functioning and coping, that may be related to aging.

racial crossover in mortality In the older years (after age 80), a crossover occurs in which the reported death rates of African Americans of both sexes fall below those of whites, a reversal from earlier in life.

reaction time The interval between the presentation of a stimulus and an individual's motor response to the stimulus. Reaction time is affected by task familiarity, task complexity, and other factors.

reactive depression A type of depression evident during the dying process that is a result of past losses (e.g., the patient may have lost a job because of an inability to work).

respite care Temporary services that use trained sitters to provide relief for caregivers of the frail elderly.

retirement Defined by Webster (1828) as "1. the art of withdrawing from company or from public notice or station; 2. the state of being withdrawn; 3. private abode; 4. private way of life."

retirement community Any living environment to which most of whose residents have relocated since retirement.

retirement test A system employed by the Social Security Administration to determine whether a person otherwise eligible for retirement benefits can be considered retired.

reverse annuity mortgage Mortgages under which a homeowner may sell some equity in his or her house and, in return, receive a fixed monthly sum based on a percentage of the current market value of the house.

rheumatoid arthritis A type of arthritis characterized by serious inflammation and joint destruction.

rites of passage Ceremonial rituals that mark an individual's move from one social position to another (e.g., single person to married person).

RNA (ribonucleic acid) Carries instructions from the DNA.

role theory One of the earliest frameworks within which researchers in gerontology attempted to understand the adjustment of the aging individual. According to the theory, role loss (e.g., retirement, widowhood, etc.) leads to maladjustment.

role transitions A timetable that society uses to order life events and transitions from one event to the next.

sarcopenia The loss of muscle that occurs with age.

savings and thrift plan The most prevalent form of defined contribution plan in which employees contribute a predetermined percentage of earnings, all or part of which the employer matches.

scenario Expectations a person has for the future.

secondary analysis A reanalysis of data produced by someone else.

self-concept The attitudes a person has about himself or herself as an object. Includes cognitive, evaluative, and conative components.

semantic (general) memory Processes whereby individuals access words, concepts, and facts, independent of context.

senescence The term used by biological gerontologists to describe all the postmaturational changes in an individual.

sensorineural hearing loss Hearing loss related to disorders of the inner ear where conducted sound vibrations are transformed into electrical impulses.

sex ratio The number of males for every 100 females ($\times$ 100).

social cohesiveness hypothesis The notion that religious involvement may influence health status by giving individuals an opportunity to participate in a "moral community."

social gerontology The study of the impact of social and sociocultural factors on the aging process.

social role A set of patterned, functionally interdependent relations between a person and his or her social circle.

Social Security   The colloquial term used to describe the Old Age Survivors, Disability, and Health Insurance (OASDHI) program administered by the federal government. The most well known aspect of this program is the public retirement pension system, which provides income support to over 90 percent of U.S. elderly.

social support   Instrumental and/or emotional assistance that is provided by professionals, family members, and/or friends.

socialization   A learning process through which one masters language, gestures, values, and beliefs of the culture into which one is born.

socioenvironmental theory   A theory that is directed at understanding the effects of the immediate social and physical environment on the activity patterns of aged individuals.

stages of dying   The most well-known conceptualization of the dying process. Prepared by Kübler-Ross, dying is seen as a five-stage process through which most persons proceed.

status passage   Process of negotiating a passage from one age-based status to another; may have both an objective and a subjective reality.

stress process framework   Hypothesizes that how an individual deals with a potential stressor depends on when the challenge occurs, the individual's unique biography, and the social and historical context.

stress proliferation   The tendency for a primary stressor (e.g., death of a spouse) to lead to secondary stressors (e.g., economic difficulties, social isolation, etc.).

structural solidarity   Opportunity for intergenerational relationships within a family (e.g., availability, geographic proximity, etc.).

substitute judgment   A legal standard that allows for the substitution of another's judgment when a person is determined to be incompetent.

Sunbelt   Made up of the southern states and southwestern regions of the United States.

Supplemental Security Income (SSI)   A federal assistance program envisioned to supplement the existing incomes of eligible aged to bring them up to a minimal income level.

symbolic interactionism   A theoretical orientation based on the premise that people behave toward objects and others according to perceptions and meanings developed through social interaction.

telomeres   The chromosomal tips of divided cells.

theodicy hypothesis   The notion that religious involvement may act to modify how individuals perceive particularly stressful situations, including hospitalization, disability, or other traumatic events.

traditional model   According to this model, religious activity declines sharply during young adulthood and, beyond age 35, posits a steady increase in religious activities until old age.

transient ischemic attack (TIA)   A small stroke (mini-stroke) that may signal the onset of a more substantial stroke.

verticalization   As a result of decreased fertility and increased longevity, the tendency for contemporary families to have living members in a greater number of generations, but fewer members in each generation, than in the past.

Vilacabamba   A village in the Andean mountains of Ecuador, where there is purported to be a high proportion of centenarians.

wear and tear theory of aging   Theorists using this biological model of aging often employ machine analogies to exemplify the theory's underlying assumption that an organism wears out with use or stress.

wisdom   One of the highest forms of knowledge and skill; it can be conceptualized as a personality characteristic, an advanced stage of intellectual development, and the ability to solve difficult life problems.

young-old   Those aged 55 to 74 years.

INDEX